GLEIM®

2017 EDITION

CPA Review

Auditing & Attestation

by

Irvin N. Gleim, Ph.D., CPA, CIA, CMA, CFM

and

William A. Hillison, Ph.D., CPA, CMA

Gleim Publications, Inc.
P.O. Box 12848
University Station
Gainesville, Florida 32604
(800) 87-GLEIM or (800) 874-5346
(352) 375-0772
Fax: (352) 375-6940
Internet: www.gleim.com
Email: admin@gleim.com

For updates to this 2017 edition of
CPA Review: Auditing and Attestation

Go To: www.gleim.com/CPAupdate

Or: Email update@gleim.com with
CPA AUD 2017-1 in the subject line. You will
receive our current update as a reply.

Updates are available until the next edition is published.

ISSN: 1547-8033

ISBN: 978-1-61854-075-1 *CPA Review: Auditing and Attestation*
ISBN: 978-1-61854-076-8 *CPA Review: Business Environment and Concepts*
ISBN: 978-1-61854-077-5 *CPA Review: Financial Accounting and Reporting*
ISBN: 978-1-61854-078-2 *CPA Review: Regulation*
ISBN: 978-1-61854-080-5 *CPA Exam Guide: A System for Success*

ACKNOWLEDGMENTS

Material from *Uniform CPA Examination, Selected Questions and Unofficial Answers*, Copyright © 1974-2016 by the American Institute of Certified Public Accountants, Inc., is reprinted and/or adapted with permission. Visit the AICPA's website at www.aicpa.org for more information.

The authors ares are indebted to the Institute of Certified Management Accountants for permission to use problem materials from past CMA examinations. Questions and unofficial answers from the Certified Management Accountant Examinations, copyright by the Institute of Certified Management Accountants, are reprinted and/or adapted with permission.

The authors are grateful for permission to reproduce Certified Internal Auditor Examination Questions, Copyright © 1991-2016 by The Institute of Internal Auditors, Inc.

Environmental Statement -- This book is printed on recyclable, environmentally friendly groundwood paper, sourced from certified sustainable forests and produced either TCF (totally chlorine-free) or ECF (elementally chlorine-free).

ABOUT THE AUTHORS

Irvin N. Gleim is Professor Emeritus in the Fisher School of Accounting at the University of Florida and is a member of the American Accounting Association, Academy of Legal Studies in Business, American Institute of Certified Public Accountants, Association of Government Accountants, Florida Institute of Certified Public Accountants, The Institute of Internal Auditors, and the Institute of Management Accountants. He has had articles published in the *Journal of Accountancy*, *The Accounting Review*, and *The American Business Law Journal* and is author/coauthor of numerous accounting books, aviation books, and CPE courses.

William A. Hillison is a Professor Emeritus of Accounting at Florida State University. His primary teaching duties included graduate and undergraduate auditing and systems courses. He is a member of the Florida Institute of Certified Public Accountants, American Accounting Association, and Institute of Certified Management Accountants. He has had articles published in many journals, including the *Journal of Accounting Research*, the *Journal of Accounting Literature*, the *Journal of Accounting Education*, *Cost and Management*, *The Internal Auditor*, *ABACUS*, the *Journal of Accountancy*, *The CPA Journal*, and *The Journal of Forecasting*.

REVIEWERS AND CONTRIBUTORS

Garrett W. Gleim, B.S., CPA (not in public practice), received a Bachelor of Science degree from The Wharton School at the University of Pennsylvania. Mr. Gleim coordinated the production staff, reviewed the manuscript, and provided production assistance throughout the project.

Grady M. Irwin, J.D., is a graduate of the University of Florida College of Law, and he has taught in the University of Florida College of Business. Mr. Irwin provided substantial editorial assistance throughout the project.

Dr. Steven A. Solieri, CPA, CGMA, CMA, CIA, CISA, CITP, CFF, CRISC, is an Associate Professor at Queens College in Flushing, New York, and is a Founding Member in the Firm of Solieri & Solieri, CPAs, PLLC, New Hyde Park, NY, where he currently practices. Dr. Solieri earned his Ph.D. from Binghamton University and holds four Masters from the University of Michigan, Pace University, Kettering University, and Binghamton University. Dr. Solieri helped develop instructor materials, multiple-choice questions, and simulations to be used in conjunction with this text.

Mark S. Modas, M.S.T., CPA, received a Bachelor of Arts in Accounting from Florida Atlantic University and a Master of Science in Taxation from Nova Southeastern University. He was the Sarbanes-Oxley project manager and internal audit department manager at Perry Ellis International, and the former Acting Director of Accounting and Financial Reporting for the School Board of Broward County, Florida. Mr. Modas provided substantial editorial assistance throughout the project.

Tatiana Cherniawsky-Walsh, M.S. in Accounting, graduated from Queens College, City University of New York. She is currently a CPA candidate and plans to begin a career in public accounting in 2017. She assisted Dr. Solieri in developing instructor materials, multiple-choice questions, and simulations to be used in conjunction with this text.

A PERSONAL THANKS

This manual would not have been possible without the extraordinary effort and dedication of Calvin Adams, Julie Cutlip, Blaine Hatton, Kelsey Olson, Bree Rodriguez, Teresa Soard, Justin Stephenson, Joanne Strong, Elmer Tucker, and Candace Van Doren, who typed the entire manuscript and all revisions and drafted and laid out the diagrams, illustrations, and cover for this book.

The authors also appreciate the production and editorial assistance of Jacob Bennett, Suzette Cook, Melody Dalton, Jim Harvin, Jessica Hatker, Kristen Hennen, Katie Larson, Diana León, Jake Pettifor, Shane Rapp, Drew Sheppard, and Alyssa Thomas.

The authors also appreciate the critical reading assistance of Felix Chen, Corey Connell, Solomon Gonite, Jared Halper, Angelica Hyde, Andrew Johnson, Jacey Johnson, Jessica Joseph, Josh Lehr, Melissa Leonard, Ross Li, Monica Metz, Sharon Sabbagh, Diana Weng, Josie Zhao, and Lily Zhao.

Finally, we appreciate the encouragement, support, and tolerance of our families throughout this project.

TABLE OF CONTENTS

DETAILED TABLE OF CONTENTS

PREFACE FOR CPA CANDIDATES

The purpose of this Gleim CPA Review study book is to help you prepare to pass the 2017 Auditing and Attestation (also referred to throughout the rest of this text as Auditing or AUD) section of the CPA examination. Our overriding consideration is to provide a comprehensive, effective, and easy-to-use study program. This book

1. Explains how to optimize your grade by focusing on the Auditing section of the CPA exam.
2. Defines the subject matter tested on the Auditing section of the CPA exam.
3. Outlines all of the subject matter tested on the Auditing section in 20 easy-to-use-and-complete study units.
4. Presents multiple-choice questions from recent CPA examinations to prepare you for questions in future CPA exams. Our answer explanations are presented to the immediate right of each question for your convenience. Use a piece of paper to cover our answer explanations as you study the questions.

The outline format, the spacing, and the question and answer formats in this book are designed to facilitate readability, learning, understanding, and success on the CPA exam. Our most successful candidates use the Gleim Premium CPA Review System,* which includes Gleim Instruct videos; our Access Until You Pass Guarantee; SmartAdapt technology; expertly authored books; the largest test bank of multiple-choice questions, Task-Based Simulations, and Written Communications; audio lectures; and the support of our team of accounting experts. This review book and all Gleim CPA Review materials are compatible with other CPA review materials and courses that follow the AICPA Blueprints.

To maximize the efficiency and effectiveness of your CPA review program, augment your studying with the *CPA Exam Guide*, which has been carefully written and organized to provide important information to assist you in passing the CPA examination.

Thank you for your interest in the Gleim CPA Review materials. We deeply appreciate the thousands of letters and suggestions received from CPA, CIA, CMA, and EA candidates during the past 5 decades.

If you use the Gleim materials, we want YOUR feedback immediately after the exam and as soon as you have received your grades. The CPA exam is NONDISCLOSED, and you will sign an attestation including, "I hereby agree that I will maintain the confidentiality of the Uniform CPA Examination. In addition, I agree that I will not divulge the nature or content of any Uniform CPA Examination question or answer under any circumstance . . ." We ask only for information about our materials, i.e., the topics that need to be added, expanded, etc. Our approach has AICPA approval.

Please go to www.gleim.com/feedbackAUD to share your suggestions on how we can improve this edition.

Good Luck on the Exam,

Irvin N. Gleim
William A. Hillison
January 2017

---

* Visit www.gleimcpa.com or call (800) 874-5346 to order.

OPTIMIZING YOUR AUDITING AND ATTESTATION SCORE

UNIFORM CPA EXAMINATION

CPA Exam Section	Auditing & Attestation	Business Environment & Concepts	Financial Accounting & Reporting	Regulation
Acronym	AUD	BEC	FAR	REG
Exam Length	4 hours	4 hours	4 hours	4 hours
Testlet 1: Multiple-Choice	36 questions	31 questions	33 questions	38 questions
Testlet 2: Multiple-Choice	36 questions	31 questions	33 questions	38 questions
Testlet 3: Task-Based Simulations	2 tasks	2 tasks	2 tasks	2 tasks
Standardized Break	Clock stops for 15 minutes			
Testlet 4: Task-Based Simulations	3 tasks	2 tasks	3 tasks	3 tasks
Testlet 5: Task-Based Simulations or Written Communications	3 tasks	3 written responses	3 tasks	3 tasks

Passing the CPA exam is a serious undertaking. Begin by becoming an expert in the content, formatting, and functionality of the AUD exam before you take it. The objective is no surprises on exam day. Also, you will save time and money, decrease frustration, and increase your probability of success by learning all you can about how to prepare for and take AUD.

Review the *CPA Exam Guide: A System for Success* at www.gleim.com/PassCPA for a complete explanation of how to prepare for and take each section of the CPA exam. You may also choose to review the Candidate Bulletin (www.gleim.com/goCPA2017), which is copublished by the AICPA and NASBA and contains information on the most important aspects of preparing to take the CPA exam. Rest assured, the Gleim *CPA Exam Guide* covers and explains everything that is contained in this official exam bulletin so there will be no surprises.

CPA Exam Pass Rates*

Percentage of Candidates			
	2014	2015	2016
AUD	46	47	46
BEC	56	57	57
FAR	48	47	46
REG	49	49	49

*Both domestic and international pass rates are included.

The implication of these pass rates for you as a CPA candidate is that you have to be, on average, in the top 45% of all candidates to pass. The major difference between CPA candidates who pass and those who do not is their preparation program. You have access to the best CPA review material; it is up to you to use it. Even if you are enrolled in a review course that uses other materials, you will benefit with the Gleim Premium CPA Review System.

GLEIM CPA REVIEW

Gleim CPA Review features the most comprehensive coverage of exam content and employs the most efficient learning techniques to help you study smarter and faster. The Gleim CPA Review System is powered by SmartAdapt technology, an innovative platform that guides you through the following steps for optimized CPA review:

Step 1:

Complete a Diagnostic Quiz. Based on your quiz results, our SmartAdapt technology will create a custom learning track.

Step 2:

Solidify your knowledge by studying the suggested Knowledge Transfer Outline(s) or watching the suggested Gleim Instruct video(s).

Step 3:

Focus on weak areas and perfect your CPA question-answering techniques by taking the adaptive quizzes and simulations that SmartAdapt directs you to.

Final Review:

After completing all study units, take the Exam Rehearsal. Then, SmartAdapt will walk you through a Final Review based on your results.

To facilitate your studies, the Gleim Premium CPA Review System uses the largest test bank of CPA exam questions on the market. Our system's content and presentation precisely mimic the whole AICPA exam environment so you feel comfortable on test day.

Learning from Your Mistakes

One of the main building blocks of the Gleim studying system is that learning from questions you answer incorrectly is very important. Each question you answer incorrectly is an **opportunity** to avoid missing actual test questions on your CPA exam. Thus, you should carefully study the answer explanations provided so you understand why the original answer you chose is wrong as well as why the correct answer indicated is correct. This learning technique is the difference between passing and failing for many CPA candidates.

The Gleim Premium CPA Review System has built-in functionality for this step. After each quiz and simulation you complete, the Gleim system directs you to study why you answered questions incorrectly so you can learn how to avoid making the same errors in the future. Reasons for answering questions incorrectly include

1. Misreading the requirement (stem)
2. Not understanding what is required
3. Making a math error
4. Applying the wrong rule or concept
5. Being distracted by one or more of the answers
6. Incorrectly eliminating answers from consideration
7. Not having any knowledge of the topic tested
8. Using a poor educated guessing strategy

SUBJECT MATTER FOR AUDITING AND ATTESTATION

The content areas from the AICPA's Blueprint for Auditing are

I. (20%) Ethics, Professional Responsibilities, and General Principles
II. (25%) Assessing Risk and Developing a Planned Response
III. (35%) Performing Further Procedures and Obtaining Evidence
IV. (20%) Forming Conclusions and Reporting

Appendix B contains the AICPA's Blueprint for AUD with cross-references to the subunits in our materials where topics are covered. Remember that we have studied and restudied the Blueprint and explain the subject matter thoroughly in our CPA Review. Accordingly, you do not need to spend time with Appendix B. Rather, it should give you confidence that Gleim CPA Review is the best review available to help you PASS the CPA exam.

The AUD section will test engagements in accordance with professional standards and/or regulations by the

- American Institute of CPAs (AICPA),
- Public Company Accounting Oversight Board (PCAOB),
- U.S. Government Accountability Office (GAO),
- Office of Management and Budget (OMB), and
- U.S. Department of Labor (DOL).

Candidates are expected to demonstrate knowledge and skills related to

- Audits of issuer and nonissuer entities;
- Attestation engagements for issuer and nonissuer entities;
- Preparation, compilation, and review engagements for nonissuer entities; and
- Reviews of interim financial information for issuer entities.

The following general topics will be tested:

- Nature and scope of engagements: (1) audit engagements and (2) non-audit engagements
- Ethics, independence, and professional conduct
- Terms of engagement
- Engagement documentation
- Communication requirements
- Quality control
- Planning the engagement
- Understanding (1) an entity and its environment and (2) internal controls over financial reporting
- Assessing risks and planning further procedures

- Performing engagement procedures and concluding on the sufficiency and appropriateness of evidence obtained
- Testing the operating effectiveness of internal controls
- Performing tests of compliance and agreed-upon procedures
- Evaluating and responding to misstatements due to error or fraud and to internal control deficiencies
- Obtaining management representations
- Performing procedures to identify and respond to subsequent events and subsequently discovered facts
- Identifying the factors that should be considered when
  - Reporting on auditing, attestation, compilation, review, or compliance engagements
  - Performing preparation engagements
  - Assisting in the preparation of reports for these engagements

WHICH PRONOUNCEMENTS ARE TESTED?

Following is the section of the AICPA's pronouncement policy that is relevant to the AUD section:

Accounting and auditing pronouncements are eligible to be tested on the Uniform CPA Examination in the later of: (1) the first testing window beginning after the pronouncement's earliest mandatory effective date or (2) the first testing window beginning six (6) months after the pronouncement's issuance date. [In either case, there is a simultaneous introduction of content related to the new pronouncement and removal of content related to the previous pronouncement.]

Note that the bracketed sentence above simply means that once a new pronouncement is testable, you will no longer be tested on the old pronouncement.

Appendix A contains a complete listing of auditing pronouncements currently tested on the AUD exam. We have also included a cross-reference to where the pronouncements can be studied in the Gleim AUD course.

AICPA's NONDISCLOSURE AGREEMENT

As part of the AICPA's nondisclosure policy and to prove each candidate's willingness to adhere to this policy, a confidentiality and nondisclosure statement must be accepted by each candidate during the introductory screens at the beginning of each exam. This statement is reproduced here to remind all CPA candidates about the AICPA's strict policy of nondisclosure, which Gleim consistently supports and upholds.

"Please read the Confidentiality and Break Policy Statement presented below. You must accept the terms and conditions to proceed.

Policy Statement and Agreement Regarding Exam Confidentiality and the Taking of Breaks

I hereby agree that I will maintain the confidentiality of the Uniform CPA Examination.

In addition, I agree that I will not:

Divulge the nature or content of any Uniform CPA Examination question or answer under any circumstances

Engage in any unauthorized communication during testing

Refer to unauthorized materials or use unauthorized equipment during testing

Remove or attempt to remove any Uniform CPA Examination materials, notes, or any other items from the examination room

I understand and agree that liability for test administration activities, including but not limited to the adequacy or accuracy of test materials and equipment, and the accuracy of scoring and score reporting, will be limited to score correction or test retake at no additional fee. I waive any and all rights to all other claims. I further agree to report to the AICPA any examination question disclosures, or solicitations for disclosure, of which I become aware.

I affirm that I have had the opportunity to read the Candidate Bulletin and I agree to all of its terms and conditions.

I understand that breaks are only allowed between testlets. I understand that I will be asked to complete any open testlet before leaving the testing room for a break. In addition, I understand that failure to comply with this Policy statement and Agreement could result in the invalidation of my scores, disqualification from future examinations, expulsion from the testing facility and possibly civil or criminal penalties."

GLEIM CPA REVIEW ESSENTIALS

Gleim CPA Review has the following features to make studying easier:

1. **Backgrounds:** In certain instances, we have provided historical background or supplemental information. This information is intended to illuminate the topic under discussion and is set off in bordered boxes with shaded headings. This material does not need to be memorized for the exam.

Background
Prior to 1984, agencies of the federal government that provided awards to state and local governments audited specific grants, contracts, subsidies, etc. This process often resulted in numerous audits of a recipient by various agencies and a wasteful duplication of effort. In other cases, large amounts of federal awards went unaudited.

2. **Examples:** Illustrative examples, both hypothetical and those drawn from actual events, are set off in shaded, bordered boxes.

EXAMPLE
If a client's prior reported sales were $120,000 in Year 1, $130,000 in Year 2, and $140,000 in Year 3, respectively, the auditor is likely to predict Year 4 sales to be approximately $150,000 based on the trend. If management's reported sales are materially different, the auditor increases the assessed risk of material misstatement (RMM) and investigates the underlying causes.

3. **Gleim Success Tips:** These tips supplement the core exam material by suggesting how certain topics might be presented on the exam or how you should prepare for an issue.

 The AICPA has increased its emphasis on quality control, and you should recognize its importance in your studies. Be conversant with the role of practice monitoring, and make certain that you understand the six elements of the AICPA's Statements on Quality Control Standards. Each element requires the CPA firm to have "policies and procedures" in place to ensure conformance with applicable standards.

4. **Memory Aids:** These mnemonic devices are designed to assist you in memorizing important concepts.

   For example, "Controls stop **CRIME**" helps candidates remember the five interrelated components of internal control: <u>C</u>ontrol activities, <u>R</u>isk assessment, <u>I</u>nformation system, <u>M</u>onitoring, and the control <u>E</u>nvironment.

5. **Detailed Table of Contents:** This information at the beginning of the book is a complete listing of all study units and subunits in the Gleim CPA Auditing Review program. Use this list as a study aid to mark off your progress and to provide jumping-off points for review.

6. **Auditing Authoritative Pronouncements Cross-References:** Appendix A lists all authoritative pronouncements and cross-references them to the Gleim study unit(s) in which they are discussed.

7. **Blueprint with Gleim Cross-References:** Appendix B contains a reprint of the AICPA Blueprint for AUD along with cross-references to the corresponding Gleim study units and subunits.

8. **Optimizing Your Task-Based Simulations (TBSs) Score:** Appendix C explains how to approach and allocate your time for the TBS testlets. It also presents several example TBSs for your review.

9. **Core Concepts:** We have also provided additional study materials to supplement the Knowledge Transfer Outlines in the digital Gleim CPA Review Course. The Core Concepts, for example, are consolidated documents providing an overview of the key points of each subunit that serve as the foundation for learning. As part of your review, you should make sure that you understand each of them.

TIME BUDGETING AND QUESTION-ANSWERING TECHNIQUES FOR AUDITING

To begin the exam, you will enter your Launch Code on the Welcome screen. If you do not enter the correct code within 5 minutes of the screen appearing, the exam session will end.

Next, you will have and additional 5 minutes to view a brief exam introduction containing two screens: the nondisclosure policy and a section information screen. Accept the policy and then review the information screen, but be sure to click the Begin Exam button on the bottom right of the screen within the allotted 5 minutes. If you fail to do so, the exam will be terminated and you will not have the option to restart your exam.

These 10 minutes, along with the 5 minutes you may spend on a post-exam survey, are not included in the 240 minutes of exam time.

Once you complete the introductory screens and begin your exam, expect two testlets of 36 multiple-choice questions (MCQs) each and three testlets of Task-Based Simulations (TBSs) (one with 2 TBSs and two with 3 TBS each). You will have 240 minutes to complete the five testlets.

1. **Budget your time.** We make this point with emphasis. Just as you would fill up your gas tank prior to reaching empty, so too should you finish your exam before time expires.

    a. Here is our suggested time allocation for Auditing:

	Minutes	Start Time	
Testlet 1 (MCQ)	45	4 hours	00 minutes
Testlet 2 (MCQ)	45	3 hours	15 minutes
Testlet 3 (TBS)	36	2 hours	30 minutes
Break	15	Clock stops	
Testlet 4 (TBS)	54	1 hour	54 minutes
Testlet 5 (TBS)	54	1 hour	0 minutes
***Extra time	6	0 hours	6 minutes

    b. Before beginning your first testlet, prepare a Gleim Time Management Sheet as recommended in the *CPA Exam Guide: A System for Success*.

    c. As you work through the individual questions, monitor your time. In Auditing, we suggest 45 minutes for each testlet of 36 multiple-choice questions. If you answer five items in 6 minutes, you are fine, but if you spend 8 minutes on five items, you need to speed up. In the TBS testlets, spend no more than 18 minutes on each TBS. For more information on TBS time budgets, refer to Appendix C, "Optimizing Your Score on the Task-Based Simulations."

    ***Remember to allocate your budgeted extra time, as needed, to each testlet. Your goal is to answer all of the items and achieve the maximum score possible. For example, research questions can probably be completed in 5-10 minutes, which will give you extra time for longer, more complex TBSs. As you practice answering TBSs in the Gleim Premium CPA Review System, you will be practicing your time management.

2. **Answer the questions in consecutive order.**

    a.   Do **not** agonize over any one item. Stay within your time budget: 1.25 minutes per MCQ and 18 minutes per TBS.

    b.   Flag for review any questions you are unsure of and return to them later as time allows.

        1)   Once you have selected the Submit Testlet option, you will no longer be able to review or change any answers in the completed testlet.

    c.   Never leave a question unanswered. **Make your best educated guess in the time allowed.** Remember that your score is based on the number of correct responses. You will not be penalized for guessing incorrectly.

3. **For each question,**

    a.   **Try to ignore the answer choices.** Do not allow the answer choices to affect your reading of the question.

        1)   In multiple-choice questions, four answer choices are presented; you know three of them are incorrect. A TBS question may even have more than four choices. These extra choices are called **distractors** for good reason. Often, distractors are written to appear correct at first glance until further analysis.

        2)   In computational items, the distractors are carefully calculated such that they are the result of making common mistakes. Be careful, and double-check your computations if time permits.

    b.   **Read the question** carefully to determine the precise requirement.

        1)   Focusing on what is required enables you to ignore extraneous information, to focus on the relevant facts, and to proceed directly to determining the correct answer.

            a)   Be especially careful to note when the requirement is an **exception**; e.g., "Which of the following is **not** a management assertion?"

    c.   **Determine the correct answer** before looking at the answer choices.

    d.   **Read the answer choices carefully.**

        1)   Even if the first answer appears to be the correct choice, do **not** skip the remaining answer choices. Questions often ask for the "best" of the choices provided. Thus, each choice requires your consideration.

        2)   Treat each answer choice as a true/false question as you analyze it.

    e.   **Click on the best answer.**

        1)   In a multiple-choice question, you have a 25% chance of answering correctly by guessing blindly. In a TBS, it depends on how many answer choices there are. Improve your odds with educated guessing.

        2)   For many questions, a few answer choices can be eliminated with minimal effort, thereby increasing your chances of choosing the correct answer with an **educated guess**.

            a)   First, rule out answers that you think are incorrect. Second, speculate on what the AICPA is looking for and/or the rationale behind the question. Third, select the best answer or guess between equally appealing answers. Your first guess is usually the most intuitive. If you cannot make an educated guess, read the question and each answer again and pick the most intuitive answer.

4. After you have answered all the items in a testlet, consult the question status list at the bottom of the screen **before** clicking the Submit Testlet button, which permanently ends the testlet.

    a. Go back to the flagged items and finalize your answer choices.
    b. Verify that all questions have been answered.
    c. Make sure you accomplish this step within your predetermined time budget per testlet.

Doing well on the **task-based simulations** requires you to be an expert on how to approach them both from a question answering and a time allocation perspective. Refer to Appendix C, "Optimizing Your Score on the Task-Based Simulations," for a complete explanation of task-based simulations and how to optimize your score on each one.

HOW TO BE IN CONTROL

Remember, you must be in control to be successful during exam preparation and execution. Perhaps more importantly, control can also contribute greatly to your personal and other professional goals. Control is the process whereby you

1. Develop expectations, standards, budgets, and plans
2. Undertake activity, production, study, and learning
3. Measure the activity, production, output, and knowledge
4. Compare actual activity with expected and budgeted activity
5. Modify the activity, behavior, or study to better achieve the expected or desired outcome
6. Revise expectations and standards in light of actual experience
7. Continue the process or restart the process in the future

Exercising control will ultimately develop the confidence you need to outperform most other CPA candidates and PASS the CPA exam!

QUESTIONS ABOUT GLEIM MATERIALS

Gleim has an efficient and effective way for candidates who have purchased the Gleim Premium CPA Review System to submit an inquiry and receive a response regarding Gleim materials **directly through their course**. This system also allows you to view your Q&A session online in your Gleim Personal Classroom.

Questions regarding the information in this introduction (study suggestions, studying plans, exam specifics) should be emailed to personalcounselor@gleim.com.

Questions concerning orders, prices, shipments, or payments should be sent via email to customerservice@gleim.com and will be promptly handled by our competent and courteous customer service staff.

For technical support, you may use our automated technical support service at www.gleim.com/support, email us at support@gleim.com, or call us at (800) 874-5346.

FEEDBACK

Please fill out our online feedback form (www.gleim.com/feedbackAUD) IMMEDIATELY after you take the CPA Auditing section so we can adapt our material based on where candidates say we need to increase or decrease coverage. Our approach has been approved by the AICPA.

STUDY UNIT ONE
ENGAGEMENT RESPONSIBILITIES

(15 pages of outline)

This study unit begins the consideration of engagement planning for attest and audit engagements. Candidates should understand the types of services performed by CPAs. The differences among preparation, compilation, review, examination or audit, and agreed-upon procedures engagements are stressed. The list below is an overview:

Preparation – no report

Compilation – disclaimer of any assurance

Review – limited assurance

Examination or audit – positive assurance or opinion expressed

Agreed-upon procedures – results of procedures but no assurance

The 11 **attestation standards** address many practitioner services. Most are considered in more detail in other study units.

Assurance services also are covered in this study unit. They are a significant enlargement of the practice of CPAs. An understanding of how these services contrast with others provided by a CPA should be obtained.

Quality control is the final subject in this study unit. The Statements on Quality Control Standards (SQCSs) address the responsibilities of a CPA firm for its accounting and auditing practice. The SQCSs, which are codified in QC Section 10, identify six specific quality control elements. Candidates must learn the elements and what each includes. This topic is receiving more attention from standards setters. For example, the AICPA's clarified SASs contain a greatly expanded treatment of quality control that includes requirements and explanatory material. The clarified statement addresses the auditor's responsibilities for quality control procedures in an audit.

1.1 ATTEST ENGAGEMENTS

1. **Applicable Pronouncements**

   a. The AICPA's **Statements on Standards for Attestation Engagements (SSAEs)** are codified in section AT of the professional standards within the framework of the 11 attestation standards. The AICPA also issues SASs (auditing services), SSARSs (accounting and review services), and SSCSs (consulting services).

      1) **SAS** = Statement on Auditing Standards issued by the Auditing Standards Board (ASB)

         SSARS = Statement on Standards for Accounting and Review Services

         SSCS = Statement on Standards for Consulting Services

      2) The **Sarbanes-Oxley Act of 2002** is federal legislation that has had a dramatic effect on the engagement responsibilities of public accounting firms. This act created the **Public Company Accounting Oversight Board (PCAOB)**. The PCAOB's standards apply to audits of issuers (companies required to file with the SEC) by public accounting firms.

2.   **Nature of an Attest Engagement**

   a.   In an **attest engagement**, a practitioner is engaged to issue or does issue an **examination**, a **review**, or an **agreed-upon procedures** report on subject matter, or an assertion about the subject matter, that is the **responsibility of another party**.

   b.   A **practitioner** is a CPA in **public practice**. Public practice is the performance of professional services for a client by a member or member's firm.

   1)   **Professional services** are all services performed for a client, an employer, or on a volunteer basis that require accountancy or related skills. Examples are (a) accounting, (b) auditing and other attest services, (c) tax, (d) consulting, and (e) other services for which standards have been issued by bodies designated by the AICPA (*Code of Professional Conduct*).

   c.   Because the attestation standards apply **only to attest engagements involving a practitioner**, they apply only to the performance by a CPA in public practice of professional services that are attest services.

   1)   However, the SSAEs provide for a compilation of prospective financial statements (AT 301).

   d.   Attest services traditionally have been limited to expressing an **opinion on historical financial statements** on the basis of an audit in accordance with U.S. generally accepted auditing standards.

   1)   But CPAs increasingly provide assurance on representations other than historical statements and in forms other than an opinion. For example, positive assurance may be provided on financial forecasts based on an **examination**, and limited (negative) assurance may be provided on historical financial statements based on a **review**.

   e.   SSAEs cover only attest engagements, not services to which specific standards apply, for example, SASs, SSARSs, and SSCSs.

   1)   Other professional services to which the SSAEs specifically do not apply include engagements in which the practitioner (a) advocates a client's position, (b) prepares tax returns or gives tax advice, (c) has the sole function of assisting the client (e.g., to prepare information other than financial statements), or (d) testifies as an expert witness given certain stipulated facts.

   f.   Some of the assurance services developed by the AICPA are considered attestation engagements, for example, **WebTrust** and **SysTrust**.

   g.   Compilations of prospective financial statements (financial forecasts and projections) are addressed in the SSAEs. These services require a disclaimer of assurance.

3.   **Attestation Standards (AT 50)**

   a.   The need to provide standards for the growing range of attest services resulted in the issuance of 11 attestation standards.

   b.   **General Standards**

   1)   *The practitioner must have adequate technical training and proficiency to perform the attestation engagement.*

   2)   *The practitioner must have adequate knowledge of the subject matter.*

   3)   *The practitioner must have reason to believe that the subject matter is capable of evaluation against criteria that are suitable and available to users.*

a) Suitable criteria have the attributes of objectivity, measurability, completeness, and relevance.

   i) For example, an engagement to attest to management's representation that "workers recorded an average of 40 hours per week on a project" could be accepted by a CPA. "Recorded" and "40 hours" are measurable and objectively determinable.

   ii) However, an engagement to attest that "workers worked very hard on the project" could not be accepted. "Very hard" is not measurable or objectively determinable.

b) Criteria should be available to users in one or more of the following ways:

   i) Publicly available

   ii) Clearly included in the presentation of the subject matter or in the assertion

   iii) Clearly included in the practitioner's report

   iv) Well understood by most users (e.g., 40 hours per week)

   v) Available only to specified parties (in which case the report should be restricted to those parties)

4) *The practitioner must maintain independence in mental attitude in all matters relating to the engagement.*

5) *The practitioner must exercise due professional care in the planning and performance of the engagement and the preparation of the report.*

c. **Standards of Field Work**

1) *The practitioner must adequately plan the work and must properly supervise any assistants.*

2) *The practitioner must obtain sufficient evidence to provide a reasonable basis for the conclusion that is expressed in the report.*

d. **Standards of Reporting**

1) *The practitioner must identify the subject matter or the assertion being reported on and state the character of the engagement in the report.*

2) *The practitioner must state the practitioner's conclusion about the subject matter or the assertion in relation to the criteria against which the subject matter was evaluated in the report.*

3) *The practitioner must state all of the practitioner's significant reservations about the engagement, the subject matter, and, if applicable, the assertion related thereto in the report.*

4) *The practitioner must state in the report that the report is intended solely for the information and use of the specified parties under the following circumstances:*

   a) *When the criteria used to evaluate the subject matter are determined by the practitioner to be appropriate only for a limited number of parties who either participated in their establishment or can be presumed to have an adequate understanding of the criteria*

   b) *When the criteria used to evaluate the subject matter are available only to specified parties*

   c) *When reporting on subject matter and a written assertion has not been provided by the responsible party*

   d) *When the report is on an attest engagement to apply agreed-upon procedures to the subject matter*

e.   The summary below is useful for learning the standards. But memorizing their order is not necessary.

SUMMARY OF THE ATTESTATION STANDARDS		
General Standards	Key Terms	Memory Aids
1. **Training** and proficiency in attestation	**T** = Training	Trisha
2. Knowledge of **subject matter**	**S** = Subject matter	Said
3. Suitable and available **criteria**	**C** = Criteria	Chris
4. **Independence** in mental attitude	**I** = Independence	Is
5. Due **professional care**	**P** = Professional care	Profane
Standards of Field Work		
1. **Planning** and supervision	**P** = Planning and supervision	Please
2. Sufficient **evidence**	**E** = Evidence	Excuse
Standards of Reporting		
1. **Character** of engagement	**C** = Character	Cousin
2. **Conclusion** about the subject matter	**C** = Conclusion	Chris's
3. Significant **reservations**	**R** = Reservations	Rude
4. Any **restrictions** on use	**R** = Restrictions	Remarks

4.   Two **levels of attest assurance** are permitted in general-distribution reports:

a.   **Positive** (high level) assurance should be given in reports that express conclusions on the basis of an **examination**.

b.   **Limited** (moderate level) assurance (sometimes termed negative assurance) should be given in reports that express conclusions on the basis of a **review**.

5.   **Scope Limitations**

a.   The practitioner may report directly on the subject matter. Nevertheless, as part of the attestation procedures for examinations and reviews, the practitioner ordinarily should obtain a **written assertion provided by the responsible party**.

b.   A failure to obtain a written assertion is considered a **scope limitation** when the responsible party is the client.

c.   In addition, a **representation letter** is typically obtained by the practitioner from the responsible party. A failure of the responsible party or client to provide written representations is normally considered a **scope limitation**.

6.   **Attest documentation** (working papers) should be prepared and maintained.

a.   Its form and content will vary with the circumstances and the practitioner's judgment.

b.   The procedures performed, evidence gathered, and the findings reached should be documented.

Stop and review! You have completed the outline for this subunit. Study multiple-choice questions 1 through 3 on page 24.

1.2 OVERALL OBJECTIVES AND CONDUCTING AN AUDIT

1.   **Overview**

a.   To make U.S. generally accepted auditing standards (GAAS) easier to read, understand, and apply, the AICPA's Auditing Standards Board (ASB) undertook a clarity project. The result was a redrafting of its standards into a new Codification of Statements on Auditing Standards. Each clarified statement states (1) objectives, (2) definitions (if relevant), (3) requirements, and (4) application and other explanatory material.

b. The new standards significantly converge with, but are not identical to, the equivalent International Standards on Auditing (ISAs) issued by the International Auditing and Assurance Standards Board. Thus, each clarified statement includes an analysis of significant differences from the equivalent ISA.

c. The clarified statements have 3-digit identification codes that correspond to those of the ISAs. Moreover, each code has the temporary prefix AU-C (C stands for "clarified"). The prefix will become AU at the AICPA's discretion. An example is AU-C 210, *Terms of Engagement*, which will become AU 210 at some time in the future.

d. The ASB's standards apply to audits of **nonissuers** (nonpublic companies). Audits of **issuers** (public companies required to file with the Securities and Exchange Commission) are regulated by the PCAOB. The Sarbanes-Oxley Act of 2002 authorized the PCAOB to establish auditing and related professional practice standards to be used by registered public accounting firms. The PCAOB reorganized their auditing standards in 2015. Each standard has an "AS" prefix followed by a 4-digit number. For example, AS 1005, *Independence*, describes the requirements of independence for auditors of issuers. However, in most cases, the PCAOB standards are similar to current ASB standards. Any significant differences are identified.

e. *Government Auditing Standards* (the Yellow Book issued by the Government Accountability Office) applies to audits of the federal government's programs. The GAO requires governmental auditors to follow the ASB standards, except as otherwise provided in the Yellow Book. Audits under the Single Audit Act also follow the Office of Budget and Management (OMB) Audit Requirements for Federal Awards (2 CFR 200).

2. An auditor is deemed to be **associated** with financial statements when the procedures applied are sufficient to report in accordance with GAAS.

3. The **purpose** of an audit is to provide financial statement users with an **opinion** by the auditor on whether the financial statements are **presented fairly**, in all material respects, in accordance with the applicable financial reporting framework (e.g., generally accepted accounting principles, cash basis, etc.).

a. The overall objectives of the auditor, in conducting an audit of financial statements, are to

1) Obtain **reasonable assurance** about whether the financial statements as a whole are free from material misstatement, whether due to fraud or error. The auditor thereby is enabled to express an opinion on whether the financial statements are presented fairly, in all material respects, in accordance with an applicable financial reporting framework.

a) Presented **fairly** means the financial statements as a whole are **free from material misstatement**, whether due to fraud or error.

b) Reasonable assurance is a high but not absolute level. It is obtained when the auditor has gathered sufficient appropriate evidence to reduce audit risk to an acceptably low level.

2) Report on the financial statements, and communicate as required by GAAS, in accordance with the auditor's findings.

3) Be independent (in most cases) and comply with other relevant ethics rules.

b. The auditor should exercise professional judgment to plan and perform an audit with **professional skepticism**, recognizing that circumstances may exist that cause the financial statements to be materially misstated.

1) Professional skepticism is an attitude that includes (a) a questioning mind, (b) alertness to conditions that may indicate material misstatement, and (c) critical assessment of audit evidence.

c.   The auditor should obtain sufficient appropriate audit evidence to reduce **audit risk** to an acceptably low level and thereby enable the auditor to draw reasonable conclusions on which to base the auditor's opinion.

d.   An auditor's **opinion** enhances the degree of confidence that intended users can place in the financial statements.

4.   **Assertions (AU-C 315)**

a.   Management implicitly or explicitly makes assertions about the recognition, measurement, presentation, and disclosure of information in the financial statements. Thus, the auditor should use **relevant** assertions in sufficient detail to assess the risks of material misstatement (RMMs) and design and perform further audit procedures. Some procedures may relate to more than one assertion. But a combination of procedures may be needed to test a relevant assertion because audit evidence from different sources or of a different nature may be relevant to the same assertion. Assertions used by the auditor to consider the types of potential misstatements may be classified as follows:

1)   **Assertions** about classes of **transactions and events** for the period (the income statement and statement of cash flows)

a)   **Occurrence** -- Recorded transactions and events actually occurred.

b)   **Completeness** -- All transactions and events that should have been recorded were recorded.

c)   **Accuracy** -- Amounts and other data were recorded appropriately.

d)   **Cutoff** -- Transactions and events were recorded in the proper period.

e)   **Classification** -- Transactions and events were recorded in the proper accounts.

2)   **Assertions** about **account balances** at period end (the balance sheet)

a)   **Existence** -- Assets, liabilities, and equity interests exist.

b)   **Rights and obligations** -- The entity holds or controls the rights to assets, and liabilities are its obligations.

c)   **Completeness** -- All assets, liabilities, and equity interests that should have been recorded were recorded.

d)   **Valuation and allocation** -- Assets, liabilities, and equity interests are included at appropriate amounts, and any valuation or allocation adjustments are appropriately recorded.

3)   **Assertions** about **presentation and disclosure** (notes to the financial statements)

a)   **Occurrence and rights and obligations** -- Disclosed transactions, events, and other matters have occurred and pertain to the entity.

b)   **Completeness** -- All disclosures that should have been included were included.

c)   **Classification and understandability** -- Financial information is appropriately presented and described, and disclosures are clearly expressed.

d)   **Accuracy and valuation** -- Information is disclosed fairly and at appropriate amounts.

b. Some assertions overlap categories. Thus, only eight separate assertions are included in the model. If these are known, they can easily be assigned to the three categories of assertions. The following memory aid is helpful for learning the assertions (envision management as a large crocodile emerging from a cave):

CAVE CROC:

C = Completeness
A = Accuracy
V = Valuation and Allocation
E = Existence

C = Cutoff
R = Rights and Obligations
O = Occurrence
C = Classification and Understandability

c. The PCAOB's AS 1105, *Audit Evidence*, describes just five assertions to be applied selectively to the financial statement transactions, balances, and disclosures. These are essentially the same as those previously described. But they do not explicitly address accuracy.

1) **Existence or occurrence** -- Assets or liabilities of the company exist at a given date, and recorded transactions have occurred during a given period.

2) **Completeness** -- All transactions and accounts that should be presented in the financial statements are so included.

3) **Valuation or allocation** -- Asset, liability, equity, revenue, and expense components have been included in the financial statements at appropriate amounts.

4) **Rights and obligations** -- The company holds or controls rights to the assets, and liabilities are obligations of the company at a given date.

5) **Presentation and disclosure** -- The components of the financial statements are properly classified, described, and disclosed.

d. An audit performed by an independent, external auditor provides assurance to external users of the financial statements of the objectivity of the auditor's opinion.

1) The auditor may make suggestions about the form or content of the financial statements or draft them based on management's information. However, the auditor's responsibility for the financial statements is confined to the **expression of an opinion**.

e. The auditor's report states, "An audit involves performing procedures to obtain audit evidence about the amounts and disclosures in the financial statements. The procedures selected depend on the auditor's judgment, including the assessment of the risks of material misstatement of the financial statements, whether due to fraud or error" (AU-C 700).

5. **Defining Professional Responsibilities**

a. GAAS and the PCAOB standards use the following categories of professional requirements to describe the degree of responsibility imposed on auditors:

1) Unconditional responsibility. The auditor must comply with an unconditional requirement whenever it is relevant. The word **must** indicates an unconditional requirement. For example, an auditor must be independent.

2) Presumptively mandatory responsibility. The auditor must comply with a presumptively mandatory requirement whenever it is relevant except in rare circumstances. The word **should** indicates a presumptively mandatory requirement. For example, an auditor should obtain an engagement letter.

   a) When the auditor judges that such a departure is necessary, (s)he should perform alternative audit procedures to achieve the intent of the requirement. A departure is expected to be needed only when a specific required procedure would be ineffective in achieving that intent.

3) Responsibility to consider. The words "may," "might," "could," or other terms and phrases describe actions and procedures that the auditor should use professional judgment in determining whether to perform.

Stop and review! You have completed the outline for this subunit. Study multiple-choice questions 4 and 5 on page 25.

1.3 ADDITIONAL PROFESSIONAL SERVICES

1. **Preparation, Compilation, and Review**

   a. The AICPA bylaws designate the Accounting and Review Services Committee as the senior technical committee authorized to issue pronouncements in connection with the unaudited financial statements or other unaudited financial information of a nonissuer (nonpublic entity).

   b. A **preparation** engagement is a **nonattest** service that does **not** require the accountant to be, or to determine whether (s)he is, **independent** of the entity. Furthermore, the accountant need **not** (1) verify the accuracy or completeness of management's information, (2) obtain evidence to express an opinion or a conclusion, or (3) report on the financial statements. The accountant's engagement **cannot** be relied upon to identify or disclose (1) misstatements, including those caused by fraud or error, or (2) wrongdoing (e.g., fraud) or noncompliance with laws and regulations. The preparation service allows accountants to use software to generate client financial statements and release them to the client or third parties without attaching a report.

   c. The objective of a **compilation** is to apply accounting and financial reporting expertise to **assist management** in the presentation of financial statements without undertaking to obtain or provide any assurance on them. Unlike a preparation service, a compilation requires the accountant to (1) determine whether (s)he is independent, (2) report on the statements, (3) disclaim any assurance, (4) disclose any lack of independence, and (5) associate his or her name with the statements. (It is included in the report.)

   d. The objective of a **review** of financial statements is to obtain **limited assurance** as a basis for reporting whether the accountant is aware of any material modifications that should be made to the statements for them to be in accordance with the reporting framework (e.g., GAAP). Thus, the accountant must be **independent**. Limited assurance also is known as **negative assurance**, in contrast with the positive assurance provided by an audit. A review is performed primarily through **inquiry** and **analytical procedures**.

2. **Agreed-Upon Procedures (AT 201)**

   a. Attest engagements include reporting on findings based on **agreed-upon procedures** performed on subject matter. The practitioner is engaged by a client to assist specified parties to evaluate the subject matter or an assertion. The report is restricted to the specified parties who have agreed to the specific procedures and taken responsibility for their sufficiency.

      1) The practitioner provides **neither positive nor limited assurance**.
      2) The practitioner must be independent.

3. **Prospective Financial Statements (PFSs) (AT 301)**

   a. PFSs consist of financial forecasts or projections, including summaries of significant assumptions and accounting policies. An accountant should examine, compile, or apply agreed-upon procedures to PFSs if they are, or reasonably might be, expected to be used by another (third) party. As with other attest services, the practitioner must be independent.

   b. A **financial forecast** consists of PFSs that present, to the best of the responsible party's knowledge and belief, an entity's expected financial position, results of operations, and cash flows. It is based on the responsible party's assumptions reflecting conditions it expects to exist and the course of action it expects to take.

   c. A **financial projection** also consists of PFSs that present, to the best of the responsible party's knowledge and belief, an entity's expected financial position, results of operations, and cash flows. But it differs from a forecast. A projection is based on the responsible party's assumptions reflecting conditions it expects would exist and the course of action it expects would be taken, given one or more **hypothetical assumptions**. A projection is sometimes prepared to present one or more hypothetical courses of action for evaluation, as in response to a question such as, "What would happen if . . .?" A projection may be expressed as a point estimate or a range.

4. **Pro Forma Financial Information (PFFI) (AT 401)**

   a. PFFI shows "what the significant effects on historical financial information would have been had a consummated or proposed transaction (or event) occurred at an earlier date."

   b. Examples of these transactions include (1) a business combination, (2) disposal of a segment, (3) change in the form or status of an entity, and (4) a change in capitalization. An independent accountant may **examine or review** PFFI.

5. **Compliance Attestation (AT 601)**

   a. The independent practitioner may perform an **examination** leading to an opinion on whether the entity is in compliance with specified requirements (e.g., covenants of a contract, either financial or nonfinancial) or the effectiveness of the entity's internal control over compliance.

   b. Also, an agreed-upon procedures engagement may be performed, but a review engagement may not.

6. **Management's Discussion and Analysis (AT 701)**

   a. Management's discussion and analysis (MD&A) may be presented in an annual report or other documents filed with the SEC. MD&A is a written assertion that may be examined or reviewed by the practitioner. However, a report on a review engagement report cannot be filed with the SEC.

   b. The practitioner must be independent.

    c.   Factors considered in planning examination include (1) attestation risk for assertions, (2) materiality, (3) items likely to require revision, and (4) conditions that may require modification of procedures.

        1)   The components of attestation risk are defined similarly to those of audit risk presented in Study Unit 3, Subunit 3.

7.   **Reporting on Controls at a Service Organization (AT 801)**

    a.   AT 801 applies to **examination** engagements undertaken by a **service auditor** to report on controls at organizations that provide services to user entities.

NOTE: The topics in this subunit are covered fully in Study Unit 19.

Stop and review! You have completed the outline for this subunit. Study multiple-choice questions 6 through 9 beginning on page 25.

1.4 ASSURANCE SERVICES

1.   **Nature of Assurance Services**

    a.   Assurance services are independent professional services that improve the quality of information, or its context, for decision makers.

    b.   Information might (1) be financial or nonfinancial, (2) be historical or prospective, (3) consist of data or relate to systems, or (4) be internal or external to the user.

    c.   Assurance services include audit and other attestation services but also nonstandard services.

    d.   Unless assurance services are covered by the AICPA's attestation standards, they do not require written assertions.

    e.   Assurance services evolved naturally from attestation services, which in turn evolved from audits. The roots of all three are in independent verification.

    f.   The form and content of assurance services differ.

        1)   Traditional audit-related services are highly structured and considered to be relevant to a large number of users.

        2)   The newer assurance services are more customized and targeted and are intended to be highly useful in more limited circumstances.

2.   Assurance services can

    a.   **Capture information.** Assurance services can capture information by using existing or improved measurement tools.

    b.   **Improve information reliability.** Raw information is refined into reliable information. Any raw information can be refined, regardless of whether it is used for decision making.

    c.   **Improve decision making.** Decision making can be improved by improving the context, such as decision models, used by the decision maker. This facet of assurance services differs from existing attestation models.

3.   Assurance services do not include **consulting services**. However, assurance and consulting services have similarities because they are delivered using a similar body of knowledge and skills.

    a.   Assurance services differ from consulting services in two ways:

        1)   They focus on improving information rather than providing advice, and

        2)   They usually involve situations in which one party wants to monitor another (often within the same entity) rather than the two-party arrangements common in consulting engagements.

4. The following table contrasts traditional attest, assurance, and consulting services:

	Attestation	Assurance	Consulting
Result	Written conclusion about subject matter or a written assertion of another party	Better information for decision makers. Recommendations might be a byproduct.	Recommendations based on the objectives of the engagement
Objective	Reliable information	Better decision making	Better outcomes
Parties to the engagement	Not specified, but generally three (the third party is usually external). CPA is generally paid by the preparer.	Generally three (although the other two might be employed by the same entity). CPA is paid by the preparer or user.	Generally two. CPA is paid by the user.
Independence	Required by standards	Included in definition	Not required
Substance of CPA output	Conformity with established or stated criteria	Assurance about reliability or relevance of information. Criteria might be established, stated, or unstated.	Recommendations; not measured against formal criteria
Form of CPA output	Written	Some form of communication	Written or oral
Critical information developed by	Asserter	Either CPA or asserter	CPA
Information content determined by	Preparer (client)	Preparer, CPA, or user	CPA
Level of assurance	Examination, review, or results of agreed-upon procedures	Flexible. For example, it might be compilation level, explicit assurance about usefulness of the information for intended purpose, or implicit from the CPA's involvement.	No explicit assurance

5. The AICPA has identified a number of services to date. Some address the needs of existing customers, but others are for new customers. Some are based on the types of data CPAs traditionally report on, but others focus on new types of data. The following examples are described subsequently:

Assurances about Risks	Assurances about Performance	Assurances about Systems
a. CPA Risk Advisory b. ElderCare (PrimePlus)	c. CPA Performance Review d. Healthcare Effectiveness	e. SysTrust f. WebTrust

    a.   **CPA risk advisory.** Managers and investors are concerned about whether entities have identified the full scope of various business risks and taken precautions to mitigate them.

    b.   **ElderCare services (PrimePlus).** ElderCare services assess whether specified goals regarding care for the elderly are being met by various care givers. Services provided to the elderly include accumulation of information, financial management, and assessment of nursing care.

    c.   **CPA performance review.** This service evaluates whether an entity's performance measurement system contains relevant and reliable measures for assessing (1) the degree to which the entity's objectives are achieved or (2) how its performance compares with that of its competitors. The review provides investors, managers, or others with a comprehensive information base and a more balanced scorecard.

    d.   **Healthcare effectiveness.** This service provides assurance about the effectiveness of healthcare services provided by HMOs, hospitals, doctors, and other providers.

e.   **SysTrust.** This service assesses whether an entity's internal information systems (financial and nonfinancial) provide reliable information for operating and financial decisions. Information systems address (1) reporting concepts and systems, (2) transaction processing systems, (3) management reporting systems, and (4) risks within a business. SysTrust is an assurance service developed under the AICPA attestation standards. SysTrust is designed to increase the comfort of management, customers, creditors, bankers, and business partners with the systems that support a business or a particular activity.

1)   The practitioner uses suitable **criteria** or benchmarks that are objective, measurable, complete, and relevant to determine whether management's assertions about any or all of the following principles are fairly stated:

a)   **Online privacy.** Personal information obtained is collected, used, disclosed, and retained as committed or agreed.

b)   **Security.** The system is protected against unauthorized access (both physical and logical).

c)   **Processing integrity.** System processing is complete, accurate, timely, and authorized.

d)   **Availability.** The system is available for operation and used as committed or agreed.

e)   **Confidentiality.** Information designated as confidential is protected as committed or agreed.

2)   Practitioners test the **policies, communications, procedures, and monitoring systems** using suitable criteria to assess the fairness of management's assertions about a particular principle. The report may address management's assertions or directly address the system.

f.   **WebTrust.** This service, developed under the AICPA attestation standards, provides Internet users, including businesses and Internet service providers, assurance about electronic commerce activities.

1)   The practitioner uses the same **criteria** as outlined for SysTrust in e.1) and 2) above.

Stop and review! You have completed the outline for this subunit. Study multiple-choice questions 10 through 13 on beginning page 26.

1.5 QUALITY CONTROL

 The AICPA has increased its emphasis on quality control, and you should recognize its importance in your studies. Be conversant with the role of practice monitoring, and make certain that you understand the six elements of the AICPA's Statements on Quality Control Standards. Each element requires the CPA firm to have "policies and procedures" in place to ensure conformance with applicable standards.

1.   **Practice-Monitoring Programs**

a.   To be admitted to or retain membership in the AICPA, practitioners who are engaged in the practice of public accounting are required to practice in firms enrolled in an AICPA-approved **practice-monitoring program** if the services performed by the firm are within the scope of the AICPA's practice-monitoring standards.

b.   A firm (or individual) enrolled in the **Center for Public Company Audit Firms Peer Review Program (Center PRP)** or the **AICPA Peer Review Program** (AICPA PRP) is deemed to be enrolled in an approved practice-monitoring program.

c.   Quality control over the audits of public companies are evaluated during periodic inspections by the **PCAOB.** The Center PRP is designed to review and evaluate those portions of a firm's accounting and auditing practice that are not inspected by the PCAOB.

    d.   Public accounting firms that are (1) without public clients and (2) required to maintain a monitoring program should enroll in the AICPA PRP.

2.   An audit firm has a responsibility to adopt a system of quality control. Thus, it should establish policies and procedures to provide reasonable assurance that (a) the firm and its personnel comply with professional standards and legal and regulatory requirements, and (b) the firm issues appropriate reports.

    a.   Quality control standards apply to the conduct of a firm's practice as a whole. Thus, quality control may affect audits.

    b.   Nevertheless, a deficiency in the system of quality control does not necessarily indicate that (1) a specific audit was not performed in accordance with professional, legal, and regulatory requirements, or (2) the auditor's report was inappropriate.

3.   **Statements on Quality Control Standards (SQCSs)**

    a.   SQCSs, codified as QC Section 10, require that a CPA firm have a system of quality control.

    b.   Other professional standards provide guidance on the quality control responsibilities of firm personnel for specific types of engagements. For example, AU-C 220 applies to audits in accordance with GAAS. It establishes requirements at the audit engagement level that are consistent with those in the SQCSs.

    c.   SQCSs apply to all CPA firms with regard to their accounting and auditing practice. This practice includes engagements to provide audit, attestation, compilation, review, and other services for which standards have been established by the Auditing Standards Board or the Accounting and Review Services Committee.

        1)   A firm is defined broadly to include "a form of organization permitted by law or regulation whose characteristics conform to resolutions of Council of the AICPA that is engaged in the practice of public accounting." This definition includes proprietorships, partnerships, and professional corporations.

    d.   The following are the six elements of a system of quality control:

        1)   **Leadership responsibilities for quality within the firm (the "tone at the top").** The firm should promote an internal culture recognizing that quality is essential in performing engagements. This requires clear, consistent, and frequent actions and messages from all levels of management that emphasize quality control policies and procedures. Emphasis also should be on (a) performing work that complies with all professional standards and legal/ regulatory requirements and (b) issuing appropriate reports.

        2)   **Relevant ethical requirements.** Policies and procedures should be established to provide reasonable assurance that the firm and personnel comply with relevant ethical requirements (e.g., the AICPA *Code of Professional Conduct*).

        3)   **Acceptance and continuance of client relationships and specific engagements.** Policies and procedures should be established to provide reasonable assurance that the firm

            a)   Has considered the client's integrity and has no information leading to a conclusion that the client lacks integrity;

            b)   Has the competence, capabilities, and resources to perform the engagement; and

            c)   Can comply with legal, regulatory, and ethical requirements.

        4)   **Human resources.** Policies and procedures should be established to provide reasonable assurance that the firm has sufficient personnel with the capabilities, competence, and commitment to ethical principles to (a) perform engagements in accordance with professional standards and legal requirements and (b) issue appropriate reports.

          a)   Matters addressed include recruitment, hiring, determining competencies, assignment of personnel, development of personnel, performance evaluation, compensation, and advancement.

          b)   An engagement partner with the appropriate competence, capabilities, and authority should be responsible for each engagement.

     5) **Engagement performance.** Policies and procedures should be established to provide reasonable assurance that engagements are consistently performed in accordance with professional standards and legal requirements and that the firm issues appropriate reports.

          a)   Matters addressed include responsibilities for consistency of performance, supervision, and review.

     6) **Monitoring.** Policies and procedures should be established to provide reasonable assurance that the policies and procedures relating to the system of quality control are relevant, adequate, operating effectively, and complied with in practice. Monitoring is an ongoing process and includes inspection and evaluation of prior engagements.

  e. **Administration of a System of Quality Control**

     1) Appropriate individuals should be responsible for designing and maintaining policies and procedures.

     2) Those policies and procedures should be communicated so as to provide reasonable assurance that they are understood and complied with.

     3) Consideration should be given to whether and to what extent policies and procedures must be documented for effective communication.

     4) The firm should appropriately document quality control policies and procedures as well as compliance with them.

     5) AU-C 220 assigns responsibility for the administration of quality control standards at the engagement level to the engagement partner.

4. **Peer Review**

  a. A peer review does not substitute for monitoring, but it is a necessary part of the practice-monitoring requirement for AICPA membership. The applicable pronouncements issued by the AICPA Peer Review Board are the Standards for Performing and Reporting on Peer Reviews (PR 100). They govern peer reviews supervised by state CPA societies of firms enrolled in the AICPA Peer Review Program.

  b. The portion of a firm's accounting and auditing practice covered by the peer review standards includes engagements under SASs, SSARSs, SSAEs, Government Auditing Standards, and PCAOB standards (for audits of non-SEC issuers).

  c. A **system review** is an on-site review required for a firm that performs the highest level of services. It provides the reviewer with a reasonable basis for expressing an opinion on the firm's system of quality control.

  d. An **engagement review** is for a firm not required to have a system review but not qualifying for a report review. It provides the reviewer with a reasonable basis for expressing limited assurance on whether (1) the financial statements or information and the accountant's reports submitted materially conform with professional standards, and (2) the firm's documentation conforms with professional standards.

5. **Sarbanes-Oxley Act of 2002**

  a. Under the federal Sarbanes-Oxley Act of 2002, a registered accounting firm (any firm having **one or more** public audit clients) must adopt quality control standards. Many of the provisions of Sarbanes-Oxley relate to improving the quality control of the audit and improving the quality of financial reporting. These standards relate to the audits of public companies.

b. A **second partner review and approval** is required of audit reports.

c. The **lead auditor** and the **reviewing partner** must be rotated off the audit every 5 years.

d. The accounting firm must supervise any **associated person** with respect to auditing or quality control standards.

e. **Independence rules have been expanded** by prohibiting the auditor from providing a variety of nonaudit services.

f. The client's CEO and CFO must certify the appropriateness of the **financial statements and disclosures**.

g. **Penalties** for destroying documents to impede an investigation have been expanded.

h. Management must **assess the effectiveness of internal control** and issue a report on its effectiveness.

i. The auditor must **audit internal control** and express an opinion on its effectiveness.

6. **The PCAOB**

   a. According to AS 1220, *Engagement Quality Review*, an **engagement quality review (EQR)** and concurring approval of issuance are required for each audit of an issuer.

   b. The **objective** of the **reviewer** is to evaluate the significant judgments made and the related conclusions reached.

   c. The reviewer must be an associated person of a registered public accounting firm. The reviewer may be from outside the firm.

      1) The reviewer must have the competence to serve as a partner on the engagement.

      2) The reviewer also must have independence, integrity, and objectivity.

      3) But an engagement partner on either of the two preceding audits ordinarily may not be the reviewer.

   d. The EQR process in an audit evaluates the **significant judgments** made.

      1) This involves discussions with the engagement partner and other team members and reviewing whether the documentation supports the conclusions reached and appropriate responses to significant risks.

   e. The reviewer should evaluate the following:

      1) Significant judgments about planning matters

      2) The assessment of, and responses to, significant risks, including those identified by the reviewer

      3) Corrected and uncorrected identified misstatements and control deficiencies

      4) The audit firm's independence

      5) The engagement completion document and whether unresolved matters are significant

      6) The statements, the internal control report, and the audit report

      7) Other information filed with the SEC

      8) Whether consultations have addressed difficult matters

      9) Whether matters have been communicated to the audit committee, management, and other parties

   f. In an audit, the reviewer may provide **concurring approval of issuance**, and the client may use the report, only if the reviewer is not aware of a significant engagement deficiency.

Stop and review! You have completed the outline for this subunit. Study multiple-choice questions 14 through 20 beginning on page 27.

QUESTIONS

1.1 Attest Engagements

1. Which of the following is a conceptual difference between the attestation standards and generally accepted auditing standards?

   A. The attestation standards provide a framework for the attest function beyond historical financial statements.

   B. The requirement that the practitioner be independent in mental attitude is omitted from the attestation standards.

   C. The attestation standards do not permit an attest engagement to be part of a business acquisition study or a feasibility study.

   D. None of the standards of field work in generally accepted auditing standards are included in the attestation standards.

Answer (A) is correct.
   REQUIRED: The conceptual difference between the attestation standards and GAAS.
   DISCUSSION: Two principal conceptual differences exist between the attestation standards and GAAS. First, the attestation standards provide a framework for the attest function beyond historical financial statements. Second, the attestation standards accommodate the growing number of attest services in which the practitioner expresses assurance below the level that is expressed for the traditional audit (an opinion).
   Answer (B) is incorrect. In any attest engagement, the practitioner must be independent in mental attitude. Answer (C) is incorrect. Attestation services may be provided in conjunction with other services provided to clients. Answer (D) is incorrect. The attestation standards and GAAS require that work be adequately planned and that assistants be properly supervised. Both also require sufficient evidence.

2. Which of the following is **not** an attestation standard?

   A. Sufficient evidence shall be obtained to provide a reasonable basis for the conclusion that is expressed in the report.

   B. The report shall identify the subject matter or the assertion being reported on and state the character of the engagement.

   C. The work shall be adequately planned and assistants, if any, shall be properly supervised.

   D. A sufficient understanding of internal control shall be obtained to plan the engagement.

Answer (D) is correct.
   REQUIRED: The item not an attestation standard.
   DISCUSSION: No attestation standard mentions internal control. However, the audit standards state, "The auditor should obtain an understanding of internal control relevant to the audit" (AU-C 315).
   Answer (A) is incorrect. The evidentiary requirement is contained in the second attestation standard of field work. Answer (B) is incorrect. The first attestation standard of reporting concerns the character of the engagement. Answer (C) is incorrect. The first attestation standard of field work concerns planning and supervision.

3. In performing an attest engagement, a CPA typically

   A. Supplies litigation support services.

   B. Assesses the risks of material misstatement.

   C. Expresses a conclusion about a written assertion.

   D. Provides management consulting advice.

Answer (C) is correct.
   REQUIRED: The CPA's usual task in an attestation engagement.
   DISCUSSION: When a CPA in the practice of public accounting performs an attest engagement, the engagement is subject to the attestation standards. An attest engagement is one in which a practitioner is engaged to issue or does issue an examination, a review, or an agreed-upon procedures report on subject matter, or an assertion about the subject matter, that is the responsibility of another party. Moreover, according to the second attestation standard of reporting, the report shall state the practitioner's conclusion about the subject matter or the assertion in relation to the criteria against which the subject matter was evaluated. However, the conclusion may refer to that assertion or to the subject matter to which the assertion relates. Furthermore, given one or more material deviations from the criteria, the practitioner should modify the report and ordinarily should express the conclusion directly on the subject matter.
   Answer (A) is incorrect. Litigation support services are consulting services. Answer (B) is incorrect. The CPA assesses the risks of material misstatement in an audit but not necessarily in all attest engagements. Furthermore, the assessment may not be at a low level. Answer (D) is incorrect. An attest engagement results in a report on subject matter or on an assertion about the subject matter.

1.2 Overall Objectives and Conducting an Audit

4. Which of the following statements is true concerning an auditor's responsibilities regarding financial statements?

A. Making suggestions that are adopted about the form and content of an entity's financial statements impairs an auditor's independence.

B. An auditor may draft an entity's financial statements based on information from management's accounting system.

C. The fair presentation of audited financial statements in conformity with GAAP is an implicit part of the auditor's responsibilities.

D. An auditor's responsibilities for audited financial statements are not confined to the expression of the auditor's opinion.

Answer (B) is correct.
    REQUIRED: The true statement about the auditor's responsibilities for financial statements.
    DISCUSSION: The independent auditor may make suggestions about the form or content of the financial statements or draft them, in whole or in part, based on information from management's accounting system. However, the auditor's responsibility for the financial statements (s)he has audited is confined to the expression of his or her opinion on them.
    Answer (A) is incorrect. Suggestions about the form and content of an entity's financial statements do not impair an auditor's independence as long as management takes responsibility for the financial statements. Answer (C) is incorrect. The presentation of the financial statements in conformity with GAAP is the responsibility of management. Answer (D) is incorrect. The auditor's responsibilities for audited financial statements are confined to the expression of the opinion.

5. When a PCAOB auditing standard indicates that an auditor "could" perform a specific procedure, how should the auditor decide whether and how to perform the procedure?

A. By comparing the PCAOB standard with related AICPA auditing standards.

B. By exercising professional judgment in the circumstances.

C. By soliciting input from the issuer's audit committee.

D. By evaluating whether the audit is likely to be subject to inspection by the PCAOB.

Answer (B) is correct.
    REQUIRED: The means of deciding whether to perform an audit procedure when a PCAOB standard indicates it "could" be performed.
    DISCUSSION: Words such as "must" and "should" indicate unconditional responsibilities and presumptively mandatory responsibilities, respectively. Words such as "might" and "could" indicate that the auditor has a responsibility to consider a matter. Thus, (s)he is expected to use professional judgment.
    Answer (A) is incorrect. PCAOB standards apply to audits of issuers, and AICPA standards apply to audits of nonissuers. Answer (C) is incorrect. The auditee should not influence what audit procedures are performed. Answer (D) is incorrect. Whether the audit is likely to be subject to inspection by the PCAOB is irrelevant to the choice of a procedure. The decision should be made on the basis of the facts and circumstances.

1.3 Additional Professional Services

6. North Co., a nonissuer, asked its tax accountant, King, a CPA in public practice, to generate North's interim financial statements on King's personal computer when King prepared North's quarterly tax return. King should not submit these financial statements to North unless, as a minimum, King complies with the provisions of

A. Statements on Standards for Accounting and Review Services.

B. Statements on Standards for Unaudited Financial Services.

C. Statements on Standards for Consulting Services.

D. Statements on Standards for Attestation Engagements.

Answer (A) is correct.
    REQUIRED: The standards appropriate for an accountant who generates interim financial statements.
    DISCUSSION: The Statements on Standards for Accounting and Review Services apply to compilations and reviews performed by practitioners. The AICPA bylaws designate the Accounting and Review Services Committee as the senior technical committee authorized to issue pronouncements in connection with the unaudited financial statements or other unaudited financial information of a nonissuer.
    Answer (B) is incorrect. These standards do not exist. Answer (C) is incorrect. The practitioner is providing compilation services, not consulting services. Answer (D) is incorrect. Statements on Standards for Attestation Engagements are appropriate whenever the practitioner is engaged in providing attestation services. A compilation, however, provides no assurance.

7. Which of the following components is appropriate in a practitioner's report on the results of applying agreed-upon procedures?

    A. A list of the procedures performed, as agreed to by the specified parties identified in the report.

    B. A statement that management is responsible for expressing an opinion.

    C. A title that includes the phrase "independent audit."

    D. A statement that the report is unrestricted in its use.

Answer (A) is correct.

    REQUIRED: The component appropriate for an agreed-upon procedures report.

    DISCUSSION: In an agreed-upon procedures engagement, the practitioner is engaged to report on the results of performing specific procedures agreed upon with specified parties. The report lists the procedures performed and provides the results of those procedures but provides no form of positive or negative assurance.

    Answer (B) is incorrect. No opinion is expressed in an agreed-upon procedures report. Answer (C) is incorrect. The report does not refer to an audit. Answer (D) is incorrect. An agreed-upon procedures report should have a statement restricting its use to the specified parties who agreed upon the procedures to be performed.

8. The party responsible for assumptions identified in the preparation of prospective financial statements is usually

    A. A third-party lending institution.

    B. The client's management.

    C. The reporting accountant.

    D. The client's independent auditor.

Answer (B) is correct.

    REQUIRED: The party usually responsible for assumptions identified in the preparation of PFSs.

    DISCUSSION: Management is usually the responsible party, that is, the person(s) responsible for the assumptions underlying PFSs. However, the responsible party may be a party outside the entity, such as a possible acquirer.

9. A financial forecast consists of prospective financial statements that present an entity's expected financial position, results of operations, and cash flows. A forecast

    A. Is based on the most conservative estimates.

    B. Presents estimates given one or more hypothetical assumptions.

    C. Unlike a projection, may contain a range.

    D. Is based on assumptions reflecting conditions expected to exist and courses of action expected to be taken.

Answer (D) is correct.

    REQUIRED: The true statement about a financial forecast.

    DISCUSSION: According to AT 301, a financial forecast consists of prospective financial statements "that present, to the best of the responsible party's knowledge and belief, an entity's expected financial position, results of operations, and cash flows." A forecast is based on "the responsible party's assumptions reflecting conditions it expects to exist and the course of action it expects to take."

    Answer (A) is incorrect. The information presented is based on expected (most likely) conditions and courses of action rather than the most conservative estimate. Answer (B) is incorrect. A financial projection (not a forecast) is based on assumptions by the responsible party reflecting expected conditions and courses of action, given one or more hypothetical assumptions (a condition or action not necessarily expected to occur). Answer (C) is incorrect. Both forecasts and projections may be stated either in point estimates or ranges.

1.4 Assurance Services

10. Assurance services are best described as

    A. Services designed for the improvement of operations, resulting in better outcomes.

    B. Independent professional services that improve the quality of information, or its context, for decision makers.

    C. The assembly of financial statements based on information and assumptions of a responsible party.

    D. Services designed to express an opinion on historical financial statements based on the results of an audit.

Answer (B) is correct.

    REQUIRED: The description of assurance services.

    DISCUSSION: The AICPA defines assurance services as "independent professional services that improve the quality of information, or its context, for decision makers." Assurance services encompass audit and other attestation services but also include nonstandard services. Assurance services do not encompass consulting services.

    Answer (A) is incorrect. Consulting services are services designed for the improvement of operations, resulting in better outcomes. Answer (C) is incorrect. Compilation services are the assembly of financial statements based on information and assumptions of a responsible party. Answer (D) is incorrect. The traditional audit consists of services designed to express an opinion on historical financial statements based on the results of an audit.

11. Assurance services differ from consulting services in that they

	Focus on Providing Advice	Involve Monitoring of One Party by Another
A.	Yes	Yes
B.	Yes	No
C.	No	Yes
D.	No	No

Answer (C) is correct.

REQUIRED: The way(s) in which assurance services differ from consulting services.

DISCUSSION: Assurance services encompass attestation services but not consulting services. Assurance services differ from consulting services in two ways: (1) They focus on improving information rather than providing advice, and (2) they usually involve situations in which one party wants to monitor another rather than the two-party arrangements common in consulting engagements.

12. SysTrust is an assurance service designed to

A. Increase the comfort of management and other stakeholders relative to an information system.

B. Provide an opinion on the fairness of an information system's output.

C. Provide the SEC with information used to administer the securities laws.

D. Allow a CPA to provide a consulting service to management relating to their information system.

Answer (A) is correct.

REQUIRED: The purpose of SysTrust.

DISCUSSION: The objective of SysTrust is an attestation report on management's assertion about the reliability of an information system that supports a business or a given activity. The CPA also may report directly on the reliability of the system. This assurance service is designed to increase the stakeholders' comfort relative to the system's satisfaction of the SysTrust principles: online privacy, security, processing integrity, availability, and confidentiality. The practitioner may provide assurance about any or all of these principles.

Answer (B) is incorrect. SysTrust does not directly address the output of a system. Answer (C) is incorrect. The report is not specifically designed for any one user. Answer (D) is incorrect. Assurance services are not classified as consulting services.

13. An entity engaged a CPA to determine whether the client's web sites comply with defined WebTrust principles and criteria. In performing this engagement, the CPA should apply the provisions of

A. Statements on Assurance Standards.

B. Statements on Standards for Attestation Engagements.

C. Statements on Standards for Management Consulting Services.

D. Statements on Auditing Standards.

Answer (B) is correct.

REQUIRED: The pronouncements that apply to WebTrust.

DISCUSSION: An attest engagement involves reporting on subject matter, or an assurance about subject matter, that is the responsibility of another party. When providing WebTrust assurance, the accountant must address written assertions by management. Thus, Statements on Standards for Attestation Engagements are applicable.

Answer (A) is incorrect. The AICPA has not issued specific Statements on Assurance Standards. Answer (C) is incorrect. WebTrust is not considered a management consulting service. Answer (D) is incorrect. Statements on Auditing Standards are applicable to audits of financial statements.

1.5 Quality Control

14. The purpose of establishing quality control policies and procedures for deciding whether to accept or continue a client relationship is to

A. Monitor the risk factors concerning misstatements arising from the misappropriation of assets.

B. Provide reasonable assurance that personnel are adequately trained to fulfill their responsibilities.

C. Minimize the likelihood of associating with clients whose management lacks integrity.

D. Document objective criteria for the CPA firm's responses to peer review comments.

Answer (C) is correct.

REQUIRED: The purpose of policies and procedures for accepting or continuing clients.

DISCUSSION: The procedures pertaining to client acceptance or continuation should provide reasonable assurance that the likelihood of association with a client whose management lacks integrity is minimized. They include consideration of the business reputation of the client's principal owners, key management, related parties, and those charged with governance.

Answer (A) is incorrect. The engagement performance element of quality control should monitor the risk factors concerning misstatements arising from the misappropriation of assets. Answer (B) is incorrect. The human resources element of quality control should provide reasonable assurance that personnel will be adequately trained to fulfill their responsibilities. Answer (D) is incorrect. Documenting objective criteria for the CPA firm's responses to peer review comments is not an objective for establishing quality control policies or procedures. However, it is a result of the monitoring aspect of a quality control system.

15. Which of the following is an element of a CPA firm's quality control system that should be considered in establishing its quality control policies and procedures?

A. Complying with laws and regulations.

B. Using statistical sampling techniques.

C. Managing human resources.

D. Considering audit risk and materiality.

Answer (C) is correct.
　REQUIRED: The element of quality control.
　DISCUSSION: The quality control element of human resources requires establishment of policies and procedures to provide reasonable assurance that only qualified persons with the required technical training and proficiency perform the work.
　Answer (A) is incorrect. The auditor considers compliance with laws and regulations. However, this consideration is not an element of quality control. Answer (B) is incorrect. An auditing firm may use statistical or nonstatistical sampling techniques in performing audits; a particular sampling technique is not an element of quality control. Answer (D) is incorrect. An auditor must consider audit risk and materiality in performing the audit, but this consideration is not an element of quality control.

16. Which of the following are elements of a CPA firm's quality control that should be considered in establishing its quality control policies and procedures?

	Human Resources	Monitoring	Engagement Performance
A.	Yes	Yes	No
B.	Yes	Yes	Yes
C.	No	Yes	Yes
D.	Yes	No	Yes

Answer (B) is correct.
　REQUIRED: The elements that should be considered in establishing quality control policies and procedures.
　DISCUSSION: The quality control element of human resources relates to providing reasonable assurance that the firm has sufficient personnel with the necessary capabilities, competence, and commitment to ethics. The quality control element of monitoring relates to providing reasonable assurance that the firm has a quality control system that is relevant, adequate, effective, and complied with. The quality control element of engagement performance relates to providing reasonable assurance that (1) engagements are consistently performed in accordance with applicable requirements and (2) issued reports are appropriate (QC 10).

17. A CPA firm should establish procedures for conducting and supervising work at all organizational levels to provide reasonable assurance that the work performed meets the firm's standards of quality. To achieve this goal, the firm most likely would establish procedures for

A. Evaluating prospective and continuing client relationships.

B. Reviewing documentation of the work performed and reports issued.

C. Requiring personnel to adhere to the applicable independence rules.

D. Maintaining personnel files containing documentation related to the evaluation of personnel.

Answer (B) is correct.
　REQUIRED: The procedure necessary to provide reasonable assurance that the work performed meets the firm's standards of quality relating to supervision.
　DISCUSSION: The engagement performance element of quality control includes policies and procedures that cover planning, performing, supervising, reviewing, documenting, and communicating the results of each engagement. Objectives of supervision include establishing procedures for (1) planning engagements, (2) maintaining the firm's standards of quality, and (3) reviewing documentation of the work performed and reports issued.
　Answer (A) is incorrect. Evaluating client relationships relates to the quality control element of acceptance and continuance of client relationships and specific engagements. Answer (C) is incorrect. Requiring adherence to independence rules relates to the quality control element of relevant ethical requirements. Answer (D) is incorrect. Evaluation of personnel relates to the quality control element of human resources.

18. All of the following are audit quality control requirements contained in the Sarbanes-Oxley Act of 2002 **except**

A. The lead audit partner must rotate off the audit every 5 years.

B. The audit report must be submitted to the Public Company Accounting Oversight Board prior to issuance.

C. The audit report must be reviewed and approved by a second partner.

D. The Public Company Accounting Oversight Board will periodically inspect registered CPA firms.

Answer (B) is correct.
　REQUIRED: The quality control issue not addressed in the Sarbanes-Oxley Act.
　DISCUSSION: Audit reports must be determined appropriate for issuance by the CPA firm but need not be approved by the PCAOB.

19. The nature and extent of a CPA firm's quality control policies and procedures depend on

	The CPA Firm's Size	The Nature of the CPA Firm's Practice	Cost-Benefit Considerations
A.	Yes	Yes	Yes
B.	Yes	Yes	No
C.	Yes	No	Yes
D.	No	Yes	Yes

Answer (A) is correct.
   REQUIRED: The factors affecting a CPA firm's quality control policies and procedures.
   DISCUSSION: The nature and extent of a firm's quality control policies and procedures depend on a number of factors, such as the firm's size, the degree of operating autonomy allowed, its human resources policies, the nature of its practice and organization, and appropriate cost-benefit considerations.

20. According to PCAOB quality control standards applying to an audit, the engagement quality reviewer evaluates

A. The documentation.

B. Only the uncorrected misstatements.

C. The audit report but not the internal control report.

D. Only the assessment of risks identified by management.

Answer (A) is correct.
   REQUIRED: The subject matter evaluated by the engagement quality reviewer (EQR).
   DISCUSSION: The EQR process in an audit evaluates the significant judgments made. This involves discussions with the engagement partner and other team members and reviewing whether the documentation supports the conclusions reached and appropriate responses to significant risks.
   Answer (B) is incorrect. The reviewer evaluates corrected and uncorrected identified misstatements and control deficiencies. Answer (C) is incorrect. The reviewer evaluates the statements, the internal control report, and the audit report. Answer (D) is incorrect. The reviewer evaluates the assessment of, and responses to, significant risks, including those identified by the reviewer.

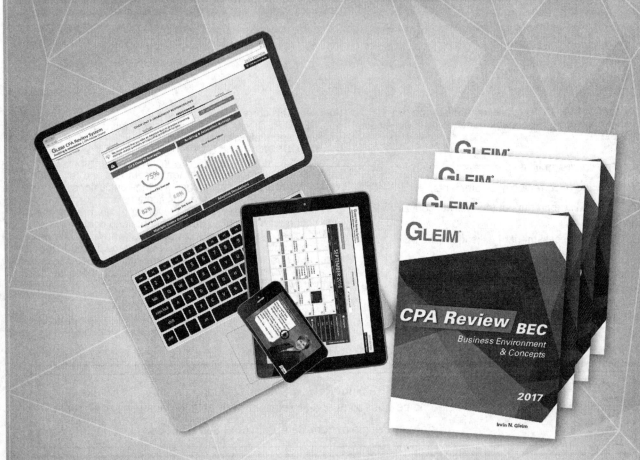

STUDY UNIT TWO
PROFESSIONAL RESPONSIBILITIES

(27 pages of outline)

The AICPA *Code of Professional Conduct* governs the performance of professional responsibilities by members of the American Institute of Certified Public Accountants (AICPA). Furthermore, accountants need to understand governmental ethical standards [e.g., *Government Auditing Standards* issued by the Government Accountability Office (GAO)] and other professional responsibilities established by the Sarbanes-Oxley Act, the PCAOB, the SEC, and the Department of Labor.

The AICPA *Code of Professional Conduct* has been reorganized, codified, and put online with new features to facilitate research. The following are the main elements of the revised *Code*:

- The **Preface** contains (1) an explanation of the structure and application of the *Code*, (2) the Principles of Professional Conduct, and (3) Definitions.
- **Part 1** contains the (1) Conceptual Framework, (2) Rules of Conduct, and (3) interpretations applying to **members in public practice**.
- **Part 2** contains the (1) Conceptual Framework, (2) Rules of Conduct, and (3) interpretations applying to **members in business**.
- **Part 3** contains the Acts Discreditable Rule and its interpretations applying to **other members** (those not in public practice or in business).

Of all ethical responsibilities, independence is the most challenging. Accordingly, it is the subject of more AICPA pronouncements than any other. That emphasis is reflected in this study unit. The need to ensure the independence of those who perform attest engagements is essential. If the accountant is not viewed as independent, an attest service has no value to the user. Thus, independence is the basis for auditing and other attestation services.

2.1 CODE OF PROFESSIONAL CONDUCT

1. **Principles and Rules**

    a. The *Code* consists of Principles, Rules of Conduct, interpretations, and other pronouncements. It guides all AICPA members in the performance of their professional responsibilities.

    1) The Principles provide the framework for the Rules and recognize responsibilities to the public, clients, and colleagues.
    2) The AICPA's bylaws require members to follow the Rules.

b. The following are the Principles:

1) **Responsibilities.** All members should exercise sensitive professional and moral judgments when carrying out their professional responsibilities.

2) **The public interest.** All members should act to benefit the public interest, honor the public trust, and demonstrate commitment to professionalism.

    a) The AICPA adopted the ethical standards because a distinguishing mark of a profession is an acceptance of responsibility to the public. That public includes clients, credit grantors, investors, and others who rely on the integrity and objectivity of members to maintain the orderly functioning of commerce.

3) **Integrity.** All members should perform all professional responsibilities with the highest sense of integrity to maintain public confidence.

    a) Integrity requires a member to be honest and candid within the limits of client confidentiality.

4) **Objectivity and independence.** All members should maintain objectivity and be free of **conflicts of interest**. Objectivity is a state of mind that lends value to a member's services and is a distinguishing feature of the profession.

    a) Thus, a member must be impartial, intellectually honest, and free of conflicts of interest.

    b) A member in public practice should be independent in **fact** and **appearance** when providing attestation services.

    c) A member **not** in public practice need not be independent.

5) **Due care.** All members should (a) follow the profession's technical and ethical standards, (b) strive for improved competence and quality services, and (c) discharge professional responsibility to the best of the member's ability.

    a) All members must adequately plan and supervise any activity for which they are responsible.

6) **Scope and nature of services.** A member in public practice should follow the Principles of the *Code of Professional Conduct* in determining the nature and scope of services.

    a) This principle is for members in public practice only.

c. All of the following Rules of Conduct apply to members **in public practice**:

1) Integrity and Objectivity [1]
2) Independence
3) General Standards [1]
4) Compliance with Standards [1]
5) Accounting Principles [1]
6) Acts Discreditable [1][3]
7) Contingent Fees
8) Commissions and Referral Fees [2]
9) Advertising and Other Forms of Solicitation
10) Confidential Client Information
11) Form of Organization and Name

[1]These Rules also apply to members **in business**.

[2]This Rule also applies in part (referrals) to **all** members and in part (commissions) to members in public practice. **Public practice** is the performance of professional services for a client by a member or a member's firm. **Professional services** are all services requiring accounting and related skills that are performed (a) for a client, (b) for an employer, or (c) as a volunteer.

[3]This Rule also applies to **other** members (those not in public practice or in business).

    d.   **Interpretations** issued by the AICPA's Professional Ethics Executive Committee provide guidelines for the scope and application of the Rules but do not limit their scope or application.

        1)   Interpretations are enforceable because they guide implementation of the Rules.

        2)   A member who departs from an interpretation must justify such action in any disciplinary hearing.

2.   **Conceptual framework for members in public practice.** This section of the *Code* (Part 1) should be consulted by members in public practice whether or not they are in business. This conceptual framework is applied when a member is confronted with a professional responsibility issue for which no specific rule governs.

    a.   **Steps in the Conceptual Framework**

        1)   **Identify threats.** Threats are relationships or circumstances that a member encounters in various engagements and work assignments that may compromise compliance with the rules.

        2)   **Evaluate the significance of a threat.** In evaluating the significance of an identified threat, the member should determine whether a threat is at an acceptable level. A threat is at an acceptable level when a reasonable and informed third party who is aware of the relevant information would be expected to conclude that the threat would not compromise the member's compliance with the rules.

        3)   **Identify and apply safeguards.** If, in evaluating the significance of an identified threat, the member concludes that the threat is not at an acceptable level, (s)he should apply safeguards to eliminate the threat or reduce it to an acceptable level.

    b.   **Types of Threats**

        1)   **Adverse interest threat.** A member may not act with objectivity because his or her interests are opposed to the client's interests. Examples:

           a)   The client has expressed an intention to commence litigation against the member.

           b)   A client or officer, director, or significant shareholder of the client participates in litigation against the member's firm.

           c)   A subrogee (e.g., an insurer) asserts a claim against the member's firm for recovery of insurance payments made to the client.

           d)   A class action lawsuit is filed against the client and its officers and directors as well as the firm and its professional accountants.

        2)   **Advocacy threat.** A member may promote a client's interests or position to the extent that his or her objectivity or independence is compromised. Examples:

           a)   A member provides forensic accounting services to a client in litigation or a dispute with third parties.

           b)   A firm acts as an investment adviser for an officer, a director, or a 10% shareholder of a client.

           c)   A firm underwrites or promotes a client's shares.

           d)   A firm acts as a registered agent for a client.

           e)   A member endorses a client's services or products.

        3)   **Familiarity threat.** Due to a long or close relationship with a client, a member may become too sympathetic to the client's interests or too accepting of the client's work or product. Examples:

           a)   A member's immediate family or close relative is employed by the client.

           b)   A member's close friend is employed by the client.

      c)   A former partner or professional employee joins the client in a key position and has knowledge of the firm's policies and practices for the professional services engagement.

      d)   Senior personnel have a long association with a client.

      e)   A member has a significant close business relationship with an officer, a director, or a 10% shareholder of a client.

4)   **Management participation threat.** A member may take on the role of client management or otherwise assume management responsibilities, e.g., during an engagement to provide nonattest services.

5)   **Self-interest threat.** A member may benefit, financially or otherwise, from an interest in, or relationship with, a client or persons associated with the client. Examples:

      a)   A member has a financial interest in a client and the outcome of a professional services engagement may affect the fair value of that financial interest.

      b)   The spouse of a member enters into employment negotiations with the client.

      c)   A firm enters into a contingent fee arrangement for a tax refund claim that is not a predetermined fee.

      d)   Excessive reliance on revenue from a single client exists.

6)   **Self-review threat.** A member may not appropriately evaluate the results of a (a) previous judgment made or (b) service performed or supervised by the member or an individual in the member's firm. The threat is that the member then may rely on that service in forming a judgment as part of another service. Examples:

      a)   A member relies on the work product of the member's firm.

      b)   A member performs bookkeeping services for a client.

      c)   A partner in a member's office was associated with the client as an employee, an officer, a director, or a contractor.

7)   **Undue influence threat.** A member may subordinate his or her judgment to an individual associated with a client or any relevant third party due to that individual's (a) reputation or expertise, (b) aggressive or dominant personality, or (c) attempts to coerce or exercise excessive influence over the member. Examples:

      a)   A firm is threatened with dismissal from a client engagement.

      b)   A client indicates that it will not award additional engagements to a firm if the firm continues to disagree with the client on an accounting or tax matter.

      c)   An individual associated with a client or any relevant third party threatens to withdraw or terminate a professional service unless the member reaches certain judgments or conclusions.

c.   **Type of safeguards.** Safeguards may partially or completely eliminate a threat or diminish the potential influence of a threat. The following are the broad categories of safeguards:

1)   **Safeguards created by the profession, legislation, or regulation.** Examples:

      a)   Education and training requirements on independence and ethics rules

      b)   External review of a firm's quality control system

      c)   Legislation establishing prohibitions and requirements for a firm or a firm's professional employees

      d)   Professional resources, such as hotlines, for consultation on ethical issues

2) **Safeguards implemented by the client.** (However, it is not possible to rely solely on safeguards implemented by the client to eliminate or reduce significant threats to an acceptable level.) Examples:

    a) The tone at the top emphasizes the client's commitment to fair financial reporting and compliance.

    b) Policies and procedures are in place to (1) address ethical conduct or (2) achieve fair financial reporting and compliance with the applicable laws, rules, regulations, and corporate governance policies.

    c) A governance structure, such as an active audit committee, is in place to ensure appropriate decision making.

3) **Safeguards implemented by the CPA firm.** These include policies and procedures implemented to follow professional and regulatory requirements. Examples:

    a) Firm leadership stressing the importance of complying with the rules and the expectation that engagement teams will act in the public interest

    b) Policies and procedures designed to implement and monitor engagement quality control or promote appropriate professional conduct

    c) Someone from senior management designated as the person responsible for overseeing the firm's quality control system and ensuring it is functioning adequately

    d) A disciplinary mechanism designed to promote compliance with policies and procedures

3. **Conceptual framework for members in business.** This section of the *Code* (Part 2) should be consulted by members in business whether or not they are in public practice.

    a. The **conceptual framework** for members in business is similar to that for members in public practice.

        1) **Identify threats.** Members may encounter various relationships or circumstances that create threats to the member's compliance with the Rules of Conduct.

        2) **Evaluate the significance of a threat.** In evaluating the significance of an identified threat, the member should determine whether a threat is at an acceptable level. Many threats fall into the same broad categories as those for members in public practice except for "**management participation threats**."

        3) **Identify and apply safeguards.** If, in evaluating the significance of an identified threat, the member concludes that the threat is not at an acceptable level, the member should apply safeguards to eliminate the threat or reduce it to an acceptable level.

    b. **Types of safeguards.** Safeguards may partially or completely eliminate a threat or diminish the potential influence of a threat. Two broad categories include

        1) **Safeguards created by the profession, legislation, or regulation.** Examples:

            a) Education and training requirements for ethics and professional responsibilities

            b) Legislation establishing prohibitions and requirements for entities and employees

            c) Competency and experience requirements for professional licensure

        2) **Safeguards implemented by the employing organization.** Examples:

            a) A tone at the top emphasizing a commitment to fair financial reporting and compliance with applicable laws, rules, regulations, and corporate governance policies

    b)   Policies and procedures addressing ethical conduct and compliance with applicable laws, rules, and regulations

    c)   Human resource policies and procedures safeguarding against discrimination or harassment, such as those related to a worker's religion, sexual orientation, gender, or disability

    d)   Policies and procedures for implementing and monitoring ethical policies

Stop and review! You have completed the outline for this subunit. Study multiple-choice questions 1 and 2 on page 58.

2.2 INDEPENDENCE

1.   **Independence Rule**

    a.   A member in public practice must be independent when performing professional services as required by standards issued by bodies designated by the AICPA Council.

        1)   These bodies include, among others, the AICPA, the Securities and Exchange Commission (SEC), the Public Company Accounting Oversight Board (PCAOB), and the GAO.

    b.   To inspire public confidence, an auditor must be not only independent (intellectually honest) but also recognized as independent (free of any obligation to, or interest in, the client, management, or owners). As defined by the professional ethics executive committee, a member must have independence of mind and independence in appearance.

        1)   **Independence of mind** (fact) "permits a member to perform an attest service without being affected by influences that compromise professional judgment, thereby allowing an individual to act with integrity and exercise objectivity and professional skepticism."

        2)   **Independence in appearance** is the "avoidance of circumstances that would cause a reasonable and informed third party who has knowledge of all relevant information, including the safeguards applied, to reasonably conclude that the integrity, objectivity, or professional skepticism of a firm or a member of the attest engagement team is compromised."

        3)   A member should determine whether influences that might compromise professional judgment create a threat to either element of independence that is not at an acceptable level.

    c.   Independence is impaired if a covered member has certain interests or relationships. A **covered member** includes

        1)   An individual (a) on the attest engagement team or (b) who can influence the engagement;

        2)   A partner (or equivalent) or manager who provides more than 10 hours of nonattest services to a client;

        3)   A partner (or equivalent) in the office where the lead engagement partner primarily practices in relation to the engagement;

        4)   The accounting firm, including the firm's employee benefit plans; and

        5)   An entity whose policies can be controlled by the foregoing parties, alone or acting together.

 Some requirements of independence relate to members in general or identified parties while other requirements relate specifically to covered members. Be alert to this distinction as you study the material. In general, the definition of covered members includes those in a position to influence the attest engagement.

2. **Impairments of Independence**

    a. Independence **is impaired** if a covered member has any **direct financial interest** in an attest client during the period of the engagement.

CONCEPT

A financial interest is ownership in an equity or debt security issued by an entity, including an option or derivative. A financial interest is direct if it is based on direct ownership, control, or beneficial ownership through an intermediary (e.g., an estate, trust, or investment vehicle controlled by the beneficiary). The restriction includes the covered member's immediate family (spouse and dependents).

EXAMPLES

A covered member must not (1) own shares in a mutual fund that is an attest client, (2) participate in an employee benefit plan sponsored by an attest client, (3) own bonds issued by an attest client, or (4) own a prepaid (529) tuition plan administered by an attest client. Also, even if shares of a client are held in a blind trust for the covered member, independence is impaired if the member has various rights, e.g., the power to amend or revoke the trust or to control the trust.

An unsolicited financial interest in a client, such as through a gift or inheritance, does not impair independence if disposed of within 30 days.

---

    b. Independence **is impaired** if a covered member has **loans to or from** an attest client or its officers, directors, or 10% (or greater) owners during the period of the engagement (with certain exceptions).

        1) Independence is **not impaired** by

            a) Certain loans from a client financial institution (e.g., bank). These include (1) auto loans and leases collateralized by the auto, (2) loans fully collateralized by the cash surrender value of insurance cash deposits, and (3) credit cards with a total outstanding balance of $10,000 or less on a current basis by the payment due date.

            b) Certain loans that are considered "grandfathered" because they were in existence before independence rules became more restrictive.

CONCEPT

Loans are considered a direct financial interest. The restriction on loans includes the covered member's immediate family (spouse and dependents).

EXAMPLE

A covered member must not borrow money from an attest client.

---

    c. Independence **is impaired** if a covered member has a **material indirect financial interest** in an attest client during the period of the engagement.

CONCEPT

A covered member (and his or her immediate family) may have some limited financial interests in clients as long as they are (1) not direct and (2) not material to the wealth of the member or the client.

EXAMPLE

A covered member or spouse may own shares in a mutual fund that holds shares of a client if the mutual fund investment is not material to the member. Ownership of 5% or less of the shares of a diversified mutual fund indicates an immaterial, indirect financial interest in the underlying investments of the mutual fund.

d.   In certain circumstances, independence **may be impaired** if a covered member is a **trustee** of a trust or **executor** of an estate that has a direct or material indirect financial interest in an attest client during the period of the engagement.

CONCEPT

A covered member must not be in a **position to make decisions** related to a trust or an estate that involves investments or other financial interests in clients.

EXAMPLE

Independence **is impaired** if (1) the member can make investment decisions for the trust or estate, (2) the trust or estate holds more than 10% of the ownership interests of a client, or (3) the value of the holding exceeds 10% of the total assets of the trust or estate.

e.   Independence **is impaired** if a covered member has a **material joint, closely held investment** with an attest client during the period of the engagement.

CONCEPT

A joint, closely held investment is an investment in property or an entity by a member and a client (or an officer, director, or owner who has significant influence over the client) that gives them control of the property or entity.

EXAMPLES

A covered member must not join with a client to develop and market a product. A covered member also must not own a vacation home jointly with a key officer or principal shareholder of a client.

f.   Independence **is impaired** if a firm partner or professional employee **owns more than 5% of an attest client** during the period of the engagement.

CONCEPT

Some members of a CPA firm, other than covered members, may have certain financial interests in clients without affecting the independence of the firm.

EXAMPLES

- A professional employee in the office that conducts an audit, who is not part of the engagement team, may own a 5% or less equity interest in a client of the firm.
- However, a partner in that office must not. (S)he is considered a covered member and must have no financial interest in the client.

g.   **Simultaneous employment or association** with an attest client of a partner or professional employee of the member's firm **impairs independence** if the service is (1) as an employee, director, officer, member of management, etc., and (2) during the period of the financial statements or the engagement.

CONCEPT

The partner or professional employee must not appear to be acting in the capacity of management or employee of the client. This status includes having the responsibility to perform any duties of employees or management.

EXAMPLE

During the period of the professional engagement, a professional employee of a firm served as campaign treasurer of a candidate for mayor of a city. If the campaign organization is an attest client, independence is impaired. But independence is not impaired if the attest client is the city or the candidate's party.

h. Independence **may be impaired** if a covered member was **formerly employed or associated** with an attest client as an officer, director, promoter, underwriter, etc.

CONCEPT

The covered member must disassociate from the client before becoming a covered member. (S)he also must not (1) participate on the engagement team or (2) be able to influence the engagement when his or her former employment or association overlaps the period of the engagement.

EXAMPLE

A member must dispose of direct or material indirect financial interests and cease to participate in most employee benefit plans before becoming a covered member.

---

i. The covered member's **immediate family** (spouse or dependents) is subject to the Independence Rule and its interpretations (with certain exceptions).

CONCEPT

The financial interests, employment relationships, and other circumstances of immediate family members are attributed to the covered member.

EXAMPLES

An immediate family member may be employed by the attest client in a nonkey position. As a result of such permitted employment, the immediate family member may participate in various employee benefit plans under limited circumstances. Thus, the immediate family member must not, among other things, (1) participate on the engagement team or be able to influence the engagement or (2) be involved in investment decisions.

---

j. Independence **is impaired** if an individual participating on the engagement team (or able to exert influence or that is a partner or equivalent in the lead partner's office) has a **close relative** (sibling, parent, or nondependent child) who holds **a key position** with, or certain financial interests in, an attest client.

CONCEPT

If a close relative has a financial interest in an attest client that (1) the individual knows or has reason to believe is material to the relative or (2) permits the relative to exert significant influence over the client, independence is impaired. Some latitude is permitted in the application of this rule based on the family relationship.

EXAMPLES

- A sibling may be a salesperson for an attest client but not the CFO or a director.
- A parent may be a production manager (nonkey position) but not the CEO or a director.

---

k. Independence of the firm **is impaired** if a former partner or professional employee of the firm is **subsequently employed or associated with** an attest client in a key position.

1) Independence is **not** impaired if the person is no longer associated or active with the CPA firm and any retirement compensation is fixed.

2) An accounting firm is not independent if a CEO, CFO, controller, or person in an equivalent position for an **issuer** was (a) employed by that firm and (b) participated in any capacity in the audit of that issuer during the year before the beginning of the audit.

CONCEPT

Third parties may believe that the person is in a position to influence the engagement.

EXAMPLE

A retired partner must not become a CFO of a client while performing consulting duties for the CPA firm or having retirement pay contingent on retaining the client.

I.   Independence of the firm **may be impaired** if certain **nonattest services** are performed for an attest client.

CONCEPT

The practitioner appears to be an advocate or a decision maker for the attest client when performing certain nonattest services. In these circumstances, (s)he is not independent.

---

1)   According to the **general requirements** for performing nonattest services, a member should not assume management responsibilities. Before performing nonattest services, the member should determine that the client has agreed to

   a)   Assume all such responsibilities,
   b)   Provide sufficient oversight of the services,
   c)   Evaluate the nonattest services for adequacy and results, and
   d)   Assume responsibility for the results.

2)   Activities that are **management responsibilities** and impair independence include the following:

   a)   Setting policies;
   b)   Hiring, terminating, or directing client employees (except when using them to provide assistance);
   c)   Authorizing or executing transactions, or otherwise having the authority to do so on behalf of the client;
   d)   Preparing source documents;
   e)   Having custody of assets;
   f)   Deciding which recommendations to implement or prioritize;
   g)   Reporting to those charged with governance on behalf of management;
   h)   Serving as a stock transfer escrow agent, registrar, or general counsel;
   i)   Accepting responsibility for the financial statements;
   j)   Accepting responsibility for a client's project;
   k)   Accepting responsibility for designing, implementing, or maintaining internal control; and
   l)   Performing ongoing evaluations of control as part of the client's monitoring activities.

EXAMPLE

During the period of the professional engagement, a professional employee of a firm engaged in the practice of public accounting served as campaign treasurer of a political candidate. If the campaign organization is a client, independence is impaired.

3) Independence **is impaired** by providing to attest clients the following services:

   a) Appraisal, valuation, or actuarial services if they involve a significant degree of uncertainty

   b) Expert witness services

   c) Management of the client's internal audit services

   d) Tax advocacy services

   e) Recruiting, hiring, terminating, or compensating employees

4) Independence is **not impaired** by providing to attest clients the following services:

   a) Business risk consulting.

   b) Corporate finance consulting. But independence is impaired if a member (1) commits the attest client to transactions (e.g., employee compensation or benefit arrangements); (2) consummates attest client transactions; (3) has custody of the attest client's securities; or (4) acts as a promoter, underwriter, broker-dealer, or guarantor of the attest client's securities.

   c) Tax preparation services.

   d) Advisory services, e.g., advice about management's decisions and strategies, interpreting financial statements and other analyses, and attending board meetings as a nonvoting advisor.

EXAMPLES

- Internal audit services must not be outsourced to the audit firm, but the audit firm may provide advice on how to improve the internal audit function.
- The auditor may prepare the client's tax return but must not testify as an advocate of the client in a tax case.

---

5) Independence is **not impaired** for attest engagements of nonissuers by providing bookkeeping, payroll processing, or other conventional recordkeeping functions. Examples are (a) preparing client financial statements based on information in a trial balance, (b) processing payroll for a client's signature based on client recordkeeping, and (c) assisting a client in drafting a stock-offering document or memorandum.

CONCEPT

The AICPA allows practitioners to perform these duties for nonissuers (typically small clients) if management functions are not performed. The PCAOB rules do not allow these services to be provided to issuers by their auditors. However, issuers are not likely to request these services. Issuers have their own recordkeeping functions.

EXAMPLE

An auditor of a nonissuer may record transactions into computer software and generate financial statements but must not provide those services for an issuer.

---

m. Independence **may be impaired** by **actual or threatened litigation** during the period of the engagement by either the covered member or the attest client.

   1) Independence is not impaired when the litigation issue is not related to the work product and is not material, for example, a dispute over billing.

   2) Independence is not necessarily impaired when shareholders or others bring a class action suit against both the client and the auditor.

CONCEPT

Legal action creates adverse interests between the parties involved. These interests can affect independence.

EXAMPLES

- The attest client may allege that the covered member was negligent, or the covered member may allege that the attest client's management committed fraud. In these circumstances, the interests of the attest client and the CPA are opposed, and independence is impaired.
- However, if a creditor or insurer files a suit that alleges reliance on the audited financial statements of an attest client, independence is not impaired.

---

n. Independence **may be impaired** if a partner or professional employee of a member's firm holds an **honorary directorship or trusteeship** of a not-for-profit organization during the period of the (1) engagement or (2) financial statements. But independence is **not impaired** if

1) The position is clearly honorary, and the individual cannot vote or participate in board or management decisions.
2) The individual is identified in a letterhead, etc., as an honorary director or trustee.

CONCEPT

CPAs may support charitable organizations without impairing independence. However, they must not have managerial responsibilities.

EXAMPLE

An auditor's name is placed on the letterhead as "Honorary Director" of a not-for-profit charity that is an attest client. If the relationship is purely honorary, the auditor is independent.

---

o. Financial interests in, and other relationships with, entities that are **affiliates** of a **financial statement attest client (client)** may impair independence. In general, members should apply the independence provisions of the *Code* to the client's affiliates. Affiliates may have many different relationships with the client. The following are affiliates of the client:

1) An entity that a client can control
2) An entity that controls the client if the client is material to the entity
3) An entity in which a client has a material direct financial interest that gives the client significant influence over the entity
4) An entity with significant influence over the client in the form of a material direct financial interest
5) A sister entity of a client if the sister entity and the client are material to the entity that controls both
6) A trustee deemed to control a trust client that is not an investment company
7) The sponsor of the plan if the client is a single-employer employee benefit plan
8) Any union or participating employer that has significant influence over a client that is a multiple or multiemployer employee benefit plan
9) An employee benefit plan sponsored by either a client or an entity controlled by the client
10) An investment advisor, general partner, or trustee of an investment company client (fund) who (a) has a material interest in the fund and (b) has significant influence or control over the fund

---

CONCEPT

Various member involvements with affiliates create an indirect interest in an attest client. Thus, some measure of materiality is considered as with other indirect interests. Significant mutual interests of a member and a financial statement attest client may cause an impairment of independence.

EXAMPLES

- A covered member may have a loan to or from an officer, director, or 10% or more owner of an affiliate of a financial statement attest client during the period of the engagement. But the covered member must not have reason to know of the individual's position with the affiliate. If the covered member has reason to know of the relationship, (s)he should evaluate the effect on independence.
- A covered member and a financial statement attest client have material investments in a startup entity. Independence is impaired.

---

p. **Alternative Practice Structures (APSs)**

1) Independence rules for an APS apply when the traditional CPA firm is closely aligned with another organization that performs other professional services.

2) In an APS, **direct superiors** of covered members are subject to the same independence rules as covered members.

3) In an APS, **indirect superiors** (including a spouse or dependents) should not have a material financial interest in an attest client of the firm that offers attest services. They also should not have significant influence over an attest client.

CONCEPT

Today's business environment has created many alternative practice structures for CPA firms. Regardless of the structure, relationships that create concern about the influence on the attest function are not permitted.

EXAMPLE

A CPA firm becomes a subsidiary of a non-CPA firm that provides nonattest services (tax, consulting, etc.). The owners and employees of the CPA firm become employees of a subsidiary and may offer nonattest services. The original owners create a **new CPA firm** to offer attest services within the structure. The relationship is represented by the following:

Figure 2-1

Majority ownership in the new firm must be held by CPAs. In this case, employees, offices, and equipment are leased from the parent, which also may provide various other services. The CPA firm and any leased or employed persons are potentially **covered members**. Any direct supervisors of activities of the new CPA firm are subject to the independence rules.

q.   **Unpaid fees** owed by an attest client to a covered member for professional services **may impair** independence.

CONCEPT

Unpaid fees may result in self-interest, undue influence, or advocacy threats to independence.

EXAMPLE

Independence is impaired if the unpaid fees relate to services performed more than 1 year prior to the date of the current-year report. But this guidance does not apply if the attest client is in bankruptcy.

---

r.   Accepting **gifts or entertainment** from an attest client during the period of the engagement **may impair** independence.

CONCEPT

Accepting a gift or entertainment may create undue influence or self-interest threats to independence.

EXAMPLES

- If a member's firm or a member of the engagement team (or someone who can influence the engagement) accepts a gift with a value clearly significant to the recipient, independence is impaired.
- A covered member's acceptance from an attest client of entertainment that is unreasonable in the circumstances impairs independence.
- Offering a gift or entertainment to an attest client during the period of the engagement that is unreasonable in the circumstances impairs independence. Whether the gift or entertainment is reasonable depends on such factors as its nature, the occasion, its cost or value, and whether it was directly associated with the conduct of business.

---

1)   Offering or accepting gifts or entertainment also may threaten compliance with the **Integrity and Objectivity Rule**.

Stop and review! You have completed the outline for this subunit. Study multiple-choice questions 3 through 6 beginning on page 58.

2.3 INTEGRITY AND OBJECTIVITY

1.   **Integrity and Objectivity Rule**

a.   A member must (1) maintain objectivity and integrity, (2) be free of conflicts of interest, (3) not knowingly misrepresent facts, and (4) not subordinate his or her judgment to others when performing professional services.

2.   **Knowing Misrepresentations of Financial Statements or Records**

a.   These include

1)   Knowingly making materially false and misleading entries in financial statements or records,

2)   Failing to correct materially false or misleading statements or records when the member has such authority, or

3)   Signing a document with materially false and misleading information.

3. **Conflicts of Interest**

    a. A conflict of interest may be permitted in certain circumstances if **disclosure** is made to, and **consent** is obtained from, the appropriate parties.

        1) However, an independence objection cannot be overcome by disclosure and consent.

EXAMPLES -- Possible Conflicts of Interest

- Performing litigation services for the plaintiff when the defendant is a client
- Representing two clients in the same matter at the same time who are in a legal dispute, e.g., a divorce or dissolution of a partnership
- Suggesting that a client invest in a business in which the member has an interest
- Providing tax or personal financial planning services to family members with conflicting interests
- Providing services to a seller and buyer in the same transaction

---

EXAMPLE

A member is a director of a fundraising organization that distributes funds to a local charity that is a client (with a significant relationship with the member). If the organization has managerial control of the charity, independence is impaired. But if (1) the organization has no managerial control, (2) the significant relationship is disclosed, and (3) consent is received from the appropriate parties; performance of services not requiring independence is allowed.

---

4. **Obligations to the Employer's External Accountant**

    a. A member in business must be candid and not knowingly misrepresent facts or fail to disclose material facts.

5. **Subordination of Member's Judgment**

    a. A member and his or her supervisor or any other person within the member's organization may have differences of opinion. These may relate to the application of (1) accounting principles, (2) auditing standards, (3) other relevant professional standards, or (4) laws or regulations. The result may be a threat to the member's integrity and objectivity.

    b. If the member concludes that the position taken by others is not in compliance but does not result in a material misrepresentation of fact or violation of laws or regulations, the threats are not considered significant. However, the member should discuss the matter with the supervisor and, if not resolved, with higher levels of management. If the matter is still not resolved, the member should consider

        1) Determining whether any additional reporting requirements exist,
        2) Consulting legal counsel, and
        3) Documenting his or her understanding of the issues and the nature of the discussions.

    c. If the member concludes that appropriate action was not taken and a material misrepresentation of fact or violation of laws or regulations exists, the member should consider ending his or her relationship with the member's organization and take appropriate steps to eliminate his or her exposure to subordination of judgment.

EXAMPLES -- Other Issues Related to Integrity and Objectivity

- A member is required to disclose the use of a third-party service provider when offering professional services to a client. If the client objects, the third-party service provider may not be used.
- A member in business must act with objectivity and integrity when providing educational services, such as teaching and research.
- A member should consider the risks to integrity and objectivity when providing services related to client advocacy.

Stop and review! You have completed the outline for this subunit. Study multiple-choice question 7 on page 59.

2.4 PROFESSIONAL STANDARDS

1. **General Standards Rule**

    a. A member shall comply with the general standards and interpretations issued by designated bodies (the PCAOB and relevant AICPA committees and boards). The following are the general standards:

        1) Undertake only those services that the member can reasonably expect to complete with **professional competence.**

        2) Exercise **due professional care** when performing professional services.

        3) Adequately **plan and supervise** performance of professional services.

        4) Obtain **sufficient relevant data** to provide a reasonable basis for conclusions or recommendations in relation to any professional service.

        NOTE: The following is a helpful memory aid:

        "Professional competence uses due professional care to plan, supervise, and obtain sufficient relevant data."

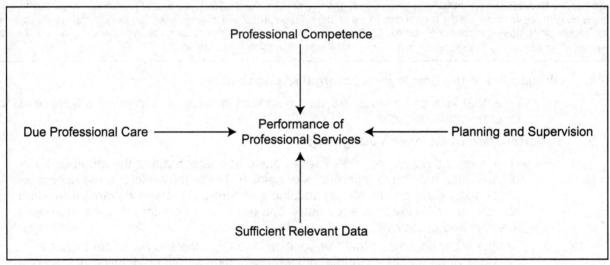

Figure 2-2

    b. **Competence**

        1) A member should complete professional services according to professional standards and with reasonable care and diligence.

            a) Competence means that the member has the technical qualifications and the ability to supervise and evaluate the work. It relates to knowledge of standards, techniques, and technical subject matter and to the ability to exercise sound judgment.

            b) In some cases, **additional research and consultation** is a normal part of performing services. However, if a member cannot gain sufficient competence, (s)he should suggest the engagement of someone competent.

c. **Consulting Services**

　　1)　The general standards apply to consulting services.

EXAMPLES

- In a consulting engagement to design and implement an IT application, a member hires a subcontractor to provide additional programming services. The member has a responsibility to ensure that the subcontractor has the professional qualifications and skills needed.
- A member plans to hire a systems analyst as a member of the firm's staff. The member is not required to be able to perform all the services of the systems analyst. But the member must be qualified to plan, supervise, and evaluate the specialist's work.

---

2. **Compliance with Standards Rule**

　　a.　A member who performs professional services shall comply with standards issued by designated bodies (the PCAOB and relevant AICPA committees and boards).

EXAMPLES

Professional services include the following:

- Audits, reviews, and compilations of financial statements
- Engagements involving special considerations, e.g., special purpose frameworks
- Attestation engagements other than traditional audits and reviews, such as engagements to report on

  - Performance of agreed-upon procedures
  - Internal control over financial reporting
  - Compliance with statutes, regulations, or contracts
  - Financial forecasts or projections

- Tax services
- Consulting services
- Valuation services
- Personal financial planning services

---

3. **Accounting Principles Rule**

　　a.　**Any material departure** from an accounting principle issued by an AICPA-designated standards setter prevents a member from

　　　　1)　Expressing an **opinion** (or stating affirmatively) that the financial statements (or other financial data) of any entity are presented in conformity with **generally accepted accounting principles (GAAP)**.

　　　　　　a)　The member cannot provide positive assurance.

　　　　2)　Stating that (s)he is **not aware** of any **material modifications** that should be made to conform with GAAP.

　　　　　　a)　The member cannot provide limited assurance.

　　　　　　NOTE: GAAP are issued by (1) the Financial Accounting Standards Board (FASB), (2) the Governmental Accounting Standards Board (GASB), (3) the International Accounting Standards Board (IASB), and (4) the Federal Accounting Standards Advisory Board (FASAB).

　　b.　This Rule applies to **all members**, whether or not in public practice, regarding any affirmative statement about conformity with GAAP.

EXAMPLES

The Accounting Principles Rule applies

- To a member who signs a report to a regulatory authority that contains an affirmation about conformity with GAAP.
- To a member in business who submits financial statements in his or her capacity as an officer, shareholder, partner, director, or employee to a third party if the communication states that they conform with the applicable financial reporting framework.

c. The prohibition against providing assurance applies if the departure has a material effect on the financial statements or data **as a whole**.

d. However, in some cases, a member may be able to provide assurance about conformity with GAAP despite a material departure.

1) The member must be able to demonstrate that, due to **unusual circumstances**, the financial statements or data would have been **misleading** without a departure from GAAP. The member must describe

a) The departure;
b) Its approximate effects, if practicable; and
c) The reasons compliance with the principle would be misleading.

2) Events that may justify departures from established accounting principles are **new legislation** or evolution of a **new form of business transaction**.

3) An unusual degree of materiality or conflicting industry practices ordinarily does not justify departures.

Stop and review! You have completed the outline for this subunit. Study multiple-choice questions 8 and 9 on page 60.

2.5 RESPONSIBILITIES TO CLIENTS

1. **Confidential Client Information Rule**

a. A member in public practice must not disclose confidential client information without the client's consent. However, this Rule does not affect the following:

1) Professional obligations under the Compliance with Standards Rule and the Accounting Principles Rule

2) The duty to comply with a valid subpoena or summons or with applicable laws and regulations

3) An official review of the member's professional practice

4) The member's right to initiate a complaint with or respond to any inquiry made by an appropriate investigative or disciplinary body

---

EXAMPLES

- A member withdrew from an engagement because of fraud on a client's tax return. If contacted by the successor, the member should suggest that the successor obtain permission from the client to reveal the reasons for leaving.

- A member reveals a client's name without permission. Disclosure violates the Confidential Client Information Rule if the client is in bankruptcy and the member specializes in bankruptcy cases. Disclosure in this situation constitutes release of confidential information.

- Knowledge and expertise obtained from a prior engagement may be used on behalf of a current client. But if (1) the information is confidential client information and (2) the current client could identify its sources, the member must obtain specific consent to disclose it.

- A member who discloses confidential client information as a result of a validly issued and enforceable subpoena (1) does not violate the Rule and (2) is not required to notify the client. But the member may want to consult legal counsel and the state board of accountancy.

- A member's service as a director, e.g., of a bank, may threaten compliance with the Confidential Client Information Rule and the Integrity and Objectivity Rule. The member's fiduciary duty to the organization may conflict with obligations under the *Code* when clients are customers of the organization. Thus, service as a consultant may be more appropriate because the member could avoid activities that threaten compliance with the *Code*.

---

b. **Review of a Member's Practice**

1) The rule against disclosure of confidential information does not prohibit the review of a member's practice as part of a purchase, sale, or merger of the practice.

2) However, appropriate precautions (e.g., a written confidentiality agreement) should be taken so that the prospective buyer does not disclose such information.

Stop and review! You have completed the outline for this subunit. Study multiple-choice questions 10 and 11 on page 60.

2.6 OTHER RESPONSIBILITIES

1. **Acts Discreditable Rule**

   a. A member must not commit an act that is discreditable to the profession.

   b. **Requests for Records**

      1) Client-provided records must be returned after a client request without exception.

         a) **Client-provided records** are "accounting or other records, including hardcopy and electronic reproductions of such records, belonging to the client that were provided to the member by, or on behalf of, the client."

      2) **Working papers** are the member's property and need not be made available to the client or others unless required by

         a) Statute,
         b) Regulation, or
         c) Contract.

      3) **Member's work products** are items (e.g., tax returns) that the member was engaged to prepare. They may be withheld if

         a) Fees are due,
         b) The work product is incomplete,
         c) The member is complying with professional standards (e.g., withholding an audit report until issues are resolved), or
         d) Litigation exists regarding the engagement or the member's work.

      4) **Member-prepared records** are records that the member was not specifically engaged to prepare. Without them, the client's financial information is incomplete.

         a) They are not otherwise available to the client.
         b) Examples are (1) journal entries and (2) supporting schedules and documents prepared as part of an engagement.
         c) Member-prepared records related to a completed and issued work product should be provided to the client unless fees are due.

      5) The following summarizes the types of records and responsibilities:

Type	Right to Withhold
Client-provided records	None
Working papers	Absolute barring legal or contractual exception
Member's work products	If fees due, work product incomplete, need to comply with standards, or litigation exists
Member-prepared records	If fees due

      6) Records also should be given to a client who suffered a loss because of an **act of war or natural disaster**. Otherwise, a member who has complied with the requirements for records requests has no further obligation.

7) In response to a request other than for working papers, the member may

    a) Charge a reasonable fee,

    b) Make and retain copies, and

    c) Provide records in any format usable by the client.

8) Compliance with a client's request usually should be within **45 days**.

EXAMPLE

If the relationship of a member who is not an owner of a firm is terminated, (s)he may not take or retain originals or copies from the firm's client files or proprietary information without permission.

---

c. **Discrimination and Harassment**

    1) When a court or administrative agency has made a final determination that a member has violated an antidiscrimination law, (s)he is deemed to have committed an act discreditable.

d. **Following the Requirements of Governmental Bodies**

    1) A member must follow the applicable financial reporting framework and the requirements of governmental bodies when preparing financial statements or related information for the purpose of reporting to such bodies.

    2) If the member performs attest services, (s)he must follow the requirements of those bodies and the applicable financial reporting framework.

    3) A material departure from the requirements is an act discreditable unless the member discloses the reasons.

e. **Governmental Audits**

    1) In a governmental audit, failure to follow applicable audit standards, guides, procedures, statutes, rules, and regulations is an act discreditable to the profession unless the report discloses the failure and the reasons.

f. **CPA Examination**

    1) A member's solicitation or knowing disclosure of CPA examination questions or answers without written permission is an act discreditable.

g. **Negligence**

    1) It is an act discreditable for negligently

        a) Making materially false and misleading entries in the financial statements or records,

        b) Failing to correct materially false and misleading statements, or

        c) Signing a document with materially false and misleading information.

h. **Failure to File a Tax Return or Pay Tax**

    1) Failing to comply with laws regarding (a) timely filing of personal or firm tax returns or (b) timely payment of taxes collected for others is an act discreditable.

i. **Indemnification and Limitation of Liability**

    1) Regulators may prohibit regulated entities from entering into certain kinds of indemnification and limitation of liability agreements in connection with attest services.

    2) Regulators also may prohibit members from providing services under such agreements.

    3) Failing to comply with such prohibitions is an act discreditable.

    j. **Confidential Information Obtained from Employment**

        1) It is an act discreditable to inappropriately disclose or use confidential employer information obtained as a result of employment or volunteer activities.

    k. **False, Misleading, or Deceptive Acts**

        1) A member who (a) promotes or markets his or her professional services or (b) makes claims about his or her experience or qualifications in a false, misleading, or deceptive manner has committed an act discreditable. Thus, representations about CPA licensure or other professional certification must comply with the requirements of the appropriate official bodies.

        2) Use of the **CPA credential** must be in accordance with the accountancy laws, rules, and regulations in the jurisdictions where the member practices.

2. **Advertising and Other Forms of Solicitation Rule**

    a. A member in public practice must not seek to obtain clients by false, misleading, or deceptive advertising or other forms of solicitation.

    b. Solicitation through coercion, overreaching, or harassing conduct is prohibited.

EXAMPLE

The designation "Personal Financial Specialists" may be used on a letterhead only when all partners or shareholders have the AICPA-awarded designation. However, the individual members holding the designation may use it after their names.

---

    c. **False, Misleading, or Deceptive Acts**

        1) Prohibited activities include the following:

            a) Creating false or unjustified expectations of favorable results

            b) Implying the ability to influence any court, regulatory agency, etc.

            c) Representing that specific services will be performed for a stated fee when it is likely at the time that the fees will be substantially increased and the client is not advised of the possibility

            d) Other representations that would cause a reasonable person to misunderstand or be deceived

    d. **Obtaining Clients through Third Parties**

        1) A member is permitted to render services to clients or customers of a third party.

        2) The member must determine that the third party's promotional efforts were within the Advertising and Other Forms of Solicitation Rule.

            a) Members must not do through others what they are prohibited from doing themselves.

3. **Contingent Fees Rule**

    a. A contingent fee is established as part of an agreement under which the amount of the fee is dependent upon the finding or result.

    b. Nevertheless, fees are not considered to be contingent if

        1) They are fixed by public authorities (e.g., courts).

        2) In tax matters, they are based on

            a) The results of judicial proceedings or

            b) The findings of governmental agencies.

c. A member in public practice must not perform for a contingent fee any of the professional services listed below. The member also must not receive a contingent fee from a client for which the member performs any of those services.

1) An audit or review of a financial statement

2) A compilation of a financial statement if

a) The member might reasonably expect that a third party will use the statement and

b) The report does not disclose the lack of independence

3) An examination of prospective financial information (a financial forecast or projection)

d. A member in public practice must not prepare for a client the following for a contingent fee:

1) An original tax return

2) An amended tax return

3) A claim for a tax refund

EXAMPLES

- A member's spouse may provide services to the member's attest client for a contingent fee provided the spouse's activities are separate from the member's practice and the member is not significantly involved. However, a conflict of interest may exist.

- A member who provides investment advisory services for an attest client for a percentage of the investment portfolio ordinarily violates the Contingent Fees Rule except when certain detailed safeguards are met.

- Providing investment advisory services to the owners, officers, or employees of an attest client for a contingent fee does not violate the Contingent Fees Rule. However, the member should consider the possible conflict of interest and also the Confidential Client Information Rule.

- A contingent fee is allowed for representation of a client (1) in an examination by a revenue agent or (2) in connection with obtaining a private letter ruling.

- A contingent fee is not allowed for the preparation of an amended income tax return for a client claiming a refund of taxes because of an inadvertent omission of a proper deduction.

- A contingent fee is allowed for filing an amended tax return claiming a refund based on a tax issue that is the subject of a test case involving a different taxpayer.

---

4. **Commissions and Referral Fees Rule**

a. **Prohibited commissions** are those received when a **member in public practice**

1) Recommends or refers

a) To a client any product or service or

b) Any product or service to be supplied by a client.

2) Also performs for that client

a) An audit,

b) A review,

c) A compilation reasonably expected to be used by a third party if the member's lack of independence is not disclosed, or

d) An examination of prospective financial information (PFI).

b. But a member's **spouse** may receive a commission for referring products or services to or from a client for whom the member has performed one of the services in 4.a.2) above.

c. A **permitted commission** must be **disclosed** to any person or entity to whom the member recommends or refers a related product or service.

d. **Referral fees** are not considered commissions and are permitted if disclosed to the client. These include

1) Acceptance of a referral fee for recommending or referring any service of a CPA to anyone and

2) Payment of a referral fee to **obtain a client**.

EXAMPLES

- A member is permitted to purchase a product and resell it to a client. Any profits collected are not considered a commission because the member had title to the product and assumed the risks of ownership.
- A member may not refer for commissions products to audit clients through distributors and agents when the member is performing any of the services described in 4.a.2) on the previous page. A member may not do through others what (s)he cannot do himself or herself. If the services are not being provided by the member, (s)he may refer the products, provided (s)he discloses the commission to the client.

---

5. **Form of Organization and Name Rule**

a. A member may practice public accounting only in a form of organization allowed by law or regulation that conforms with resolutions of the AICPA Council.

b. The firm name must not be misleading.

c. Names of past owners may be included in the name of the successor firm.

d. A firm cannot designate itself as "members of the AICPA" unless all CPA owners are members.

e. According to a Council resolution, if a firm (1) **holds itself out as CPAs** or (2) performs attest services, it must have certain characteristics. The attest services for this purpose consist of (1) audits under SASs; (2) reviews under SSARSs; (3) examinations, reviews, or agreed-upon procedures under SSAEs; or (4) engagements under PCAOB standards. The following are required characteristics:

1) CPAs own a majority of the firm's financial interests and voting rights.

2) A CPA must be responsible for all services.

3) A nonCPA owner must be active as a member of the firm or its affiliates.

4) NonCPA owners cannot hold themselves out as CPAs.

5) A member must not knowingly permit a person (s)he has the ability to control to do what is prohibited to the member by the *Code*.

a) The member also may be responsible for the acts of such a person who is an associate in the public practice.

6) NonCPA owners are not eligible to be AICPA members unless they meet the requirements for membership.

7) Owners must, at all times, be the beneficial owners of the equity attributed to them. If an owner ceases to be actively engaged as a member of the firm or its affiliates, his or her ownership should be transferred to the firm or other qualified owners within a reasonable time.

f. Members may practice not only in corporations and general partnerships but also in limited liability companies, limited liability partnerships, and other forms permitted by law or regulation.

g. **Ownership of a Separate Business**

1) A member may own an interest in a separate business that performs the services for which standards are established.

2) If the member controls the separate business, the entity and all its owners and professional employees must comply with the *Code*.

a) Absent such control, only the member is subject to the *Code*.

h.   **Alternative Practice Structures (APSs)**

1)   AICPA requirements emphasize that CPAs remain responsible, financially and otherwise, for the attest work performed to protect the public interest.

2)   However, in an APS, CPAs may own the majority of financial interests in the attest firm, but substantially all revenues may be paid to another entity for services and the lease of employees, equipment, etc.

3)   Nevertheless, given the requirements of state law and the AICPA, if the CPAs who own the attest firm remain financially responsible under state law for the firm's attest work, they are deemed to be in compliance with the financial-interests requirement.

i.   **Misleading Firm Names**

1)   A name is misleading if it contains a representation likely to cause a reasonable person to misunderstand (a) the legal form of the firm, (b) who its owners are, or (c) who its members are. An example is using the term "company" (or "Co.") when the firm is not a corporation.

j.   **Common Network Brand in Firm Name**

1)   A network is an association of entities that includes one or more public accounting firms. These entities (a) cooperate to enhance the firms' ability to provide services and (b) share at least one of certain specified characteristics (e.g., a common brand name or initials as part of the firm name, common control, profits or costs, or resources).

2)   Sharing of a common brand name or initials as part or all of the firm name is not misleading if the firm is a network firm.

EXAMPLES

- A partnership may continue to practice using a partner's name in the firm name after (s)he withdraws. If the firm later merges with another firm, the title of the new firm may include the retired partner's name.
- If a CPA becomes a partner in a firm with one or more nonCPA practitioners, the CPA is responsible for compliance with the *Code* by all of his or her professional employees.
- A CPA in partnership with nonCPAs may sign the firm name to a report and below it affix his or her name with the CPA designation. However, it must be clear that the partnership does not consist entirely of CPAs.

In addition to testing the AICPA *Code of Professional Conduct*, the CPA exam includes ethics and independence questions based on standards of the Securities and Exchange Commission (SEC), the Public Companies Accounting Oversight Board (PCAOB), the Government Accountability Office (covered in Study Unit 20), Department of Labor (DOL), and the Sarbanes-Oxley Act of 2002.

The material may appear imposing at first. However, it is important to recognize that in most cases the standards for independence from the various standard setters are very similar. Thus, use your knowledge of the AICPA *Code of Professional Conduct* as a foundation for your study. Regarding other ethics issues, you should focus on those not intuitively obvious to you. With a little effort, you should be able to gain considerable confidence in comprehending the ethics requirements.

Stop and review! You have completed the outline for this subunit. Study multiple-choice questions 12 through 14 on page 61.

2.7 OTHER PRONOUNCEMENTS ON PROFESSIONAL RESPONSIBILITIES

1. **Sarbanes-Oxley, PCAOB, the SEC, and the Department of Labor**

Background

The Sarbanes-Oxley Act of 2002 was a response to numerous financial reporting scandals involving large public companies. It contains provisions relating to corporate governance that impose new responsibilities on publicly held companies and their auditors. The Public Company Accounting Oversight Board (PCAOB) was created by the act. The act applies to issuers of publicly traded securities subject to federal securities laws. The following section addresses ethics requirements of Sarbanes-Oxley, the PCAOB, the SEC, and the Department of Labor. Most of the independence rules are parallel to the AICPA rules. Thus, the focus is on other issues not addressed in the AICPA *Code of Professional Conduct*.

---

   a. **Responsibilities and Activities of the PCAOB**

      1) Register public accounting firms

      2) Oversee the audit of public companies (issuers) that are subject to the securities laws

      3) Establish or adopt standards on auditing, quality control, ethics, and independence

      4) Inspect audit firms every 3 years (1 year if the firm is large) to

         a) Examine selected audit and review engagements;

         b) Evaluate the system of quality; and

         c) Test audit, supervisory, and quality control procedures.

      5) Conduct investigations and disciplinary proceedings involving, and impose appropriate sanctions upon, registered public accounting firms and associated persons

   b. **Preapproval of Services**

      1) Audit committees ordinarily must preapprove the services performed by accountants (permissible nonaudit services and all audit, review, and attest engagements).

         a) Approval must be either (1) explicit or (2) in accordance with detailed policies and procedures.

         b) If approval is based on detailed policies and procedures, the audit committee must be informed, and no delegation of its authority to management is allowed.

   c. **Disclosure of Fees**

      1) An issuer must disclose in its proxy statement or annual filing the fees paid to the accountant segregated into four categories:

         a) Audit,

         b) Audit-related,

         c) Tax, and

         d) All other.

      2) The disclosure is for the 2 most recent years.

   d. **Rotation of Partners**

      1) The lead and concurring (reviewing) audit partners must rotate every 5 years, with a 5-year time-out period. Other audit partners must rotate every 7 years, with a 2-year time-out.

      2) Furthermore, second partner review and approval of audit reports is required.

e. **Conflicts of Interest**

1) The act prohibits the conflict of interest that arises when the CEO, CFO, controller, chief accounting officer, or the equivalent was employed by the company's public accounting firm within 1 year preceding the audit.

f. **Working Papers**

1) Auditors must retain their audit working papers for at least 7 years.

a) It is a crime for auditors to fail to maintain all audit or review working papers for at least 5 years.

i) If retention is for more than 5 years but fewer than 7 years, sanctions that are not criminal penalties may be imposed by the PCAOB.

g. **Registration and Inspection**

1) Public accounting firms with **one or more** public audit clients must register with the PCAOB and be subject to inspection.

2) Moreover, they must adopt quality control standards and reasonably supervise any associated person with regard to auditing and quality control standards.

3) Registrants must file an annual report with the PCAOB that contains basic information about firm activities. They also must file a special report within 30 days of a reportable event, e.g., initiation of legal action against the firm.

h. **Communications with the Audit Committee**

1) The firm must include

a) All critical accounting policies and practices;

b) All material alternative accounting policies and practices within GAAP that were discussed with management; and

c) Other material written communications with management, such as representations and schedules of unadjusted audit differences.

2) These communications must be prior to filing the audit report with the SEC.

3) The firm must, before accepting an initial engagement and at least annually, (a) discuss the potential effects of the relationships that may affect independence and (b) document the discussion.

i. **Prohibited Nonaudit Services**

1) The firm is prohibited from offering certain nonaudit services to its attest clients, including

a) Appraisal and other valuation services
b) Designing and implementing financial information systems
c) Internal auditing or actuarial functions
d) Management services
e) Human resource services
f) Bookkeeping
g) Legal and expert services not pertaining to the audit
h) Investment banking or advisory services
i) Broker-dealer services

2) Preapproved compliance tax engagements and preparation of comfort letters are not prohibited. The preapproval requirement is waived with respect to acceptable nonaudit services for an issuer if

a) The aggregate amount of the services is not more than 5% of the total revenues paid by the issuer to its auditor during the fiscal year,

b) The services were not recognized by the issuer at the time of the engagement to be nonaudit services, and

        c)   The services were promptly brought to the attention of the audit committee and approved prior to the completion of the audit.

j.   **Improper Influence on Audits**

      1)   Under SOX, it is unlawful for any officer or director of an issuer to take any action to fraudulently influence, coerce, manipulate, or mislead any auditor engaged in the performance of an audit for the purpose of rendering the financial statements materially misleading.

k.   **Reporting**

      1)   In filings with the SEC, the CEO and CFO of a public company must certify that

            a)   To the best of their knowledge, the financial statements are free of material misstatements.

            b)   They are responsible for the system of internal control and have evaluated its effectiveness.

            c)   They have informed the audit committee and the independent auditors of all significant control deficiencies and any fraud, whether or not material.

l.   **PCAOB Interim Independence Standards**

      1)   The PCAOB adopted AICPA Conduct Rule 101 as it existed on April 16, 2003, as well as pronouncements of the now-defunct Independence Standards Board (ISB). It also has issued specific independence rules that apply to a registered public accounting firm (firm). However, these are similar, in most cases, to those in the AICPA *Code of Professional Conduct*.

      2)   A firm is not independent of the audit client if it provides a nonaudit service related to

            a)   Aggressive tax positions (unless they are more likely than not to be upheld) or

            b)   Confidential tax transactions (those for which a paid tax advisor places a limitation on disclosure to protect its tax strategies).

      3)   A firm is not independent of the audit client if, during the engagement period, it provides any **tax** service to a person in a **financial reporting oversight role**. Such persons include the (a) CEO, (b) president, (c) CFO, (d) COO, (e) chief accounting officer, and (f) other individuals in equivalent positions. (An exception is made for directors of the audit client and in certain narrowly defined cases.)

m.   **Fraud Issues**

      1)   Sarbanes-Oxley created a new crime for securities fraud that imposes penalties of fines and imprisonment, extends the statute of limitations on securities fraud claims, and makes it a felony to create or destroy documents to impede a federal investigation.

2.   **Department of Labor**

   a.   The DOL requires auditors to be independent for audits of pension funds administered under the Employee Retirement Income Security Act of 1974 (ERISA).

   b.   With few exceptions, the requirements for independence under the DOL rules are parallel to those of the AICPA.

3.   *Government Auditing Standards* issued by the Government Accountability Office (GAO) are covered in Study Unit 20.

Stop and review! You have completed the outline for this subunit. Study multiple-choice questions 15 through 20 beginning on page 62.

QUESTIONS

2.1 *Code of Professional Conduct*

1. A CPA who is **not** in public practice is obligated to follow which of the following rules of conduct?

- A. Independence.
- B. Integrity and objectivity.
- C. Contingent fees.
- D. Commissions.

Answer (B) is correct.

REQUIRED: The rule of conduct applicable to a CPA not in public practice.

DISCUSSION: Under the Integrity and Objectivity Rule, all members must maintain objectivity and integrity, be free of conflicts of interest, not knowingly misrepresent facts, and not subordinate his or her judgment to others when performing professional services.

Answer (A) is incorrect. The Independence Rule applies only to CPAs in public practice. Answer (C) is incorrect. The Contingent Fees Rule applies only to CPAs in public practice. Answer (D) is incorrect. The Commissions and Referral Fees Rule applies only in part (Referrals) to all members and in part (Commissions) to CPAs in public practice.

2. Under the *Code of Professional Conduct* of the AICPA, which of the following is required to be independent in fact and appearance when discharging professional responsibilities?

- A. A CPA in public practice providing tax and management advisory services.
- B. A CPA in public practice providing auditing and other attestation services.
- C. A CPA not in public practice.
- D. All CPAs.

Answer (B) is correct.

REQUIRED: The person(s) required to be independent in fact and appearance.

DISCUSSION: According to the Principles of Professional Conduct, "A member in public practice should be independent in fact and appearance when providing audit and other attestation services."

Answer (A) is incorrect. A CPA in public practice providing tax and management advisory services need not be independent unless attestation services also are performed. Answer (C) is incorrect. A CPA not in public practice need not be independent. Answer (D) is incorrect. All CPAs do not provide attestation services in public practice.

2.2 Independence

3. Under the AICPA's conceptual framework for independence, the member-client relationship is evaluated to determine whether independence in fact and appearance is jeopardized. This is considered

- A. A sufficiency of safeguards approach.
- B. An avoidance approach.
- C. A risk-based approach.
- D. A professional skepticism approach.

Answer (C) is correct.

REQUIRED: The term associated with the conceptual framework for independence standards.

DISCUSSION: The risk-based approach evaluates the risk that a CPA is not independent or is perceived by a reasonable and informed third party with knowledge of all relevant information as not independent. That risk must be reduced to an acceptable level to establish independence. Risk is acceptable when threats are acceptable. They may be acceptable because of the types of threats and their potential effect. Moreover, threats may be sufficiently mitigated or eliminated by safeguards. Threats are acceptable when it is not reasonable to expect that they will compromise professional judgment.

Answer (A) is incorrect. Safeguards are controls that mitigate the risk. Answer (B) is incorrect. The term "avoidance approach" is not meaningful in this context. Answer (D) is incorrect. Members should exercise professional skepticism, but this is not required for members to be independent.

4. The concept of materiality is **least** important to an auditor when considering the

- A. Adequacy of disclosure of a client's illegal act.
- B. Discovery of weaknesses in a client's internal control.
- C. Effects of a direct financial interest in the client on the CPA's independence.
- D. Decision whether to use positive or negative confirmations of accounts receivable.

Answer (C) is correct.

REQUIRED: The item with respect to which materiality is least important.

DISCUSSION: Independence is impaired if a CPA has any direct financial interest in a client. Whether this direct financial interest is material is irrelevant. The test of materiality is applied, however, if the financial interest is indirect.

Answer (A) is incorrect. In considering the effect of an illegal act on the financial statements and its implications for other aspects of the audit, materiality is important. Answer (B) is incorrect. An auditor who is considering internal control in a financial statement audit must make materiality judgments. Answer (D) is incorrect. Materiality is one factor considered when deciding between positive or negative confirmations.

5. A violation of the profession's ethical standards most likely would have occurred when a CPA

A. Expressed an unmodified opinion on the current year's financial statements when fees for the prior year's audit were unpaid.

B. Recommended a controller's position description with candidate specifications to an audit client.

C. Purchased a CPA firm's practice of monthly write-ups for a percentage of fees to be received over a 3-year period.

D. Made arrangements with a financial institution to collect notes issued by a client in payment of fees due for the current year's audit.

Answer (A) is correct.
REQUIRED: The violation of the ethical standards.
DISCUSSION: Audit fees that are long past due take on the characteristics of a loan. Independence is impaired if billed or unbilled fees, or a note arising from the fees, for client services rendered more than 1 year prior to the current year's report date, remain unpaid when the current year's report is issued. However, this ruling does not apply if the client is in bankruptcy. Moreover, long overdue fees do not preclude the CPA from performing services not requiring independence.
Answer (B) is incorrect. A CPA will not impair independence by recommending job position descriptions. However, the CPA will be in violation if (s)he is responsible for screening candidates or making decisions to hire. Answer (C) is incorrect. No pronouncement prohibits purchase of a bookkeeping firm for a percentage of fees. Answer (D) is incorrect. The AICPA has ruled that this practice does not violate the *Code.*

6. Various situations create threats to auditor independence. Which type of threat most likely results from an auditor's financial interest in a client?

A. Self-interest threat.

B. Self-review threat.

C. Management participation threat.

D. Advocacy threat.

Answer (A) is correct.
REQUIRED: The threat to independence created by a auditor's financial interest in a client.
DISCUSSION: Self-interest threats are benefits from a relationship with the attest client (e.g., having a financial interest in the client).
Answer (B) is incorrect. Self-review threats result when members review their own (or their firm's) nonattest work in an attest engagement. Answer (C) is incorrect. Management participation threats result from assuming management responsibilities for the attest client, such as maintaining the client's controls. Answer (D) is incorrect. Advocacy threats are actions that promote an attest client's interest, for example, representing a client in a public legal proceeding.

2.3 Integrity and Objectivity

7. Which of the following acts by a CPA who is in business most likely is a violation of the ethical standards of the profession?

A. Failing to disclose material facts when the employer's external accountant has requested written representations.

B. The member accepts a commission for selling a product.

C. The member sells a newsletter bearing his or her name.

D. Compiling the CPA's employer's financial statements and referring to the CPA's lack of independence.

Answer (A) is correct.
REQUIRED: The action by a CPA in business that violates ethical standards.
DISCUSSION: A member in business must be candid and not knowingly misrepresent facts or fail to disclose material facts. For example, this interpretation applies when the member responds to specific inquiries from the external accountant that requests written representations.
Answer (B) is incorrect. Members in business may accept commissions. Answer (C) is incorrect. A member may sell a newsletter bearing his or her name if it does not violate the prohibition against false, misleading, or deceptive advertising, or other forms of solicitation. Answer (D) is incorrect. An accountant may compile a nonissuer's financial statements if (s)he issues the appropriate report. The lack of independence should be disclosed.

2.4 Professional Standards

8. According to the standards of the profession, which of the following activities may be required in exercising due professional care?

	Consulting with Experts	Obtaining Specialty Accreditation
A.	Yes	Yes
B.	Yes	No
C.	No	Yes
D.	No	No

Answer (B) is correct.
REQUIRED: The activity(ies) that may be required in exercising due care.
DISCUSSION: A CPA should undertake only those services that (s)he reasonably expects to complete with professional competence and should exercise due professional care in performing those services. Additional research or consultation with others may be necessary to gain sufficient competence to complete a service in accordance with professional standards. However, professional standards do not require specialty accreditation, although many CPAs choose to specialize in specific services.

9. According to the profession's ethical standards, which of the following events may justify a departure from an established accounting principle?

	New Legislation	Evolution of a New Form of Business Transaction
A.	No	Yes
B.	Yes	No
C.	Yes	Yes
D.	No	No

Answer (C) is correct.
REQUIRED: The event(s), if any, that may justify departure from an established accounting principle.
DISCUSSION: In general, strict compliance with accounting principles is required. However, the Accounting Principles Rule recognizes that, due to unusual circumstances, adhering to GAAP may cause financial statements to be misleading. New legislation and the evolution of a new form of business transaction are events that may justify departure from an established accounting principle.

2.5 Responsibilities to Clients

10. A CPA is permitted to disclose confidential client information without the consent of the client to

I. Another CPA firm if the information concerns suspected tax return irregularities

II. A state CPA society voluntary peer review board

A. I only.
B. II only.
C. Both I and II.
D. Neither I nor II.

Answer (B) is correct.
REQUIRED: The event(s), if any, that allow disclosure of confidential client data without the client's consent.
DISCUSSION: Under the Confidential Client Information Rule, a CPA may reveal confidential information without the client's permission for a state board- or state society-sponsored peer review. Identifying information revealed to the review team is precluded from disclosure. However, a CPA may not disclose information to another CPA firm without the client's permission or unless pursuant to a valid subpoena.

11. To which of the following parties may a CPA partnership provide its audit documentation, without being lawfully subpoenaed or without the client's consent?

A. The IRS.
B. The FASB.
C. Any surviving partner(s) on the death of a partner.
D. A CPA before purchasing a partnership interest in the firm.

Answer (C) is correct.
REQUIRED: The true statement about records in the CPA's possession.
DISCUSSION: Audit documentation may be disclosed to another partner of the accounting firm without the client's consent because such information has not been communicated to outsiders. A partner of the CPA has a fiduciary obligation to the client not to disclose confidential information without consent.
Answer (A) is incorrect. The partnership may not provide the IRS with confidential client information without client permission, a subpoena, or a summons. Answer (B) is incorrect. The CPA or his or her firm may not disclose confidential information to the FASB without client consent. Answer (D) is incorrect. A CPA may not provide audit documentation to a prospective purchaser. However, an exception is made for a review of the practice in conjunction with a prospective purchase, sale, or merger.

2.6 Other Responsibilities

12. Which of the following is required for a CPA firm to designate itself as "Members of the American Institute of Certified Public Accountants" on its letterhead?

- A. All CPA owners must be members.
- B. The owners whose names appear in the firm name must be members.
- C. At least one of the owners must be a member.
- D. The firm must be a dues-paying member.

Answer (A) is correct.
    REQUIRED: The requirement for a CPA firm to use the designation, "Members of the AICPA."
    DISCUSSION: The Form of Organization and Name Rule states that a firm may not use the quoted designation unless all of its CPA owners are members of the AICPA.
    Answer (B) is incorrect. All CPA owners, not just certain owners, must be AICPA members. Answer (C) is incorrect. All CPA owners must be members. Answer (D) is incorrect. The CPA owners, not the firm, must be members of the AICPA.

13. Which of the following statements is (are) true regarding a CPA employee of a CPA firm taking copies of information contained in client files when the CPA leaves the firm?

I. A CPA leaving a firm may take copies of information contained in client files to assist another firm in serving that client.

II. A CPA leaving a firm may take copies of information contained in client files as a method of gaining technical expertise.

- A. I only.
- B. II only.
- C. Both I and II.
- D. Neither I nor II.

Answer (D) is correct.
    REQUIRED: The act(s), if any, considered discreditable to the profession.
    DISCUSSION: The Acts Discreditable Rule states that a member shall not commit an act discreditable to the profession. After the relationship of a member who is not an owner of the firm is terminated, the member may not take or retain copies or originals from the firm's client files or proprietary information without permission.

14. According to the ethical standards of the profession, which of the following acts generally is prohibited?

- A. Accepting a contingent fee for representing a client in connection with obtaining a private letter from the Internal Revenue Service.
- B. Retaining client-provided records after the client has demanded their return.
- C. Revealing client tax returns to a prospective purchaser of the CPA's practice.
- D. Issuing a modified report explaining the CPA's failure to follow a governmental regulatory agency's standards when conducting an attest service for a client.

Answer (B) is correct.
    REQUIRED: The act generally prohibited by the profession's ethical standards.
    DISCUSSION: Retention of client-provided records after the client has demanded their return is an act discreditable to the profession. Even if the state in which a member practices grants a lien on certain records, the ethical standard still applies.
    Answer (A) is incorrect. A contingent fee for representing a client in connection with obtaining a private letter ruling from the IRS is permitted. Answer (C) is incorrect. The disclosure of confidential information in the review of a member's professional practice is not prohibited under a purchase, sale, or merger of the practice. However, appropriate precautions (e.g., a written confidentiality agreement) should be taken so that the prospective buyer does not disclose any confidential client information. Answer (D) is incorrect. Failure to substantially follow a governmental regulatory agency's standards is an act discreditable to the profession. But the member may disclose in his or her report that such requirements were not followed and the reasons. Not following such requirements could require the member to modify the report.

2.7 Other Pronouncements on Professional Responsibilities

15. According to SEC independence regulations,

A. All audit partners must rotate every 5 years.

B. Preapproval of accountants' services may be in accord with detailed policies and procedures rather than explicit.

C. The issuer must disclose only those fees paid to the accountant for audit work.

D. No partner may sell nonaudit services to the client during the audit.

Answer (B) is correct.

REQUIRED: The true statement about SEC independence regulations.

DISCUSSION: Audit committees ordinarily must preapprove the services performed by accountants (permissible nonaudit services and all audit, review, and attest engagements). Approval must be either explicit or in accordance with detailed policies and procedures. If approval is based on detailed policies and procedures, the audit committee must be informed, and no delegation of its authority to management is allowed.

Answer (A) is incorrect. The lead and concurring (reviewing) audit partners must rotate every 5 years, with a 5-year time-out period. Other audit partners must rotate every 7 years, with a 2-year time-out. Answer (C) is incorrect. An issuer must disclose in its proxy statement or annual filing the fees paid to the accountant segregated into four categories: (1) audit, (2) audit-related, (3) tax, and (4) all other. Answer (D) is incorrect. An accountant is not independent if, during the audit and the period of the engagement, any audit partner (excluding specialty partners such as tax partners) earns or receives compensation for selling services (excluding audit, review, or attest services) to the client.

16. According to the PCAOB, an accounting firm's independence is **least** likely to be impaired if the firm

A. Provides a service to the audit client for a contingent fee.

B. Receives a commission from the audit client.

C. Has an audit client that employs a former firm professional.

D. Provides tax services to a person in a financial reporting oversight role at the audit client.

Answer (C) is correct.

REQUIRED: The circumstances least likely to impair an accounting firm's independence.

DISCUSSION: Firm independence is impaired by a client's employment of a former firm professional that could adversely affect the audit unless safeguards are established. Pre-change safeguards include removal from the audit of those negotiating with the client, and post-change safeguards include possibly modifying the audit plan.

Answer (A) is incorrect. A firm is not independent of its client if the firm or any affiliate, during the audit and engagement period, provides any service or product to the client for a contingent fee or a commission, or receives from the client a contingent fee or commission. Answer (B) is incorrect. A firm is not independent of its client if the firm or any affiliate, during the audit and engagement period, provides any service or product to the client for a contingent fee or a commission, or receives from the client a contingent fee or commission. Answer (D) is incorrect. A registered public accounting firm is not independent of its audit client if the firm or any affiliate, during the professional engagement period, provides any tax service to a person in a financial reporting oversight role at the audit client.

17. When Congress passed the Sarbanes-Oxley Act of 2002, it imposed greater regulation on public companies and their auditors and required increased accountability. Which of the following is **not** a provision of the act?

A. Executives must certify the appropriateness of the financial statements.

B. The act provides criminal penalties for fraud.

C. Auditors may not provide specific nonaudit services for their audit clients.

D. Audit firms must be rotated on a periodic basis.

Answer (D) is correct.

REQUIRED: The provision not included in the Sarbanes-Oxley Act.

DISCUSSION: The act requires rotation of the lead audit or coordinating partner and the reviewing partner on audits of public clients every 5 years. However, the act does not require the rotation of audit firms.

Answer (A) is incorrect. The CEO and CFO of a public company must provide a statement to accompany the audit report. This statement certifies the appropriateness of the financial statements and disclosures. However, a violation of this requirement must be knowing and intentional. Answer (B) is incorrect. The act creates a new crime for securities fraud with penalties of fines and imprisonment, extends the statute of limitations on securities fraud claims, and makes it a felony to create or destroy documents to impede a federal investigation. Answer (C) is incorrect. The act makes it unlawful for a registered public accounting firm to perform certain nonaudit services for audit clients, for example, bookkeeping, systems design, management functions, or any other service the Public Company Accounting Oversight Board (PCAOB) determines by regulation to be impermissible.

18. According to the PCAOB, an accounting firm is most likely to be independent of its audit client if

A. A reasonable investor would conclude that it is not objective and impartial.

B. The firm's audit professional is responsible for internal control over financial reporting.

C. The firm's audit professional implemented the client's internal control over financial reporting.

D. The firm recommended an aggressive tax position to the client that is more likely than not to be legally allowed.

Answer (D) is correct.
REQUIRED: The circumstances in which an accounting firm is most likely to be independent.
DISCUSSION: A firm is not independent of its audit client if, during the audit and engagement period, it provides any nonaudit service related to marketing, planning, or expressing an opinion in favor of the tax treatment of aggressive tax-position transactions for the purpose of tax avoidance. However, this Rule does not apply if the tax treatment is at least more likely than not to be allowable under tax law.
Answer (A) is incorrect. An auditor is not independent if (s)he is not, or a reasonable investor would conclude that (s)he is not, able to be objective and impartial. Answer (B) is incorrect. Guiding principles regarding independence include whether the auditor assumes a management role or audits his or her own work. Thus, an auditor is not independent if, for example, the auditor is responsible for internal control over financial reporting or had designed or implemented it. Answer (C) is incorrect. Designing or implementing internal control over financial reporting impairs independence.

19. According to the Sarbanes-Oxley Act of 2002, which of the following non-audit services can be provided by a registered public accounting firm to the client contemporaneously with the audit when preapproval is granted by audit committee action?

A. Internal audit outsourcing services.

B. Tax services.

C. Actuarial services related to the audit.

D. Advice on financial information system design.

Answer (B) is correct.
REQUIRED: The preapproved nonaudit services that can be provided by a registered public accounting firm at the same time as the audit.
DISCUSSION: The Sarbanes-Oxley Act of 2002 prohibits a registered public accounting firm from performing the following nonaudit services for an issuer: (1) bookkeeping or other services related to the accounting records or financial statements of the audit client; (2) design and implementation of financial information systems; (3) appraisal or valuation services, fairness opinions, or contribution-in-kind reports; (4) actuarial services; (5) internal audit outsourcing services; (6) management functions or human resource services; (7) broker or dealer, investment adviser, or investment banking services; (8) legal services and expert services unrelated to the audit; and (9) any other service that the Board determines is impermissible. But a registered public accounting firm may engage in any nonaudit service, including tax services other than those listed, if the activity is approved in advance by the audit committee of the issuer.
Answer (A) is incorrect. Internal audit outsourcing services are prohibited activities. Answer (C) is incorrect. Actuarial services related to the audit are prohibited activities. Answer (D) is incorrect. Advice on financial information system design is a prohibited activity.

20. The PCAOB has the power to

A. Inspect large firms annually.

B. Issue quality control, ethics, and accounting standards.

C. Demand the personal financial statements of audit staff.

D. Review only audit engagements of registered firms.

Answer (A) is correct.
REQUIRED: The authority of the PCAOB.
DISCUSSION: The PCAOB will inspect large firms annually and report violations to the SEC and state authorities. All attestation engagements, notably those in litigation, may be reviewed. The inspection also involves a quality control assessment. Furthermore, the inspection report must include the firm's response. The firm then has twelve months to correct the reported weaknesses.
Answer (B) is incorrect. The PCAOB has rule-making authority regarding audit standards. The FASB establishes GAAP. Answer (C) is incorrect. The PCAOB has no authority to demand personal financial statements from audit staff. Answer (D) is incorrect. All attestation engagements, notably those in litigation, may be reviewed.

STUDY UNIT THREE
PLANNING AND RISK ASSESSMENT

(22 pages of outline)

In general, the recognition and consideration of risks related to an audit have great significance on the CPA exam. The AICPA appears determined to ensure that successful candidates understand the consequences of those risks. Candidates can expect to be tested on the auditor's consideration of audit risk and its components. The interrelationship between risk and materiality is critical.

3.1 PRE-ENGAGEMENT ACCEPTANCE ACTIVITIES

1. **Preconditions for an Audit**

   a. Before agreeing to conduct an audit, the auditor should determine that management

      1) Uses an acceptable financial reporting framework (e.g., U.S. GAAP) in the preparation and fair presentation of the financial statements.

      2) Understands its responsibility for the preparation and fair presentation of the financial statements.

      3) Understands its responsibility for the design, implementation, and maintenance of internal control.

      4) Understands its responsibility to provide access to all information and persons deemed necessary for the audit.

2. **Client Acceptance**

   a. Client acceptance includes the continued evaluation of existing clients and the evaluation of new clients. Concluding that management lacks integrity causes the auditor to reject a potential client or to end a relationship with an existing client.

   b. The auditor should communicate with the **predecessor auditor** before final acceptance of the engagement (AU-C 210). The predecessor is expected to respond promptly and, absent unusual circumstances, fully.

   c. The auditor is responsible for initiating the communication.

   d. The AICPA Code of Professional Conduct requires members to protect the confidentiality of client information. Thus, both the auditor and his or her predecessor should obtain client permission to have discussions about the integrity of management and other audit-related issues.

   e. Inquiries should include

      1) Facts that are relevant to the integrity of management;

      2) Disagreements with management about accounting principles, audit procedures, or other similar matters;

      3) Communications to those charged with governance (e.g., the audit committee) about fraud and noncompliance with laws and regulations;

      4) Communications to management and those charged with governance about significant deficiencies and material weaknesses in internal control; and

      5) The predecessor's understanding as to the reason for the change in auditors.

   f.   Certain audit documentation of the auditor's predecessor normally is made available.

   g.   The client's refusal to grant permission or the predecessor auditor's failure to respond fully requires the auditor to consider the implications when deciding whether to accept the engagement.

   h.   A request by management to change the terms of the engagement should be evaluated by the auditor for reasonableness. If (1) the change is unreasonable and (2) the auditor is not permitted to continue the original engagement, the auditor should withdraw and communicate the circumstances to those charged with governance.

3.   **Terms of the Engagement**

   a.   The auditor should agree with management or those charged with governance upon the terms. The auditor accepts the engagement only if (1) the preconditions for an audit are present and (2) a common understanding of the terms has been reached.

       1)   The preconditions relate to the fundamental responsibilities of management and, if appropriate, those charged with governance. (For a statement of responsibilities, see the sample engagement letter beginning below.)

   b.   The terms should be documented in an engagement letter that states the following:

       1)   Objective and scope of the audit
       2)   Responsibilities of the auditor and management
       3)   Inherent limitations of the audit and internal control
       4)   The financial reporting framework
       5)   The expected form and content of audit reports

   c.   An engagement letter should be sent by the CPA to the prospective client on each engagement, audit or otherwise. If the client agrees to the terms by signing a copy of the letter and returning it to the CPA, a contract is formed.

4.   **Sample Engagement Letter**

   a.   The following is an example of an audit engagement letter for an audit of general purpose financial statements. This letter is not authoritative and is intended only to be a guide. Its content will vary according to individual requirements and circumstances and is drafted to refer to the audit of financial statements for a single reporting period.

EXAMPLE -- Engagement Letter

SWIFT, MARCH & COMPANY, Certified Public Accountants

January 21, 20XX
Mr. Thomas Thorp, President
Anonymous Company, Inc.
Route 32
Nowhere, New York 10000

Dear Mr. Thorp:

[The objective and scope of the audit]

You have requested that we audit the financial statements of Anonymous Company, Inc., which comprise the balance sheet as of December 31, 20XX and the related statements of income, changes in stockholders' equity, and cash flows for the year then ended as well as the related notes to the financial statements. We are pleased to confirm our acceptance and understanding of this audit engagement by means of this letter. Our audit will be conducted with the objective of our expressing an opinion on the financial statements.

-- Continued on next page --

EXAMPLE -- Continued

[The responsibilities of the auditor]

We will conduct our audit in accordance with auditing standards generally accepted in the United States of America (GAAS). Those standards require that we plan and perform the audit to obtain reasonable assurance about whether the financial statements are free from material misstatement. An audit involves performing procedures to obtain audit evidence about the amounts and disclosures in the financial statements. The procedures selected depend on the auditor's judgment, including the assessment of the risks of material misstatement of the financial statements, whether due to fraud or error. An audit also includes evaluating the appropriateness of accounting policies used and the reasonableness of significant accounting estimates made by management, as well as evaluating the overall presentation of the financial statements.

Because of the inherent limitations of an audit, together with the inherent limitations of internal control, an unavoidable risk that some material misstatements may not be detected exists, even though the audit is properly planned and performed in accordance with GAAS.

In making our risk assessments, we consider internal control relevant to the entity's preparation and fair presentation of the financial statements in order to design audit procedures that are appropriate in the circumstances but not for the purpose of expressing an opinion on the effectiveness of the entity's internal control. However, we will communicate to you in writing concerning any significant deficiencies or material weaknesses in internal control relevant to the audit of the financial statements that we have identified during the audit.

[The responsibilities of management and identification of the applicable financial reporting framework]

Our audit will be conducted on the basis that management and, when appropriate, those charged with governance acknowledge and understand that they have responsibility

    a.   For the preparation and fair presentation of the financial statements in accordance with accounting principles generally accepted in the United States of America;

    b.   For the design, implementation, and maintenance of internal control relevant to the preparation and fair presentation of financial statements that are free from material misstatement, whether due to fraud or error; and

    c.   To provide us with

        i)   Access to all information of which management is aware that is relevant to the preparation and fair presentation of the financial statements such as records, documentation, and other matters;

        ii)   Additional information that we may request from management for the purpose of the audit; and

        iii)   Unrestricted access to persons within the entity from whom we determine it necessary to obtain audit evidence.

As part of our audit process, we will request from management and, when appropriate, those charged with governance written confirmation concerning representations made to us in connection with the audit.

[Other relevant information]

[Insert other information, such as fee arrangements, billings, assistance to be provided by the client's staff, and other specific terms, as appropriate.]

[Reporting]

[Insert appropriate reference to the expected form and content of the auditor's report. Example follows:]

We will issue a written report upon completion of our audit of Anonymous Company's financial statements. Our report will be addressed to the board of directors of Anonymous Company. We cannot provide assurance that an unmodified opinion will be expressed. Circumstances may arise in which it is necessary for us to modify our opinion, add an emphasis-of-matter or other-matter paragraph(s), or withdraw from the engagement.

We also will issue a written report on [Insert appropriate reference to other auditor's reports expected to be issued.] upon completion of our audit.

Please sign and return the attached copy of this letter to indicate your acknowledgment of, and agreement with, the arrangements for our audit of the financial statements including our respective responsibilities.

SWIFT, MARCH & COMPANY, CPAs

Acknowledged and agreed on behalf of Anonymous Company, Inc., by

---

[Signed]

[Name and Title]

[Date]

| Adapted from AU-C 210 |

5.   **Representation Letter**

a.   Management is responsible for adjusting the financial statements to correct material misstatements. Furthermore, the auditor should request that management provide a written representation about whether the effects of any uncorrected misstatements are immaterial, individually or in the aggregate.

1)   A summary of the uncorrected misstatements should be included in the representation. (An example management representation letter is in Study Unit 14, Subunit 3.)

Stop and review! You have completed the outline for this subunit. Study multiple-choice questions 1 through 3 beginning on page 86.

3.2 PLANNING AN AUDIT

1.   **Overall Audit Strategy**

a.   Planning continues throughout the audit. It initially involves developing an overall audit strategy.

b.   The size and complexity of the entity, the auditor's experience with the entity, and changes in circumstances during the audit affect planning. The following are examples of other matters the auditor should consider in developing the audit strategy:

1)   Characteristics of the engagement and reporting objectives
2)   Determination of materiality (The materiality outline is in Subunit 3.3.)
3)   Areas of high risk of material misstatement
4)   Involvement of specialists and use of component auditors
5)   Management's commitment to sound internal control
6)   Relevant entity-specific, industry, or financial developments
7)   Audit resources required
8)   The results of preliminary engagement activities related to such matters as (a) continuance of the client, (b) compliance with ethical requirements, and (c) the terms of the engagement.

c.   The engagement partner is responsible for directing, supervising, and performing the audit in accordance with (1) professional standards, (2) legal and regulatory requirements, and (3) firm policies.

2.   **Audit Plans in Accordance with GAAS**

a.   An audit plan based on the audit strategy must be developed and documented for all audit engagements. It includes the nature, timing, and extent of procedures expected to reduce audit risk to an acceptably low level.

1)   Thus, the audit plan includes a description of risk assessment procedures.

a)   **Risk assessment procedures** are performed to obtain an understanding of the entity and its environment, including its internal control, to identify and assess the **risks of material misstatement (RMMs)** at the levels of (1) the financial statements as a whole and (2) relevant assertions.

i)   The RMM is the combined assessment of **inherent risk** and **control risk**. (The definitions are in Subunit 3.3.)
ii)   Risk assessment procedures are described in Subunit 3.4.

2) The plan also includes a description of **further procedures** at the relevant assertion levels for material classes of transactions, account balances, and disclosures. These procedures are to be performed in response to assessed risks and evaluations of audit evidence collected to date.

   a) This element of the plan is based on (1) the decision whether to test the operating effectiveness of controls and (2) the nature, timing, and extent of planned substantive procedures.

3) The third element of the plan describes any **other procedures** required by GAAS or the PCAOB.

b. The overall audit strategy and audit plan are likely to be adjusted as the audit progresses. For example, the auditor may change the nature, timing, and extent of further audit procedures as risk assessments are revised.

c. The overall audit strategy, the audit plan, and changes in them are documented.

d. Planning also involves determining whether and to what extent the services of IT, tax, and other **specialists** will be required. The auditor should have supervisory responsibility for specialists. Moreover, the auditor should have sufficient knowledge to

   1) Communicate his or her objectives,
   2) Evaluate whether his or her planned procedures will achieve the objectives, and
   3) Evaluate the results.

3. **Communication**

a. The auditor should discuss elements of planning with management to facilitate the performance of the audit.

   1) But the communication should not compromise the audit, for example, by making detailed procedures too predictable.

4. **Initial Audits**

a. The following are examples of additional planning considerations for initial audits:

   1) Performance of quality control procedures, e.g., those related to (a) acceptance and continuance of clients and engagements, (b) assignment of engagement teams, (c) ethical requirements, and (d) performance
   2) Communication with the predecessor auditor
   3) Major issues discussed with management
   4) Planned audit procedures regarding **opening balances** to gain assurance that

      a) Opening balances do not contain misstatements that materially affect the current period's financial statements, and

      b) Accounting policies reflected in the opening balances have been consistently applied in the current period's financial statements.

b. When the prior-period statements were audited by a **predecessor auditor**, the auditor should request management to authorize the predecessor to (1) allow a review of audit documentation and (2) respond fully to inquiries by the auditor. Thus, the auditor is provided with information to assist in planning and performing the engagement.

   1) The predecessor ordinarily permits the auditor to review audit documentation, including documentation of (a) planning, (b) risk assessment procedures, (c) further audit procedures, (d) audit results, and (e) other matters of continuing accounting and auditing significance.

      a) The predecessor's denial or limitation of access may affect (1) the auditor's assessment of risk regarding the opening balances or (2) the nature, timing, and extent of the auditor's procedures applied to the opening balances and the consistency of accounting principles.

5. **Direction and Supervision**

    a.   AU-C 220 addresses quality control for an audit. It states that direction involves informing team members about the following:

        1)   Their responsibilities, including ethical requirements and planning and performing the audit with professional skepticism

        2)   The objectives of the work

        3)   The nature of the entity's business

        4)   Risks

        5)   Potential problems

        6)   The specific approach to the engagement

    b.   Team members should hold discussions so that questions about the engagement may be raised. Furthermore, teamwork and training facilitate understanding of the objectives of the assigned work.

    c.   Supervision includes consideration of the competencies of the team members, such as whether they (1) have enough time for the work, (2) understand the instructions, and (3) carry out the work in accordance with the audit plan.

        1)   Supervision also includes (a) tracking engagement progress, (b) addressing significant findings, and (c) modifying the approach if necessary. Moreover, matters may arise that should be considered by qualified team members during the engagement.

    d.   According to AU-C 220 and QC 10, differences of opinion (1) within the engagement team, (2) with a consultant, or (3) between the engagement partner and the quality control reviewer should be resolved by following the firm's related policies and procedures.

    e.   According to QC 10, a member of the engagement team should be able to document his or her disagreement with the conclusions reached after appropriate consultation. Moreover, (1) conclusions should be documented and implemented, and (2) the report should be released only after resolution of the matter.

    f.   The PCAOB's AS 1215 requires documentation of disagreements among members of the engagement team or with consultants about final conclusions on significant accounting or auditing matters.

6.   Audit team members should be included in the discussion about the susceptibility of the statements to material misstatement due to fraud or error, but especially **fraud**. The discussion aids in understanding the entity and its environment, including its internal control, and the risks it confronts. (The outline on this topic is in Subunit 3.6.)

    a.   Moreover, the discussion should emphasize **professional skepticism**.

        1)   It is an attitude that includes a questioning mind and critical assessment of audit evidence (AU-C 200).

7. **Internal Audit Plans**

    a.   Internal audit plans differ from those written by the independent external auditor.

        1)   The independent external auditor's purpose is to express an opinion on the fairness of the financial statements, i.e., to evaluate the client's financial reporting.

2) However, the internal auditor's work is more comprehensive. According to **The Institute of Internal Auditors**, internal auditing is an independent, objective assurance **and** consulting function that adds value and improves an organization's operations. Internal auditors evaluate and improve the effectiveness of governance, risk management, and control processes. Accordingly, they evaluate risks and the adequacy and effectiveness of controls regarding (a) the reliability and integrity of financial and operational information; (b) the effectiveness and efficiency of operations; (c) the safeguarding of assets; and (d) compliance with laws, regulations, and contracts.

   a) Consequently, the internal auditor's plans are more detailed and cover areas that normally are not considered by the independent auditor.

NOTE: Independence is an organizational attribute of the internal audit activity. Individual internal auditors are employees of the entity and cannot be independent in the same sense as external auditors.

Stop and review! You have completed the outline for this subunit. Study multiple-choice questions 4 and 5 on page 87.

3.3 AUDIT RISK AND MATERIALITY

 The CPA exam can be viewed as your ticket into the profession. The AICPA uses the exam as part of its attempt to ensure that you recognize the risks associated with your new career. Thus, many questions relate to risks that accountants face. Alternatively, few questions relate to the rewards that the profession provides. Study appropriately.

1. Audit risk and materiality are considered in (a) planning and performing the audit, (b) evaluating the results, and (c) forming an opinion on the financial statements. They also are reflected in the auditor's report.

   a. Audit risk is the risk that an auditor expresses an inappropriate opinion on materially misstated financial statements.

2. **Audit Risk**

   a. Audit risk consists of the risks of material misstatement (inherent risk combined with control risk) and detection risk. The RMMs are the entity's risks, and detection risk is the auditor's risk. The components may be assessed in quantitative terms, such as percentages, or in nonquantitative terms.

      1) **Inherent risk** is the susceptibility of an assertion about a class of transaction, account balance, or disclosure to a misstatement that could be material, individually or combined with other misstatements, before consideration of related controls.

      2) **Control risk** is the risk that internal control will not timely prevent, or detect and correct, a material misstatement that could occur in an assertion.

      3) **Detection risk** is the risk that the procedures performed by the auditor to reduce audit risk to an acceptably low level will not detect a material misstatement. It is a function of the effectiveness of an audit procedure and its application by the auditor.

         a) Detection risk is the only component of audit risk that can be changed at the auditor's discretion. (Inherent risk and control risk exist independently of the audit and cannot be changed by the auditor.)

         b) The acceptable level of detection risk for a given audit risk is inversely related to the assessed RMMs at the assertion level.

3. **Materiality**

    a. Materiality is a matter of professional judgment about whether misstatements could reasonably influence the economic decisions of users as a group, given their common informational needs.

        1) Users are assumed to be knowledgeable and reasonable economic decision makers with an understanding of financial statements and their limits.

        2) Materiality judgments are made given the surrounding circumstances and depend on the size (quantitative considerations) or nature (qualitative considerations, such as whether a misstatement changes income into a loss or a loss into income) of a misstatement (or both).

            a) Thus, materiality established when planning the audit is not necessarily an amount below which uncorrected misstatements are always immaterial.

    b. Materiality is defined for planning purposes at three related levels.

        1) Materiality at the **financial statement level** as a whole is a monetary amount that results in the misstatement of the financial statements.

        2) Materiality levels also are set for particular **account balances, classes of transactions, or disclosures**. In specific circumstances, these amounts could influence users.

            a) Benchmarks often are used as a starting point in determining materiality for the financial statements.

                i) Examples might include a percentage of client income (e.g., 5%), revenues (e.g., 1%), assets (e.g., 0.5%), or some combination.

        3) **Performance materiality** is the amount(s) set by the auditor at less than the materiality for (a) the statements as a whole or (b) particular classes of transactions, balances, or disclosures.

            a) Performance materiality is an adjustment to reduce to an appropriately low level the probability that the sum of (1) uncorrected and (2) undetected misstatements (whether or not individually material) exceeds the applicable materiality.

EXAMPLE

If financial statement materiality was set at $50,000 and materiality for the accounts receivable balance was set at $10,000, performance materiality for the audit of accounts receivable might be set at $3,000 to compensate for the possibility of multiple undetected or uncorrected misstatements in accounts receivable.

---

    c. During the audit, the auditor may obtain new information that requires revision of materiality judgments.

        1) If the revised materiality is lower, the auditor considers whether to revise (a) performance materiality and (b) the nature, timing, and extent of further audit procedures.

    d. Audit risk and materiality are considered in

        1) Planning the audit;

        2) Determining the nature and extent of risk assessment procedures;

        3) Assessing RMMs;

        4) Determining the nature, timing, and extent of further audit procedures; and

> 5) Evaluating the effects of any (a) identified misstatements on the audit and (b) uncorrected misstatements on the financial statements and the audit opinion.
>
> > a) A **misstatement** is the difference between (1) the amount, classification, presentation, or disclosure of a reported item in the financial statements and (2) the amount, etc., required for the item to be presented fairly.

4. **Evaluating Findings**

   a. When evaluating audit findings, the auditor considers **uncorrected misstatements** and should **accumulate identified misstatements** (unless clearly trivial). To evaluate accumulated misstatements and communicate misstatements to appropriate parties, the auditor may classify them as factual, judgmental, and projected.

      1) No doubt exists about **factual misstatements**.
      2) **Judgmental misstatements** result from management's (a) unreasonable accounting estimates or (b) application of inappropriate accounting policies.
      3) **Projected misstatements** are the auditor's best estimates of the misstatements in populations based on audit samples.

   b. If accumulated misstatement approaches materiality, a more than acceptable risk may exist that the sum of (1) possible undetected misstatements and (2) accumulated uncorrected misstatements could exceed materiality.

   c. The auditor should promptly communicate to appropriate management all accumulated misstatements and request their correction.

      1) The auditor also may request that management

         a) Examine, based on the auditor's projected misstatement, a transaction class, balance, or disclosure and make an adjustment for the actual misstatement;
         b) Record an adjustment for factual misstatements; and
         c) Review the assumptions and methods used to develop a judgmental misstatement.

      2) Identification of a material misstatement may indicate a significant deficiency or material weakness in internal control that should be communicated to management and those charged with governance.
      3) Uncorrected misstatements should be communicated to those charged with governance.

5. **Documentation**

   a. The auditor should document

      1) The amount below which misstatements are clearly trivial,
      2) All misstatements accumulated,
      3) Whether accumulated misstatements have been corrected, and
      4) The basis for the conclusion about whether uncorrected misstatements (individually or aggregated) are material.

Stop and review! You have completed the outline for this subunit. Study multiple-choice questions 6 through 8 beginning on page 88.

3.4 UNDERSTANDING THE ENTITY AND ITS ENVIRONMENT

1. The auditor obtains an understanding of the entity and its environment, including its internal control, to identify and assess the risks of material misstatement of the financial statements, whether due to fraud or error.

    a. The understanding provides a basis for designing and implementing responses to the assessed RMMs.

2. The following are among the other reasons for obtaining the understanding:

    a. Determining materiality for planning the audit and evaluating it during the audit
    b. Considering accounting policies and disclosures
    c. Identifying areas for special audit consideration, e.g., complex financial transactions
    d. Setting expectations for results of analytical procedures
    e. Designing further audit procedures
    f. Evaluating audit evidence, e.g., that related to management's assumptions and representations

3. **Risk Assessment Procedures**

    a. Risk assessment procedures are performed to obtain the understanding. They include (1) inquiries of management, appropriate individuals in the internal audit function, and others within the entity; (2) analytical procedures; and (3) observation and inspection.

        1) The auditor also may perform other appropriate procedures, such as inquiring of external parties (e.g., legal counsel) or reviewing externally generated information (e.g., financial publications).

    b. **Inquiries within the entity** may be directed to the following:

        1) Those responsible for financial reporting
        2) Those charged with governance
        3) To evaluate accounting policies, employees involved in complex or unusual transactions
        4) Legal counsel
        5) Marketing, sales, and production managers
        6) The risk management function
        7) Information systems personnel
        8) Others at different levels of authority who may have information about the RMMs

    c. An **analytical procedures** outline is in the next subunit.

    d. **Observation and inspection** provide support for inquiries and direct evidence about the entity and its environment. Examples are

        1) Observing activities and operations;
        2) Inspecting documents and records;
        3) Reading reports, e.g., internal audit reports, interim statements, quarterly reports, and minutes of board meetings;
        4) Tours of facilities; and
        5) Tracing financial transactions through the information system (a walk-through).

4. **Obtaining the Understanding**

    a. The understanding of the entity should include the following:

        1) Industry, regulatory, and other external factors, including the accounting framework
        2) The nature of the entity, including its operating characteristics

3) Ownership and governance structures, especially complex structures such as those that include subsidiaries or multiple locations

4) Investments and investment activities, such as acquisitions, divestitures, and capital outlays

5) Financing activities

6) Selection and application of accounting principles, including any changes

7) Objectives and strategies and the related business risks, such as those related to new products, markets, or expansion

   a) A **business risk** results from (1) significant factors that could adversely affect an entity's ability to achieve objectives and execute strategies or (2) setting inappropriate objectives and strategies. The auditor should obtain an understanding of the entity's objectives and strategies and the related business risks with immediate or longer-term consequences that may result in risks of material misstatement.

      i) For example, business risks may result from developing new products that may fail.

8) Measurement and review of financial performance as an indication of what the entity considers important

5. Use of **prior-period information** about the entity and its environment (structure, nature of business, controls, and responses to prior misstatements) contributes to the understanding.

   a. But procedures should be performed to evaluate its current relevance.

6. The auditor specifically assesses the RMM due to **fraud**. (S)he considers this assessment in designing auditing procedures. (The outline on fraud risks is in Subunit 3.6.)

   a. The audit team members should discuss (1) the susceptibility of the entity's financial statements to material misstatement, whether due to fraud or error, and (2) the application of the financial reporting framework.

      1) This discussion should be documented.

7. The auditor may consider pertinent information obtained from (a) the auditor's client acceptance (or continuation) procedures, (b) previous engagements for the client, and (c) other sources.

8. **Internal Control**

   a. The auditor obtains an understanding of relevant internal controls to

      1) Determine the types of possible misstatements,
      2) Identify what affects the RMMs, and
      3) Design further procedures (tests of controls and substantive procedures).

9. **Issuers**

   a. For an audit of an issuer, the auditor should consider the following:

      1) Reading public information about the company
      2) Obtaining information from earnings calls to investors and rating agencies
      3) Gaining an understanding of compensation for senior management
      4) Obtaining information about trading activities in the company's securities
      5) Company performance measures that could create incentives or pressures on management to manipulate the financial information

10. In general, the auditor should consider the likely sources of material misstatement and ask, "What could go wrong?"

Stop and review! You have completed the outline for this subunit. Study multiple-choice questions 9 and 10 on page 89.

3.5 ANALYTICAL PROCEDURES

Background
The Auditing Standards Board (ASB) recognized that most audit procedures are fairly narrow in scope. That is, they are directed toward a particular assertion for a specific account. In some cases, auditors have failed because they "missed the forest by focusing on the trees." Analytical procedures, however, are much broader in scope. For example, the auditor might ask "Can the client's reported inventory fit in its current warehouse space?" The ASB decided that analytical procedures should be applied in every audit.

1. Analytical procedures are evaluations of financial information made by **a study of plausible relationships among financial and nonfinancial data**.

2. Plausible relationships among data are reasonably expected to exist and continue in the absence of known conditions to the contrary. Analytical procedures also include investigating fluctuations or relationships that (a) are inconsistent with other information or (b) differ significantly from expectations.

Auditor Developed Expectation of Balance or Ratio	———→	Materially Different?	←———	Management Reported Balance or Ratio

3. **Timing and Use**

   a. Analytical procedures may be applied not only as risk assessment procedures (analytical procedures used to plan the audit) but also as **substantive procedures**. These are procedures (tests of details and analytical procedures) designed to detect material misstatements at the assertion level. When applying substantive analytical procedures, the auditor should

      1) Determine their suitability for specific assertions after considering the assessed RMMs and any tests of details.
      2) Evaluate the reliability of data used to develop an expectation of an amount or ratio.
      3) Develop an expectation and determine whether it is sufficiently precise to identify a material misstatement.
      4) Use them to assist in forming an overall conclusion near the end of the audit about whether the statements are consistent with the auditor's understanding of the entity.

4. **Risk Assessment Procedures**

   a. Analytical procedures applied as risk assessment procedures at the beginning of the audit may improve the understanding of the client's business and significant transactions and events since the last audit. They also may identify unusual transactions or events and amounts, ratios, and trends that might indicate matters with audit planning implications.

      1) But when they use highly aggregated data, they provide only broad indications about the RMMs.

5. **Development of Expectations**

   a. The auditor develops expectations or predictions of recorded balances or ratios. The candidate should learn the **five sources of information** used to develop analytical procedures. They are frequently tested on the CPA exam.

1) **Financial Information from Comparable Prior Period(s)**

EXAMPLE
If a client's prior reported sales were $120,000 in Year 1, $130,000 in Year 2, and $140,000 in Year 3, respectively, the auditor is likely to predict Year 4 sales to be approximately $150,000 based on the trend. If management's reported sales are materially different, the auditor increases the assessed RMM and investigates the underlying causes.

2) **Anticipated Results**, such as budgets or forecasts prepared by management (or others) prior to the end of the period

EXAMPLE
If management's budget at the beginning of the period includes cost of sales of $100,000, the auditor expects cost of sales to approximate $100,000 at year end.
The use of standard costs and variance analysis facilitates the application of analytical procedures in this context.

3) **Relationships among Elements of Financial Information**, such as those among the balances on the financial statements

EXAMPLE
If the auditor determines that sales increased by 25% for the year, accounts receivable should increase by approximately that amount.

4) **Comparable Information from the Client's Industry**

EXAMPLE
If the usual inventory turnover ratio in the industry is 10 times per year, the auditor expects the client's turnover ratio to be approximately 10 times.

5) **Relationships between Financial and Relevant Nonfinancial Information**

EXAMPLE
If the number of hours worked increased by 30%, the auditor expects an increase in labor costs of approximately 30%.

6. **Substantive Procedures**

   a. The auditor's judgment about expected effectiveness and efficiency in reducing the assessed RMMs to an acceptable level determines the procedures chosen. For some assertions, analytical procedures alone may provide the necessary assurance. The effectiveness and efficiency of analytical procedures depend on the following factors:

   1) **Nature of the assertion.** Analytical procedures may be effective when tests of details may not indicate potential misstatements. For example, they may be effective for testing the completeness assertion.

   2) **Plausibility and predictability of the relationship.** Relationships in stable environments are more predictable than those in unstable environments, and income statement amounts tend to be more predictable than balance sheet amounts.

      a) The reason is that income statement amounts are based on transactions over a period of time, but balance sheet amounts are for a moment in time.

      b) Amounts subject to management discretion may be less predictable.

3) **Availability and reliability of the data used to develop the expectation.** Reliability is affected by the source of the data and the conditions under which they were gathered. For example, data are considered more reliable when

a) Obtained from independent sources outside the entity,

b) Obtained from sources inside the entity independent of those responsible for the amount being audited,

c) Developed under reliable internal control,

d) Subjected to audit testing in the current or prior years, and

e) Obtained from a variety of sources.

4) **Precision of the expectation.** As the expectation becomes more precise, significant differences between the expectation and management's reported number are more likely to be caused by misstatements.

a) Ordinarily, the more detailed the information, the more precise the expectation. For example, monthly data provide more precise expectations than annual data.

b. **Scanning** is a type of analytical procedure using auditor judgment to identify significant or unusual items to test.

7. **Forming an Overall Conclusion**

a. Analytical procedures used to form an overall conclusion ordinarily include reading the financial statements and considering (1) the adequacy of evidence regarding unusual or unexpected balances detected during the audit and (2) such balances or relationships not detected previously.

1) If analytical procedures detect a previously unrecognized RMM, the auditor should revise the assessments of the RMMs and modify the further planned procedures.

8. **Acceptable Differences**

a. The determination that differences between expectations and recorded amounts are acceptable without additional investigation is a function of materiality and the desired degree of assurance. It also considers that the sum of individually insignificant items may be significant.

1) As the assessed risk increases, the amount of acceptable difference decreases.

9. **Investigating Results**

a. Inconsistent fluctuations or relationships or significant differences should result in (1) inquiries of management, (2) corroboration of responses with other audit evidence, and (3) performance of any necessary other procedures. Moreover, the RMMs due to fraud should be considered.

10. **Documentation**

a. When substantive analytical procedures are performed, the auditor should document

1) The expectation,

2) The factors used to develop the expectation,

3) The results of the comparison of the expectation with the recorded amounts or ratios, and

4) Any additional auditing procedures performed to resolve differences and their results.

11. Ratio Analysis

a. Auditors apply ratio analysis in all stages of the audit as analytical procedures. An auditor should understand not only how to calculate each ratio but also the potential explanations of changes in a ratio from period to period. Many of the ratios considered here have been tested recently on the CPA exam.

1) **Current ratio**

$$\frac{Current\ assets}{Current\ liabilities}$$

   a) Changes in the ratio may be caused by changes in the components of current assets (typically cash, receivables, and inventory) and current liabilities (typically accounts payable and notes payable).

   b) If the current ratio is less than 1.0, equal increases in the numerator and denominator increase the ratio, and equal decreases decrease the ratio.

   i) However, if the current ratio is more than 1.0, equal increases in the numerator and denominator decrease the ratio, and equal decreases increase the ratio.

2) **Quick (acid-test) ratio**

$$\frac{Current\ assets\ -\ Inventory}{Current\ liabilities}$$

   a) Quick assets are convertible to cash quickly. Auditors ordinarily calculate this ratio as current assets minus inventory. Thus, changes in inventory do not affect the quick ratio, but other components of the current ratio do.

3) **Receivables turnover**

$$\frac{Net\ sales}{Average\ net\ receivables}$$

   a) Auditors often calculate this ratio using ending net receivables as the denominator because it is the balance being audited. Changes in sales or receivables affect this ratio.

   b) In principle, the numerator should be net credit sales, but this amount may not be known.

4) **Days' sales in receivables**

$$\frac{Number\ of\ days\ in\ year}{Receivables\ turnover}$$

   a) This ratio has the same components as receivables turnover and is affected by changes in sales or receivables.

   b) The number of days in a year may be 365, 360 (a banker's year), or 300 (number of business days).

5) **Inventory turnover**

$$\frac{Cost\ of\ goods\ sold}{Average\ inventory}$$

   a) Auditors often calculate this ratio using ending inventory as the denominator because it is the balance being audited. Changes in cost of goods sold or inventory affect this ratio.

   b) A high turnover implies that the entity does not hold excessive inventories that are unproductive and lessen its profitability.

   c) A high turnover also implies that the inventory is truly marketable and does not contain obsolete goods.

6) **Days' sales in inventory**

$$\frac{Number\ of\ days\ in\ year}{Inventory\ turnover}$$

a) This ratio has the same components as inventory turnover and is affected by changes in inventory or cost of sales.

b) The number of days in a year may be 365, 360 (a banker's year), or 300 (number of business days).

7) **Total asset turnover**

$$\frac{Net\ sales}{Total\ assets}$$

a) This ratio calculates how many times the total assets turn over in sales. It is affected by changes in sales and total assets.

b) The denominator also may be average total assets.

8) **Debt-to-equity ratio**

$$\frac{Total\ debt}{Total\ equity}$$

a) This ratio measures how much external parties contribute to assets relative to owners. Shifts in debt or equity affect this ratio.

b) The ratios of total assets to total equity and total assets to total debt provide similar analysis and conclusions.

9) **Times interest earned**

$$\frac{Net\ income\ +\ Interest\ expense\ +\ Income\ tax\ expense}{Interest\ expense}$$

a) Times interest earned measures the ability of an entity to pay its interest charges. Taxes are added back to net income because interest is paid before taxes. Interest is added back to net income because it is included in the calculation of net income.

b) An alternative is to exclude interest from the numerator and to add 1.0 to the quotient once the calculation is made.

c) Changes in interest and net income may affect this ratio.

d) If earnings decline sufficiently, no income tax expense will be recognized.

10) **Cost of goods sold ratio**

$$\frac{Cost\ of\ goods\ sold}{Net\ sales}$$

a) This ratio measures the percentage amount of sales consumed by cost of goods sold. Nonproportional changes in either affect the ratio.

11) **Gross margin percentage**

$$\frac{Net\ sales\ -\ Cost\ of\ goods\ sold}{Net\ sales}$$

a) The gross margin percentage measures earnings from the sale of products. Nonproportional changes in net sales and cost of goods sold affect the ratio.

12) **Net operating margin percentage**

$$\frac{Operating\ income}{Net\ sales}$$

a) Operating income is calculated before subtracting interest and taxes. Nonproportional changes in either operating income or net sales cause a change in the ratio.

13) **Return on equity**

$$\frac{Net\ income}{Total\ equity}$$

   a) This is an overall measure of a rate of return on investment. Changes in net income or changes in equity may affect this ratio.

   b) A return on average total equity or on common equity also may be calculated.

Stop and review! You have completed the outline for this subunit. Study multiple-choice questions 11 through 14 beginning on page 90.

3.6 CONSIDERATION OF FRAUD IN A FINANCIAL STATEMENT AUDIT

1. **Responsibilities**

   a. Fraud is an "intentional act by one or more individuals among management, those charged with governance, employees, or third parties, involving the use of deception that results in a misstatement in financial statements that are the subject of an audit." The auditor should plan and perform the audit to obtain reasonable assurance about whether the financial statements are free of material misstatement, whether caused by fraud or error.

   b. Those charged with governance (the board and audit committee) and management are primarily responsible for programs and controls that prevent, deter, and detect fraud. They should set the proper tone and maintain a culture of honesty.

      1) Absolute assurance is unattainable because of the characteristics of fraud and the inherent limitations of an audit. Management may override controls in unpredictable ways or alter accounting records. Fraud also may be concealed through collusion, falsifying documentation (including electronic approvals), or withholding evidence.

2. Fraud is intentional. The three conditions ordinarily present when fraud exists include **pressures or incentives** to commit fraud, an **opportunity**, and the capacity to **rationalize** misconduct.

3. The types of fraud relevant to the auditor include misstatements arising from

   a. **Fraudulent financial reporting.** These are intentional misstatements or omissions to deceive users, such as altering accounting records or documents, misrepresenting or omitting significant information, and misapplying accounting principles.

   b. **Misappropriation of assets.** These result from, for example, (1) theft of physical assets or intellectual property, (2) embezzlement (e.g., stealing collections of receivables), (3) an action that causes payment for items not received, or (4) using entity assets for personal reasons.

4. **Professional Skepticism**

   a. Professional skepticism should be maintained in considering the risk of material misstatement due to fraud **(fraud risk)**. An auditor should (1) critically assess evidence, (2) continually question whether fraud has occurred, and (3) not accept unpersuasive evidence solely because management is believed to be honest.

   b. Discussion among key engagement team members (including the engagement partner) should emphasize professional skepticism and continual alertness to potential fraud. It may occur before or during information gathering, and communication should be ongoing.

      1) The discussion should include brainstorming about (a) factors that might create the conditions for fraud, (b) how and where the statements might be misstated, (c) how assets might be misappropriated or financial reports fraudulently misstated, (d) how management could conceal fraudulent reporting, and (e) how to respond to fraud risk.

5.   **Identifying Fraud Risks**

   a.   Obtaining information for identifying fraud risks includes inquiring of (1) management, (2) those charged with governance, (3) the internal auditors, and (4) others. It also involves considering (1) fraud risk factors and (2) the results of analytical procedures performed as risk assessment procedures.

   1)   The auditor should apply analytical procedures to **revenue accounts**, e.g., by comparing recorded sales and production capacity to detect fictitious sales.

   2)   **Fraud risk factors** are events or conditions indicating possible fraud. The auditor should judge whether they are present and affect the assessment of fraud risks.

   3)   Other information may be derived from (a) discussions among audit team members, (b) procedures related to the acceptance and continuance of clients and engagements, (c) reviews of interim statements, and (d) identified inherent risks at the account-balance or class-of-transactions level.

   b.   An identifiable risk may exist when all the conditions for fraud have not been observed, especially rationalization. The extent of a condition may by itself create a fraud risk, e.g., pressure to reach an earnings goal.

   1)   Fraud risks vary with the entity's size, complexity, ownership, etc.

   2)   Fraud risks may relate to specific assertions or to the statements as a whole.

   3)   High inherent risk of an assertion about an account balance or transaction class may exist when it is susceptible to management manipulation.

   4)   Identifying fraud risks involves considering the type of risk and (a) its significance, (b) likelihood, and (c) pervasiveness.

   5)   The auditor should address the risk of **management override** of controls in all audits because of its unpredictability.

   6)   The auditor ordinarily should assume the existence of a fraud risk relating to **improper revenue recognition**. The contrary conclusion should be documented in the working papers.

   c.   Identified fraud risks are assessed at the statement and assertion levels and treated as significant. This assessment is ongoing after the initial assessment.

   1)   To the extent not done previously, the auditor should obtain an understanding of the relevant controls. Also, the auditor should evaluate whether (a) those controls have been suitably designed and implemented and (b) they reduce the risks.

6.   **Responses to Fraud Risk**

   a.   The responses to the assessment of fraud risks should reflect a critical evaluation of the audit evidence. Responses (1) may have an overall effect on the audit, (2) involve further audit procedures performed in response to assessed fraud risks at the assertion level, or (3) address management override.

   b.   One **overall effect** is to assign more experienced personnel, or individuals with special skills, or to increase supervision. A second overall effect is to consider accounting principles, especially those involving subjective measurements and complex transactions, and whether they indicate a **collective bias**. Another overall effect is to make unpredictable choices of audit procedures.

   c.   Audit procedures vary with fraud risks and the balances, transactions, and assertions affected. Procedures may (1) provide more reliable evidence or increased corroboration, (2) be performed at year end or throughout the reporting period, or (3) involve larger samples or the use of computer-assisted techniques.

    d.   The auditor should further address management override.

        1)   Material misstatements may result from inappropriate **journal entries or adjustments**, particularly those made at year end. The auditor should therefore

            a)   Understand the financial reporting process and controls

            b)   Identify, select, and test entries and adjustments after considering the risk assessments, effectiveness of controls, nature of the reporting process, and audit evidence (electronic or manual)

            c)   Choose whether to test entries during the period

            d)   Make inquiries about inappropriate or unusual activity

        2)   Fraud may result from intentional misstatement of **accounting estimates**. The auditor should perform a retrospective review of estimates in the prior-year statements that are based on sensitive assumptions or significant management judgments.

        3)   The auditor should understand **significant unusual transactions**.

7.   **Evaluating Audit Evidence**

    a.   The assessment of fraud risks should be ongoing because field work may reveal conditions that modify the judgment.

    b.   Analytical procedures performed near the end of the audit in forming an overall conclusion or as substantive procedures may detect previously unrecognized fraud risks. These procedures should be applied to revenue through year end. The auditor also should evaluate responses to inquiries about analytical relationships.

    c.   At or near the end of field work, the auditor should evaluate earlier assessments of fraud risk. The performance of additional procedures may result. Furthermore, the auditor responsible for the audit should determine that information about fraud risks has been properly communicated to team members.

    d.   The auditor should consider whether identified misstatements indicate fraud, with consequent effects on materiality judgments. If the fraud is not material, the auditor still should evaluate the implications for the audit, e.g., the management's representations and integrity.

        1)   If management (especially senior management) is involved, the auditor should (a) reevaluate the assessment of fraud risks and its effects on audit procedures and (b) consider the possibility of collusion.

        2)   If fraud risk is great, the auditor may consider withdrawing and communicating the reasons to those charged with governance and, possibly, to regulators.

8.   **Communications**

    a.   Communications about fraud are required given evidence that fraud may exist. Inconsequential fraud should be communicated to the appropriate management. Other fraud should be reported directly to those charged with governance.

    b.   In determining a responsibility to report fraud outside the entity, the auditor's legal obligation may, in some circumstances, override the duty of confidentiality.

9.   **Documentation**

    a.   Documentation of the consideration of fraud should include the following:

        1)   Decisions made during the discussions among the engagement team

        2)   Identified and assessed risks at the statement and assertion levels

        3)   Overall responses, procedures performed, and the connection to assessed risks at the assertion level

        4)   Reasons for not identifying improper revenue recognition as a fraud risk

        5)   Results of procedures, including those addressing management override

        6)   Fraud communications

Stop and review! You have completed the outline for this subunit. Study multiple-choice questions 15 through 18 beginning on page 91.

3.7 CONSIDERATION OF LAWS AND REGULATIONS IN AN AUDIT OF FINANCIAL STATEMENTS

Background
The clarified auditing standard AU-C 250, *Consideration of Laws and Regulations in an Audit of Financial Statements*, replaced AU 317, *Illegal Acts by Clients*. Although the auditor's responsibilities have not changed significantly, some terminology has been updated. The standard replaced the phrase "illegal act" with the term "noncompliance." In the prior standard, laws and regulations not expected to have a "direct effect" on the financial statements were described as having a potential "indirect effect." Those are described now as "not having a direct effect."

1.   **Noncompliance**

   a.   Noncompliance is an intentional or unintentional act or omission by the entity that is contrary to laws or regulations. It includes an act

    1)   In the name of the entity or

    2)   On its behalf by

        a)   Those charged with governance,

        b)   Management, or

        c)   Employees.

   b.   Noncompliance does not include personal misconduct by the client's personnel unrelated to their business activities.

   c.   Whether an act constitutes noncompliance is a legal determination normally beyond the auditor's competence.

   d.   Noncompliance varies in its relation to the financial statements. The further removed it is from the financial statements, the less likely the auditor is to become aware of or recognize noncompliance.

    1)   The auditor should consider laws and regulations recognized as having a **direct effect** on the determination of material amounts and disclosures, such as tax laws.

    2)   Examples of laws and regulations less likely to have a direct and material effect include those relating to environmental protection, food and drug administration, securities trading, and antitrust.

2.   **Auditor's Responsibilities**

   a.   The auditor is responsible for obtaining reasonable assurance that the financial statements as a whole are free from material misstatement, whether caused by fraud or error. Accordingly, the auditor should obtain a general understanding of (1) the legal and regulatory framework applicable to the entity and (2) how it is complying with the framework.

    1)   Thus, the auditor's primary responsibility for noncompliance is to obtain sufficient appropriate audit evidence regarding material amounts and disclosures that are determined by laws and regulations generally recognized to have a direct effect on their determination.

   b.   **Other laws and regulations** do not have a direct effect. However, compliance with them may be (1) fundamental to the entity's operations or the continuance of its business or (2) necessary to avoid material penalties.

    1)   The auditor's responsibility regarding the second category of laws and regulations is to perform specified procedures to identify noncompliance that may materially affect the financial statements.

   c.   The auditor must remain alert during the audit to the possibility that other procedures may detect noncompliance or suspected noncompliance.

3. **Audit Procedures**

    a.   The auditor should perform the following procedures that may identify noncompliance with **other laws and regulations**:

        1)   Inquiring of management and, if appropriate, those charged with governance about whether the entity is in compliance with other laws and regulations

        2)   Inspecting correspondence, if any, with the relevant licensing or regulatory authorities

    b.   An audit usually does not include audit procedures specifically designed to detect noncompliance that does **not** have direct effects. Because of (1) the inherent limitations of an audit, (2) the possibility of concealment of noncompliance, and (3) the nature of such noncompliance, a properly planned and performed audit may not detect some material misstatements resulting from such noncompliance.

        1)   However, an auditor must be aware of the possibility of such noncompliance.

    c.   The following **results of normal procedures** should raise questions about the possibility of noncompliance:

        1)   Investigations by a governmental or regulatory agency

        2)   Unauthorized or improperly recorded transactions

        3)   Unexplained payments to consultants, affiliates, employees, or government officials

        4)   Unusual payments in cash, purchases of bank checks payable to bearer, or transfers to numbered accounts

        5)   Failure to file tax returns or pay governmental fees

        6)   Excessive sales commissions on agents' fees

        7)   Violations cited in reports by regulators

    d.   If information comes to the auditor's attention indicating **noncompliance or suspected noncompliance**, the auditor should apply appropriate audit procedures. These include the following:

        1)   Obtaining (a) an understanding of the act and the circumstances in which it occurred and (b) further information to evaluate its financial statement effects

        2)   Inquiring of management at a level above those involved or, if appropriate, those charged with governance

        3)   Consulting with the entity's legal counsel or external legal counsel

4. **Auditor's Response**

    a.   The auditor's response to **detected noncompliance** is to consider the effects on the financial statements and the implications for other aspects of the audit, especially the reliability of management's representations. The auditor should

        1)   Consider the qualitative and quantitative materiality of the noncompliance,

        2)   Consider the adequacy of disclosure, and

        3)   Communicate material problems to those charged with governance.

5. **Auditor's Opinion**

    a.   If material noncompliance has not been accounted for properly, the auditor should express a qualified or adverse opinion. If unable to collect sufficient appropriate evidence, the auditor usually disclaims an opinion.

    b.   When the auditor concludes that noncompliance has or is likely to have occurred, (s)he should discuss the matter with the appropriate level of management and request that any necessary remedial actions be taken.

    c.   If the alleged noncompliance has a material effect on the financial statements, or the client does not take the necessary remedial action, the auditor should express a qualified or an adverse opinion, depending on the level of materiality, or withdraw from the engagement.

6. **Disclosure**

a. Disclosure of possible noncompliance with laws and regulations to outside parties ordinarily is not the auditor's responsibility and would violate the duty of confidentiality. Any disclosure would be the responsibility of management. However, the auditor may need to

1) Comply with certain legal and regulatory requirements;
2) Communicate with a successor auditor in accordance with auditing standards;
3) Respond to a court order; or
4) Report to a funding or other specified agency in accordance with governmental audit requirements, such as those established by the *Single Audit Act*.

Stop and review! You have completed the outline for this subunit. Study multiple-choice question 19 and 20 beginning on page 92.

QUESTIONS

3.1 Pre-Engagement Acceptance Activities

1. Before accepting an audit engagement, an auditor should make specific inquiries of the predecessor auditor regarding the predecessor's

A. Awareness of the consistency in the application of generally accepted accounting principles between periods.

B. Evaluation of all matters of continuing accounting significance.

C. Opinion of any subsequent events occurring since the predecessor's audit report was issued.

D. Understanding as to the reasons for the change of auditors.

Answer (D) is correct.

   REQUIRED: The inquiries made by an auditor of a predecessor auditor before accepting an engagement.
   DISCUSSION: According to AU-C 210, the auditor should make specific and reasonable inquiries of the predecessor auditor regarding issues bearing upon acceptance of the engagement. The inquiries should include specific questions regarding, among other things, the predecessor's understanding as to the reasons for the change of auditors.
   Answer (A) is incorrect. A specific inquiry about consistency of application of GAAP is not necessary. Answer (B) is incorrect. All matters of continuing accounting significance are not applicable to the auditor's decision to accept the engagement. Answer (C) is incorrect. The predecessor is not responsible for events subsequent to his or her report.

2. The scope and nature of an auditor's contractual obligation to a client is ordinarily set forth in the

A. Management representation letter.

B. Scope paragraph of the auditor's report.

C. Engagement letter.

D. Introductory paragraph of the auditor's report.

Answer (C) is correct.

   REQUIRED: The form of the contract with a client.
   DISCUSSION: The terms of the engagement should be documented in an engagement letter that states the (1) objective and scope of the audit, (2) responsibilities of the auditor and management, (3) inherent limitations of the audit and internal control, (4) applicable financial reporting framework, and (5) expected form and content of audit reports. An engagement letter should be sent by the CPA to the prospective client on each engagement, audit or otherwise.
   Answer (A) is incorrect. An auditor obtains a written management representation letter to complement other procedures, but it is not part of the engagement letter. Answer (B) is incorrect. The auditor's report contains an auditor's responsibility section, not a scope paragraph. The engagement letter should state the form and content of audit reports, not audit reports. Answer (D) is incorrect. The introductory paragraph (1) identifies the auditee, (2) states that the financial statements were audited, (3) identifies the title of each statement, and (4) specifies the date or period of each statement.

3. Which of the following factors most likely would cause an auditor to decline a new audit engagement?

A. An inadequate understanding of the entity's internal control.

B. The close proximity to the end of the entity's fiscal year.

C. Failure of management to satisfy the preconditions for an audit.

D. An inability to perform preliminary analytical procedures before assessing control risk.

Answer (C) is correct.
REQUIRED: The factor most likely to cause an auditor to decline a new audit engagement.
DISCUSSION: The auditor should agree with management or those charged with governance upon the terms of the engagement. The auditor accepts the engagement only if (1) the preconditions for an audit are present and (2) a common understanding of the terms has been reached. The preconditions are (1) use of an acceptable accounting framework and (2) agreement on the premise of the audit. The premise relates to the fundamental responsibilities of management and, if appropriate, those charged with governance.
Answer (A) is incorrect. The understanding of the entity's internal control is obtained subsequent to the acceptance of the engagement. Answer (B) is incorrect. Although early appointment is preferable, an independent auditor may accept an engagement near or after the close of the fiscal year. Answer (D) is incorrect. Analytical procedures are performed after the acceptance of the engagement.

3.2 Planning an Audit

4. Audit plans should be designed so that

A. Most of the required procedures can be performed as interim work.

B. The risks of material misstatement are assessed at a sufficiently low level.

C. The auditor can make constructive suggestions to management.

D. The audit evidence gathered supports the auditor's conclusions.

Answer (D) is correct.
REQUIRED: The use of audit plans.
DISCUSSION: The auditor is responsible for collecting sufficient appropriate audit evidence to be able to draw reasonable conclusions on which to base the opinion. Audit plans describe the steps involved in that process. Thus, the evidence should support the auditor's conclusions.
Answer (A) is incorrect. Depending on the assertion, work may be performed at interim dates or in the subsequent events period. Answer (B) is incorrect. The RMMs are assessed based upon the characteristics of the client. Thus, performing more effective procedures may lead to higher assessed RMMs. Answer (C) is incorrect. Suggestions to management are not required in an audit.

5. In developing written audit plans, an auditor should design specific audit procedures that relate primarily to the

A. Timing of the audit.

B. Costs and benefits of gathering evidence.

C. Financial statements as a whole.

D. Financial statement assertions.

Answer (D) is correct.
REQUIRED: The item to which specific audit procedures primarily relate.
DISCUSSION: Most audit work consists of obtaining and evaluating evidence about relevant financial statement assertions. They are management representations embodied in the financial statements that are used by the auditor to consider the types of possible material misstatements.
Answer (A) is incorrect. Timing is important in developing audit plans, but it is not the primary basis for determining the audit procedures to be performed. Answer (B) is incorrect. The costs and benefits of gathering evidence are important to the auditor but are not the primary basis for determining the audit procedures to be performed. Answer (C) is incorrect. Most audit procedures are performed at the assertion level.

3.3 Audit Risk and Materiality

6. The acceptable level of detection risk is inversely related to the

- A. Assurance provided by substantive procedures.
- B. Risk of misapplying auditing procedures.
- C. Preliminary judgment about materiality levels.
- D. Risk of failing to discover material misstatements.

Answer (A) is correct.

REQUIRED: The concept to which acceptable detection risk is inversely related.

DISCUSSION: For a given audit risk, the acceptable detection risk is inversely related to the assessed risks of material misstatement. As the RMMs increase, the acceptable detection risk decreases, and the auditor requires more persuasive audit evidence. The auditor may (1) change the types of audit procedures and their combination, e.g., confirming the terms of a contract as well as inspecting it; (2) change the timing of substantive procedures, such as from an interim date to year end; or (3) change the extent of testing, such as by using a larger sample (AU-C 330 and AS 2301).

Answer (B) is incorrect. Detection risk, not the acceptable level of detection risk, relates directly to the risk of misapplying auditing procedures. As the effectiveness of audit procedures increases, e.g., because of adequate planning, proper assignment of personnel, and supervisory review, the risk of misapplication and detection risk decrease. Answer (C) is incorrect. Preliminary judgments about materiality levels are used by the auditor to determine the acceptable level of audit risk. Materiality and overall audit risk are inversely related. However, detection risk is just one component of audit risk. Answer (D) is incorrect. The lower the acceptable level of detection risk, the greater the required persuasiveness of audit evidence. Given this additional assurance, the risk of failing to detect material misstatements (detection risk) should be decreased. Accordingly, the relationship of acceptable detection risk and the risk of failing to detect material misstatements is direct.

7. The existence of audit risk is recognized by the statement in the auditor's report that the

- A. Auditor is responsible for expressing an opinion on the financial statements, which are the responsibility of management.
- B. Financial statements are presented fairly, in all material respects, in accordance with GAAP.
- C. Audit includes examining, on a test basis, evidence supporting the amounts and disclosures in the financial statements.
- D. Auditor obtains reasonable assurance about whether the financial statements are free of material misstatement.

Answer (D) is correct.

REQUIRED: The statement that recognizes the existence of audit risk.

DISCUSSION: Audit risk is the risk that the auditor expresses an inappropriate audit opinion when the financial statements are materially misstated (AU-C 200). The high, but not absolute, level of assurance that is intended to be obtained by the auditor is described in the auditor's responsibility section of the report. Reasonable assurance means that audit risk is reduced to an acceptably low level.

Answer (A) is incorrect. The auditor's responsibility is described in the auditor's responsibility section of the report. The responsibility of management is stated in a separate paragraph. Answer (B) is incorrect. Fair presentation does not necessarily imply a reduction in audit risk. In theory, it might imply absolute assurance (elimination of audit risk). Answer (C) is incorrect. Examining all items under audit is not feasible. This limitation is one of many inherent in the audit process. However, this language is not in the report.

8. Inherent risk and control risk differ from detection risk in which of the following ways?

   A. Inherent risk and control risk are calculated by the client.

   B. Inherent risk and control risk exist independently of the audit.

   C. Inherent risk and control risk are controlled by the auditor.

   D. Inherent risk and control risk exist as a result of the auditor's judgment about materiality.

Answer (B) is correct.
   REQUIRED: The way in which inherent risk and control risk differ from detection risk.
   DISCUSSION: Audit risk consists of the risks of material misstatement (inherent risk combined with control risk) and detection risk. The RMMs are the entity's risks, and detection risk is the auditor's risk. Detection risk is the risk that the procedures performed by the auditor to reduce audit risk to an acceptably low level will not detect a material misstatement. It is a function of the effectiveness of an audit procedure and its application by the auditor. Detection risk is the only component of audit risk that can be changed at the auditor's discretion. (Inherent risk and control risk exist independently of the audit and cannot be changed by the auditor.)
   Answer (A) is incorrect. Inherent risk and control risk (the risk of material misstatement) are assessed by the auditor. Answer (C) is incorrect. Inherent risk and control risk are controlled by the entity. Answer (D) is incorrect. Inherent risk and control risk are the entity's risks. The performance of audit procedures may change the assessment of inherent risk and control risk but not the actual inherent risk and control risk.

3.4 Understanding the Entity and Its Environment

9. Prior to beginning the field work on a new audit engagement in which a CPA does **not** possess expertise in the industry in which the client operates, the CPA should

   A. Reduce audit risk by lowering initial levels of materiality.

   B. Design special substantive procedures to compensate for the lack of industry expertise.

   C. Engage financial experts familiar with the nature of the industry.

   D. Perform risk assessment procedures.

Answer (D) is correct.
   REQUIRED: The action taken by an auditor who lacks experience with the client's industry.
   DISCUSSION: The auditor should obtain an understanding of the entity and its environment, including its internal control. For this purpose, the auditor performs the following risk assessment procedures: (1) inquiries of management and others within the entity, (2) analytical procedures, and (3) observation and inspection.
   Answer (A) is incorrect. The auditor cannot make judgments about materiality levels until (s)he has a sufficient understanding of the entity. Answer (B) is incorrect. The auditor cannot design substantive procedures until (s)he has a sufficient understanding of the entity. Answer (C) is incorrect. The use of experts does not relieve the auditor of the responsibility to obtain an understanding of the entity.

10. To obtain an understanding of a continuing client in planning an audit, an auditor most likely would

   A. Perform tests of details of transactions and balances.

   B. Read internal audit reports.

   C. Read specialized industry journals.

   D. Reevaluate the risks of material misstatement.

Answer (B) is correct.
   REQUIRED: The procedure used to obtain an understanding of a continuing client.
   DISCUSSION: The auditor performs risk assessment procedures to obtain the understanding of the entity and its environment, including its internal control. These include, for example, reading (1) internal audit reports, (2) interim statements, (3) quarterly reports, and (4) minutes of board meetings.
   Answer (A) is incorrect. Tests of details are used to collect sufficient, appropriate audit evidence to support the opinion. Answer (C) is incorrect. Reading specialized industry journals would provide information about the industry, but not necessarily about the specific client. Answer (D) is incorrect. The auditor reevaluates the RMMs after updating the understanding of a continuing client.

3.5 Analytical Procedures

11. A basic premise underlying analytical procedures is that

A. These procedures cannot replace tests of balances and transactions.

B. Statistical tests of financial information may lead to the discovery of material misstatements in the financial statements.

C. The study of financial ratios is an acceptable alternative to the investigation of unusual fluctuations.

D. Plausible relationships among data may reasonably be expected to exist and continue in the absence of known conditions to the contrary.

Answer (D) is correct.
　REQUIRED: The basic premise underlying analytical procedures.
　DISCUSSION: A basic premise underlying the application of analytical procedures is that plausible relationships among data may reasonably be expected to exist and continue in the absence of known conditions to the contrary. Variability in these relationships can be explained by, for example, unusual events or transactions, business or accounting changes, misstatements, or random fluctuations.
　Answer (A) is incorrect. For some assertions, analytical procedures alone may provide the auditor with the level of assurance (s)he desires. Answer (B) is incorrect. Analytical procedures, such as simple comparisons, do not necessarily require statistical testing. Answer (C) is incorrect. The objective of analytical procedures, such as ratio analysis, is to identify significant differences for evaluation and possible investigation.

12. For all audits of financial statements made in accordance with auditing standards, the use of analytical procedures is required to some extent

	As Risk Assessment Procedures	As Substantive Procedures	To Assist in Forming an Overall Conclusion
A.	Yes	No	Yes
B.	No	Yes	No
C.	No	Yes	Yes
D.	Yes	No	No

Answer (A) is correct.
　REQUIRED: The required use(s), if any, of analytical procedures.
　DISCUSSION: Analytical procedures should be applied as risk assessment procedures to obtain an understanding of the entity and its environment, including internal control, and to assess the risks of material misstatement. They also may, but are not required to, be applied as substantive procedures. These are procedures (tests of details and analytical procedures) designed to detect material misstatements at the assertion level. Moreover, the auditor should perform analytical procedures near the end of the audit to assist in forming an overall conclusion. The purpose is to determine whether the statements are consistent with the auditor's understanding.
　Answer (B) is incorrect. Analytical procedures should be performed as risk assessment procedures and to assist in forming an overall conclusion. They need not be performed as substantive procedures. Answer (C) is incorrect. Analytical procedures should be performed as the risk assessment procedures. They need not be substantive procedures. Answer (D) is incorrect. Analytical procedures should be performed to assist in forming an overall conclusion.

13. An auditor's decision either to apply analytical procedures as substantive procedures or to perform tests of transactions and account balances usually is determined by the

A. Availability of data aggregated at a high level.

B. Auditor's determination about whether audit risk can be sufficiently reduced.

C. Timing of tests performed after the balance sheet date.

D. Auditor's familiarity with industry trends.

Answer (B) is correct.
　REQUIRED: The basis for choosing between analytical procedures and tests of details.
　DISCUSSION: For some assertions, analytical procedures alone may suffice to reduce audit risk to an acceptably low level. For example, the auditor's risk assessment may be supported by audit evidence from tests of controls. Substantive analytical procedures generally are more applicable to large transaction volumes that are predictable over time (AU-C 330). The decision is based on the auditor's professional judgment about the expected effectiveness and efficiency of the available procedures.
　Answer (A) is incorrect. Availability of data is among the factors in evaluating whether audit risk can be reduced to an acceptably low level. Answer (C) is incorrect. Timing of tests is among the factors in evaluating whether audit risk can be reduced to an acceptably low level. Answer (D) is incorrect. Familiarity with industry trends is among the factors in evaluating whether audit risk can be reduced to an acceptably low level.

14. Analytical procedures used to form an overall audit conclusion generally include

    A. Considering unusual or unexpected account balances that were not previously identified.

    B. Performing tests of transactions to corroborate management's financial statement assertions.

    C. Gathering evidence concerning account balances that have not changed from the prior year.

    D. Retesting controls that appeared to be ineffective during the assessment of control risk.

Answer (A) is correct.
    REQUIRED: The analytical procedures used to form an overall audit conclusion.
    DISCUSSION: Analytical procedures should be applied near the end of the audit. The purpose is to form an overall audit conclusion about whether the statements are consistent with the auditor's understanding of the entity. Procedures ordinarily should include reading the statements and considering (1) the adequacy of evidence regarding previously identified unusual or unexpected balances and (2) unusual or unexpected balances or relationships not previously noted (AU-C 520).
    Answer (B) is incorrect. Analytical procedures are not tests of details. Answer (C) is incorrect. The lack of change from the prior year may not be unusual or unexpected. Answer (D) is incorrect. Analytical procedures are substantive, not tests of controls.

3.6 Consideration of Fraud in a Financial Statement Audit

15. Which of the following statements reflects an auditor's responsibility for detecting fraud and errors?

    A. An auditor is responsible for detecting employee errors and simple fraud, but not for discovering fraudulent acts involving employee collusion or management override.

    B. An auditor should plan the audit to detect errors and fraud that are caused by departures from the applicable financial reporting framework.

    C. An auditor is not responsible for detecting fraud unless the application of GAAS would result in such detection.

    D. An auditor should design the audit to provide reasonable assurance of detecting fraud and errors that are material to the financial statements.

Answer (D) is correct.
    REQUIRED: The statement reflecting the auditor's responsibility for detecting fraud and errors.
    DISCUSSION: The auditor has a responsibility to plan and perform the audit to obtain reasonable assurance about whether the financial statements are free of material misstatements, whether caused by fraud or error. Thus, the auditor should (1) identify and assess the risks of material misstatement due to fraud at the financial statement and assertion levels, (2) obtain sufficient appropriate audit evidence regarding those risks through implementing responses, and (3) respond to identified fraud or suspected fraud. Moreover, the consideration of fraud should be logically integrated into the overall audit process in a manner consistent with other pronouncements, e.g., those on (1) planning and supervision, (2) audit risk and materiality, and (3) internal control.

16. What is the primary objective of the fraud brainstorming session?

    A. Determine audit risk and materiality.

    B. Identify whether analytical procedures should be applied to the revenue accounts.

    C. Assess the potential for material misstatement due to fraud.

    D. Determine whether the planned procedures in the audit plan will satisfy the general audit objectives.

Answer (C) is correct.
    REQUIRED: The primary objective of the fraud brainstorming session.
    DISCUSSION: The auditor should obtain reasonable assurance about whether the statements are free of material misstatement, whether due to fraud or error. The key members of the engagement team should discuss the potential for material misstatement. The discussion should include an exchange of ideas (brainstorming) about (1) how and where the statements might be susceptible to material misstatement due to fraud ("fraud risk"), (2) how assets might be misappropriated or financial reports fraudulently misstated, (3) how management could conceal fraudulent reporting (including override of controls), (4) how to respond to fraud risk, (5) known factors reflecting pressures/incentives/opportunities to commit fraud or an environment that permits rationalization of fraud, (6) an emphasis on the need to maintain professional skepticism, and (7) consideration of facts indicating manipulation of financial measures (e.g., earnings management).
    Answer (A) is incorrect. The auditor should determine audit risk and materiality in every audit. Answer (B) is incorrect. The auditor should apply analytical procedures to the revenue accounts to identify fraud risks in every audit. Based on the assumption that risks of fraud exist in revenue recognition, the auditor evaluates which types of revenue, revenue transactions, or assertions result in these risks. Answer (D) is incorrect. The auditor should determine whether the planned procedures in the audit plan will satisfy the general audit objectives in every audit.

17. Because of the risk of material misstatement due to fraud, an audit of financial statements in accordance with generally accepted auditing standards should be planned and performed with an attitude of

A. Objective judgment.

B. Integrity.

C. Professional skepticism.

D. Impartial conservatism.

Answer (C) is correct.

REQUIRED: The attitude required for planning and performing an audit.

DISCUSSION: The auditor should maintain professional skepticism throughout the audit. Professional skepticism is an "attitude that includes a questioning mind, being alert to conditions that may indicate possible misstatement due to fraud or error, and critical assessment of audit evidence" (AU-C 200).

Answer (A) is incorrect. Although objective judgment is a quality appropriate for practitioners, it is not required to be applied specifically in an audit. Answer (B) is incorrect. Although independent integrity is a quality appropriate for practitioners, it is not required to be applied specifically in an audit. Answer (D) is incorrect. GAAS do not require conservatism.

18. While performing an audit of the financial statements of a company for the year ended December 31, Year 1, the auditor notes that the company's sales increased substantially in December Year 1, with a corresponding decrease in January Year 2. In assessing the risk of fraudulent financial reporting or misappropriation of assets, what should be the auditor's initial indication about the potential for fraud in sales revenue?

A. There is a broad indication of misappropriation of assets.

B. There is an indication of theft of the entity's assets.

C. There is an indication of embezzling receipts.

D. There is a broad indication of financial reporting fraud.

Answer (D) is correct.

REQUIRED: The initial indication about the potential for fraud in sales revenue.

DISCUSSION: The types of fraud relevant to the auditor include misstatements arising from fraudulent financial reporting. These are intentional misstatements or omissions to deceive users, such as altering accounting records or documents, misrepresenting or omitting significant information, and misapplying accounting principles. Fraud also includes misappropriation of assets. These result from, for example, (1) theft of physical assets, (2) embezzlement (e.g., stealing collections of receivables), (3) an action that causes payment for items not received, or (4) using entity assets for personal reasons. The substantial increase in sales revenue at year end followed by a substantial decrease in January is a broad indicator of a failure to apply cut-off procedures, i.e., financial reporting fraud.

Answer (A) is incorrect. The indication of fraud involves recognition of revenue (fraudulent reporting), not misappropriation of assets. Answer (B) is incorrect. Theft of the entity's assets is a misappropriation of assets, not fraudulent reporting. Answer (C) is incorrect. Embezzling receipts is a misappropriation of assets, not fraudulent reporting.

3.7 Consideration of Laws and Regulations in an Audit of Financial Statements

19. Which of the following procedures would **least** likely result in the discovery of possible noncompliance with laws and regulations?

A. Reading the minutes of the board of directors' meetings.

B. Making inquiries of the client's management.

C. Performing tests of details of transactions.

D. Reviewing an internal control questionnaire.

Answer (D) is correct.

REQUIRED: The procedure least likely to result in the discovery of possible noncompliance with laws and regulations.

DISCUSSION: Auditors should design the audit to provide reasonable assurance of detecting noncompliance having a material effect on the financial statements. Internal control questionnaires document the auditor's understanding of internal control. Reviewing the responses to the questionnaire may reveal control deficiencies but not noncompliance.

Answer (A) is incorrect. Reading the minutes of the board of directors' meetings may provide evidence regarding noncompliance. Answer (B) is incorrect. The auditor should inquire of management about the entity's compliance with laws and regulations. Answer (C) is incorrect. Performing tests of details of transactions may provide information regarding noncompliance.

20. If specific information that implies the existence of possible noncompliance with laws and regulations that could have a material effect on the financial statements comes to an auditor's attention, the auditor should next

A. Apply audit procedures specifically directed to ascertaining whether noncompliance has occurred.

B. Seek the advice of an informed expert qualified to practice law as to possible contingent liabilities.

C. Report the matter to an appropriate level of management at least one level above those involved.

D. Discuss the evidence with the client's audit committee, or others with equivalent authority and responsibility.

Answer (A) is correct.

REQUIRED: The auditor's responsibility when (s)he becomes aware of noncompliance with laws and regulations having a material effect.

DISCUSSION: The auditor should apply audit procedures specifically directed to ascertaining whether noncompliance has occurred. When the auditor becomes aware of information about possible noncompliance, the auditor should obtain (1) an understanding of the nature of the act and the circumstances in which it occurred and (2) further information to evaluate the effect on the financial statements.

Answer (B) is incorrect. The auditor need not consult legal counsel until after determining that noncompliance has occurred. Answer (C) is incorrect. Making inquiries of management is just one possible procedure involved in determining whether noncompliance has occurred. Answer (D) is incorrect. The auditor should not discuss the evidence with those charged with governance until after determining that noncompliance has occurred.

STUDY UNIT FOUR
STRATEGIC PLANNING ISSUES

(12 pages of outline)

This study unit considers issues that are fundamental to planning an audit. Questions about the internal audit function, related parties, and accounting estimates can be expected on the exam. Moreover, most of the issues considered in this study unit have an effect on other facets of the audit, including evidence collection and reporting. We cover the additional matters here to provide comprehensive and coherent coverage.

4.1 USING THE WORK OF INTERNAL AUDITORS

1. **Internal auditors**

    a. Perform **assurance and consulting activities** designed to evaluate and improve the effectiveness of the entity's governance, risk management, and internal control processes. This may include evaluation of internal control, examination of financial and operating information, review of compliance with laws and regulation, and the assessment of fraud risk.

    b. Are **part of the organization's internal control**. The knowledge and experience of the internal audit function can inform the external auditor's understanding of the entity and its environment and identification and assessment of risks of material misstatement.

    c. Are not independent in the same manner as the external auditor (although they may be objective and unbiased).

2. The external auditor's use of the work of internal auditors includes

    a. Using the work of the internal audit function to **obtain audit evidence** and

    b. Using internal auditors to **provide direct assistance** under the direction, supervision, and review of the external auditor.

3. The external auditor may be able to use the work of the internal audit function to obtain audit evidence in a constructive and complementary manner depending on

    a. The **objectivity** of the internal auditors;

    b. The level of **competence** of the internal audit function; and

    c. Whether the function applies a **systematic and disciplined approach**, including quality control.

4. **Objectivity**, the ability to perform tasks without bias, is judged by the function's organizational status and relevant policies and procedures that support objectivity.

    a. For example, objectivity is promoted when the internal auditors (1) report to those charged with governance rather than management, (2) are free of any conflicting responsibilities, (3) work without constraints, and (4) are members of professional organizations that obligate them to be objective.

5. **Competence** is the attainment and maintenance of knowledge and skills of the function as a whole at the level required to enable assigned tasks to be performed diligently and with the appropriate level of quality. Factors that may affect the external auditor's determination about competence include whether

    a. The internal audit function is adequately and appropriately resourced relative to the size of the entity and the nature of its operations.

    b. Appropriate policies for hiring, training, and assigning internal auditors to internal audit engagements exist.

    c. The internal auditors have adequate technical training and proficiency in auditing.

    d. The internal auditors are members of relevant professional bodies or have certifications that require them to comply with the relevant professional standards, including continuing professional education requirements.

    e. The internal auditors have the required knowledge and/or experience relating to the entity's financial reporting and the applicable financial reporting framework.

    f. The internal audit function has the necessary skills (for example, industry-specific knowledge) to perform work related to the entity's financial statements.

6. Objectivity and competence are a continuum from low to high. A high level of one attribute, however, cannot compensate for a low level of the other.

7. **The external auditor has sole responsibility for the audit opinion.** That responsibility is not reduced by

    a. The external auditor's use of the work of the internal audit function to obtain audit evidence or

    b. Use of internal auditors to provide direct assistance on the engagement.

8. The function may perform audit procedures similar to those performed by the external auditor. But neither the internal audit function nor the internal auditors are independent of the entity as is required of the external auditor in an audit of financial statements.

9. In judging whether to use the internal auditors to obtain audit evidence, the external auditor should evaluate the internal auditors' objectivity, competence, and use of a systematic and disciplined approach.

    a. Attributes of objectivity and competence to be evaluated are addressed in item 4. on the previous page and item 5. above.

10. The application of a **systematic and disciplined approach** to (a) planning, (b) performing, (c) supervising, (d) reviewing, and (e) documenting internal audit activities distinguishes it from other monitoring control activities. When evaluating whether a systematic and disciplined approach is applied, the external auditor should consider

    a. The existence, adequacy, and use of documented internal audit procedures or guidance for such matters as (1) risk assessments, (2) work programs, (3) documentation, and (4) reporting. The nature and extent of this documentation should be proportionate to the nature and size of the internal audit function relative to the complexity of the entity.

    b. Whether the internal audit function has (1) appropriate quality control policies and procedures (for example, those relating to leadership, human resources, and engagement performance) or (2) quality control requirements in standards set by relevant professional bodies. Such bodies also may establish other appropriate requirements, such as conducting periodic external quality assessments.

This standard establishes the concept of a **systematic and disciplined approach** by the internal audit function. This approach is required for use of the work of the internal audit function. This issue likely will be tested on subsequent exams.

11. The external auditor **should not use** the work of the internal audit function to obtain audit evidence if the external auditor determines that

    a. The function's organizational status and relevant policies and procedures do not adequately support the objectivity of internal auditors;

    b. The function lacks sufficient competence; or

    c. The function does not apply a systematic and disciplined approach, including quality control.

12. **Internal Audit Work Used to Obtain Audit Evidence**

    a. The external auditor should consider the nature, timing, and extent of the work performed, or is planned, by the function and its relevance to the overall audit strategy and audit plan.

    b. **The external auditor should make all significant judgments** including when using the work of the internal audit function to obtain audit evidence. Significant judgments include, but are not limited to, the following:

        1) Assessing the risks of material misstatement

        2) Evaluating the sufficiency of tests performed

        3) Evaluating the appropriateness of management's use of the going concern assumption and whether substantial doubt exists about the entity's ability to continue as a going concern

        4) Evaluating significant accounting estimates

        5) Evaluating the adequacy of disclosures in the financial statements and other matters affecting the auditor's report

    c. To prevent undue use of the internal audit function to obtain audit evidence, **less** of the work should be used:

        1) The more judgment is required to plan and perform audit procedures or evaluate the audit evidence

        2) The higher the assessed risk of material misstatement at the assertion level (with special consideration given to significant risks)

        3) The less the objectivity of the internal audit function

        4) The lower the competence of the internal audit function

13. The external auditor should evaluate whether, in the aggregate, using (a) the work of the internal audit function to obtain audit evidence and (b) internal auditors to provide direct assistance results in **too little** involvement of the **external auditor** in the audit.

14. When using the work of the internal audit function to obtain audit evidence, the external auditor should

    a. Discuss the planned use of the work with the function as a basis for coordinating their activities.

    b. Read the relevant reports of the internal audit function.

    c. Perform sufficient audit procedures on the work of the function as a whole that the external auditor plans to use. The objective is to determine its adequacy for purposes of the audit, including evaluating whether

        1) Work was properly planned, performed, supervised, reviewed, and documented;

        2) Sufficient appropriate evidence was obtained to draw reasonable conclusions; and

        3) Conclusions reached were appropriate, and the reports prepared were consistent with the work performed.

15. The nature and extent of the external auditor's audit procedures should respond to the evaluation of

   a. The extent of judgment involved to perform procedures and evaluate evidence;
   b. The assessed risk of material misstatement;
   c. The objectivity of the internal auditors; and
   d. The function's competence.

16. The external auditor also should **reperform** some of the body of work of the internal audit function that the external auditor intends to use in obtaining audit evidence.

17. Before the conclusion of the audit, the external auditor should make an overall assessment of the usefulness of the internal auditor's work to obtain evidence.

18. **Direct Assistance to the External Auditor**

   a. The external auditor should **not** use an internal auditor to provide direct assistance if (s)he lacks the necessary objectivity or competence.

   b. Prior to using internal auditors to provide direct assistance, the external auditor should obtain **written acknowledgment** (e.g., in the audit engagement letter) from management or those charged with governance, as appropriate, that

     1) Internal auditors can follow the external auditor's instructions and
     2) The entity will not intervene in the work

   c. To determine the work that may be assigned to internal auditors, the external auditor should

     1) Evaluate threats to the internal auditors' objectivity, the effectiveness of the safeguards applied to reduce or eliminate the threats, and the competence of the internal auditors who will be providing such assistance;
     2) Consider the assessed risk of material misstatement; and
     3) Consider the judgment involved in (a) performing relevant audit procedures and (b) evaluating audit evidence.

   d. The external auditor should **direct, supervise, and review** the work performed by internal auditors on the engagement.

   e. The internal auditor should **not be used to perform critical procedures**.

     1) For example, internal auditors should not (a) perform inquiries of entity personnel or those charged with governance related to identifying fraud risks and determining the procedures to respond to such risks or (b) determine the use of unpredictable audit procedures.
     2) Internal auditors often perform less critical procedures, such as preparing schedules and compiling documentation.

   f. The direction, supervision, and review by the external auditor of the audit procedures performed by the internal auditors should be adequate to be satisfied that sufficient appropriate audit evidence has been obtained to support the conclusions based on that work.

   g. The external auditor should evaluate whether, in the aggregate, using (1) the work of the internal audit function to obtain audit evidence and (2) internal auditors to provide direct assistance results in **too little** involvement of the **external auditor** in the audit.

19. **Communicating with Those Charged with Governance**

   a. The external auditor should communicate how (s)he plans to use the work of the internal audit function to (1) obtain audit evidence and (2) provide direct assistance.

20. **Documentation**

    a.   If the external auditor uses the work of the internal audit function to **obtain audit evidence**, the following should be documented:

        1) The results of the evaluation of

            a) The function's organizational status and relevant policies and procedures to adequately support the objectivity of the internal auditors;

            b) The competence of the function; and

            c) The application by the function of a systematic and disciplined approach, including quality control.

        2) The nature and extent of the work used (including the period covered by, and the results of, such work)

        3) The audit procedures performed by the external auditor to evaluate the adequacy of the work used, including reperformance of some of the work of the internal audit function to obtain audit evidence

    b.   If the external auditor uses internal auditors to **provide direct assistance**, the following should be documented:

        1) The evaluation of the existence and significance of threats to the objectivity of the internal auditors, any safeguards applied to reduce or eliminate the threats

        2) The competence of the internal auditors used to provide direct assistance

        3) The basis for the decision about the nature and extent of the work performed by the internal auditors

        4) The nature and extent of the external auditor's review of the internal auditors' work (including the testing, by the external auditor, of some of the work performed by the internal auditors)

        5) The working papers prepared by the internal auditors who provided direct assistance on the audit engagement

    c.   The external auditor should document the evaluation of whether (s)he was sufficiently involved in the audit to take sole responsibility for the audit opinion expressed.

Stop and review! You have completed the outline for this subunit. Study multiple-choice questions 1 through 6 beginning on page 107.

4.2 USING THE WORK OF A SPECIALIST

1. **Types of Specialists**

    a.   An **auditor's specialist** is an individual or organization possessing expertise in a field other than accounting or auditing. The work in that field is used to assist the auditor in obtaining sufficient appropriate audit evidence.

        1) An auditor's specialist may be either (a) an internal specialist (who is a partner or staff member, including temporary staff, of the auditor's firm or a network firm) or (b) an external specialist.

    b.   A **management's specialist** is an individual or organization possessing expertise in a field other than accounting or auditing. The work in that field is used by the entity to assist the entity in preparing the financial statements.

Background

The guidance for using the work of an auditor's specialist (AU-C 620) and a management's specialist (AU-C 500) is provided in two different auditing standards because they serve two different purposes. However, the concern in each case is the consideration of the specialist's objectivity and competence. This emphasis is recognized in the outline on the following pages.

2. **Auditor's Specialist**

a. If expertise other than accounting or auditing is necessary to obtain sufficient appropriate audit evidence, the auditor should determine whether to use the work of an auditor's specialist.

    1) However, the auditor has sole responsibility for the audit opinion expressed, and that responsibility is not reduced by the auditor's use of the work of an auditor's specialist.

b. Examples of a potential specialist's expertise include the following:

    1) Valuation of complex financial instruments and nonfinancial assets and liabilities, such as land and buildings, plant and machinery, jewelry, works of art, and antiques
    2) Actuarial calculations
    3) Estimation of oil and other mineral reserves
    4) Valuation of environmental liabilities and site cleanup costs
    5) Interpretation of contracts, laws, and regulations
    6) Physical characteristics relating to quantity on hand or condition

c. The auditor should evaluate whether the auditor's specialist has the necessary **competence, capabilities, and objectivity** for the auditor's purposes.

    1) In the case of an auditor's external specialist, the evaluation of objectivity should include inquiry about interests and relationships that may threaten objectivity.

d. The auditor should obtain an **understanding** of the expertise of the auditor's specialist sufficient to

    1) Determine the nature, scope, and objectives of the work and
    2) Evaluate the adequacy of that work for the auditor's purposes.

e. The auditor should agree, in writing if appropriate, with the auditor's specialist regarding the arrangements for the services, including objectives, roles, communications, and confidentiality requirements.

f. The auditor should evaluate the adequacy of the work of the auditor's specialist, including

    1) The relevance and reasonableness of the findings and conclusions,
    2) The understanding of any significant assumptions and methods, and
    3) The use of source data significant to the work.

g. If the auditor determines that the work of the auditor's specialist is not adequate for the auditor's purposes, the auditor should consider (1) performing additional work, (2) requiring additional work by the specialist, or (3) engaging another specialist.

    1) If the auditor is unable to collect sufficient appropriate evidence, a modified opinion may be necessary.

h. The auditor should not refer to the work or findings of the auditor's specialist when expressing an **unmodified opinion**.

    1) The auditor may refer to the work of an auditor's external specialist if the reference is relevant to understanding a **modified opinion** (e.g., qualified or adverse).

        a) The report should state that the reference does not reduce the auditor's responsibility.

3. **Management's Specialist**

   a. If information to be used as audit evidence has been prepared using the work of a management's specialist, the auditor should

      1) Evaluate the competence, capabilities, and objectivity of that specialist;
      2) Obtain an understanding of the work of that specialist; and
      3) Evaluate the appropriateness of the work as audit evidence for the relevant assertion.

   b. Matters relevant to evaluating competence, capabilities, and objectivity include whether the work is subject to technical standards or professional requirements.

   c. The auditor does **not refer** to a management's specialist in an auditor's report.

Stop and review! You have completed the outline for this subunit. Study multiple-choice questions 7 through 9 beginning on page 108.

4.3 RELATED PARTIES

Background
Prior auditing standards were based on U.S. GAAP for reporting and disclosing related party transactions in financial statements. Current auditing standards apply to all financial reporting frameworks, including IFRS. However, the auditor's responsibilities and auditing procedures remain the same.

1. **Nature of Related Party Transactions**

   a. Many related party transactions are in the **normal course of business**. Thus, they may have no higher risks of material misstatement (RMMs) of the financial statements than similar transactions with unrelated parties.

   b. However, the nature of related party relationships and transactions may cause them to have higher RMMs than transactions with unrelated parties. For example,

      1) Related parties may operate through an extensive and complex range of relationships and structures,
      2) Information systems may be ineffective at identifying or summarizing transactions and outstanding balances between an entity and its related parties, and
      3) Related party transactions may not be conducted under normal market terms and conditions (for example, some related party transactions may be conducted with no exchange of consideration).

2. **Responsibilities of the Auditor**

   a. The auditor should perform audit procedures to identify, assess, and respond to the RMMs arising from the entity's failure to appropriately account for or disclose related party relationships, transactions, or balances.

   b. Because fraud may be more easily committed through related parties, an understanding of the entity's related party relationships and transactions also is relevant to the auditor's evaluation of whether fraud risk factors exist.

   c. **Risk of fraud** is increased and the auditor should act accordingly when

      1) The related party has a dominant influence over the entity.

      2)   The related party transactions are outside the normal course of business. The following are examples:

          a)   Equity transactions, such as corporate restructurings or acquisitions

          b)   Transactions with offshore entities

          c)   Leasing if no consideration is exchanged

          d)   Sales with large discounts or returns

          e)   Transactions with circular arrangements (e.g., a sale with a commitment to repurchase)

          f)   Transactions under contracts whose terms are changed

   d.   It is ordinarily not feasible to determine (1) whether a transaction would have occurred if the parties were unrelated or (2), given that it did occur, what the terms would have been. However, if management has asserted that the terms of a related party transaction were equivalent to those in an **arm's-length transaction**, the auditor should obtain sufficient appropriate audit evidence about the assertion.

      1)   Management is responsible for providing support for the assertion.

      2)   If a material assertion is not supported, or the auditor cannot collect sufficient appropriate evidence, the assertion should be removed, or the auditor's report should be modified.

3. Accounting Considerations

   a.   Because related parties are not independent of each other, financial reporting frameworks establish specific **accounting and disclosure requirements** for related party relationships, transactions, and balances to enable users of the financial statements to understand their nature and actual or potential effects on the financial statements.

   b.   Furthermore, the auditor should understand that the substance of a transaction could differ significantly from its form. Financial statements should recognize substance, not legal form.

4. Audit Procedures

   a.   Given the inherent limitations of an audit, the auditor's ability to detect material misstatements is reduced because

      1)   Management may not be aware of all related party relationships and transactions, and

      2)   Such relationships may provide a greater opportunity for collusion, concealment, or manipulation by management.

   b.   Nevertheless, the auditor should perform **risk assessment procedures** to identify RMMs associated with these relationships and transactions. They include specific consideration of the susceptibility of the statements to material misstatement due to fraud or error. The auditor should

      1)   Inquire about (a) the identity of related parties, (b) the relationship of the entity with those parties, (c) whether transactions with them have occurred, and (d) the nature and purpose of the transactions.

      2)   Obtain an understanding of any **controls** established to (a) account for and disclose related party relationships and transactions and (b) authorize and approve significant transactions and arrangements (1) with related parties or (2) outside the normal course of business.

      3)   Be alert for related party relationships and transactions when inspecting records or documents, such as bank confirmations or minutes of meetings of shareholders or those charged with governance.

      4)   Transactions that, because of their nature, may indicate the existence of related parties include the following:

          a)   Borrowing or lending on an interest-free basis or at a rate of interest significantly above or below market rates prevailing at the time of the transaction

          b)   Selling real estate at a price that differs significantly from its appraised value

          c)   Exchanging property for similar property in a nonmonetary transaction

          d)   Making loans with no scheduled terms for when or how the funds will be repaid

c.   The auditor should identify and assess the RMMs associated with related party relationships and transactions and determine whether they are **significant risks**. Significant transactions outside the normal course of business result in significant risks.

      1)   The auditor responds by performing further audit procedures to obtain sufficient appropriate evidence about the assessed RMMs.

d.   Without contrary evidence, transactions with related parties should not be assumed to be outside the normal course of business. But such transactions may have been motivated solely or largely by any of the following:

      1)   Lack of sufficient working capital or credit to continue the business
      2)   An overly optimistic earnings forecast
      3)   Dependence on one or a few products, customers, or transactions for success
      4)   A declining industry with many business failures
      5)   Excess capacity
      6)   Significant litigation, especially between shareholders and management
      7)   Significant obsolescence because the entity is in a high-technology industry

e.   **Determining the existence of related parties.** Certain relationships, such as parent-subsidiary or investor-investee, may be clearly evident. Determining the existence of others requires specific audit procedures, which may include the following:

      1)   Evaluating the entity's procedures for identifying and properly accounting for related party transactions

      2)   Requesting from management the names of all related parties and inquiring whether transactions occurred with them

      3)   Reviewing filings with the SEC and other regulatory agencies for the names of related parties and for other businesses in which officers and directors occupy directorship or management positions

      4)   Determining the names of all pensions and other trusts established for employees and the names of their officers and trustees

      5)   Reviewing shareholder listings of closely held entities to identify principal shareholders

      6)   Reviewing prior years' audit documentation for the names of known related parties

      7)   Inquiring of predecessor or other auditors of related entities concerning their knowledge of existing relationships and the extent of management involvement in material transactions

      8)   Reviewing material investment transactions during the period to determine whether they have created related parties

f. **Identifying related party transactions.** The following procedures may identify material transactions with known related parties or indicate the existence of previously unknown related parties:

1) Provide personnel performing all segments of the audit with the names of known related parties.

2) Review the minutes of meetings of the board and committees.

3) Review filings with the SEC and other regulatory agencies.

4) Review conflict-of-interest statements obtained by the entity from its management.

5) Review business transacted with major customers, suppliers, borrowers, and lenders for indications of undisclosed relationships.

6) Consider whether unrecognized transactions are occurring, such as receiving or providing accounting, management, or other services at no charge or having a major shareholder absorb entity expenses.

7) Review accounting records for large, unusual, or nonrecurring transactions or balances, especially those near the end of the period.

8) Review confirmations of compensating balance arrangements for indications that balances are or were maintained for or by related parties.

9) Review invoices from law firms.

10) Review confirmations of loans receivable and payable for guarantees.

g. **Examining related party transactions.**

1) After identifying related party transactions, the auditor should become satisfied about their purpose, nature, extent, and effect. The following should be considered:

    a) Obtain an understanding of the business purpose of the transaction.

    b) Examine invoices, executed copies of agreements, contracts, and other documents.

    c) Determine whether the transaction has been approved by those charged with governance.

    d) Test for reasonableness the compilation of amounts to be disclosed or considered for disclosure.

    e) Arrange for the audits of interentity balances to be performed as of concurrent dates, even if the fiscal years differ, and for the examination of specified, important, and representative related party transactions by the auditors for each of the parties, with appropriate exchange of relevant information.

    f) Inspect or confirm and obtain satisfaction concerning the transferability and value of collateral.

2) To fully understand a particular transaction, the auditor may

    a) Confirm the transaction amount and terms, including guarantees and other significant data, with the other parties.

    b) Inspect evidence in possession of the other parties.

    c) Confirm or discuss significant information with intermediaries, such as banks, guarantors, agents, or attorneys.

    d) Refer to financial publications, trade journals, and credit agencies.

    e) With respect to material uncollected balances, guarantees, and other obligations, obtain information about the financial capability of the other parties from audited financial statements, unaudited financial statements, income tax returns, and reports issued by credit agencies.

Stop and review! You have completed the outline for this subunit. Study multiple-choice questions 10 through 14 beginning on page 109.

4.4 ACCOUNTING ESTIMATES AND FAIR VALUE

 The more you study accounting, the more you will realize the importance of estimates. Most significant measurements in financial statements involve estimates. Be sure to understand the importance of estimates and auditors' concerns about them.

1. **Nature of Accounting Estimates**

   a. Some financial amounts cannot be measured precisely. They can only be estimated. The nature and reliability of information available to management for making estimates vary widely. The result is **estimation uncertainty**.

      1) Examples include (a) the allowance for doubtful accounts, (b) inventory obsolescence, (c) warranty obligations, (d) depreciation, (e) outcomes of long-term contracts, and (f) costs of litigation.

      2) Examples of fair value estimates include (a) complex financial instruments not traded in an active and open market; (b) share-based payments; (c) property or equipment held for disposal; and (d) certain assets or liabilities acquired in a business combination, including goodwill and intangible assets.

   b. Estimation uncertainty is the susceptibility of an estimate to a lack of precision in measurement. The degree of estimation uncertainty for an accounting estimate (1) affects its RMM and (2) may affect its susceptibility to unintentional or intentional management bias.

   c. Some accounting estimates involve relatively **low estimation uncertainty** and may result in lower RMMs. Examples include the following:

      1) Accounting estimates that are not complex

      2) Accounting estimates that are frequently made and updated because they relate to routine transactions

      3) Accounting estimates derived from readily available data, such as published interest rate data or exchange-traded prices of securities (**observable** inputs in the context of fair value estimation)

      4) Fair value accounting estimates based on a method of measurement that is simple and applied easily

      5) Fair value accounting estimates based on a well-known or generally accepted model, provided that the assumptions or inputs to the model are observable

   d. Some accounting estimates involve relatively **high estimation uncertainty** with higher RMMs, particularly when they are based on significant assumptions. Examples include the following:

      1) Accounting estimates relating to the outcome of litigation

      2) Fair value accounting estimates for derivative financial instruments not publicly traded

2. The **objective** of the auditor is to obtain sufficient appropriate audit evidence about whether accounting estimates, including fair value accounting estimates, are **reasonable** and related disclosures are **adequate**.

   a. The auditor performs **risk assessment procedures** to provide a basis for identifying and assessing the RMMs for accounting estimates. Thus, the auditor should obtain an understanding of the following:

      1) The relevant requirements of the applicable financial reporting framework

      2) How management identifies factors that create a need for estimates

      3) How management makes estimates and the data on which they are based (e.g., methods, models, controls, use of specialists, underlying assumptions, and whether and how the effects of estimation uncertainty are assessed)

    b.   The auditor also reviews **prior-period estimates** to

        1)   Understand the reasons for the differences between estimates and outcomes.

        2)   Identify intentional or unintentional **management bias**. (Intentional bias to mislead financial statement users is fraud.)

3.   **Responses to the Assessed RMMs**

    a.   The auditor should determine whether

        1)   Management has appropriately applied the applicable financial reporting framework, and

        2)   The methods for making the accounting estimates are appropriate and have been applied consistently.

    b.   The auditor should perform one or more of the following procedures:

        1)   Determining whether specialized skills or knowledge are required

        2)   Testing how management made the accounting estimate and the data on which it is based, including evaluation of the **method of measurement** and the **assumptions** used

        3)   Testing the **operating effectiveness of the controls** over how management made the estimate, together with performing **substantive procedures**

        4)   Developing a point estimate or range to evaluate management's point estimate

    c.   The auditor should respond to **significant** RMMs by evaluating

        1)   How management has considered alternative assumptions or outcomes and why it has rejected them

        2)   Whether the significant assumptions used by management are reasonable

    d.   The auditor should obtain written representations relating to the estimation process.

4.   **Evaluating Reasonableness and Determining Misstatements**

    a.   When audit evidence supports a point estimate, the difference between the auditor's estimate and management's estimate is a misstatement.

    b.   When the auditor develops a range, a management estimate outside the range is a misstatement.

    c.   Whether individual or collective misstatements are material is a matter of judgment.

    d.   The auditor should assess the appropriateness of disclosures, e.g., the assumptions, method of estimation, and sources of estimation uncertainty.

    e.   The auditor should consider the possibility of management bias.

5.   **Auditor documentation** should include

    a.   The basis for the auditor's conclusions about reasonableness for those estimates that result in significant risks

    b.   Indicators of possible management bias

Stop and review! You have completed the outline for this subunit. Study multiple-choice questions 15 through 20 beginning on page 111.

QUESTIONS

4.1 Using the Work of Internal Auditors

1. In assessing the competence and objectivity of an entity's internal auditor, an independent auditor would **least** likely consider information obtained from

A. Discussions with management personnel.

B. External quality reviews of the internal auditor's activities.

C. Previous experience with the internal auditor.

D. The results of analytical procedures.

Answer (D) is correct.

REQUIRED: The least likely procedure in assessing the competence and objectivity of an entity's internal auditor.

DISCUSSION: Analytical procedures are evaluations of financial information made by a study of plausible relationships among both financial and nonfinancial data, using models that range from simple to complex. They are substantive procedures used by the auditor to gather evidence about the fairness of the financial statements.

Answer (A) is incorrect. Discussion with management is a procedure appropriate for assessing the competence and objectivity of an internal auditor. Answer (B) is incorrect. A quality review is a procedure appropriate for assessing the competence and objectivity of an internal auditor. Answer (C) is incorrect. Consideration of previous experience is a procedure appropriate for assessing the competence and objectivity of an internal auditor.

2. For which of the following judgments may an independent auditor share responsibility with an entity's internal auditor who is assessed to be both competent and objective?

	Materiality of Misstatements	Evaluation of Significant Accounting Estimates
A.	Yes	No
B.	No	Yes
C.	Yes	Yes
D.	No	No

Answer (D) is correct.

REQUIRED: The judgment(s) for which an auditor may share responsibility with an internal auditor.

DISCUSSION: The responsibility to report on financial statements is solely the auditor's. It cannot be shared with internal auditors. Because the auditor has the ultimate responsibility to express an opinion on the financial statements, judgments about (1) assessments of RMMs, (2) materiality of misstatements, (3) sufficiency of tests performed, (4) evaluation of significant accounting estimates, and (5) other matters affecting the auditor's report always should be those of the auditor.

3. In assessing the competence of an internal auditor, an independent CPA most likely would obtain information about the

A. Quality of the internal auditor's documentation.

B. Organization's commitment to integrity and ethical values.

C. Influence of management on the scope of the internal auditor's duties.

D. Organizational levels to which the internal auditor reports.

Answer (A) is correct.

REQUIRED: The information needed to assess the competence of an internal auditor.

DISCUSSION: In assessing the competence of an internal auditor, the auditor should consider such factors as (1) educational level and professional experience; (2) professional certification and continuing education; (3) audit policies, programs, and procedures; (4) supervision and review of the internal auditor's activities; (5) practices regarding assignments; (6) quality of documentation, reports, and recommendations; and (7) evaluation of the internal auditor's performance.

Answer (B) is incorrect. The organization's commitment to integrity and ethical values relates to objectivity rather than competence. Answer (C) is incorrect. The influence of management on the scope of the internal auditor's duties relates to objectivity rather than competence. Answer (D) is incorrect. The organizational levels to which the internal auditor reports relate to objectivity rather than competence.

4. In assessing the objectivity of internal auditors, an independent auditor should

A. Evaluate the quality control program in effect for the internal auditors.

B. Examine documentary evidence of the work performed by the internal auditors.

C. Test a sample of the transactions and balances that the internal auditors examined.

D. Determine the organizational level to which the internal auditors report.

Answer (D) is correct.
 REQUIRED: The procedure performed to assess an internal auditor's objectivity.
 DISCUSSION: If the external auditor plans to use the work of the internal auditors to obtain audit evidence or to provide direct assistance, their competence and objectivity should be evaluated. Objectivity is promoted when the internal auditors (1) report to those charged with governance rather than management, (2) are free of any conflicting responsibilities, (3) work without constraints, and (4) are members of professional organizations that obligate them to be objective. The external auditor should assess each of these factors in evaluating objectivity.
 Answer (A) is incorrect. Evaluating quality control pertains to competence, not objectivity. Answer (B) is incorrect. Examining internal auditors' engagement records (documentation) pertains to competence, not objectivity. Answer (C) is incorrect. Testing details examined by internal auditors pertains to competence, not objectivity.

5. During an audit, an internal auditor may provide direct assistance to an independent CPA in

	Obtaining an Understanding of Internal Control	Performing Tests of Controls	Performing Substantive Tests
A.	No	No	No
B.	Yes	No	No
C.	Yes	Yes	No
D.	Yes	Yes	Yes

Answer (D) is correct.
 REQUIRED: The types of direct assistance an internal auditor may provide to an independent CPA.
 DISCUSSION: The auditor may request direct assistance from the internal auditor when performing the audit. Thus, the auditor may appropriately request the internal auditor's assistance in obtaining the understanding of internal control, performing tests of controls, or performing substantive procedures (AU-C 610). The internal auditor may provide assistance in all phases of the audit as long as (1) the internal auditor's competence and objectivity have been tested, and (2) the independent auditor supervises, reviews, evaluates, and tests the work performed by the internal auditor to the extent appropriate.

6. Which approach to planning, performing, supervising, reviewing, and documenting internal audit activities distinguishes it from other monitoring controls that may be performed within the entity?

A. An independent approach.

B. A balanced approach.

C. A fair and honest approach.

D. A systematic and disciplined approach.

Answer (D) is correct.
 REQUIRED: The approach of the internal audit function that distinguishes it from other controls.
 DISCUSSION: The application of a systematic and disciplined approach to planning, performing, supervising, reviewing, and documenting internal audit activities distinguishes it from other monitoring controls that may be performed within the entity.
 Answer (A) is incorrect. Internal auditors can be objective. But they are not independent in the same sense as the external auditor. Answer (B) is incorrect. Internal auditors are not distinguished by using a balanced approach. Answer (C) is incorrect. Internal auditors may take a fair and honest approach to their work, but it does not distinguish the function from other controls.

4.2 Using the Work of a Specialist

7. A management's specialist most likely is useful to

A. Assist the auditor in collecting sufficient appropriate audit evidence.

B. Provide the auditor advice on technical accounting issues.

C. Add credibility to the financial statements.

D. Assist the client in preparing the financial statements.

Answer (D) is correct.
 REQUIRED: The use of a management's specialist.
 DISCUSSION: A management's specialist is an individual or organization possessing expertise in a field other than accounting or auditing. The work in that field is used by the entity to assist in preparing the financial statements.
 Answer (A) is incorrect. An auditor's specialist may assist the auditor in collecting sufficient appropriate evidence. Answer (B) is incorrect. Both the auditor's specialists and management's specialists provide assistance on matters other than accounting. Answer (C) is incorrect. The auditor adds credibility to the financial statements.

8. An auditor referred to the findings of an auditor's external specialist in the auditor's report. This may be an appropriate reporting practice if the

    A. Auditor is not familiar with the professional certification, personal reputation, or particular competence of the specialist.

    B. Auditor, as a result of the specialist's findings, adds a paragraph emphasizing a matter regarding the financial statements.

    C. Auditor's report contains a qualified opinion.

    D. Auditor, as a result of the specialist's findings, decides to indicate a division of responsibility with the specialist for the audit opinion.

Answer (C) is correct.
    REQUIRED: The instance in which an auditor may refer to an auditor's specialist's findings.
    DISCUSSION: The auditor refers to the work of an auditor's external specialist because it is relevant to a modification of the opinion. In these circumstances, the report should indicate that the reference does not reduce the auditor's responsibility for the opinion. If the auditor's report contains an unmodified opinion, the auditor should not refer to the work of an auditor's specialist (AU-C 620). A modified opinion is a qualified opinion, an adverse opinion, or a disclaimer of opinion (AU-C 705).
    Answer (A) is incorrect. The auditor should evaluate the auditor's specialist's competence, capabilities, and objectivity regardless of whether the auditor's report refers to the specialist. Answer (B) is incorrect. An emphasis-of-matter paragraph or an other-matter paragraph may be included in the auditor's report when the opinion is unmodified or modified. Thus, an emphasis-of-matter paragraph is not a basis for referring to a specialist. Answer (D) is incorrect. The auditor has sole responsibility for the audit opinion.

9. Which of the following statements is true about the use of the work of an auditor's specialist?

    A. The specialist need not agree to the auditor's use of the specialist's findings.

    B. The auditor is required to perform substantive procedures to verify the specialist's assumptions and findings.

    C. The auditor must keep client information confidential, but the specialist is not obligated to do so.

    D. The auditor should obtain an understanding of the methods and assumptions used by the specialist.

Answer (D) is correct.
    REQUIRED: The true statement about the auditor's use of the work of an auditor's specialist.
    DISCUSSION: AU-C 620, *Using the Work of an Auditor's Specialist*, states that the auditor should evaluate the adequacy of the work of the auditor's specialist. This process includes (1) obtaining an understanding of any significant assumptions and methods used by the specialist and (2) evaluating the relevance and reasonableness of those assumptions and methods in the circumstances and in relation to the auditor's other findings and conclusions.
    Answer (A) is incorrect. The auditor should agree with the specialist, in writing if appropriate, about various matters, such as their roles and responsibilities. These may include consent for the auditor to include details of the specialist's findings or conclusions in the basis for a modified opinion paragraph in the auditor's report. Answer (B) is incorrect. The auditor should understand the assumptions and methods and evaluate their relevance and reasonableness, not verify them. But the auditor may perform corroborative procedures on the specialist's findings and conclusions, e.g., reperformance of calculations and performance of detailed analytical procedures. Answer (C) is incorrect. The auditor should establish an agreement with the specialist to maintain confidentiality.

4.3 Related Parties

10. Which of the following procedures most likely could assist an auditor in identifying related party transactions?

    A. Performing tests of controls concerning the segregation of duties.

    B. Evaluating the reasonableness of management's accounting estimates.

    C. Reviewing confirmations of compensating balance arrangements.

    D. Scanning the accounting records for recurring transactions.

Answer (C) is correct.
    REQUIRED: The procedure most likely used to identify related party transactions.
    DISCUSSION: The auditor performs procedures to identify material transactions that may be indicative of previously undetermined relationships. These procedures include reviewing confirmations of compensating balance arrangements for indications that balances are or were maintained for or by related parties (AU-C 550 and AS 2410).
    Answer (A) is incorrect. Testing segregation of duties of entity personnel is unlikely to identify related party transactions. Answer (B) is incorrect. Evaluating the reasonableness of accounting estimates has little relevance to related party transactions. The auditor should concentrate on transactions of a kind that tend to be entered into with related parties. Answer (D) is incorrect. Recurring transactions are not by their nature indicative of related party transactions.

11. An auditor searching for related party transactions should obtain an understanding of each subsidiary's relationship to the total entity because

    A. This may permit the audit of interentity account balances to be performed as of concurrent dates.

    B. Interentity transactions may have been consummated on terms equivalent to arm's-length transactions.

    C. This may reveal whether particular transactions would have taken place if the parties had not been related.

    D. The business structure may be deliberately designed to obscure related party transactions.

Answer (D) is correct.

REQUIRED: The reason for understanding parent-subsidiary relationships when searching for related party transactions.

DISCUSSION: The nature of related party relationships and transactions may result in greater risks of material misstatement than transactions with unrelated parties. Thus, related parties may operate through a complex set of relationships and structures, with increased complexity of related party transactions. For example, a transaction may involve multiple related parties in a consolidated group. Accordingly, in an audit of group statements, the group engagement team should request each component auditor to communicate with related parties not previously identified by group management or the group engagement team.

Answer (A) is incorrect. A concurrent audit is not required.

Answer (B) is incorrect. The auditor's concern is that related party transactions were not at arm's length. Answer (C) is incorrect. Determining whether a transaction would have occurred and what the terms would have been if the parties were unrelated is not normally an objective of an audit.

12. Which of the following statements is true about related party transactions?

    A. In the absence of evidence to the contrary, related party transactions should be assumed to be outside the ordinary course of business.

    B. An auditor should determine whether a particular transaction would have occurred if the parties had not been related.

    C. An auditor should substantiate that related party transactions were consummated on terms equivalent to those that prevail in arm's-length transactions.

    D. The auditor should consider whether an identified related party transaction outside the normal course of business is appropriately accounted for and disclosed.

Answer (D) is correct.

REQUIRED: The true statement about related party transactions.

DISCUSSION: The auditor should inspect any contracts or agreements to evaluate whether (1) the business purpose (or lack of a business purpose) implies that the transaction's intent was fraudulent, (2) the terms are consistent with management's explanations, and (3) the accounting and disclosure are appropriate. The auditor also should obtain evidence of appropriate authorization and approval.

Answer (A) is incorrect. In the absence of contrary evidence, related party transactions are assumed to be in the ordinary course of business. Answer (B) is incorrect. Determining whether a particular transaction would have occurred if the parties had not been related is ordinarily not an objective of the audit. Answer (C) is incorrect. The auditor should obtain sufficient appropriate evidence about a management assertion that related party transactions were conducted on terms equivalent to those that prevail in arm's-length transactions. Management is responsible for substantiating the assertion. The auditor evaluates management's support for the assertion.

13. An auditor most likely modifies the opinion if the entity's financial statements include a note on related party transactions

    A. Disclosing loans to related parties at interest rates significantly below prevailing market rates.

    B. Describing an exchange of real estate for similar property in a nonmonetary related party transaction.

    C. Stating without substantiation that a particular related party transaction occurred on terms equivalent to those that would have prevailed in an arm's-length transaction.

    D. Presenting the dollar volume of related party transactions and the effects of any change from prior periods in the method of establishing terms.

Answer (C) is correct.

REQUIRED: The procedure performed to assess risks related to accounting estimates.

DISCUSSION: The auditor should obtain sufficient appropriate evidence about a management assertion that related party transactions were conducted on terms equivalent to those that prevail in arm's-length transactions. Management is responsible for substantiating the assertion. The auditor evaluates management's support for the assertion.

14. When auditing related party transactions, an auditor places primary emphasis on

A. Confirming the existence of the related parties.

B. Verifying the valuation of the related party transactions.

C. Assessing the risks of material misstatement of related party transactions.

D. Ascertaining the rights and obligations of the related parties.

Answer (C) is correct.

REQUIRED: The primary concern of the auditor about related party transactions.

DISCUSSION: The auditor has a responsibility to perform audit procedures to identify, assess, and respond to the risks of material misstatement arising from the entity's failure to appropriately account for or disclose related party relationships, transactions, or balances.

4.4 Accounting Estimates and Fair Value

15. When performing procedures to identify and assess the risks of material misstatement for accounting estimates, the auditor should

A. Review transactions occurring prior to the date of the auditor's report that indicate variations from expectations.

B. Compare independent expectations with recorded estimates to assess management's process.

C. Obtain an understanding of how management developed its estimates.

D. Analyze historical data used in developing assumptions to determine whether the process is consistent.

Answer (C) is correct.

REQUIRED: The procedure performed to assess risks related to accounting estimates.

DISCUSSION: The auditor performs risk assessment procedures to provide a basis for identifying and assessing the RMMs for accounting estimates. Thus, the auditor obtains an understanding of the following: (1) the relevant requirements of the applicable financial reporting framework, (2) how management identifies factors that create a need for estimates, and (3) how management makes estimates and the data on which they are based (e.g., methods, models, controls, use of specialists, underlying assumptions, and whether and how the effects of estimation uncertainty are assessed).

Answer (A) is incorrect. The auditor should review transactions after obtaining an understanding of how management developed the estimates. Answer (B) is incorrect. The auditor should compare independent expectations and reported estimates after obtaining an understanding of how management developed the estimates. Answer (D) is incorrect. The auditor should analyze historical data after obtaining an understanding of how management developed the estimates.

16. In evaluating the reasonableness of an entity's accounting estimates, an auditor normally is concerned about assumptions that are

A. Susceptible to bias.

B. Consistent with prior periods.

C. Insensitive to variations.

D. Similar to industry guidelines.

Answer (A) is correct.

REQUIRED: The auditor's normal concern about assumptions used in making accounting estimates.

DISCUSSION: In evaluating the reasonableness of an estimate, the auditor normally concentrates on key factors and assumptions that are (1) significant to the accounting estimate, (2) sensitive to variations, (3) deviations from historical patterns, and (4) subjective and susceptible to misstatement and bias.

Answer (B) is incorrect. Assumptions consistent with those of prior periods are of less concern to the auditor. Answer (C) is incorrect. Assumptions insensitive to variations are of less concern to the auditor. Answer (D) is incorrect. Estimates that are similar to industry guidelines are more likely to be reasonable.

17. The auditor's evaluation of the reasonableness of accounting estimates

A. Should be in the context of individual transactions.

B. Considers that management bases its judgment on both subjective and objective factors.

C. Will be unfavorable if the estimates in the financial statements are based on assumptions about future events and transactions.

D. Should be based on an attitude of conservatism.

Answer (B) is correct.

REQUIRED: The true statement about the auditor's evaluation of the reasonableness of accounting estimates.

DISCUSSION: Estimates are based on both subjective and objective factors. Thus, control over estimates may be difficult to establish. Given the potential bias in the subjective factors, the auditor should adopt an attitude of professional skepticism toward both the subjective and objective factors.

Answer (A) is incorrect. The evaluation should be in the context of the financial statements as a whole. Answer (C) is incorrect. Estimates are often based on assumptions about the future. Answer (D) is incorrect. Estimates should be based on assumptions regarding the most likely circumstances and events. The auditor should evaluate those assumptions with professional skepticism.

18. George Karl, an auditor with extensive experience in the retail industry, is assigned to audit the reasonableness of accounting estimates in the Year 1 financial statements of Haas Company. Haas, which was formed in Year 1, markets fishing lures. Which of the following is the **least** important consideration for Karl's audit of the reasonableness of accounting estimates?

A. An inexperienced employee at Haas prepared the financial statements and was entirely responsible for the accounting estimates.

B. Karl has never been involved in an audit of a company that sells fishing lures.

C. The accounting estimates in the financial statements of Haas Company are based on numerous significant assumptions.

D. The accounting estimates in the financial statements are susceptible to significant estimation uncertainty.

Answer (B) is correct.
REQUIRED: The least important consideration in an audit of the reasonableness of accounting estimates.
DISCUSSION: The auditor evaluates the reasonableness of estimates. Among the factors considered are (1) the entity's experience in making past estimates, (2) any changes that may cause factors different from those previously considered to become significant, and (3) the need to obtain written representations from management regarding the key factors and assumptions. Karl has extensive experience in the retail industry and therefore most likely has an acceptable level of competence. If necessary, Karl may seek the help of a specialist before conducting the audit.
Answer (A) is incorrect. Preparation of the statements by an inexperienced employee who may not have the competence necessary to formulate accounting estimates suggests the need for additional audit effort. Answer (C) is incorrect. The significant assumptions underlying accounting estimates are crucial to the audit. The auditor should concentrate on the key factors and assumptions that are subjective and susceptible to misstatement and bias. Answer (D) is incorrect. Estimates that are subject to significant estimation uncertainty require additional consideration by the auditor.

19. Auditors should obtain and evaluate sufficient appropriate evidence to support significant accounting estimates. Differences between the estimates best supported by the evidence and those in the financial statements

A. Are per se unreasonable and should be treated as material misstatements.

B. May be individually reasonable but collectively indicate possible bias.

C. May be individually unreasonable, but if they collectively indicate no bias, accumulation of the differences with other identified misstatements is not required.

D. Should arouse concern only when estimates are based on hypothetical assumptions or subjective factors.

Answer (B) is correct.
REQUIRED: The true statement about differences between the estimates best supported by the evidence and those in the financial statements.
DISCUSSION: If the amount in the financial statements is not reasonable, it should be treated as fraud or error and accumulated with other identified misstatements. If the differences between the best estimates and those in the financial statements are individually reasonable but collectively indicate possible bias (for example, when the effect of each difference is to increase income), the auditor should reconsider the estimates as a whole.
Answer (A) is incorrect. No estimate is considered accurate with certainty. Hence, differences may be reasonable and not considered to be identified material misstatements. Answer (C) is incorrect. An unreasonable difference should be considered an identified misstatement and accumulated. Answer (D) is incorrect. Estimates are based on subjective as well as objective factors.

20. As part of the audit of fair value estimates and disclosures, an auditor may need to test the entity's significant assumptions. In these circumstances, the auditor should

A. Verify that the entity has used its own assumptions, not those of marketplace participants.

B. Obtain sufficient evidence to express an opinion on the assumptions.

C. Evaluate whether the assumptions individually and as a whole form a reasonable basis for the fair value estimates.

D. Apply audit effort equally to all assumptions.

Answer (C) is correct.
REQUIRED: The necessary step in an audit of fair value estimates when the auditor tests significant assumptions.
DISCUSSION: Observable market prices are not always available for fair value estimates. In this case, the entity uses valuation methods based on the assumptions that the market would employ to estimate fair values, if obtainable without excessive cost. Accordingly, GAAS require the auditor to evaluate whether the significant assumptions form a reasonable basis for the estimates. Because assumptions often are interdependent and must be consistent with each other, the auditor should evaluate them independently and as a whole.
Answer (A) is incorrect. Valuation methods should be based on the assumptions that participants in the market would use to estimate fair value without undue cost and effort. Answer (B) is incorrect. The procedures applied to the entity's assumptions are required merely to evaluate whether, in the context of the audit of the financial statements as a whole, the assumptions form a reasonable basis for the estimates. Answer (D) is incorrect. The auditor considers the sensitivity of valuations to changes in assumptions. Accordingly, the auditor considers focusing on especially sensitive assumptions.

STUDY UNIT FIVE
INTERNAL CONTROL CONCEPTS
AND INFORMATION TECHNOLOGY

(14 pages of outline)

Concepts related to the client's internal control are tested extensively. AU-C 315, *Understanding the Entity and its Environment and Assessing the Risks of Material Misstatement*, provides the basis for consideration of this topic. Emphasis also is placed on technology in the standards. Accordingly, this study unit contains definitions and concepts of great significance for exam preparation. Many of these were developed in the report of the Committee of Sponsoring Organizations of the Treadway Commission **(the COSO report)** and are reflected in AU-C 315 and other AICPA pronouncements.

Because of the Sarbanes-Oxley Act of 2002, control concepts are crucially important to entities subject to the Securities Exchange Act of 1934. PCAOB AS 2110, *Identifying and Assessing Risks of Material Misstatement*, requires consideration of internal control in a financial statement audit. Moreover, certain issuers ("accelerated filers" with $75 million in market equity) must include in their annual reports an assessment by management of whether internal control over financial reporting is effective. The auditor is required to attest to the effectiveness of internal control as part of the overall audit. However, PCAOB AS 2201 requires the auditor merely to express or disclaim an opinion on internal control, not on management's assessment of internal control.

The general concepts described in this study unit are applied specifically in the transaction processing cycles considered in Study Units 6 and 7. CPA candidates should master the material in this study unit before continuing.

5.1 INTRODUCTION TO INTERNAL CONTROL

1. **Objective of the Auditor**

   a. The objective of the auditor is to identify and assess the **risks of material misstatement** (RMMs), whether due to fraud or error, at the financial statement and relevant assertion levels. This objective is achieved through understanding the entity and its environment, including the entity's internal control, to provide a basis for designing and implementing responses to the assessed RMMs.

      1) A relevant assertion has a reasonable possibility of containing a misstatement that could cause material misstatement(s) of the financial statements. Thus, a relevant assertion has a meaningful bearing on whether the account is fairly stated.

2. **Definition of Internal Control**

   a. Internal control is a process–effected by those charged with governance, management, and other personnel–designed to provide reasonable assurance regarding the achievement of objectives related to the following:

      1) Reliability of financial reporting
      2) Effectiveness and efficiency of operations
      3) Compliance with applicable laws and regulations

3.   **Components of Internal Control**

a.   Auditing standards (and the COSO's internal control framework) define the following five interrelated components (a useful memory aid is "Controls stop **CRIME**," with E representing the control environment):

1)   **C**ontrol activities are the policies and procedures that help ensure that management directives are carried out.

2)   The **r**isk assessment process is the entity's identification and analysis of relevant risks.

3)   The **i**nformation system, including related and relevant business processes, supports the identification, capture, and exchange of information in a form and time frame that enable people to carry out their responsibilities.

4)   **M**onitoring of controls assesses the effectiveness of internal control over time.

5)   The control **e**nvironment sets the tone of an organization, influencing the control consciousness of its people.

4.   **Relevant Controls**

a.   The relationship between an entity's objectives and the components is direct. Moreover, internal control is relevant to the whole entity (or any operating unit or business function).

b.   However, an entity generally has controls relating to objectives that are not relevant to an audit and need not be considered, for example, a computerized production scheduling system.

c.   Furthermore, understanding internal control relevant to each operating unit or business function may not be needed to perform an audit.

5.   **Inherent Limitations of Internal Control**

a.   Because of the inherent limitations of internal control, it can be designed and operated to provide only **reasonable assurance** that the entity's objectives are met.

b.   Human judgment is faulty, and controls may fail because of human error. For example, an error may occur in the design of, or a change in, a control. The operation of a control also may be effective, e.g., when an individual does not understand or use an exception report.

c.   Manual or automated controls can be circumvented by collusion.

d.   Management may inappropriately override internal control.

e.   Custom, culture, the corporate governance system, and an effective control environment are not absolute deterrents to fraud. For example, if the nature of management incentives increases the RMMs, the effectiveness of controls may be reduced.

f.   An inherent limitation of an audit as well as internal control is the need to balance benefit and cost. Although the ability to provide only reasonable assurance is a primary design criterion for internal control, the precise measurement of costs and benefits is not feasible.

1)   However, costs should not exceed the benefits of control. Thus, the cost constraint limits internal control.

Stop and review! You have completed the outline for this subunit. Study multiple-choice questions 1 through 4 beginning on page 126.

5.2 INTERNAL CONTROL COMPONENTS

1. **Control Environment**

   a. This component is the foundation for the other components. It provides discipline and structure and sets the tone of the organization, including the control consciousness of its people. It includes governance and management functions and the attitudes, awareness, and actions of management and those charged with governance regarding internal control and its importance. The following are the elements of the control environment:

      1) Communication and enforcement of **integrity and ethical values.** These are essential elements of the control environment and influence the effectiveness of the other components. Standards should be effectively communicated, e.g., by management example. Management also should remove incentives and temptations for dishonest or unethical acts.

         a) Audit evidence for elements of the control environment of a small-business client may not be documented, especially when management communication with other employees is informal but effective. Thus, a small business may not have a written code of conduct.

            i) However, it may have a culture emphasizing integrity and ethical behavior by means of oral communication and management example.

      2) **Commitment to competence.** Management must consider the competence levels for particular jobs.

      3) **Participation of those charged with governance** (board of directors, audit committee, etc.). Their independence, experience, and stature are among the qualities that affect the entity's control consciousness.

      4) **Management's philosophy and operating style.** They relate to management's approach to taking and managing business risks. They also relate to management's attitudes and actions toward (a) financial reporting, (b) information processing, (c) accounting functions, and (d) personnel.

      5) **Organizational structure.** Key areas of authority and responsibility and appropriate lines of reporting should be considered. The organizational structure is depicted by an organizational chart. (This chart is presented in Study Unit 6 on page 134.)

      6) **Assignment of authority and responsibility.** This factor relates to how authority over and responsibility for operating activities are assigned and how reporting relationships and authorization hierarchies are established.

      7) **Human resource policies and practices.** These relate to recruitment, orientation, training, evaluation, counseling, promotion, compensation, and remedial action. Training policies should communicate roles, responsibilities, and expected levels of performance and behavior.

2. **Risk Assessment Process**

   a. Relevant risks include events and circumstances that may adversely affect an entity's ability to initiate, authorize, record, process, and report financial data consistent with financial statement assertions. The following factors affecting risk should be considered:

      1) **Changes in operating environment.** A shift in the regulatory or operating environment may require reconsideration of risks.

      2) **New personnel.** New employees may have a different focus on control issues.

3) **New or revamped information systems.** Automated systems are important to the risk assessment process because they provide timely information for identifying and managing risks. However, significant and rapid changes in information systems themselves may affect risk.

4) **Rapid growth.** Significant and rapid expansion may strain controls and increase risk.

5) **New technology.** Integrating new technology into production or information processes may change risk.

6) **New business models, products, or activities.** Inexperience with respect to new business areas or transactions may change risk.

7) **Corporate restructurings.** Staffing and supervision changes may change risk.

8) **Expanded foreign operations.** Expansion to foreign markets may result in changes in risk, for example, from changes in currency exchange rates.

9) **New accounting pronouncements.** Adoption or changes of principles may affect risk in statement preparation.

10) **Changes in economic conditions.** Economic change can stress an organization.

3. **Control Activities**

a. These are the policies and procedures helping to ensure that management's directives are followed. Whether automated or manual, they have various objectives and are applied at various levels.

1) **Authorization** should ensure that only valid transactions are initiated.

2) **Performance reviews** include comparisons of actual performance with budgets and prior performance.

3) **Information processing** requires checks of accuracy, completeness, and authorization of transactions. These controls include general controls and application controls.

4) **Physical controls** involve the physical security of assets, authorization of access, periodic counts, and reconciliations to create asset accountability.

5) **Segregation of duties** involves the separation of the functions of authorization, recordkeeping, and asset custody. The effect should be to minimize the opportunities for a person to be able to perpetrate and conceal fraud or errors in the normal course of his or her duties.

4. **Information Systems**

a. An information system, including the related business processes relevant to financial reporting and communication, consists of (1) physical and hardware elements (infrastructure), (2) people, (3) software, (4) data, and (5) manual and automated procedures. It often is used extensively.

b. For financial reporting, the information system (including the accounting system) encompasses automated and manual procedures and records used to initiate, authorize, record, process, and report transactions, events, and conditions and to maintain accountability for assets, liabilities, and equity.

1) Initiation may be automatic through programmed methods. Authorizing is management's approval process. Recording includes identification and capture of relevant information. Processing involves edit and validation, calculation, measurement, valuation, summarization, and reconciliation by manual or automated means. Reporting of financial and other information for use in, for example, the monitoring function, may be in a print or electronic medium.

c. An **information system**

1) Identifies and records all valid transactions,
2) Describes transactions sufficiently for proper classification,
3) Measures transactions,
4) Determines the proper reporting period for transactions, and
5) Presents transactions and related disclosures properly.

d. **Communication** includes providing an understanding to employees about their roles and responsibilities. For example, communication may be through policy manuals, financial reporting manuals, and memoranda. It also may be by electronic and oral means or by management actions.

5. **Monitoring of Controls**

a. Monitoring is management's timely assessment of internal control and the taking of corrective action so that controls operate as intended and are modified for changes in conditions. Establishing and maintaining internal control is **management's responsibility**.

b. The monitoring process involves the following:

1) Ongoing activities built into normal recurring actions such as supervision, possibly combined with separate evaluations
2) The actions of internal auditors
3) Consideration of communications from external parties

c. Monitoring information may be produced by the information system. Thus, the auditor should obtain sufficient knowledge about major monitoring activities, including the sources of related information and the basis for considering it to be reliable.

Stop and review! You have completed the outline for this subunit. Study multiple-choice questions 5 through 9 beginning on page 128.

5.3 UNDERSTANDING INTERNAL CONTROL

1. In all audits, the auditor should obtain an understanding of the five components of internal control to identify and assess the RMMs and to design further audit procedures. An understanding is obtained by performing **risk assessment procedures** to evaluate the design of controls relevant to the audit and determine whether they have been implemented.

a. Implemented at a moment in time differs from operating effectiveness over a period of time.

b. However, the auditor is not obligated to search for deficiencies in internal control, although (s)he must communicate any significant deficiencies and material weaknesses noted.

2. The risk assessment should determine whether any identified risks are **significant risks**, i.e., require special audit consideration. This judgment is made without regard to related controls but should address at least the following factors:

a. Whether risks of fraud or significant transactions with related parties are involved

b. Whether the risks relate to significant transactions outside the normal course of business (or that are otherwise unusual) or to significant recent developments

c. The complexity of the transactions or the subjectivity of the measurements

3. The understanding should be used to

a. Identify types of potential misstatements,
b. Consider factors that affect the RMMs,
c. Design tests of controls if appropriate, and
d. Design substantive procedures.

4.   **Accounting Policies**

   a.   The auditor should obtain an understanding of the selection and application of accounting policies and consider whether they are appropriate. This understanding includes the following:

   1)   Significant and unusual transactions
   2)   Significant policies applied when controversial or emerging areas lack guidance or consensus
   3)   Changes in policies
   4)   Adoption of new reporting standards, laws, and regulations

5.   **Relevant Controls**

   a.   Relevant controls ordinarily address the entity's objectives related to the preparation of fairly presented financial statements, including management of RMMs.

   1)   But assessing all such controls is not necessary, and the auditor should use professional judgment regarding what should be assessed.

   b.   The auditor determines whether a control is relevant by considering factors such as the following:

   1)   The control component
   2)   The circumstances
   3)   Materiality
   4)   The size of the entity
   5)   The nature of the business, including organizational and ownership characteristics
   6)   The diversity and complexity of operations
   7)   The nature and complexity of control systems, including the use of service organizations
   8)   Legal and regulatory concerns
   9)   The significance of the related risk

   c.   Controls over the **completeness and accuracy** of information used by the auditor are relevant if the auditor intends to use it.

   d.   **Identifying** relevant controls is facilitated by

   1)   Previous experience with the entity,
   2)   The understanding of the entity and its environment, and
   3)   Information gathered during the audit.

   e.   Controls over **operations and compliance** may be relevant if they relate to information or data involved in performance of audit procedures.

   1)   Examples are controls related to (a) nonfinancial data used in analytical procedures or (b) noncompliance with laws and regulations having a direct effect on the determination of material amounts in the statements.

   f.   Controls over **safeguarding of assets** against unauthorized acquisition, use, or disposition may include those relating to financial reporting and operations objectives.

   1)   But the auditor's consideration is usually limited to **controls relevant to financial reporting**, such as controls that limit access to the data and programs (e.g., passwords) that process cash payments.

6. **Design and Implementation**

   a. The **evaluation of design** considers whether a control (alone or with others) can effectively prevent, or detect and correct, material misstatements.

   b. A control has been **implemented** if it exists and the entity is using it.

      1) An auditor may decide not to consider implementation if the design is improper.

         a) An improper design may be a **material weakness** in internal control that the auditor should communicate to management and those charged with governance.

7. **Risk Assessment Procedures**

   a. Risk assessment procedures performed to obtain evidence about the design and implementation of relevant controls include (1) inquiries, (2) observation of the application of specific controls, (3) inspection of documents and reports, and (4) tracing transactions.

      1) Inquiries alone are not sufficient.

8. **Operating Effectiveness**

   a. Obtaining the understanding is insufficient to test the operating effectiveness of controls, unless they are automated and subject to effective general IT controls (e.g., software acquisition, access, and change controls).

   b. Operating effectiveness relates to how and by whom the control (manual or automated) was applied and the consistency of application.

9. **Understanding IT-Based Systems**

   a. IT skills may be required to (1) determine the effect of IT on the audit, (2) understand IT controls, and (3) design and perform tests of IT controls and substantive procedures.

   b. These skills may be obtained from an audit staff member or an outside professional.

      1) Whether a professional is needed depends on such factors as (a) the complexity of systems and IT controls, (b) their use in the business, (c) the extent of data sharing among systems, (d) implementation of new systems or changes in old ones, (e) the involvement in electronic commerce, (f) use of emerging technologies, and (g) audit evidence available only electronically.

      2) An outside professional may make inquiries of the entity's IT personnel, inspect documentation, observe operation of controls, and test IT controls.

      3) The auditor must have sufficient IT expertise to (a) communicate audit objectives, (b) evaluate whether the IT professional's procedures will meet those objectives, and (c) evaluate the results.

   c. The auditor should understand the **information system relevant to financial reporting**, that is, (1) the classes of significant transactions; (2) the automated and manual procedures used to initiate, authorize, record, process, and report transactions; (3) the related accounting records, supporting information, and specific accounts; (4) how the system captures other significant events and conditions; and (5) the financial reporting process, including significant accounting estimates and disclosures.

      1) Thus, the auditor should understand not only the manual procedures but also the IT systems, programs, and controls in the financial reporting process.

10. **Documentation**

    a.   Documentation of the understanding is required by GAAS. It includes the following:

        1)   Discussions among team members about the susceptibility of the statements to material misstatement and the application of the reporting framework

        2)   The understanding of the entity and its environment and each control component, the sources of information, and the risk assessment procedures performed

        3)   The assessed RMMs at the financial statement and relevant assertion levels

        4)   The significant risks identified and related controls evaluated requiring special audit consideration

    b.   The form and extent of documentation are influenced by the nature and complexity of the controls. For example, a complex information system that electronically initiates, authorizes, records, processes, and reports a large volume of transactions requires extensive documentation.

        1)   Accordingly, flowcharts, questionnaires, or decision tables may be appropriate for a complex information system, but a memorandum may suffice when little or no use is made of IT or few transactions are processed. In general, the more complex the controls and the more extensive the audit procedures, the more extensive the documentation.

    c.   **Systems (document) flowcharts** are diagrams of the client's system that track the flow of documents and processing. Advantages are that they provide a visual representation of the system and are flexible in construction. Flowcharts are introduced in Subunit 5.4 and are illustrated in Study Units 6 and 7.

    d.   **Questionnaires** consist of a series of interrelated questions about internal control policies and procedures. The questions are typically phrased so that a "Yes" indicates a control strength and a "No" indicates a potential weakness. An area is provided next to the responses for the auditor to explain the responses or cross-reference the answer with other working papers.

        1)   An advantage of the questionnaire is that it helps identify control issues.

    e.   A **narrative memorandum** is a written description of the process and flow of documents and of the control points. Its advantage is flexibility. However, following the flow from the narrative may be difficult for a complex system.

    f.   A **decision table** identifies the contingencies considered in the description of a problem and the appropriate actions to be taken in each case. Decision tables are logic diagrams presented in matrix form. Unlike flowcharts, they do not present the sequence of the actions described.

    g.   A **checklist** consists of a series of procedures to be performed.

Stop and review! You have completed the outline for this subunit. Study multiple-choice questions 10 through 13 beginning on page 129.

5.4 FLOWCHARTING

Flowcharting is a topic that many CPA candidates try to avoid. However, you should realize that flowcharting is just another auditor's tool. The good news is that it is improbable that you will be required to construct a flowchart. Any questions that you may get will likely require you to interpret a flowchart. Keep an open mind as you begin using the flowcharts in Study Units 6 and 7. Spend enough time to understand the general flow of information and documents. You will likely surprise yourself with the confidence you gain.

1.   Flowcharting is a useful tool for systems development as well as for understanding internal control. A flowchart is a pictorial diagram of the definition, analysis, or solution of a problem in which symbols are used to represent operations, data flow, documents, records, etc.

    a.   The processing is presented sequentially from the point of origin to the distribution of final output.

        1)   Processing usually flows from top to bottom and from left to right in the flowchart.

    b.   A **system flowchart** provides an overall view of the inputs, processes, and outputs of a system.

    c.   A **program flowchart** represents the specific steps in a computer program and the order in which they will be carried out.

        1)   Macro- and microflowcharts describe a program in less or greater detail, respectively.

    d.   A **document flowchart** depicts the flow of documents through an entity.

        1)   Areas of responsibility (e.g., data processing or purchasing) are usually depicted in vertical columns or areas.

2.   Flowcharts are used to understand, evaluate, and document client internal control. Many CPA questions address flowcharting itself. Other CPA questions address specific controls, audit procedures, weaknesses, etc., that are related to or are a part of internal control.

3.   Commonly used document flowchart symbols include

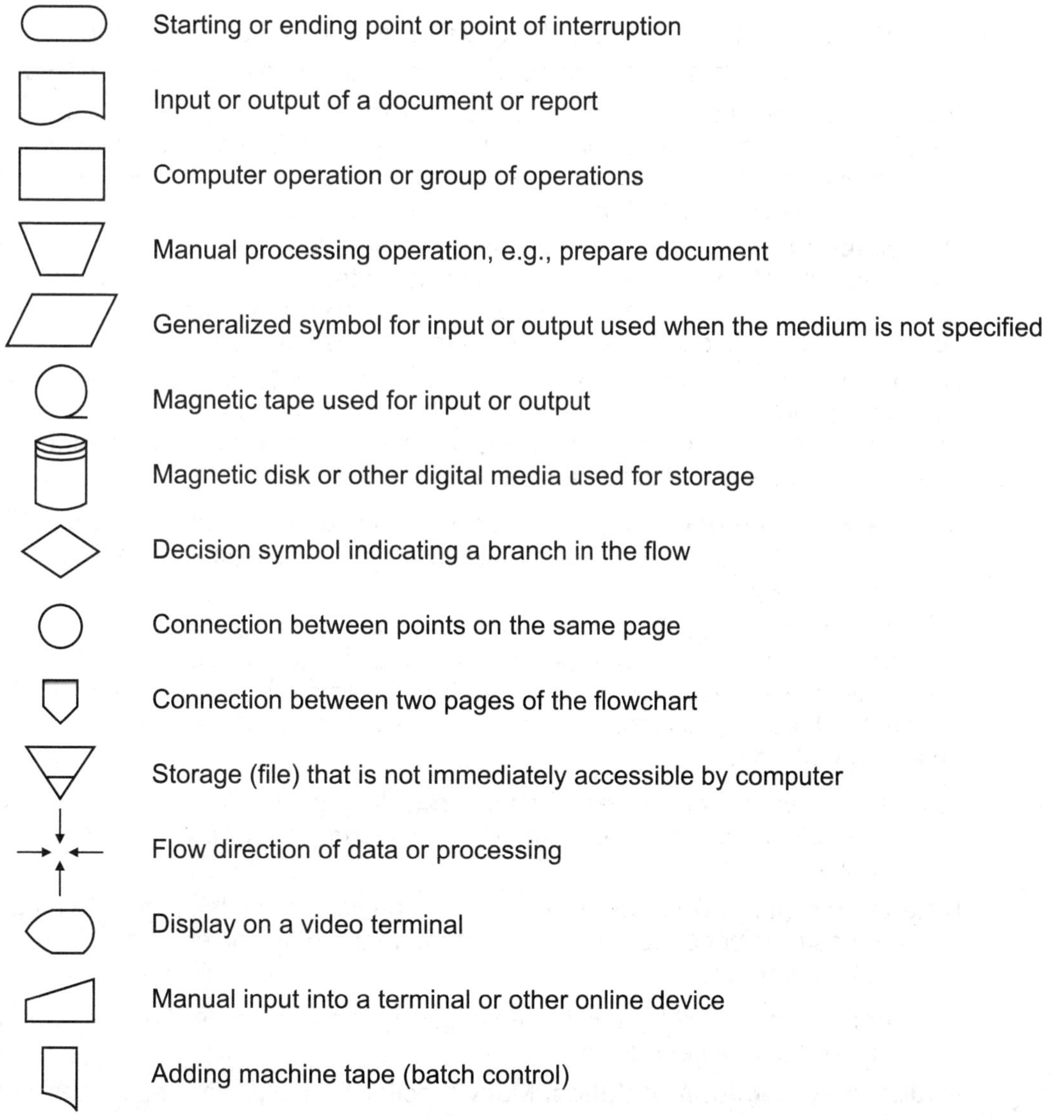

◯ (rounded)	Starting or ending point or point of interruption
▭ (document)	Input or output of a document or report
▭ (rectangle)	Computer operation or group of operations
▽ (trapezoid)	Manual processing operation, e.g., prepare document
▱ (parallelogram)	Generalized symbol for input or output used when the medium is not specified
◯ (circle/tape)	Magnetic tape used for input or output
⬠ (cylinder)	Magnetic disk or other digital media used for storage
◇ (diamond)	Decision symbol indicating a branch in the flow
◯ (circle)	Connection between points on the same page
⬠ (home plate)	Connection between two pages of the flowchart
▽ (triangle)	Storage (file) that is not immediately accessible by computer
→✛←	Flow direction of data or processing
⬡ (display)	Display on a video terminal
▱ (manual input)	Manual input into a terminal or other online device
▯ (tape)	Adding machine tape (batch control)

Figure 5-1

Stop and review! You have completed the outline for this subunit. Study multiple-choice questions 14 through 16 beginning on page 130.

5.5 INTERNAL CONTROL AND INFORMATION TECHNOLOGY

The material included in this section overlaps with the Information Technology content area representing 15% to 25% of the Business Environment and Concepts (BEC) section of the exam. We have attempted to include here those issues that are more likely to be tested on the Auditing and Attestation section of the exam. However, if you have studied for BEC, many issues should be familiar. If you have not yet studied for BEC, the following will be a good introduction to that material.

1. The objectives of a business information system are the same regardless of whether it is manual or computer-based. The risks, on the other hand, can be quite different.

    a. **System availability.** The ability to make use of any computer-based system is dependent on the following:

        1) An uninterrupted flow of electricity
        2) Protection of computer hardware from environmental hazards (e.g., fire and water)
        3) Protection of software and data files from unauthorized alteration
        4) Preservation of functioning communications channels among devices

    b. **Volatile transaction trails.** In any computer-based environment, a complete trail useful for audit purposes might exist for only a short time or in only computer-readable form. In online, real-time systems, data are entered directly into the computer, eliminating portions of the audit trail provided by source documents.

    c. **Decreased human involvement.** Because employees who enter transactions may never see the "final results," the potential for detecting errors is reduced. Also, output from a computer system often carries a mystique of infallibility, reducing the incentive of system users to closely examine reports and transaction logs.

    d. **Uniform processing of transactions.** Computer processing uniformly subjects like transactions to the same processing instructions, therefore virtually eliminating clerical error. Thus, it permits consistent application of predefined business rules and the performance of complex calculations in high volume.

        1) However, programming errors (or other similar systematic errors in either the hardware or software) will result in all like transactions being processed incorrectly.

    e. **Unauthorized access.** When accounting records were kept in pen-and-ink format, physical access to them was the only way to carry out an alteration. Once they are computer-based, however, access can be carried out from multiple work stations throughout the organization or from anywhere in the world by determined hackers using the Internet.

        1) Thus, security measures, such as firewalls and user identification-and-password combinations, are vital to maintaining security over data in an automated environment.

    f. **Data vulnerability.** Destruction of hardware devices or units of storage media could have disastrous consequences if they contain the only copies of crucial data files or application programs.

        1) For this reason, it is vital that an organization's computer files be duplicated and stored offsite periodically.

    g. **Reduced segregation of duties.** Many functions once performed by separate individuals may be combined in an automated environment.

EXAMPLE

Receiving cash, issuing a receipt to the payor, preparing the deposit slip, and preparing the journal entry may once have been performed by separate individuals. In a computer-based system, the receipt, deposit slip, and journal entry may be automatically generated by the computer. If the same employee who receives the cash is also responsible for entering the relevant data into the system, the potential for fraud or error is increased.

---

    h.   **Reduced individual authorization of transactions.** Certain transactions may be initiated automatically by a computer-based system. This is becoming ever more widespread as an increasing number of business processes become automated.

EXAMPLE

An enterprise resource planning system at a manufacturing concern may automatically generate a purchase order when raw materials inventory reaches a certain level. If the company shares an EDI system with the vendor, the purchase order may be sent to the vendor electronically without any human intervention.

---

        1)   This reduced level of oversight for individual transactions requires careful coding to ensure that computer programs accurately reflect management's objectives for business processes.

2.   **Two Basic Processing Modes of Data**

    a.   **Batch processing.** In this mode, transactions are accumulated and submitted to the computer as a single batch. In the early days of computers, this was the only way a job could be processed.

        1)   Despite huge advances in computer technology, this accumulation of transactions for processing on a delayed basis is still widely used. It is very efficient for applications (e.g., payroll) that must process large numbers of routine transactions on a regular schedule.

    b.   **Online, real-time processing.** In some systems, having the latest information available at all times is crucial to the proper functioning of the system. An airline reservation system is a common example.

        1)   In an online, real-time system, the database is updated immediately upon entry of the transaction by the operator. Such systems are **online transaction processing (OLTP)** systems.

3.   The two broad groupings of information systems control activities are **general controls** and **application controls**.

    a.   General controls are the umbrella under which the IT function operates. Because they affect the organization's entire processing environment, the auditor should achieve satisfaction about their proper operation before relying on application controls. They commonly include controls over (1) data center and network operations; (2) systems software acquisition, change, and maintenance; (3) access security; and (4) application system acquisition, development, and maintenance.

        1)   Controls over data center and network **operations** ensure efficient and effective operations of the computer activity. These include aspects of the control environment and risk assessment.

        2)   Controls over **software acquisition, change, and maintenance** ensure that proper software is available for use.

        3)   Controls over **access** encompass access to both computer hardware devices themselves (physical access) and to data and programs through the system (logical access).

b.   Application controls are particular to each of the organization's applications. Some features come built-in when applications are acquired from vendors. Software developed by the organization's own programmers must have appropriate controls incorporated in the design. Application controls may be further classified as follows:

1)   **Input controls** provide reasonable assurance that (a) data received for processing have been identified, properly authorized, and converted into machine-sensible form, and (b) data (including data transmitted over communication lines) have not been lost, added to, suppressed, duplicated, or otherwise improperly changed. Input controls also relate to rejection, correction, and resubmission of initially incorrect data.

2)   **Processing controls** provide reasonable assurance that processing has been performed as intended for the particular application. Thus, (a) all transactions should be processed as authorized, (b) no authorized transactions should be omitted, and (c) no unauthorized transactions should be added.

3)   **Output controls** ensure the accuracy of the processing result (such as account listings, reports, files, invoices, or disbursement checks) and the receipt of output by authorized personnel only.

c.   Both categories of controls are discussed in greater detail in the rest of this subunit.

4.   **General Controls -- Controls over Operations**

a.   From an audit perspective, the most significant of these general controls is the assignment of **authority and responsibility**.

1)   **Segregation of duties** is vital because a separation of functions (authorization, recording, and access to assets) may not be feasible in an IT environment. For example, a computer may print checks, record disbursements, and generate information for reconciling the account balance. These activities customarily are segregated in a manual system.

b.   **Periodic backup and offsite rotation** of computer files is the most basic part of any disaster recovery/business continuity plan.

1)   A **typical backup routine** involves duplicating all data files and application programs at least once a month. Incremental changes are then backed up and stored in an offsite location periodically, often once a week. (Application files must be backed up in addition to data because programs also are changed.)

2)   **Hot-site and cold-site backup facilities.** A hot site is a fully operational processing facility that is immediately available (e.g., a service bureau). A cold site is a shell facility where the user can quickly install equipment.

3)   **Cloud computing** is technology that allows software and data to be shared on the Internet. Thus, it provides a method for off-site backup and storage of data. However, firms using cloud computing face risks of loss or unauthorized access and should take steps, such as encryption, to protect data.

c.   **Protection against Malicious Software (Malware)**

1)   To protect against viruses, three types of controls should be implemented:

a)   **Preventive controls** include (1) establishing a formal security policy, (2) using only clean and certified copies of software, (3) not using shareware software, (4) checking new software with antivirus software, (5) restricting access, and (6) educating users.

b)   **Detective controls** include making file size and date/time stamp comparisons.

c)   **Corrective controls** include ensuring that clean backup is maintained and having a documented plan for recovery from a virus.

d. **Network Security**

1) The most important control is to install an entity-wide network security system. **User account management** involves installing a system to ensure that

a) New accounts are added correctly and assigned only to authorized users.

b) Old and unused accounts are removed promptly.

c) **Passwords** are changed periodically, and employees are taught how to choose a password that cannot be easily guessed.

5. **General Controls -- Controls over Software Acquisition, Change, and Maintenance**

a. **Controls over systems software** ensure that operating systems, utilities, and database management systems are acquired and changed only under close supervision and that vendor updates are routinely installed.

b. **Controls over application software** ensure that programs used for transaction processing (e.g., payroll and accounts receivable) are cost-effective and stable.

c. These **change controls** require proper authorization, testing, and acceptance. All changes should be properly documented.

6. **General Controls -- Access Controls**

a. Access controls prevent improper use or manipulation of data files and programs. They ensure that only those persons with a bona fide purpose and authorization have access.

7. **Application Controls -- Input**

a. **Input controls** provide reasonable assurance that data submitted for processing are (1) authorized, (2) complete, and (3) accurate. These controls vary depending on whether input is entered in online or batch mode.

b. **Online input controls** can be used when data are keyed into an input screen.

1) **Preformatting.** The data entry screen mimics a hardcopy document, forcing data entry in all necessary fields.

2) **Edit (field) checks.** The data entry screen prevents certain types of incorrect data from entering the system. For example, the system rejects any attempt to enter numerals in the Name box or letters in the Amount box. Dropdown menus can restrict the user's choices to only valid selections. Other examples of edit checks include financial totals, hash totals, reasonableness tests, check digits, sign checks, and validity checks.

3) **Limit (reasonableness) checks.** Certain amounts can be restricted to appropriate ranges, such as hours worked being limited to less than 10 per day or invoices over $100,000 requiring supervisor approval.

4) **Check digits.** An algorithm is applied to any kind of serial identifier to derive a check digit. During data entry, the check digit is recomputed by the system to ensure proper entry.

c. **Batch input controls** can be used when data are grouped for processing.

1) **Record count.** A batch is not released for processing unless the number of records in the batch, as reported by the system, matches the number calculated by the user.

2) **Financial total.** A batch is not released for processing unless the sum of the dollar amounts of the individual items as reported by the system matches the amount calculated by the user.

3) **Hash total.** The arithmetic sum of a numeric field, which has no meaning by itself, can serve as a check that the same records that should have been processed were processed. An example is the sum of all Social Security numbers.

   a) This number is much too unwieldy to be calculated by the user. But once it is calculated by the system, it can follow the batch through subsequent stages of processing.

8. **Application Controls -- Processing**

   a. Processing controls provide reasonable assurance that (1) all data submitted for processing are processed, and (2) only approved data are processed. These controls are built into the application code by programmers during the systems development process.

   b. Some processing controls repeat the steps performed by the **input controls**, such as limit checks and batch controls.

   c. **Validation.** Identifiers are matched against master files to determine existence. For example, any accounts payable transaction in which the vendor number does not match a number on the vendor master file is rejected.

   d. **Completeness.** Any record with missing data is rejected.

   e. **Arithmetic controls.** Cross-footing compares an amount with the sum of its components. Zero-balance checking adds the debits and credits in a transaction or batch to ensure that their sum is zero.

9. **Application Controls -- Output**

   a. **Output controls** provide assurance that processing was complete and accurate.

   b. A complete **audit trail** should be generated by each process: batch number, time of submission, time of completion, number of records in batch, total dollars in batch, number of records rejected, total dollars rejected, etc.

      1) The audit trail is immediately submitted to a **reasonableness check** by the user, who is most qualified to judge the adequacy of processing and the proper treatment of erroneous transactions.

   c. **Error listings** report all transactions rejected by the system. These should be corrected and resubmitted by the user.

Stop and review! You have completed the outline for this subunit. Study multiple-choice questions 17 through 20 on page 132.

QUESTIONS

5.1 Introduction to Internal Control

1. The primary objective of procedures performed to obtain an understanding of internal control is to provide an auditor with

A. Knowledge necessary for audit planning.

B. Evidence to use in assessing inherent risk.

C. A basis for modifying tests of controls.

D. An evaluation of the consistency of application of management's policies.

Answer (A) is correct.
   REQUIRED: The objective of procedures performed to obtain an understanding of internal control.
   DISCUSSION: The auditor is required to obtain an understanding of the entity and its environment, including its internal control, to assess the risks of material misstatement of the financial statements, whether due to fraud or error, to provide a basis for responding to the assessed RMMs. The auditor obtains the understanding and assesses the RMMs to plan the audit. The audit plan describes (1) the risk assessment procedures, (2) further audit procedures at the assertion level, and (3) other procedures required by GAAS.
   Answer (B) is incorrect. Inherent risk is independent of internal control. Answer (C) is incorrect. The understanding is obtained to plan all aspects of the audit, not merely tests of controls. Answer (D) is incorrect. Evaluating the consistency of application of management's policies is a test of controls.

2. An auditor uses the knowledge provided by the understanding of internal control and the assessed risks of material misstatement primarily to

A. Determine whether procedures and records concerning the safeguarding of assets are reliable.

B. Determine whether the opportunities to allow any person to both perpetrate and conceal fraud are minimized.

C. Modify the initial assessments of inherent risk and judgments about materiality levels for planning purposes.

D. Determine the nature, timing, and extent of substantive procedures for financial statement assertions.

Answer (D) is correct.
REQUIRED: The auditor's purpose in understanding internal control and assessing the risks of material misstatement.
DISCUSSION: The auditor is required to obtain an understanding of the entity and its environment, including its internal control, to assess the risks of material misstatement of the financial statements, whether due to fraud or error, to provide a basis for responding to the assessed RMMs. Regardless of the assessed RMMs, the auditor performs substantive procedures for all relevant assertions for material classes of transactions, account balances, and disclosures. Moreover, the auditor designs and performs further audit procedures whose nature, timing, and extent respond to the assessed RMMs at the relevant assertion level.
Answer (A) is incorrect. Knowledge about operating effectiveness need not be obtained as part of the understanding of internal control. Answer (B) is incorrect. Knowledge about operating effectiveness need not be obtained as part of the understanding of internal control. Answer (C) is incorrect. Inherent risk and materiality are independent of internal control.

3. Which of the following most likely would **not** be considered an inherent limitation of the potential effectiveness of an entity's internal control?

A. Incompatible duties.

B. Management override.

C. Faulty judgment.

D. Collusion among employees.

Answer (A) is correct.
REQUIRED: The item not considered an inherent limitation of internal control.
DISCUSSION: Internal control has inherent limitations. The performance of incompatible duties, however, is a failure to assign different people the functions of authorization, recording, and asset custody, not an inevitable limitation of internal control. Segregation of duties is a category of control activities.
Answer (B) is incorrect. Management establishes internal controls. Thus, it can override those controls. Answer (C) is incorrect. Human judgment in decision making may be faulty. Answer (D) is incorrect. Controls, whether manual or automated, may be circumvented by collusion among two or more people.

4. In an audit of financial statements, an auditor's primary consideration regarding an internal control is whether the control

A. Reflects management's philosophy and operating style.

B. Affects management's financial statement assertions.

C. Provides adequate safeguards over access to assets.

D. Relates to operational objectives.

Answer (B) is correct.
REQUIRED: The auditor's primary consideration regarding an internal control.
DISCUSSION: Assertions are management representations embodied in the financial statements. They are used by the auditor to consider the different potential misstatements. A relevant assertion has a reasonable possibility of containing a misstatement that could cause a material misstatement(s) of the financial statements. Thus, a relevant assertion has a meaningful bearing on whether the account is fairly stated. Tests of controls are designed to evaluate the operating effectiveness of controls in preventing, or detecting and correcting, material misstatements at the assertion level. They should be performed when (1) the auditor's assessment of the RMMs at the relevant assertion level includes an expectation of the operating effectiveness of controls, or (2) substantive procedures alone do not provide sufficient appropriate evidence at the relevant assertion level. Thus, the auditor is primarily concerned with whether a control affects relevant financial statement assertions.
Answer (A) is incorrect. Management's philosophy and operating style is just one factor in one component (the control environment) of internal control. Answer (C) is incorrect. Restricting access to assets is only one of many physical controls, which constitute one element of one component (control activities) of internal control. Answer (D) is incorrect. Many controls relating to operational objectives are not relevant to an audit.

5.2 Internal Control Components

5. An auditor would most likely be concerned with controls that provide reasonable assurance about the

    A. Efficiency of management's decision-making process.

    B. Appropriate prices the entity should charge for its products.

    C. Decision to make expenditures for certain advertising activities.

    D. Entity's ability to initiate, authorize, record, process, and report financial data.

Answer (D) is correct.
    REQUIRED: The controls about which an auditor is most likely to be concerned.
    DISCUSSION: The information system relevant to financial reporting objectives, which includes the accounting system, consists of the procedures, whether automated or manual, and records established to initiate, authorize, record, process, and report entity transactions (as well as events and conditions) and to maintain accountability for the related assets, liabilities, and equity (AU-C 315).
    Answer (A) is incorrect. The efficiency of certain management decision-making processes is not likely to be relevant to a financial statement audit. Answer (B) is incorrect. Product pricing is not likely to be relevant to a financial statement audit. Answer (C) is incorrect. Decisions about advertising are not likely to be relevant to the auditor's consideration of controls.

6. Which of the following is **not** a component of internal control?

    A. Control risk.

    B. Monitoring of controls.

    C. Information system.

    D. The control environment.

Answer (A) is correct.
    REQUIRED: The item not a component of internal control.
    DISCUSSION: Control risk is one of the elements in the audit risk model. It is the risk that a material misstatement that could occur in an assertion will not be prevented, or detected and corrected, on a timely basis by the entity's internal control. Hence, control risk is a function of the effectiveness of internal control, not a component.

7. Which of the following factors are included in an entity's control environment?

	Audit Committee Participation	Integrity and Ethical Values	Organizational Structure
A.	Yes	Yes	No
B.	Yes	No	Yes
C.	No	Yes	Yes
D.	Yes	Yes	Yes

Answer (D) is correct.
    REQUIRED: The factors in a control environment.
    DISCUSSION: The control environment is the foundation for all other control components. It provides discipline and structure, sets the tone of the organization, and influences the control consciousness of employees. Its components include (1) participation of those charged with governance, (2) integrity and ethical values, (3) organizational structure, (4) management's philosophy and operating style, (5) assignment of authority and responsibility, (6) human resource policies and practices, and (7) commitment to competence.

8. Proper segregation of duties reduces the opportunities to allow persons to be in positions both to

    A. Journalize entries and prepare financial statements.

    B. Record cash receipts and cash disbursements.

    C. Establish internal control and authorize transactions.

    D. Perpetrate and conceal fraud and error.

Answer (D) is correct.
    REQUIRED: The effects of the segregation of duties.
    DISCUSSION: Segregation of duties is a category of the control activities component of internal control. Segregating responsibilities for authorization, recording, and asset custody reduces an employee's opportunity to perpetrate fraud or error and subsequently conceal it in the normal course of his or her duties.
    Answer (A) is incorrect. Accountants typically journalize entries and prepare financial statements. Answer (B) is incorrect. Accountants may record both cash receipts and cash disbursements as long as they do not have custody of cash. Answer (C) is incorrect. Management establishes internal control and ultimately has the responsibility to authorize transactions.

9. Proper segregation of functional responsibilities to achieve effective internal control calls for separation of the functions of

A. Authorization, execution, and payment.

B. Authorization, recording, and custody.

C. Custody, execution, and reporting.

D. Authorization, payment, and recording.

Answer (B) is correct.

REQUIRED: The duties separated to achieve effective internal control.

DISCUSSION: One person should not be responsible for all phases of a transaction, i.e., for authorization of transactions, recording of transactions, and custodianship of the related assets. These duties should be performed by separate individuals to reduce the opportunities to allow any person to be in a position both to perpetrate and conceal fraud or error in the normal course of his or her duties.

Answer (A) is incorrect. Payment is a form of execution (operational responsibility). Answer (C) is incorrect. Custody of assets and execution of related transactions are often not segregated. Answer (D) is incorrect. Payments must be recorded when made.

5.3 Understanding Internal Control

10. In obtaining an understanding of internal control in a financial statement audit, an auditor is **not** obligated to

A. Determine whether the controls have been implemented.

B. Perform procedures to understand the design of internal control.

C. Document the understanding of the entity's internal control components.

D. Search for significant deficiencies in the operation of internal control.

Answer (D) is correct.

REQUIRED: The step an auditor need not take in obtaining an understanding of internal control.

DISCUSSION: In all audits, the auditor should obtain an understanding of each of the five components of internal control sufficient to plan the audit. An understanding is obtained by performing risk assessment procedures to evaluate the design of controls relevant to the audit and to determine whether they have been implemented. In addition, the auditor should obtain and document the understanding of the entity's internal control components. However, in an audit, the auditor is not obligated to search for significant deficiencies or material weaknesses (AU-C 265).

Answer (A) is incorrect. The auditor should determine whether the relevant controls are in operation. Answer (B) is incorrect. The auditor should understand the design of relevant controls. Answer (C) is incorrect. The auditor should document the understanding of each control component.

11. As part of understanding internal control relevant to the audit of a non issuer, an auditor does **not** need to

A. Consider factors that affect the risks of material misstatement.

B. Determine whether controls have been implemented.

C. Identify the risks of material misstatement.

D. Obtain knowledge about the operating effectiveness of internal control.

Answer (D) is correct.

REQUIRED: The procedure not required in obtaining the understanding of internal control of a non issuer.

DISCUSSION: Understanding internal controls relevant to the audit involves evaluating the design of the controls and determining whether they have been implemented. The auditor of a nonissuer need not obtain an understanding about operating effectiveness as part of understanding internal control. However, (1) the auditor's assessment of the risks of material misstatement (RMMs) may include an expectation of the operating effectiveness of controls, or (2) substantive procedures may not provide sufficient appropriate evidence at the relevant assertion level about operating effectiveness. In these circumstances, the auditor should test controls (AU-C 330).

Answer (A) is incorrect. The auditor performs risk assessment procedures to obtain an understanding of the entity and its environment, including its internal control, to identify and assess the RMMs, whether due to fraud or error, at the financial statement and relevant assertion levels. Answer (B) is incorrect. The understanding of internal control provides assurance that controls have been implemented. Answer (C) is incorrect. The understanding of the entity and its environment, including its internal control, involves identifying and assessing RMMs.

12. When obtaining an understanding of an entity's internal control, an auditor should concentrate on their substance rather than their form because

    A. The controls may be operating effectively but may not be documented.

    B. Management may establish appropriate controls but not enforce compliance with them.

    C. The controls may be so inappropriate that no reliance is expected by the auditor.

    D. Management may implement controls whose costs exceed their benefits.

Answer (B) is correct.
    REQUIRED: The reason an auditor should concentrate on the substance of controls, not their form.
    DISCUSSION: The auditor must concentrate on the substance rather than the form of controls because management may establish appropriate controls but not apply them. Whether controls have been implemented at a moment in time differs from their operating effectiveness over a period of time. Thus, operating effectiveness concerns not merely whether the entity is using controls but also how the controls (manual or automated) are applied, the consistency of their application, and by whom they are applied.
    Answer (A) is incorrect. An auditor is concerned with the actual operating effectiveness of controls, not with a lack of evidence about form (documentation). Answer (C) is incorrect. If controls are so inappropriate that the auditor does not expect to rely on them, their substance is irrelevant. Answer (D) is incorrect. When considering internal control in a financial statement audit, the auditor is primarily concerned with the effectiveness of controls, not their cost-benefit relationship.

13. In an audit of financial statements in accordance with generally accepted auditing standards, an auditor should

    A. Identify specific controls relevant to management's financial statement assertions.

    B. Perform tests of controls to evaluate the effectiveness of the entity's accounting system.

    C. Determine whether procedures are suitably designed to prevent, or detect and correct, material misstatement.

    D. Document the auditor's understanding of the entity's internal control.

Answer (D) is correct.
    REQUIRED: A procedure in an audit of financial statements in accordance with GAAS.
    DISCUSSION: The auditor should document (1) the understanding of the entity and its environment and the components of internal control, (2) the sources of information regarding the understanding, and (3) the risk assessment procedures performed. The form and extent of the documentation are influenced by the nature and complexity of the entity's controls (AU-C 315).

5.4 Flowcharting

14. An auditor's flowchart of a client's accounting system is a diagrammatic representation that depicts the auditor's

    A. Assessment of the risks of material misstatement.

    B. Identification of weaknesses in the system.

    C. Assessment of the control environment's effectiveness.

    D. Understanding of the system.

Answer (D) is correct.
    REQUIRED: The purpose of an auditor's flowchart.
    DISCUSSION: The auditor should document (1) the understanding of the entity and its environment and the components of internal control, (2) the sources of information regarding the understanding, and (3) the risk assessment procedures performed. The form and extent of this documentation are influenced by the nature and complexity of the entity's controls (AU-C 315). For example, documentation of the understanding of internal control of a complex information system in which many transactions are electronically initiated, authorized, recorded, processed, or reported may include questionnaires, flowcharts, or decision tables.
    Answer (A) is incorrect. The conclusions about the assessments of the RMMs should be documented. These are professional judgments of the auditor documented in the working papers. Answer (B) is incorrect. The flowchart is a tool to document the auditor's understanding of internal control, but it does not specifically identify weaknesses in the system. Answer (C) is incorrect. The auditor's judgment is the ultimate basis for concluding that controls are effective.

15. Which of the following symbolic representations indicates that new payroll transactions and the old payroll file have been used to prepare payroll checks, prepare a printed payroll journal, and generate a new payroll file?

A.

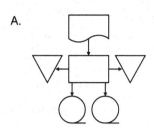

B.

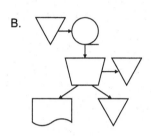

C.

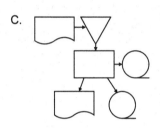

D.

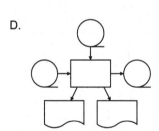

Answer (D) is correct.

REQUIRED: The symbolic representation for updating the payroll file and generating checks and a payroll journal.

DISCUSSION: The new payroll transactions and the old payroll file are represented by the magnetic tape symbols. These files are entered into the process function (the rectangle). The output is a new payroll file on magnetic tape and payroll checks and a printed payroll journal represented by the document symbols.

Answer (A) is incorrect. Two magnetically stored payroll files and two offline storage files are produced from a single document form. Answer (B) is incorrect. Two offline storage files and one document are produced (manually) from an offline storage file and a tape file. Answer (C) is incorrect. Two magnetically stored files and a document are produced from the processing of data from an offline storage file.

16. An advantage of using systems flowcharts to document information about internal control instead of using internal control questionnaires is that systems flowcharts

A. Identify internal control deficiencies more prominently.

B. Provide a visual depiction of clients' activities.

C. Indicate whether controls are operating effectively.

D. Reduce the need to observe clients' employees performing routine tasks.

Answer (B) is correct.

REQUIRED: The advantage of systems flowcharts over internal control questionnaires.

DISCUSSION: Systems flowcharts provide a visual representation of a series of sequential processes, that is, of a flow of documents, data, and operations. In many instances, a flowchart is preferable to a questionnaire because a picture is usually more easily comprehended.

Answer (A) is incorrect. A systems flowchart can present the flow of information and documents in a system, but it does not specifically identify the deficiencies. Answer (C) is incorrect. The flowchart does not provide evidence of how effectively controls are actually operating. Answer (D) is incorrect. The flowchart is useful in documenting the understanding of internal control, but it does not reduce the need for observation of employees performing tasks if those tests of controls are deemed necessary.

5.5 Internal Control and Information Technology

17. Which of the following characteristics distinguishes computer processing from manual processing?

A. Computer processing virtually eliminates the occurrence of computational error normally associated with manual processing.

B. Errors or fraud in computer processing will be detected soon after their occurrence.

C. The potential for systematic error is ordinarily greater in manual processing than in computerized processing.

D. Most computer systems are designed so that transaction trails useful for audit purposes do not exist.

Answer (A) is correct.

REQUIRED: The feature that distinguishes computer processing from manual processing.

DISCUSSION: Computer processing uniformly subjects like transactions to the same processing instructions. A computer program defines the processing steps to accomplish a task. Once the program is written and tested appropriately, it will perform the task repetitively and without error. However, if the program contains an error, all transactions will be processed incorrectly.

Answer (B) is incorrect. When an error does occur, for example, in input, it may not be discovered on a timely basis. Ordinarily, much less human intervention occurs once the transaction is processed. Answer (C) is incorrect. Systematic (repetitive) errors occur in computerized processing if an error exists in the program. Answer (D) is incorrect. Adequately designed systems maintain transaction, console, and error logs that create useful audit trails.

18. A client is concerned that a power outage or disaster could impair the computer hardware's ability to function as designed. The client desires off-site backup hardware facilities that are fully configured and ready to operate within several hours. The client most likely should consider a

A. Cold site.

B. Cool site.

C. Warm site.

D. Hot site.

Answer (D) is correct.

REQUIRED: The type of off-site backup hardware facility that is an available, fully operational processing facility.

DISCUSSION: A hot site is a service facility that is fully operational and is promptly available in the case of a power outage or disaster.

Answer (A) is incorrect. A cold site is a shell facility suitable for quick installation of computer equipment. Installing computer equipment requires more time in a cold site than in a hot site. Answer (B) is incorrect. "Cool site" is not a meaningful term in this context. Answer (C) is incorrect. A warm site provides an intermediate level of backup and causes more downtime than a hot site.

19. Which of the following is the most serious password security problem?

A. Users are assigned passwords when accounts are created, but they do not change them.

B. Users have accounts on several systems with different passwords.

C. Users copy their passwords on note paper, which is kept in their wallets.

D. Users select passwords that are not listed in any online dictionary.

Answer (A) is correct.

REQUIRED: The most serious password security problem.

DISCUSSION: Proper user authentication by means of a password requires password-generating procedures to ensure that valid passwords are known only by the proper individuals. If passwords are assigned, users should change passwords frequently so that they are the only persons with access under those identifiers.

Answer (B) is incorrect. No security issue arises when different passwords are used for accounts on different systems. Answer (C) is incorrect. Although any record of a password is potentially a security problem, storing a password online would be a greater problem. Answer (D) is incorrect. A password should not be an item in an online dictionary.

20. An entity has the following invoices in a batch:

Invoice Number	Product	Quantity	Unit Price
201	F10	150	$ 5.00
202	G15	200	10.00
203	H20	250	25.00
204	K35	300	30.00

Which of the following most likely represents a hash total?

A. FGHK80

B. 4

C. 204

D. 810

Answer (D) is correct.

REQUIRED: The example of a hash total.

DISCUSSION: Input controls in batch computer systems are used to determine that no data are lost or added to the batch. Depending on the sophistication of a particular system, control may be accomplished by using record counts, financial totals, or hash totals. The hash total is a control total without a defined meaning, such as the total of employee numbers or invoice numbers, that is used to verify the completeness of data. The hash total of the invoice numbers is 810.

Answer (A) is incorrect. A hash total is ordinarily the sum of a numeric field. Answer (B) is incorrect. The record count is four. Answer (C) is incorrect. The last invoice number is 204.

STUDY UNIT SIX
INTERNAL CONTROL --
SALES-RECEIVABLES-CASH RECEIPTS CYCLE

(10 pages of outline)

A standard approach to understanding internal control as well as designing substantive procedures is to divide the auditee's transactions, balances, and related control activities into groupings of related items. This cycle approach is consistent with how transactions are recorded in journals and ledgers. Among the relevant accounts considered are cash, trade receivables, other receivables, allowance for bad debts, sales, sales returns, and bad debt expense.

Understanding how information and documents flow through a particular cycle enables an auditor to determine what controls have been implemented and whether they are effective in safeguarding assets and preventing, or detecting and correcting, fraud and error. Auditors are required to obtain and document an understanding of internal control relevant to the audit. Thus, a knowledge of flowcharts is important in preparing for the CPA exam.

Some candidates may feel that information presented in flowcharts is difficult to master. The study materials presented here provide the foundation of understanding. They have been kept simple and straightforward. Nevertheless, they provide the information most often tested on the CPA exam. CPA candidates in the past have not been required to prepare flowcharts but have been expected to evaluate them. The narrative should be studied in conjunction with the flowcharts. Candidates should understand and not just memorize the various documents, flows, and control points. Although the basic concepts are derived from a manual system, they can be extended to a computer environment. Subunit 6.4 provides candidates with an understanding of the effect of technology on the sales cycle.

6.1 RESPONSIBILITIES/ORGANIZATIONAL STRUCTURE/FLOWCHARTS

1. **Management's Responsibility**

   a. Management is responsible for the establishment of the controls over the sales-receivables-cash receipts cycle to ensure

      1) Proper acceptance of the customer order
      2) Granting of credit approval in accordance with credit limits
      3) Safeguarding of assets associated with the sale
      4) Timely shipment of goods to customers
      5) Billing for shipments at authorized prices
      6) Accounting for and collection of receivables
      7) The recording, safeguarding, and depositing intact of cash (checks) received

2. **The Auditor's Responsibility**

   a. The auditor is required to obtain an understanding of the entity and its environment, including its internal control, to assess the risks of material misstatement and to design further audit procedures. For this purpose, the auditor performs risk assessment procedures. The plan for further audit procedures reflects (1) the auditor's decision whether to test the operating effectiveness of controls over the sales-receivables-cash receipts cycle and (2) the nature, timing, and extent of substantive procedures.

Organizational Chart

This is a standard organizational chart. To help you visualize the internal control of this typical organization, the following document flowcharts with explanations are presented for your study:

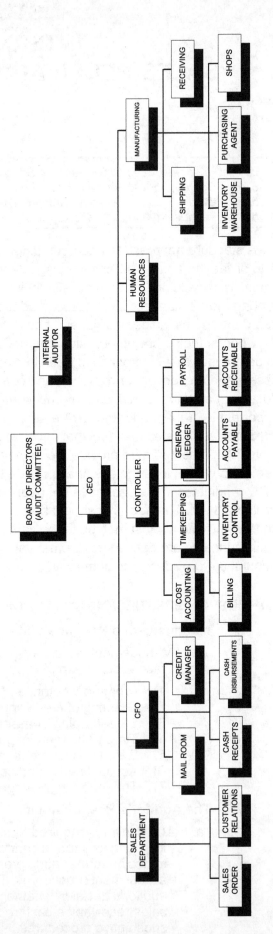

Figure 6-1

3. **Segregation of Duties**

   a. The organizational structure should segregate duties and responsibilities so that an individual is not in the position both to perpetrate and conceal fraud or error. The ideal segregation of duties is

   1) **Authorization** of the transaction

      a) **Specific authorization** may be needed for some transactions, such as unusual credit approvals, but a **general authorization** may suffice for others, such as retail cash sales.

   2) **Recording** of the transaction

   3) **Custody** of the assets (e.g., inventory, receivables, and cash) associated with the transaction

   b. However, **cost-benefit** considerations typically affect the organizational structure, and complete segregation may not be feasible. Compensating controls are likely to be established when the segregation of duties is not maintained. Typical compensating controls may include

   1) More supervision or
   2) Owner involvement in the process.

4. **Responsibilities of Personnel**

   a. The following are the responsibilities of personnel or departments in the sales-receivables-cash receipts cycle:

   1) **Sales** prepares sales orders based on customer orders.

      a) Customer Relations is commonly regarded as a separate operating unit that deals with customers after sales have been made. Thus, it is not involved in the basic transactional functions performed in the sales-receivables-cash receipts cycle.

   2) **Credit Manager**, who should report to the CFO, authorizes credit for all new customers and initiates write-off of bad debts. Credit checks should be performed before credit approval.

   3) **Inventory Warehouse** maintains physical custody of products.

   4) **Inventory Control** maintains records of quantities of products in the Inventory Warehouse.

   5) **Shipping** prepares shipping documents and ships products based on authorized sales orders.

   6) **Billing** prepares customer invoices based on goods shipped.

   7) **Accounts Receivable** maintains the accounts receivable subsidiary ledger.

   8) **Mail Room** receives mail and prepares initial cash receipts records.

   9) **Cash Receipts** safeguards and promptly deposits cash receipts.

   10) **General Ledger** maintains the accounts receivable control account and records sales. Daily summaries of sales are recorded in a sales journal. Totals of details from the sales journal are usually posted monthly to the general ledger.

   11) **Receiving** department prepares receiving reports and handles all receipts of goods or materials, including sales returns.

As you are considering the flowcharts in this and subsequent study units, remember that they are simply examples. Instead of assigning importance to the actual number of documents prepared or the document numbers, you should focus on the control provided by the division of duties and responsibilities and the control processes. Your understanding of the issues will help you answer many more CPA exam questions than just those related to flowcharting.

Sales-Receivables Manual System Flowchart

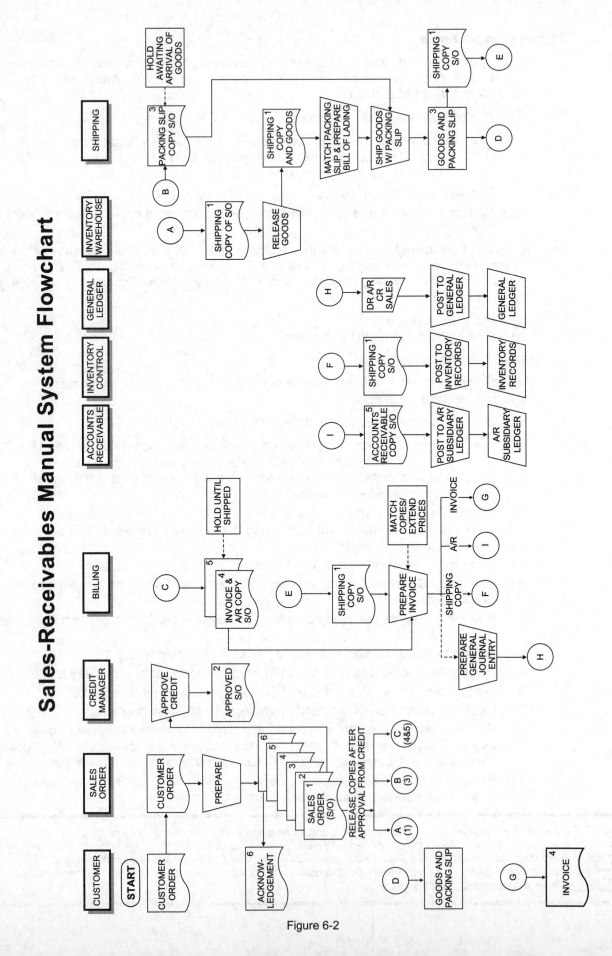

Figure 6-2

5.   **Sales-Receivables Flowchart**

a.   Study the flowchart on the previous page. Understand and visualize the sales-receivables process and controls. Read the following description as needed. Note the control activities implemented and listed in item 7. below.

6.   **The Document Flow**

a.   The process begins in the upper left corner of the flowchart marked **START**. (To simplify the presentation, the flowchart does not show the disposition of all documents, for example, by filing or other supplemental procedures.)

1)   The Sales Order department receives a customer order and prepares a multi-part sales order. Copy 2 of the sales order is sent to the Credit Manager.

2)   The Credit Manager performs a credit check and authorizes the order if appropriate. The approval is conveyed to Sales Order, and an acknowledgment (copy 6) is sent to the customer.

3)   Sales Order then releases the remaining copies of the order. Two copies, the invoice copy and accounts receivable copy (copies 4 and 5), are sent to Billing and held awaiting notification of shipment.

4)   A copy (the packing slip copy 3) is sent to Shipping pending arrival of the goods from the Inventory Warehouse.

5)   A copy (the shipping copy 1) is released to the Inventory Warehouse as authorization to release the goods to be sent to the Shipping department.

6)   When the goods and the shipping copy 1 arrive at the Shipping department, the matching packing slip copy 3 is pulled from the file, and shipping documents (e.g., a bill of lading) are prepared. The goods are packed for shipment along with the packing slip copy 3. The shipping copy 1 is marked "shipped" and forwarded to Billing.

7)   Billing pulls the matching invoice and accounts receivable copies (4 and 5). Prices are checked and extended based on the quantities shipped. The invoice (copy 4) is completed and mailed to the customer. The invoice contains a section (a remittance advice) to be returned with the customer check.

8)   Billing prepares a journal entry to be posted by the General Ledger department (credit to sales and debit to the accounts receivable control account).

9)   The accounts receivable copy 5 is forwarded to Accounts Receivable for posting to the individual account in the accounts receivable subsidiary ledger.

10) The shipping copy 1 is sent to Inventory Control for reduction of quantities for goods shipped.

7.   **Control Activities Implemented**

a.   The division of the duties of the transaction is as follows: authorization, recording, and custody of assets.

b.   Routing the sales order copy through the Credit Manager ensures that goods are shipped only to customers who are likely to pay (i.e., properly valued).

c.   Routing the shipping copy through the Inventory Warehouse helps ensure that goods are safeguarded and released only upon proper approval of the order.

d.   Matching of the packing slip copy held by Shipping can ensure that all goods released from the Inventory Warehouse are received by Shipping on a timely basis.

e.   Matching of the copies held by the Billing department can ensure that all goods shipped are invoiced to customers.

f.   Documents are prenumbered to permit detection of unrecorded or unauthorized transactions. For example, sales invoices are prenumbered and accounted for to ensure that all orders are billed.

g.   Periodic reconciliation of the accounts receivable subsidiary ledger with the general ledger can ensure that all invoices are recorded in customers' accounts.

8.   **Cash Receipts Flowchart**

   a.   Study the flowchart below. Understand and visualize the cash receipts process
        and controls. Read the description in item 9. as needed. Note the control activities
        implemented and listed in item 10. on the next page.

Cash Receipts Manual System Flowchart

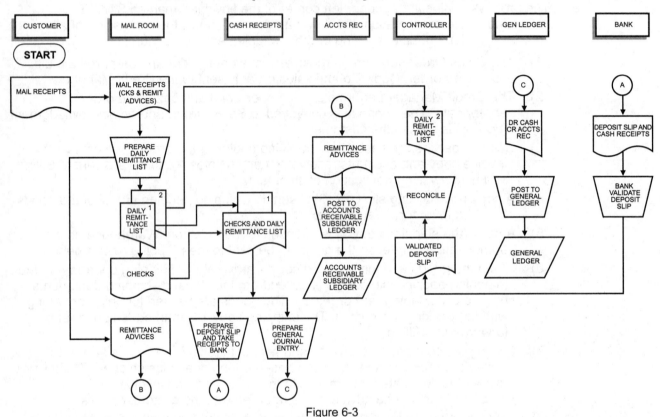

Figure 6-3

9.   **The Document Flow**

   a.   This flowchart represents the procedures and documents for cash collections from
        credit customers; cash receipts from cash sales are considered in Subunit 6.2. (To
        simplify the presentation, the flowchart does not show the disposition of documents,
        for example, by filing or other supplemental procedures.) The process begins at
        START.

       1)   The Mail Room receives all customer receipts, opens the mail, separates the
            checks from the remittance advices, and prepares a daily listing of the checks
            received (the daily remittance list). If no remittance advice is received, the mail
            clerks prepare one. A copy of the daily remittance list is sent to the Controller.

           a)   A remittance advice is part of or a copy of the sales invoice sent to a
                customer and intended to be returned with the payment. It contains the
                customer's name, the invoice number, and its amount.

       2)   Cash receipts and copy 1 of the daily remittance list are forwarded to Cash
            Receipts for preparation of the deposit ticket and recording in the cash receipts
            register.

       3)   The receipts are deposited daily by Cash Receipts. The validated (by the
            bank) deposit ticket is returned to the Controller. The Controller reconciles the
            validated deposit ticket with the daily remittance list of cash received from the
            Mail Room.

      4) A journal voucher (entry) prepared by Cash Receipts indicating the debit to cash and credit to accounts receivable is sent to the General Ledger.

      5) The remittance advices are sent to Accounts Receivable for posting the reductions in accounts receivable to the individual customers' accounts.

10. **Control Activities Implemented**

    a. Two clerks should be present in the Mail Room during the opening and recording of the receipts.

    b. Checks are endorsed "For Deposit Only into Account Number XXXX" immediately upon opening the mail.

    c. All cash is deposited intact daily. This procedure ensures that the cash received and recorded on the daily remittance list can be reconciled with the deposit ticket validated by the bank.

    d. Periodic reconciliation of the accounts receivable subsidiary ledger and the accounts receivable control account in the general ledger establishes agreement of the total amounts posted. However, the reconciliation cannot determine whether an amount was posted to the wrong account in the subsidiary ledger. Moreover, application of such a control will be ineffective if sales were not recorded in the books of original entry, e.g., the sales journal.

    e. Monthly statements are sent to customers to ensure that failure to receive and/or record payments made by customers is detected (not shown on flowchart).

    f. A **lockbox system** (not depicted in the flowchart) can ensure that cash receipts are not abstracted by mail clerks or other employees. This system provides for customer payments to be sent to a post office box and collected directly by the bank.

      1) Hence, a lockbox system prevents lapping. **Lapping** occurs when an employee with access to both the accounts receivable subsidiary ledger and customer payments steals a portion of the receipts without recording them in the customer accounts. To conceal the theft, subsequent receipts are posted to the accounts of customers whose payments were stolen. This process of using new receipts to cover a recent theft must continue indefinitely to avoid detection.

Stop and review! You have completed the outline for this subunit. Study multiple-choice questions 1 through 11 beginning on page 143.

6.2 CONTROLS IN A CASH SALE ENVIRONMENT

1. Cash sales cycles often lack the segregation of duties necessary for the proper framework of control. For example, the sales clerk often

    a. Authorizes the sale (e.g., acceptance of a check),

    b. Records the sale (i.e., enters it on the sales terminal), and

    c. Has custody of the assets related to the sale (i.e., cash and inventory).

2. Compensating controls include

    a. Use of a cash register or sales terminal to record the sale. The terminal makes a permanent record of the event that the clerk cannot erase.

    b. Assignment of one clerk to be responsible for sales recording and cash receipts during a work period. The cash drawer can be reconciled with the record of sales and accountability assigned to the clerk.

    c. Increased supervision. For example, the manager's office may be positioned to observe the clerks' sales recording and cash collection activities.

    d.   Customer audit of the transaction. Displaying the recorded transaction and providing a receipt to the customer provides some assurance that the recording process was accomplished appropriately by the clerk.

    e.   Bonding of employees responsible for handling cash. Because the bonding company investigates employees before providing the bond, some assurance is provided concerning their integrity. Also, the bond provides insurance against losses.

Stop and review! You have completed the outline for this subunit. Study multiple-choice questions 12 and 13 on page 146.

6.3 OTHER SALES-RECEIVABLES RELATED TRANSACTIONS

1.   Sales returns and allowances should have controls to assure proper approval and processing. The key controls include the following:

    a.   Approval by the sales department to return goods

    b.   Receipt of the returned goods by the receiving department and preparation of a receiving report

    c.   The separate approval of the credit memo related to a sales return or allowance, that is, approval by someone not in the sales department

2.   The write-off of bad debts requires strong controls. The key controls include

    a.   Initiation of the write-off by the credit manager and approval by the CFO or other officer. The credit manager will be evaluated, in part, on the amount of bad debts written off and will require significant evidence before initiating a write-off.

    b.   Maintenance of a separate accounting ledger for accounts written off.

Stop and review! You have completed the outline for this subunit. Study multiple-choice questions 14 through 16 beginning on page 146.

6.4 TECHNOLOGY CONSIDERATIONS

1.   Computer processing typically replaces the activities of clerks performing recording functions, e.g., recording sales and accounts receivable, updating the inventory file to reflect goods sold, and recording customer receipts by posting the amounts to the accounts receivable subsidiary file.

2.   Periodic reconciliations (weekly or monthly) of the accounts receivable subsidiary file and general ledgers are usually replaced by daily reconciliations.

3.   Sophisticated systems may replace the paper flow with computer control over authorization of the release of goods for packing and shipping.

    a.   The use of online systems expedites the response to customer orders.

    b.   Batching transactions is useful for processing large volumes of data, especially when the transactions are sorted sequentially. Batch processing is appropriate when an immediate response is not necessary.

4.   Study the flowchart on the next page. Understand and visualize the sales-receivables process and controls in a normative computer environment. Read the description in item 5. as needed. Note the control activities implemented and listed in item 6. on page 142.

Sales-Receivables Computer System Flowchart

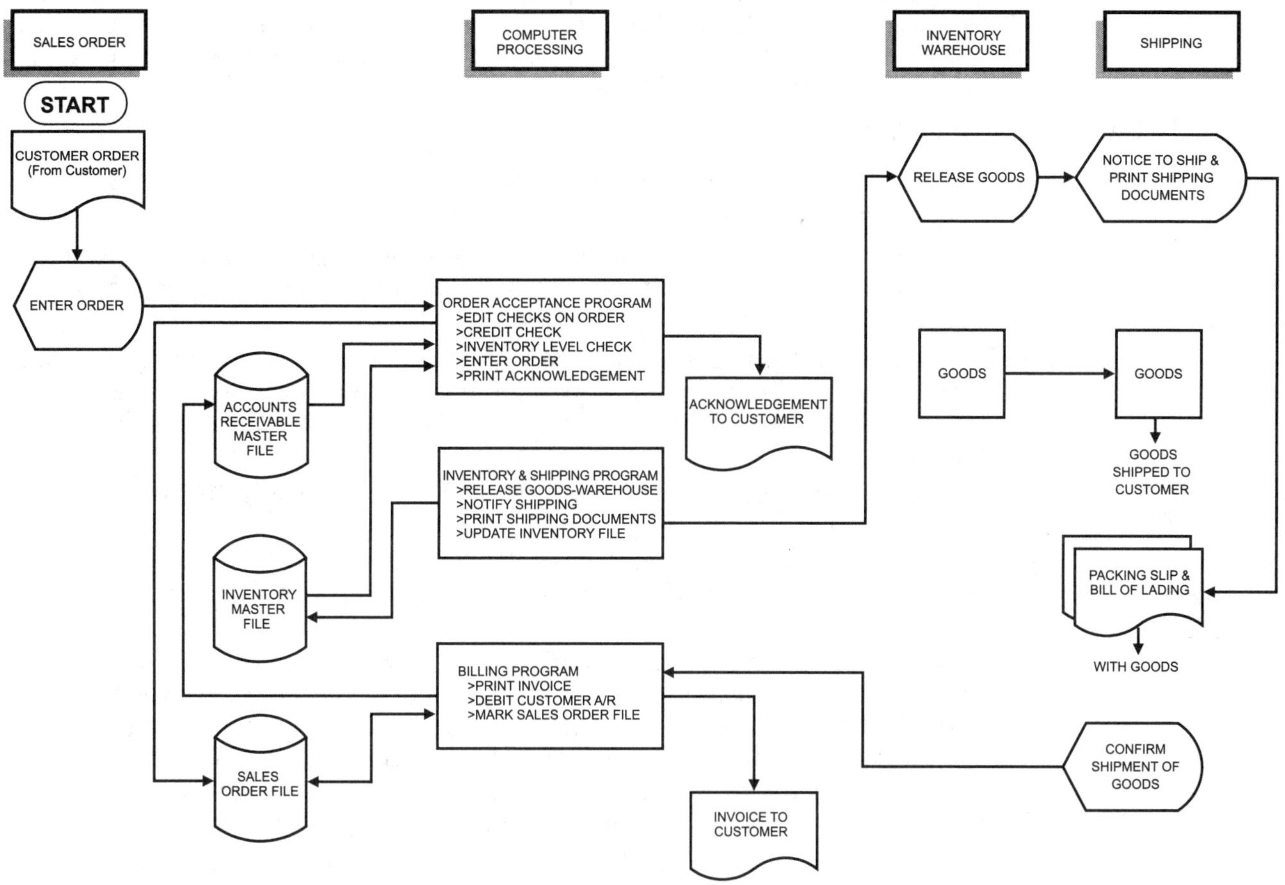

Figure 6-4

5. **The Information Flow**

a. The sales-receivables computer system flowchart above provides one view of computer processing using online systems. In this case, paper flow is replaced with electronic transmissions, and manual files and ledgers are replaced by computer files. The accounting departments (from the previous flowcharts) of Billing, Inventory Control, and Accounts Receivable are replaced by the Computer Processing department. Furthermore, routine credit decisions are replaced by a computer program.

b. The Sales Order department receives a customer order (beginning at **START** in the flowchart) and records it into the order acceptance program on a preformatted sales entry screen. Edit checks are used to ensure proper entry. The accounts receivable master file is checked for current customer information and credit limits. Inventory levels are checked for availability from the inventory master file. The accepted order, along with prices determined from the inventory master file, is entered into the sales order master file, and an acknowledgment is printed and sent to the customer.

c. Information is passed to the inventory and shipping program that sends a release authorization to the Inventory Warehouse via a computer workstation. Inventory levels are formally updated upon release of the goods from the Inventory Warehouse. An electronic shipping authorization is sent to the Shipping department. The communication also generates a packing slip and shipping documents (e.g., a bill of lading) that are printed in the Shipping department.

d.   Shipping provides the billing program with the information concerning the shipment. The billing program accesses demographic and price data from the sales order file and prepares and prints the invoice. The accounts receivable master file is also updated. (Additionally, the sale and cost of sale are recorded in the general ledger, but this step is not shown on the flowchart.)

6.   **Control Activities Implemented**

a.   Only the major controls implemented are identified. The computer-related controls identified here are those defined in Study Unit 5.

1)   Access controls, such as passwords, device authorization tables for sales and shipping personnel, and access logs, are used to prevent improper use or manipulation of data files.

2)   Preformatted screens are used to avoid data entry errors. The sales order entry screen prompts the Sales Order department to enter complete information concerning an order. Shipping must complete all information concerning a shipment.

3)   Field checks are used to test the characters in a field to verify that they are of an appropriate type for that field.

4)   Validity tests are used to determine that a customer exists in the accounts receivable master file and that ordered part numbers exist on the inventory master file.

5)   Reasonableness tests are used to test inventory quantities and billing amounts. The inventory reasonableness test can be employed in conjunction with a validity check. Thus, the inventory number can be tested against known inventory items in the inventory master file and a reasonable number determined for the reasonableness test. (For example, 100 dozen may be a reasonable order quantity for printer cartridges but not for printers.)

6)   Error listings are compiled and evaluated. Errors are corrected and reprocessed.

7.   **E-Commerce Considerations**

a.   The sales-receivables computer flowchart may be used to envision sales processing for a firm using an Internet website. Likely changes include direct entry of the order by the customer, elimination of the sales order department, and payment by credit card. Thus, accounts receivable will not be maintained. Acknowledgment of the order acceptance would be immediately communicated to the customer via an email or other Internet response. However, shipping department procedures and controls would be largely unaltered.

1)   Additional controls include the following:

a)   A **firewall** between the customer and internally stored client data

b)   **Passwords** for authorized or preferred customers

c)   **Encryption** procedures for storage and transmission of sensitive information

Stop and review! You have completed the outline for this subunit. Study multiple-choice questions 17 through 20 beginning on page 147.

QUESTIONS

6.1 Responsibilities/Organizational Structure/Flowcharts

1. At which point in an ordinary sales transaction of a wholesaling business is a lack of specific authorization of **least** concern to the auditor in the conduct of an audit?

A. Granting of credit.

B. Shipment of goods.

C. Determination of discounts.

D. Selling of goods for cash.

Answer (D) is correct.

REQUIRED: The point in an ordinary sales transaction at which specific authorization is of least concern to an auditor.

DISCUSSION: Selling goods for cash is the consummation of a transaction that is likely to be covered by a general authorization. Thus, the risk of loss arising from lack of specific authorization of cash sales is minimal.

Answer (A) is incorrect. Granting of credit in a sales transaction may require specific authorization, i.e., special consideration before approval by the appropriate person. Answer (B) is incorrect. Shipment of goods in a sales transaction may require specific authorization. Answer (C) is incorrect. Determination of discounts in a sales transaction may require specific authorization.

2. During the consideration of a small business client's internal control, the auditor discovered that the accounts receivable clerk approves credit memos and has access to cash. Which of the following controls would be most effective in offsetting this weakness?

A. The owner reviews errors in billings to customers and postings to the subsidiary ledger.

B. The controller receives the monthly bank statement directly and reconciles the checking accounts.

C. The owner reviews credit memos after they are recorded.

D. The controller reconciles the total of the detail accounts receivable accounts to the amount shown in the ledger.

Answer (C) is correct.

REQUIRED: The most effective control to compensate for an employee's performance of incompatible functions.

DISCUSSION: The clerk can both perpetrate and conceal a fraud in the normal course of his or her duties. The clerk has custody of cash, performs the recordkeeping function for accounts receivable, and authorizes credit memos. Thus, the clerk could conceal a theft of cash collected from customers on account by authorizing sales returns. In a small business, cost-benefit considerations ordinarily preclude establishment of formal control activities. In this situation, effective owner-management involvement may compensate for the absence of certain control activities. Accordingly, the owner should determine that credit memos are genuine.

Answer (A) is incorrect. The clerk could commit a theft without errors in billing and postings to the subsidiary ledger. Answer (B) is incorrect. The bank reconciliation will not detect a theft of cash concealed by improper credit memos. Cash stolen by the clerk would not be recorded. Answer (D) is incorrect. Improper credits to accounts receivable do not cause a discrepancy between the control account and the subsidiary ledger.

3. Which of the following controls most likely would help ensure that all credit sales transactions of an entity are recorded?

A. The billing department supervisor sends copies of approved sales orders to the credit department for comparison to authorized credit limits and current customer account balances.

B. The accounting department supervisor independently reconciles the accounts receivable subsidiary ledger to the accounts receivable control account monthly.

C. The accounting department supervisor controls the mailing of monthly statements to customers and investigates any differences they report.

D. The billing department supervisor matches prenumbered shipping documents with entries in the sales journal.

Answer (D) is correct.

REQUIRED: The control to detect unrecorded sales.

DISCUSSION: The sequential numbering of documents provides a standard control over transactions. The numerical sequence should be accounted for by an independent party. A major objective is to detect unrecorded and unauthorized transactions. Moreover, comparing shipments with the sales journal also will detect unrecorded transactions.

Answer (A) is incorrect. Credit approval does not ensure that sales have been recorded. Answer (B) is incorrect. The reconciliation will not detect sales that were never recorded. Answer (C) is incorrect. Customers are unlikely to report understatement of their accounts.

4. An auditor tests an entity's policy of obtaining credit approval before shipping goods to customers in support of management's financial statement assertion of

A. Valuation.

B. Completeness.

C. Occurrence.

D. Rights and obligations.

Answer (A) is correct.
    REQUIRED: The assertion related to the policy of credit approval before shipping goods to customers.
    DISCUSSION: The proper approval of credit provides assurance that the account receivable is collectible. Thus, it is related to the valuation assertion that balances are reported at appropriate amounts, e.g., accounts receivable at net realizable value.
    Answer (B) is incorrect. The completeness assertion is that all transactions, events, and balances that should have been recorded have been recorded. Answer (C) is incorrect. The occurrence assertion is that recorded transactions and events have occurred and pertain to the entity. Answer (D) is incorrect. Rights and obligations assertions relate to whether assets are rights of the entity and liabilities are obligations of the entity.

5. Which of the following activities most likely would **not** be an internal control activity designed to reduce the risk of errors in the billing process?

A. Comparing control totals for shipping documents with corresponding totals for sales invoices.

B. Using computer programmed controls over the pricing and accuracy of sales invoices.

C. Matching shipping documents with approved sales orders before invoice preparation.

D. Reconciling the control totals for sales invoices with the accounts receivable subsidiary ledger.

Answer (D) is correct.
    REQUIRED: The procedure not considered an internal control designed to reduce the risk of errors in the billing process.
    DISCUSSION: The accounts receivable subsidiary ledger contains all receivables outstanding to date. It is not feasible to attempt to reconcile current sales invoices with the accounts receivable subsidiary ledger. However, the accounts receivable subsidiary ledger should be reconciled to the general ledger control account periodically.
    Answer (A) is incorrect. The total amounts shipped should correspond to the sales invoices and can be reconciled on a daily basis. Answer (B) is incorrect. Programmed controls are appropriate in a computerized environment. Answer (C) is incorrect. The preparation of an invoice should depend on the shipment of goods.

6. Refer to the flowchart below.

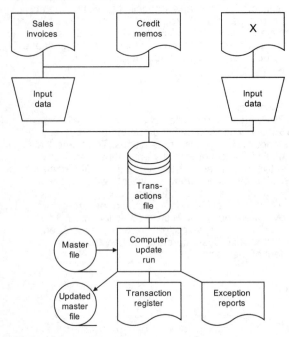

In a credit sales and cash receipts system flowchart, Symbol X could represent

A. Auditor's test data.

B. Remittance advices.

C. Error reports.

D. Credit authorization forms.

Answer (B) is correct.
    REQUIRED: The document in the credit sales and cash receipts flowchart represented by Symbol X.
    DISCUSSION: Remittance advices (Symbol X) are sent with sales invoices to customers to be returned with cash payments. Credit memos are internal documents crediting customer accounts for returns or allowances granted. These documents are processed against the master file in the updating run.
    Answer (A) is incorrect. Auditor's test data are not part of the client's processing of accounts receivable payments. Answer (C) is incorrect. Error reports are an output of the process. Answer (D) is incorrect. Credit authorization forms are documents approving credit sales. They should be distinguished from credit memos.

7. Cash receipts from sales on account have been misappropriated. Which of the following acts would conceal this defalcation and be **least** likely to be detected by an auditor?

A. Understating the sales journal.

B. Overstating the accounts receivable control account.

C. Overstating the accounts receivable subsidiary ledger.

D. Understating the cash receipts journal.

Answer (A) is correct.
REQUIRED: The act that conceals misappropriation of cash.
DISCUSSION: Not recording sales on account in the books of original entry is the most effective way to conceal a subsequent theft of cash receipts. The accounts will be incomplete but balanced, and procedures applied to the accounting records will not detect the defalcation.
Answer (B) is incorrect. The discrepancy between the control account and the subsidiary ledger indicates a misstatement. Answer (C) is incorrect. The discrepancy between the control account and the subsidiary ledger indicates a misstatement. Answer (D) is incorrect. Cash receipts will not reconcile with the credits to accounts receivable. If accounts receivable are not credited, confirmation will detect the theft.

8. Upon receipt of customers' checks in the mail room, a responsible employee should prepare a remittance listing that is forwarded to the cashier. A copy of the listing should be sent to the

A. Internal auditor to investigate the listing for unusual transactions.

B. CFO to compare the listing with the monthly bank statement.

C. Accounts receivable bookkeeper to update the subsidiary accounts receivable records.

D. Entity's bank to compare the listing with the cashier's deposit slip.

Answer (C) is correct.
REQUIRED: The use of a copy of the client's remittance listing.
DISCUSSION: The individuals with recordkeeping responsibility should not have custody of cash. Hence, they should use either the remittance advices or a listing of the remittances to make entries to the cash and accounts receivable control account and to the subsidiary accounts receivable records. Indeed, having different people make entries in the control account and in the subsidiary records is an effective control.
Answer (A) is incorrect. The internal auditors should have no ongoing control responsibilities. The investigation of unusual transactions is first conducted in the CFO's department. Answer (B) is incorrect. The monthly bank statement should be reconciled by someone outside of the treasury function. Answer (D) is incorrect. The entity's bank supplies a validated deposit slip based on the deposit for the day. Company management outside the treasury function compares the validated deposit slip with the remittance listing.

9. Evidence concerning the proper segregation of duties for receiving and depositing cash receipts ordinarily is obtained by

A. Completing an internal control questionnaire that describes the control activities.

B. Observing the employees who are performing the control activities.

C. Performing substantive procedures to verify the details of the bank balance.

D. Preparing a flowchart of the duties performed and the entity's available personnel.

Answer (B) is correct.
REQUIRED: The procedure testing segregation of duties for receiving and depositing cash.
DISCUSSION: Observation is a risk assessment procedure performed to obtain an understanding of the entity and its environment, including its controls. It is also a test of controls. Observation of entity activities and operations supports inquiries of management and provides information about the entity and its environment.
Answer (A) is incorrect. The questionnaire documents the understanding of the controls, not whether they are operating effectively. Answer (C) is incorrect. Substantive procedures directly address financial statement assertions, not controls. Answer (D) is incorrect. The flowchart documents the understanding of the controls, not whether they are operating effectively.

10. Employers bond employees who handle cash receipts because fidelity bonds reduce the possibility of employing dishonest individuals and

A. Protect employees who make unintentional errors from possible monetary damages resulting from their errors.

B. Deter dishonesty by making employees aware that insurance companies may investigate and prosecute dishonest acts.

C. Facilitate an independent monitoring of the receiving and depositing of cash receipts.

D. Force employees in positions of trust to take periodic vacations and rotate their assigned duties.

Answer (B) is correct.
REQUIRED: The purpose of bonding employees.
DISCUSSION: Effective internal control, including human resources practices that stress the hiring of trustworthy people, does not guarantee against losses from embezzlement and other fraudulent acts committed by employees. Accordingly, an employer may obtain a fidelity bond to insure against losses arising from fraud by the covered employees. Prior to issuing this form of insurance, the underwriters investigate the individuals to be covered. Also, employees should be informed that bonding companies are diligent in prosecuting bonded individuals who commit fraud.
Answer (A) is incorrect. Bonding insures employers against intentional wrongdoing. Answer (C) is incorrect. Bonding is irrelevant to monitoring the receipt and deposit of cash receipts. Answer (D) is incorrect. Bonding is irrelevant to periodic vacations and rotation of duties.

11. An entity with a large volume of customer remittances by mail most likely can reduce the risk of employee misappropriation of cash by using

    A. Employee fidelity bonds.

    B. Independently prepared mail room prelists.

    C. Daily check summaries.

    D. A bank lockbox system.

Answer (D) is correct.
    REQUIRED: The control that most likely can reduce the risk of employee misappropriation of cash.
    DISCUSSION: A lockbox system assures that cash receipts are not stolen by mail clerks or other employees. This system provides for customer payments to be sent to a post office box and collected directly by the bank.
    Answer (A) is incorrect. Bonding provides some assurance of employee honesty and has a deterrent effect, but it is less effective than eliminating employee handling of cash receipts. Answer (B) is incorrect. Prelists do not eliminate employee handling of cash. Answer (C) is incorrect. Daily check summaries do not eliminate employee handling of cash.

6.2 Controls in a Cash Sale Environment

12. Which of the following procedures would an auditor most likely perform to test controls relating to management's assertion about the completeness of cash receipts for cash sales at a retail outlet?

    A. Observe the consistency of the employee's use of cash registers and tapes.

    B. Inquire about employee's access to recorded but undeposited cash.

    C. Trace the deposits in the cash receipts journal to the cash balance in the general ledger.

    D. Compare the cash balance in the general ledger with the bank confirmation request.

Answer (A) is correct.
    REQUIRED: The test of controls for the completeness assertion.
    DISCUSSION: An assertion about completeness of transactions addresses whether all transactions that should be presented are included in the financial statements. To determine that controls are operating effectively to ensure that all cash receipts are being recorded for cash sales in a retail environment, the auditor may observe the activities of the employees. Controls should provide assurance that employees use cash registers that contain internal functions (e.g., tapes) to record all sales.
    Answer (B) is incorrect. Inquiry about employees' access to recorded cash pertains to the existence assertion. Once the sales are recorded, other controls are in place to determine that the existence of cash can be assured. Answer (C) is incorrect. Tracing cash receipts to the ledger is a substantive procedure, not a test of controls. Answer (D) is incorrect. Confirmation of cash with the bank is a substantive procedure, not a test of controls.

13. In a retail cash sales environment, which of the following controls is often absent?

    A. Competent personnel.

    B. Separation of functions.

    C. Supervision.

    D. Asset access limited to authorized personnel.

Answer (B) is correct.
    REQUIRED: The control often absent in a cash sales environment.
    DISCUSSION: In the usual retail cash sales situation, the sales clerk authorizes and records the transactions and takes custody of assets. However, management ordinarily employs other compensating controls to minimize the effects of the failure to separate functions. The cash receipts function is closely supervised, cash registers provide limited access to assets, and an internal recording function maintains control over cash receipts.

6.3 Other Sales-Receivables Related Transactions

14. Sound internal control activities dictate that defective merchandise returned by customers be presented initially to the

    A. Accounts receivable supervisor.

    B. Receiving clerk.

    C. Shipping department supervisor.

    D. Sales clerk.

Answer (B) is correct.
    REQUIRED: The individual to whom customers should return defective merchandise.
    DISCUSSION: For control purposes, all receipts of goods or materials should be handled by the receiving clerk. Receiving reports should be prepared for all items received.
    Answer (A) is incorrect. The accounts receivable supervisor has a recordkeeping function incompatible with access to assets. Answer (C) is incorrect. Shipping and receiving should be segregated. Answer (D) is incorrect. All returns of goods should be handled by an independent receiving function.

15. An auditor noted that the accounts receivable department is separate from other accounting activities. Credit is approved by a separate credit department. Control accounts and subsidiary ledgers are balanced monthly. Similarly, accounts are aged monthly. The accounts receivable manager writes off delinquent accounts after 1 year, or sooner if a bankruptcy or other unusual circumstances are involved. Credit memoranda are prenumbered and must correlate with receiving reports. Which of the following areas could be viewed as an internal control deficiency of the above organization?

    A. Write-offs of delinquent accounts.

    B. Credit approvals.

    C. Monthly aging of receivables.

    D. Handling of credit memos.

Answer (A) is correct.
    REQUIRED: The internal control deficiency.
    DISCUSSION: The accounts receivable manager has the ability to perpetrate fraud because (s)he performs incompatible functions. Authorization and recording of transactions should be segregated. Thus, someone outside the accounts receivable department should authorize write-offs.
    Answer (B) is incorrect. Credit approval is an authorization function that is properly segregated from the recordkeeping function. Answer (C) is incorrect. Monthly aging is appropriate. Answer (D) is incorrect. The procedures regarding credit memoranda are standard controls.

16. Which of the following most likely would be the result of ineffective internal control in the revenue cycle?

    A. Final authorization of credit memos by personnel in the sales department could permit an employee defalcation scheme.

    B. Fictitious transactions could be recorded, causing an understatement of revenues and an overstatement of receivables.

    C. Fraud in recording transactions in the subsidiary accounts could result in a delay in goods shipped.

    D. Omission of shipping documents could go undetected, causing an understatement of inventory.

Answer (A) is correct.
    REQUIRED: The most likely result of ineffective internal controls in the revenue cycle.
    DISCUSSION: Ineffective controls in the revenue cycle, such as inappropriate segregation of duties and responsibilities, inadequate supervision, or deficient authorization, may result in the ability of employees to perpetrate fraud. Thus, sales personnel should approve sales returns and allowances but not the related credit memos. Moreover, no authorization for the return of goods, defective or otherwise, should be considered complete until the goods are returned as evidenced by a receiving report.
    Answer (B) is incorrect. Recording fictitious sales would overstate revenues. Answer (C) is incorrect. The customers' accounts are not posted until after goods are shipped. Answer (D) is incorrect. If shipping documents are omitted, shipments of goods may not be credited to inventory, thereby overstating the account.

6.4 Technology Considerations

17. An online sales order processing system most likely would have an advantage over a batch sales order processing system by

    A. Detecting errors in the data entry process more easily by the use of edit programs.

    B. Enabling shipment of customer orders to be initiated as soon as the orders are received.

    C. Recording more secure backup copies of the database on magnetic tape files.

    D. Maintaining more accurate records of customer accounts and finished goods inventories.

Answer (B) is correct.
    REQUIRED: The advantage of an online system over a batch system.
    DISCUSSION: An online processing system can handle transactions as they are entered because of its direct connection to a computer network. Thus, shipment of customer orders may be initiated instantaneously as they are received. Batch processing is the accumulation and grouping of transactions for processing on a delayed basis.
    Answer (A) is incorrect. Both systems use edit programs. Answer (C) is incorrect. Online systems record information on direct-access memory devices. Answer (D) is incorrect. Online and batch systems provide equivalent accuracy.

18. When evaluating internal control of an entity that processes sales transactions on the Internet, an auditor would be most concerned about the

A. Lack of sales invoice documents as an audit trail.

B. Potential for computer disruptions in recording sales.

C. Inability to establish an integrated test facility.

D. Frequency of archiving and data retention.

Answer (B) is correct.

REQUIRED: The greatest concern about Internet controls.

DISCUSSION: Processing sales on the Internet (often called e-commerce) creates new and additional risks for clients. The client should use effective controls to ensure proper acceptance, processing, and storage of sales transactions. Threats include not only attacks from hackers but also system overload and equipment failure.

Answer (A) is incorrect. E-commerce sales transactions would not typically result in sales invoice documents. Answer (C) is incorrect. An integrated test facility is just one of many techniques for testing sales processing controls and transactions. Answer (D) is incorrect. Although archival and data retention are disaster recovery concerns, the question relates to controls over sales processing.

Questions 19 and 20 are based on the following information. A flowchart of a client's revenue cycle appears below.

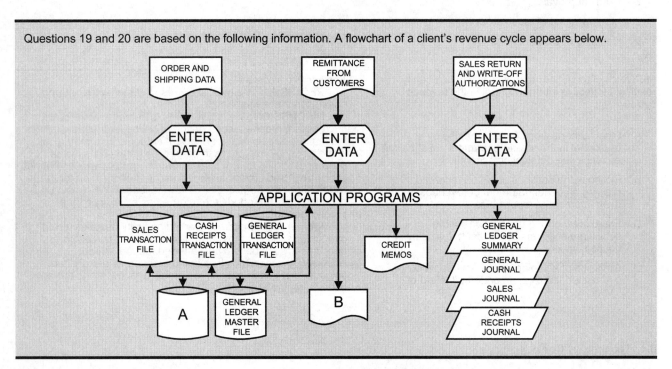

19. Symbol A most likely represents

A. Remittance advice file.

B. Receiving report file.

C. Accounts receivable master file.

D. Cash disbursements transaction file.

Answer (C) is correct.

REQUIRED: The file accessed during the processing of a client's revenue transactions.

DISCUSSION: During the processing of sales orders and remittances from customers, as well as sales returns and write-off authorizations, the accounts receivable master file is accessed and updated. Thus, symbol A represents the accounts receivable master file.

Answer (A) is incorrect. The remittance advice file is represented by the cash receipts transaction file. Answer (B) is incorrect. The receiving report file relates to the purchasing cycle. Answer (D) is incorrect. The cash disbursements transaction file relates to the purchasing cycle.

20. Symbol B most likely represents

A. Customer orders.

B. Receiving reports.

C. Customer checks.

D. Sales invoices.

Answer (D) is correct.

REQUIRED: The document represented by symbol B.

DISCUSSION: One output of the revenue cycle is the generation of sales invoices to be sent to customers.

Answer (A) is incorrect. Customer orders are entered online and not outputted from the system. Answer (B) is incorrect. Receiving reports are generated from the purchasing cycle, not the revenue cycle. Answer (C) is incorrect. Customer checks are represented by remittances from customers and entered online. However, the customer checks are safeguarded and deposited daily into the bank account.

STUDY UNIT SEVEN
INTERNAL CONTROL --
PURCHASES, PAYROLL, AND OTHER CYCLES

(15 pages of outline)

The initial sections of this study unit describe control concepts in a purchases and payment system. Their focus is on a traditional, manual voucher system that requires each payment to be vouched, or supported, prior to payment. This system has many variations, but the objectives and concepts of control are similar. The manual system presented here has most of the elements that are expected to be tested on future CPA exams.

The computer system described eliminates most of the paper flow from the manual system. However, the objectives of internal control are the same. Only the methods have changed. As always, understanding the concepts rather than attempting to memorize the material is the better approach to learning.

The primary focus of the remainder of this study unit is on payroll. Flowcharts again are used to provide a perspective on the flow of documents and information. The flowcharts are limited to essential points, particularly the payroll computer system flowchart. The narrative should be studied in conjunction with the flowcharts. Candidates should stress obtaining an understanding of the objectives of the controls.

Controls related to other accounts, not previously included in the study units, also are covered at the end of this study unit. Only the major controls are addressed, giving consideration to the questions traditionally asked on the CPA exam.

7.1 PURCHASES RESPONSIBILITIES/ORGANIZATIONAL STRUCTURE/FLOWCHART

1. **Management's Responsibility**

    a. Management is responsible for establishing the controls over the purchases-payables-cash disbursements cycle to ensure the following:

    1) Proper authorization of the purchase
    2) Ordering the proper quality and quantity of goods on a timely basis
    3) Acceptance only of goods that have been ordered
    4) Receipt of proper terms and prices from the vendor
    5) Payment only for those goods and services that were ordered, received, and properly invoiced
    6) Payment on a timely basis (e.g., to take advantage of cash discounts)

2.   **The Auditor's Responsibility**

    a.   The auditor is required to obtain an understanding of the entity and its environment, including its internal control, to assess the risks of material misstatement and to design further audit procedures. For this purpose, the auditor performs risk assessment procedures. The plan for further audit procedures reflects (1) the auditor's decision whether to test the operating effectiveness of controls over the purchases-payables-cash disbursement cycle and (2) the nature, timing, and extent of substantive procedures.

3.   **Organizational Structure**

    a.   Although some of the following information was presented in Study Unit 6, it is repeated here for your convenience.

    b.   The ideal structure segregates duties and responsibilities as follows:

        1)   Authorization of the transaction

        2)   Recording of the transaction

        3)   Custody over the assets (e.g., inventory and cash disbursements) associated with the transaction

    c.   However, cost-benefit considerations may affect the organizational structure, and complete segregation may not be feasible. Compensating controls are likely to be established when the segregation of duties is not maintained. Typical **compensating controls** may include

        1)   More supervision or

        2)   Owner involvement in the process.

4.   **Responsibilities of Personnel**

    a.   Responsibilities of personnel and departments in the purchases-payables-cash disbursements cycle include the following:

        1)   **Inventory Control** provides authorization for the purchase of goods and performs an accountability function (e.g., Inventory Control is responsible for maintaining perpetual records for inventory quantities and costs).

        2)   **Purchasing Agent** issues purchase orders for required goods.

        3)   **Receiving** department accepts goods for approved purchases, counts and inspects the goods, and prepares the receiving report.

        4)   **Inventory Warehouse** provides physical control over the goods.

        5)   **Accounts Payable** (vouchers payable) assembles the proper documentation to support a payment voucher (and disbursement) and records the account payable.

        6)   **Cash Disbursements** evaluates the documentation to support a payment voucher and signs and mails the check. This department cancels the documentation to prevent duplicate payment.

        7)   **General Ledger** maintains the accounts payable control account and other related general ledger accounts.

5.   **The Document Flow**

    a.   The organizational chart presented in Study Unit 6, Subunit 1, displays the reporting responsibilities of each function in the flowchart on the next page. To simplify the presentation, the flowchart does not show the disposition, e.g., the filing of documents, or other supplemental procedures. Some text is added to the flowchart to facilitate understanding of the flow. The flowchart begins at the point labeled **START**. Copies of documents are numbered so they may be referenced through the system.

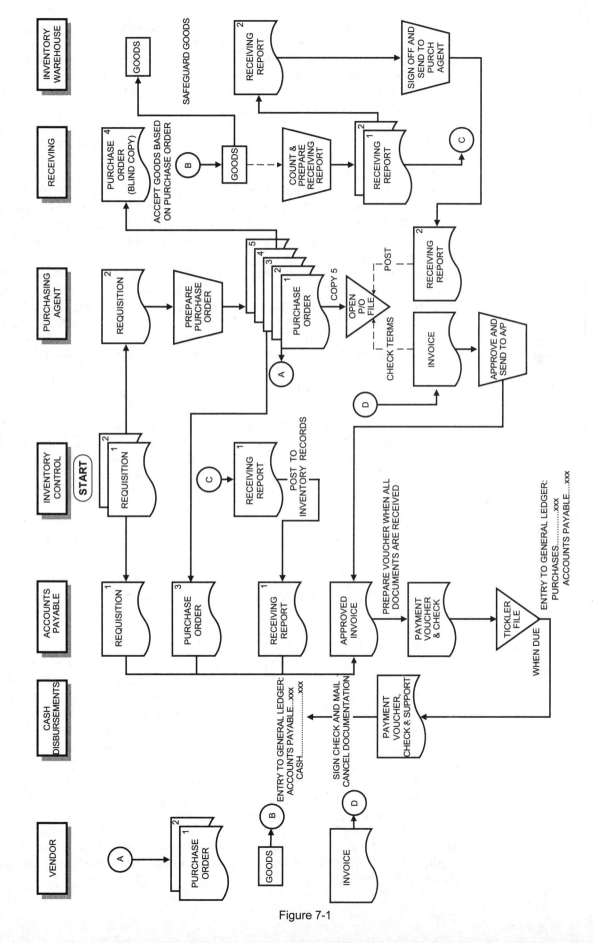

Figure 7-1

b.   Inventory Control, based on the pre-established reorder point, initiates a requisition as authorization for the purchase. The quantity authorized is the economic order quantity (EOQ). One copy of the requisition is sent to the Purchasing Agent (copy 2), and another is sent to Accounts Payable (copy 1). Inventory Control maintains a perpetual inventory by recording both reductions for sales of goods to customers and increases for receipts of goods from vendors.

c.   The Purchasing Agent provides additional authorization and determines the appropriate vendor, often through bidding, to supply the appropriate quantity and quality of goods at the optimal price. The purchasing agent then prepares a multi-part (five-part) purchase order. Copies 1 and 2 are sent to the vendor with a request to return one copy as an acknowledgment. Copy 4 of the purchase order (with the quantity omitted—a blind copy) is sent to Receiving as authorization to accept the goods when delivered. Copy 3 is sent to Accounts Payable, matched with the previously received requisition, and filed for subsequent action. Copy 5 is filed in the open purchase order file.

d.   When the goods arrive, Receiving accepts the goods based on the authorization by the Purchasing Agent (the blind copy of the purchase order). Receiving counts and inspects the goods and prepares a receiving report. A copy of the receiving report (copy 1) is sent to Inventory Control and posted to the perpetual inventory records and then sent to Accounts Payable. The copy is then matched with the requisition and purchase order being held, and the three copies are filed for subsequent action. Copy 2 of the receiving report accompanies the goods to the Inventory Warehouse.

1)   If the goods received are nonconforming, the Shipping department will return them to the vendor and notify the Purchasing Agent so arrangements can be made with the vendor for another shipment. If goods had been previously accepted and an entry had been made, the Purchasing department should send a debit memo to the Accounting department. A debit memo indicates a reduction in the amount owed to a vendor because goods have been returned. The debit memo authorizes the General Ledger to debit the appropriate payable.

e.   The Inventory Warehouse acknowledges receipt and safekeeping of the goods by signing copy 2 of the receiving report. The copy is then forwarded to the Purchasing Agent.

1)   If goods are produced rather than purchased for resale, the objective of safeguarding assets remains the same. Custody of work-in-process and finished goods should be properly maintained. Accordingly, inventories should be in the custody of a storekeeper, and transfers should be properly documented and recorded to establish accountability.

f.   The Purchasing Agent posts copy 2 of the receiving report to the open purchase order file. This file allows the Purchasing Agent to follow up with vendors concerning delivery times and terms. When a purchase order is filled (i.e., all goods and related invoices are received), it is pulled and filed in the closed purchase order file.

g.   When the invoice is received from the vendor, it is directed to the Purchasing Agent. The terms (e.g., prices and discounts) from the invoice are checked against those from the purchase order (filed in the open purchase order file). The purchasing agent approves the invoice for payment and sends it to Accounts Payable.

h.   Accounts Payable matches the invoice with the related requisition, purchase order, and receiving report, and determines its mathematical accuracy. When all four documents are received and reconciled, a payment voucher, including a check, is prepared (but the check is not signed), and an entry is forwarded to the General Ledger to debit purchases and credit accounts payable. An authorized person should approve the voucher.

i.　The voucher is then filed in a tickler file by due date based on the vendor's terms. For example, if the terms were net 30 days, the voucher would be filed so that it would be pulled just in time for the check to be signed and mailed in accordance with the terms.

j.　On the appropriate due date, the voucher is pulled from the tickler file and sent to Cash Disbursements. Cash Disbursements makes the determination that the documentation supports the voucher and check. If so, the check is signed and mailed to the vendor. At the time the check is signed, the documentation (i.e., payment voucher, approved invoice, requisition, purchase order, and receiving report) is canceled so that it cannot be used to support a duplicate payment.

k.　The check is recorded in the cash disbursements journal, and an entry is forwarded to the General Ledger to debit accounts payable and credit cash.

6.　**Controls Implemented**

a.　The segregation of duties for the transaction is as follows: authorization, recording, and custody of assets.

b.　Requisitions, purchase orders, receiving reports, payment vouchers, and checks are prenumbered and accounted for.

c.　Purchases are based only on proper authorizations. Receiving should not accept merchandise unless an approved purchase order is on hand.

d.　Receiving's copy of the purchase order omits the quantity so that employees must count the goods to determine the quantity to record on the receiving report.

e.　The Purchasing Agent compares prices and terms from the vendor invoice with requested and acknowledged terms from the vendor.

f.　Vouchers and the related journal entries are prepared only when goods are received that have been authorized, ordered, and appropriately invoiced.

g.　The tickler file permits timely payments to realize available cash discounts.

h.　Cash Disbursements ascertains that proper support exists for the voucher and check before signing the check.

i.　Two signatures may be required for checks larger than a preset limit.

j.　Cash Disbursements, which reports to the CFO, mails the checks so that no one internal to the entity can gain access to the signed checks.

k.　Cash Disbursements cancels payment documents to prevent their use as support for duplicate vouchers and checks.

l.　Periodic reconciliation of the vouchers in the tickler file with Accounts Payable ensures proper recording in the accounts payable control account.

m.　Periodic counts of inventory, independently reconciled with perpetual records, provide assurance that physical controls over inventory are effective.

　　1)　Internal verification of inventory is independent if performed by an individual who is not responsible for custody of assets or the authorization and recording of transactions.

n.　Accounts Payable examines the vendor invoice for mathematical errors.

o.　Accounts Payable compares the vendor's invoice with the receiving report, the requisition, and the purchase order to ensure that a valid transaction occurred.

7.   **Other Payment Authorizations**

    a.   This voucher-disbursement system is applicable to virtually all required payments by the entity, not just purchases of inventory as described previously. The following are additional considerations:

        1)   The authorizations may come from other departments based on a budget or policy (e.g., a utility bill might need authorization by the plant manager).

        2)   Accounts Payable would require different document(s) (e.g., a utility bill with the signature of the plant manager) to support the preparation of the payment voucher and check.

        3)   A debit other than purchases (e.g., utilities expense) would be entered on the payment voucher and recorded in the general ledger. Accounts payable would still be credited.

        4)   The use of the tickler file and the functions of Cash Disbursements would not change when other types of payments were made.

Stop and review! You have completed the outline for this subunit. Study multiple-choice questions 1 through 6 beginning on page 164.

7.2 PURCHASES TECHNOLOGY CONSIDERATIONS

1.   Computer Processing ordinarily replaces the activities of clerks performing recording functions (e.g., updating the inventory file to record goods received from vendors and updating the open purchase order file). Computer Processing is not shown on the organizational chart in Study Unit 6, but it is discussed here.

2.   No physical voucher is prepared, the tickler file is maintained by the computer, and no check is prepared until the due date.

3.   Sophisticated systems may replace the internal paper flows with electronic transmissions.

4.   Ordinarily, the manual files and ledgers are replaced by digital files.

5.   **The Information Flow**

    a.   This purchases-payables computer system flowchart (Figure 7-2) depicts one example of an online purchasing system. The accounting departments (Figure 7-1 depicts their positions in the manual system flowchart) of Inventory Control and Accounts Payable and the Purchasing Agent's open purchase order file are replaced by Computer Processing. In addition, routine order decisions are replaced by computer programs.

    b.   The shipping of inventory for sales orders and the related reduction of inventory on the inventory master file cause inventory levels to fall below the reorder point (beginning at **START** on the flowchart). As a result, a requisition request is transmitted to the Purchasing Agent. The approved vendor, economic order quantity, costs, and other relevant terms are stored in the inventory master file and provided to the Purchasing Agent. The Purchasing Agent can approve the information or make modifications based on current conditions.

    c.   Once the requisition is approved, the purchase order program prints the purchase order for mailing to the vendor, records it in the open purchase order file, and authorizes Receiving to accept the shipment.

    d.   When the goods arrive, Receiving accepts the shipment and enters the count and other relevant information into the receiving program. This step updates the open purchase order file and the inventory master file. The goods are taken to the Inventory Warehouse.

e.   When the invoice arrives, the Purchasing Agent enters the information into the invoice program, which tests the terms against those in the record in the open purchase order file. If the information is complete and the goods have been received, a record is created in the accounts payable master file. Furthermore, the General Ledger is updated for the debit to purchases and the credit to accounts payable. However, this step is not shown.

f.   The accounts payable program generates a check when the terms of the purchase require it to do so.

Purchases-Payables Computer System Flowchart

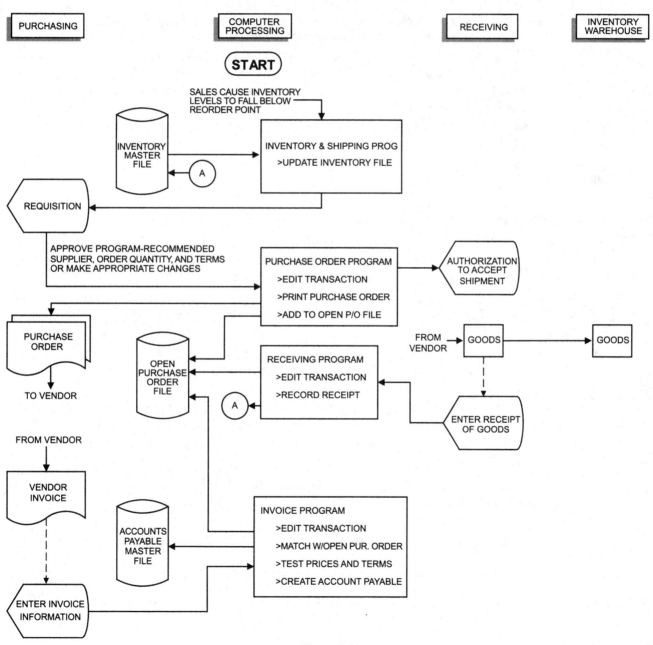

Figure 7-2

6. **Control Activities Implemented**

    a. The major computer-related controls are identified here. The controls are defined in Study Unit 5.

    b. Access to the programs and data is restricted by password and device authorization tables. For example, Receiving, even with the proper password, can access only the receiving program and can change only the fields in the records affected by the receiving transactions.

    c. Access logs are maintained that automatically record each transaction, the time of the transaction, and the identification of the person who entered the transaction.

    d. Preformatted data entry screens are used to ensure proper input. For example, Receiving's entry screen requires the quantity received to be completed (along with the other data) before the transaction is accepted.

    e. Field checks are used to test the characters in certain fields to verify that they are of an appropriate type for that field (e.g., the quantity field should contain numbers only).

    f. Validity tests are used that ensure the propriety of supplier transactional data prior to accepting the input.

    g. Reasonableness tests are used to test quantities ordered and received to determine if they are within acceptable limits.

Stop and review! You have completed the outline for this subunit. Study multiple-choice question 7 on page 166.

7.3 ELECTRONIC DATA INTERCHANGE (EDI)

1. EDI is the communication of electronic documents directly from a computer in one entity to a computer in another entity. EDI eliminates the paper documents, both internal and external, that are the traditional basis for many audit procedures.

2. Advantages include reduction of clerical errors, speed, and the elimination of repetitive clerical tasks. EDI also eliminates document preparation, processing, filing, and mailing costs.

    a. Moreover, an organization that has **reengineered** its procedures and processes to take full advantage of EDI may eliminate even the electronic equivalents of paper documents.

        1) For example, the buyer's **point-of-sale (POS) system** may directly transmit information to the seller, which delivers on a JIT (just-in-time) basis.

    b. Purchase orders, invoices, and receiving reports are replaced with a **long-term contract** establishing

        1) Quantities, prices, and delivery schedules;
        2) Production schedules;
        3) Advance shipment notices;
        4) Evaluated receipts settlements (periodic payment authorizations transmitted to the trading partner); and
        5) Payments by **electronic funds transfer (EFT)**.

            a) EFT is a process based on EDI that transfers money from one account to another by computer.

3. **Audit Procedures**

   a.   Accordingly, auditors must seek **new forms of evidence** to support assertions about EDI transactions, whether the evidence exists at the auditee, the trading partner, or a third party (e.g., a value-added network).

      1)   Examples of such evidence are

         a)   The EDI long-term contract,

         b)   An electronic completed production schedule image, and

         c)   Internal and external evidence of evaluated receipts settlements sent to the trading partner.

   b.   Auditors should evaluate **electronic signatures and reviews** when testing controls.

   c.   Auditors may need to consider **other subsystems** when testing a particular system.

      1)   Thus, production cycle evidence may be needed to test the expenditure cycle.

   d.   Auditing an EDI application requires consideration of the **audit trail**. In addition to the elements listed above, an essential element of an EDI audit trail is an **activity log**.

      1)   Because an audit trail allows for the **tracing** of a transaction from initiation to disposition, an activity log provides a key link in the process. Such a log provides information about the

         a)   Users who have accessed the system,
         b)   Files accessed,
         c)   Processing accomplished,
         d)   Time of access, and
         e)   Amount of time the processing required.

4. **Value-Added Networks (VANs)**

   a.   EDI often uses a VAN as a **third-party service provider**, and **controls** provided by the VAN may be critical.

   b.   VANs are privately owned telecommunications carriers that sell capacity to outside users.

   c.   Among other things, a VAN provides a **mailbox service** permitting EDI messages to be sent, sorted, and held until needed in the recipient's computer system.

      1)   **Encryption** of such messages that is performed by physically secure **hardware** is more secure than encryption performed by software.

5.   Successful implementation of EDI begins with identifying the work processes and flows that support the entity's objectives.

   a.   The initial phase of EDI implementation includes understanding the entity's **mission** and an analysis of its **activities** as part of an integrated solution to its needs.

Stop and review! You have completed the outline for this subunit. Study multiple-choice questions 8 and 9 on page 166.

7.4 PAYROLL RESPONSIBILITIES/ORGANIZATIONAL STRUCTURE/FLOWCHART

1. **Management's Responsibility**

   a. Management should establish controls to ensure the following:

      1) Proper authorization of the payroll
      2) Appropriate calculation of the payroll
      3) Safeguarding of assets associated with the payment of payroll
      4) Proper distribution of the payroll
      5) Proper accounting for the payroll transactions

2. **The Auditor's Responsibility**

   a. The auditor must obtain an understanding of the entity and its environment, including its internal control, to assess the risks of material misstatement and to design further audit procedures. For this purpose, the auditor performs risk assessment procedures. The plan for further audit procedures reflects (1) the auditor's decision whether to test the operating effectiveness of controls over the payroll cycle and (2) the nature, timing, and extent of substantive procedures.

3. **Organizational Structure**

   a. Although the following information is similar to that in the previous flowchart discussions, it has been repeated for your convenience.

   b. The structure should segregate duties and responsibilities as follows:

      1) Authorization of payroll transactions
      2) Recording of payroll transactions
      3) Custody of the assets (e.g., payroll checks) associated with payroll transactions

   c. Duties and responsibilities for payroll have traditionally been appropriately segregated. However, cost-benefit considerations may affect the organizational structure, and complete segregation may not be feasible. **Compensating controls** are likely to be established when segregation of duties is not maintained. They may include

      1) More supervision or
      2) Owner involvement in the payroll process.

   d. The following are the responsibilities of organizational subunits in the payroll cycle:

      1) **Human Resources** provides an authorized list of employees and associated pay rates, deductions, and exemptions.
      2) **Payroll** is an accounting function responsible for calculating the payroll (i.e., preparing the payroll register) based on authorizations from Human Resources and the authorized time records from Timekeeping.
      3) **Timekeeping** is an accounting function that oversees the employees' recording of hours on time cards (using the time clock) and that receives and reconciles the job time tickets from Manufacturing.
      4) **Cost Accounting** is an accounting function that accumulates direct materials, direct labor, and overhead costs on job order cost sheets to determine the costs of production.
      5) **Accounts Payable** prepares the payment voucher based on the payroll register prepared by Payroll.
      6) **Cash Disbursements** signs and deposits a check based on the payment voucher into a separate payroll account, prepares individual employee paychecks, and distributes paychecks.

e.   Study the flowchart on the next page. Understand and visualize the payroll process and controls. The organizational chart in Study Unit 6 displays the reporting responsibilities of each function in the flowchart. Read the following description as needed. Note the control activities implemented.

4.   **The Document Flow**

a.   To simplify the presentation, the flowchart does not show the disposition, e.g., the filing of documents, or other supplemental procedures. The process begins at the point labeled **START**.

b.   Human Resources provides authorizations of employees, pay rates, and deductions to Payroll just prior to calculation of the payroll.

c.   Employees punch the time clock with their time cards in Timekeeping before and after each shift.

d.   The shop supervisor assigns employees production-order tasks to be performed, and each employee completes a job time ticket for each task performed. Indirect labor (e.g., down time, cleaning machines, and setup) is also reported on job time tickets. At the end of the shift, the shop supervisor determines that employees have submitted job time tickets to account for all time worked. The job time tickets are then forwarded to Timekeeping.

e.   Timekeeping reconciles the time clock cards with the job time tickets to ensure that employees were present and working. Time clock cards are approved (e.g., initialed) by Timekeeping.

f.   Time clock cards are forwarded to Payroll as authorization of the hours worked. The authorized employees, rates, and deductions from Human Resources, together with the authorized hours from Timekeeping, are used to calculate the payroll for the period. A payroll register is prepared listing each employee, gross pay, all deductions, and net pay. The payroll register is then sent to Accounts Payable.

g.   Accounts Payable uses the payroll register as authorization to prepare a payment voucher and check for the payroll equal to the total of the net pay to employees. (Actually, a number of separate vouchers and checks will be prepared for each required payment generated from the payroll. For example, a check will be prepared with the IRS as payee for withholding taxes, and a check may be prepared with the union as payee for withheld union dues, etc.)

h.   The check, voucher, and supporting documentation will be sent to Cash Disbursements (CFO) for signing. The check for the net payroll drawn on the general cash account is deposited in a separate payroll account. Checks drawn on this special account are prepared for each employee; that is, an imprest payroll checking account is used. The checks are distributed to the employees.

i.   The job time tickets, once used by Timekeeping, are sent to Cost Accounting to charge the work-in-process recorded on job cost sheets for the direct labor used in production. The nonproductive labor is accumulated and reported as overhead incurred (not shown on the flowchart).

j.   The accounting entries are forwarded to the General Ledger (not shown on the flowchart). The entry to record the debit to work-in-process is from Cost Accounting. An entry to credit a payable comes from Accounts Payable. When the check based on the payment voucher is signed, Cash Disbursements forwards the entry to the General Ledger to debit accounts payable and credit cash.

Payroll Manual System Flowchart

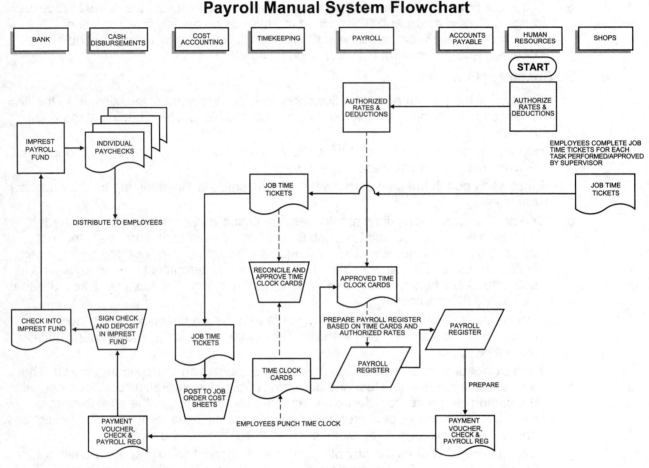

Figure 7-3

5. **Control Activities Implemented**

a. Human Resources has no functional responsibility other than authorization of employees, pay rates, and deductions.

b. Supervisors approve (authorize) work performed (executed) by employees.

c. The Timekeeping reconciliation of the time clock cards and job time tickets ensures that employees are present and working. Punching another person's time clock card would be detected because of the absence of job time tickets.

d. Payroll accounting calculates pay only. It does not authorize transactions or handle (take custody of) assets.

e. Cash Disbursements signs the check but does not authorize, prepare, or account for the transaction.

f. Paychecks are distributed by Cash Disbursements, usually by the paymaster. This individual has no other functions relative to payroll. Supervisors should not distribute paychecks because they have an authorization function.

g. Unclaimed paychecks are safeguarded by the CFO.

h. A separate payroll account allows for ease in reconciling bank statements.

Stop and review! You have completed the outline for this subunit. Study multiple-choice questions 10 through 12 on page 167.

7.5 PAYROLL TECHNOLOGY CONSIDERATIONS

1.   Most information may be collected directly by computer.

2.   Physical preparation, handling, and safeguarding of checks can be avoided. Direct deposit into employees' bank accounts is a typical control.

3.   Digital files and data transmission replace the file cabinets and forms.

4.   Several of the accounting clerk's functions are replaced by computer programs. These include some of the duties of Timekeeping and Payroll. Computer Processing is not shown on the organizational chart in Study Unit 6 because it assumes a manual system.

5.   The objectives of control, however, do not change.

6.   The daily processing is immediate because the files are updated as the activities are recorded. However, the calculation of the payroll is normally batch-oriented because checks to employees are prepared periodically (e.g., weekly).

Payroll Computer System Flowchart

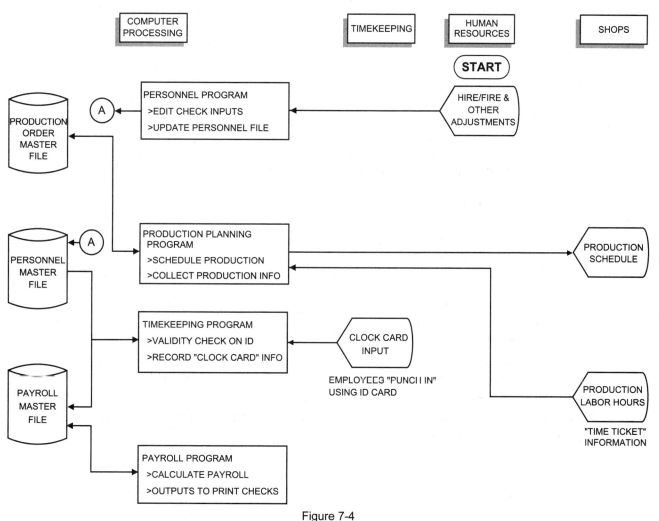

Figure 7-4

7.   **Payroll Computer System Flowchart**

a.   Study the flowchart on the previous page. Understand and visualize the payroll process and controls in a computer environment. Read the following description as needed. Note the control activities that are implemented.

b.   The payroll computer system flowchart illustrates a system that eliminates virtually all of the paper flow found in the manual system.

c.   Human Resources makes authorized changes in the personnel master file.

d.   As the employee enters the plant, a time clock card record is initiated by passing an ID card through a terminal that contains the timekeeping program.

e.   Production orders, based on the production schedule, are released to the shops via terminal. Shop supervisors assign production employees to the tasks. Prior to beginning, the production employee logs in to the system using his or her ID card. When the production job is complete, the employee logs out, thereby updating the production record. Information is passed to the timekeeping program to be reconciled with the time records and to update the payroll master file.

f.   Periodically (e.g., weekly), information from the payroll master file is matched with wage rate, deduction, and exemption information to calculate the payroll. The checks are printed (or deposits are sent to employees' banks), and the general ledger is updated (not shown on flowchart).

8.   **Control Activities Implemented**

a.   The major computer-related controls are identified here. The controls are defined in Study Unit 5.

b.   Access controls are used, requiring passwords and identification numbers. Only Human Resources has access to the personnel master file and can make changes. Other departments are limited to the changes that can be made to files. Each shop employee is issued an identification card used as input to initiate timekeeping transactions.

c.   Preformatted data entry screens are used for inputs.

d.   Validity checks are made to ensure that an employee record exists on the personnel file before any transactions are accepted.

e.   Time records from Timekeeping are automatically reconciled with the production time logged in the shops.

f.   Reasonableness tests are made when appropriate, e.g., testing at the end of the week to ensure that total hours recorded for an employee are not in excess of 40 hours or the acceptable limit.

g.   Exception reports are printed, identifying all questionable and potentially incorrect transactions. These transactions are investigated, and any corrections are made for reprocessing.

Stop and review! You have completed the outline for this subunit. Study multiple-choice questions 13 and 14 on page 168.

7.6 OTHER CYCLES

1. Other cycles follow the basic pattern of the segregation of duties illustrated in the previous discussions of controls. Flowcharts are not presented for the other cycles discussed here. However, certain basic controls are identified.

2. **Property, Plant, and Equipment Cycle -- Typical Controls**

    a. Formal budgeting process with subsequent variance analysis
    b. Written policies for acquisition and retirement of fixed assets
    c. Written authorizations for acquisition and retirement of fixed assets

        1) Moreover, the same individual should not both approve removal work orders (authorization) and dispose of equipment (asset custody).

    d. Segregation of recordkeeping and accountability (controller) from physical custody (user departments)
    e. Limited physical access to assets when feasible
    f. Periodic reconciliation of subsidiary records and the general ledger control account
    g. Periodic comparisons of physical assets with subsidiary records

3. **Investing Cycle -- Typical Controls**

    a. Written authorizations from the board of directors (or appropriate oversight committee)
    b. Segregation of recordkeeping and accountability (controller) from physical custody (CFO)
    c. Physical safeguards over assets, e.g., a safe-deposit box requiring two signatures to gain admittance
    d. Specific identification of certificate numbers when possible
    e. Periodic reconciliation of subsidiary records and the general ledger control account
    f. Periodic comparisons of physical assets with subsidiary records

4. **Financing Cycle**

    a. The financing cycle concerns obtaining and repaying capital through noncurrent debt and shareholders' equity transactions. These major transactions are authorized by the board of directors or other ultimate authority.

5. **Inventory and Warehousing Cycle**

    a. Transfers of raw materials, finished goods, and costs are subject to cost accounting internal control activities.
    b. The objectives of internal control include safeguarding assets and promoting the reliability of financial reporting. Thus, internal control includes (1) physical controls over storage, (2) assignment of custody to specific individuals, (3) use of prenumbered documents for authorization of transfers, and (4) perpetual inventory records.

        1) For example, requisitions and other documents should have proper authorizations, quantities, descriptions, and dates. Subsidiary ledgers should be independently reconciled with control accounts.

Stop and review! You have completed the outline for this subunit. Study multiple-choice questions 15 through 20 beginning on page 168.

QUESTIONS

7.1 Purchases Responsibilities/Organizational Structure/Flowchart

1. Which of the following controls is most effective in providing assurance that recorded purchases are free of material errors?

    A. The receiving department compares the quantity ordered on purchase orders with the quantity received on receiving reports.

    B. Vendors' invoices are compared with purchase orders by an employee who is independent of the receiving department.

    C. Receiving reports require the signature of the individual who authorized the purchase.

    D. Purchase orders, receiving reports, and vendors' invoices are independently matched in preparing vouchers.

Answer (D) is correct.
    REQUIRED: The most effective control to provide assurance that recorded purchases are free of material errors.
    DISCUSSION: A voucher should not be prepared for payment until the vendor's invoice has been matched against the corresponding purchase order and receiving report (and often the requisition). This procedure provides assurance that a valid transaction has occurred and that the parties have agreed on the terms, such as price and quantity.
    Answer (A) is incorrect. The receiving department should receive a blind copy of the purchase order. Answer (B) is incorrect. Receiving reports (and possibly requisitions) also should be examined. Before paying an invoice, an independent person should determine that what has been received matches what has been ordered. Answer (C) is incorrect. The receiving report is prepared by the receiving department.

2. Which of the following describes a weakness in accounts payable procedures?

    A. The accounts payable clerk files invoices and supporting documentation after payment.

    B. The accounts payable clerk manually verifies arithmetic on the vendor invoice.

    C. The accounts payable system compares the receiving report to the vendor invoice.

    D. The accounts payable manager issues purchase orders.

Answer (D) is correct.
    REQUIRED: The weakness in accounts payable procedures.
    DISCUSSION: To maintain a proper segregation of duties, the purchasing agent, not the accounts payable manager, should issue purchase orders. The accounts payable manager performs a recording function. (S)he should not be able to authorize transactions or have custody of assets.
    Answer (A) is incorrect. The approved vendor invoice and supporting documentation (requisition, purchase order, and receiving report) are retained by the accounts payable function after the payment voucher (and an unsigned check) is prepared and sent to the cash disbursements function. Answer (B) is incorrect. The purchasing agent approves the invoice for payment and sends it to the accounts payable function. The accounts payable clerk matches the invoice with the related requisition, purchase order, and receiving report and determines its mathematical accuracy. Answer (C) is incorrect. The accounts payable clerk matches the invoice with the related requisition, purchase order, and receiving report and determines its mathematical accuracy.

3. In a well-designed internal control system, the same employee may be permitted to

    A. Mail signed checks and also cancel supporting documents.

    B. Prepare receiving reports and also approve purchase orders.

    C. Approve vouchers for payment and also have access to unused purchase orders.

    D. Mail signed checks and also prepare bank reconciliations.

Answer (A) is correct.
    REQUIRED: The functions the same employee may be permitted to perform in a well-designed control system.
    DISCUSSION: The cash disbursements department has an asset custody function. Consequently, this department is responsible for signing checks after verification of their accuracy by reference to the supporting documents. The supporting documents should then be canceled and the checks mailed. Cancelation prevents the documentation from being used to support duplicate payments. Moreover, having the party who signs the checks place them in the mail reduces the risk that they will be altered or diverted.
    Answer (B) is incorrect. The receiving department should not know how many units have been ordered. Answer (C) is incorrect. Accounts is responsible for approving vouchers, and purchasing is the only department with access to the purchase orders. The same employee should not approve the purchase and approve payment. Answer (D) is incorrect. The bank reconciliation is performed by someone with no asset custody function.

4. Which of the following situations most likely could lead to an embezzlement scheme?

A. The accounts receivable bookkeeper receives a list of payments prepared by the cashier and personally makes entries in the customers' accounts receivable subsidiary ledger.

B. Each vendor invoice is matched with the related purchase order and receiving report by the vouchers payable clerk who personally approves the voucher for payment.

C. Access to blank checks and signature plates is restricted to the cash disbursements bookkeeper who personally reconciles the monthly bank statement.

D. Vouchers and supporting documentation are examined and then canceled by the CFO who personally mails the checks to vendors.

Answer (C) is correct.

REQUIRED: The situation that could most likely lead to embezzlement.

DISCUSSION: Sufficient segregation of duties should exist to prevent embezzlement (a fraudulent appropriation to one's own use of property entrusted to one's care). The cash disbursements bookkeeper has an asset custody function. (S)he signs checks prepared by the accounts payable function after inspecting the supporting documents. (S)he then cancels those documents and mails the checks. The cash disbursements bookkeeper's access to blank checks and ability to reconcile the monthly bank statement are inappropriate. (S)he can perpetrate and conceal fraud.

Answer (A) is incorrect. An accounts receivable bookkeeper's responsibility is to record entries into the accounts receivable subsidiary ledger. Answer (B) is incorrect. Vendor invoices should be matched with the related requisition, purchase order, and receiving report by the vouchers payable clerk. (S)he then prepares a payment voucher, including a check. The voucher and unsigned check are then placed in the tickler file. Thus, the vouchers payable bookkeeper may approve vouchers as long as (s)he has no access to any other elements of the transaction, for example, approval of purchase orders. Answer (D) is incorrect. Vouchers and supporting documentation should be examined and canceled by the CFO, a person with responsibility for cash payments, to prevent duplicate payments. It is the CFO's duty to have custody of assets. (S)he should personally mail the checks to vendors.

5. In a well-designed internal control system, employees in the same department most likely would approve purchase orders, and also

A. Reconcile the open invoice file.

B. Inspect goods upon receipt.

C. Authorize requisitions of goods.

D. Negotiate terms with vendors.

Answer (D) is correct.

REQUIRED: The task appropriately performed by employees who approve purchase orders.

DISCUSSION: To prevent or detect fraud or error in the performance of assigned responsibilities, duties are often segregated. Approving purchase orders and negotiating terms with vendors are part of the authorization process performed by the purchasing department.

Answer (A) is incorrect. Reconciling the open invoice file is the accounting department's function. Answer (B) is incorrect. Inspection of goods upon receipt is the receiving department's function. Answer (C) is incorrect. Authorization of the requisition is inventory control's function.

6. Which of the following controls most likely would assist in reducing the risks of material misstatement related to the existence or occurrence of manufacturing transactions?

A. Perpetual inventory records are independently compared with goods on hand.

B. Forms used for direct materials requisitions are prenumbered and accounted for.

C. Finished goods are stored in locked limited-access warehouses.

D. Subsidiary ledgers are periodically reconciled with inventory control accounts.

Answer (A) is correct.

REQUIRED: The control most likely to reduce the RMMs related to the existence or occurrence assertion.

DISCUSSION: The recorded accountability for assets should be compared with existing assets at reasonable intervals. If assets are susceptible to loss through fraud or error, the comparison should be made independently. An independent comparison is one made by persons not having responsibility for asset custody or the authorization or recording of transactions.

Answer (B) is incorrect. Accounting for prenumbered forms relates more to the completeness assertion than the existence or occurrence assertion. This control provides assurance that all transactions were recorded. Answer (C) is incorrect. Although limitation of access is appropriate for safeguarding certain assets, it does not establish accountability, and locking raw materials and work-in-process inventories in limited-access warehouses may not be feasible. Answer (D) is incorrect. Periodic reconciliation of subsidiary ledgers with control accounts is related to the completeness assertion.

7.2 Purchases Technology Considerations

7. In the accounting system of Apogee Company, the quantities counted by the receiving department and entered at a terminal are transmitted to the computer, which immediately transmits the amounts back to the terminal for display on the terminal screen. This display enables the operator to

A. Establish the validity of the account number.

B. Verify that the amount was entered accurately.

C. Verify the authorization of the disbursement.

D. Prevent the overpayment of the account.

Answer (B) is correct.
 REQUIRED: The effect of displaying the amounts entered at a terminal.
 DISCUSSION: The display of the amounts entered is an input control that permits visual verification of the accuracy of the input by the operator. This is termed closed-loop verification.

7.3 Electronic Data Interchange (EDI)

8. Many entities use the Internet as a network to transmit electronic data interchange (EDI) transactions. An advantage of using the Internet for electronic commerce rather than a traditional value-added network (VAN) is that the Internet

A. Permits EDI transactions to be sent to trading partners as transactions occur.

B. Automatically batches EDI transactions to multiple trading partners.

C. Possesses superior characteristics regarding disaster recovery.

D. Converts EDI transactions to a standard format without translation software.

Answer (A) is correct.
 REQUIRED: The advantage of using the Internet to transmit EDI transactions.
 DISCUSSION: VAN services have typically used a proprietary network or a network gatewayed with a specific set of other proprietary networks. A direct Internet connection permits real-time computer-to-computer communication for client-server applications, so transactions can be sent to trading partners as they occur.
 Answer (B) is incorrect. The Internet does not automatically batch EDI transactions, although multiple trading partners are possible. Answer (C) is incorrect. The use of the Internet affects the entity's disaster recovery plan. Answer (D) is incorrect. Regardless of the network used to transmit transactions, they first must be translated into a standard format for transmission.

9. Which of the following statements is correct concerning internal control in an electronic data interchange (EDI) system?

A. Preventive controls generally are more important than detective controls in EDI systems.

B. Control objectives for EDI systems generally are different from the objectives for other information systems.

C. Internal controls in EDI systems rarely permit the risks of material misstatement to be assessed at an acceptably low level.

D. Internal controls related to the segregation of duties generally are the most important controls in EDI systems.

Answer (A) is correct.
 REQUIRED: The true statement about EDI controls.
 DISCUSSION: In general, preventive controls are more important than detective controls because the benefits typically outweigh the costs. In electronic processing, once a transaction is accepted, the opportunity to apply detective controls is often limited. Thus, preventing fraud or error is important.
 Answer (B) is incorrect. The basic control objectives are the same regardless of the nature of the processing: to ensure the integrity of the information and to safeguard the assets. Answer (C) is incorrect. To gather sufficient evidence in a sophisticated computer system, testing controls is often necessary. The RMMs may be assessed at an acceptably low level if relevant controls are identified and tested and if the resulting evidence provides the degree of assurance desired regarding operating effectiveness. Answer (D) is incorrect. The level of segregation of duties achieved in a manual system is usually not feasible in a computer system.

7.4 Payroll Responsibilities/Organizational Structure/Flowchart

10. The purpose of segregating the duties of hiring personnel and distributing payroll checks is to segregate the

A. Authorization of transactions from the custody of related assets.

B. Operational responsibility from the record-keeping responsibility.

C. Human resources function from the controllership function.

D. Administrative controls from the internal accounting controls.

Answer (A) is correct.
    REQUIRED: The purpose of segregating the duties of hiring personnel and distributing payroll checks.
    DISCUSSION: In principle, the payroll function should be divided into its authorization, recording, and custody functions. Authorization of hiring, wage rates, and deductions is provided by human resources. Authorization of hours worked (executed by employees) is provided by production. Based upon these authorizations, accounting calculates and records the payroll. Based on the calculated amounts, the CFO prepares and distributes payroll checks.
    Answer (B) is incorrect. Neither hiring personnel (authorization) nor distributing checks (asset custody) is a recordkeeping activity. Answer (C) is incorrect. Controllership is a recordkeeping activity. Neither the controller nor the human resources department should distribute checks. Answer (D) is incorrect. The professional standards no longer recognize the distinction between administrative controls and internal accounting controls.

11. In meeting the control objective of safeguarding of assets, which department should be responsible for

	Distribution of Paychecks	Custody of Unclaimed Paychecks
A.	CFO	CFO
B.	Payroll	CFO
C.	CFO	Payroll
D.	Payroll	Payroll

Answer (A) is correct.
    REQUIRED: The department(s) responsible for the distribution of paychecks and the custody of unclaimed paychecks.
    DISCUSSION: Segregating paycheck preparation from distribution makes it more difficult for fictitious employees to receive payment. In principle, the payroll function should be divided into its authorization, recording, and custody functions. Authorization of hiring, wage rates, and deductions is provided by human resources. Authorization of hours worked is provided by production. Based upon these authorizations, accounting (the payroll department) calculates and records the payroll and prepares checks. The CFO signs and distributes payroll checks. Consistent with its asset custody function, the CFO should distribute paychecks or cash in a manual system (or make electronic funds transfers in a computerized system) so as to prevent payments to fictitious employees. Furthermore, the CFO, not the payroll department, should receive unclaimed paychecks or cash for safeguarding, and incomplete EFTs should not be returned to any of the other functions.

12. Which of the following departments most likely would approve changes in pay rates and deductions from employee salaries?

A. Human resources.

B. CFO.

C. Controller.

D. Payroll.

Answer (A) is correct.
    REQUIRED: The department most likely to approve changes in pay rates and deductions.
    DISCUSSION: The human resources department provides the authorization for payroll-related transactions, e.g., hiring, termination, and changes in pay rates and deductions.
    Answer (B) is incorrect. The CFO performs a custody function for payroll-related transactions. Answer (C) is incorrect. The payroll department, which is overseen by the controller, has a recordkeeping function for payroll-related transactions. Answer (D) is incorrect. The payroll department, which is overseen by the controller, has a recordkeeping function for payroll-related transactions.

7.5 Payroll Technology Considerations

13. Which of the following activities most likely would detect whether payroll data were altered during processing?

A. Monitoring authorized distribution of data control sheets.

B. Using test data to verify the performance of edit routines.

C. Examining source documents for approval by supervisors.

D. Segregating duties between approval of hardware and software specifications.

Answer (B) is correct.
  REQUIRED: The activity most likely to detect alteration of payroll data during processing.
  DISCUSSION: The test data approach uses the computer to test the processing logic and controls within the system and the records produced. The auditor prepares a set of dummy transactions specifically designed to test the control activities that management claims to have incorporated into the processing programs. The auditor can expect the controls to be applied to the transactions in the prescribed manner. Thus, the auditor is testing the effectiveness of the controls over the payroll data.
  Answer (A) is incorrect. Monitoring authorized distribution of data control sheets detects alteration of data outside the computer, not during processing. Answer (C) is incorrect. Examining source documents for approval by supervisors detects alteration of data outside the computer, not during processing. Answer (D) is incorrect. Segregating duties between hardware and software approval does not affect data during processing.

14. Matthews Corp. has changed from a system of recording time worked on time clock cards to a computerized payroll system in which employees record time in and out with magnetic cards. The computer system automatically updates all payroll records. Because of this change

A. A generalized computer audit program must be used.

B. Part of the audit trail is altered.

C. The potential for payroll-related fraud is diminished.

D. Transactions must be processed in batches.

Answer (B) is correct.
  REQUIRED: The effect of computerization of a payroll system.
  DISCUSSION: In a manual payroll system, a paper trail of documents would be created to provide audit evidence that controls over each step in processing were operating effectively. One element of a computer system that differentiates it from a manual system is that a transaction trail useful for auditing purposes might exist only for a brief time or only in computer-readable form.
  Answer (A) is incorrect. Use of generalized audit software is only one of many ways of auditing through a computer. Answer (C) is incorrect. Conversion to a computer system may actually increase the chance of fraud by eliminating segregation of incompatible functions and other controls. Answer (D) is incorrect. Automatic updating indicates that processing is not in batch mode.

7.6 Other Cycles

15. Which of the following internal control activities most likely justifies reducing the assessment of the risks of material misstatement for plant and equipment acquisitions?

A. Periodic physical inspection of plant and equipment by the internal audit staff.

B. Comparison of current-year plant and equipment account balances with prior-year actual balances.

C. The review of prenumbered purchase orders to detect unrecorded trade-ins.

D. Approval of periodic depreciation entries by a supervisor independent of the accounting department.

Answer (A) is correct.
  REQUIRED: The internal control activity that justifies reducing the assessed RMMs.
  DISCUSSION: A periodic physical inspection by the internal audit staff is the best activity for verifying the existence of plant and equipment. Direct observation by an independent, competent, and objective internal audit staff helps to reduce the potential for fictitious acquisitions or other fraudulent activities. The result is a lower assessment of the RMMs.
  Answer (B) is incorrect. Comparing records of assets may not detect nonexistent assets. Answer (C) is incorrect. Reviewing purchase orders is less effective than direct verification. Answer (D) is incorrect. Depreciation is based on recorded amounts. If they are misstated, depreciation also is misstated.

16. Equipment acquisitions that are misclassified as maintenance expense most likely would be detected by an internal control activity that provides for

A. Segregation of duties for employees in the accounts payable department.

B. Independent verification of invoices for disbursements recorded as equipment acquisitions.

C. Investigation of variances within a formal budgeting system.

D. Authorization by the board of directors of significant equipment acquisitions.

Answer (C) is correct.

   REQUIRED: The control activity to detect misclassification of equipment acquisitions as maintenance expense.

   DISCUSSION: A formal planning and budgeting system that estimates maintenance expense at a certain level will report a significant variance if capital expenditures are charged to the account. Investigation of the variance is likely to disclose the misclassification.

   Answer (A) is incorrect. Accounts payable assembles the required payment documentation but is unlikely to question the classification of the expenditure. Answer (B) is incorrect. Testing the population of recorded equipment acquisitions will not detect items misclassified as maintenance expense. Answer (D) is incorrect. The misclassification would occur subsequent to authorization.

17. Which of the following questions would an auditor most likely include on an internal control questionnaire for notes payable?

A. Are assets that collateralize notes payable critically needed for the entity's continued existence?

B. Are two or more authorized signatures required on checks that repay notes payable?

C. Are the proceeds from notes payable used for the purchase of noncurrent assets?

D. Are direct borrowings on notes payable authorized by the board of directors?

Answer (D) is correct.

   REQUIRED: The question most likely included on an internal control questionnaire for notes payable.

   DISCUSSION: Control is enhanced when different persons or departments authorize, record, and maintain custody of assets for a class of transactions. Authorization of notes payable transactions is best done by the board of directors.

   Answer (A) is incorrect. The importance of specific assets to the entity is an operational matter and not a primary concern of an auditor when (s)he is considering internal control. Answer (B) is incorrect. Questions about the payment function are likely to be on the questionnaire relating to cash disbursements. Answer (C) is incorrect. The use of funds is an operating decision made by management and is not a primary concern of the auditor when considering internal control.

18. Which of the following controls would an entity most likely use in safeguarding against the loss of trading securities?

A. An independent trust company that has no direct contact with the employees who have record-keeping responsibilities has possession of the securities.

B. The internal auditor verifies the trading securities in the entity's safe each year on the balance sheet date.

C. The independent auditor traces all purchases and sales of trading securities through the subsidiary ledgers to the general ledger.

D. A designated member of the board of directors controls the securities in a bank safe-deposit box.

Answer (A) is correct.

   REQUIRED: The most likely control over trading securities.

   DISCUSSION: Assigning custody of trading securities to a bank or trust company provides the greatest security because such an institution normally has strict controls over assets entrusted to it and access to its vaults.

   Answer (B) is incorrect. Verification of the existence of securities does not prevent their removal between the verification dates, for example, to be used as collateral for unauthorized loans. Answer (C) is incorrect. The independent auditor's procedures are not part of the client's internal control. Answer (D) is incorrect. Access to a safe-deposit box should require the presence of two authorized persons.

19. Which of the following internal control activities would an entity most likely use to assist in satisfying the completeness assertion related to long-term investments?

    A. Senior management verifies that securities in the bank safe-deposit box are registered in the entity's name.

    B. The internal auditor compares the securities in the bank safe-deposit box with recorded investments.

    C. The CFO vouches the acquisition of securities by comparing brokers' advices with canceled checks.

    D. The controller compares the current market prices of recorded investments with the brokers' advices on file.

Answer (B) is correct.

    REQUIRED: The control activity to assist in satisfying the completeness assertion for long-term investments.

    DISCUSSION: The items being tested consist of the assets in the safe-deposit box. This population should be compared with the records of the investments to provide assurance that the balance is complete, that is, contains all long-term investments.

    Answer (A) is incorrect. Verification that securities are registered in the entity's name relates to the rights assertion. Answer (C) is incorrect. Comparing canceled checks with brokers' advices pertains to the rights assertion. Answer (D) is incorrect. Comparing market prices with brokers' advices relates most directly to the valuation assertion.

20. In obtaining an understanding of a manufacturing entity's internal control concerning inventory balances, an auditor most likely would

    A. Analyze the liquidity and turnover ratios of the inventory.

    B. Perform analytical procedures designed to identify cost variances.

    C. Review the entity's descriptions of inventory policies and procedures.

    D. Perform test counts of inventory during the entity's physical count.

Answer (C) is correct.

    REQUIRED: The activity for understanding a manufacturer's controls relevant to inventory.

    DISCUSSION: The auditor makes inquiries of personnel, observes activities and operations, and reviews an entity's documentation of controls relevant to the management of inventories to obtain an understanding of internal control.

    Answer (A) is incorrect. Analytical procedures relate to substantive testing, not the evaluation of controls. Answer (B) is incorrect. Analytical procedures relate to substantive testing, not the evaluation of controls. Answer (D) is incorrect. Test counts relate to substantive testing, not internal controls.

STUDY UNIT EIGHT
RESPONSES TO ASSESSED RISKS

(13 pages of outline)

To reduce audit risk to an acceptable level, the auditor makes overall responses to the assessed risks of material misstatement at the financial statement level. At the relevant assertion level, the auditor responds by designing and performing further audit procedures (tests of controls and substantive procedures).

If candidates have difficulty understanding the conceptual issues in this study unit, they should review the material in Study Units 5 through 7 before continuing.

8.1 ASSESSING RISKS OF MATERIAL MISSTATEMENT

1. The risk of material misstatement (RMM) is the combined assessment of inherent risk and control risk.

2. Before designing and performing further audit procedures, the auditor identifies and assesses the RMMs at the financial statement and relevant assertion levels. Thus, when obtaining the understanding of the entity and its environment, the auditor identifies risks and the controls related to those risks that are relevant to the audit. For this purpose, the auditor considers the classes of transactions, balances, and disclosures.

   a. Risks should be related to the threats at the relevant assertion level.

   b. The auditor considers the magnitude of the risks and the likelihood of material misstatement.

   c. As a basis for the risk assessment, the auditor uses audit evidence gathered from performing **risk assessment procedures**, including that from

      1) Evaluating the design of controls and
      2) Determining whether they have been implemented.

   d. The risk assessment is used to determine the nature, timing, and extent of further audit procedures.

   e. If the risk assessment is based on the expectation that controls are operating effectively at the relevant assertion level, the auditor tests suitably designed controls.

   f. The auditor determines whether the risks relate to

      1) Specific relevant assertions or
      2) The statements as a whole.

         a) Risks at the statement level may indicate a deficient control environment.

            i) Such a deficiency may affect numerous relevant assertions, and an overall response may be necessary.

   g. The auditor identifies controls related to risks and specific relevant assertions.

      1) Some controls may specifically and directly affect an assertion. Others may reduce a risk only indirectly and in conjunction with numerous other controls.

         a) For example, controls over handling of cash receipts directly affect the completeness assertion.

            i) However, a condensed report on merchandise sales is less directly related to the valuation assertion than requiring credit approval by an appropriate manager.

3. **Significant Risks**

    a. As part of the assessment of RMMs, an auditor identifies the risks that require special audit consideration.

        1) For example, the auditor should obtain an understanding of significant operating transactions.

    b. The auditor's professional judgment about significance excludes the effect of identified controls.

    c. A risk is more likely to be significant when it involves the following:

        1) A risk of fraud
        2) Recent significant developments (e.g., economic)
        3) A complex transaction
        4) A related party transaction
        5) A high degree of subjectivity or uncertainty in a financial measure, e.g., an accounting estimate
        6) A transaction outside the normal course of business, i.e., a nonroutine (unusual and infrequent) transaction

    d. Significant risks frequently result from nonroutine transactions and matters requiring significant judgment. But these are less likely to be subject to routine controls.

        1) RMMs related to significant nonroutine transactions may be greater if they result from, among other things, the following:

            a) Increased manual intervention for data processing
            b) Increased management intervention to determine accounting practices
            c) Complex accounting principles or calculations
            d) Transactions with related parties
            e) Transactions for which implementing controls is difficult

        2) RMMs related to significant judgments may be greater if they involve accounting estimates resulting from, among other things, the following:

            a) Accounting principles subject to different interpretations
            b) Subjective or complex judgments
            c) Significant assumptions

    e. The auditor performs substantive procedures that specifically respond to a significant risk.

        1) The auditor also obtains an understanding of the controls relevant to the risk. (S)he then evaluates whether the controls have been suitably designed and implemented.

4. **Insufficiency of Substantive Procedures**

    a. The auditor may be unable to obtain sufficient appropriate audit evidence about some relevant assertions by applying substantive procedures alone.

        1) For example, routine transactions may be highly automated, and audit evidence may not exist in manual form. Thus, tests of controls may be essential.

5. The assessment of RMMs at the relevant assertion level may need to be revised as more audit evidence is gathered.

Stop and review! You have completed the outline for this subunit. Study multiple-choice questions 1 through 4 beginning on page 183.

8.2 AUDITOR'S RESPONSE TO RISKS

1. **Financial Statement Level**

   a. **Overall responses** apply to the assessed RMMs at the financial statement level. The following are examples of overall responses:

      1) An emphasis on professional skepticism in evidence gathering and evaluation
      2) Increased supervision
      3) Assignment of staff with greater experience or expertise
      4) Greater unpredictability in the choice of further audit procedures
      5) Changing the nature, timing, and extent of audit procedures, such as modifying the nature of a procedure to obtain more persuasive evidence

   b. The assessment of the RMMs depends on the understanding of the control environment.

      1) An effective control environment increases the reliability of internally generated audit evidence.
      2) The following are examples of responses to deficiencies in the control environment:

         a) Obtaining more evidence from substantive procedures
         b) Performing more audit procedures at the end of the period
         c) Expanding the engagement's scope to audit more locations

   c. Overall responses relate to the general approach to the audit. Thus,

      1) A substantive audit approach emphasizes substantive procedures.
      2) A combined audit approach applies tests of controls and substantive procedures.

2. **Relevant Assertion Level**

   a. The nature, timing, and extent of the auditor's further audit procedures should respond to the assessed RMMs at the relevant assertion level.
   b. The further procedures and the assessed RMMs should be clearly connected.
   c. The most important factor in the response is the nature of the procedures.
   d. The design of further audit procedures should consider the following, among other things:

      1) Level of the assessed risk
      2) Likelihood of a material misstatement
      3) Characteristics of the transaction class, balance, or disclosure
      4) Whether the auditor intends to rely on the operating effectiveness of controls

3. **Audit Approach**

   a. The assessment of risks is a basis for choosing the audit approach.
   b. The auditor may decide that the substantive approach is appropriate for specific assertions. Thus, the auditor excludes the effect of controls from the risk assessment. For example, the risk assessment procedures may not identify effective controls for the relevant assertion, or testing controls may be inefficient. In these cases, the auditor does not intend to rely on controls.

      1) The combined approach is appropriate if, for example, the business is conducted without documentation of transactions except through the IT system. In this case, an effective response requires testing of controls.

    c.   Regardless of the assessment of the RMMs, the auditor should design and perform substantive procedures for all relevant assertions related to each material transaction class, balance, or disclosure.

        1)   Tests of controls by themselves are insufficient because (a) the assessments of the RMMs are judgments that may not identify all RMMs and (b) internal control has inherent limitations.

        2)   Analytical procedures applied as substantive procedures also may be insufficient.

4.   **Nature of Further Procedures**

    a.   The nature of further procedures is a function of their purpose and type.

        1)   Substantive procedures and tests of controls have different purposes.

        2)   Types of procedures include inspection, observation, inquiry, confirmation, recalculation, reperformance, or analytical procedures.

    b.   The choice of audit procedures depends on the following:

        1)   The relevant assertion

            a)   For example, a test of controls may be preferable for the completeness assertion about sales.

        2)   The RMMs

            a)   For higher RMMs, the evidence should be more persuasive. Thus, the auditor increases the quantity of evidence or obtains evidence that is more relevant or reliable. For example, the auditor may seek external confirmation in addition to inspecting internally generated documents and inquiring of management.

        3)   Reasons for Assessing RMMs

            a)   For example, a lower RMM for a transaction class because of its characteristics (without regard to related controls) may justify performing only substantive analytical procedures.

            b)   But if a lower RMM is based on the effectiveness of controls, and the design of substantive procedures reflects that RMM, tests of controls should be performed.

5.   **Timing of Further Procedures**

    a.   Timing relates to when a procedure is performed or the date or period of the audit evidence. The greater the RMMs, the more likely that tests of controls or substantive procedures will be performed at the end of the period or at unpredictable times.

        1)   However, earlier performance of procedures may identify significant issues in time to permit their resolution either (a) with the aid of management or (b) by designing an effective audit approach.

    b.   The timing of procedures is based on considerations such as the following:

        1)   The relevant period or date
        2)   Availability of information
        3)   Nature of the risk
        4)   The control environment

    c.   Substantive procedures may be performed at an **interim** date. The auditor then should cover the remaining period by performing substantive procedures and tests of controls (if substantive procedures do not suffice) to provide a reasonable basis for extending conclusions. For example, tests of details, substantive analytical procedures, and reconciliation should be performed.

1) If unexpected misstatements are detected, the auditor may conclude that the planned procedures for the remaining period need to be modified. Modification may include extending or repeating at period end the procedures performed at the interim date.

2) If no misstatements for an account are identified at the interim date, the auditor does not perform substantive procedures on the account at period end for the entire year under audit.

   d. Some procedures are performed only at or after the end of the period, for example, (1) cutoff procedures, (2) comparing financial statement amounts with accounting records, or (3) examining adjustments of the statements.

6. **Extent of Further Procedures**

   a. The extent of a procedure is its quantity, such as the number of sampled items. The extent of a procedure ordinarily increases as the RMMs increase. The auditor's judgment about extent is based on

     1) The desired level of assurance,
     2) The assessed RMM, and
     3) Materiality.

   b. The use of computer-assisted audit techniques (CAATs) may increase the extent of procedures. For example, they may be applied to the whole population of relevant items.

     1) But sampling often is appropriate if statistically sound methods are used. Study Unit 15 addresses audit sampling.

7. **Tests of Controls**

   a. The auditor tests suitably designed controls at the relevant assertion level when

     1) The risk assessment is based on the expectation that controls are operating with some degree of effectiveness (i.e., the auditor intends to rely on the controls).

       a) The greater the reliance on controls, the more persuasive the evidence of their effectiveness should be.

     2) Substantive procedures alone are inadequate to obtain sufficient appropriate evidence.

       a) Tests of controls are necessary for IT processing of routine, high-volume transactions with little manual intervention or hardcopy documentation.

   b. Performing risk assessment procedures to obtain an **understanding** of the entity and its environment involves, among other things, evaluating the **design** of controls and determining whether they have been **implemented**.

     1) Testing controls takes the additional step of obtaining evidence about their **operating effectiveness**. The evidence addresses such matters as the following:

       a) How controls were applied at relevant times
       b) By whom they were applied
       c) The consistency of their application

   c. The procedures for evaluating design and determining implementation also may test operating effectiveness.

     1) For example, if IT general controls are effective, determining that an IT processing control has been implemented also tests effectiveness.

   d. **Dual-purpose testing** involves performing (1) a test of details and (2) a test of controls on the same transaction. An example is examining an invoice to obtain evidence of (1) the occurrence of a transaction and (2) its approval by a supervisor.

e.   The auditor considers whether the controls to be tested (direct controls) depend upon the effectiveness of indirect controls.

1)   For example, the control group's review of an exception report is a direct control over IT processing supported by indirect controls (general controls and application controls).

8.   **Nature of Tests of Controls**

a.   The audit approach may be based primarily on tests of controls. They typically include the following:

1)   Inquiry
2)   Inspection (e.g., of electronic files)
3)   Observation
4)   Reperformance
5)   Recalculation

b.   Inquiry alone is **not** sufficient to test the operating effectiveness of controls. The auditor should perform other audit procedures in combination with inquiry.

1)   A combination of procedures consisting of inquiry and reperformance, recalculation, or inspection normally provides more assurance than inquiry and observation.

c.   The nature of the control affects the selection of a procedure.

1)   For example, documentation may be inspected.

a)   But in its absence, such as when a control is performed by a computer, inquiry may need to be combined with observation or CAATs.

d.   Misstatements detected by substantive procedures may imply that controls are ineffective.

1)   But nondetection of misstatements is not evidence of effectiveness.

9.   **Timing of Tests of Controls**

a.   Timing depends on whether controls are tested (1) at a moment in time or (2) over a period.

1)   For example, a year-end test of controls over property, plant, and equipment may be sufficient.

2)   However, a test at a moment in time of a programmed control over transactions reported in the income statement ordinarily should be combined with other tests. These include procedures to verify consistent operation for the reporting period, e.g., tests of change controls or monitoring controls.

b.   When tests are performed at an interim period, the auditor should determine procedures to be performed during the remaining period. The auditor considers the following:

1)   Assessed RMMs
2)   Controls tested
3)   The evidence about operating effectiveness
4)   The duration of the remaining period
5)   Any intended reduction of substantive procedures
6)   The control environment
7)   Significant changes in the controls since they were last tested

c.   Procedures should be performed to determine the relevance of audit evidence from prior audits.

1)   For example, the auditor should verify that changes in an effective control have not been made that impair its functioning.

2) Furthermore, the auditor may not rely on evidence from a prior audit about a control intended to reduce a significant risk.

3) If the auditor plans to rely on controls that have not changed (other than those related to significant risks), they should be tested at least once every third audit.

   a) At least some controls should be tested every year to provide information about the continuing effectiveness of the control environment.

4) To determine whether to rely on audit evidence from a prior audit, the auditor considers matters such as the following:

   a) The RMMs and extent of reliance on the control
   b) Other elements of internal control (e.g., the control environment)
   c) IT general controls

10. **Extent of Tests of Controls**

   a. The following are considered in determining extent:

      1) Frequency of use of the control
      2) Expected rate of control deviations
      3) Relevance and reliability of needed evidence
      4) Evidence from tests of other controls
      5) Planned reliance on the control
      6) Time during the period for which reliance is sought

   b. Audit sampling should be considered when a control is used frequently.

   c. The extent of tests of controls increases with increases in the following:

      1) Reliance on their operating effectiveness in the assessment of RMMs
      2) The expected deviation rate

         a) But if this rate is high, tests of controls for the specific assertion may not suffice to reduce the audit risk.

11. **Substantive Procedures**

   a. Substantive procedures are performed to detect material misstatements at the relevant assertion level.

   b. The auditor should apply substantive procedures to all relevant assertions about material transaction classes, balances, and disclosures.

   c. Procedures related to the statement closing process include

      1) Examining material entries and other adjustments made in statement preparation.

      2) Reconciling the statements with the accounting records.

   d. Substantive procedures should be performed that respond specifically and reliably to **significant risks**.

      1) For example, management may have an incentive to recognize revenue prematurely. The specific response may be to (a) seek external confirmation of the terms of sales agreements (e.g., dates, delivery information, and rights of return) and (b) inquire of nonfinancial employees about changes in such agreements.

12. **Nature of Substantive Procedures**

   a. They consist of tests of details (transaction classes, balances, and disclosures) and substantive analytical procedures.

      1) **Tests of details** normally should be applied to certain assertions about balances, e.g., existence, occurrence, and valuation.

      2) **Analytical procedures** are most often applied to high-volume, relatively predictable transactions.

         a) Study Unit 3, Subunit 5, has a full outline.

b.   Analytical procedures alone may suffice to reduce audit risk to an acceptable level.

   1)   For example, the assessed RMMs may have been reduced by tests of controls.
   2)   The best responses in other cases may be to perform (a) tests of details only or (b) a combination of other substantive procedures.

c.   To test the existence or occurrence assertion, the auditor chooses items from a financial statement amount.

d.   To test the completeness assertion, the auditor obtains evidence that an item should be and is included in a financial statement amount.

   1)   For example, an auditor may compare cash payments with accounts payable to test for unrecorded liabilities.

e.   The auditor should consider **tests of controls** over the data used to perform analytical procedures.

   1)   The risk of **management override** of controls is especially pertinent. It may affect the relationship on which such procedures are based.

      a)   Thus, analytical procedures may not detect certain frauds.

   2)   The auditor also may consider whether the accuracy and completeness of the data have been audited, especially data generated by the entity's information system.

13. **Timing of Substantive Procedures**

a.   An auditor who performs procedures at an **interim date** should cover the remaining period.

   1)   For this purpose, the auditor performs

      a)   Further substantive procedures or
      b)   A combination of substantive procedures and tests of controls.

   2)   If neither option suffices, substantive procedures should be performed at the end of the period.

b.   The longer the remaining period, the greater the risk resulting from performing procedures at an interim date. Accordingly, the auditor should consider, among other things, the following:

   1)   Relevant controls, including the control environment
   2)   Availability of information at the end of the remaining period
   3)   Purpose of the procedure
   4)   Assessed RMMs
   5)   Nature of the transaction class or balance and relevant assertions
   6)   Ability to reduce the risk that misstatements at the end of the period will not be detected

c.   When an auditor has identified RMMs due to **fraud**, (s)he may decide that substantive procedures should not be performed at an interim date.

d.   The auditor may compare interim-date and period-end amounts and perform **analytical procedures** for the remaining period to identify anomalies.

   1)   The auditor should consider

      a)   The predictability of ending balances
      b)   The entity's procedures for interim-date adjustments and accounting cutoffs
      c)   Whether the information system will produce the information about balances and transactions necessary to an analytical investigation

e. Detection of **misstatements** at an interim date may result in modification of risk assessments and planned procedures.

f. Audit evidence from a prior audit's substantive procedures provide little evidence usable in the current period.

14. **Extent of Substantive Procedures**

a. The greater the RMMs, the greater the extent of relevant procedures.

1) The extent of substantive procedures may be reduced if controls are effective.

b. For tests of details, the extent is usually a function of sampling. Sampling is the subject of Study Unit 15.

c. For analytical procedures, the auditor considers the acceptable variation from the expectation.

1) This variation relates to performance materiality and the desired assurance.

15. **Documentation**

a. The auditor should document the following:

1) Overall responses to assessed RMMs at the statement level

2) Nature, timing, and extent of further audit procedures and their connection with assessed risks at the relevant assertion level

3) Results of audit procedures

4) Conclusions if not clear

5) Conclusions about use of prior-audit evidence with respect to the operating effectiveness of controls

Considerable detail has been presented in the previous two subunits. However, do not lose sight of the big picture. In planning the audit, the auditor assesses the risks of material misstatement (RMMs) by performing risk assessment procedures. The RMMs can be assessed at a lower level if controls are operating effectively. Thus, the auditor may perform tests of controls to make this lower assessment. Finally, based on the assessed RMMs, the auditor designs appropriate substantive procedures to identify potential misstatements. Conceptually, this should make sense to you.

Stop and review! You have completed the outline for this subunit. Study multiple-choice questions 5 through 13 beginning on page 185.

8.3 ASSESSING RISK IN A COMPUTER ENVIRONMENT

1. **Similarities**

a. The process of assessing RMMs in a computer environment and in a manual system have many similarities. The candidate's review should begin with the similarities. Most of the terms used in this subunit are defined in Study Unit 5.

b. The **objectives** are the same. The RMMs are assessed by the auditor to help determine the nature, timing, and extent of the substantive procedures and tests of controls appropriate to support the opinion regardless of the nature of the system.

c. The **concept** is the same. The auditor obtains an understanding of the entity and its environment, including its internal control, and determines that the controls have been implemented. The auditor then considers whether testing the effectiveness of the controls and relying on them is more efficient than performing only substantive procedures. However, the auditee's use of IT requires the auditor to consider whether omitting tests of controls enables him or her to provide the necessary assurance.

1) The conventional procedure is first to assess the RMMs relative to the control environment (often referred to as the general controls). If the control environment is ineffective, the auditor should not rely on individual controls (application controls).

d. Many **procedures** are the same. Numerous controls in a computer environment are outside the computer system and can be tested using procedures applicable to a manual system. These procedures include the following:

1) Inquiries of entity personnel
2) Inspection of documents, reports, and files
3) Observation of the application of specific controls
4) Reperformance by the auditor

e. Computer controls to which traditional tests of controls apply include those found in the control environment and control activities components of internal control.

f. **The Control Environment**

1) **Organizational structure.** The auditor inspects documentation and observes operations demonstrating that the IT function has no custody of assets or transaction authority and is actually

a) Operating as a service department independently of users and
b) Reporting to senior-level management.

2) **Assignment of authority and responsibility.** The auditor inquires and observes whether the following employees are performing functions consistent with their assigned responsibilities (and have no incompatible responsibilities):

a) Systems analyst
b) Programmer
c) Computer (console) operator
d) Data conversion (key) operator
e) Librarian
f) Data control group

g. **Control Activities**

1) **Information processing.** The auditor

a) Observes the backup copies of files and programs to determine that they are safeguarded;
b) Inspects the written security policy concerning virus protection and observes the existence of available anti-virus software;
c) Inspects program acquisition and development requests for the proper authorization, assignment of responsibility for design and coding, testing, and acceptance; and
d) Inspects program documentation to determine whether it is complete and up to date.

2) The auditor tests **access controls** by

a) Attempting to sign on to the computer system using various passwords and ID numbers,
b) Inspecting the system access log for completeness and appropriate use and follow-up (passwords consistent with employees' responsibilities), and
c) Observing that disposal of sensitive documents and printouts is controlled so that unauthorized persons cannot gain information concerning passwords or ID numbers.

2. **Differences**

a. Certain controls relating to the input, processing, and output of data are internal to the computer system. They should be tested by procedures that are not traditionally performed in a manual environment. Such methods have been called auditing around the computer or auditing through the computer.

   b.   **Auditing around the computer** is not appropriate when systems are sophisticated or the major controls are included in the computer programs. It may be appropriate for very simple systems that produce appropriate printed outputs.

   1)   The auditor manually processes transactions and compares the results with the client's computer-processed results.

   2)   Because only a small number of transactions can ordinarily be tested, the effectiveness of the tests of controls must be questioned.

   3)   The computer is treated as a black box, and only inputs and outputs are evaluated.

   c.   **Auditing through the computer** uses the computer to test the processing logic and controls within the system and the records produced. The following are examples:

   1)   Processing test data
   2)   Parallel simulation
   3)   Creation of an integrated test facility
   4)   Programming embedded audit modules

3.   **Test Data Approach**

   a.   The auditor prepares a set of dummy transactions specifically designed to test the control activities that management claims to have incorporated into the processing programs. The auditor can expect the controls to be applied to the transactions in the prescribed manner. Thus, the auditor is testing the effectiveness of the controls.

EXAMPLE

Management may have represented that the following edit checks were included in the payroll processing program:

1)   Field checks for all numeric and alphabetic fields
2)   Reasonableness test of hours worked over 40 hours
3)   Validity check of employee numbers compared with known employees in the personnel master file
4)   Error listings of all transactions that fail a test

The auditor's test transactions include some that should pass the edit checks and be processed and some that should fail the edit checks and be printed on the error listing. Because processing is uniform, only one transaction for each control tested needs to be included.

---

   b.   The primary advantage of this method is that it directly tests the controls.

   c.   The primary disadvantage is that it tests processing at only one moment in time. That is, the auditor does not have assurance that the program tested is the one used throughout the year to process client transactions.

   d.   The following illustrates a test data approach in flowchart form:

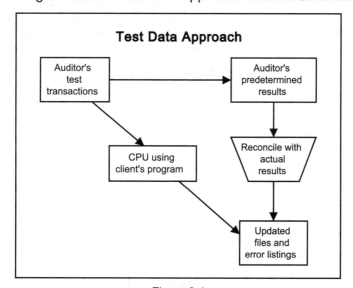

Figure 8-1

4.   **Parallel Simulation**

a.   Parallel simulation uses a controlled program to reprocess sets of client transactions and compares the auditor-achieved results with those of the client. The key is for the auditor's program to include the client's edit checks. Thus, the client's results of processing, rejected transactions, and error listing should be the same as the auditor's.

b.   The auditor's controlled program may be a copy of the client's program that has been tested. An expensive alternative is for the auditor to write a program that includes management's controls. Also, a program may be created from generalized audit software.

c.   The primary advantage of parallel simulation is that transactions from throughout the period may be reprocessed. The results can then be compared with the client's results to provide assurance that the edit checks (controls) have been applied during the period.

d.   The primary disadvantages of this method are the cost of obtaining the program and the coordination effort required to obtain transactions to reprocess.

e.   The following illustrates the parallel simulation method in flowchart form:

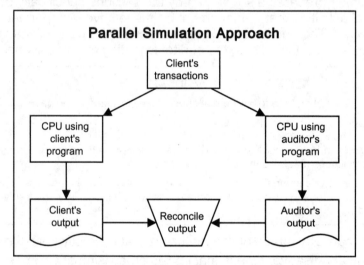

Figure 8-2

5.   **Integrated Test Facility Method**

a.   Using the **integrated test facility (ITF)** method, the auditor creates a dummy record within the client's actual system (e.g., a fictitious employee in the personnel and payroll file). Dummy and actual transactions are processed (e.g., time records for the dummy employee and for actual employees). The auditor can test the edit checks by altering the dummy transactions and evaluating error listings.

b.   The primary advantage of this method is that it tests the actual program in operation.

c.   The primary disadvantages are that the method requires considerable coordination, and the dummy transactions must be purged prior to internal and external reporting. Thus, the method is not used extensively by external auditors.

d.   The following illustrates the ITF method in flowchart form:

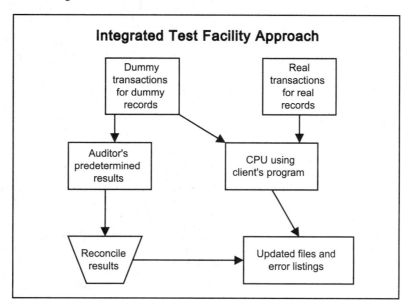

Figure 8-3

6.   **Embedded Audit Module**

a.   An embedded audit module is an integral part of an application system that is designed to identify and report actual transactions and other information that meet criteria having audit significance.

b.   An advantage is that it permits continuous monitoring of online, real-time systems.

c.   A disadvantage is that **audit hooks** must be programmed into the operating system and applications programs to permit the use of audit modules.

d.   Upon completion of the tests of computer controls, the auditor assesses computer control risk and relates it to specific financial statement assertions. This risk assessment is a primary factor in determining the appropriate substantive procedures.

Stop and review! You have completed the outline for this subunit. Study multiple-choice questions 14 through 20 beginning on page 187.

QUESTIONS

8.1 Assessing Risks of Material Misstatement

1. The risks of material misstatement (RMMs) should be assessed in terms of

A.   Specific controls.

B.   Types of potential fraud.

C.   Financial statement assertions.

D.   Control environment factors.

Answer (C) is correct.
  REQUIRED: The approach used in assessing the RMMs.
  DISCUSSION: The auditor's objective is to identify and assess the RMMs, whether due to fraud or error, at the financial statement and relevant assertion levels. This objective is achieved through understanding the entity and its environment, including its internal control. The understanding provides a basis for designing and implementing responses to the assessed RMMs (AU-C 315 and AS 2110).
  Answer (A) is incorrect. Relevant controls should relate to the identified RMMs, and the RMMs are identified and assessed at the financial statement and relevant assertion levels. Answer (B) is incorrect. The auditor should use information obtained from the understanding to identify types of potential misstatements. Answer (D) is incorrect. The auditor considers the control environment in assessing the RMMs but does not assess risk in terms of control environment factors.

2. The ultimate purpose of understanding the entity and its environment and assessing the risks of material misstatement is to contribute to the auditor's assessment of the risk that

    A. Tests of controls may fail to identify procedures relevant to assertions.

    B. Material misstatements may exist in the financial statements.

    C. Specified controls requiring segregation of duties may be circumvented by collusion.

    D. Entity policies may be inappropriately overridden by senior management.

Answer (B) is correct.
    REQUIRED: The purpose of understanding the entity and its environment and assessing the RMMs.
    DISCUSSION: The auditor's objective is to identify and assess the RMMs, whether due to fraud or error, at the financial statement and relevant assertion levels. This objective is achieved through understanding the entity and its environment, including its internal control. The understanding provides a basis for designing and implementing responses to the assessed RMMs (AU-C 315 and AS 2110). Moreover, the auditor's overall objectives in an audit include obtaining reasonable assurance about whether the statements as a whole are free from material misstatement (AU-C 200).
    Answer (A) is incorrect. An auditor should obtain an understanding of controls relevant to the audit. Thus, the auditor should evaluate their design and determine whether they have been implemented. The evaluation of design considers whether the controls can effectively prevent, or detect and correct, material misstatements (AU-C 315 and AS 2110). The auditor then tests relevant controls to obtain sufficient appropriate evidence about their operating effectiveness if (1) the auditor intends to rely on them in determining the nature, timing, and extent of substantive procedures or (2) substantive procedures alone cannot provide sufficient appropriate evidence at the relevant assertion level (AU-C 330 and AS 2301). Answer (C) is incorrect. Collusion is an inherent limitation of internal control. Answer (D) is incorrect. Inappropriate management override is an inherent limitation of internal control.

3. The auditor should perform tests of controls when the auditor's assessment of the risks of material misstatement includes an expectation of the operating effectiveness of internal control or when

    A. Substantive procedures alone cannot provide sufficient appropriate audit evidence at the relevant assertion level.

    B. Tests of details and substantive analytical procedures provide sufficient appropriate audit evidence to support the assertion being evaluated.

    C. The auditor is not able to obtain an understanding of internal controls.

    D. The owner-manager performs virtually all the functions of internal control.

Answer (A) is correct.
    REQUIRED: The reason to test controls.
    DISCUSSION: For some RMMs, the auditor may determine that it is not feasible to obtain sufficient appropriate audit evidence only from substantive procedures. These RMMs may relate to routine, significant transactions subject to highly automated processing with no documentation except what is recorded in the IT system. In such circumstances, the controls over the RMMs are relevant to the audit. Thus, the auditor should obtain an understanding of, and test, the controls.
    Answer (B) is incorrect. When evidence obtained from substantive procedures is sufficient and appropriate to support an assertion, the auditor need not test controls. Answer (C) is incorrect. The auditor should obtain an understanding of controls relevant to the audit. The understanding includes an evaluation of their design and a determination of whether they have been implemented. Answer (D) is incorrect. In small organizations, when the owner-manager performs many or most control activities, tests of controls ordinarily are not necessary.

4. When assessing the risks of material misstatement at a low level, an auditor is required to document the auditor's

	Understanding of the Entity's Control Environment	Overall Responses to Assessed Risks
A.	Yes	No
B.	No	Yes
C.	Yes	Yes
D.	No	No

Answer (C) is correct.
    REQUIRED: The item(s) that should be documented when assessing the RMMs at a low level.
    DISCUSSION: The understanding of the components of internal control, including the control environment, should be documented regardless of the degree of risk (AU-C 315). The overall responses to the assessed RMMs at the financial statement level also should be documented (AU-C 330).

8.2 Auditor's Response to Risks

5. Which of the following is a step in an auditor's decision to rely on internal controls?

- A. Apply analytical procedures to both financial data and nonfinancial information to detect conditions that may indicate weak controls.

- B. Perform tests of details of transactions and account balances to identify potential fraud and error.

- C. Identify specific controls that are likely to prevent, or detect and correct, material misstatements and perform tests of controls.

- D. Document that the additional audit effort to perform tests of controls exceeds the potential reduction in substantive testing.

Answer (C) is correct.
    REQUIRED: The step necessary to rely on internal controls.
    DISCUSSION: An auditor should obtain an understanding of controls relevant to the audit. Thus, the auditor should evaluate their design and determine whether they have been implemented. The evaluation of design considers whether the controls can effectively prevent, or detect and correct, material misstatements (AU-C 315 and AS 2110). The auditor then tests relevant controls to obtain sufficient appropriate evidence about their operating effectiveness if (1) the auditor intends to rely on them in determining the nature, timing, and extent of substantive procedures, or (2) substantive procedures alone cannot provide sufficient appropriate evidence at the relevant assertion level (AU-C 330 and AS 2301).
    Answer (A) is incorrect. Analytical procedures are substantive procedures. The auditor should perform tests of controls to rely on internal controls. Answer (B) is incorrect. Tests of details are substantive procedures. The auditor should perform tests of controls to rely on internal controls. Answer (D) is incorrect. If the effort to perform tests of controls exceeds the potential reduction in substantive testing, the auditor need not rely on controls.

6. An auditor may decide to perform only substantive procedures for certain assertions because the auditor believes

- A. Controls are not relevant to the assertions.

- B. The entity's control components are interrelated.

- C. Sufficient appropriate audit evidence to support the assertions is likely to be available.

- D. More emphasis on tests of controls than substantive tests is warranted.

Answer (A) is correct.
    REQUIRED: The reason an auditor may decide to perform only substantive procedures.
    DISCUSSION: The auditor's risk assessment procedures may not have identified any suitably designed and implemented controls that are relevant to the assertions. Another possibility is that testing of controls may be inefficient. But the auditor needs to be satisfied that performing only substantive procedures will be effective in reducing audit risk to an acceptable level.
    Answer (B) is incorrect. The integration of control components may be a valuable consideration in performing tests of controls as well as substantive procedures. Answer (C) is incorrect. The auditor tests controls when sufficient appropriate audit evidence is not provided by substantive procedures. Answer (D) is incorrect. The auditor's decision to perform only substantive procedures is a decision not to perform procedures to obtain evidence about the effectiveness of controls.

7. After gaining an understanding of a client's computer processing internal control, a financial statement auditor may decide not to test the effectiveness of the computer processing control procedures. Which of the following is **not** a valid reason for choosing to omit tests of controls?

- A. The controls duplicate operative controls existing elsewhere in the system.

- B. Risk assessment procedures have not identified relevant effective controls.

- C. The time and dollar costs of testing exceed the time and dollar savings in substantive testing if the tests of controls show the controls to be effective.

- D. The assessment of the risks of material misstatement permits the auditor to rely on the controls.

Answer (D) is correct.
    REQUIRED: The invalid reason for omitting tests of controls.
    DISCUSSION: Although controls appear to be effective based on the understanding of internal control, the auditor should perform tests of controls when the assessment of the RMMs at the relevant assertion level includes an expectation of their operating effectiveness. This expectation reflects the auditor's intention to rely on the controls in determining the nature, timing, and extent of substantive procedures.
    Answer (A) is incorrect. Compensating controls may appropriately limit the RMMs. Answer (B) is incorrect. Performing only substantive procedures is appropriate for certain assertions, e.g., when (1) testing controls is inefficient or (2) effective controls relevant to the assertions have not been identified. Answer (C) is incorrect. Difficulty, time, and cost do not justify (1) omitting an audit procedure for which no alternative exists or (2) being satisfied with less than persuasive audit evidence. But users of financial statements expect that the auditor will (1) form an opinion within a reasonable time and (2) balance benefit and cost (AU-C 200).

8. To test the effectiveness of controls, an auditor ordinarily selects from a variety of techniques, including

- A. Inquiry and analytical procedures.
- B. Reperformance and observation.
- C. Comparison and confirmation.
- D. Inspection and verification.

Answer (B) is correct.
REQUIRED: The procedures associated with tests of controls.
DISCUSSION: Inquiry alone is not sufficient to test the operating effectiveness of controls. Other audit procedures performed in combination with inquiry may include inspection, recalculation, and reperformance of a control that pertains to an assertion.
Answer (A) is incorrect. Analytical procedures are more closely associated with substantive procedures. Answer (C) is incorrect. Comparison and confirmation are more closely associated with substantive procedures. Answer (D) is incorrect. Verification is more closely associated with substantive procedures.

9. The objective of tests of details of transactions performed as tests of controls is to

- A. Monitor the design and use of entity documents such as prenumbered shipping forms.
- B. Determine whether internal controls have been implemented.
- C. Detect material misstatements in the account balances of the financial statements.
- D. Evaluate whether internal controls operated effectively.

Answer (D) is correct.
REQUIRED: The objective of tests of details of transactions performed as tests of controls.
DISCUSSION: The auditor may use tests of details of transactions concurrently as tests of controls (i.e., as dual-purpose tests). As substantive procedures, their objective is to support relevant assertions or detect material misstatements in the financial statements. As tests of controls, their objective is to evaluate whether a control operated effectively.
Answer (A) is incorrect. The client's controls should monitor the use of entity documents. Answer (B) is incorrect. Determination of whether controls have been implemented is made in conjunction with the auditor's understanding of internal control. Answer (C) is incorrect. The objective of substantive procedures is to support relevant assertions or detect material misstatements in the account balances.

10. When an auditor increases the assessment of the risks of material misstatement because certain controls were determined to be ineffective, the auditor will most likely increase the

- A. Extent of tests of details.
- B. Assessed inherent risk.
- C. Extent of tests of controls.
- D. Acceptable detection risk.

Answer (A) is correct.
REQUIRED: The effect of an increase in the assessment of the RMMs.
DISCUSSION: An auditor should obtain an understanding of internal control to assess the RMMs. The greater (lower) the assessment of the RMMs, the lower (greater) the acceptable detection risk for a given level of audit risk. In turn, the acceptable audit risk affects substantive testing. For example, as the acceptable audit risk decreases, the auditor changes the nature, timing, or extent of substantive procedures to increase the reliability and relevance of the evidence they provide.
Answer (B) is incorrect. Inherent risk is not affected by the auditor's procedures. Answer (C) is incorrect. Once controls are determined to be ineffective, further tests of controls are unnecessary. Answer (D) is incorrect. The acceptable detection risk for a given level of audit risk decreases when the assessment of the RMMs increases.

11. When numerous property and equipment transactions occur during the year, an auditor who assesses the risks of material misstatement at a low level usually performs

- A. Tests of controls and extensive tests of property and equipment balances at the end of the year.
- B. Analytical procedures for current-year property and equipment transactions.
- C. Tests of controls and limited tests of current-year property and equipment transactions.
- D. Analytical procedures for property and equipment balances at the end of the year.

Answer (C) is correct.
REQUIRED: The procedures performed when an auditor assesses the RMMs at a low level.
DISCUSSION: The auditor usually performs tests of controls and substantive procedures (the combined audit approach). The auditor must make decisions about the nature, timing, and extent of substantive procedures that are most responsive to the assessment of the RMMs. These decisions are affected by whether the auditor has tested controls. Thus, the extent of relevant substantive procedures may be reduced when control is found to be effective.
Answer (A) is incorrect. The extent of substantive procedures may be reduced. Answer (B) is incorrect. When numerous transactions are subject to controls, and the RMMs are low, the auditor may rely on tests of controls. Answer (D) is incorrect. When numerous transactions are subject to effective controls, and the RMMs are low, the auditor may rely on tests of controls.

12. A client maintains perpetual inventory records in both quantities and dollars. If the assessment of the risks of material misstatement is high, an auditor will probably

A. Apply gross profit tests to ascertain the reasonableness of the physical counts.

B. Increase the extent of tests of controls relevant to the inventory cycle.

C. Request the client to schedule the physical inventory count at the end of the year.

D. Insist that the client perform physical counts of inventory items several times during the year.

Answer (C) is correct.
 REQUIRED: The auditor's action if the assessment of the RMMs for inventory is high.
 DISCUSSION: If the assessment of the RMMs is high, the acceptable detection risk for a given level of audit risk decreases. The auditor should change the nature, timing, or extent of substantive procedures to increase the reliability and relevance of the evidence they provide. Thus, extending work done at an interim date to year end might be inappropriate. Observation of inventory at year end provides more reliable and relevant evidence.
 Answer (A) is incorrect. Comparing the gross profit test results with those of the prior year provides evidence about sales and cost of goods sold but not inventory. Answer (B) is incorrect. If the auditor believes controls are unlikely to be effective, e.g., because the assessment of the RMMs is high, tests of controls may not be performed. However, the auditor needs to be satisfied that performing only substantive procedures will reduce audit risk to an acceptably low level. Answer (D) is incorrect. The risk is that year-end inventory is misstated.

13. An auditor may compensate for a high assessed risk of material misstatement by

A. Increasing the acceptable level of detection risk.

B. Eliminating tests of controls.

C. Decreasing the preliminary judgment about audit risk.

D. Increasing the extent of substantive analytical procedures.

Answer (D) is correct.
 REQUIRED: The method an auditor may use to compensate for high assessed RMMs.
 DISCUSSION: When designing further audit procedures, the auditor obtains more persuasive evidence the higher the risk assessment. Thus, the auditor may increase the quantity of evidence or obtain more relevant or reliable evidence. Furthermore, the extent of audit procedures generally increases as the RMMs increase. For example, the auditor may increase sample sizes or perform more detailed substantive analytical procedures (AU-C 330).
 Answer (A) is incorrect. The acceptable level of detection risk decreases for a given level of audit risk when the assessment of the RMMs increases. Answer (B) is incorrect. The auditor may need to increase the extent of tests of controls or change their nature or timing. Answer (C) is incorrect. The auditor obtains sufficient appropriate audit evidence to reduce audit risk to an acceptably low level. This risk is not necessarily changed because of a high assessment of the RMMs.

8.3 Assessing Risk in a Computer Environment

14. To obtain evidence that online access controls are properly functioning, an auditor most likely will

A. Create checkpoints at periodic intervals after live data processing to test for unauthorized use of the system.

B. Examine the transaction log to discover whether any transactions were lost or entered twice because of a system malfunction.

C. Enter invalid identification numbers or passwords to ascertain whether the system rejects them.

D. Vouch a random sample of processed transactions to assure proper authorization.

Answer (C) is correct.
 REQUIRED: The procedure an auditor most likely performs to obtain evidence that user online access controls are functioning as designed.
 DISCUSSION: Employees with access authority to process transactions that change records should not also have asset custody or program modification responsibilities. The auditor should determine that password authority is consistent with other assigned responsibilities. The auditor can directly test whether password controls are working by attempting entry into the system by using invalid identifications and passwords.
 Answer (A) is incorrect. Checkpoints are used as a recovery procedure in batch processing applications. Answer (B) is incorrect. Testing for missing or duplicate transactions will not determine whether online access controls were functioning effectively. Answer (D) is incorrect. Unauthorized transactions may be entered by someone having knowledge of valid passwords, etc.

15. To obtain evidence that user identification and password controls are functioning as designed, an auditor should

    A. Review the online transaction log to ascertain whether employees using passwords have access to data files and computer programs.

    B. Examine a sample of password holders and access authority to determine whether they have access authority incompatible with their other responsibilities.

    C. Extract a random sample of processed transactions and ensure that transactions are appropriately authorized.

    D. Observe the file librarian's activities to discover whether other systems personnel are permitted to operate computer equipment without restriction.

Answer (B) is correct.
    REQUIRED: The procedure an auditor should perform to obtain evidence that user identification and password controls are functioning as designed.
    DISCUSSION: Employees with access authority to process transactions that change records should not also have asset custody or program modification responsibilities. The auditor should determine that password authority is consistent with other assigned responsibilities. In addition, the auditor can directly test whether password controls are working by attempting entry into the system by using invalid identifications and passwords.
    Answer (A) is incorrect. Password assignment properly provides employees with access to files and programs. Answer (C) is incorrect. Testing transactions for proper authorization does not ensure that user identification controls were functioning effectively. Answer (D) is incorrect. The file librarian oversees the physical protection of files, programs, and documentation, not the operation of computer equipment.

16. Which of the following computer-assisted auditing techniques allows fictitious and real transactions to be processed together without the knowledge of client operating personnel?

    A. Integrated test facility (ITF).

    B. Input controls matrix.

    C. Parallel simulation.

    D. Data entry monitor.

Answer (A) is correct.
    REQUIRED: The method that processes fictitious and actual transactions without the knowledge of client personnel.
    DISCUSSION: The ITF or minicompany technique is a development of the test data method. It permits dummy transactions to be processed at the same time as live transactions but requires additional programming to ensure that programs will recognize the specially coded test data. The test transactions may be submitted without the computer operators' knowledge.
    Answer (B) is incorrect. Input controls matrix is not a method typically used by auditors to test a client's computer systems. Answer (C) is incorrect. Parallel simulation reprocesses only real, not fictitious, transactions. Answer (D) is incorrect. Data entry monitor is not a method typically used by auditors to test a client's computer systems.

17. Which of the following statements is **not** true of the test data approach to testing an accounting system?

    A. Test data are processed by the client's computer programs under the auditor's control.

    B. The test data need consist of only those valid and invalid conditions that interest the auditor.

    C. Only one transaction of each type need be tested.

    D. The test data must consist of all possible valid and invalid conditions.

Answer (D) is correct.
    REQUIRED: The false statement about the test data approach.
    DISCUSSION: The test data approach includes preparation of dummy transactions by the auditor. These transactions are processed by the client's computer programs under the auditor's control. The test data consist of one transaction for each valid and invalid condition that interests the auditor. Consequently, the test data need not consist of all possible valid and invalid conditions.
    Answer (A) is incorrect. The test data are processed by the client's computer programs under the control of the auditor. Answer (B) is incorrect. Only those controls deemed important to the auditor need be tested. Answer (C) is incorrect. The computer processes all similar transactions in the same way. Accordingly, only one transaction needs to be tested to determine whether a control is working effectively.

18. A client maintains a large data center where access is limited to authorized employees. How may an auditor best determine the effectiveness of this control activity?

    A. Inspect the policy manual establishing this control activity.

    B. Ask the chief technology officer about known problems.

    C. Observe whether the data center is monitored.

    D. Obtain a list of current data center employees.

Answer (C) is correct.
    REQUIRED: The best procedure to determine the effectiveness of a control activity.
    DISCUSSION: Physically observing that the data center is being monitored provides direct evidence that the control is in place and is being utilized effectively. The auditor will be able to see, first hand, if the control is preventing unauthorized access.
    Answer (A) is incorrect. Inspecting the policy manual will ensure that a control has been established but will not test the effectiveness of this control. Answer (B) is incorrect. Inquiry will help the auditor understand the control but will not test its effectiveness. Answer (D) is incorrect. Obtaining a list of current employees does not provide evidence of who has been accessing the data center.

19. In parallel simulation, actual client data are reprocessed using an auditor software program. An advantage of using parallel simulation, instead of performing tests of controls without a computer, is that

    A. The test includes all types of transaction errors and exceptions that may be encountered.

    B. The client's computer personnel do not know when the data are being tested.

    C. There is no risk of creating potentially material errors in the client's data.

    D. The size of the sample can be greatly expanded at relatively little additional cost.

Answer (D) is correct.
    REQUIRED: The advantage of parallel simulation.
    DISCUSSION: Parallel simulation uses a controlled program to reprocess sets of client transactions and compares those results with those of the client. The primary disadvantages are the initial cost of obtaining the software and the need for coordination with client personnel to gain access to transactions. However, the auditors have the freedom to process transactions (1) at their convenience, (2) using their own equipment, and (3) taking as long as necessary. Thus, the auditors can greatly increase the sample size at relatively little marginal cost.
    Answer (A) is incorrect. Parallel simulation tests for errors and exceptions that occur only as a result of the software being tested. Answer (B) is incorrect. Whether the computer personnel know when the data are tested is not a concern when the test is at the auditor's own facilities. Answer (C) is incorrect. Use of actual data poses some risk of contamination.

20. The following flowchart depicts

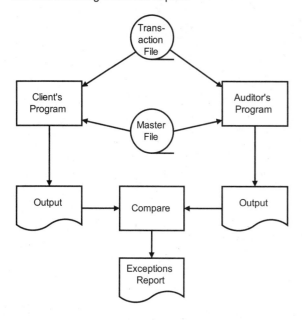

    A. Program code checking.

    B. Parallel simulation.

    C. Integrated test facility.

    D. Test data approach.

Answer (B) is correct.
    REQUIRED: The audit method depicted by the flowchart.
    DISCUSSION: Parallel simulation is a test of the controls in a client's application program. An auditor-developed program is used to process actual client data and compare the output and the exceptions report with those of the client's application program. If the client's programmed controls are operating effectively, the two sets of results should be reconcilable.
    Answer (A) is incorrect. Program code checking refers to checking the client's application program code to determine if it contains the appropriate controls. Answer (C) is incorrect. An ITF introduces dummy records into the client's files and then processes dummy transactions to update the records. The auditor can test the controls by including various types of transactions to be processed. Answer (D) is incorrect. Using the test data approach, the auditor prepares a set of dummy transactions specifically designed to test the control activities.

STUDY UNIT NINE
INTERNAL CONTROL COMMUNICATIONS AND REPORTS

(21 pages of outline)

This study unit applies to various auditor communications and reports, most involving internal control. During the conduct of an audit, the auditor may observe control deficiencies. If so, the auditor has a responsibility to communicate significant deficiencies and material weaknesses to management and those charged with governance (AU-C 265, *Communicating Internal Control Related Matters Identified in an Audit*). Other issues relating to the audit also should be communicated to management and those charged with governance. Some of these issues are closely related to internal control, but others relate to the audit in general (AU-C 260, *The Auditor's Communication with Those Charged with Governance* and AS 1301, *Communications with Audit Committees*). Public companies (issuers) are required by the Sarbanes-Oxley Act of 2002 to provide a management assessment of the effectiveness of internal control over financial reporting in annual reports. The PCAOB's AS 2201, *An Audit of Internal Control over Financial Reporting That Is Integrated with an Audit of Financial Statements*, provides guidance on the required process and reporting. For example, it requires the auditor to express an opinion, or disclaim an opinion, on internal control. For other entities (nonissuers), the CPA may be engaged to provide a report on the effectiveness of an entity's internal control over financial reporting. This service and the reports issued are governed by the AICPA's AU-C 940, *An Audit of an Entity's Internal Control over Financial Reporting That Is Integrated with an Audit of Its Financial Statements*. The CPA may be either a user or a preparer of a report prepared in accordance with AU-C 402, *Audit Considerations Relating to an Entity Using a Service Organization*, and AT 801, *Reporting on Controls at a Service Organization*. Such a report may affect the user CPA's assessment of a client's risks of material misstatement.

9.1 COMMUNICATING INTERNAL CONTROL RELATED MATTERS IDENTIFIED IN AN AUDIT

1. The financial statement auditor is **not** required to perform procedures specifically to identify deficiencies in internal control or to express an opinion on internal control.

2. But, in each audit, the auditor should report **significant deficiencies** and **material weaknesses** in internal control over financial reporting that have been identified.

3. The communication should be **in writing** and directed to **management** and **those charged with governance** (e.g., a board of directors).

4. A **deficiency** in internal control exists when the **design or operation** of a control does not allow management or employees, in the normal course of their assigned functions, to prevent, or detect and correct, misstatements on a timely basis.

5. A **significant deficiency** is a deficiency, or combination of deficiencies, in internal control that is less severe than a material weakness but that merits attention by those charged with governance.

6. A **material weakness** is a deficiency, or combination of deficiencies, in internal control that results in a **reasonable possibility** that a **material misstatement** of the financial statements will not be prevented or timely detected and corrected.

    a.   A reasonable possibility means that the likelihood of the event is **more than remote**.

7. **Evaluating Control Deficiencies**

a. The auditor should evaluate each deficiency to determine whether, individually or in combination, it is a significant deficiency or a material weakness. The **severity of a deficiency** depends on

1) The magnitude of the potential misstatement and
2) Whether a reasonable possibility exists that the controls will fail.

b. Severity does not depend on actual occurrence of a misstatement.

c. The **magnitude** of a misstatement depends on, among other things,

1) The financial statement amounts or transactions involved and
2) The activity in the relevant balance or transaction class.

d. The maximum **overstatement** ordinarily is the recorded amount, but the **understatement** is unlimited.

1) The auditor need not quantify the **probability** of misstatement.
2) A small misstatement often is more likely than a large misstatement.

e. **Risk factors** may indicate whether a reasonable possibility exists that one or more deficiencies will result in a misstatement. The following are examples of risk factors:

1) Accounts, transaction classes, disclosures, and assertions involved (e.g., overstatement of revenues and understatement of expenses)
2) Cause and frequency of exceptions
3) Susceptibility of the related asset or liability to loss or fraud
4) Degree of judgment required to determine the amount involved
5) Relationship of the control with other controls
6) Interaction among deficiencies
7) Possible consequences of the deficiency
8) Importance to financial reporting

f. Controls may operate individually or in combination, e.g., manual and IT controls over a significant account, disclosure, or assertion. Thus, a deficiency by itself may not be significant.

1) But a combination of deficiencies affecting a significant account, etc., may increase the RMMs sufficiently to create a deficiency that should be communicated.

g. **Indicators of material weaknesses** include the following:

1) Identification of any fraud by senior management
2) Restatement of financial statements to correct a material misstatement due to fraud or error
3) Identification by the auditor of a material misstatement that would not have been detected by internal control
4) Ineffective oversight of financial reporting and internal control by those charged with governance

h. The auditor considers whether prudent officials, having the same knowledge, would agree with the auditor that one or more deficiencies are **not** a material weakness.

i. The following are examples of possible deficiencies, significant deficiencies, or material weaknesses related to **design**:

1) Inadequate design of internal control over financial statement preparation
2) Inadequate design of controls over a significant account or process
3) Inadequate documentation of the components of internal control
4) Insufficient control consciousness
5) Absent or inadequate segregation of duties or controls

6) An ineffective control environment, risk assessment process, or response to significant risks over the safeguarding of assets

7) Inadequate design of IT general and application controls

8) Employees or management who lack the proper qualifications and training

9) Inadequate design of monitoring controls

10) The absence of an internal process to report deficiencies on a timely basis

j. The following are examples of deficiencies, significant deficiencies, or material weaknesses related to **operational failures**:

1) Failures in the operation of effectively designed controls over a significant account or process

2) Failure of the information and communication component of internal control to provide timely, complete, and accurate information

3) Failure of controls designed to safeguard assets

4) Failure to perform reconciliations of significant accounts

5) Undue bias or lack of objectivity by those responsible for accounting decisions

6) Misrepresentation by client personnel to the auditor

7) Management override of controls

8) Failure of an application control caused by deficient design or operation of an IT general control

9) An excessive observed deviation rate in a test of controls

8. **Communication**

a. The auditor should **communicate in writing significant deficiencies** and **material weaknesses** to management and those charged with governance.

1) The communication also should describe these conditions and explain their potential effects.

b. The communication is best made by the **audit report release date**, but **no later than 60 days** after.

c. Communication of **significant and urgent matters** during the audit need not be in writing. But the auditor ultimately should communicate significant deficiencies and material weaknesses in writing even if they have been corrected.

d. Management or those charged with governance may explicitly decide, e.g., because of the cost, not to correct significant deficiencies or material weaknesses. However, the auditor should communicate them regardless of such decisions.

1) If the communication was made in a prior audit, it should be repeated in the current audit if the condition has not been remedied.

e. The auditor should communicate to management other deficiencies that merit attention but are not significant deficiencies or material weaknesses. This communication may be made orally or in writing.

f. The **written communication** should

1) State that the purpose of the audit was to express an opinion on the financial statements.

2) State that the audit considered internal control to design audit procedures, not to express an opinion, and that the auditor is not expressing an opinion on the effectiveness of internal control.

3) State that the auditor's consideration of internal control was **not** designed to identify all deficiencies that might be significant deficiencies or material weaknesses.

4) Include the definition of a material weakness and, if relevant, the definition of a significant deficiency.

5) Describe significant deficiencies and material weaknesses.
6) Explain the potential effects of each significant deficiency and material weakness.
7) Restrict the use of the communication to (a) management, (b) those charged with governance, and (c) others within the entity (and possibly governmental agencies).

EXAMPLE -- Communications of Significant Deficiencies and Material Weaknesses

To Management and the Board of Directors:

In planning and performing our audit of the financial statements of ABC Company (the "Company") as of and for the year ended December 31, Year 1, in accordance with auditing standards generally accepted in the United States of America, we considered the Company's internal control over financial reporting (internal control) as a basis for designing auditing procedures that are appropriate in the circumstances for the purpose of expressing our opinion on the financial statements, but not for the purpose of expressing an opinion on the effectiveness of the Company's internal control. Accordingly, we do not express an opinion on the effectiveness of the Company's internal control.

Our consideration of internal control was for the limited purpose described in the preceding paragraph and was not designed to identify all deficiencies in internal control that might be *[significant deficiencies or material weaknesses]* and therefore, *[significant deficiencies or material weaknesses]* may exist that were not identified. However, as discussed below, we identified certain deficiencies in internal control that we consider to be *[material weaknesses or significant deficiencies]*.

A deficiency in internal control exists when the design or operation of a control does not allow management or employees, in the normal course of performing their assigned functions, to prevent, or detect and correct, misstatements on a timely basis. A material weakness is a deficiency, or a combination of deficiencies, in internal control, such that there is a reasonable possibility that a material misstatement of the entity's financial statements will not be prevented, or detected and corrected, on a timely basis. *[We consider the following deficiencies in the Company's internal control to be material weaknesses:]*

[Describe the material weaknesses that were identified and explain their potential effects.]

[A significant deficiency is a deficiency, or a combination of deficiencies, in internal control, that is less severe than a material weakness, yet important enough to merit attention by those charged with governance. We consider the following deficiencies in the Company's internal control to be significant deficiencies:]

[Describe the significant deficiencies that were identified and explain their potential effects.]

This communication is intended solely for the information and use of management, *[identify the body or individuals charged with governance]*, others within the organization, *[identify any governmental authorities]* and is not intended to be and should not be used by anyone other than these specified parties.

Auditor's signature
Auditor's city and state
Date

---

g. A client may ask the auditor to issue a written communication for the client stating that **no material weaknesses** were identified. A communication similar to the example above is appropriate, with the following paragraph added:

EXAMPLE

Our consideration of internal control was for the limited purpose described in the first paragraph and was not designed to identify all deficiencies in internal control that might be material weaknesses. Given these limitations, during our audit we did not identify any deficiencies in internal control that we consider to be material weaknesses. However, material weaknesses may exist that have not been identified.

---

h. An auditor should **not** issue a written communication stating that **no significant deficiencies** were identified.
i. Management may wish to prepare a written response to the auditor's communication. If one is included in the communication document, the auditor should disclaim an opinion on the response.

Stop and review! You have completed the outline for this subunit. Study multiple-choice questions 1 through 6 beginning on page 211.

9.2 THE AUDITOR'S COMMUNICATION WITH THOSE CHARGED WITH GOVERNANCE

1. Those charged with governance are responsible for oversight of the entity's strategic direction and accountability, including the **financial reporting process**. The **board of directors** and the **audit committee** are typical governance bodies. In smaller organizations, owners or management may be those charged with governance.

    a. **Two-way communication** is expected and should provide those charged with governance with information about matters relevant to their responsibilities, including an overview of the audit process and of the auditor's responsibilities.

        1) It also should allow the auditor to obtain information relevant to the audit.

    b. Communication may be either **oral or in writing** and should be **documented**.

        1) The auditor communicates significant findings from the audit in writing when (s)he judges that oral communication is inadequate.

            a) A written communication should indicate that it is for the **sole use** of those charged with governance.

    c. Communication should be on a **timely basis** to enable those charged with governance to meet their responsibilities for oversight of financial reporting. For example, communications about planning should be early in the engagement.

    d. It may be appropriate for **management** to communicate certain matters to those charged with governance, and the auditor should be satisfied that such communication has occurred.

        1) Many matters are discussed with management during the audit. But certain discussions may be inappropriate, e.g., those related to management's integrity.

    e. Before communicating with a subgroup (e.g., an audit committee) of those charged with governance, the auditor may consider such matters as (1) the responsibilities of the subgroup and the governing body, (2) the nature of the matter, (3) legal or regulatory requirements, (4) whether the subgroup can (a) act on the information and (b) provide further information and explanations the auditor may need, and (5) whether the auditor is aware of potential conflicts of interest between the subgroup and other members of the governing body.

2. **Matters to be communicated** include (a) the auditor's responsibilities in accordance with GAAS, (b) an overview of the audit, and (c) significant and relevant findings.

3. **Auditor's Responsibilities under GAAS**

    a. The auditor may provide a copy of the **engagement letter** to those charged with governance (Study Unit 3, Subunit 1, includes a sample engagement letter). Among other things, the engagement letter states that

        1) The auditor is responsible for forming and expressing an opinion about whether the financial statements are presented fairly.

        2) The audit does not relieve management or those charged with governance of their responsibilities for fair reporting.

4. **Planned Scope and Timing of the Audit**

    a. An **overview** should be provided, but it should in no way compromise the effectiveness of the audit. The auditor should never discuss details of procedures to be used. Issues to be addressed include

        1) How the auditor proposes to address the risks of material misstatement, whether due to fraud or error;

        2) Issues related to internal control and the internal audit function; and

        3) Materiality in planning and performing the audit.

5. **Qualitative Aspects of the Entity's Significant Accounting Practices**

    a. The auditor should inform those charged with governance about the following:

    1) The auditor's views on the entity's significant accounting practices, including policies, estimates, and disclosures

    2) The reasons that the entity should not use a significant accounting practice that is acceptable under the applicable reporting framework

    3) Management's process for making sensitive accounting estimates (including fair value estimates) and the basis for the auditor's conclusions about their reasonableness

    4) Management's selection of, changes in, and application of significant accounting policies

    5) Management's methods used to account for significant, unusual transactions

    6) The effects of significant accounting policies in controversial or emerging areas that lack authoritative guidance or consensus, such as revenue recognition, off-balance-sheet financing, and accounting for equity investments

6. Those charged with governance should be informed of **significant difficulties** encountered in dealing with management, such as delays in providing required information and unnecessary time constraints on the audit. Other significant problems may include unavailability of information and management-imposed restrictions.

7. **Uncorrected misstatements**, other than those not accumulated by the auditor because they are clearly trivial, and their effect on the opinion should be communicated to those charged with governance.

    a. The auditor also should communicate

    1) The effect of uncorrected misstatements from prior periods on the statements as a whole and relevant transaction classes, etc.;

    2) Material, corrected misstatements communicated to management; and

    3) Written representations requested by the auditor.

    b. The auditor may communicate immaterial, corrected misstatements that recur frequently and may indicate a bias in the statements.

    c. The auditor should discuss with those charged with governance the implications of not correcting misstatements.

8. Management and the auditor may disagree about (a) the application of accounting principles, (b) the basis for accounting estimates, (c) the scope of the audit, (d) disclosures, and (e) the auditor's report.

    a. The auditor and those charged with governance should discuss any disagreements about matters significant to the statements or the audit report.

9. When the auditor is aware of consultations between management and other accountants, (s)he should communicate to those charged with governance his or her views about the significant matters involved.

10. The auditor should communicate to those charged with governance discussions with management about significant matters such as (a) business conditions affecting the entity, (b) plans and strategies affecting the RMMs, (c) the initial or recurring retention of the auditors, and (d) the application of accounting principles.

11. Discussions may be appropriate about circumstances or relationships (e.g., financial interests, business or family relationships, or nonaudit services) that, in the auditor's professional judgment,

    a. May reasonably bear on **independence** and

    b. Were given significant consideration by the auditor in reaching the conclusion that independence has not been impaired.

12. **Sarbanes-Oxley Act of 2002**

    a. The act requires the auditor to report the following to those charged with governance:

        1) All critical accounting policies and practices to be used

        2) All material alternative treatments of financial information within GAAP discussed with management

        3) Ramifications of the use of alternative disclosures and treatments

        4) The treatment preferred by the auditor

Stop and review! You have completed the outline for this subunit. Study multiple-choice questions 7 through 12 beginning on page 213.

9.3 REPORTING ON AN ENTITY'S INTERNAL CONTROL

1. Both the AICPA (AU-C 940) and the PCAOB (AS 2201) have issued an auditing standard titled, *An Audit of Internal Control over Financial Reporting that is Integrated with an Audit of Financial Statements*. These standards are very similar. Each provides guidance regarding the audit of and reports on internal control over financial reporting (ICFR).

    a. The PCAOB's standard provides guidance for the audits of accelerated-filer **issuers** (public companies) required to obtain an opinion on the effectiveness of ICFR. (An accelerated filer is a company reporting to the SEC with market equity of at least $75 million).

    b. The AICPA's standard provides guidance for the audits of **nonissuers** (nonpublic entities) that may request to have an opinion expressed on the effectiveness of ICFR.

    c. An audit of ICFR must be integrated with the audit of the financial statements.

    d. Differences between AU-C 940 and AS 2201 are noted farther in the outline.

2. Every nonissuer who requires an audit of ICFR and every issuer regardless of whether an audit of ICFR is required must provide **management's written assessment** of the design and effectiveness of ICFR.

    a. The assessment should be performed using suitable **control criteria**, such as Internal Control – Integrated Framework published by the Committee of Sponsoring Organizations (COSO). The components of ICFR are outlined in Study Unit 5, Subunit 2.

    b. The assessment is to be included in the annual report prepared by an **issuer**.

    c. The same control criteria used by management should be used by the auditor in the audit of ICFR.

3. The objectives of an audit of ICFR are to

    a. Obtain reasonable assurance about whether material weaknesses exist as of the date specified in management's assessment about the effectiveness of ICFR,

    b. Express an opinion on the effectiveness of ICFR in a written report, and

    c. Communicate findings to management and those charged with governance.

4. The auditor must plan and perform the audit to obtain sufficient appropriate evidence to provide **reasonable assurance** that no **material weaknesses** exist in ICFR at the date of management's assessment.

    a. The auditor expresses an opinion directly on the effectiveness of ICFR.

        1) If a material weakness exists, the auditor expresses an **adverse opinion**.

        2) If management's assessment does not include an existing material weakness, the audit report is modified to state that the weakness was not included in the assessment.

    b. The auditor also may express an opinion on management's assessment.

5.   **Integrating the Audits**

    a.   The audit of ICFR should be integrated with the audit of the financial statements. The integrated audit should achieve the objectives of both.

        1)   The auditor should design **tests of controls** to obtain sufficient appropriate evidence to support the auditor's opinion on ICFR at a moment in time (e.g., at year end) and taken as a whole (i.e., addressing the effectiveness of selected controls over all relevant assertions).

        2)   The auditor should obtain evidence that ICFR has operated effectively for a sufficient period of time, which may be less than the entire period (ordinarily 1 year) covered by the entity's financial statements.

        3)   The audit of ICFR typically involves testing controls not tested in a financial statement audit.

6.   **Planning the Audit**

    a.   The integrated audit should be properly planned. The auditor should evaluate how the following affect the examination of ICFR:

        1)   Knowledge of ICFR obtained during other engagements or from the predecessor's working papers

        2)   Industry issues, such as financial reporting practices, economic conditions, laws and regulations, and technological changes

        3)   Matters related to the business, e.g., operating characteristics, capital structure, and organization

        4)   Recent changes in the entity's operations or ICFR

        5)   Preliminary judgments about materiality, risk, and other factors relating to the determination of material weaknesses

        6)   Control deficiencies previously communicated to those charged with governance

        7)   Legal or regulatory matters

        8)   The type and extent of available evidence related to the effectiveness of ICFR

        9)   Preliminary judgments about ICFR

        10)   Public information relevant to the likelihood of material misstatements and the effectiveness of ICFR

        11)   The relative complexity of operations

        12)   Knowledge about risks obtained from the client acceptance and retention evaluation

7.   A direct relationship exists between the degree of risk that a material weakness could exist and the audit effort made regarding the risk.

    a.   Risk assessment underlies the audit, including the determination of (1) significant accounts and disclosures, (2) relevant assertions, (3) controls to test, and (4) the evidence necessary to assess the effectiveness of a given control.

    b.   When an audit of ICFR is integrated with an audit, the same risk assessment process supports both engagements.

        1)   But the auditor must test the effectiveness of the design and operation of a control before concluding on its effectiveness.

8.   The size and complexity of the company, its business processes, and business units may affect the way in which the company achieves many of its **control objectives**. Size and complexity also affect risks and related controls.

    a.   Thus, **scaling** is an extension of the risk-based approach.

9. **Addressing the Risk of Fraud**

   a. The auditor should (1) consider the results of the fraud risk assessment and (2) evaluate (a) whether controls sufficiently address the identified risks of material fraud and (b) controls over the risk of management override. The following controls address these risks:

      1) Controls over significant, unusual transactions, particularly those that result in late or unusual journal entries
      2) Controls over journal entries and adjustments made in the period-end financial reporting process
      3) Controls over related party transactions
      4) Controls related to significant management estimates
      5) Controls that mitigate incentives for, and pressures on, management to falsify or inappropriately manage financial results

10. **Using the Work of Others**

    a. The auditor may use the work performed by, or receive direct assistance from, internal auditors, company personnel, and third parties working under the direction of management or the audit committee that provides evidence about the effectiveness of ICFR.

    b. The auditor should assess the competence and objectivity of the persons whose work the auditor plans to use. The higher the degree of competence and objectivity, the greater use the auditor may make of the work.

11. The same **materiality** considerations apply in the audit of ICFR as in planning the audit of the annual financial statements.

12. **Using a Top-Down Approach**

    a. The auditor begins an integrated audit at the financial statement level by understanding overall risks to ICFR and focusing on **entity-level controls**. (S)he then performs procedures on significant classes of transactions, account balances, disclosures, and their relevant assertions. The following are examples of entity-level controls:

       1) The control environment
       2) Controls over management override
       3) Monitoring of the results of operations
       4) Controls over the period-end financial reporting process
       5) Monitoring of other controls, including activities of internal auditing, the audit committee, and self-assessment programs
       6) The risk assessment process
       7) Policies that address significant business control and risk management practices

    b. The auditor should evaluate the **control environment** by assessing whether

       1) Management's philosophy and operating style promote effective ICFR.
       2) Sound integrity and ethical values, particularly of management, are developed and understood.
       3) The board or audit committee understands and exercises oversight responsibility over financial reporting and ICFR.

    c.   The auditor should evaluate the **period-end financial reporting process**, including procedures

        1)   Used to enter transaction totals into the general ledger;

        2)   Related to the selection and application of accounting policies;

        3)   Used to initiate, authorize, record, and process journal entries;

        4)   Used to record recurring and nonrecurring adjustments to the annual and quarterly financial statements; and

        5)   For preparing annual and quarterly financial statements and related disclosures.

13. **Identifying Significant Classes of Transactions, Account Balances, Disclosures, and Their Relevant Assertions**

    a.   The following are risk factors related to significant classes of transactions, account balances, and disclosures:

        1)   Size and composition of the account

        2)   Susceptibility to misstatement due to fraud or error

        3)   Volume of activity, complexity, and homogeneity of the transactions

        4)   Nature of the account or disclosure

        5)   Accounting and reporting complexities

        6)   Exposure to losses in the account

        7)   Possibility of significant contingent liabilities arising from the activities reflected in the account or disclosure

        8)   Existence of related party transactions in the account

        9)   Changes from the prior period or disclosure characteristics

14. A **walkthrough** (following transactions through a process) often is an effective way of achieving the following objectives related to understanding the likely **sources of potential misstatement**:

    a.   Understanding the flow of transactions related to relevant assertions, including how transactions are initiated, authorized, processed, and recorded

    b.   Identifying the points within the company's processes at which a material misstatement, including a misstatement due to fraud, could arise

    c.   Identifying the controls that management has implemented to address these potential misstatements

    d.   Identifying the controls that management has implemented for the prevention or timely detection of unauthorized acquisition, use, or disposition of assets

15. **Testing Controls**

    a.   **Evaluating Design Effectiveness**

        1)   The auditor should determine whether controls, if they are operated as prescribed by persons with the necessary authority and competence to perform them effectively, (a) satisfy the control objectives and (b) can effectively prevent, or detect and correct, fraud or error that could result in material misstatements in the financial statements.

        2)   Procedures include (a) inquiry of appropriate personnel, (b) observation of operations, and (c) inspection of relevant documentation. Walkthroughs that include these procedures ordinarily are sufficient to evaluate design effectiveness.

b. **Testing Operating Effectiveness**

1) The auditor should determine whether (a) a control is operating as designed and (b) the person performing the control possesses the necessary authority and competence to perform the control effectively.

2) Procedures the auditor performs to test operating effectiveness include a mix of (a) inquiry of appropriate personnel, (b) observation of operations, (c) inspection of relevant documentation, and (d) reperformance of the control.

c. **Relationship of Risk to the Evidence to Be Obtained**

1) More risk requires more testing and more competent evidence.

2) Generally, a conclusion that a control is not operating effectively can be supported by less evidence than is necessary to support a conclusion that a control is operating effectively.

3) Different combinations of the **nature, timing, and extent of testing** may provide sufficient evidence.

   a) **Nature** of tests of controls. The following tests are presented in order of the evidence that they ordinarily produce, from least to most: (1) inquiry, (2) observation, (3) inspection of relevant documentation, and (4) reperformance of a control. Inquiry alone does not provide sufficient evidence to support a conclusion about the effectiveness of a control.

   b) **Timing** of tests of controls. Testing controls over a greater period of time provides more evidence of the effectiveness of controls than testing over a shorter period of time. Moreover, testing closer to the date of management's assessment provides more evidence than testing earlier in the year.

   c) **Extent** of tests of controls. The more extensively a control is tested, the greater the evidence obtained from that test.

   d) **Roll-forward procedures.** To roll forward the results of interim work, the auditor should consider (1) the specific controls, their associated risks, and the test results; (2) the sufficiency of evidence obtained at the interim date; (3) the length of the remaining period; and (4) the possibility of changes.

16. **Evaluating Identified Deficiencies**

a. A **control deviation** occurs when a control does not operate as designed. Control deviations are evaluated when determining whether a **deficiency** in ICFR exists. Effective ICFR cannot provide absolute assurance of achieving the entity's control objectives. Thus, an individual control does not necessarily have to operate without any deviation to achieve the entity's control objectives and to be considered effective.

b. The auditor should evaluate each deficiency in ICFR to determine whether, individually or in combination, they are **significant deficiencies or material weaknesses** as of the date of management's assessment.

c. The severity of a deficiency, or a combination of deficiencies, in ICFR depends on (1) the **magnitude of the potential misstatement** resulting from the deficiency or deficiencies and (2) whether a **reasonable possibility** exists that the entity's controls will fail to prevent, or detect and correct, a misstatement.

d. In evaluating the magnitude of the potential misstatement, the maximum amount by which an account balance or total of transactions can be overstated is generally the recorded amount. But understatements could be larger.

e. Although compensating controls can mitigate the effects of a deficiency in ICFR, they do not eliminate the deficiency.

The terms for deficiency, significant deficiency, and material weakness are those used consistently in other sections of the AICPA and PCAOB standards, including in government auditing standards. Knowing the following definitions is important because they are popular topics on the CPA exam:

A **deficiency** exists when the design or operation of a control does not allow management or employees, in the normal course of performing their assigned functions, to prevent, or detect and correct, misstatements on a timely basis,

A **significant deficiency** is a deficiency, or a combination of deficiencies, in ICFR that is less severe than a material weakness yet important enough to merit attention by those charged with governance,

A **material weakness** is a deficiency, or a combination of deficiencies, in ICFR such that a reasonable possibility exists that a material misstatement of the entity's financial statements will not be prevented, or detected and corrected, on a timely basis.

    f.   The auditor is not required to search for deficiencies that, individually or in combination, are **less severe than a material weakness**.

    g.   The **severity of a deficiency** does not depend on whether a misstatement actually has occurred but rather on whether a reasonable possibility exists that the controls will fail to prevent, or detect and correct, a misstatement.

17.   The following are **indicators of material weaknesses** in ICFR:

    a.   Identification of fraud, whether or not material, on the part of senior management

    b.   Restatement of previously issued financial statements to reflect the correction of a material misstatement

    c.   Identification by the auditor of a material misstatement in the current period in circumstances that indicate that the misstatement would not have been detected by ICFR

    d.   Ineffective oversight by the audit committee of external financial reporting and ICFR

18.   **Forming an Opinion**

    a.   The auditor should **form an opinion** on the effectiveness of ICFR by evaluating evidence obtained from all sources, including (1) the auditor's testing of controls, (2) misstatements detected during the financial statement audit, and (3) any identified control deficiencies.

    b.   The auditor may obtain knowledge about conditions that did not exist as of the date of management's assessment but arose subsequent to that date and before the release of the auditor's report. If this information has a material effect on the entity's ICFR, the auditor should include in the auditor's report

        1)   An emphasis-of-matter paragraph directing the reader's attention to the subsequently discovered fact and its effects as disclosed in management's report or

        2)   An other-matter paragraph describing the subsequently discovered fact and its effects.

    c.   After forming an opinion on the effectiveness of the entity's ICFR, the auditor should evaluate management's assessment report, which will accompany the auditor's report. The auditor should determine whether it contains

        1)   A statement regarding management's responsibility for ICFR;

        2)   An identification of ICFR as the subject matter of the audit;

        3)   An identification of the criteria against which ICFR is measured;

        4)   Management's assessment about ICFR;

        5)   A description of the material weakness(es), if any; and

        6)   The date as of which management's assessment about ICFR is made.

    d.   If the auditor determines that any required element of management's report is incomplete or improperly presented, the auditor should request management to revise its report.

19. The auditor should obtain **written representations** from management

    a. Acknowledging management's responsibility for establishing and maintaining effective ICFR

    b. Stating that management has performed an evaluation and made an assessment of the effectiveness of the ICFR and specifying the control criteria (e.g., the COSO model)

    c. Stating that management did not use the auditor's procedures performed during the audits of ICFR or the financial statements as part of the basis for management's assessment of the effectiveness of ICFR

    d. Stating management's conclusion about the effectiveness of ICFR based on the control criteria at a specified date

    e. Stating that management has disclosed to the auditor all deficiencies in ICFR identified in its evaluation

    f. Describing any material fraud and any other fraud involving senior management or management or other employees who have a significant role in ICFR

    g. Stating whether control deficiencies identified and communicated to the audit committee during previous engagements have been resolved

    h. Stating whether, subsequent to the date being reported on, any changes occurred in ICFR or other factors that might significantly affect ICFR

20. **Communicating Certain Matters**

    a. The auditor should communicate, in writing, to management and those charged with governance all **material weaknesses** and **significant deficiencies** identified during the audit. The communication should include those remediated during the audit and those previously communicated but not remediated.

    b. The written communication should be made prior to the release date of the auditor's report.

    c. The auditor should communicate to management, in writing, **all deficiencies** in ICFR in addition to material weaknesses and significant deficiencies no later than 60 days following the report release date.

    d. Because the integrated audit does not provide the auditor with reasonable assurance that the auditor has identified all deficiencies less severe than a material weakness, the auditor should not issue a report stating that no such deficiencies were identified during the integrated audit.

21. **Reporting on Internal Control**

    a. The report may be a separate report, or it may be combined with the opinion on the financial statements.

    b. The auditor should date the audit report no earlier than the date on which the auditor has obtained sufficient competent evidence to support the auditor's opinion. The dates of the report on the financial statements and the report on ICFR should be the same.

    c. The auditor's report on an audit of ICFR for a nonissuer includes the following elements:

        1) A title that includes the word "**independent**"

        2) An addressee as required by the circumstances of the engagement

        3) An introductory paragraph that includes the following:

            a) Identification of the entity audited

            b) A statement that the entity's ICFR has been audited

            c) Identification of the "as of" date

            d) Identification of the criteria against which ICFR is measured

4) A section headed **Management's Responsibility for Internal Control Over Financial Reporting** that includes the following:

   a) A statement that management is responsible for designing, implementing, and maintaining effective ICFR

   b) A statement that management is responsible for its assessment about the effectiveness of ICFR

   c) A reference to management's report on ICFR

5) A section headed **Auditor's Responsibility** that includes the following:

   a) A statement that the auditor's responsibility is to express an opinion on the entity's ICFR based on the audit

   b) A statement that the audit was conducted in accordance with auditing standards generally accepted in the United States of America

   c) A statement that such standards require that the auditor plan and perform the audit to obtain reasonable assurance about whether effective ICFR was maintained in all material respects

   d) A description of the audit stating that (1) an audit of ICFR involves performing procedures to obtain audit evidence about whether a material weakness exists; (2) the procedures selected depend on the auditor's judgment, including the assessment of the risks that a material weakness exists; and (3) an audit includes obtaining an understanding of ICFR and testing and evaluating the design and operating effectiveness of ICFR based on the assessed risk

   e) A statement about whether the auditor believes that the audit evidence the auditor has obtained is sufficient and appropriate to provide a basis for the audit opinion

6) A section headed **Definition and Inherent Limitations of Internal Control Over Financial Reporting** that includes the following:

   a) A definition of ICFR (the auditor should use the same description of the entity's ICFR as management uses in its report)

   b) A paragraph stating that because of inherent limitations, ICFR may not prevent, or detect and correct, misstatements and that projections of any assessment of effectiveness to future periods are subject to the risk that controls may become inadequate because of changes in conditions, or that the degree of compliance with the policies or procedures may deteriorate

7) A section headed **Opinion** that includes the auditor's opinion on whether the entity maintained, in all material respects, effective ICFR as of the specified date, based on the criteria

8) The manual or printed signature of the auditor's firm

9) The city and state where the auditor practices

10) The date of the auditor's report

22. **Examples of Reports on an Entity's Internal Control**

 a.   Below is an audit report expressing an unmodified opinion of the effectiveness of ICFR for nonissuers (private entities). The differences from the report on the next page include (1) the title, (2) use of paragraph headings, (3) identification of applicable standards, and (4) other minor wording changes. However, the **essence** of the report is the same.

<u>EXAMPLE</u> -- AU-C 940 Auditor's Unmodified Report on Internal Control

<u>Independent Auditor's Report</u>

To the Board of Directors and Shareholders of Z Company:

Report on Internal Control Over Financial Reporting

We have audited Z Company's internal control over financial reporting as of December 31, 20X1, based on Internal Control – Integrated Framework issued by the Committee of Sponsoring Organizations of the Treadway Commission (COSO) [or other appropriate criteria].

Management's Responsibility for Internal Control Over Financial Reporting

Management is responsible for designing, implementing, and maintaining effective internal control over financial reporting and for its assessment about the effectiveness of internal control over financial reporting, included in the accompanying [*title of management's report*].

Auditor's Responsibility

Our responsibility is to express an opinion on the entity's internal control over financial reporting based on our audit. We conducted our audit in accordance with auditing standards generally accepted in the United States of America. Those standards require that we plan and perform the audit to obtain reasonable assurance about whether effective internal control over financial reporting was maintained in all material respects.

An audit of internal control over financial reporting involves performing procedures to obtain audit evidence about whether a material weakness exists. The procedures selected depend on the auditor's judgment, including the assessment of the risks that a material weakness exists. An audit includes obtaining an understanding of internal control over financial reporting and testing and evaluating the design and operating effectiveness of internal control over financial reporting based on the assessed risk.

We believe that the audit evidence we have obtained is sufficient and appropriate to provide a basis for our audit opinion.

Definition and Inherent Limitations of Internal Control Over Financial Reporting

An entity's internal control over financial reporting is a process effected by those charged with governance, management, and other personnel, designed to provide reasonable assurance regarding the preparation of reliable financial statements in accordance with accounting principles generally accepted in the United States of America [*or other applicable financial reporting framework*]. An entity's internal control over financial reporting includes those policies and procedures that (1) pertain to the maintenance of records that, in reasonable detail, accurately and fairly reflect the transactions and dispositions of the assets of the entity; (2) provide reasonable assurance that transactions are recorded as necessary to permit preparation of financial statements in accordance with accounting principles generally accepted in the United States of America, and that receipts and expenditures of the entity are being made only in accordance with authorizations of management and those charged with governance; and (3) provide reasonable assurance regarding prevention, or timely detection and correction, of unauthorized acquisition, use, or disposition of the entity's assets that could have a material effect on the financial statements.

Because of its inherent limitations, internal control over financial reporting may not prevent, or detect and correct, misstatements. Also, projections of any assessment of effectiveness to future periods are subject to the risk that controls may become inadequate because of changes in conditions, or that the degree of compliance with the policies or procedures may deteriorate.

Opinion

In our opinion, Z Company maintained, in all material respects, effective internal control over financial reporting as of December 31, 20X1, based on Internal Control – Integrated Framework issued by the Committee of Sponsoring Organizations of the Treadway Commission (COSO).

Report on Financial Statements

We also have audited, in accordance with auditing standards generally accepted in the United States of America, the [*identify financial statements*] of Z Company, and our report dated [*date of report, which should be the same as the date of the report on the audit of ICFR*] expressed an unmodified opinion.

Auditor's Signature
Auditor's City and State
Date

b.   The following is an audit report expressing an unmodified opinion on the effectiveness of ICFR for issuers (public companies):

EXAMPLE -- PCAOB AS 2201 Auditor's Unmodified Report on Internal Control

Report of the Independent Registered Public Accounting Firm

To The Board of Directors and Shareholders of W Company:

We have audited W Company's internal control over financial reporting as of December 31, 20X1, based on criteria established in Internal Control—Integrated Framework issued by the Committee of Sponsoring Organizations of the Treadway Commission (COSO). W Company's management is responsible for maintaining effective internal control over financial reporting and for its assessment of the effectiveness of internal control over financial reporting included in the accompanying Management's Annual Report on Internal Control over Financial Reporting. Our responsibility is to express an opinion on the effectiveness of the company's internal control over financial reporting based on our audit.

A company's internal control over financial reporting is a process designed to provide reasonable assurance regarding the reliability of financial reporting and the preparation of financial statements for external purposes in accordance with generally accepted accounting principles. A company's internal control over financial reporting includes those policies and procedures that (1) pertain to the maintenance of records that, in reasonable detail, accurately and fairly reflect the transactions and dispositions of the assets of the company; (2) provide reasonable assurance that transactions are recorded as necessary to permit preparation of financial statements in accordance with generally accepted accounting principles, and that receipts and expenditures of the company are being made only in accordance with authorizations of management and directors of the company; and (3) provide reasonable assurance regarding prevention or timely detection of unauthorized acquisition, use, or disposition of the company's assets that could have a material effect on the financial statements.

We conducted our audit in accordance with the standards of the Public Company Accounting Oversight Board (United States). Those standards require that we plan and perform the audit to obtain reasonable assurance about whether effective internal control over financial reporting was maintained in all material respects. Our audit included obtaining an understanding of internal control over financial reporting, evaluating management's assessment, testing and evaluating the design and operating effectiveness of internal control, and performing such other procedures as we considered necessary in the circumstances. We believe that our audit provides a reasonable basis for our opinion.

Because of its inherent limitations, internal control over financial reporting may not prevent or detect misstatements. Also, projections of any evaluation of effectiveness to future periods are subject to the risk that controls may become inadequate because of changes in conditions, or that the degree of compliance with the policies or procedures may deteriorate.

In our opinion, W Company maintained, in all material respects, effective internal control over financial reporting as of December 31, 20X1, based on criteria established in Internal Control—Integrated Framework issued by the Committee of Sponsoring Organizations of the Treadway Commission (COSO).

We have also audited, in accordance with the standards of the Public Company Accounting Oversight Board (United States), the [identify financial statements] of W Company and our report dated [date of report, which should be the same as the date of the report on the effectiveness of internal control over financial reporting] expressed an unmodified opinion.

Auditor's Signature
Auditor's City and State or Country
Date

---

23.   The auditor should **modify the report** on ICFR in any of the following circumstances:

a.   A **material weakness** requires an **adverse opinion**.

1)   The report must include the definition of a material weakness.

b.   Elements of management's annual report on ICFR are incomplete or improperly presented.

c.   The scope of the engagement is restricted.

d.   The auditor decides to refer to the report of other auditors as the basis, in part, for the auditor's own report.

e.   The auditor uses a service auditor's report.

f.   Other information is contained in management's annual report on ICFR.

24. The PCAOB's AS 6115, *Reporting on Whether a Previously Reported Material Weakness Continues to Exist*, addresses management requests to the auditor to provide a new opinion on whether one or more material weaknesses, which caused an adverse opinion, have been remediated.

   a. The auditor is allowed to reaudit the control based on management's assertion that the deficiency has been corrected and to provide an opinion relative to the control.

   b. Similar standards apply to the new engagement as for the initial reporting engagement on ICFR.

Stop and review! You have completed the outline for this subunit. Study multiple-choice questions 13 through 17 beginning on page 215.

9.4 SERVICE ORGANIZATIONS

Background

AT 801, *Reporting on Controls at a Service Organization*, provides guidance for a service auditor's reports on a service organization's internal control. AU-C 402, *Audit Considerations Relating to an Entity Using a Service Organization*, provides guidance to a user auditor when the user entity uses a service organization. An auditor is required to obtain an understanding of controls in all cases and to determine that they are effective if they are relied on. These requirements apply whether the relevant controls are the client's or the service provider's. For example, the client may outsource payroll processing, with certain controls over payroll maintained by the service provider. The auditor should consider the controls at the payroll processing service in the audit of the client. The user auditor may directly consider the controls at the service organization or use a service auditor's report to obtain the understanding and, if appropriate, determine whether the controls are effective.

---

1. **Nature of a Service Organization**

   a. A service organization's services and controls are part of the client's information system relevant to financial reporting if they have an effect on

      1) The significant classes of transactions in the user entity's operations;

      2) The systems, both IT and manual, that initiate, authorize, record, process, correct, and report the user entity's transactions;

      3) How the user entity's information system captures significant events and conditions, other than transactions; or

      4) The process used to prepare statements, including significant estimates and disclosures.

   b. If the user auditor is unable to obtain a sufficient understanding of the controls from the user entity, the user auditor should obtain that understanding from one or more of the following procedures:

      1) Obtaining and reading a service auditor's report, if available (This subunit relates to this option.)

      2) Contacting the service organization, through the user entity, to obtain specific information

      3) Performing procedures at the service organization to provide the necessary information about its relevant controls

      4) Using another auditor to perform procedures to provide the necessary information about the relevant controls at the service organization

2. **Definitions**

   a. The **user entity** uses a service organization. The user entity's financial statements are being audited.

   b. The **user auditor** audits and reports on the financial statements of the user entity.

   c. The **service organization** provides services to users that are relevant to their internal control over financial reporting.

    d.   The **service auditor** reports on controls at a service organization in one of the following reports:

        1)   Report on management's description of a service organization's system and the suitability of the design of controls (a **type 1 report**)

        2)   Report on management's description of a service organization's system, the suitability of the design of the controls, and operating effectiveness of controls (a **type 2 report**)

    e.   A **subservice organization** is used by another service organization to perform some of the services provided to user entities that are relevant to their internal control over financial reporting.

    f.   **Complementary user entity controls** are those that management of the service organization assumes, in the design of its service, will be implemented by user entities to achieve the control objectives.

    g.   **Tests of controls** are designed to evaluate the operating effectiveness of controls in achieving the control objectives stated in management's description of the service organization's system.

3.   **Objectives of the User Auditor (AU-C 402)**

    a.   The user auditor should

        1)   Obtain an understanding of the nature and significance of the services provided by the service organization and their effect on the user entity's internal control relevant to the audit. The understanding should be sufficient to identify and assess the risks of material misstatement.

        2)   Design and perform audit procedures responsive to those risks.

4.   **Understanding a Service Organization's Services and Internal Control**

    a.   The user auditor should consider the following:

        1)   The nature of the services provided by the service organization and their significance to the user entity, including their effect on the user entity's internal control

        2)   The nature and materiality of the transactions processed (or accounts or financial reporting processes affected) by the service organization

        3)   The degree of interaction between the service organization and the user entity

        4)   The nature of the relationship between the user entity and the service organization, including the relevant contractual terms

5.   **Using a Type 1 or Type 2 Report to Support the User Auditor's Understanding**

    a.   The user auditor should be satisfied as to

        1)   The service auditor's professional competence and independence from the service organization and

        2)   The adequacy of the standards under which the report was issued.

    b.   If the user auditor plans to use a type 1 or type 2 report, the user auditor should

        1)   Evaluate whether the report is appropriate for the user auditor's purposes;

        2)   Evaluate the sufficiency and appropriateness of the evidence provided by the report for understanding the user entity's relevant internal control; and

        3)   Determine whether complementary user entity controls identified by the service organization are relevant to the RMMs relating to the relevant assertions in the user entity's financial statements and, if so, obtain an understanding of whether the user entity has designed and implemented such controls.

6. **Reliance on Controls**

    a. When the user auditor's risk assessment includes an expectation that controls at the service organization are **operating effectively**, the user auditor should obtain audit evidence about the operating effectiveness of those controls from one or more of the following:

        1) Obtaining and reading a type 2 report
        2) Performing appropriate tests of controls at the service organization
        3) Using another auditor to perform tests of controls at the service organization

7. **Fraud, Noncompliance, and Uncorrected Misstatements**

    a. The user auditor should inquire of management of the user entity about whether the user entity is aware of any (1) fraud, (2) noncompliance with laws and regulations, or (3) uncorrected misstatements at the service organization affecting the financial statements of the user entity.

    b. The user auditor should evaluate how such matters, if any, affect the nature, timing, and extent of the user auditor's further audit procedures, including the effect on the user auditor's conclusions and report.

8. **Reporting by the User Auditor**

    a. The user auditor should express a qualified opinion or disclaim an opinion if (s)he cannot obtain sufficient appropriate audit evidence regarding the services provided by the service organization relevant to the audit of the user entity.

    b. The user auditor should not refer to the work of a service auditor in the user auditor's report containing an unmodified opinion.

    c. If a reference to the work of a service auditor is relevant to understanding a modification of the opinion, the report should indicate that the reference does not reduce the user auditor's responsibility.

9. **Responsibilities of a Service Auditor (AT 801)**

    a. The service auditor should be **independent** of the service organization but not necessarily of each user organization.

    b. As in other audit engagements, the service auditor should consider the following issues and apply the applicable standards or make the appropriate judgments:

        1) Whether to accept a new client or continue with existing clients
        2) Whether to agree to a request for a change in the scope of the engagement
        3) Use of appropriate materiality judgments in planning and performing the audit
        4) Consideration of the cause and nature of any discovered deviations
        5) Whether to use the work of an internal auditor
        6) The need to read other information contained in management's description of the system
        7) Effects of subsequent events after the date of the service auditor's report
        8) The need to document the engagement

    c. The service auditor **should obtain and read management's description** of the service organization's system and should evaluate whether the information is presented fairly. Thus, the service auditor considers whether, among other things,

        1) The control objectives are reasonable
        2) Controls were implemented
        3) The major aspects of the service provided are addressed
        4) The description is sufficiently detailed and complete

    d.   The service auditor should assess whether the controls have been **suitably designed** by determining whether

        1)   The risks that threaten the achievement of the control objectives have been identified.

        2)   The controls, if operating effectively, mitigate those risks.

    e.   For type 1 and type 2 reports, the service auditor should obtain sufficient appropriate evidence to support

        1)   The assessment of management's description of the service organization's system and whether those controls described **have been implemented**

        2)   The opinion that the controls are **suitably designed**

    f.   For type 2 reports, the service auditor also should obtain sufficient appropriate audit evidence to support

        1)   The opinion that the controls **operated effectively** throughout the period.

    g.   The service auditor should **obtain a representation letter** from management dated as of the date of the service auditor's report.

    h.   The service organization may use a subservice organization. The service auditor may test and report on those controls **(inclusive method)** or disclaim an opinion on those controls **(carve-out method)**.

10. **Reports of the Service Auditor**

    a.   The service auditor may provide two types of **examination** reports that express opinions:

        1)   A **type 1 report** expresses an opinion on the fair presentation of management's description and whether the controls are suitably designed at the specified date.

            a)   Suitable design means the controls can attain the control objectives if they operate effectively.

        2)   A **type 2 report** expresses not only the type 1 opinions but also an opinion on whether the controls were operating effectively (meeting the control objectives).

            a)   Type 2 opinions relate to design and effectiveness throughout the period rather than at a specific date.

    b.   **Content of a Service Auditor's Type 1 Report**

        1)   A title that includes the word "independent"

        2)   An addressee

        3)   Identification of management's description of the system

        4)   A reference to management's assertion and a statement of management's responsibility for the controls

        5)   A statement that the service auditor's responsibility is to express an opinion on the fairness of management's description of the system and the suitability of the design of the controls in meeting the objectives

        6)   A statement that the report was conducted in accordance with the AICPA attestation standards

        7)   A statement that the service auditor did not test the effectiveness of the controls

        8)   Statements about the scope of the service auditor's procedures

        9)   A statement about the inherent limitations of controls

        10) An opinion on whether, in all material respects, management's description of the system is fairly stated and whether the controls are suitably designed

        11) A statement restricting the use of the report to management of the service organization, user entities, and auditors of user entities

        12) The date of the report

        13) The name, city, and state of the service auditor

    c.   **Content of a Service Auditor's Type 2 Report**

        1)   The type 2 report includes the same basic information as a type 1 report except it includes an opinion on the operating effectiveness of the controls throughout the specified period. Thus, the statement in a type 1 report that the service auditor did not test the effectiveness of controls is excluded.

    d.   **Modified opinions.** The opinion should be modified if

        1)   Management's description of the service organization's system is not fairly presented,

        2)   The controls are not suitably designed,

        3)   The controls did not operate effectively in the case of a type 2 report, or

        4)   The service auditor was not able to obtain sufficient appropriate evidence.

    e.   If the service auditor becomes aware of (1) fraud, (2) uncorrected errors that are not clearly trivial, or (3) noncompliance with laws and regulations that may affect the user entity, (s)he should determine the effects and whether the information has been communicated to user entities. If not, the service auditor should inform those charged with governance of the service organization. If (s)he is not satisfied with the response, the service auditor may consider obtaining legal advice or withdrawing from the engagement.

Stop and review! You have completed the outline for this subunit. Study multiple-choice questions 18 through 20 beginning on page 216.

QUESTIONS

9.1 Communicating Internal Control Related Matters Identified in an Audit

1. Management may already know of the existence of significant deficiencies or material weaknesses in internal control. Which of the following is a true statement about the auditor's communication in this situation?

A. The auditor should communicate these control conditions orally, but need not communicate them in writing.

B. The auditor need not communicate these control conditions if management is already aware of them.

C. The auditor need not communicate these control conditions if they were communicated in prior periods.

D. The auditor should communicate these control conditions in writing regardless of a decision by management and those charged with governance not to remedy them.

Answer (D) is correct.
    REQUIRED: The true statement about communication of significant deficiencies or material weaknesses in internal control.
    DISCUSSION: The auditor's responsibility is to communicate in writing significant deficiencies and material weaknesses regardless of a decision by management and those charged with governance not to remedy them because of cost-benefit considerations or other factors. These should be communicated to management and those charged with governance each period within 60 days after the report release date (AU-C 265).

2. An auditor's written communication of internal control related matters identified in an audit would be addressed to "those charged with governance," which would include the

A. Board of directors.

B. Director of internal auditing.

C. Chief financial officer.

D. Chief accounting officer.

Answer (A) is correct.
    REQUIRED: The recipient of the auditor's written communication of internal control related matters identified in an audit.
    DISCUSSION: In many organizations, governance is provided by the board of directors (and its related audit committee). However, the communication may be made to individuals at an equivalent level of authority and responsibility if the organization does not have a board.

3. Which of the following statements is true about the auditor's communication of a material weakness in internal control?

    A.   A weakness that management refuses to correct should be included in a separate paragraph of the auditor's report on the financial statements.

    B.   The auditor should request management to include a written response in the auditor's communication.

    C.   Suggested corrective action for management's consideration concerning a material weakness need not be communicated to the client.

    D.   The auditor should test the controls that constitute a material weakness before communicating it to the client.

Answer (C) is correct.
    REQUIRED: The true statement about the communication of a material internal control weakness.
    DISCUSSION: Although the auditor should communicate material weaknesses to management and those charged with governance, suggested corrective action need not be communicated.
    Answer (A) is incorrect. A weakness that management refuses to correct is not, by itself, sufficient to require an emphasis-of-matter or other-matter paragraph. Answer (B) is incorrect. In some instances, management may choose to include a written response. The auditor should include a disclaimer of opinion on the response in the communication. Answer (D) is incorrect. The auditor should communicate material weaknesses of which (s)he becomes aware. Testing controls is not a prerequisite of the communication.

4. Which of the following statements about an auditor's communication of internal control related matters identified in an audit of a nonissuer is true?

    A.   The auditor may issue a written report to management and those charged with governance that no significant deficiencies were noted.

    B.   Significant deficiencies or material weaknesses need not be recommunicated each year if the audit committee has acknowledged its understanding of such deficiencies.

    C.   Significant deficiencies or material weaknesses may not be communicated in a document that contains suggestions regarding activities that concern other topics such as business strategies or administrative efficiencies.

    D.   The auditor should communicate significant internal control related matters no later than 60 days after the report release date.

Answer (D) is correct.
    REQUIRED: The true statement about an auditor's communication of internal control related matters identified in an audit.
    DISCUSSION: Timely communication of significant deficiencies or material weaknesses should be made no later than 60 days after the report release date. But the communication is best made by the report release date. However, early communication may be important because of the significance of the matters noted and the urgency of corrective action.
    Answer (A) is incorrect. AU-C 265 prohibits issuance of a report declaring that no significant deficiencies were noted. However, a report can be issued stating that no material weaknesses were detected if it states that material weaknesses may exist and not be identified. Answer (B) is incorrect. Significant deficiencies and material weaknesses that previously were communicated and have not yet been remediated should continue to be communicated. Answer (C) is incorrect. Items beneficial to the client may be communicated even though they are not control related.

5. Which of the following circumstances would be inappropriate for the auditor to communicate to those charged with governance?

    A.   A material misstatement was noted by the auditor and corrected by management.

    B.   No significant deficiencies in internal control exist that would affect the financial statements.

    C.   The auditor is requesting representations regarding the financial statements from management.

    D.   Management has consulted with other accountants about accounting and auditing matters during the period under audit.

Answer (B) is correct.
    REQUIRED: The matter not communicated to those charged with governance.
    DISCUSSION: An auditor may issue a written communication stating that no material weaknesses were identified if the auditor complies with the applicable requirements for such communications. But a written communication stating that no significant deficiencies were identified is prohibited. It might be misunderstood or misused (AU-C 265).
    Answer (A) is incorrect. Unless all those charged with governance are managers, the auditor should communicate material, corrected misstatements that were brought to management's attention (AU-C 260). Answer (C) is incorrect. Unless all those charged with governance are managers, the auditor should communicate written representations requested by the auditor (AU-C 260). Answer (D) is incorrect. Unless all those charged with governance are managers, the auditor should communicate his or her views on significant accounting and auditing matters about which management consulted other accountants (AU-C 260).

6. During consideration of internal control in a financial statement audit, an auditor is **not** obligated to

A. Search for significant deficiencies in the operation of internal control.

B. Understand the internal control environment.

C. Determine whether the control activities relevant to audit planning have been implemented.

D. Perform procedures to understand the design of internal control.

Answer (A) is correct.

REQUIRED: The task not required during the auditor's consideration of the entity and its environment, including its internal control.

DISCUSSION: The auditor should obtain an understanding of the entity and its environment, including its internal control, and assess the risks of material misstatement. The limited purpose of this consideration does not include the search for significant deficiencies or material weaknesses.

Answer (B) is incorrect. The auditor should obtain an understanding of the five components of internal control. Answer (C) is incorrect. The understanding includes determining whether relevant controls have been implemented. Answer (D) is incorrect. Obtaining the understanding of controls includes evaluating the design of the relevant controls.

9.2 The Auditor's Communication with Those Charged with Governance

7. An auditor would **least** likely initiate a discussion with a client's audit committee concerning

A. The methods used to account for significant unusual transactions.

B. The maximum dollar amount of misstatements that could exist without causing the financial statements to be materially misstated.

C. Indications of fraud committed by a corporate officer that were discovered by the auditor.

D. Disagreements with management as to accounting principles that were resolved during the current year's audit.

Answer (B) is correct.

REQUIRED: The item least likely to be discussed with the audit committee.

DISCUSSION: The auditor is responsible for determining the levels of materiality appropriate in the audit of a client's financial statements. Only the general nature of materiality need be discussed.

Answer (A) is incorrect. Methods used to account for significant unusual transactions are communicated to those charged with governance. Answer (C) is incorrect. Fraud is an item communicated to those charged with governance. Answer (D) is incorrect. Disagreements with management are communicated to those charged with governance.

8. Which of the following is true about the auditor's communication with those charged with governance?

A. It should be explained that the auditor is responsible for the fairness of the financial statements.

B. The communication should be a two-way discourse between the auditor and those charged with governance.

C. Specific audit procedures should be described to those charged with governance.

D. The auditor should limit the communication to only those issues required to be communicated.

Answer (B) is correct.

REQUIRED: The true statement about the auditor's communication with those charged with governance.

DISCUSSION: Two-way communication is expected and should provide those charged with governance an overview of the audit process and of the auditor's responsibilities. It should also allow the auditor to obtain information relevant to the audit.

Answer (A) is incorrect. Management is responsible for the fairness of the financial statements. Answer (C) is incorrect. The description of specific audit procedures could compromise the audit. Answer (D) is incorrect. Nothing precludes the auditor from communicating other information to those charged with governance.

9. In an audit engagement, should an auditor communicate the following matters to those charged with governance?

	Auditors' Judgments About the Quality of the Client's Accounting Principles	Issues Discussed with Management Prior to the Auditor's Retention
A.	Yes	Yes
B.	Yes	No
C.	No	Yes
D.	No	No

Answer (A) is correct.

REQUIRED: The matter(s), if any, to be communicated to those charged with governance.

DISCUSSION: The matters to be discussed with those charged with governance include the quality of the accounting principles used by management. Management is normally a participant in the discussion. Matters covered may include the auditor's views on the entity's significant accounting practices, e.g., policies, estimates, and disclosures. Furthermore, in any audit engagement, the auditor and those charged with governance should discuss any major issues discussed with management in connection with the initial or recurring retention of the auditors, for example, issues concerning the application of accounting principles and auditing standards.

10. Which of the following statements is true about an auditor's communication to those charged with governance?

A. Any matters communicated to those charged with governance also should be communicated to the entity's management.

B. The auditor is required to inform those charged with governance about misstatements discovered by the auditor and not subsequently corrected by management.

C. Disagreements with management about the application of accounting principles are required to be communicated in writing to those charged with governance.

D. Issues previously reported to those charged with governance are required to be communicated to the audit committee after each subsequent audit.

Answer (B) is correct.
REQUIRED: The true statement about an auditor's communication to those charged with governance.
DISCUSSION: The matters to be communicated to those charged with governance include uncorrected misstatements, other than those not accumulated by the auditor because they are clearly trivial. The auditor communicates uncorrected misstatements and the effect they may have, individually or aggregated, on the opinion. Furthermore, material uncorrected misstatements should be identified individually. Also, the auditor should communicate to those charged with governance the effect of uncorrected misstatements related to prior periods (AU-C 260).
Answer (A) is incorrect. Certain information should be communicated to those charged with governance, for example, information relating to the integrity of management. Answer (C) is incorrect. Communication with those charged with governance may be oral or written. Answer (D) is incorrect. Communication of recurring matters ordinarily need not be repeated.

11. Which of the following statements is true about an auditor's communication with those charged with governance?

A. This communication is required to occur at the same time as the auditor's report on the financial statements is issued.

B. This communication should include management changes in the application of significant accounting policies.

C. Any significant matter communicated to those charged with governance also should be communicated to management.

D. Audit adjustments proposed by the auditor, whether or not recorded by management, need not be communicated to those charged with governance.

Answer (B) is correct.
REQUIRED: The true statement about an auditor's communication with those charged with governance.
DISCUSSION: The auditor should communicate to those charged with governance, among other things, management's selection of and changes in significant accounting policies or their application. The auditor also should determine that those charged with governance are informed about the methods used to account for significant unusual transactions and the effects of significant accounting policies in controversial or emerging areas (AU-C 260).
Answer (A) is incorrect. The communication should be on a timely basis. Answer (C) is incorrect. The communication is required to be made only to those with oversight authority. Answer (D) is incorrect. Uncorrected misstatements and material corrected misstatements should be communicated to those charged with governance.

12. Which of the following statements is true about an auditor's communication with those charged with governance?

A. This communication should include disagreements with management about audit adjustments, whether or not satisfactorily resolved.

B. If matters are communicated orally, it is necessary to repeat the communication of recurring matters each year.

C. If matters are communicated in writing, the report is required to be distributed to both the audit committee and management.

D. This communication is required to occur after the auditor's report on the financial statements is released.

Answer (A) is correct.
REQUIRED: The true statement about an auditor's communication with those charged with governance.
DISCUSSION: The matters to be discussed with those charged with governance include (1) the auditors' responsibility under GAAS; (2) significant accounting policies; (3) sensitive accounting estimates; (4) uncorrected and material corrected misstatements; (5) the quality of the accounting principles used by management; (6) auditor disagreements with management, whether or not satisfactorily resolved; (7) management's consultations with other accountants; (8) issues discussed with management prior to the auditors' retention; and (9) any serious difficulties the auditors may have had with management during the audit.
Answer (B) is incorrect. The oral or written communication of recurring matters ordinarily need not be repeated. Answer (C) is incorrect. Communications with management are neither required nor precluded. Answer (D) is incorrect. The communication is to be made on a timely basis.

9.3 Reporting on an Entity's Internal Control

13. Firms subject to the reporting requirements of the Securities Exchange Act of 1934 are required by the Foreign Corrupt Practices Act of 1977 to maintain satisfactory internal control. Moreover, the Sarbanes-Oxley Act of 2002 requires that annual reports include (1) a statement of management's responsibility for establishing and maintaining adequate internal control and procedures for financial reporting, and (2) management's assessment of their effectiveness. The role of the registered auditor relative to the assessment made by management is to

A. Express an opinion on the assessment.

B. Report clients with unsatisfactory internal control to the SEC.

C. Express an opinion on whether the client is subject to the Securities Exchange Act of 1934.

D. Determine whether management's report is complete and properly presented.

Answer (D) is correct.
    REQUIRED: The role of the auditor relative to the assessment by management of internal control.
    DISCUSSION: According to PCAOB AS 2201, the auditor must express (or disclaim) an opinion on the effectiveness of internal control. Moreover, if the auditor determines that elements of management's annual report on internal control over financial reporting are incomplete or improperly presented, the auditor should modify his or her report to describe the reasons for this determination.
    Answer (A) is incorrect. According to PCAOB AS 2201, the auditor must express (or disclaim) an opinion on internal control but not necessarily on management's assessment. Answer (B) is incorrect. The auditor's report on internal control is issued with the audit report on the financial statements. Answer (C) is incorrect. Issuers must report to the SEC, but the auditor need not express an opinion on whether the client is subject to the Securities Exchange Act of 1934.

14. An auditor is auditing internal control in conjunction with the audit of financial statements for an issuer. The auditor is considering the appropriate materiality level for planning the audit of internal control. Relative to the materiality level for the audit of the financial statements, materiality levels for the audit of internal control are

A. Larger.

B. Smaller.

C. The same.

D. Cannot determine.

Answer (C) is correct.
    REQUIRED: The materiality for an audit of internal control relative to the materiality for an audit of financial statements.
    DISCUSSION: Auditing standards indicate that the auditor should use the same materiality considerations in the audit of internal control over financial reporting that (s)he would use in planning the audit of annual financial statements.
    Answer (A) is incorrect. The materiality levels should be the same. Answer (B) is incorrect. The materiality levels should be the same. Answer (D) is incorrect. The materiality levels for the audit of internal control are based on those for the financial statement audit.

15. In an audit of internal control over financial reporting, which deficiencies in control should be communicated in writing to those charged with governance?

A. All deficiencies.

B. Only material weaknesses.

C. Only significant deficiencies.

D. Both material weaknesses and significant deficiencies.

Answer (D) is correct.
    REQUIRED: The deficiencies in control required to be communicated in writing to those charged with governance.
    DISCUSSION: The auditor should communicate, in writing, to management and to those charged with governance all material weaknesses and significant deficiencies identified during the audit. The written communication should be made prior to the report release date. The auditor also should communicate to management, in writing, all lesser deficiencies in internal control and inform those charged with governance when such a communication has been made.
    Answer (A) is incorrect. Material weaknesses and significant deficiencies should be communicated. Answer (B) is incorrect. Significant deficiencies also should be communicated. Answer (C) is incorrect. Material weaknesses also should be communicated.

16. During the audit of internal controls integrated with the audit of the financial statements, the auditor discovered a material weakness in internal control. The auditor most likely will express a(n)

A. Adverse opinion on internal control.

B. Qualified opinion on internal control.

C. Unmodified opinion on internal control.

D. Disclaimer of opinion on internal control.

Answer (A) is correct.
    REQUIRED: The type of opinion expressed because of discovery of a material weakness.
    DISCUSSION: Material weaknesses are significant control deficiencies that result in more than a remote chance that a material misstatement will result in the financial statements. A material weakness requires the auditor to express an adverse opinion on the effectiveness of internal control.
    Answer (B) is incorrect. A qualified opinion (or disclaimer of opinion) is expressed if there is a scope limitation. Answer (C) is incorrect. An unmodified opinion is not expressed if a material weakness exists. Answer (D) is incorrect. Disclaimer of opinion (or qualified opinion) is expressed if there is a scope limitation.

17. An auditor is conducting an integrated audit of internal control with the audit of a nonissuer's financial statements. In applying the top-down approach, the auditor first

    A. Focuses on entity-level controls and then significant classes of transactions, account balances, and disclosures.

    B. Communicates material weaknesses and significant deficiencies to those charged with governance.

    C. Determines the type of opinion to be expressed.

    D. Applies substantive procedures to test financial statement assertions.

Answer (A) is correct.
    REQUIRED: The meaning of the top-down approach.
    DISCUSSION: The top-down approach to evaluating internal control begins at the financial statement level by understanding overall risks, focusing on entity-level controls, and then working down to significant classes of transactions, account balances, and disclosures. Examples of entity-level controls are controls (1) related to the control environment, (2) over management override, (3) to monitor results of operations, (4) over the period-end financial reporting process, and (5) to monitor other controls.
    Answer (B) is incorrect. Communication is at the end of the examination, when findings are available. Answer (C) is incorrect. The type of opinion to be expressed cannot be determined until the audit is completed. Answer (D) is incorrect. Substantive procedures are used to test financial statement assertions, not internal controls.

9.4 Service Organizations

18. AU-C 402, *Audit Considerations Relating to an Entity Using a Service Organization*, applies to a financial statement audit of an entity that uses services of another organization as part of its information system. For this purpose, the user auditor may need to obtain a service auditor's report. Which of the following is a true statement about a service auditor's report?

    A. It provides the user auditor with assurance regarding whether control procedures have been implemented at the user organization.

    B. It should include an opinion.

    C. If it proves to be inappropriate for the user auditor's purposes, (s)he must personally perform procedures at the service organization.

    D. A user auditor need not be concerned about the service auditor's professional competence.

Answer (B) is correct.
    REQUIRED: The true statement about a service auditor's report regarding internal control.
    DISCUSSION: A service auditor's report should be helpful in providing a sufficient understanding to plan the audit of the user organization. The service auditor's report may express an opinion on the fairness of the description of the controls implemented at the service organization and whether they were suitably designed. If the service auditor also has tested controls, the report may express an opinion on the operating effectiveness of the controls.
    Answer (A) is incorrect. A service auditor's report is helpful to the user auditor in obtaining an understanding of internal control at the service organization, but it does not provide assurance regarding conditions at the user organization. Answer (C) is incorrect. Audit procedures at the service organization may be applied by the service auditor at the request of (and under the direction of) the user auditor. Answer (D) is incorrect. The user auditor should be satisfied about the service auditor's independence and professional competence.

19. Lake, CPA, is auditing the financial statements of Gill Co. Gill uses the EDP Service Center, Inc., to process its payroll transactions. EDP's financial statements are audited by Cope, CPA, who recently issued a report on EDP's internal control. Lake is considering Cope's report on EDP's internal control in assessing control risk on the Gill engagement. What is Lake's responsibility concerning making reference to Cope as a basis, in part, for Lake's own unmodified opinion?

    A. Lake may refer to Cope only if Lake is satisfied as to Cope's professional reputation and independence.

    B. Lake may refer to Cope only if Lake relies on Cope's report in restricting the extent of substantive procedures.

    C. Lake may refer to Cope only if Lake's report indicates the division of responsibility.

    D. Lake may not refer to Cope under the circumstances above.

Answer (D) is correct.
    REQUIRED: The reference, if any, in an auditor's report to a service auditor's report on internal control.
    DISCUSSION: The service auditor was not responsible for examining any portion of the user entity's financial statements. Hence, the user auditor should not refer to the service auditor's report as a basis in part for his or her own unmodified opinion on those financial statements. If the user auditor's opinion is modified, the service auditor's work may be referred to if it is relevant to understanding the modification (AU-C 402).
    Answer (A) is incorrect. Although the user auditor should become satisfied about the service auditor's professional competence and consider the service auditor's independence, no reference to the service auditor normally should be made in the user auditor's report. Answer (B) is incorrect. The user auditor should not refer to the service auditor's report even if (s)he uses that report in assessing RMMs and in determining the nature, timing, and extent of further audit procedures. Answer (C) is incorrect. The user auditor should not divide responsibility with the service auditor.

20. Computer Services Company (CSC) processes payroll transactions for schools. Drake, CPA, is engaged to report on CSC's controls implemented as of a specific date. These controls are relevant to the schools' internal control, so Drake's report will be useful in providing the schools' independent auditors with information necessary to plan their audits. Drake's report expressing an opinion on CSC's controls implemented as of a specific date should contain a(n)

A. Description of the scope and nature of Drake's procedures.

B. Statement that CSC's management has disclosed to Drake all design deficiencies of which it is aware.

C. Opinion on the operating effectiveness of CSC's controls.

D. Paragraph indicating the basis for Drake's assessment of the risks of material misstatement.

Answer (A) is correct.
   REQUIRED: The item in a service auditor's report on controls implemented.
   DISCUSSION: The report expressing an opinion on the description of controls implemented and their design (type 1 report) includes (1) a title that includes the word *independent*; (2) an addressee; (3) identification of management's description of the system; (4) a reference to management's assertion and a statement of management's responsibility for the controls; (5) a statement that the service auditor's responsibility is to express an opinion on the fairness of management's description of the system and the suitability of the design of the controls in meeting the objectives; (6) a statement that the report was conducted in accordance with the AICPA attestation standards; (7) a statement that the service auditor did not test the effectiveness of the controls; (8) statements about the scope of the service auditor's procedures; (9) a statement about the inherent limitations of controls; (10) an opinion on whether, in all material respects, management's description of the system is fairly stated and whether the controls are suitably designed; (11) a statement restricting the use of the report to management of the service organization and user entities; (12) the date of the report; and (13) the name, city, and state of the service auditor.
   Answer (B) is incorrect. The service auditor need not state whether management has disclosed all design deficiencies. Answer (C) is incorrect. A type 1 report does not contain an opinion on operating effectiveness. Answer (D) is incorrect. A type 1 report contains no assessment of RMMs, only an opinion on the description of the controls implemented and their design.

Access the Gleim CPA Premium Review System featuring SmartAdapt for exam-emulating multiple-choice questions and simulations with detailed answer explanations.

Learn more: gleim.com/CPApremium | 800.874.5346

STUDY UNIT TEN
EVIDENCE -- OBJECTIVES AND NATURE

(13 pages of outline)

The auditor should design and perform audit procedures to obtain sufficient appropriate audit evidence. The objective is to be able to draw reasonable conclusions as a basis for the auditor's opinion on whether the financial statements are fairly presented in all material respects. Thus, most audit work involves obtaining and evaluating audit evidence.

Generally accepted auditing standards (GAAS) require the auditor to obtain **reasonable assurance** about whether the statements as a whole are free from material misstatement, whether due to fraud or error. Reasonable assurance is a high but not absolute level of assurance. It is obtained when sufficient appropriate evidence reduces audit risk to an acceptably low level. **Audit risk** is the risk of expressing an inappropriate audit opinion when the statements are materially misstated.

10.1 NATURE, SUFFICIENCY, AND APPROPRIATENESS

You should recognize that the collection and documentation of evidence are keys to the audit. Be sure to understand these processes and, if necessary, review the role of management assertions that were addressed in Study Unit 1, Subunit 2.

1. **Nature of Audit Evidence**

    a. Audit evidence is all information used by the auditor in arriving at the conclusions on which the audit opinion is based. Audit evidence includes the accounting records underlying the financial statements.

    1) But accounting records alone do not provide sufficient appropriate audit evidence. Thus, the auditor should obtain other information.

    b. **Accounting records** include

    1) Initial entries (manual or electronic).
    2) Supporting records. Examples are (a) checks, (b) electronic funds transfers (EFTs), (c) invoices, (d) contracts, (e) the general and subsidiary ledgers, (f) journal entries, (g) worksheets, (h) spreadsheets, and (i) reconciliations.

    c. Sources of information other than accounting records include (1) minutes of meetings; (2) external confirmations; (3) analysts' reports; (4) comparable data about competitors; and (5) information obtained by the auditor from (a) inquiries (e.g., management's written representations), (b) observation, (c) inspection, (d) recalculation, (e) reperformance, and (f) analytical procedures.

    d. The auditor typically relies on persuasive, rather than conclusive, evidence because of the inherent limitations of the audit:

    1) The nature of financial reporting (e.g., use of accounting estimates dependent on forecasts)
    2) The nature of audit procedures (e.g., the possibility of fraud involving collusion or the failure of management to provide all the information requested)

3) The need to perform the audit (a) within a reasonable period of time and (b) to achieve a balance between benefit and cost

   a) However, the difficulty, time, or cost of obtaining evidence is not a valid reason for (1) omitting an audit procedure for which no alternative exists or (2) being satisfied with evidence that is less than persuasive.

2. **Assertions**

   a. Management implicitly or explicitly makes assertions about the recognition, measurement, presentation, and disclosure of information in the financial statements.

      1) Thus, the auditor should use relevant assertions in sufficient detail to assess the risks of material misstatement (RMMs) and design and perform further audit procedures.

   b. Some procedures may relate to more than one assertion. But a combination of procedures may be needed to test a relevant assertion because audit evidence from different sources or of a different nature may be relevant to the same assertion.

   c. The AICPA's and the PCAOB's **assertions models** are in Study Unit 1, Subunit 2.

3. **Sufficiency and Appropriateness**

   a. Sufficiency is the measure of the **quantity** of evidence.

      1) The greater the assessed RMMs, the more evidence is likely to be required.
      2) The higher the quality of evidence, the less evidence may be required.

   b. Appropriateness is the measure of the **quality** of evidence.

      1) Quality depends on relevance and reliability in supporting the auditor's conclusions. Relevance is the logical connection of information with, or bearing upon, the purpose of the audit procedure and any assertion considered.

      2) The **reliability** of information used as audit evidence is affected by (a) its source, (b) its nature, and (c) how it is obtained. These circumstances include controls over its preparation and maintenance. Evidence is generally more reliable when it is

         a) Obtained from knowledgeable independent sources outside the entity,
         b) Generated internally by the entity under effective internal control,
         c) Obtained directly by the auditor,
         d) In documentary form (in any medium), and
         e) Represented by original documents (rather than photocopies).

4. **Audit Procedures**

   a. **Risk assessment procedures** are performed to obtain an understanding of the entity and its environment, including internal control. The understanding permits the auditor to assess the RMMs at the financial statement and relevant assertion levels.

   b. **Further audit procedures** include tests of controls and substantive procedures.

      1) **Tests of controls** test the operating effectiveness of controls in preventing, or detecting and correcting, material misstatements at the relevant assertion level. Study Unit 8 contains the relevant outline. They are required when

         a) The auditor's risk assessment is based on an expectation of the operating effectiveness of controls or

         b) Substantive procedures alone do not provide sufficient appropriate evidence.

2) **Substantive procedures** are used to detect material misstatements at the relevant assertion level. They include (a) tests of details and (b) substantive analytical procedures.

   a) They should be performed for **all** relevant assertions about each material (1) transaction class, (2) account balance, and (3) disclosure.

c.   A **management's specialist** is an individual or organization having expertise in a field other than accounting or auditing that assists in preparing the financial statements. The client may rely on a management's specialist to prepare information used as audit evidence. An example is estimation of the fair value of securities. (Use of specialists is the subject of Study Unit 4, Subunit 2.)

   1) The auditor should (a) evaluate the competence, capabilities, and objectivity of such specialists; (b) obtain an understanding of their work relevant to the audit; and (c) evaluate its appropriateness.

5.   **Types of Audit Procedures**

   a.   The auditor should use the following, singly or in combination, as risk assessment procedures, tests of controls, or substantive procedures:

   1) **Inspection of records or documents** is the examination of records or documents, whether internal or external, in paper, electronic, or other media.
   2) **Inspection of tangible assets** is the physical examination of assets to test existence. For example, it is combined with observation of inventory counts.
   3) **Observation** is looking at a process or procedure being performed.
   4) **Inquiry** seeks financial or nonfinancial information from knowledgeable persons within the entity or outside the entity.
   5) **External confirmation** obtains audit evidence as a direct, written response to the auditor from a third party, e.g., confirmation of account balances or the terms of agreements. (Additional discussion is in Subunit 10.2.)
   6) **Recalculation** is checking mathematical accuracy.
   7) **Reperformance** is the independent execution of procedures or controls.
   8) **Analytical procedures** are evaluations of financial data made by a study of plausible relationships among both financial and nonfinancial data. (Additional discussion is in Study Unit 3, Subunit 5.)

      a) **Scanning** is a type of analytical procedure used to review accounting data to identify significant or unusual items for testing.

6.   **Electronic Environments**

   a.   Some information may exist only in electronic form or only at a certain moment (or period) of time.

   1) For example, transactions in **electronic commerce** may occur solely by exchange of electronic messages.
   2) Moreover, **image processing systems** may convert documents to electronic images with no retention of source documents.
   3) In electronic environments, substantive procedures alone may be insufficient to reduce audit risk to an acceptable level.

   b.   The auditor's responses may include the following:

   1) Performing audit procedures using **computer-assisted audit techniques (CAATs)**
   2) Requesting the entity to retain certain information
   3) Performing audit procedures at the moment when information exists

7.   **Direction of Testing**

   a.   The direction of testing is important in evaluating certain assertions. The direction of testing for existence (or occurrence) and completeness assertions is illustrated as follows:

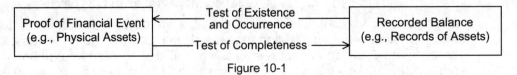

Figure 10-1

   b.   In essence, the auditor collects evidence that the economic events of the entity are fairly reflected in the financial statement assertions. The diagram below illustrates (1) how those events flow to the assertions and (2) the direction of testing for the completeness, existence, and occurrence assertions.

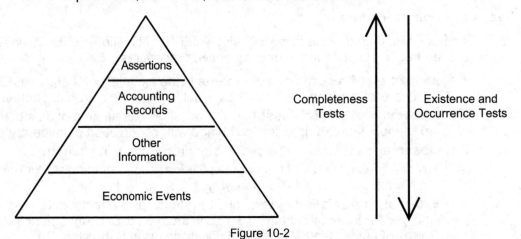

Figure 10-2

   c.   For example, to test for completeness that all sales were recorded, an auditor might select a sample of shipping documents (economic event of a sale) and trace them through the recording process to determine that they were included in the sales account.

      1)   To test that recorded sales occurred, the auditor might select a sample of recorded sales from the sales account and vouch them back through the records to determine that shipments to customers were made.

Stop and review! You have completed the outline for this subunit. Study multiple-choice questions 1 through 6 beginning on page 231.

10.2 EXTERNAL CONFIRMATIONS

1.   In general, audit evidence is more reliable (and persuasive) when it is (a) obtained from independent sources external to the entity, (b) obtained directly, or (c) in documentary form (paper, electronic, or other medium).

   a.   Thus, external confirmations may be more reliable than evidence generated internally by the entity.

2.   The auditor is required to consider whether external confirmation procedures should be performed as substantive procedures. External confirmations provide audit evidence as **direct written responses** from a third (confirming) party. They are in documentary form.

   a.   An example is providing the auditor with electronic access codes to data held by the confirming party on a secure website.

3. The external confirmation process includes

    a. Determining the information to be confirmed or requested;

    b. Selecting the appropriate confirming parties;

    c. Designing confirmation requests, including determining that they (1) are directed to the appropriate confirming parties and (2) provide for direct responses to the auditor; and

    d. Sending the requests, including follow-up requests when applicable, to the confirming parties.

4. The higher the assessed risks of material misstatement, the more persuasive the audit evidence obtained should be.

    a. For example, the auditor may decide to obtain more evidence directly from third parties by performing external confirmation procedures.

        1) These procedures may provide evidence at the higher level of reliability required for responding to **significant** RMMs, including those due to fraud.

5. External confirmation requests often address assertions about account balances.

    a. **Accounts receivable** are the entity's claims against customers resulting from the sale of goods or services in the normal course of business.

        1) They include the loans of a financial institution.

        2) Displaying the details of the balance (e.g., the items or invoices) may increase the response rate by helping the customer to reconcile the balance with his or her records.

    b. External confirmation of accounts receivable is required except when

        1) They are immaterial;

        2) Confirmation would be ineffective; or

        3) The assessed RMMs are low, and other substantive procedures address the assessed risks.

    c. An auditor should document the basis for not using external confirmations of accounts receivable when the balance is material.

    d. Confirmation of accounts receivable also is covered in Study Unit 11.

6. External confirmation also may be relevant to other items, such as terms of contracts or other agreements.

    a. External confirmation may provide relevant evidence about, for example,

        1) Bank balances,

        2) Inventories held by third parties,

        3) Investments held by brokers, or

        4) Accounts payable and loan balances.

    b. External confirmation provides more relevant evidence about the existence assertion than about the recoverability of receivables.

7. **Designing Confirmation Requests**

    a. The following factors affecting the design of the request directly relate to the response rate and the reliability of the evidence obtained:

        1) The assertions addressed

        2) Specific RMMs, including fraud risks

        3) Presentation of the request and method of communication

        4) Management's authorization to confirming parties

        5) Prior experience on the audit

        6) Ability of the confirming parties to confirm or provide the information (e.g., a total balance instead of an invoiced amount)

b. A **positive confirmation request** asks for a reply in all cases. It may ask the confirming parties to state whether they agree with the information given or to provide information.

    1) Positive confirmation requests obtain evidence only when responses are received.

    2) **Blank confirmation requests** are used to reduce the risk that recipients will respond without verifying the information. They omit the amount or other information to be confirmed and ask the confirming parties to fill in the information.

        a) The disadvantage is a lower response rate because of the additional effort required.

c. **Negative confirmation requests** ask confirming parties to respond only if they disagree with the stated information.

    1) Negative confirmation requests are not used as the only substantive procedure addressing an assessed RMM at the assertion level unless

        a) The assessed RMM is low,

        b) The auditor has obtained sufficient appropriate evidence about the effectiveness of relevant controls,

        c) The population consists of many small homogeneous items,

        d) The expected exception rate is very low, and

        e) The auditor has no reason to believe that recipients will not consider the requests.

    2) **Unreturned negative confirmation requests** provide less persuasive evidence than responses to positive confirmation requests.

        a) An unreturned negative confirmation request provides some evidence of existence because it has not been returned marked *Return to Sender* with an indication that the addressee is unknown. However, it provides no explicit evidence that the intended recipient verified the information.

d. The auditor may consider information from **prior years' audits** or audits of similar entities when determining the effectiveness and efficiency of using external confirmations.

e. When designing requests, the auditor should consider the **types of information** to confirm. The nature of the information may directly affect the reliability of the evidence obtained and the response rate.

    1) Understanding the substance of the client's arrangements and transactions with third parties is fundamental to determining the information to be confirmed. The auditor also should consider the following:

        a) Requesting confirmation of the terms of unusual agreements or transactions as well as the amounts

        b) Determining whether oral modifications have been made to agreements

f. The auditor should direct the confirmation request to the appropriate **confirming party**.

    1) This party should be knowledgeable about the information, e.g., a bank official with knowledge of specific transactions, assets, or liabilities.

8. The auditor may need to (a) consider the effects on the assessed RMMs (including the risk of fraud) and (b) perform alternative procedures when

    a. Responses to confirmation requests are unreliable or
    b. No response to a confirmation request is made.

9. **Management's Refusal to Allow the Auditor to Perform External Confirmation Procedures**

    a. If management does not allow the auditor to perform confirmation procedures, the auditor should

        1) Inquire about management's reasons for the refusal and seek audit evidence about their validity and reasonableness.
        2) Evaluate the implications of management's refusal on the auditor's assessment of the relevant RMMs, including the risk of fraud, and on the nature, timing, and extent of other audit procedures.
        3) Perform alternative audit procedures designed to obtain relevant and reliable audit evidence.

    b. Management's refusal to allow the auditor to perform external confirmation procedures may be unreasonable, or the auditor may be unable to obtain relevant and reliable audit evidence from alternative audit procedures.

        1) In these cases, the auditor should (a) communicate with those charged with governance and (b) determine the implications for the audit and the opinion.

            a) A management-imposed limitation should result in a disclaimer or withdrawal from the engagement if the possible effects of undetected misstatements are material and pervasive.

10. An **oral response** to a confirmation is not an external confirmation.

    a. But if a direct written response to a positive confirmation is not necessary, the auditor may consider the oral response when determining the alternative procedures to be performed for nonresponses.

11. The auditor may not be able to obtain sufficient appropriate evidence without a written response to a **positive confirmation**. When alternative procedures will not obtain the required evidence, the auditor considers the implications for the audit and the opinion.

12. The auditor should evaluate the evidence provided by external confirmations and alternative procedures to determine whether sufficient appropriate evidence has been obtained. Responses to external confirmation requests may be classified as

    a. Indicating agreement
    b. Unreliable
    c. Nonresponses
    d. Indicating an exception

        1) Exceptions should be investigated because they may be **misstatements**.
        2) If a misstatement is identified, the auditor is required to determine whether it indicates fraud.
        3) Exceptions also may suggest deficiencies in internal control.

Stop and review! You have completed the outline for this subunit. Study multiple-choice questions 7 through 10 beginning on page 233.

10.3 AUDIT DOCUMENTATION

1. Sufficient appropriate audit documentation **(working papers)** should be prepared on a timely basis. Documentation records the work performed (including the nature, timing, extent, and results of audit procedures), the audit evidence obtained, and the conclusions reached. Audit documentation should provide

    a. A sufficient and appropriate record of the basis for the auditor's report.
    b. Evidence that the audit was planned and performed in accordance with GAAS and legal and regulatory requirements.

2. The auditor should document

    a. The characteristics of what was tested.
    b. Who performed the audit work and the date such work was complete.
    c. Who reviewed the audit work and the date and extent of the review.

3. Audit documentation serves other purposes, including the following:

    a. Assisting the audit team to plan and perform the audit
    b. Assisting new auditors to understand the work performed
    c. Assisting audit supervisors
    d. Demonstrating the accountability of the audit team
    e. Retaining a record of matters of continuing significance to future audits
    f. Assisting inspectors, peer reviewers, and quality control reviewers
    g. Assisting a successor auditor

4. Documentation should be assembled into an **audit file** (physical or electronic). It should enable an experienced auditor to understand the following:

    a. The procedures performed under GAAS or other requirements
    b. The results and evidence obtained
    c. Significant findings or issues, the conclusions drawn, and the judgments made

5. The **form, content, and extent** of documentation are determined by the following:

    a. Risks of material misstatement
    b. Extent of judgment involved in performing the work and evaluating the results
    c. Nature of the auditing procedures
    d. Significance of the evidence obtained
    e. Nature and extent of exceptions identified
    f. Need to document a conclusion or the basis for a conclusion not readily determinable from other documentation of the work
    g. Size and complexity of the entity
    h. Audit methods

6. **Tickmarks** document work performed and issues uncovered during the field work. A legend should define the tickmarks used on that working paper. For example, the # mark next to the sum of a column of numbers may be defined in the legend as "# -- Footed the column." The same tickmark may be used on different working papers to mean different things as long as it is defined in the legend on that page.

7. Each page in a working paper should be given a **unique reference number** that identifies its use and location. For example, working paper "C-1" may be for Cash in Bank. These are also used to cross-reference information on other working papers.

You are expected to be competent in evaluating working papers, including understanding the use of tick marks and cross-reference numbers. Be certain you can complete the practice task-based simulations on this topic that we provide in our online courses. Most simulations relating to working papers have been similar to the Gleim examples.

8. **Examples of documentation** include (a) audit plans, (b) analyses, (c) issues memoranda, (d) confirmations, (e) representation letters, (f) abstracts or copies of documents (e.g., copies of contracts), (g) summaries of significant findings or issues (completion memoranda that describe how the identified items were addressed), (h) discussions of significant findings or issues with management or those charged with governance, (i) how the auditor addressed information inconsistent with a significant final conclusion, (j) justification for departing from a presumptively mandatory audit requirement, (k) checklists, and (l) correspondence (including email). Documentation may be on paper or other media (e.g., digital, audio, or video).

    a. A **working trial balance** ordinarily is used to record the year-end ledger balances prior to audit. Reclassifications and adjustments are accumulated on the trial balance to reflect the final audited balances.

    b. **Lead schedules** are summaries of detailed schedules. For example, a cash lead schedule may summarize findings recorded on the cash in bank, petty cash, and count-of-cash-on-hand detail schedules.

    c. **Permanent files** are schedules, documents, and records with continuing audit significance for a specific client. These may include, for example, the articles of incorporation, bylaws, and contracts.

    d. **Current files** include schedules and analyses that relate to the current year under audit. For example, results of substantive procedures, such as confirmations and inventory observation and test counts, are kept in the current files.

9. **Significant audit findings or issues** to be documented include the following:

    a. Matters resulting in significant risks

    b. Selection, application, and consistency of significant accounting practices, for example,

        1) Accounting for complex or unusual transactions or
        2) Treatment of estimates and uncertainties (and any related assumptions)

    c. Evidence that the financial statements or disclosures may be materially misstated

    d. Evidence of a need to revise the assessments of RMMs and the responses to them

    e. Difficulty in applying necessary auditing procedures

    f. Other findings that could result in modification of the report

---

Background

Rules over the preparation and maintenance of audit documentation were augmented after claims that documents may have been shredded and evidence destroyed in the Enron case.

---

10. The auditor should complete the assembly of the final audit file within 60 days following the report release date (documentation completion date). (Under AS 1215, the period is 45 days after the report release date.)

    a. The auditor should not delete or discard audit documentation after the documentation completion date prior to the end of the retention period.

    b. The auditor may modify existing documentation or add to the audit file after the documentation completion date. Moreover, (s)he should include the reasons for the change, who made the change, and the date of the change.

11. **Ownership and Confidentiality**

    a.   Audit documentation is the **property of the auditor**.

    b.   Copies of documentation may be made available to the entity if the validity and independence of the audit are not undermined.

    c.   The auditor should retain audit documentation for a period of time sufficient to meet the needs of his or her practice and to satisfy any applicable legal or regulatory requirements for records retention. The minimum period is **5 years** from the report release date.

    d.   An auditor should take reasonable steps to preserve the **confidentiality** of documented client information, including prevention of unauthorized access.

12. **Sarbanes-Oxley Act of 2002**

    a.   The act provides further documentation guidance for registered public accountants. The PCAOB's AS 1215, *Audit Documentation*, which applies to audit engagements and reviews of interim financial information of **issuers**, reflects these considerations.

    b.   Audit documentation must contain sufficient information to enable an **experienced auditor**, having no previous connection with the engagement, to understand the work performed and conclusions reached and to determine who performed and reviewed the work and the relevant dates.

        1)   Audit documentation must not only support final conclusions but also must include auditor-identified information about significant findings and issues that is inconsistent with or contradicts the auditor's final conclusions.

    c.   The auditor must identify all **significant findings or issues** in an **engagement completion document**, including (1) corrections of misstatements (audit adjustments) that the auditor proposed or should have proposed, (2) significant disagreements among the engagement team, and (3) significant deficiencies or material weaknesses in internal control.

    d.   Audit documentation must be retained for **at least 7 years** from the report release date. This requirement only applies to issuers, but the AICPA 5-year requirement applies to nonissuers.

    e.   A complete and final set of audit documentation should be assembled for retention as of a date **(the documentation completion date)** not more than **45 days** after the report release date.

    f.   Audit documentation must **not** be deleted or discarded after the documentation completion date. However, information may be added.

    g.   AS 1215 does not address whether audit documentation is the property of the auditor or the confidentiality of audit documentation.

    NOTE: The PCAOB adopted as interim ethics standards only the AICPA's provisions in its *Code of Professional Conduct* on (1) independence and (2) integrity and objectivity. Thus, the AICPA's Confidential Client Information Rule, is not a PCAOB standard.

13. Still **other documentation standards** may apply, for example, those of the SEC regarding retention of memoranda, communications (sent or received), other documents, and records related to engagements.

Stop and review! You have completed the outline for this subunit. Study multiple-choice questions 11 through 16 beginning on page 234.

10.4 THE COMPUTER AS AN AUDIT TOOL

1. **Computer-Assisted Audit Techniques**

   a. Most auditors use personal computers (PCs) to perform audit functions more efficiently and effectively. For this purpose, auditors must select tasks appropriate for personal computer capabilities and the software for those tasks. The uses of software by the auditor are called computer-assisted audit techniques (CAATs).

   b. **Advantages of CAATs**

      1) The auditor can work independently of the auditee.
      2) The confidentiality of auditor procedures can be maintained.
      3) Audit work does not depend on the availability of auditee personnel.
      4) The auditor has access to records at remote sites.

   c. **Disadvantages of CAATs**

      1) The auditor must have a working understanding of the computer system, e.g., a complicated database system (also may be an advantage).
      2) Supervisory review may be more difficult.

   d. **Audit procedures** include the following:

      1) Directly accessing the entity's database (interrogation)
      2) Scanning files for certain types of records, items, etc.
      3) Building and using predictive models to identify high-risk areas
      4) Applying statistical sampling item selection and analysis routines
      5) Using input/output routines to provide hard copy and to reformat data (extraction)
      6) Preparing financial statements and other reports with spreadsheet routines
      7) Illustrating analyses with graphs and other pictorial displays
      8) Writing customized audit plans
      9) Storing audit plans, routines, and results electronically
      10) Implementing other types of audit procedures and analyses electronically
      11) Preparing and storing audit documentation
      12) Communicating data through networks
      13) Using specialized audit software to, among other things, compare source code with object code to detect unauthorized program changes, analyze unexecuted code, or generate test data
      14) Embedding code in the entity's programs to routinely extract/select certain transactions or details to be recorded in a file accessible only by the auditor
      15) Using expert systems software to automate the knowledge and logic of experts in a certain field to help an auditor with decision making and risk analysis

2. **Generalized Audit Software (GAS)**

   a. GAS is useful for both **tests of controls** and **substantive procedures**. It is software that is written to interface with many different client systems.

   b. GAS may be used to perform **audit tasks** such as the following:

      1) Sampling and selecting items (e.g., confirmations)
      2) Testing extensions, footings, and calculations
      3) Examining records (e.g., accounts receivable for amounts in excess of credit limits)
      4) Summarizing and sorting data
      5) Performing analytical procedures (e.g., comparing inventory records with transaction details)
      6) File access and file reorganization

   c.   **Advantages of GAS**

      1)   It is independent of the client's programs and personnel. Thus, information can be accessed without detailed knowledge of the client's hardware and software.

      2)   Less computer expertise is needed compared with writing original programs.

      3)   It can run on a variety of systems.

   d.   **Disadvantages of GAS**

      1)   Some software packages may process only sequential files.

      2)   Modifications may be necessary for a specific audit.

      3)   Audit software cannot examine items not in machine-readable form.

      4)   It has limited application in an online, real-time system.

   e.   Outlines of the test data approach, parallel simulation, and integrated test facilities are presented in Study Unit 8, Subunit 3.

   f.   The leading GAS software packages are currently Audit Command Language (ACL) and Interactive Data Extraction and Analysis (IDEA) software. These software packages, designed specifically for use in auditing, perform the following **major functions**:

      1)   Aging. An auditor can test the aging of accounts receivable.

      2)   Duplicate identification. Duplicate data can be organized by data field and subsequently identified.

      3)   Exportation. Data can be transferred to other software.

      4)   Extraction. Data can be extracted for exception analysis.

      5)   Gap identification. Gaps in information can be automatically noted.

      6)   Joining and merging. Two separate data files can be joined or merged to combine and match information.

      7)   Sampling. Samples of the data can be prepared and analyzed.

      8)   Sorting. Information can be sorted by any data field.

      9)   Stratification. Large amounts of data can be organized by specific factors, thereby facilitating analysis.

     10)   Summarization. Data can be organized to identify patterns.

     11)   Total fields. Totals for numeric fields can be quickly and accurately calculated.

3.   **Artificial Intelligence (AI).** AI is computer software designed to perceive, reason, and understand.

   a.   Business applications of AI are called **expert systems**. Expert systems in taxation, financial accounting, managerial accounting, and auditing have long been in use in major CPA firms.

      1)   An expert system is **interactive**. It asks a series of questions and uses knowledge gained from a human expert to analyze answers and make a decision.

      2)   Expert systems allow auditors and accountants to perform their duties in less time and with more uniformity. The result is that different decision makers are more likely to reach the same conclusions given the same set of facts.

      3)   An expert system can be used to (a) choose an audit plan, (b) select a test sample type and size, (c) determine the level of misstatement, (d) perform analytical procedures, and (e) make a judgment based on the findings.

   b.   **Neural networks** are another form of AI. The software learns from experience because it changes its knowledge database when informed of mistakes.

   c.   An expert system imitates a human expert and relies on many programmed rules, but a neural network has a generalized learning capacity.

4. **Specialized Audit Software**

   a. Specialized audit software is written to fulfill a specific set of audit tasks. The purposes and users of the software are well defined before the software is written.

   b. Auditors develop specialized audit software for the following reasons:

      1) Unavailability of alternative software
      2) Functional limitations of alternative software
      3) Efficiency considerations
      4) Increased understanding of systems
      5) Opportunity for easy implementation
      6) Increased auditor independence and prestige

Stop and review! You have completed the outline for this subunit. Study multiple-choice questions 17 through 20 beginning on page 235.

QUESTIONS

10.1 Nature, Sufficiency, and Appropriateness

1. Which of the following statements about audit evidence is true?

A. To be appropriate, audit evidence should be either persuasive or relevant but need not be both.

B. The sufficiency and appropriateness of audit evidence is a matter of professional judgment.

C. The difficulty and expense of obtaining audit evidence about an account balance is a valid basis for omitting the test.

D. A client's accounting records can be sufficient audit evidence to support the financial statements.

Answer (B) is correct.
  REQUIRED: The true statement about audit evidence.
  DISCUSSION: The auditor exercises professional judgment when forming a conclusion about whether sufficient appropriate audit evidence has been obtained to reduce audit risk to an acceptably low level. Sufficiency measures the quantity of audit evidence. Appropriateness measures its quality (relevance and reliability). To form this conclusion, the auditor considers all relevant evidence, regardless of whether it corroborates or contradicts the assertions in the statements.
  Answer (A) is incorrect. To be appropriate, audit evidence should be relevant and reliable. Also, because of the inherent limitations of the audit, most audit evidence is persuasive rather than conclusive. Answer (C) is incorrect. Although the cost of obtaining evidence and its usefulness should be rationally related, the matter of difficulty, time, or cost is not in itself a valid basis for (1) omitting a procedure when no alternative exists or (2) being satisfied with less than persuasive evidence. Answer (D) is incorrect. Accounting records should be supported by corroborating information.

2. The objective of tests of details of transactions performed as substantive procedures is to

A. Comply with generally accepted auditing standards.

B. Attain assurance about the reliability of the accounting system.

C. Detect material misstatements at the relevant assertion level.

D. Evaluate whether management's policies and procedures operated effectively.

Answer (C) is correct.
  REQUIRED: The objective of tests of details.
  DISCUSSION: Substantive procedures are (1) tests of the details of transaction classes, balances, and disclosures and (2) substantive analytical procedures. They are performed to detect material misstatements at the relevant assertion level. The auditor performs substantive procedures as a response to the related assessment of the RMMs (AU-C 330).
  Answer (A) is incorrect. The auditor may use a variety of techniques and is not required to use tests of the details of transactions to comply with GAAS. Answer (B) is incorrect. Tests of controls test the operating effectiveness of internal control. Internally generated audit evidence is generally more reliable when relevant controls are effective. Answer (D) is incorrect. Tests of controls are used to determine whether policies or procedures operated effectively.

3. In determining whether transactions have been recorded, the direction of the audit testing should begin from the

A. General ledger balances.

B. Adjusted trial balance.

C. Original source documents.

D. General journal entries.

Answer (C) is correct.
REQUIRED: The direction of testing to determine whether transactions have been recorded.
DISCUSSION: Determining whether transactions have been recorded is a test of the completeness assertion. Thus, beginning with the original source documents and tracing the transactions to the appropriate accounting records determines whether they were recorded.

4. Which of the following presumptions is **least** likely to relate to the reliability of audit evidence?

A. The more effective internal control is, the more assurance it provides about the accounting data and financial statements.

B. An auditor's opinion is formed within a reasonable time to achieve a balance between benefit and cost.

C. Evidence obtained from independent sources outside the entity is more reliable than evidence secured solely within the entity.

D. The auditor's direct personal knowledge obtained through observation and inspection is more persuasive than information obtained indirectly.

Answer (B) is correct.
REQUIRED: The presumption not relating to the reliability of audit evidence.
DISCUSSION: Appropriate audit evidence is relevant and reliable. Evidence is usually more reliable when it (1) is obtained from independent sources; (2) is generated internally under effective internal control; (3) is obtained directly by the auditor; (4) is in documentary form, whether paper, electronic, or other medium; and (5) consists of original documents. However, the need for (1) reporting to be timely and (2) maintaining a balance between benefit and cost are inherent limitations of the audit. Thus, for the opinion to be relevant, it must be formed within a reasonable period of time.
Answer (A) is incorrect. The more effective internal control is, the more assurance it provides about the reliability of the accounting data and financial statements. Answer (C) is incorrect. Evidence obtained from independent sources outside an entity provides greater assurance of reliability than evidence secured solely within the entity. Answer (D) is incorrect. The auditor's direct personal knowledge obtained through physical examination, observation, computation, and inspection is more persuasive than information obtained indirectly.

5. Which statement about audit evidence is **false**?

A. The auditor is seldom convinced beyond all doubt with respect to all aspects of the statements being audited.

B. The auditor should not perform a procedure that provides persuasive evidence rather than conclusive evidence.

C. The auditor evaluates the degree of risk involved in deciding the kind of evidence to gather.

D. The auditor balances the benefits of the evidence and the cost to obtain it.

Answer (B) is correct.
REQUIRED: The false statement about audit evidence.
DISCUSSION: In most cases, evidence that is obtained to enable an auditor to draw reasonable conclusions on which to base the opinion is necessarily persuasive rather than conclusive. The cost of obtaining conclusive evidence may outweigh the benefits. But the difficulty, time, or cost is not in itself a valid reason (1) to omit an audit procedure for which no alternative exists or (2) to be satisfied with less than persuasive evidence (AU-C 200).
Answer (A) is incorrect. The auditor is seldom persuaded beyond all doubt given the high cost of absolute certainty. Answer (C) is incorrect. The auditor should assess the risks of material misstatement before determining the kind and amount of evidence necessary to form an opinion. Answer (D) is incorrect. A rational relationship should exist between the cost and benefits of evidence.

6. Each of the following might, by itself, form a valid basis for an auditor to decide to omit a procedure **except** for the

A. Difficulty and cost involved in testing a particular item.

B. Assessment of the risks of material misstatement at a low level.

C. Inherent risk involved.

D. Relationship between the cost of obtaining evidence and its usefulness.

Answer (A) is correct.
REQUIRED: The consideration not a valid reason for omission of an audit procedure.
DISCUSSION: The costs and benefits of obtaining evidence should have a rational relationship. However, the difficulty, time, or cost required to perform a procedure is not in itself a valid reason for its omission if no alternative is available. Such matters also do not justify being satisfied with audit evidence that is less than persuasive (AU-C 500).
Answer (B) is incorrect. The lower the RMMs, the higher the acceptable audit risk and the greater the justification for omitting a substantive procedure. Answer (C) is incorrect. A procedure might be omitted if the susceptibility to material misstatement of an assertion before consideration of related controls is slight. Answer (D) is incorrect. The cost of obtaining evidence and its usefulness should have a rational relationship.

10.2 External Confirmations

7. Which of the following statements is correct concerning the use of negative confirmation requests?

A. Unreturned negative confirmation requests rarely provide significant explicit evidence.

B. Negative confirmation requests are effective when audit risk is low.

C. Unreturned negative confirmation requests indicate that alternative procedures are necessary.

D. Negative confirmation requests are effective when understatements of account balances are suspected.

Answer (A) is correct.
REQUIRED: The true statement about negative confirmation requests.
DISCUSSION: Unreturned negative confirmation requests rarely provide significant evidence about assertions other than certain aspects of existence. Additionally, unreturned negative confirmations do not provide explicit evidence that the intended parties received the requests and verified the information provided.
Answer (B) is incorrect. When the acceptable audit risk is low, positive confirmations are more effective. Answer (C) is incorrect. The auditor assumes the account is fairly stated when negative confirmations are not returned, indicating that alternative procedures are not necessary. Answer (D) is incorrect. Positive confirmations are more effective when understatements of account balances are suspected.

8. Which of the following strategies most likely could improve the response rate of the confirmation of accounts receivable?

A. Including a list of items or invoices that constitute the account balance.

B. Restricting the selection of accounts to be confirmed to those customers with relatively large balances.

C. Requesting customers to respond to the confirmation requests directly to the auditor by fax or email.

D. Notifying the recipients that second requests will be mailed if they fail to respond in a timely manner.

Answer (A) is correct.
REQUIRED: The strategy that most likely improves the response rate of confirmations.
DISCUSSION: One factor in the design of external confirmation requests is the layout and presentation. Thus, for an account receivable, displaying the details of the balance most likely helps the customer to reconcile the amount and may increase the response rate.
Answer (B) is incorrect. Restricting the selection of accounts to be confirmed to those customers with relatively large balances precludes a random sample without necessarily improving the response rate. Moreover, the sum of the relatively small balances may be material. Answer (C) is incorrect. Electronic responses may be unreliable because the origin or identity of the confirmer may be difficult to determine, and alteration may be difficult to detect. Answer (D) is incorrect. Threatening a second request is less likely to improve the response rate than facilitating the customer's response.

9. In which of the following circumstances would the use of the negative form of accounts receivable confirmation most likely be justified?

A. A substantial number of accounts may be in dispute, and the accounts receivable balance arises from sales to a few major customers.

B. A substantial number of accounts may be in dispute, and the accounts receivable balance arises from sales to many customers with small balances.

C. A small number of accounts may be in dispute, and the accounts receivable balance arises from sales to a few major customers.

D. A small number of accounts may be in dispute, and the accounts receivable balance arises from sales to many customers with small balances.

Answer (D) is correct.
REQUIRED: The circumstances in which negative accounts receivable confirmations are most likely justified.
DISCUSSION: Negative confirmation requests may be used to reduce audit risk to an acceptably low level when (1) the assessed risk of material misstatement is low, (2) a large number of small homogeneous balances is involved, (3) a very low exception rate is expected, (4) the auditor has no reason to believe that the recipients of the requests are unlikely to consider them, and (5) the auditor has obtained sufficient appropriate evidence about the effectiveness of relevant controls (AU-C 505).

10. The confirmation of customers' accounts receivable rarely provides reliable evidence about the completeness assertion because

- A. Many customers merely sign and return the confirmation without verifying its details.
- B. Recipients usually respond only if they disagree with the information on the request.
- C. Customers may not be inclined to report understatement errors in their accounts.
- D. Auditors typically select many accounts with low recorded balances to be confirmed.

Answer (C) is correct.
   REQUIRED: The reason confirmations rarely provide evidence about completeness.
   DISCUSSION: Confirmations do not address all assertions with equal effectiveness. For example, confirmations of accounts receivable do not necessarily provide reliable evidence about the completeness assertion because customers may not report understatements. Also, confirmations may not be designed to provide assurance about information not given in the request forms.
   Answer (A) is incorrect. A customer ordinarily confirms the balance, not its details. Moreover, many confirmation requests do not contemplate a response unless the customer disagrees with the entity's recorded amount. Answer (B) is incorrect. Positive confirmations ask the customer to return the confirmation form whether it is correct or not. Answer (D) is incorrect. Auditors typically select accounts with material balances. The existence assertion is normally tested by confirmation.

10.3 Audit Documentation

11. The current file of the auditor's audit documentation ordinarily should include

- A. A flowchart of the internal control procedures.
- B. Organization charts.
- C. A copy of the financial statements.
- D. Copies of bond and note indentures.

Answer (C) is correct.
   REQUIRED: The item included in the current file of the auditor's audit documentation.
   DISCUSSION: The current file of the auditor's audit documentation includes all working papers applicable to the current year under audit. A copy of the financial statements must be included in the current file because the amounts included in these statements are the focus of the audit.
   Answer (A) is incorrect. A flowchart of the internal control procedures would be included in the permanent file. Answer (B) is incorrect. Organization charts would be included in the permanent file. Answer (D) is incorrect. Copies of bond and note indentures would be included in the permanent file.

12. Audit documentation

- A. Is the property of the client.
- B. Serves as a substitute for the client's accounting records.
- C. Is unnecessary if the auditor expresses an adverse opinion.
- D. Provides evidence that the audit was performed in accordance with GAAS.

Answer (D) is correct.
   REQUIRED: The true statement about audit documentation.
   DISCUSSION: The objectives of audit documentation are to provide (1) a sufficient and appropriate record of the basis of the auditor's report and (2) evidence that the audit was performed in accordance with GAAS and other requirements. Audit documentation is the record of (1) the audit procedures performed, (2) relevant evidence obtained, and (3) conclusions reached.
   Answer (A) is incorrect. The audit documentation is the property of the auditor. Answer (B) is incorrect. The audit documentation is not a substitute for the client's accounting records. Answer (C) is incorrect. The audit documentation is necessary even if the auditor expresses an adverse opinion.

13. Which of the following factors would **least** likely affect the form, content, and extent of audit documentation?

- A. The risks of material misstatement.
- B. The extent of exceptions identified.
- C. The nature of the auditing procedures.
- D. The medium in which it is recorded and maintained.

Answer (D) is correct.
   REQUIRED: The least likely factor affecting the form, content, and extent of audit documentation.
   DISCUSSION: The medium used to prepare and maintain the audit documentation, e.g., paper or digital, does not affect its nature and extent. The form, content, and extent of documentation are determined by (1) the risks of material misstatement, (2) the extent of judgment involved in performing the work and evaluating the results, (3) the nature of the auditing procedures, (4) the significance of the evidence obtained, (5) the nature and extent of exceptions identified, (6) the need to document a conclusion or the basis for a conclusion, (7) audit methods, and (8) size and complexity of the entity.

14. Although the quantity and content of audit documentation vary with each engagement, an auditor's permanent files most likely include

    A. Schedules that support the current year's adjusting entries.

    B. Prior years' accounts receivable confirmations that were classified as exceptions.

    C. Documentation indicating that the audit work was adequately planned and supervised.

    D. Analyses of capital stock and other owners' equity accounts.

Answer (D) is correct.
    REQUIRED: The component of the permanent section of audit documentation.
    DISCUSSION: The permanent section of audit documentation usually contains copies of important client documents. They may include (1) the articles of incorporation, stock options, contracts, and bylaws; (2) the engagement letter, the contract between the auditor and the client; (3) analyses from previous audits of accounts of special importance to the auditor, such as noncurrent debt, PP&E, and equity; and (4) information concerning internal control, e.g., flowcharts, organization charts, and questionnaires.
    Answer (A) is incorrect. Schedules that support the current year's adjusting entries are not carried forward in the permanent file. They are unlikely to have continuing significance. Answer (B) is incorrect. Prior years' accounts receivable confirmations that were classified as exceptions are not carried forward in the permanent file. They are unlikely to have continuing significance. Answer (C) is incorrect. Documentation indicating that the audit work was adequately planned and supervised is always included in the current files.

15. Which of the following documentation is required for an audit in accordance with PCAOB standards?

    A. A flowchart or an internal control questionnaire that evaluates the effectiveness of the entity's internal controls.

    B. A list of alternative procedures that were considered but not used in the audit.

    C. An indication that the accounting records agree or reconcile with the financial statements.

    D. The manner in which management considered trivial errors discovered in the audit.

Answer (C) is correct.
    REQUIRED: The audit documentation required by the PCAOB.
    DISCUSSION: Audit documentation should (1) demonstrate that the engagement complied with PCAOB standards, (2) support the basis for conclusions about all relevant assertions, and (3) demonstrate that the accounting records agree or reconcile with the financial statements.
    Answer (A) is incorrect. Although an auditor must document that a sufficient understanding of internal control has been obtained, a flowchart or questionnaire is not required. Answer (B) is incorrect. Procedures not employed need not be documented. Answer (D) is incorrect. Errors judged as trivial need not be considered by management.

16. Which of the following statements concerning audit documentation is **false**?

    A. An auditor may support an opinion by other means in addition to audit documentation.

    B. The form of audit documentation should be designed to meet the circumstances of a particular engagement.

    C. Audit documentation is the property of the client.

    D. Audit documentation should show that the auditor has obtained an understanding of internal control.

Answer (C) is correct.
    REQUIRED: The false statement about audit documentation.
    DISCUSSION: Audit documentation is the property of the auditor. Copies of documentation may be made available to the client if the validity and independence of the audit are not undermined.
    Answer (A) is incorrect. Audit documentation supports the auditor's conclusions, but additional means may be used to support an opinion. Answer (B) is incorrect. The form, content, and extent of audit documentation vary with the circumstances. Answer (D) is incorrect. Among other things, the auditor should document the understanding of the components of internal control.

10.4 The Computer as an Audit Tool

17. An auditor would **least** likely use computer software to

    A. Construct parallel simulations.

    B. Access data files.

    C. Prepare spreadsheets.

    D. Assess risk.

Answer (D) is correct.
    REQUIRED: The task least likely to be done with computer software.
    DISCUSSION: The auditor is required to obtain an understanding of the entity and its environment, including its internal control, and to assess the risk of material misstatement to plan the audit. This assessment is a matter of professional judgment that cannot be accomplished with a computer.
    Answer (A) is incorrect. Parallel simulation involves using an auditor's program to reproduce the logic of the client's program. Answer (B) is incorrect. Computer software makes accessing client files much faster and easier. Answer (C) is incorrect. Many audit spreadsheet programs are available.

18. The two requirements crucial to achieving audit efficiency and effectiveness with a personal computer are selecting

- A. The appropriate audit tasks for personal computer applications and the appropriate software to perform the selected audit tasks.
- B. The appropriate software to perform the selected audit tasks and audit procedures that are generally applicable to several clients in a specific industry.
- C. Client data that can be accessed by the auditor's personal computer and audit procedures that are generally applicable to several clients in a specific industry.
- D. Audit procedures that are generally applicable to several clients in a specific industry and the appropriate audit tasks for personal computer applications.

Answer (A) is correct.
REQUIRED: The two requirements necessary to achieve audit efficiency and effectiveness using a personal computer.
DISCUSSION: The question relates to using the computer as an audit tool. To use a personal computer for this purpose effectively and efficiently, the auditor must have the appropriate hardware and software.
Answer (B) is incorrect. Selection of standardized procedures for the industry does not relate directly to the efficient and effective use of a personal computer. Answer (C) is incorrect. Access to the client's records and selection of standardized audit procedures pertain more to the use of generalized audit software to perform substantive tests than to using the personal computer as an audit tool. Answer (D) is incorrect. Selection of standardized procedures for the industry does not relate directly to the efficient and effective use of a personal computer.

19. A primary advantage of using generalized audit software packages to audit the financial statements of a client that uses a computer system is that the auditor may

- A. Consider increasing the use of substantive tests of transactions in place of analytical procedures.
- B. Substantiate the accuracy of data through self-checking digits and hash totals.
- C. Reduce the level of required tests of controls to a relatively small amount.
- D. Access information stored on computer files while having a limited understanding of the client's hardware and software features.

Answer (D) is correct.
REQUIRED: The advantage of using generalized audit software (GAS).
DISCUSSION: These packages permit the auditor to audit through the computer; e.g., to extract, compare, analyze, and summarize data; and to generate output for use in the audit. Although generalized audit software requires the auditor to provide certain specifications about the client's records, computer equipment, and file formats, a detailed knowledge of the client's system may be unnecessary because the audit package is designed to be used in many environments.
Answer (A) is incorrect. The auditor is required to apply analytical procedures in the planning and overall review phases of the audit. Answer (B) is incorrect. Self-checking digits and hash totals are application controls used by clients. Answer (C) is incorrect. Audit software may permit far more comprehensive tests of controls than a manual audit.

20. Which of the following is an engagement attribute for an audit of an entity that processes most of its financial data in electronic form without any paper documentation?

- A. Discrete phases of planning, interim, and year-end fieldwork.
- B. Increased effort to search for evidence of management fraud.
- C. Performance of audit tests on a continuous basis.
- D. Increased emphasis on the completeness assertion.

Answer (C) is correct.
REQUIRED: The engagement attribute for auditing in an electronic environment.
DISCUSSION: The audit trail for transactions processed in electronic form may be available for only a short period of time. The auditor may conclude that it is necessary to time audit procedures so that they correspond to the availability of the evidence. Thus, audit modules may be embedded in the client's software for this purpose.
Answer (A) is incorrect. This engagement attribute would be appropriate for any type of client. Answer (B) is incorrect. Processing transactions in electronic form does not inherently increase the risk of management fraud. Answer (D) is incorrect. No inherent additional concern arises about the completeness assertion as a result of processing transactions in electronic form.

Access the Gleim CPA Premium Review System featuring SmartAdapt for exam-emulating multiple-choice questions and simulations with detailed answer explanations.

Learn more: gleim.com/CPApremium | 800.874.5346

STUDY UNIT ELEVEN
EVIDENCE -- THE SALES-RECEIVABLES-CASH CYCLE

(9 pages of outline)

The primary purpose of the collection of evidence is to test relevant assertions about the transaction classes, balances, and disclosures in the financial statements. The auditor uses these assertions as a basis for assessing risks of material misstatement (RMMs) and designing and performing further audit procedures.

Many audit procedures performed in accordance with the risk assessment are intended to detect overstatement of sales, receivables, and cash. This study unit presents a comprehensive audit plan for the sales-receivables-cash cycle. The plan includes the customary procedures assuming no unusual risks. Some of the CPA questions that follow the study outlines in this study unit relate to special risks that require modification of the audit plan. The candidate should consider those questions and practice the modification of audit plans to address special risks.

The approach to audit plan development described in the outlines may be used in answering CPA exam questions. Application of the AICPA's **assertions model** ensures that all assertions are tested. However, other formats for presentation of the procedures are acceptable, for example, the PCAOB's assertions model. These models are addressed in Study Unit 1, Subunit 2.

11.1 SUBSTANTIVE TESTING OF SALES AND RECEIVABLES

1. **Accounts receivable** are the entity's claims against customers that have arisen from the sale of goods or services in the normal course of business or from a financial institution's loans.

2. **Revenues** result from an entity's ongoing major or central operations, for example, sales of goods or services.

   a. Testing assertions about accounts receivable also results in evidence relevant to the assertions about sales revenues. Thus, testing for the completeness of receivables also tests the completeness of sales. A credit to sales ordinarily is accompanied by a debit to receivables, an entry that is recorded in the sales journal. **Special journals** record a large volume of similar items. Entries not suitable for one of the special journals are recorded in the **general journal**.

   b. Special sales-related accounts are covered in item 4. of this subunit.

 Study Units 11 through 13 have sections on testing relevant assertions. They describe examples of procedures an auditor may use to test the assertions. You need not memorize them, but after reading the description you should understand why the procedure would be useful in testing the assertion. You will not be required to draft an audit program on the CPA Exam, but you may be required to identify procedures useful in testing specific assertions.

3. **Testing relevant assertions.** The following is a standard audit plan for sales and receivables that tests relevant assertions (CAVE CROC).

   a. **Completeness.** Do sales and receivables reflect all recordable transactions for the period?

      1) Compare (reconcile) the total recorded amounts in the **subsidiary ledger** with the accounts receivable amount recorded in the **general ledger**.

2) **Analytical procedures.** Use the appropriate sources of data (e.g., prior experience, budgets prepared by management at the beginning of the period, nonfinancial data, industry information, and interrelationships) to develop expectations to compare with management's presentations. Calculate and compare ratios for the current period, for example, the **accounts receivable turnover ratio** (net credit sales ÷ average accounts receivable), with those of prior periods and industry norms.

3) Account for the **numerical sequence** of sales-related documents, such as sales orders, shipping documents, and invoices.

4) Compare **shipping documents** with sales invoices and journal entries to test whether the related sales were recorded at the time of sale.

b.   **Accuracy.** Have transactions and events been recorded appropriately?

1) Obtain a **management representation letter** that includes assertions relating to sales and receivables.

2) Evaluate management's disclosures about **reportable operating segments** and related information, including products and services, geographic areas, and major customers.

3) Compare the general ledger balances with the balances on the financial statements.

c.   **Valuation and allocation.** Are accounts receivable measured in accordance with the applicable financial reporting framework, e.g., net realizable value (gross accounts receivable – allowance for uncollectible accounts)?

1) **Age the accounts receivable.** Classify the receivables by age, and compare percentages within classifications with those of the prior year.

2) **Trace subsequent cash receipts.** Cash receipts after the balance sheet date provide the best evidence of collectibility. By the end of the field work, the auditor should be able to judge the likely collections of the outstanding balances and determine whether the allowance for uncollectibles is sufficient to properly measure the year-end balance of receivables.

3) Review delinquent customers' **credit ratings**. This procedure provides evidence for assessing collectibility.

d.   **Existence.** Are the accounts receivable valid assets?

1) **Confirm accounts receivable** (also tests the rights and valuation assertions).

a)   External confirmation of accounts receivable is a generally accepted auditing procedure. Moreover, confirmation at year end provides greater assurance than at an interim date. The auditor confirms accounts receivable unless (1) they are immaterial, (2) confirmation would be ineffective, or (3) RMM based on other procedures is judged to be sufficiently low.

b)   An oral response to a confirmation request does not meet the definition of an external confirmation.

c)   An auditor who has not confirmed accounts receivable should **document** how (s)he overcame this presumption.

d)   Confirming receivables may detect lapping because the entity's and customer's records of lapped accounts will differ. **Lapping** is the theft of a cash payment from one customer concealed by crediting that customer's account when a second customer makes a payment.

e)   Confirmation requests also may detect an **improper cutoff**. The client might have held open the sales journal after year end and improperly recorded sales and receivables for the period under audit rather than for the subsequent period. In this case, responses to confirmations would indicate that amounts owed by debtors at year end are smaller than the recorded amounts.

f)   A **negative confirmation** request contains the recorded balance of the receivable. The debtor is requested to respond only if the amount is incorrect. A **positive confirmation** request asks the debtor to respond whether the amount is incorrect or not. The **blank form** of a positive confirmation request asks that the debtor fill out the amount owed to the entity being audited.

g)   When customers fail to answer a **second request** for a positive confirmation, the accounts may be in dispute, uncollectible, or fictitious. The auditor should then apply alternative procedures (examination of subsequent cash receipts, shipping documents, and other client documentation of existence) to obtain evidence about the validity of nonresponding accounts.

h)   The auditor should be convinced that confirmations received via email, fax, or other electronic media were sent by the debtor and not by an impostor.

2)   **Vouch recorded accounts receivable to shipping documents.** Because shipment of goods is typically the event creating the sale and receivable, vouching recorded receivables to shipping documents, such as bills of lading, tests for existence.

e.   **Cutoff.** Have transactions been recorded in the proper period?

1)   **Sales cutoff test.** Test to determine that a sale and receivable were recorded when title passed to the customer, which often occurs when goods are shipped (i.e., when terms are **FOB shipping point**). Shipping documents are traced to the accounting records for several days prior to and after year end to determine proper recognition in the appropriate period. This test detects inflated sales.

2)   **Cash receipts cutoff test.** Test the recording of the receipts of cash and the associated reduction in accounts receivable. Inspection and tracing of the items on the **daily remittance list** for several days prior to and after year end provides evidence of proper recording.

f.   **Rights and obligations.** Does the entity have the right to collect receivables?

1)   **Inquiries of management.** Consider the motivation and opportunity for factoring or selling the receivables, and inquire of management as to whether such transactions have occurred.

2)   **Track cash receipts** to determine that the entity is collecting and depositing the proceeds into bank accounts it controls.

3)   Determine whether sales have been made with a **right of return** and what the expected and actual returns are after year end.

g.   **Occurrence.** Did sales occur?

1)   **Vouch a sample of recorded sales** to customer orders and shipping documents. Large and unusual sales should be included in the sample selected for testing. This test is useful for detecting overstatements.

h. **Classification and understandability.** Are sales and receivables appropriately described and disclosures fairly and clearly expressed?

1) **Inspect the income statement** to determine that sales are reported as a revenue, minus returns and allowances. **Inspect the balance sheet** to determine that accounts receivable are presented as a current asset, minus the allowance for uncollectible accounts.

2) **Evaluate note disclosures** to determine that **accounting policies** are disclosed (e.g., accounts receivable should be presented at net realizable value). **Pledges of accounts receivable** should be disclosed. Any significant sales or receivables transactions with **related parties** also should be disclosed.

4. **Testing Relevant Assertions about Related Accounts**

a. **Sales returns and allowances.** The auditor should test all assertions. But if the risk of material misstatement is low, the primary tests will address the existence and occurrence assertions. Was there a proper authorization for the return of goods, and were those goods actually returned?

1) The auditor ordinarily tests the **documentation** that supports the return. This procedure determines whether proper **authorization** exists, and the credit to the customer's account was supported by a receiving report representing the return of goods.

b. **Write-off of bad debts.** If the risk of material misstatement is relatively low, the audit plan for accounts receivable described above should provide sufficient appropriate evidence. However, if controls are ineffective, for example, if the accounting function (the accounts receivable bookkeeper) is allowed to approve write-offs, the auditor will perform specific procedures to reduce detection risk to an acceptably low level.

1) Thus, the auditor might decide to attempt to confirm the receivables previously written off. If the write-offs were legitimate, most requests will be marked *Return to Sender* because the debtors will probably not be in business.

Stop and review! You have completed the outline for this subunit. Study multiple-choice questions 1 through 14 beginning on page 245.

11.2 SUBSTANTIVE TESTING OF CASH

1. **Cash** includes cash on hand, demand accounts, and other asset accounts held in financial institutions.

2. Substantive testing of cash addresses assertions related to the **balance sheet**.

3. **Testing Relevant Assertions**

a. **Completeness.** Does the balance at the end of the accounting period reflect all cash transactions?

1) For cash **receipts**, trace the **daily remittance list** to the last validated deposit ticket for the period. For cash **disbursements**, determine the **last check written** for the period and trace the effect to the accounting records. Determine that all outstanding checks have been listed on the **bank reconciliation**.

2) Use of **analytical procedures** is not typically as effective for cash as for most other accounts because it is a managed account. However, the auditor may be able to use management's budget, prepared at the beginning of the period, as an expectation with which to compare the year-end balance.

    b.   **Accuracy.** Has cash been recorded accurately?

       1) Compare a sample of daily remittance lists with deposits, journal entries, and ledger postings.

       2) Compare the general ledger balances with the balances on the financial statements.

    c.   **Valuation and allocation.** Is cash valued in accordance with the applicable reporting framework?

       1) U.S. currency has low inherent risk relative to this assertion. However, special circumstances, such as holdings of foreign currency, may require additional testing.

    d.   **Existence.** Does cash exist? Because **inherent risk** is high for cash, most audit procedures are directed toward existence.

       1) **Count cash on hand.**

          a) Control all cash and negotiable securities to protect against substitution.

          b) Determine that all received checks are payable to the client.

          c) Determine that all received checks are endorsed "For Deposit Only into Account Number XXXX."

       2) **Bank confirmation.** The AICPA *Standard Form to Confirm Account Balance Information with Financial Institutions* is used for specific deposits and loans.

          a) A confirmation request is **authorized by the client**, but it should be **sent by the auditor** to any bank with which the client has had business during the period.

          b) The form confirms the account name and number, interest rate, and balance for deposits.

          c) For **direct liabilities on loans**, the form confirms account number/ description, balance, due date, interest rate, date through which interest is paid, and description of collateral.

          d) To confirm other transactions and written or oral arrangements, such as contingent liabilities, lines of credit, compensating balances, and security agreements, auditors send a **separate letter signed by the client** to an official responsible for the financial institution's relationship with the client.

          e) The standard form (and separate letter) is designed to substantiate only the information that is stated on the confirmation request. Thus, the auditor should be aware that the standard form is **not** intended to elicit evidence about the **completeness assertion**.

             i) Nevertheless, the standard form requests any additional information about other deposit and loan accounts that may have come to the attention of the financial institution.

       3) **Bank reconciliation.** Inspect or prepare bank reconciliations for each account.

          a) A bank reconciliation verifies the **agreement** of the bank statements obtained directly from the institution and the amount of cash reported in the financial statements. These amounts should be equal after adjustment for deposits in transit, outstanding checks, bank charges, etc.

STANDARD FORM TO CONFIRM ACCOUNT
BALANCE INFORMATION WITH FINANCIAL INSTITUTIONS

ORIGINAL
To be mailed to accountant

CUSTOMER NAME

Financial
Institution's   [   ]
Name and
Address

[   ]

We have provided to our accountants the following information as of

the close of business on _____, 20 _____,
regarding our deposit and loan balances. Please confirm the
accuracy of the information, noting any exceptions to the information
provided. If the balances have been left blank, please complete this
form by furnishing the balance in the appropriate space below.*
Although we do not request or expect you to conduct a
comprehensive, detailed search of your records, if, during the process
of completing this confirmation, additional information about other
deposit and loan accounts we may have with you comes to your
attention, please include such information below. Please use the
enclosed envelope to return the form directly to our accountants.

1. At the close of business on the date listed above, our records indicated the following deposit balance(s):

ACCOUNT NAME	ACCOUNT NO.	INTEREST RATE	BALANCE*

2. We were directly liable to the financial institution for loans at the close of business on the date listed above as follows:

ACCOUNT NO./ DESCRIPTION	BALANCE*	DATE DUE	INTEREST RATE	DATE THROUGH WHICH INTEREST IS PAID	DESCRIPTION OF COLLATERAL

_____   _____
(Customer's Authorized Signature)   (Date)

The information presented above by the customer is in agreement with our records. Although we have not conducted a comprehensive,
detailed search of our records, no other deposit or loan accounts have come to our attention except as noted below.

_____   _____
(Financial Institution Authorized Signature)   (Date)

_____
(Title)

EXCEPTIONS AND/OR COMMENTS

Please return this form directly to our accountants: [   ]

[   ]

*Ordinarily, balances are intentionally left blank if they are not
available at the time the form is prepared.

Approved 1990 by American Bankers Association, American Institute of Certified Public Accountants, and Bank Administration
Institute. Additional forms available from: AICPA - Order Department, P.O. Box 1003, NY, NY 10108-1003

D451 5951

EXAMPLE OF LETTER TO CONFIRM OTHER FINANCIAL INSTITUTION INFORMATION

[*Date*]
Financial Institution Official
First United Bank
Anytown, USA 00000

Dear Financial Institution Official:

In connection with an audit of the financial statements of [*name of customer*] as of [*balance sheet date*] and for the [*period*] then ended, we have advised our independent auditors of the information listed below, which we believe is a complete and accurate description of our contingent liabilities, including oral and written guarantees, with your financial institution. Although we do not request nor expect you to conduct a comprehensive, detailed search of your records, if during the process of completing this confirmation additional information about other contingent liabilities, including oral and written guarantees, between [*name of customer*] and your financial institution comes to your attention, please include such information below.

Name of Maker	Date of Note	Due Date	Current Balance
Interest Rate	Date Through Which Interest Is Paid	Description of Collateral	Description of Purpose of Note

Information related to oral and written guarantees is as follows:

_____

_____

_____

Please confirm whether the information about contingent liabilities presented above is correct by signing below and returning this directly to our independent auditors [*name and address of CPA firm*].

Sincerely,

[*name of customer*]

_____

By: _____
                    (*Authorized Signature*)

Dear CPA Firm:

The above information listing contingent liabilities, including oral and written guarantees, agrees with the records of this financial institution. Although we have not conducted a comprehensive, detailed search of our records, no information about other contingent liabilities, including oral and written guarantees, came to our attention. [Note exceptions below or in an attached letter.]

_____

_____

_____

                                                     _____
                                                              (*Name of Financial Institution*)

                            By: _____ _____
                                           (*Officer and Title*)   (*Date*)

4) **Cutoff bank statement.** This should be requested directly from the bank for the period 7 to 10 days after year end. Use this statement to test reconciling items on the year-end bank reconciliation, e.g., deposits in transit and outstanding checks.

   a) Search for checks written before year end but **not listed as outstanding** on the bank reconciliation. These checks are often evidence of **kiting**, a fraud resulting from an improper recording of a bank transfer.

      i) To cover a shortage of cash (cash is recorded in the accounting records but not in the bank's records), an employee writes a check just prior to year end on the disbursing bank but does not record the disbursement in the accounting records in the current year. Furthermore, the check also does not appear as a disbursement on the year-end statement issued by the disbursing bank because it would not have cleared. However, the receipt is recorded by the receiving bank (at least as a deposit in transit), thereby covering the shortage. In the short term, the cash balance will appear to reconcile.

      ii) To uncover the fraud, the auditor should match the returned checks written prior to year end listed on the cutoff bank statement with the outstanding checks listed on the bank reconciliation for the disbursing bank. Because the kited check was not recorded, it will not be listed as outstanding.

   b) Consider the **number of checks returned** listed on the cutoff bank statement. This procedure may provide evidence of window dressing, that is, trying to improve the **current ratio**. The client may write checks to pay current liabilities but not mail them until the next accounting period.

5) **Schedule of interbank transfers.** Preparing this schedule can help detect errors in transfers but may not be effective to detect kiting if a disbursement has not been recorded. For this procedure to be effective, the auditor should be assured that all transfers have been identified.

6) **Proof of cash.** When internal control over a transaction process is not effective, a proof of cash may be prepared. It provides direct evidence that amounts recorded by the bank (beginning and ending balances, deposits, and disbursements) reconcile with amounts recorded by the entity for a period of time, typically a month.

e. **Cutoff.** Have transactions been recorded in the proper period?

   1) Inspect and trace the daily remittance lists for several days prior to and after year end.

   2) Identify and trace the last check written for the year into the records.

f. **Rights and obligations.** Does the entity have ownership right to the cash?

   1) In most cases, risks related to ownership are low, and few specific procedures are applied. However, confirmations related to the existence assertion provide evidence for the rights and obligations assertion. Inquiries of management are also appropriate.

g. **Occurrence.** Did the cash transactions occur?

   1) **Vouch** a sample of recorded cash receipts to accounts receivable and customer orders.

   2) Vouch a sample of recorded cash disbursements to approved vouchers.

h. **Classification and understandability.** Is cash appropriately described, and are disclosures fairly and clearly expressed?

1) **Inquire of management about disclosure.** Include references to cash in the management representation letter.

2) Determine that **restricted cash** (e.g., sinking funds and compensating balances) is reported in the noncurrent asset section of the balance sheet.

3) **Assess statement of cash flows.**

a) Determine proper presentation: direct or indirect method.

b) Reconcile information with income statement and balance sheet presentations.

c) Examine elements of statement of cash flows classifications: operating activities, investing activities, and financing activities.

4) Evaluate financial statement note disclosures.

Stop and review! You have completed the outline for this subunit. Study multiple-choice questions 15 through 20 beginning on page 249.

QUESTIONS

11.1 Substantive Testing of Sales and Receivables

1. Which of the following comparisons would be most useful to an auditor in evaluating the results of an entity's operations?

A. Prior-year accounts payable to current-year accounts payable.

B. Prior-year payroll expense to budgeted current-year payroll expense.

C. Current-year revenue to budgeted current-year revenue.

D. Current-year warranty expense to current-year contingent liabilities.

Answer (C) is correct.
  REQUIRED: The best comparison for evaluating the results of operations.
  DISCUSSION: Revenues result from an entity's ongoing major or central operations. These operations reflect numerous activities and affect many accounts. Consequently, comparing current-year revenue with the budgeted current-year revenue provides evidence as to the completeness of revenue. Revenue is a broad measure of the effects of the entity's main activities and is a primary component of the results of operations.
  Answer (A) is incorrect. The change in accounts payable is too narrow a measure to be useful in this evaluation. Answer (B) is incorrect. Payroll expense is too narrow a measure to be useful in this evaluation. Answer (D) is incorrect. The relationship of warranty expense with contingent liabilities is too narrow a measure to be useful in this evaluation.

2. An auditor most likely would limit substantive audit tests of sales transactions when the risks of material misstatement are assessed as low for the existence and occurrence assertions concerning sales transactions and the auditor has already gathered evidence supporting

A. Opening and closing inventory balances.

B. Cash receipts and accounts receivable.

C. Shipping and receiving activities.

D. Cutoffs of sales and purchases.

Answer (B) is correct.
  REQUIRED: The evidence related to the existence and occurrence assertions for sales transactions.
  DISCUSSION: Cash receipts and accounts receivable have a direct relationship with sales. A cash sale results in a debit to cash and a credit to sales. A sale on account results in a debit to accounts receivable and a credit to sales. Thus, evidence related to cash receipts and accounts receivable provides assurances about sales.
  Answer (A) is incorrect. The opening and closing inventory balances do not directly affect the sales transactions. Answer (C) is incorrect. Although shipping activities are related to sales, receiving activities are not. Answer (D) is incorrect. Although cutoffs of sales provide evidence as to sales transactions, cutoffs of purchases do not.

3. If the objective of a test of details is to detect overstatements of sales, the auditor should compare transactions in the

   A. Cash receipts journal with the sales journal.

   B. Sales journal with the cash receipts journal.

   C. Source documents with the accounting records.

   D. Accounting records with the source documents.

Answer (D) is correct.
   REQUIRED: The appropriate test to detect overstatement of sales.
   DISCUSSION: Overstatements of sales likely result from entries with no supporting documentation. The proper direction of testing is to sample entries in the sales account and vouch them to the shipping documents. The source documents represent the valid sales.
   Answer (A) is incorrect. The cash receipts journal and the sales journal are books of original entry, not source documents. Answer (B) is incorrect. The cash receipts journal and the sales journal are books of original entry, not source documents. Answer (C) is incorrect. The proper direction of testing is from the accounting records to the source documents.

4. Tracing shipping documents to prenumbered sales invoices provides evidence that

   A. No duplicate shipments or billings occurred.

   B. Shipments to customers were properly invoiced.

   C. All goods ordered by customers were shipped.

   D. All prenumbered sales invoices were accounted for.

Answer (B) is correct.
   REQUIRED: The evidence provided by tracing shipping documents to prenumbered sales invoices.
   DISCUSSION: The direction of testing to determine that shipments to customers were properly invoiced is from the shipping documents to the sales invoices.
   Answer (A) is incorrect. Tracing a sample of customer orders to the shipping documents provides evidence about duplicate shipments. Answer (C) is incorrect. Tracing sales orders to shipping documents provides evidence that all goods ordered by customers were shipped. Answer (D) is incorrect. Accounting for all the numbered invoices provides assurance that no invoices were lost or misplaced.

5. An auditor most likely would review an entity's periodic accounting for the numerical sequence of shipping documents and invoices to support management's financial statement assertion of

   A. Occurrence.

   B. Rights and obligations.

   C. Valuation and allocation.

   D. Completeness.

Answer (D) is correct.
   REQUIRED: The assertion supported by reviewing the numerical sequence of shipping documents and invoices.
   DISCUSSION: The completeness assertion concerns whether all transactions (or assets, liabilities, and equity interests) that should be recorded are recorded. Testing the numerical sequence of shipping documents and invoices is a means of detecting omitted items.
   Answer (A) is incorrect. The occurrence assertion addresses whether recorded transactions have occurred and pertain to the entity. Answer (B) is incorrect. The rights and obligations assertion concerns whether assets are the rights of the entity and liabilities are obligations at a given date. Answer (C) is incorrect. The valuation and allocation assertion concerns whether assets, liabilities, and equity interests have been included at appropriate amounts.

6. An entity's financial statements were misstated over a period of years because large amounts of revenue were recorded in journal entries that involved debits and credits to an illogical combination of accounts. The auditor could most likely have been alerted to this fraud by

   A. Scanning the general journal for unusual entries.

   B. Performing a revenue cutoff test at year end.

   C. Tracing a sample of journal entries to the general ledger.

   D. Examining documentary evidence of sales returns and allowances recorded after year end.

Answer (A) is correct.
   REQUIRED: The procedure to detect misstatement of revenue as a result of illogical entries.
   DISCUSSION: The general journal is a book of original entry used for transactions not suitable for recording in the special journals (sales, purchases, cash receipts, cash disbursements). Entries involving unusual combinations of accounts are more likely to appear in the general journal than in one of the special journals, which are designed to record large numbers of similar items. For example, credit sales (debit accounts receivable, credit sales) are entered in the sales journal.
   Answer (B) is incorrect. A revenue cutoff is a test of the timing of recognition. Moreover, it applies to transactions at year end only. Answer (C) is incorrect. Tracing journal entries will only test whether recorded transactions were posted to the ledger. Answer (D) is incorrect. This procedure applies to year-end transactions only.

7. Which of the following might be detected by an auditor's review of the client's sales cutoff?

A. Excessive goods returned for credit.

B. Unrecorded sales discounts.

C. Lapping of year-end accounts receivable.

D. Inflated sales for the year.

Answer (D) is correct.
REQUIRED: The condition that might be detected by review of the client's sales cutoff.
DISCUSSION: Sales cutoff tests are designed to detect the client's manipulation of sales. By examining recorded sales for several days before and after the balance sheet date and comparing them with sales invoices and shipping documents, the auditor may detect the recording of a sale in a period other than that in which title passed.
Answer (A) is incorrect. Sales returns are not examined in the sales cutoff test. Answer (B) is incorrect. Examination of cash receipts would reveal unrecorded discounts. Answer (C) is incorrect. Lapping may be detected by the confirmation of customer balances and tracing amounts received according to duplicate deposit slips to the accounts receivable subsidiary ledger.

8. The auditing standards define external confirmation as "a direct written response to the auditor from a third party (the confirming party), either in paper form or by electronic or other medium." The assertions for which confirmation of accounts receivable balances provides primary evidence are

A. Completeness and valuation.

B. Valuation and rights and obligations.

C. Rights and obligations and existence.

D. Existence and completeness.

Answer (C) is correct.
REQUIRED: The assertions tested by confirming receivables.
DISCUSSION: Confirmation by means of direct (independent) communication with debtors is the generally accepted auditing procedure for accounts receivable. Properly designed requests may address any assertion in the financial statements, but they are most likely to be effective for the existence and rights and obligations assertions. Thus, confirmation provides evidence that (1) receivables are valid, (2) the client has ownership of the accounts and the right of collection, and (3) the debtor has the obligation to pay.
Answer (A) is incorrect. Confirmation is not effective for the completeness assertion. It is unlikely to detect unrecorded accounts. Answer (B) is incorrect. Confirmation is less effective for the valuation assertion than for the existence and rights and obligations assertions. Answer (D) is incorrect. Confirmation is less effective for the completeness assertion than for the existence and rights and obligations assertions.

9. An auditor confirms a representative number of open accounts receivable as of December 31 and investigates respondents' exceptions and comments. By this procedure, the auditor would be most likely to learn of which of the following?

A. One of the cashiers has been covering a personal embezzlement by lapping.

B. One of the sales clerks has not been preparing charge slips for credit sales to family and friends.

C. One of the computer control clerks has been removing all sales invoices applicable to his account from the data file.

D. The credit manager has misappropriated remittances from customers whose accounts have been written off.

Answer (A) is correct.
REQUIRED: The fraud most likely to be detected by confirming receivables.
DISCUSSION: Lapping is the theft of a cash payment from one customer concealed by crediting that customer's account when a second customer makes a payment. When lapping exists at the balance sheet date, the confirmation of customer balances will probably detect the fraud because the customers' and entity's records of lapped accounts will differ.
Answer (B) is incorrect. If a charge slip has not been prepared, no accounts receivable balance will exist to be confirmed. Answer (C) is incorrect. If a sales invoice is not processed, no account balance will appear in the records. Answer (D) is incorrect. Once the account has been written off, the account is no longer open.

10. To reduce the risks associated with accepting fax responses to requests for confirmations of accounts receivable, an auditor most likely would

A. Examine the shipping documents that provide evidence for the existence assertion.

B. Verify the sources and contents of the faxes in telephone calls to the senders.

C. Consider the faxes to be nonresponses and evaluate them as unadjusted differences.

D. Inspect the faxes for forgeries or alterations and consider them to be acceptable if none are noted.

Answer (B) is correct.

REQUIRED: The procedure to reduce the risk of accepting false confirmations by fax.

DISCUSSION: Because establishing the source of a fax is often difficult, the auditor should ensure that the confirmations returned by fax are genuine. One way is to verify the sources by following up with telephone calls to the senders.

Answer (A) is incorrect. The purpose of the confirmation is to test the existence of the receivable by direct communication with the debtor. Answer (C) is incorrect. A fax is considered a valid response if the source can be verified. Answer (D) is incorrect. Faxes may not be signed. Furthermore, the auditor is unlikely to be qualified to recognize forgeries.

11. An auditor who has confirmed accounts receivable may discover that the sales journal was held open past year end if

A. Positive confirmation requests sent to debtors are not returned.

B. Negative confirmation requests sent to debtors are not returned.

C. Most of the returned negative confirmation requests indicate that the debtor owes a larger balance than the amount being confirmed.

D. Most of the returned positive confirmation requests indicate that the debtor owes a smaller balance than the amount being confirmed.

Answer (D) is correct.

REQUIRED: The result of confirmation indicating that the sales journal was held open past year end.

DISCUSSION: When the majority of the returned positive confirmation requests indicate smaller balances at year end than those in the client's records, the client may have held open the sales journal after year end. Thus, the client debited customers' accounts for the period under audit rather than for the subsequent period. The effect is to overstate sales and receivables.

Answer (A) is incorrect. The failure to receive replies to positive confirmation requests may cause the auditor concern about the existence assertion. Answer (B) is incorrect. Nonresponses to negative confirmation requests provide some evidence about the existence assertion. Answer (C) is incorrect. Replies indicating balances larger than those confirmed suggest that the sales journal was closed prior to year end.

12. An auditor confirmed accounts receivable as of an interim date, and all confirmations were returned and appeared reasonable. Which of the following additional procedures most likely should be performed at year end?

A. Send confirmation requests for all new customer balances incurred from the interim date to year end.

B. Resend confirmation requests for any significant customer balances remaining at year end.

C. Review supporting documents for new large balances occurring after the interim date, and evaluate any significant changes in balances at year end.

D. Review cash collections subsequent to the interim date and the year end.

Answer (C) is correct.

REQUIRED: The year-end procedure most likely performed after receivables were confirmed at an interim date.

DISCUSSION: If incremental RMMs can be controlled, procedures to cover the remaining period ordinarily include (1) comparing information at the interim date with information at the balance sheet date to identify and investigate unusual amounts (e.g., new large balances) and (2) other analytical procedures or tests of details.

Answer (A) is incorrect. Sampling is normally used in confirming receivables. Answer (B) is incorrect. Second confirmation requests are normally not sent when initial confirmations were returned. Answer (D) is incorrect. Verification of subsequent collections is an alternative procedure used when the response rate to confirmation requests is low.

13. When an auditor does **not** receive replies to positive requests for year-end accounts receivable confirmations, the auditor most likely would

- A. Inspect the allowance account to verify whether the accounts were subsequently written off.
- B. Increase the assessed risks of material misstatement for the valuation and completeness assertions.
- C. Send the customer a second confirmation request.
- D. Increase the assessed risks of material misstatement for the revenue cycle.

Answer (C) is correct.
   REQUIRED: The auditor action when positive confirmation requests are not returned.
   DISCUSSION: When first requests for positive confirmation are not returned, the auditor should consider second requests. The requests should be authorized by the client and should ask the debtor to respond directly to the auditor.
   Answer (A) is incorrect. It is premature to conclude that the account is uncollectible. Answer (B) is incorrect. The auditor should collect sufficient appropriate evidence to reduce audit risk to an acceptably low level. Answer (D) is incorrect. Increasing the assessed RMMs is premature. The auditor should send second requests or perform alternative procedures.

14. Which of the following procedures would an auditor most likely perform for year-end accounts receivable confirmations when the auditor did **not** receive replies to second requests?

- A. Review the cash receipts journal for the month prior to year end.
- B. Intensify the study of internal control concerning the revenue cycle.
- C. Increase the assessed level of detection risk for the existence assertion.
- D. Inspect the shipping records documenting the merchandise sold to the debtors.

Answer (D) is correct.
   REQUIRED: The most appropriate audit procedure when customers fail to reply to second request forms.
   DISCUSSION: When customers fail to answer a second request for a positive confirmation, the accounts may be in dispute, uncollectible, or fictitious. The auditor should then apply alternative procedures (examination of subsequent cash receipts, shipping documents, and other client documentation of existence) to obtain evidence about the validity of nonresponding accounts.
   Answer (A) is incorrect. Previous collections cannot substantiate year-end balances. Answer (B) is incorrect. Nonresponse to a confirmation request is not proof of ineffective controls. Nonresponses do occur and are expected. Answer (C) is incorrect. RMMs are assessed, but detection risk is not. However, the acceptable level of detection risk may be decreased if the assessment of RMMs is increased as a result of nonresponses to confirmation requests.

11.2 Substantive Testing of Cash

15. An auditor ordinarily sends a standard confirmation request to all banks with which the client has done business during the year under audit, regardless of the year-end balance. A purpose of this procedure is to

- A. Provide the data necessary to prepare a proof of cash.
- B. Request that a cutoff bank statement and related checks be sent to the auditor.
- C. Detect kiting activities that may otherwise not be discovered.
- D. Seek information about other deposit and loan amounts that come to the attention of the institution in the process of completing the confirmation.

Answer (D) is correct.
   REQUIRED: The reason confirmations are sent to all banks used by the client.
   DISCUSSION: The AICPA *Standard Form to Confirm Account Balance Information with Financial Institutions* is used to confirm specifically listed deposit and loan balances. Nevertheless, the standard confirmation form contains this language: "Although we do not request or expect you to conduct a comprehensive, detailed search of your records, if, during the process of completing this confirmation, additional information about other deposit and loan accounts we may have with you comes to your attention, please include such information below."
   Answer (A) is incorrect. The information for a proof of cash is in the month-end bank statement. Answer (B) is incorrect. A cutoff bank statement is for some period subsequent to the balance sheet date. Answer (C) is incorrect. The auditor should compare the returned checks in the cutoff bank statement with those listed as outstanding on the bank reconciliation, as well as prepare a bank transfer schedule for a few days before and after the balance sheet date.

16. An independent auditor asked a client's internal auditor to assist in preparing a standard financial institution confirmation request for a payroll account that had been closed during the year under audit. After the internal auditor prepared the form, the controller signed it and mailed it to the bank. What was the major flaw in this procedure?

A. The internal auditor did not sign the form.

B. The form was mailed by the controller.

C. The form was prepared by the internal auditor.

D. The account was closed, so the balance was zero.

Answer (B) is correct.
 REQUIRED: The flaw in the confirmation request to a financial institution about a closed payroll account.
 DISCUSSION: The AICPA *Standard Form to Confirm Account Balance Information with Financial Institutions* is used for specific deposits and loans. A confirmation is signed (requested) by the client, but it should be sent by the auditor. Thus, the auditor should control confirmation requests and responses. Control means direct communication between the intended recipient and the auditor to minimize possible bias of the results because of interception and alteration of the requests or responses.
 Answer (A) is incorrect. The internal auditor need not sign the form. Answer (C) is incorrect. The auditor may request direct assistance from the internal auditors when performing an audit. Answer (D) is incorrect. The auditor must still obtain evidence about the account even though it has been closed.

Questions 17 and 18 are based on the following information. The following was taken from the bank transfer schedule prepared during the audit of Fox Co.'s financial statements for the year ended December 31, Year 1. Assume all checks are dated and issued on December 30, Year 1.

Check No.	Bank Accounts		Disbursement Date		Receipt Date	
	From	To	Per Books	Per Bank	Per Books	Per Bank
101	National	Federal	Dec. 30	Jan. 4	Dec. 30	Jan. 3
202	County	State	Jan. 3	Jan. 2	Dec. 30	Dec. 31
303	Federal	American	Dec. 31	Jan. 3	Jan. 2	Jan. 2
404	State	Republic	Jan. 2	Jan. 2	Dec. 31	Jan. 2

---

17. Which of the following checks might indicate kiting?

A. #101 and #303.

B. #202 and #404.

C. #101 and #404.

D. #202 and #303.

Answer (B) is correct.
 REQUIRED: The checks that might indicate kiting.
 DISCUSSION: Kiting is the recording of a deposit from an interbank transfer in the current period while failing to record the related disbursement until the next period. It is a fraud that exploits the lag (float period) between the deposit of a check in one account and the time it clears the bank on which it is drawn. Checks #202 and #404 may indicate kiting. They were recorded as receipts on the books in the current period. However, they were recorded as disbursements on the books in the next year.
 Answer (A) is incorrect. Checks #101 and #303 were recorded as received after year end. Answer (C) is incorrect. Check #101 was recorded as received after year end. Answer (D) is incorrect. Check #303 was recorded as received after year end.

18. Which of the following checks illustrate deposits or transfers in transit at December 31, Year 1?

A. #101 and #202.

B. #101 and #303.

C. #202 and #404.

D. #303 and #404.

Answer (B) is correct.
 REQUIRED: The checks indicating deposits or transfers in transit.
 DISCUSSION: A deposit or transfer in transit is one recorded in the entity's books as a receipt by the balance sheet date but not recorded as a deposit by the bank until the next period. Check #101 is a deposit or transfer in transit because the check was recorded in the books before the end of the year but not recorded by either bank until January. Check #303 is also a deposit or transfer in transit because the check was deducted from Federal's balance in December but was not added to American's balance until January.
 Answer (A) is incorrect. Check #202 was recorded in the books after the balance sheet date. Answer (C) is incorrect. Checks #202 and #404 were recorded in the books after the balance sheet date. Answer (D) is incorrect. Check #404 was recorded in the books after the balance sheet date.

19. An auditor should test bank transfers for the last part of the audit period and first part of the subsequent period to detect whether

A. The cash receipts journal was held open for a few days after year end.

B. The last checks recorded before year end were actually mailed by year end.

C. Cash balances were overstated because of kiting.

D. Any unusual payments to or receipts from related parties occurred.

Answer (C) is correct.
REQUIRED: The reason for testing bank transfers at year end.
DISCUSSION: Kiting is the recording of a deposit from an interbank transfer in the current period while failing to record the related disbursement until the next period. It is a fraud that exploits the lag (float period) between the deposit of a check in one account and the time it clears the bank on which it is drawn. To detect kiting, the auditor should examine a schedule of bank transfers for a period covering a few days before and after the balance sheet date. For the procedure to be effective, however, the auditor should be assured that all transfers have been identified.
Answer (A) is incorrect. A cutoff bank statement should be examined to determine whether the cash receipts journal was held open for a few days after year end. Answer (B) is incorrect. A cutoff bank statement should be examined to determine whether the last checks recorded before year end were actually mailed by year end. Answer (D) is incorrect. Unusual payments to or receipts from related parties can occur at any time of the year.

20. Which of the following cash transfers results in a misstatement of cash at December 31, Year 1?

Bank Transfer Schedule

	Disbursement		Receipt	
	Recorded in Books	Paid by Bank	Recorded in Books	Received by Bank
A.	12/31/Yr 1	1/4/Yr 2	12/31/Yr 1	12/31/Yr 1
B.	1/4/Yr 2	1/5/Yr 2	12/31/Yr 1	1/4/Yr 2
C.	12/31/Yr 1	1/5/Yr 2	12/31/Yr 1	1/4/Yr 2
D.	1/4/Yr 2	1/11/Yr 2	1/4/Yr 2	1/4/Yr 2

Answer (B) is correct.
REQUIRED: The interbank cash transfer that indicates an error in cash cutoff.
DISCUSSION: An error in cash cutoff occurs if one half of the transaction is recorded in the current period and one half in the subsequent period. Inspection of the Recorded in Books columns indicates the transfer was recorded as a receipt on 12/31/Yr 1 but not as a disbursement until 1/4/Yr 2. This discrepancy is an error in cutoff called a kite, and it overstates the cash balance.

STUDY UNIT TWELVE
EVIDENCE --
THE PURCHASES-PAYABLES-INVENTORY CYCLE

(6 pages of outline)

The primary purpose of the collection of evidence is to test relevant assertions about the transaction classes, balances, and disclosures in the financial statements. The auditor uses these assertions as a basis for assessing risks of material misstatement (RMMs) and designing and performing further audit procedures.

In general, most testing in the inventory-acquisition process is applied to accounts payable and inventory. The emphasis is on (1) understatement of accounts payable and (2) overstatement of inventory. Evidence about the debit in the payables transaction (inventory in a perpetual system and purchases in a periodic system) is gathered when the credit (accounts payable) is tested. The relationship is apparent in the opposite direction as well. As the debit is tested, evidence about the credit also is produced.

This study unit presents a comprehensive audit plan for the accounts payable and inventory accounts. The plan includes the customary procedures assuming no unusual risks. Some of the questions at the end of this study unit relate to special risks that require modification of the audit plan. The candidate should consider those questions and practice the modification of programs to address special risks.

The approach to audit plan development described in the outlines may be used in answering CPA exam questions. Application of the AICPA's **assertions model** ensures that all assertions are tested. However, other formats for presentation of the procedures are acceptable, for example, the PCAOB's assertions model. These models are addressed in Study Unit 1, Subunit 2.

12.1 SUBSTANTIVE TESTING OF ACCOUNTS PAYABLE AND PURCHASES

1. Testing assertions about accounts payable provides evidence about **purchases** and ultimately **cost of goods sold**. Purchases obviously result in ending inventory, but because inventory is a significant item on the balance sheet, a separate audit plan is typically developed for the account. An audit plan for inventory follows in Subunit 12.2.

    a. Candidates should understand the interrelationship of these accounts and the overlap of the audit procedures.

2. **Accounts payable**, sometimes termed trade payables, represent the most significant current liability of most firms.

3. **Testing Relevant Assertions.** The following is a standard audit plan for accounts payable and purchases that tests relevant assertions (recall CAVE CROC from Study Unit 1):

    a. **Completeness.** Do the balances contain all transactions for the period? (This is typically the major detection risk for the auditor in testing payables.)

        1) **Reconcile** the accounts payable ledger with the general ledger control account. Compare the total recorded amounts in the subsidiary ledger with the amount recorded in the general ledger.

2) **Analytical procedures.** The auditor should use appropriate sources of data (e.g., prior-period financial data, budgets prepared by management at the beginning of the period, nonfinancial information, industry data, and interrelationships) to form expectations with which to compare management's presentations. Ratios may be calculated and used (e.g., the **accounts payable turnover ratio**). Unexpected findings should be investigated.

3) **Trace subsequent payments** to recorded payables. A primary test is to match the payments (checks) issued after year end with the related payables. Checks should be issued only for recorded payables. Any checks that cannot be matched are likely indications of **unrecorded liabilities**.

   a) Management may be motivated to delay recording of liabilities to improve the current ratio. However, unrecorded accounts payable must still be paid, and financial statements that fail to report all liabilities at year end are misstated.

4) **Search for unvouchered payables.** The accounts payable function prepares and records a voucher (with a debit to purchases and a credit to accounts payable) when all the supporting documentation is assembled. The auditor should search the suspense files for unmatched documents to determine whether relevant documents have been lost, misplaced, or misfiled.

   a) A **suspense file** contains transactions, the classification and treatment of which are in doubt, for example, because of missing documents.

   b) For example, a requisition, receiving report, and invoice may be held by the accounts payable department, but no voucher is prepared or entry made if the purchase order has not been matched with the other documents. This situation results in an unrecorded liability.

b. **Accuracy.** Have the amounts been recorded appropriately?

   1) Obtain a management **representation letter** with assertions related to purchases and payables.

   2) Compare the general ledger balances to the balances on the financial statements.

c. **Valuation and allocation.** Are accounts payable measured in accordance with the applicable reporting framework? U.S. GAAP require that debts be stated at the amount necessary to satisfy the obligation.

   1) Detection risk for this assertion is reduced if the other assertions are tested in accordance with GAAS. The valuation or allocation assertion is interrelated with those for **existence and completeness**.

d. **Existence.** Do the recorded accounts payable represent valid liabilities at the balance sheet date?

   1) **Confirmation** is not a generally accepted auditing procedure because it is not likely to disclose unrecorded payables. Normally, the auditor can become satisfied as to the existence of recorded payables using evidence available directly from the client.

      a) If confirmation is undertaken, small and zero balances should be sampled as well as larger balances. The auditor should use the **activity in the account** as a basis for selection. That is, if orders are placed with a vendor on a consistent basis, a confirmation should be sent to that vendor regardless of the recorded balance due at year end.

      b) The **blank form of positive confirmations** should be used. It requests that the balance due be provided by the creditor (e.g., the vendor).

e.   **Cutoff.** Have transactions been recorded in the proper period?

1) **Purchases cutoff test.** Determine that all goods for which title has passed to the client at year end are recorded in inventory and accounts payable.

a)   Goods shipped **FOB shipping point** by the vendor should be recorded in the period of shipment to the client. Thus, receipts for several days after year end should be evaluated to determine whether the goods should be recorded in the current year.

b)   Goods shipped **FOB destination** by the vendor should be recorded in the period received by the client. Receiving documents are traced to the accounting records by the auditor for several days prior to and after year end to determine proper recognition of inventory and accounts payable.

2) **Cash disbursements cutoff test.** Test the recording of cash disbursements and the associated reduction in accounts payable. Inspecting the last check written and tracing it to the accounts payable subsidiary ledger will provide evidence of proper recording.

f.   **Rights and obligations.** Does the balance of accounts payable reflect the liability of this entity? Because the risk is relatively low that management would report liabilities of others, the procedures testing this assertion are not as consequential as those for other assertions.

1) **Inquiries.** Obtain management representations about the nature of the recorded payables.

g.   **Occurrence.** Did purchases occur?

1) **Vouch recorded payables to documentation.** A sample of recorded payables should be reconciled with documentary support (e.g., requisitions, purchase orders, receiving reports, and approved invoices).

h.   **Classification and understandability.** Are (1) purchases and payables appropriately described and (2) disclosures fairly and clearly expressed?

1) **Inspect the financial statements.** Accounts payable should be presented as a current liability on the balance sheet. Purchases should be used in the determination of cost of sales for the income statement.

2) **Evaluate note disclosures.** Any unusual significant transactions or events should be described by management in the notes (e.g., significant accounts payable to related parties).

Stop and review! You have completed the outline for this subunit. Study multiple-choice questions 1 through 10 beginning on page 258.

Background
Recent auditing standards emphasize the importance of understanding clients and their businesses. This understanding always has been an issue for audits of inventory. Auditors often have been deceived by their clients about the amount or measurement of inventory because clients have more knowledge than the auditor. This is particularly true of certain types of inventory, for example, bulk or liquid inventory, high-tech products, or manufactured parts. Current auditing standards require some physical contact (observe and test count) to reduce the risks associated with verifying the existence of inventory, but significant risks remain.

12.2 SUBSTANTIVE TESTING OF INVENTORY

1.   The primary purpose of the collection of evidence for inventory is to test management's assertions about the presentation of the balance and disclosures in the financial statements.

2.   **Inventory** consists of the goods held for resale by the client and is presented as a current asset on the balance sheet.

3.   **Testing Relevant Assertions.** The following is a standard audit plan that tests relevant assertions (CAVE CROC) about the inventory balance:

a.   **Completeness.** Does the inventory balance contain all inventory owned by the entity at year end?

   1)   **Analytical procedures.** The calculation of amounts and ratios and their comparison with expectations can identify unusual findings indicative of misstatements.

      a)   The **inventory turnover ratio** (cost of sales ÷ average or ending inventory) should be compared with that of the prior period and industry averages.

      b)   **Vertical analysis** (e.g., the percentage of inventory to total assets), using industry information, can identify unusual conditions.

      c)   Information from the client's previously prepared **budgets** can provide the basis for expectations.

      d)   **Nonfinancial information** (e.g., the volume, in boxes or pounds) may provide expectations about the flow of inventory as well as sales and receivables.

b.   **Accuracy.** Have the amounts been recorded appropriately?

   1)   Compare the general ledger balance to the balance on the financial statements.

c.   **Valuation and allocation.** Is inventory recorded at **lower of cost or market**?

   1)   **Compare recorded costs with current cost to replace the goods.** Current vendor price lists should be compared with recorded inventory costs to determine that current prices are not less than recorded costs.

   2)   **Calculate the turnover ratio.** An applicable analytical procedure is to calculate the inventory turnover ratio for the individual inventory items. Excessive inventory results in small turnover ratios and provides evidence of potentially obsolete items.

   3)   **Test costs of manufactured items.** Manufactured goods should be costed to include direct materials, direct labor, and an allocation of overhead. The overhead allocation rate should be tested for reasonableness.

d.   **Existence.** Does the inventory exist at a given date?

   1)   **Observation** of inventories is generally required. The auditor should observe and make test counts but is not responsible for taking inventory.

      a)   If the entity uses the **periodic inventory method**, test counts should be made at or very close to year end because the counted inventory is used to calculate cost of sales.

      b)   If the entity uses the **perpetual inventory method**, test counts may be made at interim dates if records are well kept. If the RMMs are high, inventory counts should be done at year end.

         i)   The client may use methods, including **statistical sampling**, that are sufficiently reliable to make an annual count of all items unnecessary. The auditor must be assured these methods are reasonable and statistically valid and have been properly applied. Observations and test counts must still be performed.

      c)   Observations should encompass all **significant inventory locations**.

         i)   The auditor should observe and make test counts even if inventory is taken by **management specialists** (i.e., businesses that perform inventory counts as their service).

    2) The client's plan for taking inventory should make effective use of, and exercise control over, **prenumbered inventory tags** and **summary sheets**.

        a) The plan should include provisions for handling receipts and shipments during the count.

        b) Goods not owned by the client, such as goods held on consignment, should be separated.

        c) Appropriate instructions and supervision should be given to employees conducting the count.

    3) **Performing tests of the count** should include the following:

        a) Observing employees following the plan

        b) Assuring that all items are tagged

        c) Evaluating control over the movement of inventory before, during, and after the count

        d) Observing employees making counts and recording amounts on tags

        e) Determining that tags and inventory summary sheets are controlled

        f) Making test counts, comparing test counts with amounts recorded on the tags and summary sheets, and reconciling amounts with records

        g) Being alert for empty boxes, empty squares (i.e., boxes stacked to suggest the block of boxes is solid when the middle does not contain boxes), and inventory defects (e.g., damaged or dirty items)

        h) Establishing a cutoff by documenting the last receiving report and shipping document

    4) The performance of procedures should be **documented**.

    5) The auditor should confirm or investigate inventories held by **public warehouses** or other third parties.

        a) The auditor ordinarily obtains confirmation by direct communication with the custodian. When a significant portion of current or total assets is held in a public warehouse, the auditor should consider testing the client's procedures by (1) evaluating the warehouser, (2) obtaining an independent accountant's report on the warehouser's internal control, (3) visiting the warehouse and observing physical counts, and (4) investigating the use of warehouse receipts (e.g., whether they are being used for collateral). The auditor should confirm with lenders the details of any pledged receipts.

  e. <u>Cutoff.</u> Have transactions been recorded in the proper period?

    1) **Purchases and sales cutoff tests**. Test recording of transactions subject to the terms (FOB shipping point or FOB receiving point) of both purchase and sale of inventory.

  f. <u>Rights and obligations.</u> Does the entity own the inventory reported on the balance sheet?

    1) **Vouch recorded purchases to documentation.** Vouch a sample of recorded inventory items to payment records. Payment vouchers for inventory should have supporting documentation (e.g., requisition, purchase order, receiving report, and vendor invoice) and canceled checks (if payment has been made).

2) **Consider the industry or client practices for consigned goods.** The nature of the client or industry suggests the possibility of consignment transactions (e.g., the client has held or shipped consigned goods in the past). The auditor should review the client's correspondence, evaluate sales and receivables records, and consider the results of vouching purchases to detect unrecognized consignment activity.

    a) For example, if the client has inappropriately recorded consignment shipments as sales, the auditor most likely will find a pattern of large sales on account and many small, periodic cash receipts for the receivables.

g. **Occurrence.** Did the inventory transactions occur?

1) Vouch a sample of recorded purchases to documentation.
2) Vouch a sample of recorded cost of sales to documentation.

h. **Classification and understandability.** Are inventories properly displayed as current assets, and has cost of sales been properly reflected in the income statement? Have adequate disclosures been made concerning inventory measurement, cost flow assumptions, and significant transactions, such as pledging of inventory?

1) **Read financial statements.** The auditor should read the financial statements to determine that accounts are properly reflected and notes adequately informative.

2) **Inquire of management.** The auditor should inquire of management about (a) consigned goods, (b) major purchase commitments, (c) pledging of inventory, and (d) other significant transactions or events.

3) Obtain a **management representation letter** that includes assertions relating to inventory and cost of sales.

Stop and review! You have completed the outline for this subunit. Study multiple-choice questions 11 through 20 beginning on page 261.

QUESTIONS

12.1 Substantive Testing of Accounts Payable and Purchases

1. Which of the following is a substantive procedure that an auditor most likely would perform to verify the existence and valuation assertions about recorded accounts payable?

A. Investigating the open purchase order file to ascertain that prenumbered purchase orders are used and accounted for.

B. Receiving the client's mail, unopened, for a reasonable period of time after year end to search for unrecorded vendor's invoices.

C. Vouching selected entries in the accounts payable subsidiary ledger to purchase orders and receiving reports.

D. Confirming accounts payable balances with known suppliers who have zero balances.

Answer (C) is correct.
   REQUIRED: The substantive procedure for the existence and valuation assertions about recorded accounts payable.
   DISCUSSION: Vouching a sample of recorded accounts payable to purchase orders and receiving reports provides evidence that the obligations exist at a given date. The purchase orders evidence the initiation of the transactions, and the receiving reports indicate that goods were received and that liabilities were thereby incurred. Thus, these documents provide evidence that amounts are owed to others, that the transactions occurred, and that the liabilities have been included at appropriate amounts.
   Answer (A) is incorrect. Ascertaining that prenumbered documents are used and accounted for relates most directly to the completeness assertion. Answer (B) is incorrect. Searching for unrecorded liabilities relates most directly to completeness. Answer (D) is incorrect. Confirming payables with known suppliers having zero balances is a procedure for detecting unrecorded liabilities. Thus, it relates most directly to completeness.

2. To determine whether accounts payable are complete, an auditor performs a test to verify that all merchandise received is recorded. The population of documents for this test consists of all

- A. Payment vouchers.
- B. Receiving reports.
- C. Purchase requisitions.
- D. Vendors' invoices.

Answer (B) is correct.

REQUIRED: The population of documents for a test to verify that all merchandise received is recorded.

DISCUSSION: The population to be tested consists of receiving reports. An accounts payable record should be available for each receiving report.

Answer (A) is incorrect. A payment voucher is prepared for each account payable. A payment voucher would not exist for an unrecorded payable. Answer (C) is incorrect. The goods requisitioned may not have been ordered. If ordered, they may not have been received. Hence, a payable may not exist for each requisition. Answer (D) is incorrect. A vendor's invoice does not provide evidence that the goods have been received and a liability incurred. Thus, a payable need not exist for every vendor's invoice.

3. When performing a substantive test of a random sample of cash disbursements, an auditor is supplied with a photocopy of vendor invoices supporting the disbursements for one particular vendor rather than the original invoices. The auditor is told that the vendor's original invoices have been misplaced. What should the auditor do in response to this situation?

- A. Increase randomly the number of items in the substantive test to increase the reliance that may be placed on the overall test.
- B. Reevaluate the risk of fraud and design alternate tests for the related transactions.
- C. Increase testing by agreeing more of the payments to this particular vendor to the photocopies of its invoices.
- D. Count the missing original documents as misstatements, and project the total amount of the error based on the size of the population and the dollar amount of the errors.

Answer (B) is correct.

REQUIRED: The auditor's response to finding a photocopy of an invoice in support of a disbursement.

DISCUSSION: Several issues should cause the auditor to be suspicious. First, how could the client lose the original? Second, how did the client obtain a photocopy if the original was lost? Finally, and most importantly, photocopies are much less credible given the ease with which they can be altered. Thus, the auditor should reevaluate the risk of fraud.

Answer (A) is incorrect. The auditor should resolve this issue. The change in audit plan depends on the disposition of this transaction. Answer (C) is incorrect. More tests of this vendor may be in order, but the auditor should insist on obtaining originals of the documents. Answer (D) is incorrect. This may or may not be a misstatement. However, the transaction could be fraudulent with much broader implications.

4. An auditor performs a test to determine whether all merchandise for which the client was billed was received. The population for this test consists of all

- A. Merchandise received.
- B. Vendors' invoices.
- C. Canceled checks.
- D. Receiving reports.

Answer (B) is correct.

REQUIRED: The population for a test to determine whether all merchandise for which the client was billed was received.

DISCUSSION: Vendors' invoices are the billing documents received by the client. They describe the items purchased, the amounts due, and the payment terms. The auditor should trace these invoices to the related receiving reports.

Answer (A) is incorrect. Testing merchandise received will not detect merchandise billed but not received. Answer (C) is incorrect. Tracing canceled checks to the related receiving reports tests whether goods paid for, not goods billed, were received. Answer (D) is incorrect. Tracing receiving reports to vendors' invoices tests whether all goods received were billed.

5. In auditing accounts payable, an auditor's procedures most likely will focus primarily on the relevant assertion about

- A. Existence.
- B. Classification and understandability.
- C. Completeness.
- D. Valuation and allocation.

Answer (C) is correct.

REQUIRED: The assertion that is the focus of an audit of accounts payable.

DISCUSSION: The primary audit risk for accounts payable is understatement of the liability. Thus, the auditor will most likely focus on the completeness assertion.

Answer (A) is incorrect. The existence assertion concerns whether liabilities exist at a given date. The audit risk for accounts payable is not great for that assertion. Answer (B) is incorrect. The risk of inappropriate classification and understandability on the financial statements is not as great as the risk that some items are not included. Answer (D) is incorrect. The risk that accounts payable are not measured in accordance with the applicable reporting framework is lower than the risk that the balance may not be complete.

6. An auditor's purpose in reviewing the renewal of a note payable shortly after the balance sheet date most likely is to obtain evidence concerning relevant assertions about

A. Existence.

B. Classification and understandability.

C. Completeness.

D. Valuation and allocation.

Answer (B) is correct.
REQUIRED: The auditor's purpose in reviewing the renewal of a note payable shortly after year end.
DISCUSSION: Events such as the renewal of the note payable do not require adjustment of the financial statements but may require disclosure. Accordingly, the auditor should determine that the renewal had essentially the same terms and conditions as the recorded debt at year end. A significant change may affect the classification of notes payable (e.g., as current or noncurrent), the understandability of the statements, and the required disclosures.

7. When using confirmations to provide evidence about the completeness assertion for accounts payable, the appropriate population most likely is

A. Vendors with whom the entity has previously done business.

B. Amounts recorded in the accounts payable subsidiary ledger.

C. Payees of checks drawn in the month after the year end.

D. Invoices filed in the entity's open invoice file.

Answer (A) is correct.
REQUIRED: The appropriate population when confirmations of accounts payable are used to test the completeness assertion.
DISCUSSION: When sending confirmations for accounts payable, the population of accounts should include small and zero balances as well as large balances. The auditor should use the activity in the account as a gauge for sample selection. That is, if orders are placed with a vendor on a consistent basis, a confirmation should be sent to that vendor regardless of the recorded balance due.
Answer (B) is incorrect. The auditor, in testing the completeness assertion, is concerned with balances that have not been recorded or invoices that have not been filed. Answer (C) is incorrect. The payees of checks are not an appropriate population for the confirmation process. Payments in the month after year end do not necessarily reflect year-end liabilities. Answer (D) is incorrect. The auditor, in testing the completeness assertion, is concerned with balances that have not been recorded or invoices that have not been filed.

8. An auditor suspects that certain client employees are ordering merchandise for themselves over the Internet without recording the purchase or receipt of the merchandise. When vendors' invoices arrive, one of the employees approves the invoices for payment. After the invoices are paid, the employee destroys the invoices and the related vouchers. In gathering evidence regarding the fraud, the auditor most likely would select items for testing from the file of all

A. Cash disbursements.

B. Approved vouchers.

C. Receiving reports.

D. Vendors' invoices.

Answer (A) is correct.
REQUIRED: The file tested to determine whether checks are being issued for unauthorized expenditures.
DISCUSSION: The best procedure to test whether any checks have been issued without supporting vouchers, purchase orders, and receiving reports is to select an appropriate sample of canceled checks (cash disbursements) and trace them to the related supporting documentation.
Answer (B) is incorrect. The approved vouchers relating to the fraudulent transactions have been destroyed and therefore could not be chosen for audit. Answer (C) is incorrect. The receipt of the merchandise is not recorded. Answer (D) is incorrect. The vendors' invoices relating to the fraudulent transactions have been destroyed and therefore could not be chosen for audit.

9. Tests designed to detect purchases made before the end of the year that have been recorded in the subsequent year most likely would provide assurance about the relevant assertion regarding

A. Valuation and allocation.

B. Existence.

C. Cutoff.

D. Classification and understandability.

Answer (C) is correct.
REQUIRED: The purpose of an audit procedure.
DISCUSSION: The cutoff assertion is that transactions and events have been recorded in the proper period. To determine that all goods for which title has passed to the client at year end are recorded in inventory and accounts payable, a purchases cutoff test is appropriate.
Answer (A) is incorrect. The procedure does not directly test the assertion of valuation and allocation. Answer (B) is incorrect. The procedure does not directly test the assertion of existence. Answer (D) is incorrect. The procedure does not directly test the assertion of classification and understandability.

10. An internal control narrative indicates that an approved voucher is required to support every check request for payment of merchandise. Which of the following procedures provides the greatest assurance that this control is operating effectively?

A. Select and examine vouchers and ascertain that the related canceled checks are dated no later than the vouchers.

B. Select and examine vouchers and ascertain that the related canceled checks are dated no earlier than the vouchers.

C. Select and examine canceled checks and ascertain that the related vouchers are dated no earlier than the checks.

D. Select and examine canceled checks and ascertain that the related vouchers are dated no later than the checks.

Answer (D) is correct.
REQUIRED: The procedure giving the greatest assurance that approved vouchers support check requests.
DISCUSSION: Payment vouchers bearing the required approvals should be supported by a properly authorized purchase requisition, a purchase order executing the transaction, a receiving report indicating all goods ordered have been received in good condition, and a vendor invoice confirming the amount owed. To determine that check requests are valid, the appropriate audit procedure is therefore to compare checks and the related vouchers. The direction of testing should be from a sample of checks to the approved vouchers. If the date of a voucher is later than the date of the related check, the inference is that a check was issued without proper support.
Answer (A) is incorrect. Tracing from vouchers to canceled checks does not give assurance that all checks are supported by approved vouchers. This test will not detect canceled checks unsupported by approved vouchers, although it will permit comparison of the dates of the respective documents. Answer (B) is incorrect. Tracing from vouchers to canceled checks does not give assurance that all checks are supported by approved vouchers. This test will not detect canceled checks unsupported by approved vouchers, although it will permit comparison of the dates of the respective documents. Answer (C) is incorrect. The checks should be dated no earlier than the vouchers. Each voucher should be dated earlier than (or have the same date as) the related check.

12.2 Substantive Testing of Inventory

11. The element of the audit-planning process most likely to be agreed upon with the client before implementation of the audit strategy is the determination of the

A. Evidence to be gathered to provide a sufficient basis for the auditor's opinion.

B. Procedures to be undertaken to discover litigation, claims, and assessments.

C. Pending legal matters to be included in the inquiry of the client's attorney.

D. Timing of inventory observation procedures to be performed.

Answer (D) is correct.
REQUIRED: The element of audit planning most likely agreed upon with the client before implementation.
DISCUSSION: The client is responsible for taking the physical inventory. The auditor is responsible for observing this process and performing test counts. The audit procedures are dependent upon management's plans. Thus, the auditor must coordinate the collection of this evidence with management.
Answer (A) is incorrect. The evidence to be gathered is a matter of professional judgment to be determined solely by the auditor. Answer (B) is incorrect. The procedures performed to discover litigation, claims, and assessments are matters of professional judgment to be determined solely by the auditor. Answer (C) is incorrect. Pending legal matters to be included in the inquiry of the client's attorney are matters of professional judgment to be determined solely by the auditor.

12. When auditing inventories, an auditor would **least** likely verify that

A. All inventory owned by the client is on hand at the time of the count.

B. The client has used proper inventory pricing.

C. The financial statement presentation of inventories is appropriate.

D. Damaged goods and obsolete items have been properly accounted for.

Answer (A) is correct.
REQUIRED: The procedure not performed in an audit of inventories.
DISCUSSION: An auditor does not expect all inventory to which the auditee has title to be on hand at the date of the count. Some purchased goods may still be in transit at that time. Also, some inventory may be on consignment or in public warehouses although properly included in the count.
Answer (B) is incorrect. The auditor should test relevant assertions about valuation of inventory. Answer (C) is incorrect. The auditor should test relevant assertions about presentation in the financial statements. Answer (D) is incorrect. The auditor should test relevant assertions about valuation of inventory.

13. To gain assurance that all inventory items in a client's inventory listing schedule are valid, an auditor most likely would vouch

- A. Inventory tags noted during the auditor's observation to items listed in the inventory listing schedule.
- B. Inventory tags noted during the auditor's observation to items listed in receiving reports and vendors' invoices.
- C. Items listed in the inventory listing schedule to inventory tags and the auditor's recorded count sheets.
- D. Items listed in receiving reports and vendors' invoices to the inventory listing schedule.

Answer (C) is correct.
REQUIRED: The step to provide assurance that all inventory items in a client's inventory listing are valid.
DISCUSSION: Validity relates to the existence assertion. To determine that the items exist, the direction of testing should be from the schedule to the inventory tags and ultimately to the auditor's count sheet.
Answer (A) is incorrect. Tracing tags to the inventory listing schedule should provide evidence of completeness. That is, all items counted are included on the listing sheet. Answer (B) is incorrect. Tracing inventory tags to receiving reports and vendors' invoices should provide information useful in determining whether inventory was recorded at cost. Answer (D) is incorrect. Tracing inventory items on receiving reports and vendors' invoices to the inventory listing schedule is not an effective test. Many items received are sold by the inventory date.

14. An auditor selected items for test counts while observing a client's physical inventory. The auditor then traced the test counts to the client's inventory listing. Tracing test counts most likely obtained evidence concerning the relevant assertion about

- A. Rights and obligations.
- B. Completeness.
- C. Existence.
- D. Valuation.

Answer (B) is correct.
REQUIRED: The assertion relevant to tracing test counts to the client's inventory listing.
DISCUSSION: Tracing the details of test counts to the final inventory schedule assures the auditor that items in the observed physical inventory are included in the inventory records. The auditor should compare the inventory tag sequence numbers in the final inventory schedule with those in the records of his or her test counts made during the client's physical inventory.
Answer (A) is incorrect. The reconciliation of the test counts with the inventory listing does not provide assurance that the inventory is owned by the client. Answer (C) is incorrect. Although the observation of inventory provides evidence as to existence, specifically tracing test counts to the inventory listing provides evidence of completeness. Answer (D) is incorrect. The valuation assertion is tested by determining whether inventory items are included in inventory at lower of cost or market.

15. While observing a client's annual physical inventory, an auditor recorded test counts for several items and noticed that certain test counts were higher than the recorded quantities in the client's perpetual records. This situation could be the result of the client's failure to record

- A. Purchase discounts.
- B. Purchase returns.
- C. Sales.
- D. Sales returns.

Answer (D) is correct.
REQUIRED: The transaction class not recorded when test counts are greater than recorded quantities.
DISCUSSION: Failure to record sales returns for goods returned to the physical inventory will result in test counts greater than the quantities reported by the perpetual inventory system.
Answer (A) is incorrect. Purchase discounts relate to the measurement of inventory, not to the quantity. Answer (B) is incorrect. Failure to record purchase returns results in lower quantities in the physical inventory than in the perpetual records. Answer (C) is incorrect. Failure to record sales results in lower quantities in the physical inventory than in the perpetual records.

16. An auditor most likely would analyze inventory turnover rates to obtain evidence concerning relevant assertions about

- A. Existence.
- B. Rights and obligations.
- C. Classification and understandability.
- D. Valuation and allocation.

Answer (D) is correct.
REQUIRED: The assertion about which analysis of inventory turnover rates provides evidence.
DISCUSSION: Assertions about valuation and allocation address whether (1) assets, liabilities, and equity interests are included in the financial statements at appropriate amounts and (2) resulting adjustments are properly recorded. An examination of inventory turnover pertains to identifying slow-moving, excess, defective, and obsolete items included in inventories. This audit procedure tests the valuation and allocation assertion.
Answer (A) is incorrect. Analysis of inventory turnover does not test existence. Answer (B) is incorrect. Analysis of inventory turnover does not test whether the entity has rights to the inventory. Answer (C) is incorrect. The classification and understandability assertion concerns whether financial information is properly presented and described and disclosures are clear.

17. To measure how effectively an entity employs its resources, an auditor calculates inventory turnover by dividing average inventory into

    A. Net sales.

    B. Cost of goods sold.

    C. Operating income.

    D. Gross sales.

Answer (B) is correct.
    REQUIRED: The calculation of the inventory turnover ratio.
    DISCUSSION: Inventory turnover equals cost of goods sold divided by average inventory. It provides a measure of how many times inventory requires replacement.

18. An auditor most likely would make inquiries of production and sales personnel concerning possible obsolete or slow-moving inventory to support the relevant assertion about

    A. Valuation and allocation.

    B. Rights and obligations.

    C. Existence.

    D. Classification and understandability.

Answer (A) is correct.
    REQUIRED: The assertion tested when considering obsolete or slow-moving inventory.
    DISCUSSION: The valuation and allocation assertion is directed towards whether inventory is recorded at lower of cost or market. The discovery of slow-moving, excess, defective, or obsolete inventory suggests that the cost of inventory be written down to market.

19. An auditor concluded that no excessive costs for an idle plant were charged to inventory. This conclusion most likely related to the auditor's objective to obtain evidence about the relevant assertions regarding inventory, including presentation and disclosure and

    A. Valuation and allocation.

    B. Completeness.

    C. Occurrence.

    D. Rights and obligations.

Answer (A) is correct.
    REQUIRED: The assertion related to the conclusion that no excessive costs for an idle plant were inventoried.
    DISCUSSION: Inventory should properly include the costs of direct labor, direct materials, and manufacturing overhead. Thus, to be properly measured, an appropriate amount of manufacturing overhead should be charged to inventory. Costs of an idle plant should not be included in manufacturing overhead.

20. Which of the following auditing procedures most likely would provide assurance regarding a manufacturing entity's relevant assertions about inventory valuation?

    A. Testing the entity's computation of standard overhead rates.

    B. Obtaining confirmation of inventories pledged under loan agreements.

    C. Reviewing shipping and receiving cutoff procedures for inventories.

    D. Tracing test counts to the entity's inventory listing.

Answer (A) is correct.
    REQUIRED: The procedure that provides assurance about a manufacturing entity's inventory measurement.
    DISCUSSION: Manufactured goods should be recorded at cost, including direct materials, direct labor, and an allocation of overhead. The overhead allocation rate should be tested for reasonableness.
    Answer (B) is incorrect. Obtaining confirmation of inventories pledged under loan agreements tests the assertion of rights and obligations. Answer (C) is incorrect. Reviewing shipping and receiving cutoff procedures tests the assertion of cutoff. Answer (D) is incorrect. Tracing test counts to the inventory listing tests the assertion of completeness.

STUDY UNIT THIRTEEN
EVIDENCE --
OTHER ASSETS, LIABILITIES, AND EQUITIES

(10 pages of outline)

This study unit presents comprehensive audit plans for accounts not previously considered. Each plan includes the customary procedures assuming no unusual risks. The candidate also should consider whether audit plans and procedures need to be modified to address special risks.

The approach to audit plan development described in the outlines may be used in answering CPA exam questions. Application of the AICPA's assertions model ensures that all assertions are tested. However, other formats for presentation of the procedures are acceptable, for example, the PCAOB's assertions model. These models are addressed in Study Unit 1, Subunit 2.

13.1 SUBSTANTIVE TESTING OF PROPERTY, PLANT, AND EQUIPMENT

1. **Scope**

   a. The following balances are included in this audit plan:

      1) Buildings, equipment, improvements, and vehicles including associated depreciation expense, repairs and maintenance, and accumulated depreciation
      2) Land
      3) Capital leases and associated amortization expense

2. **Testing Relevant Assertions.** The following is a standard audit plan for property, plant, and equipment that tests relevant assertions (CAVE CROC):

   a. **Completeness.** Are all transactions affecting property, plant, and equipment for the period reflected in the balance?

      1) **Perform analytical procedures.** The five sources of information for analytical procedures (covered in Study Unit 3, Subunit 5) can be used to develop expectations. Typical ratios include rate of return on plant assets and plant assets to total assets.

      2) **Reconcile subsidiary and general ledgers.** The client usually maintains records for individual assets or classes of assets. The subsidiary records, including cost, current depreciation expense, and accumulated depreciation, should reconcile with the general ledger and the amounts to be included on the financial statements.

         a) A schedule of fixed assets is typically prepared from the subsidiary records to be used in testing and is included in the audit documentation.

      3) **Analyze repairs and maintenance.** The auditor should vouch significant debits from the repairs and maintenance expense account to determine whether any should have been capitalized.

         a) Vouching additions to property, plant, and equipment also tests the completeness assertion because debits may have been for non-capital items.

b. **Accuracy.** Have the amounts for the specific accounts been recorded appropriately?

    1) Include amounts and classifications in the management representation letter.
    2) Compare the general ledger balances with the financial statement balances.

c. **Valuation and allocation.** Are balances of property, plant, and equipment reported in accordance with the applicable reporting framework [assumed to be U.S. GAAP in this study unit (historical cost – accumulated depreciation)]?

    1) **Inspect records of purchases.** The purchase of fixed assets should result in payments. Vouching the entries to the payment records supports the rights and obligations assertion as well as the valuation assertion.

    2) **Vouch additions and disposals.** These are tests of the details of transactions. In a continuing audit, the prior year's balance of property, plant, and equipment is an audited balance. If the auditor tests the details of the transactions that changed the balance, (s)he has made significant progress in obtaining evidence about the valuation assertion (as well as other assertions such as completeness and existence).

    3) **Test depreciation.** Fixed assets (except certain nondepreciable assets such as land) are usually measured at cost minus accumulated depreciation. The depreciation methods and their application should be tested to determine that they are generally accepted and applied consistently.

d. **Existence.** Do the assets reflected in property, plant, and equipment exist at the balance sheet date?

    1) **Inspect plant additions.** The focus is on additions to property, plant, and equipment.

        a) The auditor vouches a sample from the recorded asset additions by examining the supporting documents and inspecting the physical assets. Testing in the opposite direction, i.e., by tracing from the supporting documentation to the general ledger, does not provide evidence that recorded assets exist.

        b) Initial audits require inspection of significant assets reflected in the beginning balance as well as additions.

e. **Cutoff.** Have transactions relating to property, plant, and equipment been recorded in the proper period?

    1) **Test the cutoff.** Additions and disposals near year end should be tested to ensure recording in the proper periods.

f. **Rights and obligations.** Does the entity have ownership rights in the reported property, plant, and equipment?

    1) **Examine titles and leases.** Certain property (e.g., autos and trucks) should have certificates of title. For leased assets, contracts should allow the auditor to determine whether leases have been properly recorded as either capital or operating leases.

    2) **Inspect insurance policies.** The entity should insure its assets. Vouching the recorded assets to insurance policies supports the rights assertion.

        a) When liens are placed on equipment or property, the lienholder often requires that the assets be insured and that the lienholder be named as the beneficiary. Hence, the policy is likely to be held by the lienholder even though the client is required to pay the premiums.

    3) **Inspect property tax records.** Many states assess property tax on certain fixed assets. Payment of taxes is evidence that the client has rights in the assets.

g. **Occurrence.** Did the transactions relating to property, plant, and equipment occur?

1) The auditor should test the authorization, execution, recording, and custody aspects of a sample of transactions.

h. **Classification and understandability.** Is the balance of property, plant, and equipment reflected on the balance sheet in the noncurrent section? Are adequate disclosures presented for methods of depreciation, commitments of assets, and capital lease terms?

1) **Read financial statements.** The auditor should determine that property, plant, and equipment is presented as a noncurrent asset. Depreciable assets and land should be reported at cost minus accumulated depreciation and cost, respectively. Notes to the financial statements should describe classes of assets, lease agreements, depreciation methods, and any property mortgaged or used as collateral for loans.

2) **Make inquiries of management about disclosures and other reporting issues.** Significant items should be included in the management representation letter.

Stop and review! You have completed the outline for this subunit. Study multiple-choice questions 1 through 4 beginning on page 274.

13.2 SUBSTANTIVE TESTING OF INVESTMENTS AND DERIVATIVES

1. **Scope**

a. The following balances are included in this audit plan:

1) **Noncurrent items.** These include (a) capital stock or other equity interests reported using the fair value or equity methods, (b) bonds and similar debt instruments, (c) loans and advances that are essentially investments, and (d) goodwill.

2) **Current items.** These include trading, held-to-maturity, and available-for-sale securities classified as current.

3) **Derivatives and hedges.** A derivative is an unperformed contract that results in cash flow between two counterparties based on (derived from) the change in some other indicator of value. Hedges are defensive strategies to protect an entity against the risk of adverse price or interest rate movements on certain assets, liabilities, or anticipated transactions.

4) **Revenues** generated from investments.

b. According to U.S. GAAP, the appropriate classification of investments depends on (1) management's **intent** in purchasing and holding the investment, (2) the entity's actual investment activities, and (3), for certain debt securities, the entity's **ability** to hold the investment to maturity. The auditor should obtain an understanding of the process used by management to classify investments before determining the nature, timing, and extent of further audit procedures.

c. AU-C 501, *Audit Evidence -- Specific Consideration for Selected Items*, provides guidance for planning and performing audit procedures to test assertions about investments in securities and derivatives.

2.   **Securities Valued Based on Investee Financial Results**

    a.   In accordance with AU-C 501, the following procedures should be performed to support the investee's financial results (excluding equity method investments, which are accounted for as components under AU-C 600):

        1)   Read the investee's statements and related audit report and determine whether the other auditor's report is satisfactory.

            a)   These statements may be unaudited, or the other auditor's report may be unsatisfactory. In this case, apply the procedures to the statements that are appropriate given the investment's materiality to the investor.

        2)   Obtain evidence to support (a) an investment carrying amount based on factors not in the investee's statements or (b) fair values materially different from the investee's carrying amounts.

        3)   Determine whether the entity has properly considered a **lack of comparability**, resulting from a difference between the dates of the investor's and investee's statements. For example, a significant transaction occurring between those dates may have a material effect on the entity's statements.

    b.   The auditor should (1) read interim statements of the investee and (2) make inquiries of investor management to identify **subsequent events and transactions** of the investee that may be material to the investor.

3.   **Derivatives and Securities Measured at Fair Value**

    a.   The auditor should

        1)   Determine whether the applicable reporting framework specifies the method for measuring fair value

        2)   Evaluate whether the measurement is consistent with the method

    b.   Fair value estimates may be obtained from a third-party source (e.g., a broker-dealer). The auditor should understand the method used by the source to make the estimate and consider the significance of the work of the management's specialist.

        1)   If the entity has used a valuation model, the auditor applies AU-C 540, *Auditing Accounting Estimates, including Fair Value Accounting Estimates, and Related Disclosures.*

4.   **Impairment Losses**

    a.   The auditor

        1)   Evaluates management's conclusion about recognition of a loss for a decline in fair value below cost or carrying amount

        2)   Obtains support for the amount of the recorded adjustment, including compliance with the reporting framework

5.   **Unrealized Appreciation or Depreciation**

    a.   The auditor should obtain sufficient appropriate evidence about the unrealized amount of a derivative's fair value that is recognized or disclosed because a hedge is ineffective.

6. **Testing Relevant Assertions.** The following is a standard audit plan for investments that tests relevant assertions (CAVE CROC):

    a. **Completeness.** Are all transactions affecting investments for the period reflected in the balance?

        1) **Perform analytical procedures.** Prior-period amounts held should be compared with current amounts. The expected return on investments held can be compared with actual recorded amounts.

        2) **Reconcile the subsidiary ledger with the control accounts.** The auditor should prepare a schedule from the subsidiary ledger and reconcile the amounts with the balances in the general ledger and financial statements.

        3) **Evaluate contracts and agreements.** The auditor should determine whether all securities, derivatives, and hedges have been identified and reported.

    b. **Accuracy.** Have the balances for specific accounts been recorded appropriately?

        1) **Recalculate interest revenue.** The auditor should determine that interest revenue, based on stated rates for recorded investments, has been properly recorded.

        2) Compare the general ledger balances with the financial statement balances.

    c. **Valuation and allocation.** Are balances reported in accordance with the applicable reporting framework?

        1) **Vouch recorded amounts for trading securities and available-for-sale securities to market quotations if available.** When market quotations are unavailable, the auditor can obtain fair-value estimates from broker-dealers and other third-party sources who derive the fair value of a security by using modeling or a similar technique. The auditor should evaluate the appropriateness of the valuation models and the variables and assumptions used in the model.

        2) **Determine that unrealized gains and losses (changes in fair value) are properly accounted for.** Unrealized gains and losses on trading securities are included in earnings. Unrealized gains and losses on available-for-sale securities are reported in other comprehensive income until realized. (An exception is provided for all or part of the unrealized gain or loss on an available-for-sale security designated as hedged in a fair-value hedge.)

        3) **Vouch recorded costs for held-to-maturity securities to market quotations.** The entity should measure these securities at amortized cost only if it has the positive intent and ability to hold them to maturity. The auditor also should recalculate the premium or discount.

        4) **Determine that transfers between categories of investments are at fair value.**

        5) **Inspect relevant records and documents and make appropriate inquiries about nontemporary declines in fair value.** Individual available-for-sale or held-to-maturity securities may suffer a nontemporary decline in fair value below their cost basis. The securities should be written down to fair value reflecting the new cost basis, and the amount of the write-down should be included in earnings.

        6) **Obtain audited financial statements from the investees if investments are accounted for by the equity method.** The investment accounts should be based on percentage ownership in the investee and reported income or loss of the investee.

        7) **Evaluate goodwill for potential impairments.** If management cannot provide evidence to support the value, it should be written off.

d. **Existence.** Do investments reported at the balance sheet date exist?

    1) **Physically inspect and count securities in the client's possession.** Serial numbers should be recorded and compared with the entity's records. Inspection and counting also should be performed when counting other liquid assets (e.g., cash). The client's representative should be available to acknowledge that the securities have been returned intact.

    2) **Confirm securities.** Confirmation requests may be made to the issuer, custodian, counterparty, or broker-dealer for unsettled transactions.

e. **Cutoff.** Have transactions relating to investments been recorded in the proper period?

    1) **Test the cutoff.** The auditor should test transactions made near year end to ensure they are reflected in the proper period.

f. **Rights and obligations.** Does the entity own the reported investments?

    1) **Trace dividend and interest revenue.** The auditor should determine that revenue has been properly recorded.

g. **Occurrence.** Did the transactions relating to investments occur?

    1) **Vouch recorded costs to documentation.** The cost of recorded securities can be established by comparing recorded amounts with broker invoices, canceled checks, and other evidence of purchase.

h. **Classification and understandability.** Are balances related to investments reflected on the balance sheet in the current or noncurrent section depending on management expectations?

    1) **Read financial statements.** Determine that individual trading, available-for-sale, and held-to-maturity securities are reported as current or noncurrent as appropriate. Determine whether derivatives, hedges, and other financial instruments are adequately described in the notes to the financial statements.

    2) **Make inquiries of management about intentions to dispose of investments.** Classification often is based on the actions of management. The responses should be documented in the management representation letter. Also, the auditor should consider whether investment activities corroborate or conflict with management's stated intent.

Stop and review! You have completed the outline for this subunit. Study multiple-choice questions 5 through 12 beginning on page 276.

13.3 SUBSTANTIVE TESTING OF NONCURRENT DEBT

1. **Scope**

    a. The following balances are included in this audit plan:

        1) Noncurrent notes payable, mortgages payable, and bonds payable
        2) Related interest expense

2. **Testing Relevant Assertions.** The following is a standard audit plan for noncurrent debt that tests relevant assertions (CAVE CROC):

    a. **Completeness.** Are all transactions affecting noncurrent debt reflected in the balances for the period?

        1) **Perform analytical procedures.** Prior-period amounts recorded should be compared with current amounts. A key procedure to detect unrecorded debt is to recalculate interest expense based on recorded debt and compare it with recorded interest expense. Significant unexpected interest expense recorded in the general ledger suggests the existence of unrecorded debt. The debt-to-equity ratio, which equals total liabilities divided by total equity, can also be calculated and compared with previous periods.

      2) **Reconcile the subsidiary ledger with the control accounts.** The auditor should prepare a schedule from the subsidiary ledger and reconcile the amounts with the balances in the general ledger and financial statements.

  b. **Accuracy.** Have the balances for specific accounts been recorded appropriately?

      1) **Make inquiries of management.** Questions about the sources and uses of the recorded debt may be addressed to management.

      2) Compare the general ledger balances with financial statement balances.

  c. **Valuation and allocation.** Are balances reported in accordance with GAAP?

      1) **Vouch recorded debt to debt instruments.** Bonds should be recorded at their face amounts, with separate recognition of premium or discount. Debt due in the next year should be reclassified as current (also a classification issue).

      2) **Test amortization.** Recorded debt premium or discount should be recalculated to determine that it is being amortized using appropriate GAAP (the interest method).

  d. **Existence.** Does noncurrent debt reported at the balance sheet date exist?

      1) **Confirm debt.** Debt is confirmed with investment bankers, lenders, and bond trustees. Noncurrent notes payable may be confirmed directly with the holders of the notes. Study Unit 11, Subunit 2, contains the AICPA *Standard Form to Confirm Account Balance Information with Financial Institutions.*

  e. **Cutoff.** Have transactions relating to noncurrent debt been recorded in the proper period?

      1) **Test the cutoff.** Consider transactions near year end.

  f. **Rights and obligations.** Does the entity owe the noncurrent debt?

      1) **Evaluate existing agreements.** The auditor should obtain evidence that the debt is the obligation of the auditee.

      2) **Examine bond trust indentures.** The auditor should obtain evidence that the client is meeting the conditions of the contract and is in compliance with the law. Thus, the client should have obtained an attorney's opinion. The indenture contains information about contractual arrangements with bondholders, such as (a) the face amount of the bonds, (b) interest rates, (c) payment dates, (d) descriptions of collateral, (e) provisions for conversion or retirement, (f) trustee duties, and (g) sinking-fund requirements.

  g. **Occurrence.** Did the transactions relating to noncurrent debt occur?

      1) **Review contracts and agreements.** Debt transactions should be supported by appropriate documentation identifying (a) interest rates, (b) payment dates, (c) collateral, and (d) other terms.

  h. **Classification and understandability.** Are balances properly reflected in the balance sheet, is interest expense properly reported on the income statement, and are adequate disclosures provided?

      1) **Evaluate financial statements.** Determine that noncurrent and current debt are properly classified.

      2) **Inspect disclosures.** Appropriate disclosures should be made about the terms of the debt and collateral securing the debt.

Stop and review! You have completed the outline for this subunit. Study multiple-choice questions 13 and 14 on page 278.

13.4 SUBSTANTIVE TESTING OF EQUITY

1. **Scope**

   a. The following typical balances for a corporation are included in this audit plan:

      1) Common and preferred stock
      2) Additional paid-in capital
      3) Retained earnings
      4) Treasury stock
      5) Accumulated other comprehensive income

2. **Testing Relevant Assertions.** The following is a standard audit plan for equity that tests relevant assertions (CAVE CROC):

   a. **Completeness.** Are all transactions affecting equity included in the balances for the period?

      1) **Perform analytical procedures.** Prior-period amounts recorded should be compared with current amounts.

      2) **Reconcile the subsidiary ledger with the control accounts.** The auditor should prepare a schedule from the subsidiary ledger and reconcile the amounts with the balances in the general ledger and financial statements.

   b. **Accuracy.** Have the balances for the specific accounts been recorded appropriately?

      1) The auditor should inquire of management about the actions, activities, and balances related to equity.

      2) Compare the general ledger balances with the financial statement balances.

   c. **Valuation and allocation.** Are balances reported in accordance with GAAP?

      1) **Trace entries to equity accounts.** The closing entries should be tested to determine that net income has been closed to retained earnings. Any designations (appropriations) of retained earnings should be traced to the related account.

      2) **Test sales of treasury stock.** Differences between the carrying amounts and the amounts received on the sale of treasury stock are recognized directly in the equity section of the balance sheet, not in earnings.

   d. **Existence.** Do the shares reported as outstanding or treasury stock exist at the balance sheet date?

      1) **Confirm shares issued and outstanding with the registrar and transfer agent.** The auditor should have direct communication with external parties responsible for contact with the shareholders to request information about the number of shares issued and outstanding and payment of dividends.

      2) **Inspect stock certificates held in treasury.** Treasury stock should be counted.

      3) **Inspect stock certificate book.** If the client keeps its own stock records, the shares outstanding and stubs should be reconciled.

   e. **Cutoff.** Have transactions relating to equity been recorded in the proper period?

      1) The auditor should consider whether transactions near year end have been recognized in the proper period.

   f. **Rights and obligations.** Do equity balances reflect owners' interests?

      1) **Inspect the articles of incorporation and bylaws of the corporation.** These documents provide evidence about the legal status of the shareholders and their relationship(s) to the entity. The auditor should include copies in the working papers.

   g. **Occurrence.** Did the transactions relating to equity occur?

      1) **Vouch entries to supporting documents.** Documentation should exist for each equity transaction.

    h.   **Classification and understandability.** Are balances appropriately presented, and are adequate disclosures provided?

        1) **Read minutes of meetings of the board of directors.** Authorizations of actions related to equity (e.g., issuances of additional shares, purchases or sales of treasury shares, and declarations of dividends) should be documented in the minutes. Many of these issues have implications for disclosure.

        2) **Inspect disclosures about treasury stock.** The auditor should determine the proper use of the method (cost or par value) to report treasury stock.

        3) **Search for restrictions.** Restrictions on retained earnings may arise from loans, agreements, or state law. The auditor should determine that disclosure is appropriate.

Stop and review! You have completed the outline for this subunit. Study multiple-choice questions 15 through 17 beginning on page 278.

13.5 SUBSTANTIVE TESTING OF PAYROLL

  1. **Scope**

    a. The following balances are included in this audit plan:

        1) Payroll expense
        2) Inventories (for manufacturing firms)
        3) Accrued payroll and vacation
        4) Payroll tax liability
        5) Pension costs and other post-employment benefit (OPEB) costs

    b. Payroll processing has traditionally included controls that have allowed the auditor to assess the RMM at a low level and thereby reduce the audit effort devoted to substantive testing. Most entities recognize that the benefits of controls exceed the costs related to the payroll processing system.

        1) One key control is a division of duties that includes the establishment of a **separate human resources department**. This control separates authorization from recordkeeping by the payroll department.

  2. **Testing Relevant Assertions.** The following is a standard audit plan for payroll and related accounts that tests relevant assertions (CAVE CROC):

    a. **Completeness.** Are all transactions affecting payroll reflected in the balances for the period?

        1) **Perform analytical procedures.** The auditor should compare current expense with expectations from prior periods and management-prepared budgets from the beginning of the period with actual results. Total hours worked should be used to develop an expectation for total payroll expense. This expectation is compared with recorded expense. Industry percentages for labor-related ratios also should be compared with the client's results.

        2) **Reconcile payroll tax expense with payroll tax returns** (income tax, FICA, and unemployment taxes).

    b. **Accuracy.** Have the balances for specific accounts been recorded appropriately?

        1) **Make inquiries** of management. Questions include those relating to the reporting and disclosure of contractual arrangements with officers, union contracts, and pension and OPEB agreements.

        2) Compare the general ledger balances with the financial statement balances.

    c. **Valuation and allocation.** Are balances reported in accordance with GAAP?

        1) **Trace costs to inventories (for manufacturing firms).** The auditor should determine that they contain direct labor costs.

        2) **Recalculate pension and OPEB costs.** Appropriate amounts should have been recorded and funded based on the appropriate agreements.

   d.   **Existence.** Do the accounts and balances exist at the balance sheet date?

   1)   **Observe the distribution of paychecks.** A surprise observation of the distribution will provide assurance that only bona fide employees are being paid.

   e.   **Cutoff.** Have transactions relating to payroll been recorded in the proper period?

   1)   **Test payroll cutoff.** Amounts to be accrued for the period should be recalculated from the last payroll date to year end. Also, amounts should have been recorded as payroll expense and accrued payroll.

   f.   **Rights and obligations.** Are the assets (capitalized in inventory), expenses, and payables those of the entity?

   1)   **Inspect canceled checks.** These checks indicate payment to employees, government, and others relating to payroll.

   g.   **Occurrence.** Did the transactions relating to payroll occur?

   1)   **Vouch a sample of employee transactions.** These should be sampled from the payroll-related balances and compared with the supporting documentation, including approved time cards, time tickets, and notations in the human resources records. The purpose is to verify that employees worked the number of hours for which they were paid.

   h.   **Classification and understandability.** Are payroll costs properly reflected as an expense in the income statement (or properly allocated to inventory and cost of sales for manufacturing firms)? Are liabilities properly displayed as current or noncurrent on the balance sheet, and are disclosures presented adequately?

   1)   **Read the financial statements and disclosures.** The auditor should determine the appropriate presentation of balances. Disclosures should include a description of accounting policies and pension-related transactions.

You should have now completed Study Units 11 through 13. They address the auditor's substantive procedures performed in response to the assessment of the risks of material misstatement in the various accounting cycles. You should understand the relationship between management's assertions about the transactions, balances, and disclosures and the auditor's tests of the assertions. If you are having difficulty understanding this relationship or the role of management's assertions, review Study Unit 1, Subunit 2, which defines the assertions and the auditor's responsibility. Even if you have a solid understanding, a refreshed look at that material will likely help you.

Stop and review! You have completed the outline for this subunit. Study multiple-choice questions 18 through 20 beginning on page 279.

QUESTIONS

13.1 Substantive Testing of Property, Plant, and Equipment

1. Which of the following combinations of procedures would an auditor most likely perform to obtain evidence about fixed asset additions?

A. Inspecting documents and physically examining assets.

B. Recomputing calculations and obtaining written management representations.

C. Observing operating activities and comparing balances with prior-period balances.

D. Confirming ownership and corroborating transactions through inquiries of client personnel.

Answer (A) is correct.
   REQUIRED: The combination of procedures most likely to obtain evidence about fixed asset additions.
   DISCUSSION: The auditor's direct observation of fixed assets is one means of determining whether additions have been made. Tracing to the detailed records determines whether additions have been recorded. Inspection of deeds, lease agreements, insurance policies, invoices, canceled checks, and tax notices may also reveal additions.
   Answer (B) is incorrect. Recomputations are based on recorded amounts and will not reveal unrecorded additions. Answer (C) is incorrect. Analytical procedures may not detect additions offset by disposals. Answer (D) is incorrect. The auditor must become aware of additions before confirming ownership or corroborating transactions.

2. In testing plant and equipment balances, an auditor may inspect new additions listed on the analysis of plant and equipment. This procedure is designed to obtain evidence concerning relevant assertions about

	Existence	Classification and Understandability
A.	Yes	Yes
B.	Yes	No
C.	No	Yes
D.	No	No

Answer (B) is correct.

REQUIRED: The relevant assertion(s), if any, tested by inspection of new additions of plant and equipment.

DISCUSSION: Assertions about existence address whether assets or liabilities of the entity exist at a particular date. Assertions about classification and understandability concern whether financial statement components are appropriately presented, described, and disclosed (AU-C 315). Thus, inspection by the auditor provides direct evidence that new plant and equipment assets exist but is irrelevant to the classification and understandability assertions. Reading the financial statements and related notes provides evidence about these assertions.

3. Which of the following explanations most likely would satisfy an auditor who questions management about significant debits to accumulated depreciation accounts in the current year?

A. Prior years' depreciation expenses were erroneously understated.

B. Current year's depreciation expense was erroneously understated.

C. The estimated remaining useful lives of plant assets were revised upward.

D. Plant assets were retired during the current year.

Answer (D) is correct.

REQUIRED: The satisfactory explanation about significant debits to accumulated depreciation accounts in the current year.

DISCUSSION: If plant assets were retired during the current year, their carrying amount is removed from the accounts. Accordingly, the asset (plant assets) is credited, accumulated depreciation is debited, and any consideration received and gain or loss are recognized.

Answer (A) is incorrect. The correction of an error for the prior period requires restatement of those statements. The effects of the adjustment are not recognized currently. Furthermore, a prior-period restatement of an understatement of depreciation increases the credit balance of accumulated depreciation. Answer (B) is incorrect. The current-year correction of an understatement of depreciation increases the credit balance of accumulated depreciation. Answer (C) is incorrect. A change in estimate is accounted for prospectively. Thus, no previously recognized depreciation is derecognized when the estimated remaining useful lives of plant assets are revised upward.

4. An auditor analyzes repairs and maintenance accounts primarily to obtain evidence in support of the relevant assertion that all

A. Noncapitalizable expenditures for repairs and maintenance have been recorded in the proper period.

B. Expenditures for property and equipment have been recorded in the proper period.

C. Noncapitalizable expenditures for repairs and maintenance have been properly charged to expense.

D. Expenditures for property and equipment have not been charged to expense.

Answer (D) is correct.

REQUIRED: The reason an auditor analyzes repairs and maintenance expense.

DISCUSSION: The auditor should vouch significant debits from the repairs and maintenance expense account to determine whether any should have been capitalized.

Answer (A) is incorrect. An improper cutoff of repairs and maintenance expenses is not typically a major risk. Answer (B) is incorrect. The repairs and maintenance expense accounts are not the appropriate sources of evidence regarding the cutoff of expenditures for property and equipment. Answer (C) is incorrect. Vouching additions to plant, property, and equipment provides evidence of whether any expense has been inappropriately charged as a capital item.

13.2 Substantive Testing of Investments and Derivatives

5. Which of the following pairs of accounts would an auditor most likely analyze on the same working paper?

- A. Notes receivable and interest income.
- B. Accrued interest receivable and accrued interest payable.
- C. Notes payable and notes receivable.
- D. Interest income and interest expense.

Answer (A) is correct.
REQUIRED: The pairs of accounts that an auditor most likely analyzes on the same working paper.
DISCUSSION: The auditor analyzes information and presents the analysis for related accounts on the same working paper. Notes receivable and interest on them are such related accounts.
Answer (B) is incorrect. Interest receivable and interest payable are independent of one another and are not likely to be analyzed on the same working paper. Answer (C) is incorrect. Notes payable and notes receivable are independent of one another and are not likely to be analyzed on the same working paper. Answer (D) is incorrect. Interest income and interest expense are independent of one another and are not likely to be analyzed on the same working paper.

6. An auditor would most likely verify the interest earned on bond investments by

- A. Verifying the receipt and deposit of interest checks.
- B. Confirming the bond interest rate with the issuer of the bonds.
- C. Recomputing the interest earned on the basis of face amount, interest rate, and period held.
- D. Testing internal controls relevant to cash receipts.

Answer (C) is correct.
REQUIRED: The method most likely used to verify bond interest earned.
DISCUSSION: The audit plan for investments includes making an independent computation of revenue (such as dividends and interest). For example, the auditor may use information from bond certificates (interest rates, payment dates, issue date, and face amount) to recalculate bond interest earned. This amount includes uncollected accruals.
Answer (A) is incorrect. Verifying the receipt and deposit of interest checks does not consider accrued interest. Answer (B) is incorrect. Confirming the rate would not, by itself, verify interest earned, which must be recomputed. Answer (D) is incorrect. Verification of interest earned requires substantive testing, not tests of controls.

7. In performing a count of negotiable securities, an auditor records the details of the count on a security count worksheet. What other information is usually included on this worksheet?

- A. An acknowledgment by a client representative that the securities were returned intact.
- B. An analysis of realized gains and losses from the sale of securities during the year.
- C. An evaluation of the client's internal control concerning physical access to the securities.
- D. A description of the client's procedures that prevent the negotiation of securities by just one person.

Answer (A) is correct.
REQUIRED: The information usually included on a security count worksheet.
DISCUSSION: A securities count worksheet should include a record of all the significant information from the securities, such as names, amounts, and interest rates. Also, to ensure a clear chain of custody, it should contain an acknowledgment by a client representative that the securities were returned intact when the count was complete.

8. In confirming with an outside agent, such as a financial institution, that the agent is holding investment securities in the client's name, an auditor most likely gathers evidence in support of relevant financial statement assertions about existence or occurrence and

- A. Valuation and allocation.
- B. Rights and obligations.
- C. Completeness.
- D. Classification and understandability.

Answer (B) is correct.
REQUIRED: The assertion tested by confirming investments to determine whether they are in the client's name.
DISCUSSION: External confirmations may be designed to test any financial statement assertion (AU-C 505). However, a given confirmation request does not test all assertions equally well. For example, if the issue is whether securities are being held in the client's name by an outside agent, the completeness assertion with regard to the investment account is not adequately addressed by a confirmation request. Other agents may be holding securities for the client. Moreover, the agent may be holding other securities not specified in the request. Thus, the request tends to be most effective for testing the existence (whether the assets exist at a given date) assertion and the rights (whether the client has a specified ownership interest in the assets) assertion.

9. An auditor inspects a client's investment records to determine that any transfers between categories of investments have been properly recorded. The primary purpose of this procedure is to obtain evidence concerning relevant financial statement assertions about

    A. Rights and obligations, and existence.

    B. Valuation and allocation, and rights and obligations.

    C. Existence or occurrence, and classification and understandability.

    D. Classification and understandability, and valuation and allocation.

Answer (D) is correct.

    REQUIRED: The assertions tested by inspecting reclassification of investments.

    DISCUSSION: Assertions about classification and understandability address whether the information is appropriately presented and described and disclosures are clear. For example, U.S. GAAP require that a debt security be reclassified as available for sale if the entity (1) does not have the positive intent and ability to hold it to maturity but (2) does not intend to sell it in the near term. Inspecting the client's records just prior to and just after year end could help the auditor determine whether investment classifications are appropriate. Assertions about valuation address whether reported amounts conform with U.S. GAAP. Classification affects valuation. For example, held-to-maturity securities are measured at cost, and available-for-sale and trading securities are measured at fair value. Thus, inspecting transfers between categories also helps determine whether the investments are recorded at proper amounts.

10. An auditor testing investments would ordinarily use analytical procedures to ascertain the reasonableness of the

    A. Existence of unrealized gains or losses.

    B. Completeness of recorded investment income.

    C. Classification as available-for-sale or trading securities.

    D. Valuation of trading securities.

Answer (B) is correct.

    REQUIRED: The use of analytical procedures when an auditor tests investments.

    DISCUSSION: The auditor may develop expectations regarding the completeness assertion for recorded investment income from stocks by using dividend records published by standard investment advisory services to recompute dividends received. Interest income from bond investments can be calculated from interest rates and payment dates noted on the certificates. Income from equity-based investments can be estimated from audited financial statements of the investees. Thus, applying an expected rate of return to the net investment amount may be an effective means of estimating total investment income.

    Answer (A) is incorrect. Unrealized gains or losses are dependent on the fair values of specific securities and cannot be calculated based on plausible relationships among the data. Answer (C) is incorrect. Available-for-sale securities may meet the definition of current assets. Answer (D) is incorrect. Individual trading securities may meet the definition of current assets.

11. Auditors may need to plan and perform auditing procedures for financial statement assertions about derivatives and hedging activities. Which of the following substantive procedures most clearly tests the completeness assertion about derivatives?

    A. Assessing the reasonableness of the use of an option-pricing model.

    B. Determining whether changes in the fair value of derivatives designated and qualifying as hedging instruments have been reported in earnings or in other comprehensive income.

    C. Requesting counterparties to provide information about them, such as whether side agreements have been made.

    D. Physically inspecting the derivative contract.

Answer (C) is correct.

    REQUIRED: The substantive procedure that most clearly tests the completeness assertion about derivatives.

    DISCUSSION: An audit of the completeness assertion addresses whether balances and transactions related to derivatives and hedging activities that should be recorded are recorded. A substantive procedure for the completeness assertion about derivatives and hedging activities is a request to the counterparty to a derivative for information about it, for example, whether an agreement exists to repurchase securities sold or whether side agreements have been made.

    Answer (A) is incorrect. Assessing the reasonableness of the use of an option-pricing model tests the valuation assertion. Answer (B) is incorrect. Determining whether changes in the fair value of derivatives designated and qualifying as hedging instruments have been reported in earnings or in other comprehensive income tests the classification and understandability assertion. Answer (D) is incorrect. Physically inspecting the derivative contract tests the existence assertion.

12. To test the valuation assertion when auditing an investment accounted for by the equity method, an auditor most likely would

   A. Inspect the stock certificates evidencing the investment.

   B. Examine the audited financial statements of the investee company.

   C. Review the broker's advice or canceled check for the investment's acquisition.

   D. Obtain market quotations from financial newspapers or periodicals.

Answer (B) is correct.
   REQUIRED: The procedure to test the valuation assertion for an equity-based investment.
   DISCUSSION: The equity method recognizes undistributed income arising from an investment in an investee. Under the equity method, investor income is recorded as the investee reports income. Consequently, the audited financial statements of the investee provide the auditor with the undistributed income from the investee.
   Answer (A) is incorrect. Inspection of stock certificates provides evidence about existence, not valuation. Answer (C) is incorrect. Reviewing the broker's advice or canceled check provides evidence about rights. Answer (D) is incorrect. Equity-based investments are not accounted for at fair value.

13.3 Substantive Testing of Noncurrent Debt

13. An audit plan for noncurrent debt should include steps that require

   A. Examining bond trust indentures.

   B. Inspecting the accounts payable subsidiary ledger.

   C. Investigating credits to the bond interest income account.

   D. Verifying the existence of the bondholders.

Answer (A) is correct.
   REQUIRED: The procedure to be included in the audit plan for noncurrent debt.
   DISCUSSION: The bond trust indenture contains information about contractual arrangements made with bondholders, such as (1) the face amount of the bonds, (2) interest rates, (3) payment dates, (4) descriptions of collateral, (5) provisions for conversion or retirement, (6) trustee duties, and (7) sinking fund requirements. The auditor should examine any bond trust indenture to determine that the client is meeting the conditions of the contract and is in compliance with the law.
   Answer (B) is incorrect. Accounts payable are current liabilities, not noncurrent debt. Answer (C) is incorrect. Credits to bond interest income do not pertain to noncurrent debt (income relates to investments, not debt). Answer (D) is incorrect. The existence of bondholders is implied by the reporting of bonded debt.

14. In auditing for unrecorded noncurrent bonds payable, an auditor most likely will

   A. Perform analytical procedures on the bond premium and discount accounts.

   B. Examine documentation of assets purchased with bond proceeds for liens.

   C. Compare interest expense with the bond payable amount for reasonableness.

   D. Confirm the existence of individual bondholders at year end.

Answer (C) is correct.
   REQUIRED: The appropriate procedure for testing noncurrent bonds payable.
   DISCUSSION: The recorded interest expense should reconcile with the outstanding bonds payable. If interest expense appears excessive relative to the recorded bonds payable, unrecorded noncurrent liabilities may exist.
   Answer (A) is incorrect. Performing analytical procedures on bond premium and discount are not likely to uncover unrecorded payables. Answer (B) is incorrect. The examination of documentation related to asset additions is considered in the audit of assets, not bonds payable. Answer (D) is incorrect. The greatest risk is that the bonds payable balance is not complete.

13.4 Substantive Testing of Equity

15. During an audit of a company's equity accounts, the auditor determines whether restrictions have been imposed on retained earnings resulting from loans, agreements, or state law. This audit procedure most likely is intended to verify relevant assertion about

   A. Existence or occurrence.

   B. Completeness.

   C. Valuation and allocation.

   D. Classification and understandability.

Answer (D) is correct.
   REQUIRED: The assertion that the auditor tests relative to restrictions on retained earnings.
   DISCUSSION: The presentation and disclosure assertions include assertions about classification and understandability. Financial information should be properly presented and disclosed, and disclosures should be clear (AU-C 315 and AS 1105). Hence, when restrictions have been placed on retained earnings, the auditor should determine that they are properly disclosed in the notes to the financial statements.
   Answer (A) is incorrect. Restrictions on retained earnings have little relevance to the existence or occurrence assertion. Answer (B) is incorrect. Restrictions on retained earnings have little relevance to the completeness assertion. Answer (C) is incorrect. Restrictions on retained earnings have little relevance to the valuation assertion.

16. An auditor usually obtains evidence of a company's equity transactions by reviewing its

    A. Minutes of board of directors meetings.

    B. Transfer agent's records.

    C. Canceled stock certificates.

    D. Treasury stock certificate book.

Answer (A) is correct.
    REQUIRED: The source of evidence about equity transactions.
    DISCUSSION: Equity transactions are typically few in number and large in amount. They require authorization by the board of directors. Thus, an auditor reviews the minutes of the board meetings to identify transactions.
    Answer (B) is incorrect. Although the auditor might confirm certain transactions with the client's transfer agent, the agent's records are not typically made available to the auditor. Answer (C) is incorrect. Canceled stock certificates represent only those shares that were retired. Answer (D) is incorrect. Treasury stock records include only those transactions involving reacquisition and resale of the entity's own stock.

17. When a client's company does not maintain its own stock records, the auditor should obtain written confirmation from the transfer agent and registrar concerning

    A. Restrictions on the payment of dividends.

    B. The number of shares issued and outstanding.

    C. Guarantees of preferred stock liquidation value.

    D. The number of shares subject to agreements to repurchase.

Answer (B) is correct.
    REQUIRED: The information confirmed by the transfer agent and registrar.
    DISCUSSION: The independent stock registrar is a financial institution employed to prevent improper issuances of stock, especially over-issuances. The transfer agent maintains detailed shareholder records and facilitates transfer of shares. Both are independent and reliable sources of evidence concerning total shares issued and outstanding.
    Answer (A) is incorrect. The payment of dividends is confirmed, but dividend restrictions are found in the articles of incorporation, bylaws, and minutes of directors' and shareholders' meetings. Answer (C) is incorrect. Guarantees of preferred stock liquidation value are not made by the transfer agent and registrar. Answer (D) is incorrect. The number of shares subject to agreements to repurchase is not the concern of the transfer agent and registrar.

13.5 Substantive Testing of Payroll

18. An auditor vouched data for a sample of employees in a payroll register to approved clock card data to provide assurance that

    A. Payments to employees are computed at authorized rates.

    B. Employees work the number of hours for which they are paid.

    C. Segregation of duties exists between the preparation and distribution of the payroll.

    D. Internal controls relating to unclaimed payroll checks are operating effectively.

Answer (B) is correct.
    REQUIRED: The purpose of vouching payroll register information to approved clock card data.
    DISCUSSION: To test that payroll events actually occurred, an auditor vouches a sample of employee transactions recorded in the payroll-related balances to supporting documentation, including approved time cards, time tickets, and notations in personnel records. The purpose is to verify that employees work the hours for which they are paid.
    Answer (A) is incorrect. The auditor compares the pay rates used in calculating payments to employees with the authorized rates in the personnel files to determine whether they were authorized. Answer (C) is incorrect. The auditor tests segregation of duties by inquiry and observation. Answer (D) is incorrect. The auditor observes the activities of the treasurer to determine whether unclaimed payroll checks were being properly controlled.

19. In auditing payroll when control risk is assessed as low, an auditor most likely will

    A. Verify that checks representing unclaimed wages are mailed.

    B. Trace individual employee deductions to entity journal entries.

    C. Observe entity employees during a payroll distribution.

    D. Compare payroll costs with entity standards or budgets.

Answer (D) is correct.
    REQUIRED: The procedure most likely performed during the audit of payroll.
    DISCUSSION: Comparing payroll costs with budgeted amounts is a standard analytical procedure that is performed in most audits of payroll.
    Answer (A) is incorrect. Checks representing unclaimed wages should be maintained by the CFO until claimed by the appropriate employees. Answer (B) is incorrect. The individual employee deductions do not result in entity journal entries, but cumulative journal entries record the sum of the payroll. Answer (C) is incorrect. Observation of payroll distribution may not be necessary when the RMMs are low.

20. Which of the following circumstances most likely will cause an auditor to suspect an employee payroll fraud scheme?

    A. There are significant unexplained variances between standard and actual labor cost.

    B. Payroll checks are disbursed by the same employee each payday.

    C. Employee time cards are approved by individual departmental supervisors.

    D. A separate payroll bank account is maintained on an imprest basis.

Answer (A) is correct.

    REQUIRED: The circumstance most likely to cause the auditor to suspect an employee payroll fraud scheme.

    DISCUSSION: Analytical procedures, such as variance analysis, alert the auditor when actual results were not anticipated. Thus, the auditor should consider the possibility that payroll is fraudulently overstated.

    Answer (B) is incorrect. The payroll checks should be disbursed by the paymaster each pay period. Answer (C) is incorrect. Supervisors should approve individual time cards. Answer (D) is incorrect. A separate payroll account using an imprest basis provides additional control over payroll.

Access the Gleim CPA Premium Review System featuring SmartAdapt for exam-emulating multiple-choice questions and simulations with detailed answer explanations.

Learn more: gleim.com/CPApremium | 800.874.5346

STUDY UNIT FOURTEEN
EVIDENCE -- KEY CONSIDERATIONS

(14 pages of outline)

This study unit covers topics related to the collection of evidence. Of these issues, (1) inquiry of the client's legal counsel, (2) an entity's ability to continue as a going concern, and (3) client representations have been tested most consistently on recent exams. But all topics presented here are likely subjects of future multiple-choice questions.

14.1 CONSIDERATION OF LITIGATION, CLAIMS, AND ASSESSMENTS

1. Management is responsible for adopting policies and procedures to identify, evaluate, and account for **litigation, claims, and assessments (LCA)**. Accordingly, it is the primary source of information about LCA.

   a. The applicable accounting principles are those relevant to **contingencies** and contingent liabilities.

2. The auditor should **obtain evidence** relevant to the following:

   a. Circumstances indicating an uncertainty as to possible loss from LCA

      1) Under U.S. GAAP, the outcomes of an uncertainty are classified as (a) remote, (b) reasonably possible, or (c) probable.

         a) This language need not be used by legal counsel to evaluate the outcomes of LCA. However, legal counsel's descriptions are sufficiently clear for the auditor's purposes if they can be used to classify outcomes in the three categories established by U.S. GAAP.

   b. The period in which the underlying cause for legal action occurred

   c. The probability of an unfavorable outcome

   d. The amount or range of potential loss

3. The **auditor's procedures** include the following:

   a. Inquiring about, and discussing with management and in-house legal counsel, the policies and procedures for identifying, evaluating, and accounting for LCA that may result in a risk of material misstatement (RMM).

   b. Obtaining from management a description and evaluation of LCA at period end, and from then to the date the information is provided, including an identification of matters referred to legal counsel.

      1) The auditor also should obtain **written representations** from management that all actual and possible LCA that should be considered in preparing the statements have been (a) disclosed to the auditor and (b) accounted for and disclosed in accordance with the applicable reporting framework.

   c. Examining documents in the entity's possession (e.g., legal expense accounts and invoices from, and correspondence with, external legal counsel).

    d.   Applying related procedures. An audit normally includes procedures undertaken for other purposes that also might produce evidence about LCA. Some examples are the following **risk assessment** procedures performed to obtain an understanding of the entity and its environment:

        1)   Reading minutes of meetings of shareholders, directors, and appropriate committees held during, and subsequent to, the period being audited

        2)   Reading contracts, loan agreements, leases, correspondence from governmental agencies, and similar documents

        3)   Obtaining information about guarantees from bank confirmations

        4)   Inspecting other documents for possible guarantees by the client

4.   If the auditor concludes that no actual or potential LCA exist that indicate RMMs, **no direct communication** with the entity's legal counsel is required. This decision should be documented in the working papers.

    a.   Otherwise, the auditor should send a letter of inquiry prepared by the entity's management requesting that legal counsel communicate directly with the auditor. Thus, the auditor should request that management authorize legal counsel to discuss relevant matters.

5.   **Communication with Legal Counsel**

    a.   A **letter of inquiry** to external legal counsel is the auditor's primary means of obtaining corroboration of the information provided about material LCA by management. An auditor usually cannot make legal judgments.

        1)   Evidence provided by in-house counsel may corroborate management's information.

    b.   The letter of inquiry includes the following:

        1)   Identification of the entity and its subsidiaries and the date of the audit

        2)   A management list (or a request by management that legal counsel prepare a list) that describes and evaluates **pending** or **threatened** LCA with respect to which legal counsel has performed substantive legal services on behalf of the entity

            a)   For each matter, legal counsel should be requested either to provide the following information or to comment on disagreements with management:

               i)   The nature of the matter, the progress of the case, and the entity's intended action

               ii)   The probability of an unfavorable outcome and an estimate, if possible, of the amount or range of loss

               iii)   Omission of any pending or threatened LCA from management's list

        3)   A management list that describes and evaluates **unasserted** claims and assessments that (a) management considers to be probable and (b) have at least a reasonable possibility of an unfavorable outcome, with respect to which legal counsel has performed substantive legal services on behalf of the entity

            a)   Also included is a request that legal counsel comment on those matters that are the basis for disagreements with management.

        4)   A statement that management understands that legal counsel will advise the client when an unasserted claim or assertion with respect to which (s)he has provided legal services requires the entity to disclose or consider disclosure in accordance with the applicable reporting framework

            a)   The letter of inquiry should request legal counsel to confirm this understanding.

5) A request that legal counsel explain any limitation on, and specify the effective date of, his or her response

c. An example of the text of a letter of inquiry to legal counsel is presented below.

EXAMPLE -- Audit Inquiry Letter to Legal Counsel

In connection with an audit of our financial statements at (balance sheet date) and for the (period) then ended, management of the Company has prepared and furnished to our auditors (name and address of auditors) a description and evaluation of certain contingencies, including those set forth below involving matters with respect to which you have been engaged and to which you have devoted substantive attention on behalf of the Company in the form of legal consultation or representation. These contingencies are regarded by management of the Company as material for this purpose (management may indicate a materiality limit if an understanding has been reached with the auditor). Your response should include matters that existed at (balance sheet date) and during the period from that date to the date of your response.

Pending or Threatened Litigation (Excluding Unasserted Claims)

[Ordinarily, the information would include the following: (1) the nature of the litigation, (2) the progress of the case to date, (3) how management is responding or intends to respond to the litigation (for example, to contest the case vigorously or to seek an out-of-court settlement), and (4) an evaluation of the likelihood of an unfavorable outcome and an estimate, if one can be made, of the amount or range of potential loss.] This letter will serve as our consent for you to furnish our auditor all the information requested herein. Accordingly, please furnish to our auditors such explanation, if any, that you consider necessary to supplement the foregoing information, including an explanation of those matters for which your views may differ from those stated and an identification of the omission of any pending or threatened litigation, claims, and assessments or a statement that the list of such matters is complete.

Unasserted Claims and Assessments (Considered by Management to be Probable of Assertion and That, if Asserted, Would Have at Least a Reasonable Possibility of an Unfavorable Outcome)

[Ordinarily, management's information would include the following: (1) the nature of the matter, (2) how management intends to respond if the claim is asserted, and (3) an evaluation of the likelihood of an unfavorable outcome and an estimate, if one can be made, of the amount or range of potential loss.] Please furnish to our auditors such explanation, if any, that you consider necessary to supplement the foregoing information, including an explanation of those matters for which your views may differ from those stated.

We understand that whenever, in the course of performing legal services for us with respect to a matter recognized to involve an unasserted possible claim or assessment that may call for financial statement disclosure, if you have formed a professional conclusion that we should disclose or consider disclosure concerning such possible claim or assessment, as a matter of professional responsibility to us, you will so advise us and will consult with us concerning the question of such disclosure and the applicable requirements of Accounting Standards Codification (ASC) 450, *Contingencies*. Please specifically confirm to our auditors that our understanding is correct.

Please specifically identify the nature of and reasons for any limitation on your response.

[The auditor may request the client to inquire about additional matters, for example, unpaid or unbilled charges or specified information on certain contractually assumed obligations of the company, such as guarantees of indebtedness of others.]

[The letter should be signed by the client.]

---

6. **Limitations on the Scope of Legal Counsel's Response**

a. Legal counsel may limit the response to matters to which **substantive attention** has been given.

b. Legal counsel's response may be limited to matters considered **individually or collectively material**, for example, when (1) the entity and auditor agree on the limits of materiality for this purpose, and (2) management has communicated the agreement to legal counsel.

1) These limits are not limits on the audit scope.

c. Legal counsel may not be able to reach a conclusion about the probability of an unfavorable outcome or the amount or range of loss because of **inherent uncertainties**.

7. **Modification of the Opinion**

    a. The opinion in the auditor's report is modified if

        1) Legal counsel refuses to respond appropriately to the letter of inquiry, and the auditor cannot obtain sufficient appropriate evidence by performing alternative procedures, or

        2) Management refuses permission for the auditor to communicate or meet with external legal counsel.

    b. External legal counsel's refusal to provide (orally or in writing) information requested in a letter of inquiry may be a scope limitation sufficient to preclude an unmodified opinion.

        1) However, the need for confidentiality of client communications with legal counsel protects some matters from disclosure even to the auditor.

Stop and review! You have completed the outline for this subunit. Study multiple-choice questions 1 through 6 beginning on page 294.

14.2 SUBSEQUENT EVENTS AND SUBSEQUENTLY DISCOVERED FACTS

> The Clarified Standards do not contain the accounting guidance that was previously included in the auditing standards covered in this subunit because it is included in the accounting standards. In the future, the CPA exam is not likely to test accounting for subsequent events in the auditing section, but you should still know the relevant accounting principles. In general, subsequent events that relate to conditions that existed at the balance sheet date should be reflected in the balances of the financial statements. Those that occur after the balance sheet date may require disclosure in the financial statements. Several questions at the end of this study unit consider these issues to demonstrate the contrast between accounting and auditing issues.

1. **Definitions**

    a. **Subsequent events** occur between the date of the financial statements and the date of the auditor's report.

    b. **Subsequently discovered facts** become known to the auditor after the date of the auditor's report. Had they been known to the auditor at that date, they might have caused the auditor to revise the auditor's report.

2. **Subsequent Events**

    a. The auditor should perform audit procedures designed to obtain sufficient appropriate audit evidence that all subsequent events that require adjustment of, or disclosure in, the financial statements have been identified.

    b. The following procedures should be performed as near as practicable to the report date:

        1) Understanding management's procedures for identifying subsequent events.

        2) Reading the latest subsequent interim financial statements, if any.

        3) Inquiring of management and those charged with governance about the current status of items accounted for using preliminary or inconclusive data.

        4) Inquiring specifically about whether

            a) New commitments, borrowings, or guarantees have been entered into.

            b) Sales or acquisitions of assets have occurred or are planned.

            c) Increases in capital or issuance of debt have occurred, or an agreement to merge or liquidate has been made or is planned.

            d) Any assets have been appropriated by the government or destroyed (for example, by fire or flood).

            e) Any developments regarding contingencies have occurred.

            f) Any unusual accounting adjustments have been made or are contemplated.

g) Any events have occurred or are likely to occur that affect the appropriateness of accounting policies.

h) Any events have occurred that are relevant to the measurement of estimates or provisions made in the financial statements.

i) Any events have occurred that are relevant to the recoverability of assets.

5) Reading the available **minutes** of meetings of owners, those charged with governance, and management after the date of the statements.

6) Sending, if appropriate, a letter of inquiry prepared by management to **legal counsel** requesting direct communication about litigation, claims, and assessments.

7) Obtaining **written representations**, dated as of the date of the auditor's report, from appropriate management stating that adjustments or disclosures have been made for any subsequent events requiring such treatment. This is one of many written representations obtained from the entity. Representations are discussed in Subunit 14.3.

c. The auditor should determine whether any subsequent events identified have been properly accounted for and disclosed.

d. The accounting treatment of subsequent events depends on whether they provide evidence of conditions that

1) Existed at the date of the financial statements.

a) These events require adjustments of the financial statements.

2) Did **not** exist at the date of the financial statements.

a) These events may require disclosure in the financial statements but not recognition.

3. **Subsequently Discovered Facts That Become Known to the Auditor before the Report Release Date**

a. The auditor is not required to perform any audit procedures regarding the financial statements after the date of the auditor's report. However, if a subsequently discovered fact becomes known to the auditor before the report release date, the auditor should

1) Discuss the matter with management and, if appropriate, those charged with governance.

2) Determine whether the financial statements need revision and, if so, inquire how management intends to address the matter.

b. If management revises the financial statements, the auditor should perform the necessary audit procedures on the revision. The auditor also should either

1) Date the auditor's report as of a later date and extend the audit procedures to the new date of the auditor's report, including obtaining an update of the management representation letter, or

2) Include an additional date in the auditor's report on the revised statements that is limited to the revision (that is, dual-date the auditor's report). Dual-dating indicates that the auditor's procedures subsequent to the original date are limited solely to the relevant note to the statements. The auditor also should request written representations from management as of the additional date in the auditor's report about whether

a) The previous representations should be modified.

b) Any other events have occurred subsequent to the date of the statements.

c. If management does not revise the statements that need revision, the auditor should modify the opinion (express a qualified opinion or an adverse opinion).

4. **Unaudited events** occurring after the date of the auditor's report may be disclosed by management to prevent the statements from being misleading.

    a. If the event is described in a separate note labeled as **unaudited**, the auditor need not perform procedures on the revision of the statements, and the report date is not changed.

5. **Subsequently Discovered Facts That Become Known to the Auditor after the Report Release Date**

    a. If a subsequently discovered fact becomes known to the auditor after the report release date, the auditor should

        1) Discuss the matter with management and, if appropriate, those charged with governance.

        2) Determine whether the financial statements need revision and, if so, inquire how management intends to respond.

    b. Management may revise the financial statements before they have been made available to third parties. In this case, the auditor should apply the appropriate procedures and either extend the date of the audit or dual-date the report for the revision.

    c. However, the unrevised audited statements may have been made available to third parties. In this case, the auditor should assess whether the steps taken by management were timely and appropriate. The auditor should ensure that anyone who has received the statements is informed of the situation, including that the audited statements are not to be relied upon.

        1) When revised statements are issued, and the auditor's opinion on the revised statements differs from the opinion the auditor previously expressed, the following matters should be disclosed in an other-matter paragraph:

            a) The date of the auditor's previous report

            b) The type of opinion previously expressed

            c) The substantive reasons for the different opinion

            d) That the auditor's opinion on the revised statements is different from the auditor's previous opinion

    d. Management may not take the necessary steps to ensure that anyone who has received the audited statements is informed of the situation. In this case, the auditor should notify management and those charged with governance that the auditor will seek to prevent future reliance on the auditor's report. If, despite such notice, the necessary steps are still not taken, the auditor should take appropriate action to seek to prevent reliance on the auditor's report. Unless the auditor's legal counsel recommends otherwise, the auditor may take the following steps to the extent applicable:

        1) Notify management and those charged with governance that the auditor's report is not to be relied upon.

        2) Notify regulatory agencies having jurisdiction over the entity that the auditor's report is not to be relied upon. This notice should include a request that the agency take appropriate steps to make the necessary disclosure.

        3) If feasible, notify anyone known to the auditor to be relying on the statements that the auditor's report is not to be relied upon.

Stop and review! You have completed the outline for this subunit. Study multiple-choice questions 7 through 11 beginning on page 296.

14.3 WRITTEN REPRESENTATIONS

1. **Audit Evidence**

   a. The auditor is required to obtain written representations from management. (In this study unit, management includes those charged with governance.)

   b. Written representations confirm certain matters or support other evidence. They complement other procedures but do **not** provide sufficient appropriate evidence. They also do not affect the nature or effect of other procedures.

   c. Written representations should be in a letter addressed to the auditor and dated as of the date of the auditor's report.

      1) The auditor should possess this letter before release of the auditor's report.
      2) The CEO and CFO usually should sign the letter.

2. **Specific Representations**

   a. Among other things, written representations are based on the **premise** of the audit. It relates to management's responsibilities for (1) preparing and fairly presenting the financial statements; (2) internal control relevant to the statements; and (3) providing access to (a) information relevant to the statements, (b) other information requested for audit purposes, and (c) persons within the entity.

   b. The auditor should request the following written representations:

      1) Management is responsible for the preparation and fair presentation of the financial statements and for internal control relevant to their preparation.

      2) Management has provided all relevant information and access, and all transactions have been recorded and reflected in the statements.

      3) Management is responsible for internal controls to prevent and detect fraud and has disclosed to the auditor its knowledge of fraud, suspected fraud, and allegations of fraud.

      4) All instances of noncompliance with laws and regulations that should be considered in preparing the statements have been disclosed to the auditor.

      5) Management states whether the effects of uncorrected misstatements are immaterial and that a list is attached to the representation letter.

      6) All known actual or possible litigation and claims that should be considered in preparing the statements have been disclosed to the auditor.

      7) The significant assumptions used to make estimates are reasonable.

      8) Management has disclosed to the auditor the identities of related parties, related party relationships, and related party transactions.

      9) Subsequent events have been disclosed to the auditor, and required adjustments or disclosures have been made.

      10) Management has provided additional written representations (a) required by GAAS or (b) requested by the auditor to support other audit evidence or specific assertions.

3.   **Representation Letter**

Background
The example representation letter in the auditing standards is a one-page document. It affirms management's responsibilities to the auditor and for the fairness of the financial statements. In practice, letters often are much longer than the AICPA's example letter. Many CPA firms require management to affirm each key assertion for each major account as well as the other affirmations from the example letter. This should not be too surprising because representation is synonymous with assertion.

a.   The example representation letter on the next page is taken from AU-C 580. Although addressed to the auditor, the letter is drafted by the auditor. It should be signed by management with overall responsibility for financial and operating matters, including preparation and fair presentation of the statements.

b.   Management's representations may be limited to matters that are considered **material** to the financial statements, either individually or collectively, provided that management and the auditor have reached an understanding on materiality for this purpose. But materiality does not apply to

   1)   Management's responsibility for internal control to prevent or detect fraud or
   2)   Representations not directly related to financial statement amounts.

c.   The auditor may determine, based on the circumstances, that other matters should be specifically included among the written representations.

d.   If the auditor reports on **consolidated** statements, the representations obtained from the parent should specify that they pertain to the consolidated statements and, if applicable, to the parent's separate statements.

e.   The written representations should be

   1)   Addressed to the auditor,
   2)   Dated as of the date of the audit report, and
   3)   Signed by responsible and knowledgeable members of management. The chief executive officer and the chief financial officer usually should sign the representations.

f.   The auditor may want to obtain written representations from other individuals, such as the completeness of the minutes of meetings from the person responsible for the minutes.

EXAMPLE -- Management Representation Letter

Date of the Auditor's Report
To Independent Auditor (Named)

This representation letter is provided in connection with your audit of the financial statements of ABC Company, which comprise the balance sheet as of December 31, 20XX, and the related statements of income, changes in stockholders' equity, and cash flows for the year then ended, and the related notes to the financial statements, for the purpose of expressing an opinion on whether the financial statements are presented fairly, in all material respects, in accordance with accounting principles generally accepted in the United States (U.S. GAAP).

Certain representations in this letter are described as being limited to matters that are material. Items are considered material, regardless of size, if they involve an omission or misstatement of accounting information that, in the light of surrounding circumstances, makes it probable that the judgment of a reasonable person relying on the information would be changed or influenced by the omission or misstatement.

Except where otherwise stated below, immaterial matters less than $[insert amount] collectively are not considered to be exceptions that require disclosure for the purpose of the following representations. This amount is not necessarily indicative of amounts that would require adjustment to or disclosure in the financial statements.

Financial Statements

- We have fulfilled our responsibilities, as set out in the terms of the audit engagement dated [insert date], for the preparation and fair presentation of the financial statements in accordance with U.S. GAAP.
- We acknowledge our responsibility for the design, implementation, and maintenance of internal control relevant to the preparation and fair presentation of financial statements that are free from material misstatement, whether due to fraud or error.
- We acknowledge our responsibility for the design, implementation, and maintenance of internal control to prevent and detect fraud.
- Significant assumptions used by us in making accounting estimates, including those measured at fair value, are reasonable.
- Related party relationships and transactions have been appropriately accounted for and disclosed in accordance with the requirements of U.S. GAAP.
- All events subsequent to the date of the financial statements and for which U.S. GAAP requires adjustment or disclosure have been adjusted or disclosed.
- The effects of uncorrected misstatements are immaterial, both individually and in the aggregate, to the financial statements as a whole. A list of the uncorrected misstatements is attached to the representation letter.
- The effects of all known actual or possible litigation and claims have been accounted for and disclosed in accordance with U.S. GAAP.

Information Provided

- We have provided you with:
    - Access to all information of which we are aware that is relevant to the preparation and fair presentation of the financial statements such as records, documentation and other matters;
    - Additional information that you have requested from us for the purpose of the audit; and
    - Unrestricted access to persons within the entity from whom you determined it necessary to obtain audit evidence.
- All transactions have been recorded in the accounting records and are reflected in the financial statements.
- We have disclosed to you the results of our assessment of the risk that the financial statements may be materially misstated as a result of fraud.
- We have [no knowledge of any] [disclosed to you all information that we are aware of regarding] fraud or suspected fraud that affects the entity and involves:
    - Management;
    - Employees who have significant roles in internal control; or
    - Others when the fraud could have a material effect on the financial statements.
- We have [no knowledge of any] [disclosed to you all information that we are aware of regarding] allegations of fraud, or suspected fraud, affecting the entity's financial statements communicated by employees, former employees, analysts, regulators or others.
- We have disclosed to you all known instances of non-compliance or suspected non-compliance with laws and regulations whose effects should be considered when preparing financial statements.
- We [have disclosed to you all known actual or possible] [are not aware of any pending or threatened] litigation, claims, and assessments whose effects should be considered when preparing the financial statements [and we have not consulted legal counsel concerning litigation, claims, or assessments]
- We have disclosed to you the identity of the entity's related parties and all the related party relationships and transactions of which we are aware.

[Include other representations unique to the entity and related to specific accounts and assertions.]

(Name of Chief Executive Officer and Title)　　　　　　　　(Name of Chief Financial Officer and Title)

4. **Unreliable or Omitted Representations**

    a.   The auditor disclaims an opinion or withdraws from the engagement if

        1)   Management does not provide the representations regarding the premise of the audit (**management's responsibilities** for the audit), or

        2)   The auditor concludes that such representations are unreliable because of doubts about management's integrity.

    b.   Management's refusal to provide other written representations also often precludes an unmodified opinion.

        1)   The auditor should consider the effects of the refusal on his or her (a) evaluation of management's integrity and (b) ability to rely on other representations.

        2)   Furthermore, failure to provide representations about certain matters (fraud, noncompliance, misstatements, litigation and claims, estimates, related parties, and subsequent events) may cause the auditor to disclaim an opinion or withdraw from the engagement. But circumstances may permit expression of a qualified opinion.

5. **Other Pronouncements**

    a.   The PCAOB's AS 2201 requires that an audit of an **issuer's** internal control over financial reporting be integrated with the financial statement audit. The AICPA's AU-C 940 provides for the **optional** performance of a similar service for a **nonissuer**. Additional representations required by AS 2201 include the following:

        1)   Management has evaluated internal control, specified the control criteria, and stated its conclusion about the effectiveness of internal control.

        2)   Management has disclosed to the auditor all deficiencies in internal control.

        3)   Deficiencies identified and communicated to those charged with governance during previous engagements have been resolved, and unresolved deficiencies have been identified.

        4)   Management has stated certain changes subsequent to the date reported on. These are changes in factors that might significantly affect internal control over financial reporting.

Stop and review! You have completed the outline for this subunit. Study multiple-choice questions 12 through 17 beginning on page 297.

14.4 AUDITOR'S CONSIDERATION OF AN ENTITY'S ABILITY TO CONTINUE AS A GOING CONCERN

1.   The auditor should evaluate whether a **substantial doubt** exists about an entity's ability to continue as a **going concern** for a **reasonable period of time**.

    a.   For U.S. GAAP, a reasonable period is **1 year after the date that the financial statements are issued or are available to be issued**. (Hereafter, the term "substantial doubt" reflects this language.)

    b.   Continuation as a going concern is assumed in financial reporting, absent significant contrary information. Such information relates to the inability to continue to meet obligations as they become due without, for example, one of the following:

        1)   Substantial disposal of assets outside the ordinary course of business
        2)   Debt restructuring
        3)   Externally forced revisions of operations

    c.   This standard applies to all audits of financial statements except audits of statements prepared on the **liquidation basis**.

        1)   Thus, it applies to audits of financial statements prepared in accordance with a general purpose or a special purpose framework.

2. **Evaluating Whether Substantial Doubt Exists**

   a. The evaluation is based on relevant conditions and events as of the date of the report.

      1) Necessary information is obtained by applying the auditing procedures planned and performed to test the assertions in the financial statements.

   b. The following is the process of evaluation:

      1) The auditor considers whether the results of normal auditing procedures identify **conditions and events** that, in the aggregate, indicate that substantial doubt could exist (hereafter, "conditions and events").

         a) Additional information about the conditions and events, as well as evidence supporting information that mitigates the substantial doubt, may need to be gathered.

      2) If the auditor believes a substantial doubt exists, (s)he should obtain information about **management's plans** to mitigate the effect of such conditions or events and assess the likelihood that the plans will be effective.

      3) The auditor then determines whether (s)he has a substantial doubt.

         a) If so, (s)he should

            i) Consider the adequacy of disclosure about the going concern issue.
            ii) Include an **emphasis-of-matter** paragraph (immediately after the opinion paragraph) in the audit report. Also, a disclaimer of opinion is possible.

         b) If not, (s)he should still consider the need for disclosure but need not include an emphasis-of-matter paragraph in the audit report.

   c. Because of the inherent limitations of an audit, the entity's **failure to continue as a going concern**, even within the year after the date of the issuance of the statements, does not, in itself, indicate inadequate auditor performance.

      1) Thus, omission of the reference to substantial doubt provides no assurance of continuation as a going concern.

3. **Audit Procedures**

   a. Procedures need not be designed solely to identify conditions and events because typical audit procedures should be sufficient. Such procedures may include the following:

      1) Analytical procedures
      2) Review of subsequent events
      3) Review of compliance with debt and loan agreements
      4) Reading minutes of meetings of shareholders, the board, and committees
      5) Inquiry of legal counsel about litigation, claims, and assessments
      6) Confirmation with related and third parties of arrangements for financial support

4. **Conditions and Events**

   a. The significance of conditions and events depends on the circumstances, and some may be significant only in conjunction with others. Such conditions and events include the following:

      1) **Negative trends**, e.g., (a) recurring operating losses, (b) working capital deficiencies, (c) negative cash flows from operations, and (d) adverse key financial ratios

      2) **Financial difficulties**, e.g., (a) default on loans, (b) unpaid dividends, (c) denial of normal trade credit by suppliers, (d) debt restructuring, (e) noncompliance with statutory capital requirements, and (f) the need to seek new financing or to dispose of substantial assets

      3) **Internal matters**, e.g., (a) labor difficulties, (b) substantial dependence on the success of one project, (c) uneconomic long-term commitments, and (d) the need to revise operations significantly

      4) **External matters**, e.g., (a) litigation, legislation, or similar matters jeopardizing operating ability; (b) loss of a key franchise, license, or patent; (c) loss of a principal customer or supplier; and (d) an uninsured or underinsured catastrophe, such as a drought, earthquake, or flood

5. **Written Representations**

   a. If the auditor believes that a substantial doubt exists before considering management's plans, discussed in item 6. below, (s)he should obtain written representations from management

      1) About its plans to mitigate the adverse effects of conditions or events and the likelihood that those plans can be effectively implemented and

      2) That the statements disclose all the matters of which management is aware that are relevant to the going concern issue, including principal conditions or events and management's plans.

6. **Management's Plans**

   a. Given substantial doubt, the auditor should (1) consider management's plans for responding to the adverse effects of the conditions and events, (2) obtain information about the plans, and (3) consider the likelihood that the adverse effects will be mitigated and the plans can be effectively implemented.

   b. These considerations may include the following:

      1) **Disposing of assets**

         a) Restrictions such as those in loan agreements or interests held by other parties (e.g., mortgages or security interests)

         b) Marketability of the assets to be sold

         c) Direct or indirect effects

      2) **Borrowing money or restructuring debt**

         a) Availability of debt financing, including credit arrangements, such as lines of credit, factoring of receivables, or sale-leasebacks

         b) Arrangements to restructure or subordinate debt or to guarantee loans to the entity

         c) Existing restrictions on borrowing or the sufficiency of available collateral

      3) **Reducing or delaying expenditures**

         a) Feasibility of plans to reduce overhead or administrative expenses, postpone maintenance or R&D, or lease rather than purchase

         b) Direct or indirect effects

      4) **Increasing ownership equity**

         a) Feasibility of such plans, including arrangements to obtain capital

         b) Arrangements to reduce dividends or accelerate cash receipts from affiliates or other investors

   c. The elements of plans that are particularly significant to overcoming the adverse effects should be identified and procedures performed to obtain evidence about them, for example, about the ability to obtain **additional financing**.

   d. **Prospective financial information (PFI)** may be important to management's plans, and the auditor should request such information and consider the adequacy of support for significant underlying **assumptions**.

       1)   Special attention should be given to assumptions that are

          a)   Material,

          b)   Especially sensitive or susceptible to change, and

          c)   Inconsistent with historical trends.

       2)   The auditor should have knowledge of the entity, its business, and its management. The auditor should

          a)   Read the PFI and assumptions.

          b)   Compare PFI for prior periods with results and, for the current period, with results to date.

       3)   If the effects of certain factors are not reflected in the PFI, the auditor should discuss them with management and, if necessary, request revision.

7. **Financial Statement Effects**

   a.   After considering management's plans, the auditor may decide that a substantial doubt exists and should consider the possible effects on the statements and the **adequacy of disclosure.**

   b.   Information disclosed may include the following:

       1)   The conditions and events on which the substantial doubt is based, their possible effects, and management's evaluation of their significance and of any mitigating factors

       2)   Possible discontinuance of operations

       3)   Management's plans, including PFI

          a)   The information need not meet guidelines for PFI, and the consideration need not go beyond that required by GAAS.

       4)   Information about recoverability or classification of recorded assets or the amounts or classification of liabilities

   c.   The auditor may decide, primarily because of the consideration of management's plans, that the substantial doubt is mitigated. (S)he then should consider **disclosure** of (1) the principal conditions and events that led to the substantial doubt; (2) their possible effects; and (3) any mitigating factors, including management's plans.

8. **Effects on the Auditor's Report**

   a.   If the auditor has a substantial doubt, the audit report should include an **emphasis-of-matter** paragraph immediately following the opinion paragraph. (Emphasis of a matter is covered more fully in Study Unit 17, Subunit 3.) The wording of the auditor's conclusion should include the phrases **substantial doubt** and **going concern.**

   b.   If disclosure is inadequate, the auditor may modify the opinion.

   c.   Also, the auditor is not precluded from **disclaiming** an opinion in cases involving uncertainties.

9. **Documentation**

   a.   If the auditor has a substantial doubt (even if that doubt is mitigated by management actions), the following should be documented in the working papers:

       1)   The conditions or events causing the substantial doubt

       2)   The significant elements of management's plans to overcome the problem considered by the auditor

       3)   The auditing procedures performed and evidence obtained

       4)   The auditor's conclusions about whether the substantial doubt remains, including any effects on the financial statements or disclosures and any effect on the audit report

10. **Communications**

a.   An auditor who has a substantial doubt should communicate the following to **those charged with governance**:

1)   Nature of identified conditions and events
2)   Financial statement effects
3)   Adequacy of disclosure
4)   Audit report effects

Stop and review! You have completed the outline for this subunit. Study multiple-choice questions 18 through 20 beginning on page 299.

QUESTIONS

14.1 Consideration of Litigation, Claims, and Assessments

1. The primary source of information to be reported about litigation, claims, and assessments is the

A.   Client's legal counsel.

B.   Court records.

C.   Client's management.

D.   Independent auditor.

Answer (C) is correct.
   REQUIRED: The primary source of information to be reported about litigation, claims, and assessments.
   DISCUSSION: According to AU-C 501, "Management is responsible for adopting policies and procedures to identify, evaluate, and account for litigation, claims, and assessments as a basis for the preparation of financial statements in accordance with the requirements of the applicable financial reporting framework." The auditor should discuss with management its policies and procedures for identifying and evaluating these matters.
   Answer (A) is incorrect. The client's legal counsel is the auditor's primary source of evidence to corroborate the information furnished by management. Answer (B) is incorrect. The auditor does not ordinarily examine court records. Answer (D) is incorrect. The auditor collects evidence to support management's assertions about litigation, claims, and assessments.

2. Legal counsel's response to an auditor's inquiry about litigation, claims, and assessments may be limited to matters that are considered individually or collectively material to the client's financial statements. Which parties may reach an understanding on the limits of materiality for this purpose that are stated in the letter of inquiry?

A.   The auditor and the client's management.

B.   The client's audit committee and legal counsel.

C.   The client's management and legal counsel.

D.   Legal counsel and the auditor.

Answer (A) is correct.
   REQUIRED: The parties responsible for setting materiality limits stated in the letter of inquiry about litigation, claims, and assessments.
   DISCUSSION: The letter of inquiry is prepared by management and sent by the auditor to the entity's legal counsel. Among other things, the letter requests a statement about the nature of, and reasons for, any limitation on legal counsel's response. Legal counsel may limit the response to matters to which (s)he has given substantive attention in the form of legal consultation or representation. Furthermore, legal counsel's response may be limited to those matters that are considered individually or collectively material to the financial statements, such as when the entity and the auditor have agreed on materiality limits, and management has stated the limits in the letter of inquiry (AU-C 501). NOTE: According to the American Bar Association's statement of policy, the lawyer may wish to reach an understanding with the auditor about the test of materiality. However, the lawyer need not do so if (s)he assumes responsibility for the criteria.
   Answer (B) is incorrect. Legal counsel and the audit committee do not draft the letter of inquiry or agree on its terms. Answer (C) is incorrect. Legal counsel may reach an understanding with the auditor about materiality but does not draft the letter of inquiry. Moreover, the auditor ultimately must make materiality judgments relevant to the audit. Answer (D) is incorrect. Legal counsel does not determine the content of the letter of inquiry.

3. Which of the following procedures would best detect a liability omission by management?

A. Inquiry of senior support staff and recently departed employees.

B. Review and check mathematical accuracy of financial statements.

C. Review articles of incorporation and corporate bylaws.

D. Review purchase contracts and other legal documents.

Answer (D) is correct.
REQUIRED: The procedure to detect a liability omission by management.
DISCUSSION: The auditor's search for unrecorded liabilities should include reading contracts, loan agreements, leases, correspondence from governmental agencies, and any legal documents in the client's possession.
Answer (A) is incorrect. The support staff and departed employees do not likely have knowledge about devious actions of management. Answer (B) is incorrect. The omitted liabilities would not be included in the financial statements. Answer (C) is incorrect. The articles of incorporation and the bylaws will not address litigation or liabilities.

4. The primary reason an auditor requests letters of inquiry be sent to a client's legal counsel is to provide the auditor with

A. The probable outcome of asserted claims and pending or threatened litigation.

B. Corroboration of the information furnished by management about litigation, claims, and assessments.

C. Legal counsel's opinion of the client's historical experiences in recent similar litigation.

D. A description and evaluation of litigation, claims, and assessments that existed at the balance sheet date.

Answer (B) is correct.
REQUIRED: The primary reason that letters of inquiry are sent to a client's legal counsel.
DISCUSSION: A letter of inquiry to a client's external legal counsel is the auditor's primary means of corroborating information furnished by management about litigation, claims, and assessments. If in-house legal counsel is primarily responsible for the entity's litigation, claims, and assessments, the auditor should send a similar letter of inquiry to in-house legal counsel. But the letter to in-house legal counsel is not a substitute for direct communication with external legal counsel.
Answer (A) is incorrect. Management provides information about the probable outcome of asserted claims and impending or threatened litigation. Answer (C) is incorrect. The auditor is concerned with current litigation, not recent similar litigation. Answer (D) is incorrect. Management provides a description and evaluation of litigation, claims, and assessments that existed at the balance sheet date. The letter of inquiry corroborates that information.

5. The refusal of a client's legal counsel to provide information requested in an inquiry letter generally is considered

A. Grounds for an adverse opinion.

B. A limitation on the scope of the audit.

C. Reason to withdraw from the engagement.

D. A significant deficiency in internal control.

Answer (B) is correct.
REQUIRED: The nature of the refusal of a client's legal counsel to provide information requested.
DISCUSSION: Legal counsel's refusal to furnish the information requested in an inquiry letter either in writing or orally may be a limitation on the scope of the audit sufficient to preclude an unmodified opinion.
Answer (A) is incorrect. A scope limitation never requires an adverse opinion. Answer (C) is incorrect. The refusal is not immediate grounds for withdrawal from an engagement. The auditor should attempt to become satisfied by alternative means. Answer (D) is incorrect. Consideration of internal control is related to the client, not the client's legal counsel.

6. Which of the following statements about litigation, claims, and assessments extracted from a letter from a client's legal counsel is most likely to cause the auditor to request clarification?

A. "I believe that the possible liability to the company is nominal in amount."

B. "I believe that the action can be settled for less than the damages claimed."

C. "I believe that the plaintiff's case against the company is without merit."

D. "I believe that the company will be able to defend this action successfully."

Answer (B) is correct.
REQUIRED: The statement by legal counsel most likely causing an auditor's request for clarification.
DISCUSSION: The letter of inquiry requests, among other things, that legal counsel evaluate the likelihood of pending or threatened litigation, claims, and assessments. It also requests that legal counsel estimate, if possible, the amount or range of potential loss. Thus, the auditor is concerned about the amount of the expected settlement as well as the likelihood of the outcome. The statement that the action can be settled for less than the damages claimed is an example given in AU-C 501 of an evaluation that is unclear about the likelihood of an unfavorable outcome.
Answer (A) is incorrect. Legal counsel's statement that the amount of possible liability will not be material states an amount or range of loss. Answer (C) is incorrect. Legal counsel has stated that no liability is expected. Answer (D) is incorrect. Legal counsel has stated that no liability is expected.

14.2 Subsequent Events and Subsequently Discovered Facts

7. Which of the following procedures should an auditor ordinarily perform regarding subsequent events?

A. Read the latest subsequent interim financial statements.

B. Send second requests to the client's customers who failed to respond to initial accounts receivable confirmation requests.

C. Communicate material weaknesses in internal control to the client's audit committee.

D. Review the cutoff bank statements for several months after the year end.

Answer (A) is correct.

REQUIRED: The subsequent events procedure.

DISCUSSION: Subsequent events procedures include (1) reading the latest subsequent interim statements, if any; (2) inquiring of management and those charged with governance about the occurrence of subsequent events and various financial and accounting matters; (3) reading the minutes of meetings of owners, management, and those charged with governance; (4) obtaining a letter of representations from management; (5) inquiring of client's legal counsel; and (6) obtaining an understanding of management's procedures for identifying subsequent events.

Answer (B) is incorrect. Second confirmation requests do not disclose subsequent events. Answer (C) is incorrect. Communication of material weaknesses is not a subsequent events procedure. Answer (D) is incorrect. Cutoff bank statements are requested from banks 7 to 10 days after year end. They are used to verify the client's bank reconciliations and detect kiting.

8. Wilson, CPA, obtained sufficient appropriate audit evidence on which to base the opinion on Abco's December 31, Year 1, financial statements on March 6, Year 2, the date of the auditor's report. A subsequently discovered fact requiring revision of the Year 1 financial statements occurred on April 10, Year 2, and came to Wilson's attention on April 24, Year 2. If the fact became known prior to the report release date, and the revision is made, Wilson's report ordinarily should be dated

A. March 6, Year 2.

B. April 10, Year 2.

C. April 24, Year 2.

D. Using dual-dating.

Answer (D) is correct.

REQUIRED: The date of the report if the statements are adjusted for a subsequently discovered fact.

DISCUSSION: A subsequently discovered fact (1) becomes known to the auditor after the report date and (2) may cause the auditor to revise the report. The report date is no earlier than the date when sufficient appropriate evidence is obtained. If such a fact becomes known to the auditor before the report release date, the auditor should (1) discuss the matter with management and (2) determine whether the statements need revision (adjustment or disclosure). If management revises the statements, the auditor should perform the necessary procedures on the revision. The auditor also (1) dates the report as of a later date or (2) dual-dates the report. Dual-dating indicates that the procedures performed subsequent to the original date are limited to the revision. Unless the auditor extends subsequent events procedures to a new date (one presumably later than April 24, Year 2, the date when the subsequently discovered fact became known), the auditor should dual-date the report.

Answer (A) is incorrect. March 6, Year 2, is the original report date. Answer (B) is incorrect. April 10, Year 2, is inappropriate because the discovery of a fact requiring revision of the report did not occur until later. Answer (C) is incorrect. The new (or additional) date is presumably later than April 24, Year 2, the date when the subsequently discovered fact became known.

9. Zero Corp. suffered a loss having a material effect on its financial statements as a result of a customer's bankruptcy that rendered a trade receivable uncollectible. This bankruptcy occurred suddenly because of a natural disaster 10 days after Zero's balance sheet date but 1 month before the issuance of the financial statements and the auditor's report. Under these circumstances, the

	Financial Statements Should Be Adjusted	Event Requires Financial Statement Disclosure, but No Adjustment	Auditor's Report Should Be Modified for a Lack of Consistency
A.	Yes	No	No
B.	Yes	No	Yes
C.	No	Yes	Yes
D.	No	Yes	No

Answer (D) is correct.

REQUIRED: The effect on the financial statements and the auditor's report of a subsequent event.

DISCUSSION: Certain subsequent events may provide evidence about conditions at the date of the balance sheet and require adjustment of the statements in accordance with the applicable financial reporting framework. For example, U.S. GAAP require recognition in the statements of the effects of a subsequent event providing additional evidence about conditions at the balance sheet date, including accounting estimates. Other subsequent events provide evidence about conditions not existing at the date of the balance sheet but arising subsequent to that date. These events may require disclosure but do not require adjustment of financial statement balances. In this case, the financial statements should not be adjusted, but disclosure should be made. The report is unaffected if disclosure is made.

10. Which of the following procedures will an auditor most likely perform to obtain evidence about the occurrence of subsequent events?

A. Recomputing a sample of large-dollar transactions occurring after year end for arithmetic accuracy.

B. Investigating changes in equity occurring after year end.

C. Inquiring of the entity's legal counsel concerning litigation, claims, and assessments arising after year end.

D. Confirming bank accounts established after year end.

Answer (C) is correct.

REQUIRED: The auditing procedure for the subsequent events period.

DISCUSSION: Subsequent events procedures include (1) reading the latest subsequent interim statements, if any; (2) inquiring of management and those charged with governance about the occurrence of subsequent events and various financial and accounting matters; (3) reading the minutes of meetings of owners, management, and those charged with governance; (4) obtaining a letter of representations from management; (5) inquiring of client's legal counsel; and (6) obtaining an understanding of management's procedures for identifying subsequent events.

Answer (A) is incorrect. Testing the arithmetic accuracy of known events does not obtain evidence about the occurrence of a subsequent event. Answer (B) is incorrect. The auditor should inquire of officers and other executives as to significant changes in equity, but an investigation of such changes is less likely than the inquiry of legal counsel. Answer (D) is incorrect. A bank account established after year end is not an asset that existed at the balance sheet date.

11. After the date of the report, an auditor has no obligation to make continuing inquiries or perform other procedures concerning the audited financial statements, **unless**

A. Information, which existed at the report date and may affect the report, comes to the auditor's attention.

B. The control environment changes after the date of the report.

C. Information about an event that occurred after the date of the report comes to the auditor's attention.

D. Final determinations or resolutions are made of contingencies that had been disclosed in the financial statements.

Answer (A) is correct.

REQUIRED: The basis for the obligation to perform procedures after the report date.

DISCUSSION: Although the auditor may need to extend subsequent events procedures when issuers make filings under the Securities Act of 1933 (AU-C 925, *Filings with the U.S. Securities and Exchange Commission Under the Securities Act of 1933*), (s)he ordinarily need not apply any procedures after the date of the report. However, facts may be discovered by the auditor after the report release date that, if known at that date, might have caused the auditor to revise the report. In this case, the auditor should (1) discuss the matter with management and (2) determine whether the statements should be revised and, if so, how management intends to address the matter in the statements (AU-C 560).

Answer (B) is incorrect. Additional audit procedures are ordinarily not necessary prior to reissuing a report. Answer (C) is incorrect. The subsequent event must have occurred prior to the date of the auditor's report (ordinarily, the date of the completion of field work) for the auditor to have additional responsibilities. Answer (D) is incorrect. The auditor has no continuing responsibility to monitor disclosed contingencies.

14.3 Written Representations

12. A purpose of a management representation letter is to reduce

A. Audit risk to an aggregate level of misstatement that could be considered material.

B. An auditor's responsibility to detect material misstatements only to the extent that the letter is relied on.

C. The possibility of a misunderstanding concerning management's responsibility for the financial statements.

D. The scope of an auditor's procedures concerning related party transactions and subsequent events.

Answer (C) is correct.

REQUIRED: The purpose of written representations by management.

DISCUSSION: Management's written representations should be in the form of a representation letter addressed to the auditor. The auditor should have possession of the letter before release of the auditor's report. Among other things, the auditor should request that management provide a written representation that it has met its responsibilities stated in the terms of the audit engagement. These responsibilities include those for (1) the preparation and fair presentation of the statements in accordance with the applicable reporting framework and (2) the design, implementation, and maintenance of the relevant internal control.

Answer (A) is incorrect. Written representations by management complement but do not affect the procedures necessary to enable an auditor to obtain sufficient appropriate evidence to draw reasonable conclusions on which to base the opinion. Answer (B) is incorrect. Written representations by management do not affect other audit procedures. Answer (D) is incorrect. Written representations by management do not pertain only to related party transactions and subsequent events and do not affect other procedures.

13. Which of the following documentation is required for an audit in accordance with generally accepted auditing standards?

    A.   An internal control questionnaire.

    B.   An organization chart.

    C.   A planning memorandum or checklist.

    D.   A management representation letter.

Answer (D) is correct.
    REQUIRED: The requirement of an audit made in accordance with GAAS.
    DISCUSSION: AU-C 580 requires that the auditor obtain certain written representations from management. The written representations confirm certain matters (e.g., oral representations) or support other audit evidence. They complement other audit procedures but do not provide sufficient appropriate evidence or affect the other procedures.

14. To which of the following matters would an auditor **not** apply materiality limits when obtaining specific written management representations?

    A.   Disclosure of compensating balance arrangements involving restrictions on cash balances.

    B.   Information concerning related party transactions and related amounts receivable or payable.

    C.   The absence of errors and unrecorded transactions in the financial statements.

    D.   Fraud involving employees with significant roles in internal control.

Answer (D) is correct.
    REQUIRED: The matter to which an auditor does not apply materiality limits.
    DISCUSSION: Management's representations may be limited to matters that are considered individually or collectively material if management and the auditor have reached an understanding about materiality for this purpose. Materiality considerations do not apply to certain representations not directly related to amounts in the financial statements, for example, representations about the premise of the audit (i.e., acknowledgment of responsibility for fair presentation, internal control, and auditor access to information and people). Materiality also does not apply to knowledge of fraud or suspected fraud affecting the entity involving (1) management, (2) employees with significant roles in internal control, or (3) others if the fraud could materially affect the statements (AU-C 580).

15. To which of the following matters would materiality limits **not** apply in obtaining written management representations?

    A.   The availability of minutes of shareholders' and directors' meetings.

    B.   Losses from purchase commitments at prices in excess of fair value.

    C.   The disclosure of compensating balance arrangements involving related parties.

    D.   Reductions of obsolete inventory to net realizable value.

Answer (A) is correct.
    REQUIRED: The matter to which materiality limits do not apply when obtaining written management representations.
    DISCUSSION: Materiality does not apply to representations not directly related to amounts in the financial statements. The availability of minutes of shareholders' meetings and directors' meetings is independent of amounts in the financial statements. Thus, materiality limits do not apply.

16. Key Co. plans to present comparative financial statements for the years ended December 31, Year 1 and Year 2, respectively. Smith, CPA, audited Key's financial statements for both years and plans to report on the comparative financial statements on May 1, Year 3. Key's current management team was not present until January 1, Year 2. What period of time should be covered by Key's management representation letter?

    A.   January 1, Year 1, through December 31, Year 2.

    B.   January 1, Year 1, through May 1, Year 3.

    C.   January 1, Year 2, through December 31, Year 2.

    D.   January 1, Year 2, through May 1, Year 3.

Answer (B) is correct.
    REQUIRED: The dates to be covered by a management representation letter.
    DISCUSSION: The auditor is concerned with events occurring through the date of his or her report that may require adjustment of, or disclosure in, the financial statements. Thus, the representations should be made (1) as of a date no earlier than the date of the auditor's report and (2) for all periods referred to in the report. Moreover, if current management was not present during all periods covered by the auditor's report, the auditor should nevertheless obtain written representations from current management for all such periods (AU-C 580).

17. An auditor finds several misstatements in the financial statements that the client prefers not to correct. The auditor determines that the misstatements are not material in the aggregate. Which of the following actions by the auditor is most appropriate?

A. Document all misstatements accumulated during the audit and the conclusion about whether uncorrected misstatements are material.

B. Document the conclusion that the misstatements do not cause the financial statements to be misstated, but do not accumulate uncorrected misstatements in the audit documentation.

C. Accumulate the uncorrected misstatements in the working papers, but do not document whether they cause the financial statements to be misstated.

D. Do not accumulate the uncorrected misstatements in the audit documentation, and do not document a conclusion about whether the uncorrected misstatements cause the financial statements to be misstated.

Answer (A) is correct.
REQUIRED: The most appropriate auditor action when uncorrected misstatements are not material in the aggregate.
DISCUSSION: The auditor should document (1) the amount below which misstatements are clearly trivial; (2) all misstatements accumulated during the audit and whether they were corrected; and (3) the conclusion about whether uncorrected misstatements are material, individually or aggregated, and the basis for the conclusion (AU-C 450). Furthermore, the representation letter should have an accompanying list of uncorrected misstatements. The letter should include a sentence stating, "The effects of the uncorrected misstatements are immaterial, both individually and in the aggregate, to the financial statements as a whole."

14.4 Auditor's Consideration of an Entity's Ability to Continue as a Going Concern

18. An auditor has substantial doubt about the entity's ability to continue as a going concern for a reasonable period of time because of negative cash flows and working capital deficiencies. Under these circumstances, the auditor would be most concerned about the

A. Control environment factors that affect the organizational structure.

B. Correlation of detection risk and inherent risk.

C. Effectiveness of the entity's internal control activities.

D. Possible effects on the entity's financial statements.

Answer (D) is correct.
REQUIRED: The auditor's priority given substantial doubt about the entity's ability to continue as a going concern for a reasonable period of time.
DISCUSSION: If an auditor has substantial doubt about the entity's ability to continue as a going concern for a reasonable period of time, (s)he should assess the possible effects on the entity's financial statements, including the adequacy of disclosure of uncertainties related to the going-concern issue. The auditor also should include in the auditor's report an emphasis-of-matter paragraph.
Answer (A) is incorrect. The control environment factors that affect the organizational structure have a lower audit priority than a substantial doubt about the entity's ability to continue as a going concern for a reasonable period of time. Answer (B) is incorrect. The correlation of detection risk and inherent risk is considered in every audit. For a given audit risk, the acceptable detection risk is inversely related to the assessed risks of material misstatement (combined inherent risks and control risks). Answer (C) is incorrect. The auditor sometimes may obtain sufficient appropriate evidence without testing controls.

19. Which of the following auditing procedures most likely would assist an auditor in identifying conditions and events that may indicate substantial doubt about an entity's ability to continue as a going concern?

A. Inspecting title documents to verify whether any assets are pledged as collateral.

B. Confirming with third parties the details of arrangements to maintain financial support.

C. Reconciling the cash balance per books with the cutoff bank statement and the bank confirmation.

D. Comparing the entity's depreciation and asset capitalization policies to other entities in the industry.

Answer (B) is correct.
REQUIRED: The audit procedure that may identify conditions indicating substantial doubt about an entity's continuation as a going concern.
DISCUSSION: The procedures typically employed to identify going-concern issues include (1) analytical procedures, (2) review of subsequent events, (3) review of compliance with debt and loan agreements, (4) reading minutes of meetings, (5) inquiry of legal counsel, and (6) confirmation with related and third parties of arrangements for financial support.
Answer (A) is incorrect. Searching for pledged assets is related to disclosure issues. Answer (C) is incorrect. Reconciling the cash balance with cutoff bank statements and the bank confirmation tests the existence of cash. Answer (D) is incorrect. This comparison might identify conditions needing additional consideration but would not provide evidence about going-concern issues.

20. Cooper, CPA, believes there is substantial doubt about the ability of Zero Corp. to continue as a going concern for a reasonable period of time. In evaluating Zero's plans for dealing with the adverse effects of future conditions and events, Cooper most likely will consider, as a mitigating factor, Zero's plans to

- A. Discuss with lenders the terms of all debt and loan agreements.
- B. Strengthen internal controls over cash disbursements.
- C. Purchase production facilities currently being leased from a related party.
- D. Postpone expenditures for research and development projects.

Answer (D) is correct.

REQUIRED: The managerial action that mitigates adverse effects of future conditions and events.

DISCUSSION: Once an auditor has identified conditions and events indicating that substantial doubt exists about an entity's ability to continue as a going concern, the auditor should first obtain written representations and then consider management's plans to mitigate their adverse effects. The auditor should consider plans to dispose of assets, borrow money or restructure debt, reduce or delay expenditures, and increase equity.

Answer (A) is incorrect. Discussion with lenders is not a sufficient action to mitigate the circumstances. Answer (B) is incorrect. Internal control improvements do not increase cash flows or postpone expenditures. Answer (C) is incorrect. The purchase of facilities may worsen the company's problems.

Access the Gleim CPA Premium Review System featuring SmartAdapt for exam-emulating multiple-choice questions and simulations with detailed answer explanations.

Learn more: gleim.com/CPApremium | 800.874.5346

STUDY UNIT FIFTEEN
EVIDENCE -- SAMPLING

(20 pages of outline)

The first subunit defines terms, describes the purpose of and approach to sampling, and presents the basic concepts traditionally tested on the CPA exam. A study of these fundamentals is an effective way to prepare for most sampling-related questions. However, some comprehensive questions may be asked, including those requiring basic calculations or the consideration of tables.

The remaining three subunits contain study materials related to more extensive questions and simulations. They describe specific sampling methods in more detail and provide several examples. Although more comprehensive than the first subunit, they are not intended to be an exhaustive treatment of sampling. These sections are based on concepts that have been tested in the past or are likely to be tested on future CPA exams. They are based on the AICPA Audit Guide, *Audit Sampling* (2013).

15.1 SAMPLING FUNDAMENTALS

No one can accurately predict what will be on the exam you take. But we can give you some facts to help you make informed decisions about your study strategy. Sampling is included in the Auditing and Attestation section of the Uniform CPA Examination blueprint in Area III – Performing Further Procedures and Obtaining Evidence. Between 30% and 40% of the section's content will be based on Area III. Only 2 of the 39 representative tasks in Area III relate to sampling. When the exam was disclosed, sampling questions normally accounted for about 3% to 4% of the questions, but occasionally more. Many, if not most, of those questions could have been answered with a solid understanding of the material in Subunit 15.1. Understand all you can about the exam and your strengths and weaknesses; then decide how much time to invest in studying more specialized sampling topics.

1. **Audit Sampling**

   a. Audit sampling selects and evaluates fewer than 100% of the items in the relevant audited population.

      1) The population is the entire data set (a) from which a sample is selected and (b) about which conclusions are to be drawn.

      2) The auditor expects the sample (items selected) to (a) represent the population and (b) provide a reasonable basis for conclusions about it.

         a) The sample is representative if, subject to sampling risk, conclusions are similar to those drawn if the same procedures were applied to every item in the population.

   b. Sampling may be nonstatistical or statistical.

      1) **Nonstatistical (judgment) sampling** uses the auditor's subjective judgment to determine the sample size (number of items to examine) and sample selection (which items to examine).

         a) Subjectivity is not always a weakness. The auditor, based on other audit work, may be able to test the most material and risky transactions and emphasize the types subject to high risk of material misstatement.

   b)   Although sample results can be extrapolated to the population, statistical sampling theory cannot be used to quantify the confidence level of precision. Item 2)a) below has definitions for these terms.

   2)   **Statistical sampling** (a) **randomly** selects sample items and (b) uses an appropriate statistical method to evaluate the results, including measurement of sampling risk.

   a)   Accordingly, statistical sampling is an objective method of determining sample size and selecting the items to be examined. Unlike nonstatistical sampling, it also provides a means of quantitatively assessing the confidence level and precision.

   i)   The **confidence level**, also called the reliability level, is the percentage of times the sample should adequately reflect the population. It is the complement of the applicable sampling risk factor. For a test of controls, if the allowable risk of overreliance is 5%, the auditor's desired confidence level is 95% (100% − 5%). For a test of details, if the risk of incorrect rejection is 5%, the auditor's desired confidence level is 95% (100% − 5%).

   ii) **Precision** (allowance for sampling risk) is a measure of how closely the sample represents the population.

   b)   **Random selection** includes (1) simple random sampling; (2) stratified random sampling; (3) probability-weighted, including monetary-unit, sampling; and (4) systematic random sampling.

   c)   Statistical sampling helps the auditor to (1) design an efficient sample, (2) measure the sufficiency of the evidence obtained, and (3) evaluate the results.

   d)   Auditors must obtain sufficient appropriate evidence. Sufficiency is the measure of the quantity of evidence. Thus, it relates to the design and size of the sample.

   i)   Statistical sampling permits the auditor to measure **sampling risk** and design more efficient samples (the minimum samples necessary to provide sufficient appropriate evidence).

c.   Statistical sampling applies to **tests of controls** (attribute sampling) and **tests of details** (variables sampling).

2.   The auditor must address uncertainties due to sampling (sampling risk) and uncertainties due to factors other than sampling (nonsampling risk).

3.   **Sampling Risk**

a.   Sampling risk is the risk that the auditor's conclusion based on a sample may differ from the conclusion when the same procedure is applied to the entire population. Two types of erroneous conclusions may be drawn:

   1)   **Controls** are more effective than they actually are (overreliance), or a **material misstatement** does not exist when in fact it does exist (incorrect acceptance).

   a)   This type of error affects audit effectiveness and is more likely to result in an inappropriate opinion.

   2)   **Controls** are less effective than they actually are (underreliance), or a **material misstatement** exists when in fact it does not exist (incorrect rejection).

   a)   This type of error affects audit efficiency and results in more work.

3) The following table is helpful in understanding sampling risk:

	Tests of Controls (Attribute Sampling)	Tests of Details (Variables Sampling)
Audit Efficiency Error	Controls are less effective than they actually are. (Unnecessary audit effort)	A material misstatement exists when in fact it does not exist. (Unnecessary audit effort)
Audit Effectiveness Error	Controls are more effective than they actually are. (Potential audit failure)	A material misstatement does not exist when in fact it does exist. (Potential audit failure)

4. **Nonsampling Risk**

   a. Nonsampling risk is the risk of an erroneous conclusion caused by a factor not related to sampling risk. For example, the auditor may (1) apply inappropriate procedures, (2) misinterpret audit evidence, or (3) not recognize misstatements or control deviations.

   b. Adequate **planning** and effective **quality control** decrease nonsampling risk.

5. **Sample Design, Size, and Selection**

   a. The auditor considers the purpose of the audit procedure(s) and the characteristics of the population.

      1) The auditor (a) defines the nature of a control deviation or misstatement, (b) chooses the population to be sampled, and (c) determines whether it is complete.

      2) For tests of controls, the auditor assesses the expected deviation rate based on the understanding of internal control. If the rate is unacceptably high, controls ordinarily are not tested.

      3) For tests of details, the auditor assesses the expected misstatement. If the expected misstatement is high, an increased sample size or a 100% audit may be needed.

      4) The characteristics of the population may be appropriate for stratification or value-weighted selection.

   b. **Sample size** is inversely related to the acceptable sampling risk. The following factors determine sample size:

      1) **Tests of controls**

         a) The tolerable rate of deviation in the population

         b) The expected rate of deviation in the population

         c) The desired level of assurance **(complement of the risk of overreliance)** that the actual rate of deviation is **not** greater than the tolerable rate

            i) The desired assurance (confidence level) may be based on the extent of the reliance on the relevant controls.

         d) The number of individual items (sampling units) in the population (if the population is very small)

2) **Tests of details**

    a) The desired level of assurance **(complement of the risk of incorrect acceptance)** that actual misstatement is **not** greater than tolerable misstatement. The desired level (confidence level) may be based on the following:

        i) Assessed risks of material misstatement

        ii) Evidence provided by other substantive procedures performed on the same assertion

        iii) Tolerable misstatement

        iv) Expected misstatement

        v) If relevant, stratification of the population and the sampling units in each stratum

    NOTE: For tests of details, auditors also consider a measure of **variance** (e.g., the standard deviation). Furthermore, auditors may directly consider the **risk of incorrect rejection**. Computer programs used to calculate sample size commonly require the auditor to enter the risk of incorrect rejection and the desired allowance for risk of incorrect rejection (precision). Subunit 15.3 contains a relevant table (Table 3). It is based on factors used to determine an amount of precision that is appropriate to give the specified protection against incorrect acceptance.

6. If the appropriate (or alternative) procedures cannot be performed on a sample item, the auditor treats the item as a misstatement or a control deviation.

    a. In some cases, the auditor may select a **replacement item** if (s)he is satisfied that the initially selected item is not a misstatement or a control deviation.

7. The auditor should investigate the causes and evaluate the effects of identified misstatements and control deviations.

    a. They may have a **common feature** (e.g., type of transaction or period of time), and the auditor may wish to examine all items with that feature.

        1) The presence of a common feature also may indicate **fraud** if intentional.

    b. The auditor also evaluates the **qualitative** aspects of misstatements, e.g., whether they are (1) differences in accounting principles or their application or (2) caused by fraud.

        1) Another qualitative aspect is the potential effect on other parts of the audit.

8. The auditor should project the results of sampling to the population. The projection for tests of

    a. Details is the **projected misstatement**.

    b. Controls is the **sample deviation rate**.

9. **Evaluation of Results**

    a. The auditor should evaluate the results of sampling, including sampling risk, and whether the results provide a reasonable basis for conclusions about the population.

        1) Without other audit evidence,

            a) An unexpectedly high deviation rate for a test of controls may require higher assessed risks of material misstatement.

        b)   An unexpectedly high misstatement amount may indicate that a transaction class or account balance is materially misstated.

            i)   The closer projected misstatement is to tolerable misstatement, the more likely that actual misstatement is greater than tolerable misstatement.

            ii)   If expected misstatement used to calculate sample size is less than projected misstatement, it is more likely that sampling risk is unacceptable.

    2)   If sampling does not provide a reasonable basis for conclusions, the auditor may

        a)   Ask management to investigate misstatements and make needed adjustments or

        b)   Perform further audit procedures, for example, increasing sample size.

10. **Basic Steps in a Statistical Plan**

    a.   **Determine the objectives of the plan.**

        1)   For a test of controls, an example is to conclude that control is reasonably effective.

        2)   For a test of details, an example is to conclude that a balance is not misstated by more than an immaterial amount.

    b.   **Define the population.** This step includes defining the sampling unit (an individual item in the population) and considering the completeness of the population.

        1)   For tests of controls, the period covered is defined.

        2)   For tests of details, individually significant items may be defined.

    c.   **Determine acceptable levels of sampling risk** (e.g., 5% or 10%).

    d.   **Calculate the sample size** using tables or sample-size formulas.

        1)   In some cases, it is efficient to divide the population into subpopulations or strata. The primary objective of **stratification** is to minimize variability.

            a)   The variance within each subpopulation or stratum is lower than in the population as a whole. Thus, the auditor may sample a smaller number of items while holding the allowance for sampling risk (precision) and the confidence level constant.

        2)   Stratification also allows the auditor to apply more audit effort to larger elements or more risky parts of the population.

        3)   For example, when auditing sales revenue, an auditor could divide the population into strata of dollar increments. The auditor could test transactions under $500, between $501 and $2,000, and $2,001 and above.

    e.   **Select the sampling approach**, e.g., random number, systematic, or block.

        1)   In **random sampling**, each item in the population has an equal and nonzero probability of selection. Selection may be by (a) generating random numbers from a random number table or computer program and (b) tracing them to associated documents or items in the population.

        2)   **Systematic sampling** begins with selecting a random start and then taking every *n*th item in the population. The value of *n* is computed by dividing the population by the number of sampling units. The random start should be in the first interval.

            a)   The sampling method requires only counting in the population. Accordingly, random numbers and the items in the population need not correspond as in random number sampling.

b) A systematic sampling plan assumes the items are arranged randomly in the population. If they are not, a random selection method should be used.

EXAMPLE

If the population contains 8,200 items and a sample of 50 is required, every 164th item is selected (8,200 ÷ 50). After a random start in the first interval (1 to 164), every additional 164th item is selected. For example, if the 35th item is the first selected randomly, the next is the 199th (35 + 164). The third item is the 363rd (199 + 164). The process is continued until the 50 items are identified.

---

3) **Block sampling** (cluster sampling) randomly selects groups of items as the sampling units rather than individual items. An example is the inclusion in the sample of all cash payments for May and September.

a) One problem is that the variability of items within the blocks may not be representative of the variability within the population.

b) The advantage of block sampling is that it avoids assigning random numbers to individual items in the population. Instead, blocks (clusters) are randomly selected.

f. **Take the sample.** The auditor selects the items to be evaluated.

g. **Evaluate the sample results.** The auditor draws conclusions about the population.

h. **Document the sampling procedures.** The auditor prepares appropriate working papers.

11. **Overview of Attribute Sampling**

a. Attribute sampling is used to test the effectiveness of controls (tests of controls).

EXAMPLE

The auditor tests the effectiveness of the approval process of purchase orders. (S)he selects a sample of purchase orders from the population of all purchase orders issued during the year and inspects each one in the sample for the required approval.

---

b. The deviation (failure) rate in the application of the control in the sample is used to project the deviation rate to the whole population.

c. By specifying a tolerable deviation rate, a preliminary expected deviation rate, and the risk of overreliance, the auditor can determine the appropriate sample size by consulting a table.

12. **Primary Methods of Variables Sampling**

a. Variables sampling applies to dollar values or other quantities for tests of details.

1) Attribute sampling tests binary propositions.

b. **Mean-per-unit** averages the audit amounts of the sample items and multiplies the average by the number of items in the population to estimate the population amount. An allowance for sampling risk (achieved precision at the desired level of confidence based on the normal distribution) is then calculated.

c. **Difference estimation** (of population misstatement) (1) determines differences between the audit and recorded amounts of items in the sample, (2) adds the differences, (3) calculates the mean difference, and (4) multiplies the mean by the number of items in the population. An allowance for sampling risk (achieved precision at the desired level of confidence based on the normal distribution) is then calculated.

1) **Ratio estimation** is similar to difference estimation except that it estimates the population misstatement by multiplying the recorded amount of the population by the ratio of the total audit amount of the sample items to their total recorded amount.

d. **Monetary-unit sampling (MUS)**, also known as probability-proportional-to-size (PPS) or dollar-unit sampling (DUS), uses the dollar or another monetary unit as the sampling unit. MUS is appropriate for testing account balances (typically assets) for **overstatement** when some items may be far larger than others in the population. In effect, it stratifies the population because the larger account balances have a greater chance of being selected. MUS is most useful if few misstatements are expected.

1) Also, the method does **not** require the use of a measure of variance (e.g., standard deviation or expected deviation rate) to determine sample size or interpret the results.

Stop and review! You have completed the outline for this subunit. Study multiple-choice questions 1 through 6 beginning on page 320.

15.2 STATISTICAL SAMPLING IN TESTS OF CONTROLS (ATTRIBUTE SAMPLING)

1. **Attribute sampling** tests binary (yes/no or error/nonerror) questions. It tests the effectiveness of controls because it can estimate a rate of occurrence of control deviations in a population.

   a. Attribute sampling requires evidence indicating performance of the control being tested (e.g., a control indicating that the purchasing agent has signed all purchase orders before sending them to the vendor). It is most helpful for a large population of documentary evidence.

   1) In general, the performance of any task that leaves evidence of its execution is suitable for attribute sampling. In such cases, the auditor can form conclusions about the population by examining a sample.

   b. The following are examples of activities subject to controls that may be tested using attribute sampling:

   1) Billing
   2) Voucher processing
   3) Payroll
   4) Inventory pricing

2. **Steps for Testing Controls**

   a. **Define the objectives of the plan.** The auditor should clearly state what is to be accomplished, for example, to determine that the deviation rate from an approval process for a transaction is at an acceptable level.

   b. **Define the population.** The population is the focus of interest. The accountant wants to reach conclusions about all of the items (typically documents) in the population.

   1) The **sampling unit** is the individual item included in the sample. Thus, the population may consist of all the transactions for the fiscal year. The sampling unit is each document representing a transaction and containing the required evidence that a control was performed (e.g., an approval signature).

   c. **Define the deviation conditions.** The characteristic indicative of performance of a control is the attribute of interest, for example, the supervisor's signature of approval on a document. Careful definition of the attribute is important so that deviations (departures) from the control may be determined and the sample items properly evaluated.

   1) For example, is it acceptable for another person to sign for the supervisor during vacation periods, and must the signature be in a certain place on the form for it to be considered approved?

d. **Determine the sample size.** Tables ordinarily are used to calculate the appropriate sample size based on the factors below. Tables 1 and 2 below and on the next page are derived from Appendix A of the AICPA Audit Guide, *Audit Sampling* (2013). The sample sizes in the tables are based on the assumption that the population is large.

1) **Allowable risk of overreliance.** This risk has an inverse effect on sample size. The higher the allowable risk, the smaller the sample size. The usual risk specified by auditors is 5% or 10%. The auditor can specify other levels of risk, but the tables most often presented use only these two.

2) **Tolerable deviation rate.** This is the maximum rate of deviations from the prescribed control that the auditor is willing to accept without altering the assessed risk of material misstatement. Deviations increase the likelihood of misstatements in the accounting records but do not always cause misstatements.

a) If the auditor cannot tolerate any deviations, sampling is inappropriate, and the whole population must be investigated.

3) **Expected population deviation rate.** An estimate of the deviation rate in the current population is necessary to determine the appropriate sample size. This estimate can be based on the prior year's findings or a pilot sample of approximately 30 to 50 items.

a) The expected rate should be less than the tolerable rate. Otherwise, tests of the control should be omitted, and the auditor should not rely on the effectiveness of the control.

Table 1 -- Sample Sizes for Tests of Controls -- 5% Risk of Overreliance									
Expected Population Deviation Rate	Tolerable Deviation Rate								
	2%	3%	4%	5%	6%	7%	8%	9%	10%
0.00%	149	99	74	59	49	42	36	32	29
.25	236	157	117	93	78	66	58	51	46
.50	313	157	117	93	78	66	58	51	46
.75	386	208	117	93	78	66	58	51	46
1.00	590	257	156	93	78	66	58	51	46
1.25	1,030	303	156	124	78	66	58	51	46
1.50	*	392	192	124	103	66	58	51	46
1.75	*	562	227	153	103	88	77	51	46
2.00	*	846	294	181	127	88	77	68	46
2.25	*	1,466	390	208	127	88	77	68	61
2.50	*	*	513	234	150	109	77	68	61
2.75	*	*	722	286	173	109	95	68	61
3.00	*	*	1,098	361	195	129	95	84	61
3.25	*	*	1,936	458	238	148	112	84	61
3.50	*	*	*	624	280	167	112	84	76
3.75	*	*	*	877	341	185	129	100	76
4.00	*	*	*	1,348	421	221	146	100	89
5.00	*	*	*	*	1,580	478	240	158	116
6.00	*	*	*	*	*	1,832	532	266	179
7.00	*	*	*	*	*	*	*	585	298
8.00	*	*	*	*	*	*	*	*	649

Table 2 -- Results Evaluation for Tests of Controls -- Upper % Limits at 5% Risk of Overreliance										
Sample Size	Actual Number of Deviations Found									
	0	1	2	3	4	5	6	7	8	9	10
20	14.0	21.7	28.3	34.4	40.2	45.6	50.8	55.9	60.7	65.4	69.9
25	11.3	17.7	23.2	28.2	33.0	37.6	42.0	46.3	50.4	54.4	58.4
30	9.6	14.9	19.6	23.9	28.0	31.9	35.8	39.4	43.0	46.6	50.0
35	8.3	12.9	17.0	20.7	24.3	27.8	31.1	34.4	37.5	40.6	43.7
40	7.3	11.4	15.0	18.3	21.5	24.6	27.5	30.4	33.3	36.0	38.8
45	6.5	10.2	13.4	16.4	19.2	22.0	24.7	27.3	29.8	32.4	34.8
50	5.9	9.2	12.1	14.8	17.4	19.9	22.4	24.7	27.1	29.4	31.6
55	5.4	8.4	11.1	13.5	15.9	18.2	20.5	22.6	24.8	26.9	28.9
60	4.9	7.7	10.2	12.5	14.7	16.8	18.8	20.8	22.8	24.8	26.7
65	4.6	7.1	9.4	11.5	13.6	15.5	17.5	19.3	21.2	23.0	24.7
70	4.2	6.6	8.8	10.8	12.7	14.5	16.3	18.0	19.7	21.4	23.1
75	4.0	6.2	8.2	10.1	11.8	13.6	15.2	16.9	18.5	20.1	21.6
80	3.7	5.8	7.7	9.5	11.1	12.7	14.3	15.9	17.4	18.9	20.3
90	3.3	5.2	6.9	8.4	9.9	11.4	12.8	14.2	15.5	16.9	18.2
100	3.0	4.7	6.2	7.6	9.0	10.3	11.5	12.8	14.0	15.2	16.4
125	2.4	3.8	5.0	6.1	7.2	8.3	9.3	10.3	11.3	12.3	13.2
150	2.0	3.2	4.2	5.1	6.0	6.9	7.8	8.6	9.5	10.3	11.1
200	1.5	2.4	3.2	3.9	4.6	5.2	5.9	6.5	7.2	7.8	8.4

4) **Population size.** The total number of sampling units in the population should be known. However, the sample size is relatively insensitive to size changes in large populations. For populations over 2,000, a standard table (e.g., Table 1, which assumes a large population) can be used.

    a) Use of standard tables (based on the assumption of large populations) for sampling plans based on a smaller population size is a conservative approach because it overstates the sample size. Thus, the risk of overreliance is not affected.

    b) A change in the size of the population has a very small effect on the required sample size when the population is large.

EXAMPLE

Assume the risk of overreliance is 5%, the tolerable rate is 6%, the expected population deviation rate is 2.5%, and the population size is over 5,000. Given these data, the sample size determined from Table 1 is 150. This is the intersection of the 6% Tolerable Deviation Rate column and the 2.50% Expected Population Deviation Rate row.

---

e. **Perform the sampling plan.** A random sample should be taken. Each item in the population should have an equal and nonzero chance of being selected. A random number table or a computer program can be used to identify the items to be selected if the random number and the item in the population correspond.

    1) Sampling may be **with** or **without** replacement. The tables are designed for sampling with replacement, resulting in a conservative sample size because a slightly larger sample size than necessary is selected.

        a) In practice, auditors normally sample without replacement. No additional evidence is obtained by choosing the same item more than once.

    2) Sampling without replacement means that a population item cannot be selected twice.

f.   **Evaluate and document sample results.** The steps include calculating the sample deviation rate and determining the achieved upper deviation limit.

1)   **Sample deviation rate.** The number of deviations observed is divided by the sample size to determine the sample deviation rate. This rate is the best estimate of the population deviation rate.

a)   For example, if three deviations were discovered in a sample of 150, the auditor's best estimate of the population deviation rate is 2% (3 ÷ 150).

b)   The auditor cannot state with certainty that the sample rate is the population rate because the sample may not be representative of the population. But, (s)he can state at a specified confidence level that the deviation rate is not likely to be greater than a specified upper limit.

2)   **Achieved upper deviation limit.** The achieved upper deviation limit is based on the sample size and the number of deviations discovered. Table 2 on the previous page is used. The intersection of the sample size and the number of deviations indicates the achieved upper deviation limit. Accordingly, if the auditor discovers 3 deviations in a sample of 150, (s)he can state at a 95% confidence level (the complement of a 5% risk of overreliance) that the true occurrence rate is not greater than 5.1%.

a)   The difference between the achieved upper deviation limit determined from a standard table and the sample rate is the allowance for sampling risk (achieved precision). In the example, it is 3.1% (5.1% – 2%).

b)   When the sample deviation rate exceeds the expected population deviation rate, the achieved upper deviation limit exceeds the tolerable rate at the given risk of overreliance. In that case, the sample does not support the planned reliance on the control.

c)   When the sample deviation rate does not exceed the expected population deviation rate, the achieved upper deviation limit does not exceed the tolerable rate at the given risk level. Thus, the sample supports the planned reliance on the control. In the example, the sample deviation rate (2%) does not exceed the expected population rate (2.5%). Thus, the achieved upper deviation limit (5.1%) does not exceed the tolerable rate (6%).

3)   Each deviation should be analyzed to determine its nature, importance, and probable cause. Obviously, some are much more significant than others. Sampling provides a means of forming a conclusion about the overall population but should not be used as a substitute for good judgment.

3.   **Analysis of Results**

a.   The following presentation is a popular method for testing sampling concepts related to tests of controls. It is used to explain how to analyze the information. Many questions can be answered based on the analysis.

b.   The table below depicts the possible combinations of the sample results and the true state of the population.

Auditor's Estimate Based on Sample Results	**True State of Population**	
	Deviation rate is less than tolerable rate.	Deviation rate exceeds tolerable rate.
Deviation rate is less than tolerable rate.	I. Correct	III. Incorrect
Deviation rate exceeds tolerable rate.	II. Incorrect	IV. Correct

c. The following definitions and explanations should be understood:

1) The true state of the population is the actual rate of deviations in the population.

2) If the true deviation rate is less than the tolerable rate, the auditor should have an expectation of the effectiveness of the control tested.

3) If the true deviation rate exceeds the tolerable rate, the auditor should not have an expectation of the effectiveness of the control tested.

4) The auditor's estimate based on the sample is the auditor's conclusion about the deviation rate in the population based on taking and evaluating a sample.

5) Cell I is a correct decision to have an expectation of the effectiveness of the control tested. The population actually has a deviation rate less than the tolerable rate.

6) Cell II is an incorrect decision not to have an expectation of the effectiveness of the control tested. The population has an acceptable deviation rate. But, because of sampling risk, the sample indicates that the population deviation rate is greater than the tolerable rate.

a) This mistake requires the auditor to expand substantive testing even though the control is effective. Thus, it relates to the efficiency rather than the effectiveness of the audit.

7) Cell III is an incorrect decision (and a critical one) to have an expectation of the effectiveness of the control tested. The population has a greater-than-acceptable deviation rate, but the sample indicates that the deviation rate is less than the tolerable rate.

a) Because the auditor expects the control to have some degree of effectiveness, substantive testing is reduced, and an audit failure could result.

8) Cell IV is a correct decision not to have an expectation of the effectiveness of the control tested. The population has an unacceptable deviation rate, and the sample properly reflects this condition.

d. A CPA exam question may be in many forms, but the following is representative:

1) As a result of tests of a control, the auditor does not have an expectation of the effectiveness of the control and increases substantive testing. This is illustrated by which situation? Answer: Cell II.

Stop and review! You have completed the outline for this subunit. Study multiple-choice questions 7 through 13 beginning on page 322.

15.3 CLASSICAL VARIABLES SAMPLING (MEAN-PER-UNIT)

1. **Sampling for Tests of Details**

a. Sampling for tests of details provides evidence about whether a financial statement assertion about an account balance is materially misstated.

1) For example, the recorded balance of accounts receivable is expected to represent the true balance of the receivables, which is not known (and will never be known without a 100% audit). After taking a sample and drawing a conclusion about the population, the auditor either accepts or rejects the reported number.

b. The following are examples:

1) Is management's recorded balance of accounts receivable measured at net realizable value?

2) Is management's recorded balance of inventory measured at lower of cost or market?

2.   **Steps for Mean-per-Unit Sampling**

    a.   **Define the objectives of the plan.** The auditor intends to estimate the carrying amount of the population, for example, an accounts receivable balance.

    b.   **Define the population and the sampling unit.** This is the balance or class of transactions and the supporting detail under audit.

EXAMPLE

The population consists of 4,000 accounts receivable with a reported carrying amount of $3,500,000. Each customer account is a sampling unit.

The material immediately following is technical. However, it is not likely that you will need to know the formula for the sample size. The AICPA Audit Guide, *Audit Sampling* (2013), states, "Because auditors generally use computer programs to assist them in determining sample sizes and evaluating sample results for classical variables sampling applications, it is not essential for auditors to know mathematical formulas to use these methods." However, we present the formula and an example to help you understand the relationship of the factors.

---

    c.   **Determine the sample size.** The following is the sample size formula for mean-per-unit variables sampling:

$$n = \left[\frac{C \times S \times N}{A} \right]^2$$

If: n = Sample size
    C = Confidence coefficient or number of standard deviations related to the required confidence level (1 − the risk of incorrect rejection)
    S = Standard deviation of the population (an estimate based on a pilot sample or from the prior year's sample)
    N = Number of items in the population
    A = Allowance for sampling risk. This allowance is a total. In some representations, the allowance (precision) is stated in the denominator on a per-item basis ($A \div N$), and N would not be included in the formula.

       1)   The **allowance for sampling risk**, also called the **precision or confidence interval**, is an interval around the sample statistic that is expected to include the true balance of the population at the specified confidence level. When using classical variables sampling, the allowance for sampling risk is calculated based on the normal distribution.

           a)   This allowance is a function of the **tolerable misstatement** determined by the auditor. It is the maximum misstatement that may exist without causing the financial statements to be materially misstated.

               i)   Tolerable misstatement is an expression of **performance materiality**. This measure of materiality is an amount estimated to reduce the probability that the sum of uncorrected and undetected misstatements exceeds materiality for the statements as a whole.

               ii)   Tolerable misstatement may be equal to or less than performance materiality.

b) The allowance for sampling risk is a function of materiality to control the risk of incorrect acceptance. *C* in the formula is based on the risk of incorrect rejection, but the more important risk to the auditor is incorrect acceptance.

   i) The allowance for sampling risk equals the product of tolerable misstatement and a ratio determined in accordance with Table 3 below. This ratio is based on the allowable risk of incorrect acceptance and the risk of incorrect rejection. Both are specified by the auditor.

Table 3 -- Ratio of Desired Allowance for Sampling Risk of Incorrect Rejection to Tolerable Misstatement				
Risk of Incorrect Acceptance	Risk of Incorrect Rejection (Two Sided)			
	.20	.10	.05	.01
.01	.355	.413	.457	.525
.025	.395	.456	.500	.568
.05	.437	.500	.543	.609
.075	.471	.532	.576	.641
.10	.500	.561	.605	.668
.15	.533	.612	.653	.712
.20	.603	.661	.700	.753
.25	.653	.708	.742	.791
.30	.707	.756	.787	.829
.35	.766	.808	.834	.868
.40	.831	.863	.883	.908
.45	.907	.926	.937	.953
.50	1.000	1.000	1.000	1.000

2) The confidence coefficient, *C*, is derived from the standard normal distribution and is based on the risk of incorrect rejection.

Risk of Incorrect Rejection	Confidence Level	Confidence Coefficient
20%	80%	1.28
10%	90%	1.64
5%	95%	1.96
1%	99%	2.58

EXAMPLE

The number of sampling units is 4,000, the estimated population standard deviation is $125 based on a pilot sample, and the number of standard deviations related to the desired 90% confidence level (10% risk of incorrect rejection) is 1.64. Assuming tolerable misstatement of $100,000 and a risk of incorrect acceptance of 5%, the desired allowance for sampling risk (precision) can be determined using Table 3. The intersection of the 10% risk of incorrect rejection and 5% risk of incorrect acceptance is .500. The result is a $50,000 allowance for sampling risk ($100,000 tolerable misstatement × .500).

Thus, the sample size is

$$n = \left[\frac{C \times S \times N}{A} \right]^2$$

$$= \left[\frac{1.64 \times \$125 \times 4,000}{\$50,000} \right]^2$$

$$= 268.96 \text{ or } 269$$

d. **Select the sample, execute the plan, and evaluate and document the results.**

1) Randomly select and audit the accounts, e.g., send confirmations.
2) Calculate the average confirmed accounts receivable amount (assume $880).
3) Calculate the sample standard deviation (assume $125).
4) Evaluate the sample results.

   a) The best estimate of the population balance equals the average accounts receivable amount based on the sample times the number of items in the population. Thus, the amount estimated is determined as follows:

   Estimated balance = Average sample amount × Items in population

   = $880 × 4,000

   = $3,520,000

   b) The calculated allowance for sampling risk (achieved precision) is determined by solving the sample size formula for A.

   $$A = \frac{C \times S \times N}{\sqrt{n}}$$

   $$= \frac{1.64 \times \$125 \times 4,000}{\sqrt{269}}$$

   $$= \$820,000 \div 16.4 = \$50,000$$

      i) C, S, and N have the same values used to calculate the original sample size, n. Thus, the allowance for sampling risk, A, is the same as planned, or $50,000. A is different only when the standard deviation of the sample, S, differs from the estimate used to calculate n. This difference can result in changes in the levels of risk faced by the auditor, but these issues are beyond the scope of the materials presented here (and are usually not covered on the CPA exam).

   c) The audit conclusion is that the auditor is 90% confident that the true balance is $3,520,000 plus or minus $50,000, an interval of $3,470,000 to $3,570,000. If the carrying amount is $3,500,000, the auditor cannot reject the hypothesis that it is not materially misstated. Because the carrying amount is within the interval, the auditor accepts it as fair.

Stop and review! You have completed the outline for this subunit. Study multiple-choice questions 14 through 17 on page 324.

15.4 MONETARY-UNIT SAMPLING (MUS)

1. The **monetary-unit-sampling (MUS)** approach to variables sampling differs from the classical approach. It is a hybrid method that uses attribute sampling methods to estimate monetary amounts. MUS is based on the Poisson distribution, used in attribute sampling to approximate the binomial distribution.

2. MUS uses a monetary unit (e.g., a dollar) as the sampling unit. The classical approach uses items themselves (e.g., invoices, checks, etc.) as the sampling units.

   a. MUS gives each monetary unit in the population an equal chance of selection. In practice, the auditor does not examine an individual monetary unit but uses it to identify an entire transaction or balance to audit (the logical sampling unit).

    b.   MUS is appropriate for account balances that may include only a few overstated items, such as may be expected in inventory and receivables.

        1)   MUS is useful only for tests of **overstatements** (e.g., of assets) because a **systematic selection** method is applied (every *n*th monetary unit is selected).

            a)   Accordingly, the larger the transaction or balance, the more likely it will be selected. This method is inappropriate for testing a population (e.g., liabilities) when understatement is the primary audit consideration.

    c.   MUS is used to reach a conclusion regarding the probability of overstating an account balance by a specified monetary amount.

3.   **Advantages** of MUS include the following:

    a.   The largest items are selected for testing (i.e., the population is stratified).

    b.   It is ideal for testing for overstatement.

    c.   Small sample sizes may be appropriate, especially when no misstatements are expected.

    d.   It is relatively easy to apply, especially if no misstatements are discovered.

    e.   The sample size and sample evaluation can be calculated without dependence on the estimated variation (standard deviation) of the population.

    f.   The sample selection process may begin even before the complete population is available for testing.

4.   **Disadvantages** of MUS include the following:

    a.   Items with zero or negative balances have no chance of selection.

    b.   It is useful only for detecting overstatement errors.

    c.   Sample sizes become relatively large if a significant amount of misstatement is expected.

    d.   The calculated allowance for sampling risk tends to be overstated when a significant amount of misstatement is found in the sample.

5.   **Steps for MUS**

    a.   The steps in MUS are similar to those of other sampling methods:

        1)   Determine the objective of the plan.
        2)   Define the population and sampling unit.
        3)   Determine the sampling interval and sample size.
        4)   Select the sample.
        5)   Execute the sampling plan.
        6)   Evaluate and document the results.

Two examples are provided, one simple and one more complex. It is probably more important that you understand the uses of MUS, the advantages and disadvantages of MUS, and the steps involved in the process than the illustrations presented. The formulas and factors are specified, so you need not know how they were derived. Try to follow the logic and concepts rather than the details.

6.   Simple Example

a.   Below is a simple example of the application of MUS. In the next section, the example is extended to the case in which overstatement errors are detected.

EXAMPLE -- Simple

The following assumptions apply in an audit of Seminole, Inc.:

- The auditor's objective is to test the assertion that the $900,000 accounts receivable balance is fairly stated. Tolerable misstatement is $35,000.
- The population contains 900,000 sampling units and over 1,000 individual accounts receivable (logical sampling units), all with debit balances.
- The risk of incorrect acceptance specified by the auditor is 5%. Thus, the auditor desires to be 95% confident that the recorded balance is not overstated by more than $35,000.

The **sample size** is determined by the following formula:

$$Sample\ size = Recorded\ amount\ of\ population \div Sampling\ interval$$

The **sampling interval (SI)** is a function of the **risk of incorrect acceptance** and **tolerable misstatement (TM)**. SI is determined by dividing tolerable misstatement by a **confidence factor (CF)** associated with the risk level.

$$SI = TM \div CF$$

The following are CFs taken from Appendix C of the AICPA Audit Guide, *Audit Sampling* (2013):

Risk of Incorrect Acceptance	CF
5%	3.00
10%	2.31
15%	1.90

Because the risk of incorrect acceptance is 5%, the CF is 3.00. Thus, the SI is

$$SI = TM \div CF$$
$$= \$35,000 \div 3.00$$
$$= \$11,667$$

The sample size (n) is

$$n = Recorded\ amount\ of\ population \div SI$$
$$= \$900,000 \div \$11,667$$
$$= 77$$

The auditor uses **systematic sampling** (discussed in the extension of the example that follows) to select 77 dollars (actually 77 account balances) to audit.

If **no misstatements are discovered**, the auditor can form the following conclusion: "I am 95% confident that the recorded accounts receivable balance of $900,000 is not overstated by more than $35,000." The risk is 5% that the account balance is overstated by more than $35,000.

The **allowance for sampling risk** (also known as precision or confidence interval) is $35,000. Because the sample contains no misstatements, the conclusion is that the population has no misstatements. But, because the sample may not be perfectly representative of the population, an allowance for sampling risk must be considered. Thus, the more accurate conclusion is that the auditor is 95% confident that the misstatements are not greater than the allowance for sampling risk.

Given that the allowance for sampling risk is less than or equal to the TM, the objective of the audit test has been met.

7. **Extended Example**

a. The Seminole, Inc., example is extended below and on the next three pages to consider **anticipated misstatements** and to demonstrate the extrapolation of the sample results to the population when misstatements are discovered in the sampling units.

EXAMPLE -- Extended

Objective, population, and sampling unit. In this example, the basic information remains the same. However, the auditor anticipates misstatements (overstatements) in the population to be $10,000 based on the prior audit.

Determining the sampling interval and sample size. When no misstatements are expected, the SI equals TM divided by the CF. However, any anticipated misstatements must be considered in the determination of the SI. Moreover, the **anticipated misstatement (AM)** must be multiplied by an **expansion factor (EF)** appropriate for the risk of incorrect acceptance. The revised SI calculation is given below. The CF is the same as when no overstatements are expected.

$$SI = [TM - (AM \times EF)] \div CF$$

The following are EFs taken from Appendix C of the AICPA Audit Guide, *Audit Sampling* (2013):

Risk of Incorrect Acceptance	EF
5%	1.6
10%	1.5
15%	1.4

Accordingly, the revised SI is

$$
\begin{aligned}
SI &= [TM - (AM \times EF)] \div CF \\
&= [\$35,000 - (\$10,000 \times 1.6)] \div 3.00 \\
&= \$6,333
\end{aligned}
$$

As before, the sample size is calculated as

$$
\begin{aligned}
\text{Sample size} &= \text{Recorded amount of population} \div SI \\
&= \$900,000 \div \$6,333 \\
&= 142
\end{aligned}
$$

The effects of changes in the factors in the sample size formula should be understood. For example, the greater the auditor's allowable risk of incorrect acceptance, the smaller the sample size. Also, the larger the anticipated misstatement, the larger the sample size.

Selecting the sample. The SI is used to select logical sampling units (in this example, accounts receivable) from the population.

A monetary unit (in this example, a dollar) identifies a logical sampling unit. If every 6,333rd cumulative dollar is selected from the population of $900,000, the sample will consist of 142 items. The auditor therefore should start randomly between $1 and $6,333. Given a random start at the 2,733rd cumulative dollar, the sample will include the following:

- The first dollar selected will be $2,733.
- The next dollar will be $9,066 ($2,733 + $6,333).
- The third dollar will be $15,399 ($9,066 + $6,333).
- The fourth dollar will be $21,732 ($15,399 + $6,333).
- Each subsequent dollar will equal the prior dollar selected plus $6,333.

Table 4 on the next page demonstrates the selection process. When the **cumulative balance** is equal to or greater than the dollar selected, the account is selected because it contains the sampling unit. If an account contains two or more logical sampling units, for example, an account receivable of $15,000, it is selected, but it is given no special consideration. The ultimate sample of logical sampling units may contain fewer items than the calculated *n*.

-- Continued on next page --

EXAMPLE -- Continued

Table 4 -- Systematic Selection				
Customer Number	A/R Recorded Amount	Cumulative Balance	Dollar Selected	Recorded Amount of Sample Item
001	$ 2,000	$ 2,000		
002	1,225	3,225	2,733	1,225
003	3,500	6,725		
004	2,500	9,225	9,066	2,500
005	10,000	19,225	15,399	10,000
006	915	20,140		
etc.	etc.	etc.	etc.	etc.
Total	$900,000			

Executing the sampling plan. The auditor performs procedures on the sampled items (e.g., confirming the accounts). The auditor identifies **overstatement** errors. (Any **understatement** errors require special consideration, but the issue is beyond the scope of this outline.)

Evaluating and documenting the results. The evaluation process depends on whether any misstatements are found in the sample. The following summarizes that process:

- Project the misstatement from the sample to the population.
- Determine the allowance for sampling risk.

$$Allowance\ for\ sampling\ risk = Basic\ precision\ (BP) + Incremental\ allowance\ (IA)$$

- Calculate the upper misstatement limit (UML).

$$UML = Projected\ misstatement + Allowance\ for\ sampling\ risk$$

If **no overstatement errors** are discovered, the UML equals BP because

- The projected misstatement to the population is $0.
- The allowance for sampling risk equals BP (i.e., the IA is $0).

The calculation for **BP** is

$$BP = SI \times CF$$

Assuming no misstatements are found, BP (and the UML) is

$$BP = \$6,333 \times 3.00$$
$$= \$18,999$$

The conclusion is that the auditor is 95% confident that the balance of accounts receivable is not overstated by more than $18,999. This amount is within the TM of $35,000. Moreover, $18,999 is the allowance for sampling risk.

If **some overstatement errors** are discovered, the evaluation process is more involved but follows that presented above.

Project the sample results to the population if misstatements are discovered. Table 5 on the next page illustrates the projection of misstatements to the population.

Tainting. Because each selected dollar represents a group of dollars (the SI), the percentage of misstatement in the logical sampling unit (the account selected) is the percentage of misstatement in the SI. This is called tainting. However, if the recorded amount of a logical sampling unit (the account selected) **equals or exceeds** the SI, the projected misstatement is the actual misstatement for the SI, and no tainting is calculated.

For each logical sampling unit with a recorded amount (RA) **less than** the SI, calculate the **tainting percentage**.

$$Tainting\ \% = \frac{(RA - AA)}{RA} \qquad If:\ AA = Audit\ amount$$

$$Projected\ misstatement = SI \times Tainting\ \%$$

-- Continued on next page --

EXAMPLE -- Continued

Add the individual projected misstatements to determine the projected population misstatement.

Table 5 -- Calculation of Projected Misstatement				
Recorded Amount	Audit Amount	Tainting % = (RA – AA) ÷ RA	SI	Projected Misstatement
$ 1,000	$ 800	20%	$6,333	$ 1,267
10,000	6,000	N/A	N/A	4,000
300	0	100%	6,333	6,333
$11,300	$6,800			$11,600

The first and third projected misstatements equal the tainting percentage times SI because the RA of the logical unit sampled is less than the SI. The second projected misstatement included is the actual misstatement. The RA of the logical unit sampled is greater than the SI. The total projected misstatement to the population is $11,600, but the allowance for sampling risk must be added to derive the UML.

Calculate the **allowance for sampling risk** and the UML.

Allowance for sampling risk has two components: BP and IA.

BP is the same as when no misstatements are found (i.e., SI × CF).

IA is based on projected misstatements related to logical sampling units less than SI. (The misstatements related to logical sampling units greater than SI are not considered in the calculation of IA in Table 5 above.)

Projected misstatements are ranked by size (but only for misstatements related to logical sampling units less than SI). Each projected misstatement is multiplied by a factor that gives greater weights to the larger amounts. The first few factors for the 5% risk of incorrect acceptance, sufficient to calculate the allowance for sampling risk for this example, are presented in Table 6 below. Each factor equals the incremental change in the confidence factor minus one. Given a 5% risk of incorrect acceptance, the confidence factors for 0, 1, 2, and 3 misstatements are 3.00, 4.75, 6.30, and 7.76, respectively.

In this example, two misstatements are related to logical sampling units less than the SI of $6,333.

The ranked projected misstatements are multiplied by the factors from Table 6 and added to determine IA in Table 7.

Table 6 -- Misstatement Factors 5% Risk of Incorrect Acceptance		
Misstatement Number	Change in Confidence Factor	Change in CF – 1.0
1	1.75 (4.75 – 3.00)	.75
2	1.55 (6.30 – 4.75)	.55
3	1.46 (7.76 – 6.30)	.46
etc.	etc.	etc.

Table 7 -- Calculation of the IA		
Ranked Projected Misstatements	Factor	Incremental Allowance
$6,333	.75	$4,750
1,267	.55	697
Total IA (rounded)		$5,447

The allowance for sampling risk is the sum of BP and IA.

$$\text{Allowance for sampling risk} = \$18,999 + \$5,447$$
$$= \$24,446$$

-- Continued on next page --

EXAMPLE -- Continued

The total projected misstatement (PM) plus the allowance for sampling risk equals the upper misstatement limit (UML).

$$\text{UML} = \text{PM} + \text{Allowance for sampling risk}$$

$$= \$11,600 + \$24,446$$

$$= \$36,046$$

The **auditor's conclusion** is that (s)he is 95% confident that the balance of accounts receivable is not overstated by more than $36,046. However, TM is only $35,000. Thus, the auditor cannot conclude within the acceptable level of risk that the balance is fairly presented. (The auditor would likely require the client to make adjustments downward to the account before presentation on the balance sheet.)

Stop and review! You have completed the outline for this subunit. Study multiple-choice questions 18 through 20 on page 325.

QUESTIONS

15.1 Sampling Fundamentals

1. An advantage of statistical sampling over nonstatistical sampling is that statistical sampling helps an auditor to

A. Minimize the failure to detect errors and fraud.

B. Eliminate the risk of nonsampling errors.

C. Reduce the level of audit risk and materiality to a relatively low amount.

D. Measure the sufficiency of the evidence obtained.

Answer (D) is correct.
REQUIRED: The advantage of statistical sampling over nonstatistical sampling.
DISCUSSION: Statistical sampling helps the auditor to design an efficient sample, to measure the sufficiency of the evidence obtained, and to evaluate the sample results. Auditors are required to obtain sufficient appropriate evidence. Sufficiency is the measure of the quantity of evidence. It relates to the design and size of the sample.
Answer (A) is incorrect. In some circumstances, professional judgment may indicate that nonstatistical methods are preferable to minimize the failure to detect errors and fraud. Answer (B) is incorrect. Statistical sampling is irrelevant to nonsampling errors. Answer (C) is incorrect. Statistical sampling is irrelevant to materiality. Moreover, nonstatistical methods may be used to reduce audit risk.

2. A principal advantage of statistical methods of attribute sampling over nonstatistical methods is that they provide a scientific basis for planning the

A. Risk of overreliance.

B. Tolerable deviation rate.

C. Expected population deviation rate.

D. Sample size.

Answer (D) is correct.
REQUIRED: The item for which statistical methods provide a scientific basis for planning.
DISCUSSION: Statistical theory permits the auditor to measure sampling risk and to restrict it to an acceptable level. Statistical methods determine the sample size that will accomplish the auditor's objectives.
Answer (A) is incorrect. The risk of overreliance is the risk of believing a control is effective when it is not. Answer (B) is incorrect. The tolerable deviation rate is a function of the auditor's judgment about the assessed risks and the desired degree of assurance to be provided by the evidence, not of the statistical methods used. Answer (C) is incorrect. The expected population deviation rate prior to sampling is a function of auditor judgment.

3. The risk of underreliance is the risk that the sample selected to test controls

A. Indicates that the controls are less effective than they actually are.

B. Contains misstatements that could be material to the financial statements when aggregated with misstatements in other account balances or transactions classes.

C. Contains proportionately fewer deviations from prescribed internal controls than exist in the balance or class as a whole.

D. Does not support the tolerable misstatement for some or all financial statement assertions.

Answer (A) is correct.
REQUIRED: The risk of underreliance.
DISCUSSION: One aspect of sampling risk in performing tests of controls is the risk of underreliance. It is the risk that the sample indicates that the controls are less effective than they actually are.
Answer (B) is incorrect. Tests of details are directed towards misstatements in assertions. Answer (C) is incorrect. If the sample deviation rate is lower than the population rate, the risk is overreliance. Answer (D) is incorrect. Tests of details are directed toward misstatements in assertions.

4. An advantage of statistical over nonstatistical sampling methods in tests of controls is that the statistical methods

A. Afford greater assurance than a nonstatistical sample of equal size.

B. Provide an objective basis for quantitatively evaluating sample risks.

C. Can more easily convert the sample into a dual-purpose test useful for substantive testing.

D. Eliminate the need to use judgment in determining appropriate sample sizes.

Answer (B) is correct.
REQUIRED: The advantage of statistical over nonstatistical sampling methods.
DISCUSSION: The results of statistical (probability) sampling are objective and subject to the laws of probability. Hence, sampling risk can be quantified and controlled, and the degree of reliability desired (the confidence level) can be specified. Sampling risk is the risk that the sample selected does not represent the population.
Answer (A) is incorrect. A nonstatistical method may permit the auditor to test the most material and risky transactions and therefore may provide equal or greater assurance. However, that assurance cannot be quantified. Answer (C) is incorrect. Statistical sampling provides no advantage for converting to dual-purpose testing. Answer (D) is incorrect. Sample size is subject to judgments about the sampling plan factors.

5. While performing a test of details during an audit, the auditor determined that the sample results supported the conclusion that the recorded account balance was materially misstated. It was, in fact, not materially misstated. This situation illustrates the risk of

A. Incorrect rejection.

B. Incorrect acceptance.

C. Overreliance.

D. Underreliance.

Answer (A) is correct.
REQUIRED: The risk of erroneously concluding that a balance is materially misstated.
DISCUSSION: An auditor is concerned with two aspects of sampling risk in performing substantive tests of details: the risk of incorrect acceptance and the risk of incorrect rejection. The second is the risk that the sample supports the conclusion that the recorded account balance is materially misstated when it is not materially misstated.
Answer (B) is incorrect. The risk of incorrect acceptance is the risk that an auditor will erroneously conclude that a balance is not materially misstated. Answer (C) is incorrect. The risk of overreliance is an aspect of sampling risk for tests of controls. Answer (D) is incorrect. The risk of underreliance is an aspect of sampling risk for tests of controls.

6. Which of the following statements about audit sampling risks is correct for a nonissuer?

A. Nonsampling risk arises from the possibility that, when a substantive test is restricted to a sample, conclusions might be different than if the auditor had tested each item in the population.

B. Nonsampling risk can arise because an auditor failed to recognize misstatements.

C. Sampling risk is derived from the uncertainty in applying audit procedures to specific risks.

D. Sampling risk includes the possibility of selecting audit procedures that are not appropriate to achieve the specific objective.

Answer (B) is correct.
REQUIRED: The true statement about audit sampling risks for a nonissuer.
DISCUSSION: Nonsampling risk is the risk that the auditor may draw an erroneous conclusion for any reason not related to sampling risk. Examples include the use of inappropriate audit procedures or misinterpretation of audit evidence and failure to recognize a misstatement or deviation. Nonsampling risk may be reduced to an acceptable level through such factors as adequate planning and proper conduct of a firm's audit practice in accordance with the quality control standards (AU-C 530).
Answer (A) is incorrect. Sampling risk is the risk that the auditor's conclusion based on a sample may differ from the conclusion if the same audit procedure were applied to every item in the population. Answer (C) is incorrect. Sampling risk results from not performing an audit procedure on every sampling unit in a population. Answer (D) is incorrect. Nonsampling risk includes the use of inappropriate audit procedures.

15.2 Statistical Sampling in Tests of Controls (Attribute Sampling)

7. Which of the following combinations results in a decrease in sample size in an attribute sample?

	Allowable Risk of Overreliance	Tolerable Rate	Expected Population Deviation Rate
A.	Increase	Decrease	Increase
B.	Decrease	Increase	Decrease
C.	Increase	Increase	Decrease
D.	Increase	Increase	Increase

Answer (C) is correct.
　　REQUIRED: The combination that results in a decrease in size in an attribute sample.
　　DISCUSSION: To determine the sample size for a test of controls, the auditor considers (1) the tolerable rate of deviations from the control being tested, (2) the expected actual rate of deviations, and (3) the allowable risk of overreliance. An increase in the allowable risk of overreliance, an increase in the tolerable rate, and a decrease in the expected rate each has the effect of reducing the required sample size.

8. In determining the number of documents to select for a test to obtain assurance that all sales returns have been properly authorized, an auditor should consider the tolerable rate of deviation from the control activity. The auditor should also directly consider the

I. Likely rate of deviations
II. Allowable risk of underreliance

　　A. I only.

　　B. II only.

　　C. Both I and II.

　　D. Either I or II.

Answer (A) is correct.
　　REQUIRED: The factor(s) in determining sample size.
　　DISCUSSION: The factors necessary to determine sample size in an attribute sampling plan for a large population include (1) the tolerable deviation rate, (2) the acceptable risk of overreliance, and (3) the expected deviation rate.

9. For which of the following audit tests would an auditor most likely use attribute sampling?

　　A. Making an independent estimate of the amount of a LIFO inventory.

　　B. Examining invoices in support of the measurement of fixed asset additions.

　　C. Selecting accounts receivable for confirmation of account balances.

　　D. Inspecting employee time cards for proper approval by supervisors.

Answer (D) is correct.
　　REQUIRED: The appropriate use of attribute sampling.
　　DISCUSSION: The auditor uses attribute sampling to test the effectiveness of controls. Attribute sampling enables the auditor to estimate the occurrence rate of deviations and to determine its relation to the tolerable deviation rate. Thus, a control, such as proper approval of time cards by supervisors, can be tested for effectiveness using attribute sampling.
　　Answer (A) is incorrect. Variables sampling is useful in estimating the amount of inventory. Answer (B) is incorrect. Examining invoices in support of the measurement of fixed asset additions is a substantive test for which variables sampling is appropriate. Answer (C) is incorrect. The selection of accounts receivable for confirmation is a substantive test.

10. Which of the following statements is true concerning statistical sampling in tests of controls?

　　A. As the population size increases, the sample size should increase proportionately.

　　B. Deviations from specific control activities increase the likelihood of misstatements but do not always cause misstatements.

　　C. There is an inverse relationship between the expected population deviation rate and the sample size.

　　D. In determining the tolerable deviation rate, an auditor considers detection risk and the sample size.

Answer (B) is correct.
　　REQUIRED: The true statement about statistical sampling in tests of controls.
　　DISCUSSION: Deviations from a specific control increase the risk of misstatements in the accounting records but do not always result in misstatements. Thus, deviations from a specific control at a given rate ordinarily result in misstatements at the financial statement level at a lower rate.
　　Answer (A) is incorrect. As population size increases, the required sample size increases at a decreasing rate. Answer (C) is incorrect. The relationship between the expected population deviation rate and the required sample size is direct. Answer (D) is incorrect. The tolerable rate depends on the planned assessed risk of material misstatement and the assurance to be provided by the evidence in the sample.

11. Which of the following statements is true concerning statistical sampling in tests of controls?

A. The population size has little or no effect on determining sample size except for very small populations.

B. The expected population deviation rate has little or no effect on determining sample size except for very small populations.

C. As the population size doubles, the sample size also should double.

D. For a given tolerable rate, a larger sample size should be selected as the expected population deviation rate decreases.

Answer (A) is correct.
    REQUIRED: The true statement about statistical sampling.
    DISCUSSION: A change in the size of the population has a very small effect on the required sample size when the population is large. Tables are available for smaller population sizes providing appropriate smaller sample sizes.
    Answer (B) is incorrect. The expected population deviation rate is a variable in the sample size formula. Answer (C) is incorrect. The population size and the sample size are not proportionate. Answer (D) is incorrect. A lower expected population deviation rate results in a smaller sample size.

12. In addition to evaluating the frequency of deviations in tests of controls, an auditor should also consider certain qualitative aspects of the deviations. The auditor most likely would give broader consideration to the implications of a deviation if it was

A. The only deviation discovered in the sample.

B. Identical to a deviation discovered during the prior year's audit.

C. Caused by an employee's misunderstanding of instructions.

D. Initially concealed by a forged document.

Answer (D) is correct.
    REQUIRED: The aspect of a control deviation requiring broader consideration.
    DISCUSSION: The discovery of a fraud ordinarily requires broader consideration than the discovery of an error. The discovery of an initially concealed forged document indicates that the integrity of employees may be in doubt.
    Answer (A) is incorrect. A single deviation discovered in a sample may not cause major concern. Answer (B) is incorrect. Deviations are often repetitive. Discovery of an identical deviation in a subsequent year is not unusual. Answer (C) is incorrect. A misunderstanding is an error rather than fraud and does not necessarily arouse concern.

13. The diagram below depicts the auditor's estimated maximum deviation rate compared with the tolerable deviation rate and also depicts the true population deviation rate compared with the tolerable deviation rate.

Auditor's Estimate Based on Sample Results	True State of Population	
	Deviation rate is less than tolerable rate.	Deviation rate exceeds tolerable rate.
Maximum deviation rate is less than tolerable rate.	I. Correct	III. Incorrect
Maximum deviation rate exceeds tolerable rate.	II. Incorrect	IV. Correct

As a result of testing controls, the auditor underrelies on the controls and increases substantive testing. This is illustrated by situation

A. I.

B. II.

C. III.

D. IV.

Answer (B) is correct.
    REQUIRED: The situation that involves underreliance.
    DISCUSSION: The risk of underreliance (situation II) is one aspect of sampling risk in testing controls. It is the risk that the controls are more effective than indicated by the sample. Like the risk of incorrect rejection in substantive testing, the risk of underreliance relates to the efficiency, not effectiveness, of the audit. It ordinarily leads to application of further audit procedures and ultimate arrival at the correct conclusion.
    Answer (A) is incorrect. In situation I, the auditor properly should rely on the controls. Answer (C) is incorrect. In situation III, the sample might lead to overreliance. Answer (D) is incorrect. In situation IV, the auditor properly should not rely on the controls.

15.3 Classical Variables Sampling (Mean-per-Unit)

14. An auditor examining inventory most likely would use variables sampling rather than attributes sampling to

- A. Identify whether inventory items are properly priced.
- B. Estimate whether the dollar amount of inventory is reasonable.
- C. Discover whether misstatements exist in inventory records.
- D. Determine whether discounts for inventory are properly recorded.

Answer (B) is correct.
  REQUIRED: The purpose of using variables sampling rather than attribute sampling in an audit of inventory.
  DISCUSSION: Variables sampling is used by auditors to estimate quantities or dollar amounts in substantive testing. Attribute sampling applies to tests of controls and is used to estimate a deviation rate (occurrence rate) for a population. Thus, an auditor who wants to estimate whether the dollar amount of inventory is reasonable uses variables sampling.
  Answer (A) is incorrect. An auditor who wants to determine whether inventory items are properly priced uses attribute sampling, as an item is either properly priced or not. Answer (C) is incorrect. An auditor who wants to discover whether misstatements exist in inventory records uses attribute sampling. Answer (D) is incorrect. An auditor who wants to determine whether discounts for inventory are properly recorded uses attribute sampling, as an item is either properly recorded or not.

15. When planning a sample for a substantive test of details, an auditor should consider tolerable misstatement for the sample. This consideration should

- A. Be related to the auditor's business risk.
- B. Not be adjusted for qualitative factors.
- C. Be related to preliminary judgments about materiality levels.
- D. Not be changed during the audit process.

Answer (C) is correct.
  REQUIRED: The true statement about the consideration of tolerable misstatement.
  DISCUSSION: When planning a sample for a test of details, the auditor should consider how much monetary misstatement in the related account balance or class of transactions may exist without causing the financial statements to be materially misstated. This maximum misstatement is the tolerable misstatement for the sample. It is used in audit planning to determine the necessary precision and sample size. Tolerable misstatement, combined for the entire audit plan, should not exceed the auditor's preliminary judgments about materiality.
  Answer (A) is incorrect. The auditor's business risk is irrelevant. Answer (B) is incorrect. Qualitative factors should be considered, for example, the nature and cause of misstatements and their relationship to other phases of the audit. Answer (D) is incorrect. If sample results suggest that planning assumptions were incorrect, the auditor should take appropriate action.

16. How would an increase in tolerable misstatement and an increase in the risk of material misstatement (RMM) affect the sample size in a substantive test of details?

	Increase in Tolerable Misstatement	Increase in the RMM
A.	Increase sample size	Increase sample size
B.	Increase sample size	Decrease sample size
C.	Decrease sample size	Increase sample size
D.	Decrease sample size	Decrease sample size

Answer (C) is correct.
  REQUIRED: The effects of increases in tolerable misstatement and the assessed RMM.
  DISCUSSION: An increase in tolerable misstatement or the level of materiality decreases the sample size necessary to collect sufficient appropriate audit evidence. An increase in the RMM increases the assurance to be provided by substantive procedures and therefore the necessary sample size.

17. An auditor is determining the sample size for an inventory observation using mean-per-unit estimation, which is a variables sampling plan. To calculate the required sample size, the auditor usually determines the

	Variability in the Dollar Amounts of Inventory Items	Risk of Incorrect Rejection
A.	Yes	Yes
B.	Yes	No
C.	No	Yes
D.	No	No

Answer (A) is correct.
  REQUIRED: The factor(s), if any, used to determine a mean-per-unit sample size.
  DISCUSSION: Four factors are considered in determining the sample size for mean-per-unit estimation. Those factors include (1) the population size, (2) an estimate of population variation (the standard deviation), (3) the risk of incorrect rejection (its complement is the confidence level), and (4) the tolerable misstatement (the desired allowance for sampling risk is a percentage thereof, and this percentage is a function of the risk of incorrect rejection and the allowable risk of incorrect acceptance).

15.4 Monetary-Unit Sampling (MUS)

18. Which of the following statements is true concerning monetary-unit sampling (MUS), also known as probability-proportional-to-size sampling?

A. The sampling distribution should approximate the normal distribution.

B. Overstated units have a lower probability of sample selection than units that are understated.

C. The auditor controls the risk of incorrect acceptance by specifying that risk level for the sampling plan.

D. The sampling interval is calculated by dividing the number of physical units in the population by the sample size.

Answer (C) is correct.
REQUIRED: The true statement about MUS.
DISCUSSION: MUS is one technique whereby the auditor can measure and control the risks associated with observing less than 100% of the population. The auditor can quantify and measure the risk of accepting a client's recorded amount as fair when it is materially misstated.
Answer (A) is incorrect. MUS is most closely associated with the Poisson distribution. Answer (B) is incorrect. As the size of the units in the population increases, so does the probability of selection. Answer (D) is incorrect. The sampling interval is calculated by dividing the total dollars, not units, in the population by the sample size. Every n^{th} dollar is then selected after a random start.

19. In a monetary-unit sample with a sampling interval of $10,000, an auditor discovered that a selected account receivable with a recorded amount of $5,000 had an audited amount of $4,000. If this were the only misstatement discovered by the auditor, the projected misstatement of this sample is

A. $1,000

B. $2,000

C. $5,000

D. $10,000

Answer (B) is correct.
REQUIRED: The projected misstatement of the monetary-unit sample.
DISCUSSION: MUS is a commonly used method of statistical sampling for tests of details of balances because it provides a simple statistical result expressed in dollars. Given that only one misstatement was detected, the projected misstatement for this sample is the product of the tainting percentage and the sampling interval. The tainting percentage is calculated as the difference between the recorded amount and the audited amount, divided by the recorded amount. In this sample, the tainting percentage is 20% [($5,000 – $4,000) ÷ $5,000]. Multiplying this number by the sampling interval results in a projected misstatement based on the sample of $2,000 ($10,000 × 20%).

20. Which of the following most likely would be an advantage in using classical variables sampling rather than monetary-unit sampling?

A. An estimate of the standard deviation of the population's recorded amounts is not required.

B. The auditor rarely needs the assistance of a computer program to design an efficient sample.

C. Inclusion of zero and negative balances usually does not require special design considerations.

D. Any amount that is individually significant is automatically identified and selected.

Answer (C) is correct.
REQUIRED: The advantage of using classical variables sampling rather than MUS.
DISCUSSION: MUS is most useful if few misstatements are expected, and overstatement is the most likely kind of misstatement. One disadvantage of MUS is that it is designed to detect overstatements. It is not effective for estimating understatements. The smaller the item, the less likely it will be selected in the sample, but the more likely the item is understated.
Answer (A) is incorrect. The sample size formula for estimation of variables includes the standard deviation of the population. Answer (B) is incorrect. A computer program is helpful in many sampling applications. Answer (D) is incorrect. In classical variables sampling, every item has an equal and nonzero probability of selection.

Access the Gleim CPA Premium Review System featuring SmartAdapt for exam-emulating multiple-choice questions and simulations with detailed answer explanations.

Learn more: gleim.com/CPApremium | 800.874.5346

STUDY UNIT SIXTEEN
REPORTS --
OPINIONS AND DISCLAIMERS

(15 pages of outline)

This study unit presents interrelated reporting issues. Subunit 16.2 should be studied carefully. Most reporting guidance is based on the auditor's report expressing an unmodified opinion on financial statements. The other subunits of this study unit and all of Study Unit 17 outline the requirements for wording changes in the auditor's report. Special reporting considerations (Study Unit 18), many matters considered in Study Unit 19, and governmental audit reports (Study Unit 20) are variations of the auditor's report.

16.1 THE AUDITOR'S REPORTING RESPONSIBILITY

1. **Objectives**

   a. The purpose of an audit is to provide the users of the financial statements with an opinion as to whether the financial statements are presented fairly, in all material respects, in accordance with the applicable financial reporting framework (the **framework**).

   b. The auditor's objectives are to (1) **form an opinion** on the fairness of the statements based on an evaluation of the audit evidence obtained and (2) clearly express that opinion through a written report (hard copy or electronic) that describes the basis for that opinion.

   c. The framework ordinarily is U.S. generally accepted accounting principles (U.S. GAAP). But another framework may apply, for example, International Financial Reporting Standards (IFRS) issued by the International Accounting Standards Board. IFRS are used in many countries.

2. **Forming an Opinion**

   a. Presented **fairly** means the financial statements as a whole are **free from material misstatement**, whether due to fraud or error.

      1) The auditor should conclude whether (s)he has obtained **reasonable assurance** regarding fair presentation.

      2) Reasonable assurance is a high but not absolute standard. It is achieved when the auditor obtains sufficient appropriate evidence that audit risk is acceptably low. Audit risk is the risk of expressing an inappropriate opinion when the statements are materially misstated.

b.   The evaluation of fairness should include consideration of the **qualitative aspects** of the entity's accounting practices, including indicators of possible bias in management's judgments. In particular, the auditor should **evaluate** whether, given the requirements of the framework,

  1)   The statements adequately disclose the significant accounting policies.

  2)   The accounting policies selected and applied are consistent with the framework and are appropriate.

  3)   Management's accounting estimates are reasonable.

  4)   The information in the statements is relevant, reliable, comparable, and understandable.

  5)   The statements provide adequate disclosures to enable the intended users to understand the effect of material transactions and events.

  6)   The terminology used, including the title of each statement, is appropriate.

  7)   The statements adequately refer to or describe the framework.

c.   The auditor's evaluation of fair presentation also should consider the following:

  1)   The overall presentation, structure, and content of the statements

  2)   Whether the statements, including the related notes, represent the underlying transactions and events in a manner that achieves fair presentation

3.   **Form of Opinion**

a.   The auditor should express an **unmodified opinion** when (s)he concludes that the statements are presented fairly, in all material respects, in accordance with the framework.

Background

Standards superseded by the AICPA's Clarified Auditing Standards used the term "unqualified" for an opinion that expressed positive assurance that the financial statements were free of material misstatements or on which the auditor had no reservations as to scope. You should expect to encounter the term "unmodified" for this type of audit opinion, but be aware of the superseded terminology.

---

b.   If the auditor concludes that the statements are not fairly presented, (s)he should **discuss the matter with management**. Depending on how the matter is resolved, the auditor should determine whether the opinion should be modified.

c.   A modified opinion is a qualified opinion, an adverse opinion, or a disclaimer of opinion. The opinion is modified if the auditor

  1)   Concludes that, based on the audit evidence obtained, the financial statements as a whole **are materially misstated** (qualified or adverse opinion) or

  2)   Is **unable to obtain sufficient appropriate audit evidence** to conclude that the financial statements as a whole are free from material misstatement (qualified opinion or disclaimer of opinion).

Stop and review! You have completed the outline for this subunit. Study multiple-choice questions 1 and 2 on page 342.

16.2 THE AUDITOR'S REPORT

Background

The AICPA's Clarified Auditing Standards change the format of the auditor's report for nonissuers. However, the PCAOB's Auditing Standards continue to use a form for issuers based on prior AICPA standards. The basic difference is that the AICPA's new format uses headings for all the sections of the report other than the introductory paragraph. The basic content of the report is the same based on both AICPA and PCAOB standards. Any specific differences are noted in the subsequent materials presented here.

 We recommend that you learn as much about the auditor's reports as you can. You will not be required to draft a report on the exam, but questions often relate to how a report may change based on audit findings. Having a firm grasp of the reports will serve you well.

---

1. The report for an audit of a nonissuer in accordance with GAAS (AICPA standards) should include the following:

   a. **Title.** The auditor's report should have a title that includes the word **independent** to clearly indicate that it is the report of an independent auditor.

   b. **Addressee.** The auditor's report should be addressed as required by the circumstances of the engagement. (Subunit 16.3 covers addressing the report.)

   c. **Introductory paragraph.** This paragraph should

      1) Identify the entity audited,
      2) State that the financial statements have been audited,
      3) Identify the title of each statement, and
      4) Specify the date or period covered by each statement.

      NOTE: No heading is required for the introductory paragraph, but the other major parts of the report should have appropriate headings or subtitles.

   d. **Management's responsibility for the financial statements.** This paragraph should describe management's responsibility for

      1) Preparation and fair presentation of the statements and
      2) The design, implementation, and maintenance of internal control relevant to their preparation and fair presentation.

   e. **Auditor's responsibility.** This section should

      1) State that the responsibility of the auditor is to express an opinion on the financial statements based on the audit.
      2) State that the audit was conducted in accordance with auditing standards generally accepted in the United States of America. (The PCAOB's report for an issuer refers to "the standards of the Public Company Accounting Oversight Board," not GAAS.)
      3) Explain that those standards require that the auditor plan and perform the audit to obtain reasonable assurance about whether the statements are free from material misstatement.

4) Describe an audit by stating the following:

    a) An audit involves performing procedures to obtain audit evidence about the amounts and disclosures in the financial statements.

    b) The procedures selected depend on the auditor's judgment, including the assessment of the risks of material misstatement of the financial statements, whether due to fraud or error.

    c) In making risk assessments, the auditor considers internal control relevant to the entity's preparation and fair presentation of the financial statements. The purpose is to design audit procedures that are appropriate in the circumstances, not to express an opinion on the effectiveness of the entity's internal control. Accordingly, no such opinion is expressed. (If the auditor is also responsible for expressing an opinion on internal control, the caveat is omitted.)

    d) An audit also includes (1) evaluating the appropriateness of the accounting policies used, (2) the reasonableness of significant accounting estimates made by management, and (3) the overall presentation of the financial statements.

    e) The auditor believes that the audit evidence obtained is sufficient and appropriate to provide a basis for the opinion.

f. **Opinion.** When expressing an unmodified opinion, the auditor should state that the financial statements present fairly, in all material respects, the financial position of the entity as of the balance sheet date and the results of its operations and its cash flows for the period then ended in accordance with the applicable financial reporting framework. (The framework typically is U.S. GAAP.)

g. **Signature of the auditor.** The report should include the manual or printed signature of the auditor's firm.

h. **Auditor's address.** The report should name the city and state where the auditor practices.

i. **Date of the auditor's report.** The report should be dated no earlier than the date on which the auditor has obtained sufficient appropriate audit evidence on which to base the opinion, including evidence that

1) The audit documentation has been reviewed;

2) All of the financial statements, including the related notes, have been prepared; and

3) Management has asserted its responsibility for those statements.

2. **Separate Statement by Management**

a. The description of management's responsibility for the financial statements in the auditor's report should **not** refer to a separate statement by management about such responsibilities if the statement is included in a document containing the auditor's report.

1) For example, if a section of the annual report describes management's responsibility for internal control, the auditor's report should not refer to that section. The reference may lead users to believe the auditor is providing assurance about the description.

3. **Example of an Auditor's Report for a Nonissuer (AICPA Standards)**

   a. The following is an auditor's report on consolidated comparative financial statements prepared in accordance with U.S. GAAP. The report expresses an unmodified opinion for all years presented. (If only single-year financial statements are presented, the report is adjusted to refer only to those statements.)

EXAMPLE -- Auditor's Unmodified Report for a Nonissuer (AICPA Standards)

Independent Auditor's Report

To: <----------- Addressed to the Board of Directors and/or Shareholders

We have audited the accompanying consolidated financial statements of X Company and its subsidiaries, which comprise the consolidated balance sheets as of December 31, 20X1 and 20X0, and the related consolidated statements of income, changes in stockholders' equity, and cash flows for the years then ended, and the related notes to the financial statements.

Management's Responsibility for the Financial Statements

Management is responsible for the preparation and fair presentation of these consolidated financial statements in accordance with accounting principles generally accepted in the United States of America; this includes the design, implementation, and maintenance of internal control relevant to the preparation and fair presentation of consolidated financial statements that are free from material misstatement, whether due to fraud or error.

Auditor's Responsibility

Our responsibility is to express an opinion on these consolidated financial statements based on our audits. We conducted our audits in accordance with auditing standards generally accepted in the United States of America. Those standards require that we plan and perform the audit to obtain reasonable assurance about whether the consolidated financial statements are free from material misstatement.

An audit involves performing procedures to obtain audit evidence about the amounts and disclosures in the consolidated financial statements. The procedures selected depend on the auditor's judgment, including the assessment of the risks of material misstatement of the consolidated financial statements, whether due to fraud or error. In making those risk assessments, the auditor considers internal control relevant to the entity's preparation and fair presentation of the consolidated financial statements in order to design audit procedures that are appropriate in the circumstances, but not for the purpose of expressing an opinion on the effectiveness of the entity's internal control. Accordingly, we express no such opinion. An audit also includes evaluating the appropriateness of accounting policies used and the reasonableness of significant accounting estimates made by management, as well as evaluating the overall presentation of the consolidated financial statements.

We believe that the audit evidence we have obtained is sufficient and appropriate to provide a basis for our audit opinion.

Opinion

In our opinion, the consolidated financial statements referred to above present fairly, in all material respects, the financial position of X Company and its subsidiaries as of December 31, 20X1 and 20X0, and the results of their operations and their cash flows for the years then ended in accordance with accounting principles generally accepted in the United States of America.

Auditor's signature   <----------- May be manual or printed
Auditor's address   <----------- City and state
Date   <----------- No earlier than the date that sufficient appropriate audit evidence was obtained

---

4. **The report for an audit in accordance with PCAOB standards**

   a. The auditor's report identifies the financial statements audited in an opening (introductory) paragraph, describes the nature of an audit in a scope paragraph, and expresses the auditor's opinion in a separate opinion paragraph.

   b. The three paragraphs have no headings.

   c. The scope paragraph includes the statement "We conducted our audits in accordance with the standards of the Public Company Accounting Oversight Board (United States)" rather than referring to "auditing standards generally accepted in the United States of America."

   d. The report would also refer the **audit of internal control** for an integrated audit if a separate report on internal control is not presented (See Study Unit 9.3).

e. The following is an auditor's report on consolidated comparative financial statements prepared in accordance with U.S. GAAP based on an audit using PCAOB standards. The report expresses an unmodified opinion for the years presented. (If only single-year financial statements are presented, the report is adjusted to refer only to those statements.)

EXAMPLE -- Auditor's Unmodified Report for an Issuer (PCAOB Standards)

Report of Independent Registered Public Accounting Firm

To: <----------- Addressed to the Board of Directors and/or Shareholders

We have audited the accompanying balance sheets of Y Company as of December 31, 20X2 and 20X1, and the related statements of income, retained earnings, and cash flows for the years then ended. These financial statements are the responsibility of the Company's management. Our responsibility is to express an opinion on these financial statements based on our audits.

We conducted our audits in accordance with the standards of the Public Company Accounting Oversight Board (United States). Those standards require that we plan and perform the audit to obtain reasonable assurance about whether the financial statements are free of material misstatement. An audit includes examining, on a test basis, evidence supporting the amounts and disclosures in the financial statements. An audit also includes assessing the accounting principles used and significant estimates made by management, as well as evaluating the overall financial statement presentation. We believe that our audits provide a reasonable basis for our opinion.

In our opinion, the financial statements referred to above present fairly, in all material respects, the financial position of Y Company as of December 31, 20X2 and 20X1, and the results of its operations and its cash flows for the years then ended in conformity with accounting principles generally accepted in the United States of America.

Auditor's signature   <----------- May be manual or printed
Auditor's address   <----------- City and state
Date   <----------- No earlier than the date that sufficient appropriate audit evidence was obtained

---

5. **Other Reporting Responsibilities**

a. If an audit of financial statements is conducted in accordance with the standards of the PCAOB and the audit is not within the jurisdiction of the PCAOB, the auditor is required also to conduct the audit in accordance with GAAS. In such circumstances, when the auditor refers to the standards of the PCAOB in addition to GAAS in the auditor's report, the auditor should use the form of report required by the standards of the PCAOB. The report should be amended to state that the audit also was conducted in accordance with GAAS. For example, "We conducted our audit in accordance with the auditing standards of the Public Company Accounting Oversight Board (United States) and in accordance with auditing standards generally accepted in the United States of America."

b. In some cases, the auditor may report on matters in addition to the fair presentation of the statements. For example, for audits conducted under *Government Auditing Standards*, the auditor may be required to report on internal control over financial reporting.

1) These other reporting responsibilities are addressed in a separate section of the auditor's report following the opinion paragraph. The section is subtitled *Report on Other Legal and Regulatory Requirements* (if appropriate).

a) The form and content vary depending on the nature of the auditor's other reporting responsibilities.

b) If this separate section is included, the preceding headings, statements, and explanations should be under the subtitle *Report on the Financial Statements* preceding the introductory paragraph.

6. **Overview of Opinions**

    a. An **unmodified opinion** is the conclusion that the financial statements are presented fairly, in all material respects, in accordance with the framework.

    b. A **qualified opinion** is the conclusion that, except for the matter(s) described in the basis for qualified opinion paragraph, the financial statements are presented fairly, in all material respects, in accordance with the framework.

        1) If the auditor has obtained sufficient appropriate audit evidence, misstatements are material but not pervasive.

        2) If the auditor has not obtained sufficient appropriate audit evidence, the possible effects of undetected misstatements are material but not pervasive.

    c. An **adverse opinion** is the conclusion that, because of the significance of the matter(s) described in the basis for adverse opinion paragraph, the financial statements are not presented fairly.

        1) The auditor has obtained sufficient appropriate audit evidence, but the misstatements are material and pervasive.

    d. A **disclaimer of opinion** is the conclusion that, because of the significance of the matter(s) described in the basis for disclaimer of opinion paragraph, the auditor has not been able to obtain sufficient appropriate audit evidence. Accordingly, the auditor does not express an opinion on the financial statements.

        1) The possible effects of undetected misstatements are material and pervasive.

7. The auditor may choose to include, or be required to include, an **emphasis-of-matter** or **other-matter** paragraph in the auditor's report.

    a. The matters addressed do not affect the type of opinion expressed. This subject is discussed in further detail in Study Unit 17.

8. **Summary of Modified Opinions**

Reason for the Modification	Auditor's Judgment About the Pervasiveness of the Effects or Possible Effects on the Statements	
	Material but Not Pervasive	*Material and Pervasive*
Financial statements are materially misstated	Qualified opinion	Adverse opinion
Inability to obtain sufficient appropriate audit evidence	Qualified opinion	Disclaimer of opinion

    a. **Pervasive effects** on the statements

        1) Are not limited to specific elements, accounts, or items of the statements;

        2) Represent or could represent a substantial proportion of the statements if limited to specific elements, accounts, or items; and

        3) Are, with regard to disclosures, fundamental to users' understanding of the statements.

    b. A **misstatement** arises from fraud or error. It is a difference between (1) the amount, classification, presentation, or disclosure of a financial statement item and (2) the amount, etc., required for it to be presented fairly.

Stop and review! You have completed the outline for this subunit. Study multiple-choice questions 3 through 6 beginning on page 343.

16.3 ADDRESSING AND DATING THE REPORT

1. The auditor's report should be addressed to those for whom the report is prepared. It may be addressed to the entity whose statements are being audited or to those charged with governance. If the client is an unincorporated entity, the report should be addressed as circumstances dictate, e.g., to the partners or the proprietor.

   a. If an auditor is retained to audit the financial statements of an entity that is **not the client**, the report customarily is addressed to the client and not to those charged with governance. For example, if a bank engages an auditor to audit a loan applicant, the report is addressed to the bank.

2. **The Date of the Auditor's Report**

   a. The date of the audit report is **no earlier than the date on which the auditor has obtained sufficient appropriate evidence** to support the opinion. This date is important because users expect the auditor to perform subsequent events procedures. They are intended to detect events occurring between the date of the statements and the date of the report that materially affect the statements.

      1) The auditor is ordinarily not responsible for making inquiries or carrying out any audit procedures after the date of the report.

   b. When a **subsequent event** disclosed in the financial statements occurs after the date of the report but before the report release date, the auditor may use **dual-dating**. (S)he may use the original date of the report except for the matters affected by the subsequent event, which are assigned the appropriate later date.

      1) In that case, the auditor's responsibility for events after the original date of the report is limited to the specific event.

      2) If the auditor is willing to accept responsibility to the later date and accordingly extends subsequent events procedures to that date, the auditor may choose the later date as the date for the entire report.

   c. Use of the original date by a predecessor auditor in a **reissued report** removes any implication that records, transactions, or events after such date have been audited or reviewed. However, the predecessor auditor should perform the following procedures to determine whether the report is still appropriate: (1) read the statements of the subsequent period, (2) compare the prior statements with the current statements, and (3) obtain written representations from management and the auditor about information obtained or events that occurred subsequent to the original date of the report.

      1) An exception exists for filings under the Securities Act of 1933. This exception is covered in AU-C 925. (Study Unit 18, Subunit 3, covers SEC filings.)

Stop and review! You have completed the outline for this subunit. Study multiple-choice questions 7 and 8 on page 344.

16.4 QUALIFIED OPINIONS

1. A qualified opinion should be expressed if the auditor

    a. Has obtained sufficient appropriate audit evidence and concludes that **misstatements**, individually or aggregated, are **material but not pervasive** to the financial statements or

    b. Is **unable** to obtain sufficient appropriate audit evidence but concludes that the possible effects on the financial statements of undetected misstatements, if any, could be **material but not pervasive**.

2. Financial statements may be fairly presented **except for** the effects or possible effects of a certain matter. If the opinion is qualified because of such effects, the auditor should describe the matter(s) resulting in the qualification.

    a. This description is included in a **basis for qualified opinion** paragraph **preceding the opinion** paragraph.

    b. The opinion paragraph should contain qualifying language and refer to the basis for qualified opinion paragraph.

        1) The opinion paragraph should include the words "except for."

        2) "Subject to," "with the foregoing explanation," and similar phrases lack clarity and forcefulness and should **not** be used.

        3) Notes are part of the statements, and language such as "fairly presented when read in conjunction with Note 1" should **not** be used because of the likelihood of misunderstanding.

3. **Inability to Obtain Sufficient Appropriate Evidence**

    a. The inability to obtain sufficient appropriate evidence that is material but not pervasive (also called a scope limitation) may result from the following:

        1) Circumstances not controlled by the entity, such as destruction or government seizure of accounting records

        2) Circumstances related to the nature or timing of the work, such as not being able to observe inventory due to the late appointment of the auditor or determining that controls are ineffective

        3) Limitations imposed by management, such as preventing the auditor from (a) observing inventory or (b) confirming receivables

    b. A **precondition** of the audit is management's agreement to provide the auditor with access to information relevant to preparing and fairly presenting the financial statements.

        1) Management also should agree to provide

            a) Additional information requested for the purpose of the audit and
            b) Unrestricted access to persons having necessary audit evidence.

        2) Accordingly, if a limitation on the scope of the engagement is imposed that will result in a disclaimer of opinion, the auditor should not accept the engagement.

    c. However, the auditor may become aware of a management-imposed scope limitation after accepting the engagement that is likely to result in a qualified opinion or a disclaimer of opinion.

        1) The auditor should request removal of the limitation.

        2) If it is not removed, the auditor should communicate with those charged with governance and determine whether alternative procedures can be performed.

        3)   If the auditor cannot obtain sufficient appropriate evidence because of the limitation, (s)he should determine whether the possible effects of undetected misstatements could be material and pervasive.

           a)   If they are, the auditor should disclaim an opinion or withdraw from the engagement.

    d.   When a qualified opinion results from an inability to obtain sufficient appropriate evidence, the auditor describes the matter in the basis for qualified opinion paragraph, **not** in a note to the statements.

        1)   The description of the audit scope is the responsibility of the auditor, not management.

    e.   The opinion paragraph should indicate that the qualification pertains to the **possible effects** on the financial statements, not to the scope limitation itself.

        1)   The wording ". . . except for the limitation on the scope of the audit . . ." is unacceptable.

        2)   The wording ". . . except for the possible effects of the matter described in the basis for qualified opinion paragraph . . ." is appropriate.

    f.   The following are the effects on the auditor's report when the opinion is qualified due to an inability to obtain sufficient appropriate evidence with possible effects that are material but not pervasive:

        1)   The introductory paragraph is unchanged.

        2)   The management's responsibility paragraph is unchanged.

        3)   The auditor's responsibility section ends with the sentence, "We believe that the audit evidence we have obtained is sufficient and appropriate to provide a basis for our qualified audit opinion."

    g.   The following are examples of the basis for qualified opinion and opinion paragraphs:

EXAMPLE -- Opinion Qualified for a Material but Not Pervasive Scope Limitation

Basis for Qualified Opinion

ABC Company's investment in XYZ Company, a foreign affiliate acquired during the year and accounted for under the equity method, is carried at $XXX on the balance sheet at December 31, 20X1, and ABC Company's share of XYZ Company's net income of $XXX is included in ABC Company's net income for the year then ended. We were unable to obtain sufficient appropriate audit evidence about the carrying amount of ABC Company's investment in XYZ Company as of December 31, 20X1, and ABC Company's share of XYZ Company's net income for the year then ended because we were denied access to the financial information, management, and the auditors of XYZ Company. Consequently, we were unable to determine whether any adjustments to these amounts were necessary.

Qualified Opinion

In our opinion, except for the possible effects of the matter described in the Basis for Qualified Opinion paragraph, the financial statements referred to above present fairly, in all material respects, the financial position of ABC Company as of December 31, 20X1, and the results of its operations and its cash flows for the year then ended in accordance with accounting principles generally accepted in the United States of America.

---

    4.   **Material Misstatements**

        a.   A material misstatement may result from

        1)   Inappropriate selection or application of accounting principles or policies.

        2)   Inappropriate presentation of the statements.

        3)   Inappropriate or inadequate disclosure. For example, management may (a) not comply with the requirements for a change in accounting policies or (b) not apply those policies consistently from period to period.

        4)   Omission of required disclosures, such as when a required statement (e.g., a statement of cash flows) is not reported.

5. **Misstatement of Specific Amounts**

   a. If a material misstatement relates to **specific amounts**, the basis for a qualified opinion paragraph should describe the financial effects. It also should include a quantification of the effects, if practicable. Practicable means

      1) Reasonably obtainable from the accounts and records and
      2) Not putting the auditor in the position of a preparer.

   b. The auditor is not expected to prepare a basic statement. Moreover, the basis paragraph may be shortened by referring to a note (if any) that contains such information.

   c. The following are the effects on the auditor's report when the opinion is qualified due to a material but not pervasive misstatement:

      1) The introductory paragraph is unchanged.
      2) The management's responsibility paragraph is unchanged.
      3) The auditor's responsibility section ends with the sentence, "We believe that the audit evidence we have obtained is sufficient and appropriate to provide a reasonable basis for our qualified audit opinion."

   d. The following are examples of the basis for qualified opinion and opinion paragraphs:

EXAMPLE -- Opinion Qualified for a Material but Not Pervasive Misstatement

Basis for Qualified Opinion

The Company has stated inventories at cost in the accompanying balance sheets. Accounting principles generally accepted in the United States of America require inventories to be stated at the lower of cost or market. If the Company stated inventories at the lower of cost or market, a write down of $XXX and $XXX would have been required as of December 31, 20X1 and 20X0, respectively. Accordingly, cost of sales would have been increased by $XXX and $XXX, and net income, income taxes, and stockholders' equity would have been reduced by $XXX, $XXX, and $XXX, and $XXX, $XXX, and $XXX, as of and for the years ended December 31, 20X1 and 20X0, respectively.

Qualified Opinion

In our opinion, except for the effects of the matter described in the Basis for Qualified Opinion paragraph, the financial statements referred to above present fairly, in all material respects, the financial position of ABC Company as of December 31, 20X1 and 20X0, and the results of its operations and its cash flows for the year then ended in accordance with accounting principles generally accepted in the United States of America.

---

6. **Misstatement Based on Inadequate Disclosure**

   a. If a material misstatement relates to narrative disclosures, the auditor includes in the basis paragraph an explanation of the misstatement.

   b. If information required to be presented or disclosed is omitted, the auditor describes the nature of the information in the basis paragraph. (S)he also includes the information, if practicable, and discusses the omission with those charged with governance.

   c. The following are the effects on the auditor's report when the opinion is qualified due to inadequate disclosure:

      1) The introductory paragraph is unchanged.
      2) The management's responsibility paragraph is unchanged.
      3) The auditor's responsibility section ends with the sentence, "We believe that the audit evidence we have obtained is sufficient and appropriate to provide a reasonable basis for our qualified audit opinion."

d.   The following are examples of the basis for qualified opinion and opinion paragraphs:

EXAMPLE -- Opinion Qualified for Inadequate Disclosure

Basis for Qualified Opinion

The Company's financial statements do not disclose [describe the nature of the omitted information that is not practicable to present in the auditor's report]. In our opinion, disclosure of this information is required by accounting principles generally accepted in the United States of America.

Qualified Opinion

In our opinion, except for the omission of the information described in the Basis for Qualified Opinion paragraph, the financial statements referred to above present fairly, in all material respects, the financial position of ABC Company as of December 31, 20X1 and 20X0, and the results of its operations and its cash flows for the year then ended in accordance with accounting principles generally accepted in the United States of America.

---

7.   **Summary of Qualified Opinions**

a.   A qualified opinion is expressed because of

1)   An inability to obtain sufficient appropriate evidence that could result in material but not pervasive undetected misstatements or

2)   Misstatements that are material but not pervasive. Examples of misstatements include the following:

a)   Inappropriate selection of accounting principles
b)   Inappropriate application of accounting principles
c)   Unjustified change in accounting principles
d)   Inadequate disclosure
e)   Failure to provide a basic financial statement, e.g., statement of cash flows

Stop and review! You have completed the outline for this subunit. Study multiple-choice questions 9 through 12 beginning on page 345.

16.5 ADVERSE OPINIONS

1.   The auditor should express an adverse opinion when, having obtained sufficient appropriate audit evidence, (s)he concludes that **misstatements**, individually or combined, are **material and pervasive** to the financial statements.

2.   The auditor should include a **basis for adverse opinion** paragraph **preceding the opinion** paragraph that describes the matter resulting in the modification.

a.   If misstatements relate to specific amounts in the financial statements (including quantitative disclosures), the auditor should include a description and quantification of the financial effects, if practicable. If it is not practicable to quantify the financial effects, the auditor should so state.

3.   The opinion should state that, because of the significance of the matter(s) described in the basis for adverse opinion paragraph, the financial statements are **not presented fairly** in accordance with the framework.

4. **Example of an Adverse Opinion**

   a. The following are other effects on the auditor's report when an adverse opinion is expressed:

      1) The introductory paragraph is unchanged.
      2) The management's responsibility paragraph is unchanged.
      3) The auditor's responsibility section is changed to state, "We believe that the audit evidence we have obtained is sufficient and appropriate to provide a basis for our adverse audit opinion."

   b. The following are examples of the basis for adverse opinion and opinion paragraphs:

EXAMPLE -- Adverse Opinion Due to a Material and Pervasive Misstatement

Basis for Adverse Opinion

As described in Note X, the Company has not consolidated the financial statements of subsidiary XYZ Company that it acquired during 20X1 because it has not yet been able to ascertain the fair values of certain of the subsidiary's material assets and liabilities at the acquisition date. This investment is therefore accounted for on a cost basis by the Company. Under accounting principles generally accepted in the United States of America, the subsidiary should have been consolidated because it is controlled by the Company. Had XYZ Company been consolidated, many elements in the accompanying consolidated financial statements would have been materially affected. The effects on the consolidated financial statements of the failure to consolidate have not been determined.

Adverse Opinion

In our opinion, because of the significance of the matter discussed in the Basis for Adverse Opinion paragraph, the consolidated financial statements referred to above do not present fairly the financial position of ABC Company and its subsidiaries as of December 31, 20X1, or the results of their operations or their cash flows for the year then ended.

Stop and review! You have completed the outline for this subunit. Study multiple-choice questions 13 through 15 on page 346.

16.6 DISCLAIMERS OF OPINION

1. The auditor disclaims an opinion due to an **inability to obtain sufficient appropriate audit evidence** when the auditor concludes that the possible effects on the financial statements of undetected misstatements, if any, could be **material and pervasive**. The inability to obtain sufficient appropriate audit evidence may result from the following:

   a. Circumstances not controlled by the entity, such as destruction or government seizure of accounting records.
   b. Circumstances related to the nature or timing of the work, such as not being able to observe inventory due to the late appointment of the auditor, determining that controls are ineffective, or not being able to obtain audited financial statements of a long-term investor.
   c. Limitations imposed by management, such as preventing the auditor from (1) observing inventory or (2) confirming receivables.

2. The following are the effects on the auditor's report when an opinion is disclaimed:

   a. The introductory paragraph is changed to state, "We were engaged to audit . . ."
   b. The management's responsibility paragraph is unchanged.
   c. Because an audit has not been conducted, the auditor's responsibility section is changed to consist only of (1) a one-sentence description of the auditor's responsibility and (2) a statement that the auditor could not obtain sufficient appropriate audit evidence to express an opinion because of the matters described in the basis for disclaimer of opinion paragraph.

3.   The following is an example of a disclaimer of opinion:

EXAMPLE -- Disclaimer of Opinion

Independent Auditor's Report

To: <----------- Addressed to the Board of Directors or Shareholders

We were engaged to audit the accompanying financial statements of ABC Company, which comprise the balance sheet as of December 31, 20X1, and the related statements of income, changes in stockholders' equity, and cash flows for the year then ended, and the related notes to the financial statements.

Management's Responsibility for the Financial Statements

Management is responsible for the preparation and fair presentation of these financial statements in accordance with accounting principles generally accepted in the United States of America; this includes the design, implementation, and maintenance of internal control relevant to the preparation and fair presentation of financial statements that are free from material misstatement, whether due to fraud or error.

Auditor's Responsibility

Our responsibility is to express an opinion on these financial statements based on conducting the audit in accordance with auditing standards generally accepted in the United States of America. Because of the matters described in the Basis for Disclaimer of Opinion paragraph, however, we were not able to obtain sufficient appropriate audit evidence to provide a basis for an audit opinion.

Basis for Disclaimer of Opinion

We were not engaged as auditors of the Company until after December 31, 20X1, and, therefore, did not observe the counting of physical inventories at the beginning or end of the year. We were unable to satisfy ourselves by other auditing procedures concerning the inventory held at December 31, 20X1, which is stated in the balance sheet at $XXX. In addition, the introduction of a new computerized accounts receivable system in September 20X1 resulted in numerous misstatements in accounts receivable. As of the date of our audit report, management was still in the process of rectifying the system deficiencies and correcting the misstatements. We were unable to confirm or verify by alternative means accounts receivable included in the balance sheet at a total amount of $XXX at December 31, 20X1. As a result of these matters, we were unable to determine whether any adjustments might have been found necessary in respect of recorded or unrecorded inventories and accounts receivable, and the elements making up the statements of income, changes in stockholders' equity, and cash flows.

Disclaimer of Opinion

Because of the significance of the matters described in the Basis for Disclaimer of Opinion paragraph, we have not been able to obtain sufficient appropriate audit evidence to provide a basis for an audit opinion. Accordingly, we do not express an opinion on these financial statements.

Auditor's signature   <----------- May be manual or printed
Auditor's address   <----------- City and state
Date   <----------- Date disclaimer signed

---

4.   **Auditor Not Independent but Required to Report**

a.   An auditor who is not independent may be required by law or regulation to report on the financial statements. The auditor should disclaim an opinion and should specifically state that (s)he is not independent.

1)   The auditor may or may not provide the reasons for the lack of independence. However, if the reasons are provided, the auditor should include all the reasons.

5. **Reporting on a Single Financial Statement**

    a.   The auditor may, in appropriate circumstances, express an unmodified opinion on one basic financial statement (e.g., the balance sheet). References in the introductory and opinion paragraphs of the report are made only to the one statement. The other sections of the report are essentially unaffected.

    b.   A **piecemeal opinion** is an expression of opinion on a specific element in the financial statements when the auditor has disclaimed an opinion or expressed an adverse opinion on the statements as a whole. This type of assurance is inappropriate because it would contradict the disclaimer or adverse opinion.

6. **Accountant Associated with the Unaudited Financial Statements of an Issuer**

    a.   The PCAOB's AS 3320 requires a disclaimer to be attached to the financial statements of an issuer (public company) when an accountant is associated with those statements and has not audited or reviewed them.

        1)   Association means that the accountant has consented to the use of his or her name in a report, document, or written communication containing the statements.

        2)   It also may mean that the accountant has submitted financial statements that (s)he prepared or assisted in preparing.

        3)   An accountant might become associated by performing consulting services for a nonaudit client, for example, structuring a purchase transaction for a new subsidiary.

    b.   The following relate to the disclaimer:

        1)   Each page of the financial statements should be marked as **unaudited**.

        2)   The accountant has no responsibility to apply any procedures beyond reading the statements for obvious material misstatements. Any procedures that may have been performed should not be described.

        3)   If the accountant has reservations about fair presentation in accordance with GAAP (e.g., that management has elected to omit substantially all disclosures), (s)he should suggest revision. Failing that, the matter should be disclosed.

        4)   The report has no title or salutation.

    c.   The following is an example of a disclaimer on unaudited financial statements of an issuer:

EXAMPLE -- Disclaimer of Opinion When Associated with Unaudited Financial Statements of an Issuer

The accompanying balance sheet of X Company as of December 31, Year 1, and the related statements of income, retained earnings, and cash flows for the year then ended were not audited by us and, accordingly, we do not express an opinion on them.

Signature
Date

---

    d.   Accountants providing nonaudit services to **nonissuers** should follow the guidance in *Statements on Standards for Accounting and Review Services* or Statements on Standards for Attestation Engagements. (These matters are covered in detail in Study Unit 19.)

Stop and review! You have completed the outline for this subunit. Study multiple-choice questions 16 through 20 beginning on page 347.

QUESTIONS

16.1 The Auditor's Reporting Responsibility

1. The objective of the audit of GAAP-based financial statements is to

A. Make suggestions as to the form or content of the financial statements or to draft them in whole or in part.

B. Express an opinion on the fairness with which the statements present financial position, results of operations, and cash flows in accordance with generally accepted accounting principles.

C. Ensure adoption of sound accounting policies and the establishment and maintenance of internal control.

D. Express an opinion on the accuracy with which the statements present financial position, results of operations, and cash flows in accordance with generally accepted accounting principles.

Answer (B) is correct.
   REQUIRED: The objective of an audit.
   DISCUSSION: Based on an audit, the auditor expresses an opinion (or a disclaimer of opinion) on the fairness, in all material respects, of the presentation of financial statements, i.e., on whether they will be misleading to users.
   Answer (A) is incorrect. The auditor may make suggestions about the statements or help prepare them, but (s)he is responsible only for expressing an opinion as to their fairness. The statements remain the representations of management. Answer (C) is incorrect. Management is responsible for adopting sound accounting policies and establishing and maintaining internal control. Answer (D) is incorrect. The auditor expresses an opinion on the fairness of financial statements, not their accuracy.

2. Which of the following statements best describes the distinction between the auditor's responsibilities and management's responsibilities?

A. Management has responsibility for maintaining and adopting sound accounting policies, and the auditor has responsibility for internal control.

B. Management has responsibility for the basic data underlying financial statements, and the auditor has responsibility for drafting the financial statements.

C. The auditor's responsibility is confined to the audited portion of the financial statements, and management's responsibility is confined to the unaudited portions.

D. The auditor's responsibility is confined to expressing an opinion, but the financial statements remain the responsibility of management.

Answer (D) is correct.
   REQUIRED: The statement that best distinguishes between the auditor's and management's responsibilities for audited financial statements.
   DISCUSSION: The auditor is responsible for the opinion on financial statements, but management is responsible for the representations made in the financial statements.
   Answer (A) is incorrect. Management has responsibility for establishing and maintaining internal control. Answer (B) is incorrect. Management is responsible for preparing the financial statements. Answer (C) is incorrect. The auditor expresses an opinion on the financial statements as a whole, and management is responsible for all the assertions in the financial statements.

16.2 The Auditor's Report

3. Which of the following statements is a basic element of the auditor's report for a nonissuer?

A. The disclosures provide reasonable assurance that the financial statements are free of material misstatement.

B. The auditor evaluated management decisions.

C. The procedures used depend on the auditor's judgment.

D. The financial statements are consistent with those of the prior period.

Answer (C) is correct.
    REQUIRED: The statement that is an element of the auditor's report for a nonissuer.
    DISCUSSION: The auditor's responsibility section states, "The procedures selected depend on the auditor's judgment . . ."
    Answer (A) is incorrect. The audit is planned and performed to obtain reasonable assurance about whether the statements are free from material misstatement. Answer (B) is incorrect. The audit addresses the fair presentation of the statements, not the quality of most management decisions. Answer (D) is incorrect. The auditor evaluates the appropriateness (not necessarily the consistency) of the accounting policies used.

4. The existence of audit risk is recognized by the statement in the auditor's report that the auditor

A. Obtains reasonable assurance about whether the financial statements are free of material misstatement.

B. Evaluates the accounting policies used.

C. Realizes some matters, either individually or in the aggregate, are important, while other matters are not important.

D. Is responsible for expressing an opinion on the financial statements.

Answer (A) is correct.
    REQUIRED: The statement in the auditor's report that relates to audit risk.
    DISCUSSION: The existence of audit risk is recognized by the statement in the auditor's report that the auditor obtained reasonable assurance about whether the financial statements are free of material misstatement. Audit risk is the risk that the auditor expresses an inappropriate audit opinion when the financial statements are materially misstated. Audit risk exists because the assurance is not absolute. Reasonable assurance is obtained when the auditor has obtained sufficient appropriate evidence to reduce audit risk to an acceptably low level (AU-C 200).
    Answer (B) is incorrect. The statement about evaluating accounting policies relates to whether the accounting principles selected and applied are consistent with the applicable framework and are appropriate. Answer (C) is incorrect. Materiality is mentioned in the auditor's report, but a statement defining materiality is not. Answer (D) is incorrect. The statement about the responsibilities of the auditor does not pertain to audit risk.

5. When single-year financial statements are presented, an auditor ordinarily expresses an unmodified opinion if the

A. Auditor is unable to obtain audited financial statements supporting the entity's investment in a foreign affiliate.

B. Entity declines to present a statement of cash flows with its balance sheet and related statements of income and retained earnings.

C. Auditor is not independent but judges that an unmodified opinion is appropriate.

D. Prior year's financial statements were audited by another CPA whose report, which expressed an unmodified opinion, is not presented.

Answer (D) is correct.
    REQUIRED: The condition for expressing an unmodified opinion on single-year financial statements.
    DISCUSSION: When single-year financial statements are presented, the auditor's reporting responsibility is limited to those statements. If the prior year's financial statements are not presented for comparative purposes, the current-year auditor should not refer to the prior year's statements and the report thereon. Furthermore, the failure to present comparative statements is not a basis for modifying the opinion.
    Answer (A) is incorrect. An inability to obtain audited financial statements supporting an entity's material investment in a foreign affiliate is a scope limitation requiring either a qualified opinion or a disclaimer of opinion. Answer (B) is incorrect. If the entity declines to present a statement of cash flows, the auditor should express a qualified opinion. Answer (C) is incorrect. The auditor should not express an opinion if (s)he is not independent.

6. Does an auditor make the following representations explicitly or implicitly in the opinion paragraph when expressing an unmodified opinion?

	Conformity with the Applicable Financial Reporting Framework	Adequacy of Disclosure
A.	Explicitly	Explicitly
B.	Implicitly	Implicitly
C.	Implicitly	Explicitly
D.	Explicitly	Implicitly

Answer (D) is correct.

REQUIRED: The explicit and implicit representations an auditor makes when expressing an unmodified opinion.

DISCUSSION: The opinion paragraph of the auditor's report explicitly states whether the financial statements are in accordance with the applicable financial reporting framework, e.g., U.S. GAAP or IFRS. The adequacy of disclosure is implicit in the auditor's report. Adequacy of disclosure is implied if the report does not mention disclosure.

Answer (A) is incorrect. Adequacy of disclosure is implied if the report does not mention disclosure. Answer (B) is incorrect. Presentation in accordance with the applicable financial reporting framework is explicitly stated. Answer (C) is incorrect. Presentation in accordance with the applicable financial reporting framework is explicitly stated, and adequacy of disclosure is implied if the report does not mention disclosure.

16.3 Addressing and Dating the Report

7. In May Year 3, an auditor reissues the auditor's report on the Year 1 financial statements at a former client's request. The Year 1 financial statements are to be presented comparatively with subsequent audited statements. They are not restated, and the auditor does not revise the wording of the report. The auditor should

A. Dual-date the reissued report.

B. Use the release date of the reissued report.

C. Use the original report date on the reissued report.

D. Use the current-period auditor's report date on the reissued report.

Answer (C) is correct.

REQUIRED: The date of a reissued report.

DISCUSSION: Use of the original date in a reissued report removes any implication that records, transactions, or events after such date have been audited or reviewed. However, the predecessor auditor should perform the following procedures to determine whether the report is still appropriate: (1) read the statements of the subsequent period, (2) compare the prior statements with the current statements, and (3) obtain written representations from management and the successor auditor about information obtained or events that occurred subsequent to the original date of the report.

Answer (A) is incorrect. The report is dual-dated only if it has been revised since the original reissue date. Answer (B) is incorrect. The release date of the reissued report implies that additional audit procedures have been applied. Answer (D) is incorrect. Use of the current report date implies that the report has been updated for additional audit procedures applied between the original issue date and the current auditor's report date.

8. An auditor released an audit report that was dual-dated for a subsequently discovered fact occurring after the date of the auditor's report but before issuance of the related financial statements. The auditor's responsibility for events occurring subsequent to the original report date was

A. Limited to the specific event referenced.

B. Limited to include only events occurring before the date of the last subsequent event referenced.

C. Extended to subsequent events occurring through the date of issuance of the related financial statements.

D. Extended to include all events occurring since the original report date.

Answer (A) is correct.

REQUIRED: The auditor's responsibility for events occurring subsequent to the original report date when the report is dual-dated.

DISCUSSION: Subsequent to the original report date, the auditor is responsible only for the specific subsequently discovered fact for which the report was dual-dated. (S)he is responsible for other events only up to the original report date.

Answer (B) is incorrect. After the original report date, the auditor's responsibility extends only to the specified event. Answer (C) is incorrect. The date(s) of the report determines the auditor's responsibility. Answer (D) is incorrect. After the original report date, the auditor's responsibility extends only to the specified subsequent event.

16.4 Qualified Opinions

9. An auditor may express a qualified opinion for which of the following reasons?

	Circumstances Related to the Work	Limitations Imposed by Management
A.	Yes	Yes
B.	Yes	No
C.	No	Yes
D.	No	No

Answer (A) is correct.

REQUIRED: The reasons for which the auditor may express a qualified opinion.

DISCUSSION: An auditor may express a qualified opinion due to an inability to obtain sufficient appropriate audit evidence if the possible effects are material but not pervasive. The inability to obtain sufficient audit evidence (also called a scope limitation) may result from (1) circumstances not controlled by the entity, such as destruction or government seizure of accounting records; (2) circumstances related to the nature or timing of the work, such as not being able to (a) observe inventory due to the late appointment of the auditor, (b) obtain an investee's financial information, or (c) determine that controls are ineffective; or (3) limitations imposed by management, such as preventing the auditor from observing inventory or confirming receivables (AU-C 705).

Answer (B) is incorrect. Limitations imposed by management may require expression of a qualified opinion. Answer (C) is incorrect. Circumstances related to the nature or timing of the work may require expression of a qualified opinion. Answer (D) is incorrect. Circumstances related to the nature or timing of the work and limitations imposed by management may require expression of a qualified opinion.

10. In which of the following situations would an auditor ordinarily choose between expressing a qualified opinion and an adverse opinion?

A. The auditor did not observe the entity's physical inventory and is unable to become satisfied about its balance by other auditing procedures.

B. Conditions that cause the auditor to have substantial doubt about the entity's ability to continue as a going concern are inadequately disclosed.

C. There has been a change in accounting principles that has a material effect on the comparability of the entity's financial statements.

D. The auditor is unable to apply necessary procedures concerning an investor's share of an investee's earnings recognized in accordance with the equity method.

Answer (B) is correct.

REQUIRED: The situation ordinarily involving a choice between a qualified opinion and an adverse opinion.

DISCUSSION: When the auditor concludes that substantial doubt exists about an entity's ability to continue as a going concern for a reasonable period of time, (s)he should include an emphasis-of-matter paragraph (following the opinion paragraph) in the auditor's report to describe the uncertainty. By itself, this doubt does not require a modification of the opinion. However, if the entity's disclosures about the issue are inadequate, the misstatement may result in a qualified or an adverse opinion.

Answer (A) is incorrect. A scope limitation requires the auditor to choose between a qualified opinion and a disclaimer of opinion. Answer (C) is incorrect. A justified change in accounting principle requires the auditor to add an emphasis-of-matter paragraph to the report but not to modify the opinion. Answer (D) is incorrect. A scope limitation requires the auditor to choose between a qualified opinion and a disclaimer of opinion.

11. An auditor decides to express a qualified opinion on an entity's financial statements because a major inadequacy in its computerized accounting records prevents the auditor from applying necessary procedures. The opinion paragraph of the auditor's report should state that the qualification pertains to

A. A client-imposed scope limitation.

B. A departure from generally accepted auditing standards.

C. The possible effects on the financial statements.

D. Inadequate disclosure of necessary information.

Answer (C) is correct.

REQUIRED: The wording in the opinion paragraph when the opinion is qualified because of a scope limitation.

DISCUSSION: When an auditor qualifies his or her opinion because of a scope limitation, the wording in the opinion paragraph should indicate that the qualification pertains to the possible effects on the financial statements and not to the scope limitation itself.

Answer (A) is incorrect. The qualification should not pertain to the scope limitation. Answer (B) is incorrect. The auditor apparently has followed GAAS in the conduct of the audit. Answer (D) is incorrect. Inadequate disclosure is a misstatement, not a lack of sufficient appropriate evidence.

12. An auditor concludes that a client's noncompliance with laws and regulations, which has a material effect on the financial statements, has not been properly accounted for or disclosed. Depending on how pervasive the effect is on the financial statements, the auditor should express either a(n)

A. Adverse opinion or a disclaimer of opinion.

B. Qualified opinion or an adverse opinion.

C. Disclaimer of opinion or an unmodified opinion with a separate explanatory paragraph.

D. Unmodified opinion with a separate emphasis-of-matter paragraph or a qualified opinion.

Answer (B) is correct.
    REQUIRED: The opinion(s) expressed when noncompliance has not been properly accounted for or disclosed.
    DISCUSSION: When noncompliance with laws and regulations having a material effect on the financial statements has been detected but not properly reported, the auditor should insist upon revision of the financial statements. Failure to revise the statements precludes an unmodified opinion. Depending on the pervasiveness of the misstatement, the auditor should express either a qualified opinion or an adverse opinion.
    Answer (A) is incorrect. A disclaimer of opinion is inappropriate. The auditor has concluded that the statements are materially misstated. Answer (C) is incorrect. A disclaimer of opinion is inappropriate. The auditor has concluded that the statements are materially misstated. Answer (D) is incorrect. An unmodified opinion is inappropriate for materially misstated financial statements.

16.5 Adverse Opinions

13. An auditor's report includes the following statement: "The financial statements referred to above do not present fairly the financial position, results of operations, or cash flows in conformity with U.S. generally accepted accounting principles." This auditor's report was most likely issued in connection with financial statements that are

A. Inconsistent.

B. Based on prospective financial information.

C. Misleading.

D. Affected by a material uncertainty.

Answer (C) is correct.
    REQUIRED: The nature of the financial statements on which the quoted report was issued.
    DISCUSSION: The language quoted states an adverse opinion. The essence of an adverse opinion is that the statements reported on, as a whole, are materially and pervasively misstated. If financial statements fail to meet the standards, they are misleading.
    Answer (A) is incorrect. An inconsistency, by itself, results in no modification of the opinion paragraph. Answer (B) is incorrect. The accountant's examination report on a financial forecast or projection refers to guidelines for the presentation of a forecast (or projection) established by the AICPA, not to U.S. GAAP (AT 301). Answer (D) is incorrect. A material uncertainty, if properly disclosed, does not require modification of the opinion.

14. When an auditor expresses an adverse opinion, the opinion paragraph should include

A. The effects of the material misstatement.

B. A direct reference to a separate paragraph disclosing the basis for the opinion.

C. The financial effects of the misstatement.

D. A description of the uncertainty or scope limitation that prevents an unmodified opinion.

Answer (B) is correct.
    REQUIRED: The matter included in the opinion paragraph when an adverse opinion is expressed.
    DISCUSSION: An adverse opinion states that the financial statements are not fairly presented in accordance with the applicable financial reporting framework. When an adverse opinion is expressed, the opinion paragraph should directly refer to a basis for adverse opinion paragraph that discloses the basis for the adverse opinion. This paragraph should precede the opinion paragraph (AU-C 705).
    Answer (A) is incorrect. The effects of the material misstatement, if practicable, should be stated in the basis for adverse opinion paragraph. Answer (C) is incorrect. The financial effects of the misstatement should be stated in the basis paragraph. Answer (D) is incorrect. An adverse opinion is not expressed as a result of an uncertainty or scope limitation.

15. In which of the following circumstances would an auditor be most likely to express an adverse opinion?

A. Information comes to the auditor's attention that raises substantial doubt about the entity's ability to continue as a going concern.

B. The chief executive officer refuses the auditor access to minutes of board of directors' meetings.

C. Tests of controls show that the entity's internal control is so poor that it cannot be relied upon.

D. The financial statements are not in conformity with the FASB Codification's guidance regarding the capitalization of leases.

Answer (D) is correct.
    REQUIRED: The basis for an adverse opinion.
    DISCUSSION: An adverse opinion is expressed when, in the auditor's judgment, the financial statements as a whole are not presented fairly in conformity with GAAP. The FASB Accounting Standards Codification is authoritative with regard to U.S. GAAP.
    Answer (A) is incorrect. Substantial doubt about the entity's ability to continue as a going concern requires an emphasis-of-matter paragraph following the opinion paragraph, not an adverse opinion. Answer (B) is incorrect. A client-imposed scope limitation ordinarily results in a disclaimer of opinion. Answer (C) is incorrect. Lack of an expectation of the effectiveness of internal control may affect the nature, timing, and extent of substantive procedures but is not a basis for an adverse opinion. Ineffective internal control does not, by itself, indicate that the financial statements are not fairly presented.

16.6 Disclaimers of Opinion

16. Under which of the following circumstances might an auditor disclaim an opinion?

A. The financial statements contain a material misstatement.

B. Material related party transactions are disclosed in the financial statements.

C. There has been a material change between periods in the method of application of accounting principles.

D. The auditor is unable to obtain sufficient appropriate evidence to support management's assertions concerning an uncertainty.

Answer (D) is correct.
　REQUIRED: The reason for a disclaimer.
　DISCUSSION: Based on the audit evidence that is, or should be, available, the auditor assesses whether the audit evidence is sufficient to support managements' assertions about an uncertainty. When the auditor cannot obtain sufficient appropriate evidence, (s)he expresses a qualified opinion if the possible effects are material but not pervasive. If the possible effects are material and pervasive, (s)he disclaims an opinion.
　Answer (A) is incorrect. The auditor should express a qualified or an adverse opinion when the statements contain a material misstatement. Answer (B) is incorrect. It is appropriate to disclose related party transactions. Answer (C) is incorrect. If the auditor concurs in the change, lack of consistency requires only an emphasis-of-matter paragraph.

17. Due to a scope limitation, an auditor disclaimed an opinion on the financial statements as a whole, but the auditor's report included a statement that the current asset portion of the entity's balance sheet was fairly stated. The inclusion of this statement is

A. Not appropriate because it may tend to overshadow the auditor's disclaimer of opinion.

B. Not appropriate because the auditor is prohibited from reporting on only one basic financial statement.

C. Appropriate, provided the auditor's responsibility section adequately describes the scope limitation.

D. Appropriate, provided the statement is in the basis for disclaimer of opinion paragraph preceding the disclaimer of opinion paragraph.

Answer (A) is correct.
　REQUIRED: The suitability of a statement in an auditor's disclaimer about whether an element was stated fairly.
　DISCUSSION: A piecemeal opinion is an expression of an opinion on a specific element of a financial statement when the auditor has disclaimed an opinion or expressed an adverse opinion on the financial statements as a whole. This type of assurance is inappropriate because it would contradict a disclaimer of opinion or an adverse opinion (AU-C 705).
　Answer (B) is incorrect. The auditor may report on one basic financial statement and not on the others. Such a limited reporting engagement is acceptable. Answer (C) is incorrect. A piecemeal opinion is inappropriate in this circumstance. Answer (D) is incorrect. A piecemeal opinion is inappropriate in this circumstance.

18. A CPA concludes that the unaudited financial statements of an issuer on which the CPA is disclaiming an opinion are not in conformity with generally accepted accounting principles (GAAP) because management has failed to capitalize leases. The CPA suggests appropriate revisions to the financial statements, but management refuses to accept the CPA's suggestions. Under these circumstances, the CPA ordinarily would

A. Express limited assurance that no other material modifications should be made to the financial statements.

B. Restrict the distribution of the CPA's report to management and the entity's board of directors.

C. Issue a qualified opinion or adverse opinion depending on the materiality of the departure from GAAP.

D. Describe the nature of the departure from GAAP in the CPA's report and state the effects on the financial statements, if practicable.

Answer (D) is correct.
　REQUIRED: The appropriate action when the CPA suggests revisions to the financial statements but management refuses to accept them.
　DISCUSSION: An accountant planning to disclaim an opinion on an issuer's financial statements may discover a material departure from GAAP. Under PCAOB standards, the accountant should disclose the departure in the disclaimer, including its effects if they have been determined by management or by the accountant's procedures.
　Answer (A) is incorrect. A disclaimer should provide no assurance. Answer (B) is incorrect. The disclaimer should not be restricted in use. Answer (C) is incorrect. A disclaimer of opinion is necessary when the CPA has not audited the statements.

19. If an issuer releases financial statements that purport to present its financial position and results of operations but omits the statement of cash flows, the auditor ordinarily will express a(n)

   A. Disclaimer of opinion.

   B. Qualified opinion.

   C. Review report.

   D. Unmodified opinion with a separate emphasis-of-matter paragraph.

Answer (B) is correct.
   REQUIRED: The opinion expressed when a client fails to present a statement of cash flows.
   DISCUSSION: An entity that reports financial position and results of operations should provide a statement of cash flows. Thus, the omission of the cash flow statement is normally a basis for modifying the opinion. If the statements fail to disclose required information, the auditor should provide the information in the report, if practicable. However, the auditor is not required to prepare a basic financial statement. Accordingly, (s)he should qualify the opinion and explain the reason in a basis for qualified opinion paragraph.
   Answer (A) is incorrect. The question concerns disclosure rather than an inability to obtain sufficient appropriate audit evidence. Answer (C) is incorrect. The engagement is an audit. Answer (D) is incorrect. A material omission of disclosures normally requires modification of the opinion.

20. Morris, CPA, suspects that a pervasive scheme of illegal bribes exists throughout the operations of Worldwide Import-Export, Inc., a new audit client. Morris notified the audit committee and Worldwide's legal counsel, but neither would assist Morris in determining whether the amounts involved were material to the financial statements or whether senior management was involved in the scheme. Under these circumstances, Morris most likely should

   A. Express an unmodified opinion with an other-matter paragraph.

   B. Disclaim an opinion on the financial statements.

   C. Express an adverse opinion on the financial statements.

   D. Issue a special report regarding the illegal bribes.

Answer (B) is correct.
   REQUIRED: The auditor action when (s)he cannot determine the amounts involved in material noncompliance with laws or regulations or the extent of management's involvement.
   DISCUSSION: Bribery is a violation of laws or governmental regulations. If the auditor is precluded by management or those charged with governance (e.g., the audit committee) from obtaining sufficient appropriate evidence to evaluate whether material noncompliance with laws or regulations has (or is likely to have) occurred, the auditor should disclaim an opinion or express a qualified opinion.
   Answer (A) is incorrect. An unmodified opinion is not justified. Answer (C) is incorrect. An adverse opinion is expressed only when the financial statements are not presented fairly. Answer (D) is incorrect. Special reports as defined in AU-C 805 are not issued on such topics.

Access the Gleim CPA Premium Review System featuring SmartAdapt for exam-emulating multiple-choice questions and simulations with detailed answer explanations.

Learn more: gleim.com/CPApremium | 800.874.5346

STUDY UNIT SEVENTEEN
REPORTS -- OTHER MODIFICATIONS

(13 pages of outline)

This study unit covers additional language modifying the auditor's report. These modifications normally do not affect the auditor's opinion on the financial statements. They permit the users of the financial statements and readers of the auditor's report to better understand the responsibility assumed by the auditor. They also provide information about the client's financial statements that the auditor considers important. The following table summarizes these modifications:

Basis for Modifying the Report	Modification
Group auditor's report refers to the audit of the component auditor	Auditor's responsibility section and opinion paragraph
Material accounting change affects consistency	Emphasis-of-matter paragraph
Substantial going-concern doubt	Emphasis-of-matter paragraph
Prior-period opinion changed in comparative statements	Emphasis-of-matter paragraph or other-matter paragraph
Predecessor auditor's report not presented in comparative statements	Other-matter paragraph
Drawing attention to matter presented or not presented	Emphasis-of-matter paragraph or other-matter paragraph, respectively

A candidate who is unfamiliar with emphasis-of-matter or other-matter paragraphs may want to study Subunit 17.5 before proceeding.

17.1 GROUP AUDITS AND COMPONENT AUDITORS

1. **Nature of Group Audits**

   a. GAAS apply to audits of group financial statements. Part of the audit may be performed by a component auditor.

      1) A **component** is an entity or business activity for which group or component management prepares financial information required by the reporting framework to be included in the group statements.

         a) A component may be a subsidiary, joint venture, or equity-method investee.

      2) A **component auditor** performs work on the financial information that will be used as audit evidence for the group audit.

      3) A component auditor may be a member of the group engagement partner's firm, a network firm of that partner's firm, or another firm.

b.   The **group engagement partner**

1)   Is responsible for the group engagement, its performance, and the report on the group statements.

2)   Is responsible for deciding, individually for each component, either to

a)   **Not assume responsibility** for, and accordingly refer to, the audit of a component auditor in the auditor's report on the group financial statements or

b)   **Assume responsibility** for, and thus be required to be involved in, the work of a component auditor to the extent that work relates to the expression of an opinion on the group financial statements. Involvement may include

i)   Performing risk assessment procedures,
ii)   Performing further procedures, and
iii) Reviewing the component auditor's documentation.

3)   Is required to be satisfied that those performing the group audit engagement, including component auditors, collectively possess the **appropriate competence and capabilities**.

a)   This requirement applies whether or not the group engagement partner assumes responsibility for the work of a component auditor.

4)   Is responsible for the direction, supervision, and performance of the group audit engagement performed by the engagement team.

5)   Should determine whether sufficient appropriate audit evidence can reasonably be expected to be obtained regarding the consolidation process (e.g., for investments accounted for under the equity method).

c.   This standard may be applied and adapted as necessary when an auditor involves other auditors in the audit of financial statements that are **not group** financial statements.

1)   For example, an auditor may involve another auditor to observe the inventory count or inspect physical fixed assets at a remote location.

d.   If the auditor decides to act as the auditor of the group financial statements, the **objectives** are to

1)   Obtain **sufficient appropriate audit evidence** regarding the financial information of the components and the consolidation process to express an opinion about whether the group statements are prepared, in all material respects, in accordance with the applicable financial reporting framework (typically U.S. GAAP);

2)   **Communicate** clearly with component auditors; and

3)   Determine **whether to refer** to the audit of a component auditor in the auditor's report on the group financial statements.

e.   If the auditor concludes it is **not** possible to serve as the group auditor because of restrictions imposed by management, the auditor should

1)   Not accept a new engagement or
2)   Withdraw from a continuing engagement.

    f.   The group engagement team should establish an overall **group audit strategy** and develop a **group audit plan**. The strategy and plan should be approved by the group engagement partner.

        1)   The team should assess (a) the extent to which it will use the work of component auditors and (b) whether the group audit report will refer to the audit of a component auditor.

        2)   The strategy and plan should recognize that detection risk for the group audit includes the detection risk of component auditors.

    g.   The group engagement team should obtain an understanding of the components that is sufficient to

        1)   Confirm or revise its initial identification of components that are likely to be significant.

        2)   Assess the risks of material misstatement of the group financial statements, whether due to fraud or error.

    h.   **Materiality** should be established by the group engagement team.

        1)   Component materiality should be lower than materiality for the group statements as a whole. The purpose is to reduce the risk that the sum of uncorrected and undetected misstatements in the group statements is greater than materiality for the group statements as a whole.

2.   **Reference to a Component Auditor**

    a.   The group engagement team should obtain an understanding of the component auditor's professional competence and compliance with ethical requirements (especially independence).

    b.   The group auditor's report should **not refer** to the audit of a component auditor unless the following requirements are met:

        1)   The component auditor has audited the statements of the component in accordance with GAAS or auditing standards of the PCAOB (if required by law or regulation).

            a)   However, the component auditor's report may not have stated that the component audit was in accordance with GAAS or PCAOB standards. In this case, if the group auditor determines that the component auditor performed additional procedures to comply with GAAS, reference may be made to the component auditor. The report should indicate

                i)   The set of standards used by the component auditor and

                ii)   That additional procedures were performed.

        2)   The component auditor has issued an auditor's report that is not restricted as to use.

    c.   When the group engagement partner decides to refer to the audit of a component auditor, the report on the group statements should clearly indicate that the component was **not audited** by the group auditor but by the component auditor.

        1)   The magnitude of the portion of the statements audited by the component auditor (by dollar amounts or percentages of an appropriate criterion, such as total assets or revenues) should be included.

    d.   If certain conditions are met, the group auditor's report may refer to the component auditor even if the **reporting frameworks** of the component and the group statements differ. Thus, the group auditor's report should disclose

        1)   The framework used by the component and

        2)   That responsibility is taken for evaluating the adjustments needed to convert from one framework to another.

3.   **No Reference to a Component Auditor**

   a.   The group auditor assumes responsibility for the work of the component auditor by not making reference.

   b.   When responsibility is assumed, the type of work performed on the financial information of a component depends on whether the component is significant.

   1)   A **significant component** is

   a)   Of individual financial significance to the group or

   b)   Likely to include significant risks of material misstatement (RMMs) of the group statements.

   2)   When the component has individual financial significance, the group engagement team, or a component auditor on its behalf, audits the financial information, using appropriate component materiality.

   a)   When significance depends on RMMs, the response may be (1) an audit of the financial information or one or more balances, transaction classes, or disclosures or (2) the performance of specified audit procedures.

   3)   When the group auditor assumes responsibility for components that are **not significant**, the group engagement team should perform **analytical procedures** at the group level.

   c.   In summary, when the auditor of the group financial statements assumes responsibility for the work of a component auditor, the component auditor is not referred to in the report on the group audit. To do so may cause a reader to misinterpret the degree of responsibility being assumed.

4.   **Other Issues**

   a.   A reference in the auditor's report on the group financial statements to a component auditor **is not a qualification** of the opinion. Rather, it is intended to communicate that

   1)   The auditor of the group financial statements is not assuming responsibility for the work of the component auditor and

   2)   The component auditor is the source of the audit evidence with respect to those components for which the reference is made.

   b.   Regardless of whether the component auditor is referred to in the report, the group engagement partner is responsible for the overall group audit opinion.

   c.   The component auditor's report may include (1) a modified opinion, (2) an emphasis-of-matter paragraph, or (3) an other-matter paragraph that does not affect the report on the group statements. If the component auditor's report is not presented, the group auditor need not refer to those paragraphs in the auditor's report.

   1)   If the component auditor's report is presented, the group auditor may refer to those paragraphs and their disposition.

   d.   The group engagement team should **communicate** its requirements to the component auditor clearly, effectively, and on a timely basis.

   1)   The group engagement team should communicate to group management (a) fraud and (b) material weaknesses and significant deficiencies in internal control.

   a)   It should also request that group management communicate to component management significant matters discovered during the group audit that may affect the component's statements.

e.   A component auditor may not meet the **independence** requirements that are relevant to the group audit. In this case, the group engagement team should obtain sufficient appropriate audit evidence relating to the financial information of the component without

1)   Referring to the audit of the component auditor in the auditor's report or
2)   Using that auditor's work.

5.   **Report Making Reference**

a.   The following is an example of the two paragraphs from the auditor's report that are changed by the reference to a component auditor.

EXAMPLE

Auditor's Responsibility

Our responsibility is to express an opinion on these consolidated financial statements based on our audits. We did not audit the financial statements of B Company, a wholly-owned subsidiary, which statements reflect total assets constituting 20 percent and 22 percent, respectively, of consolidated total assets at December 31, 20X1 and 20X0, and total revenues constituting 18 percent and 20 percent, respectively, of consolidated total revenues for the years then ended. Those statements were audited by other auditors, whose report has been furnished to us, and our opinion, insofar as it relates to the amounts included for B Company, is based solely on the report of the other auditors. We conducted our audits in accordance with auditing standards generally accepted in the United States of America. Those standards require that we plan and perform the audit to obtain reasonable assurance about whether the consolidated financial statements are free from material misstatement.

[The remainder of the Auditor's Responsibility section is unchanged.]

Opinion

In our opinion, based on our audit and the report of the other auditors, the consolidated financial statements referred to above present fairly, in all material respects, the financial position of ABC Company and its subsidiaries as of December 31, 20X1 and 20X0, and the results of their operations and their cash flows for the years then ended in accordance with accounting principles generally accepted in the United States of America.

Stop and review! You have completed the outline for this subunit. Study multiple-choice questions 1 through 3 on page 362.

17.2 CONSISTENCY OF FINANCIAL STATEMENTS

1.   **Evaluation of Consistency**

a.   The auditor should evaluate whether the comparability of the financial statements between or among periods has been materially affected by

1)   A change in accounting principle or
2)   Adjustments to correct a material misstatement in previously issued financial statements.

b.   If the auditor's report does not state otherwise, it implies that comparability between or among periods has not been materially affected by such changes or corrections.

c.   The **periods covered** in the auditor's evaluation of consistency depend on the periods covered by the auditor's opinion.

1)   For initial audits, the auditor should obtain sufficient appropriate audit evidence about whether the accounting policies reflected in the opening balances have been consistently applied in the current period's financial statements.

2)   When the auditor reports only on the current period, (s)he should evaluate whether the current-period statements are consistent with those of the preceding period, regardless of whether they are presented.

3)   When the auditor's opinion covers two or more periods, (s)he should evaluate consistency between or among such periods.

4)   The auditor also evaluates the consistency of the earliest period covered by the opinion with the period preceding it, if such prior period is presented.

   a)   For example, assume that an entity presents comparative statements for 3 years and has a change in auditors.

   i)   In the current year (20X3), the auditor evaluates consistency between the year on which (s)he reports (20X3) and the immediately preceding year (20X2).

   ii)   In the next year (20X4), the auditor evaluates consistency between (a) the 2 years on which (s)he reports (20X3 and 20X4), and (b) those years and the earliest year presented (20X2).

5)   The auditor also should evaluate whether the statements for the periods reported on are consistent with previously issued financial statements for the relevant periods.

2.   **Change in Accounting Principle**

   a.   A change in principle is a change from one principle in accordance with the applicable financial reporting framework to another such principle when (1) two or more principles apply or (2) the principle used previously is no longer in accordance with the framework.

   b.   A change in the method of applying a principle also is a change in principle.

   c.   A change from a principle that is not in accordance with the applicable framework to one that is in accordance is a **correction of a misstatement**.

   d.   The applicable framework usually states the method of accounting for the effects of a change in principle and the related disclosures. The auditor should evaluate a change in principle to determine whether

   1)   The new principle and the method of accounting for the effect of the change are in accordance with the applicable framework,

   2)   The disclosures related to the change are adequate, and

   3)   The entity has justified that the alternative principle is preferable.

   e.   The issuance of an accounting pronouncement that (1) requires use of a new principle, (2) interprets an existing principle, (3) expresses a preference for a principle, or (4) rejects a specific principle is **sufficient justification** for a change if it is in accordance with the applicable framework.

   f.   If the criteria stated in 2.d. above are met, and the change in principle is material, the auditor should include an **emphasis-of-matter** paragraph in the report. This paragraph

   1)   Describes the change,

   2)   Refers to the entity's disclosures, and

   3)   Follows the opinion paragraph.

   g.   If the criteria stated in 2.d. are **not** met, the auditor evaluates whether the change results in a material misstatement. If it does, the opinion should be modified.

   h.   If the change is expected to have a material effect only in later periods, the current-period auditor's report need not recognize the change.

   i.   An emphasis-of-matter paragraph is included in the auditor's report for the period of change and in later periods until the new principle is applied in all periods presented.

   j.   The auditor should evaluate and report on a change in **accounting estimate** that is inseparable from the effect of a related change in principle like other changes in principle.

   1)   An example is a change in a method of depreciation, amortization, or depletion of a long-lived nonfinancial asset.

k. A change in the **reporting entity** results in statements that are effectively those of a different entity.

    1) The auditor does **not** recognize the change by including an emphasis-of-matter paragraph in the report if the change results from a transaction or event.

        a) A **transaction or event** is the creation, cessation, or complete or partial purchase or disposition of a subsidiary or other business unit.

    2) An emphasis-of-matter paragraph **is** required if the change is **not** from a transaction or event. Examples include

        a) Presenting consolidated or combined statements in place of the statements of individual entities,

        b) Changing the subsidiaries included in consolidated statements, or

        c) Changing the entities included in combined statements.

l. If an entity's statements contain an investment accounted for by the equity method, the auditor's evaluation of consistency considers the investee.

    1) If the investee makes a change in principle that is material to the investor, the auditor's report should include an emphasis-of-matter paragraph.

3. **Correction of a Material Misstatement in Previously Issued Financial Statements**

a. This correction should be recognized in the auditor's report by including an emphasis-of-matter paragraph.

b. The paragraph is included only in the period when the statements are restated.

c. Certain disclosures are required relating to such misstatements in previously issued statements. If the disclosures are not adequate, the auditor may need to modify the opinion.

d. Correction of a material misstatement also includes a change from a principle not in accordance with the applicable framework to one that is.

4. **Change in Classification**

a. Changes in classification, for example, changing "Cash in Bank" to "Cash," in previously issued statements do not require recognition in the auditor's report unless the change is

    1) The correction of a material misstatement or
    2) A change in principle.

b. For example, certain reclassifications, such as debt from long term to short term or cash flows from operating activities to financing activities, might occur because those items were incorrectly classified. In such situations, the reclassification also is the correction of a misstatement and requires an emphasis-of-matter paragraph.

5. **Example of Reporting on the Change in Accounting Principle**

a. The following is an emphasis-of-matter paragraph that follows an opinion paragraph for a change in principle.

EXAMPLE -- Paragraph Added to Auditor's Report for a Change in Principle

Emphasis of Matter

As discussed in Note X to the financial statements, the Company changed its method of computing depreciation in Year 3. Our opinion is not modified with respect to this matter.

Stop and review! You have completed the outline for this subunit. Study multiple-choice questions 4 through 7 beginning on page 363.

17.3 UNCERTAINTIES AND GOING CONCERN

1. **Uncertainties**

   a. Conclusive audit evidence about the outcome of uncertainties is not expected to exist at the date of the audit. Accordingly, management is responsible for

      1) Estimating the effect of future events on the financial statements or
      2) Determining that a reasonable estimate is not possible and making required disclosures.

   b. The auditor may be able to conclude that sufficient appropriate audit evidence supports (1) management's assertions about an uncertainty and (2) its presentation and disclosure. In these circumstances, an **unmodified** opinion ordinarily is appropriate and an emphasis-of-matter paragraph is not required.

      1) But a qualified opinion or a disclaimer of opinion is expressed if the auditor is unable to obtain such evidence. Thus, Study Unit 16, Subunits 4 and 6, respectively, also are relevant.

2. **Going-Concern Issues**

   a. The auditor should evaluate whether substantial doubt exists about an entity's ability to continue as a going concern for a reasonable period. (Under U.S. GAAP, this period is 1 year from the date the statements are issued or available to be issued.) An **emphasis-of-matter** paragraph should be added following the opinion paragraph if a substantial doubt exists.

      1) The auditor's emphasis-of-matter paragraph should include the terms **substantial doubt** and **going concern**.
      2) In the emphasis-of-matter paragraph, the auditor should not use conditional language, such as, "If the company is unable to obtain refinancing, there may be substantial doubt about the company's ability to continue as a going concern."

   b. By itself, the substantial doubt ordinarily does not require a modified opinion, but the auditor is not precluded from disclaiming an opinion.

   c. The following is an example of an emphasis-of-matter paragraph.

EXAMPLE -- Paragraph Added to Auditor's Report
Expressing Substantial Doubt about Going Concern

Emphasis of Matter

The accompanying financial statements have been prepared assuming that the Company will continue as a going concern. As discussed in Note X to the financial statements, the Company has suffered recurring losses from operations and has a net capital deficiency that raises substantial doubt about its ability to continue as a going concern. Management's plans in regard to these matters are also described in Note X. The financial statements do not include any adjustments that might result from the outcome of this uncertainty.

---

   d. If disclosures are inadequate, the misstatement may result in a qualified or an adverse opinion.

   e. Substantial doubt arising in the current period does not imply that such doubt existed in the prior period and should not affect the report on the prior-period statements.

      1) If substantial doubt existed at the date of prior-period statements and that doubt has been removed in the current period, the emphasis-of-matter paragraph in the report for the prior period should not be repeated.

Stop and review! You have completed the outline for this subunit. Study multiple-choice questions 8 through 12 beginning on page 364.

17.4 COMPARATIVE FINANCIAL STATEMENTS

1. **General Considerations**

   a. A continuing auditor should **update** the report for the one or more prior periods presented in comparative form.

      1) An updated report is not a reissuance of a previous report.
      2) Updated reports consider information from the audit of the current-period statements and are issued with the report on those statements and dated as of the latest audit.

   b. The auditor's report

      1) Should refer to each period for which financial statements are presented and on which an audit opinion is expressed.
      2) Should not be dated earlier than the date on which the auditor has obtained sufficient appropriate audit evidence on which to support the opinion for the most recent audit.

   c. If audit firms merge and the new firm becomes the auditor of a former client of one of the merged firms, the new firm may accept responsibility as a continuing auditor.

      1) The new firm's report may indicate that a merger occurred and name the firm that was merged with it.
      2) If the new firm does not express an opinion on the prior statements, the guidance for the reissuance of reports by a predecessor auditor applies.

   d. The report applies to individual financial statements, so an auditor may (1) express a qualified or an adverse opinion, (2) disclaim an opinion, or (3) include an emphasis-of-matter or other-matter paragraph for one or more statements for one or more periods while issuing a different report on the other statements.

   e. During the audit, the auditor **should be alert** for circumstances or events affecting the **prior-period** financial statements presented and should consider their effects when updating the report.

2. **Comparative Information**

   a. An auditor need not report on comparative information, which consists of condensed statements or summarized prior-period information.

      1) For example, state and local governmental units and not-for-profit entities often present total-all-funds information rather than information by individual funds.
      2) If the client requests an opinion on the prior period(s), the auditor should consider whether the information contains sufficient detail for a fair presentation.
      3) To avoid modification of the report, additional columns or separate detail by fund will usually be needed.

3. **Opinion on Prior-Period Financial Statements Different from the Opinion Previously Issued**

   a. An auditor may become aware of circumstances or events affecting the statements of a prior period and should consider them when updating the report.

      1) For example, if the opinion was modified because of a material misstatement and the statements are revised in the current period, the updated report should express an unmodified opinion.
      2) An emphasis-of-matter or other-matter paragraph should disclose

         a) All substantive reasons for the different opinion,
         b) The date of the previous report,
         c) The type of opinion previously expressed, and
         d) That the updated opinion differs from the previous opinion.

       3)   The introductory paragraph, management's responsibility paragraph, and auditor's responsibility section are not modified in the updated report.

4.   **Report of Predecessor Auditor**

    a.   A predecessor auditor ordinarily can **reissue** the report for a prior period at the request of the former client if (1) satisfactory arrangements are made to perform this service and (2) certain procedures are performed.

    b.   Before reissuing the report, the predecessor auditor should consider whether the report is still appropriate given the current form or presentation of the prior-period statements and any subsequent events. The predecessor auditor should

       1)   Read the current-period statements.

       2)   Compare the prior-period statements reported on with those to be presented comparatively.

       3)   Obtain a representation letter from the auditor stating whether the audit revealed matters that might materially affect, or require disclosure in, the statements reported on by the predecessor auditor.

       4)   Obtain a representation letter from management stating whether (a) any new information has caused management to believe that previous representations should be modified, and (b) any events have occurred after the date of the latest prior-period statements reported on by the predecessor auditor that would require adjustment of, or disclosure in, those financial statements.

    c.   Because a predecessor auditor's knowledge of the former client is limited, (s)he should use the **date of the previous report** to avoid implications that (s)he has examined any records, transactions, or events after that date.

       1)   If the report is revised or the statements are restated, the report should be dual-dated with a second date relating to those items changed or revised.

    d.   In certain circumstances, a predecessor auditor's report may not be reissued (e.g., because the CPA is no longer in public practice).

       1)   When the predecessor auditor's report is **not** presented, the auditor's report should include an **other-matter** paragraph that states the following:

          a)   The prior-period statements were audited by a predecessor auditor. (But the auditor should not name the predecessor auditor unless the predecessor's practice was acquired by, or merged with, that of the auditor.)

          b)   The date of the predecessor's report.

          c)   The type of opinion expressed by the predecessor and the reasons for any modification.

          d)   The nature of any emphasis-of-matter or other-matter paragraph in the predecessor's report.

       2)   An auditor's report when the predecessor's report is not reissued includes an other-matter paragraph similar to the example that follows.

EXAMPLE -- Other-Matter Paragraph Added to Auditor's Report to Reference Predecessor's Report

Other Matter

The financial statements of ABC Company as of December 31, Year 1, were audited by other auditors whose report dated March 31, Year 2, expressed an unmodified opinion on those statements.

---

3) If the predecessor's report contained an emphasis-of-matter paragraph, the following is an example of an other-matter paragraph.

EXAMPLE -- Other-Matter Paragraph of Auditor's Report to Reference Predecessor's Modified Report

Other Matter

The financial statements of ABC Company as of December 31, Year 1, were audited by other auditors whose report on those statements, dated March 1, Year 2, included an emphasis-of-matter paragraph that described the change in the Company's method of computing depreciation discussed in Note X to the financial statements.

---

4) The statements audited by a predecessor auditor whose report is not reissued may have been restated. An auditor who has audited the adjustments includes an other-matter paragraph indicating that a predecessor reported on them before restatement. Also, if the auditor becomes satisfied as to the propriety of the restatement, (s)he also may report on the restatement.

EXAMPLE -- Other-Matter Paragraph of Auditor's Report to Reference Prior Financial Statements that Have Been Restated

Other Matter

(Paragraph stating information about the predecessor auditor's report)

As part of our audit of the Year 2 financial statements, we also audited the adjustments described in Note X that were applied to restate the Year 1 financial statements. In our opinion, such adjustments are appropriate and have been properly applied. We were not engaged to audit, review, or apply any procedures to the Year 1 financial statements of the Company other than with respect to the adjustments, and, accordingly, we do not express an opinion or any other form of assurance on the Year 1 financial statements as a whole.

---

5. **Prior-Period Financial Statements Not Audited**

   a. Current-period statements may be audited and presented in comparative form with compiled or reviewed financial statements for the prior period. If the report on the prior period is not reissued, the auditor should include an **other-matter paragraph** in the current-period auditor's report that includes the following:

      1) The service performed in the prior period
      2) The date of the report on that service
      3) A description of any material modifications noted in that report
      4) A statement that the service was less in scope than an audit and does not provide a basis for the expression of an opinion on the financial statements

   b. If the prior-period financial statements were not audited, reviewed, or compiled, the financial statements should be clearly marked to indicate their status. Moreover, the auditor's report should include an other-matter paragraph to indicate that (1) the auditor has not audited, reviewed, or compiled the prior-period financial statements, and (2) the auditor assumes no responsibility for them.

Stop and review! You have completed the outline for this subunit. Study multiple-choice questions 13 through 16 beginning on page 366.

17.5 EMPHASIS-OF-MATTER AND OTHER-MATTER PARAGRAPHS

Background

Prior auditing standards referred to emphasis-of-matter and other-matter paragraphs as simply "explanatory paragraphs." Current PCAOB Auditing Standards continue to use the term. The use and content of the paragraph is the same for both the AICPA and the PCAOB reports, but the paragraph in the PCAOB audit report for issuers is not titled.

---

1. An **emphasis-of-matter** paragraph is used in the auditor's report to draw users' attention to a matter **appropriately** presented or disclosed in the financial statements that is of such importance that it is fundamental to **users' understanding** of the **financial statements**.

    a. When the auditor includes an emphasis-of-matter paragraph in the auditor's report, the auditor should do all of the following:

        1) Include it immediately after the opinion paragraph in the auditor's report

        2) Use the heading **Emphasis of Matter** or another appropriate heading

        3) Include in the paragraph a clear reference to the matter being emphasized and to where relevant disclosures that fully describe the matter can be found in the financial statements

        4) Indicate that the auditor's opinion is not modified with respect to the matter emphasized

    b. Certain auditing standards require the auditor to include an emphasis-of-matter paragraph. These sections are covered in various study units and include the following:

        1) AU-C 560, *Subsequent Events and Subsequently Discovered Facts* -- If the auditor's opinion on revised financial statements changes after the original report date, the new report should include either an emphasis-of-matter or other-matter paragraph.

        2) AU-C 570, *The Auditor's Consideration of an Entity's Ability to Continue as a Going Concern* -- If the auditor has substantial doubt about an entity's ability to continue as a going concern, an emphasis-of-matter paragraph should be included in the report.

        3) AU-C 708, *Consistency of Financial Statements* -- A material change in principle or the correction of a material misstatement in previously issued statements requires the auditor to include an emphasis-of-matter paragraph in the report.

        4) AU-C 800, *Special Considerations—Audits of Financial Statements Prepared in Accordance With Special Purpose Frameworks* -- Reports on special purpose financial statements require the auditor to add an emphasis-of-matter paragraph to the report.

    c. In addition to the required emphasis-of-matter paragraphs, the following are examples of circumstances when the auditor may consider inclusion of an emphasis-of-matter paragraph to be necessary:

        1) An uncertainty relating to the future outcome of unusually important litigation or regulatory action

        2) A major catastrophe that has had, or continues to have, a significant effect on the entity's financial position

        3) Significant transactions with related parties

        4) Unusually important subsequent events

2. An **other-matter** paragraph is used in the auditor's report to draw users' attention to any matter relevant to users' understanding of the **auditor's (a) audit, (b) responsibilities, or (c) report**.

    a. The other matter is **not** required to be presented or disclosed in the financial statements.

        1) The paragraph also does **not**

            a) Include information required to be provided by management.
            b) State a basis for expressing a qualified or an adverse opinion.

        2) But an other-matter paragraph may be used to explain why an auditor cannot withdraw from the engagement.

    b.   The paragraph should be titled **Other Matter** or use another appropriate heading.

        1)   The auditor normally includes this paragraph immediately after the opinion paragraph and any emphasis-of-matter paragraph.

        2)   However, conditions may warrant placing the other-matter paragraph elsewhere in the auditor's report.

            a)   For example, the content of the other-matter paragraph may be relevant to the section of the report addressing other legal and regulatory requirements.

    c.   Certain auditing standards require the auditor to include an other-matter paragraph. These sections are covered in various study units and include the following:

        1)   AU-C 560, *Subsequent Events and Subsequently Discovered Facts* -- If the auditor's opinion on revised financial statements changes after the original report date, the new report should include either an emphasis-of-matter or other-matter paragraph.

        2)   AU-C 700, *Forming an Opinion and Reporting on Financial Statements* -- If prior-period financial statements presented in comparative form were (a) audited by a predecessor auditor or (b) reviewed or compiled and the report is not reissued, the auditor should include an other-matter paragraph.

        3)   AU-C 720, *Other Information in Documents Containing Audited Financial Statements* -- Material inconsistencies in the other information presented along with audited financial statements require the auditor to include an other-matter paragraph.

        4)   AU-C 725, *Supplementary Information in Relation to the Financial Statements as a Whole* -- The auditor may report on the supplementary information in an other-matter paragraph or in a separate report.

        5)   AU-C 730, *Required Supplementary Information* -- The auditor reports on the required supplementary information in an other-matter paragraph in the report.

        6)   AU-C 800, *Special Considerations—Audits of Financial Statements Prepared in Accordance With Special Purpose Frameworks* -- If a report on such financial statements restricts the use of the report, it should contain an other-matter paragraph.

        7)   AU-C 806, *Reporting on Compliance With Aspects of Contractual Agreements or Regulatory Requirements in Connection With Audited Financial Statements* -- If a report on compliance is included in the auditor's report on the financial statements, the compliance report should be presented in an other-matter paragraph.

    d.   An auditor who expects to include an emphasis-of-matter or other-matter paragraph in the report should communicate with those charged with governance regarding this expectation and the proposed wording of any paragraph.

3.   **Summary of Paragraphs that Draw Attention to Certain Matters**

	Emphasis of Matter	Other Matter
Relation to statements	Issue appropriately presented or disclosed in the statements	Issue not presented or disclosed in the statements
Standard for use	Fundamental to users' understanding of the statements	Relevant to users' understanding of the auditor's audit, responsibilities, or report

Stop and review! You have completed the outline for this subunit. Study multiple-choice questions 17 through 20 beginning on page 367.

QUESTIONS

17.1 Group Audits and Component Auditors

1. Pell, CPA, is the group engagement partner in the audit of the financial statements of Tech Consolidated, Inc. Smith, CPA, audits one of Tech's subsidiaries. In which situation(s) should Pell refer to Smith's audit?

I.   Pell reviews Smith's audit documentation and assumes responsibility for Smith's work but expresses a qualified opinion on Tech's financial statements.

II. Pell is unable to review Smith's audit documentation but reads the financial statements and gains an understanding that Smith has an excellent reputation for professional competence and integrity.

A. I only.

B. II only.

C. Both I and II.

D. Neither I nor II.

Answer (B) is correct.
   REQUIRED: The situation, if any, in which a group auditor should refer to a component auditor's audit.
   DISCUSSION: Regardless of the decision to make reference, the group engagement team should obtain an understanding of the component auditor's professional competence and compliance with ethical requirements (especially independence). The understanding also addresses (1) the extent of the team's involvement in the component auditor's work, (2) whether (s)he operates under regulatory oversight, and (3) whether the team will be able to obtain information about the consolidation process from the component auditor. Serious concerns about (1) compliance with ethical requirements or (2) lack of competence preclude a reference to the audit of the component auditor. Moreover, the group engagement partner's assumption of responsibility for the component auditor's audit indicates a decision not to refer to the audit of the component auditor.
   Answer (A) is incorrect. Assumption of responsibility reflects a decision not to refer. Answer (C) is incorrect. Assumption of responsibility reflects a decision not to refer. Answer (D) is incorrect. The component auditor's (1) compliance with ethical requirements and (2) professional competence generally permit a reference.

2. An auditor may issue an unmodified audit report when the

A. Auditor refers to the findings of an auditor's specialist.

B. Financial statements are derived from audited financial statements but contain less detail.

C. Financial statements are prepared on the cash receipts and disbursements basis of accounting chosen by management.

D. Group engagement partner assumes responsibility for the work of a component auditor.

Answer (D) is correct.
   REQUIRED: The situation in which an auditor's report may be unmodified.
   DISCUSSION: If the group engagement partner assumes responsibility for the work of the component auditor, the component auditor is not referred to in the report on the group financial statements.
   Answer (A) is incorrect. The auditor does not refer to an auditor's specialist unless (s)he departs from an unmodified opinion. Answer (B) is incorrect. The report on summary financial statements varies in many respects, e.g., it identifies the summary financial statements and the audited financial statements. Answer (C) is incorrect. A modification of the report is appropriate. The cash basis generally is not an acceptable reporting framework.

3. In which of the following situations will a group auditor be most likely to refer to a component auditor who audited a subsidiary of the entity?

A. The component auditor performed an audit in accordance with PCAOB standards.

B. The component auditor issued a restricted use report.

C. The financial statements audited by the component auditor are prepared using a financial reporting framework different from that used in the group statements.

D. The component auditor is not independent.

Answer (A) is correct.
   REQUIRED: The situation in which a group auditor is most likely to refer to a component auditor.
   DISCUSSION: The group engagement partner may not refer to the audit of the component auditor unless the component auditor performed an audit in accordance with (1) GAAS or (2), if required by law or regulation, PCAOB auditing standards.
   Answer (B) is incorrect. Reference to the audit of the component auditor is not made unless the component auditor has issued an unrestricted report. Answer (C) is incorrect. When the reporting frameworks differ, no reference is made unless certain conditions are met. Moreover, the group auditor's report should disclose that responsibility is taken for evaluating the adjustments needed to convert from one framework to the other. Answer (D) is incorrect. When the component auditor is not independent or the group engagement team has serious concerns about other ethical issues or professional competence, no reference is made.

17.2 Consistency of Financial Statements

4. The following additional paragraph was included in an auditor's report to indicate a lack of consistency:

"As discussed in note T to the financial statements, the company changed its method of computing depreciation in Year 1."

How should the auditor report on this matter if the auditor concurred with the change?

	Type of Opinion	Location of Additional Paragraph
A.	Unmodified	Before Opinion paragraph
B.	Unmodified	After Opinion paragraph
C.	Qualified	Before Opinion paragraph
D.	Qualified	After Opinion paragraph

Answer (B) is correct.
REQUIRED: The reporting of a lack of consistency.
DISCUSSION: A change in accounting principle meeting certain criteria and having a material effect on the financial statements requires the auditor to refer to the change in an emphasis-of-matter paragraph of the report. This paragraph should follow the opinion paragraph, describe the change, and refer to the entity's disclosure.

5. For which of the following events would an auditor issue a report that omits any reference to a change in accounting principle or correction of a material misstatement?

A. A change in the method of accounting for inventories.

B. A change from an accounting principle that is not in accordance with the applicable reporting framework to one that is.

C. A change in the useful life used to calculate the provision for depreciation expense.

D. Management's lack of reasonable justification for a material change in accounting principle.

Answer (C) is correct.
REQUIRED: The event not requiring a reference to a change in accounting principle or correction of a material misstatement in the auditor's report.
DISCUSSION: A change in estimate is neither a change in accounting principle nor the correction of a material misstatement in previously issued financial statements. Thus, it requires no modification of the opinion or other recognition in the report. However, an exception is a change in estimate that is inseparable from a change in principle. The auditor evaluates and reports on this change as a change in principle.
Answer (A) is incorrect. A change in the method of accounting for inventory, for example, from FIFO to LIFO, is a change in accounting principle. It requires an emphasis-of-matter paragraph in the auditor's report that describes the new accounting guidance. Answer (B) is incorrect. A correction of a material misstatement, e.g., a change from an accounting principle that is not in accordance with the applicable reporting framework to one that is, requires an emphasis-of-matter paragraph that includes a statement that previously issued statements have been restated to correct a material misstatement. Answer (D) is incorrect. Lack of justification for a material change in accounting principle requires the auditor to express a qualified or an adverse opinion. The basis for modification paragraph describes the matter.

6. When the auditor concurs with a change in accounting principle that materially affects the comparability of the comparative financial statements, the auditor should

	Concur Explicitly with the Change	Express a Qualified Opinion	Refer to the Change in an Additional Paragraph
A.	No	No	Yes
B.	Yes	No	Yes
C.	Yes	Yes	No
D.	No	Yes	No

Answer (A) is correct.
REQUIRED: The appropriate report when the auditor concurs with a change in accounting principle.
DISCUSSION: A material change in accounting principle raises a consistency issue. Thus, a report with an emphasis-of-matter paragraph is required if the auditor's evaluation concludes that certain criteria have been met: (1) the new principle and the method of accounting for it are in accordance with the applicable framework, (2) related disclosures are appropriate, and (3) the entity has justified that the principle is preferable. The opinion is modified for a material change in principle only if the criteria are not met. Furthermore, the auditor's concurrence is implied by the inclusion of an emphasis-of-matter paragraph. This paragraph is included only if the opinion is not modified with regard to the matter.

7. When management does **not** provide reasonable justification for a change in accounting principle, and it presents comparative financial statements, the auditor should express a qualified opinion

    A. Only in the year of the accounting principle change.

    B. Each year that the financial statements initially reflecting the change are presented.

    C. Each year until management changes back to the accounting principle formerly used.

    D. Only if the change is to an accounting principle that is not generally accepted.

Answer (B) is correct.
    REQUIRED: The year(s) or circumstance in which an unjustified accounting change requires a qualified opinion.
    DISCUSSION: If (1) the new principle and the method of accounting for the effect of the change are in accordance with the applicable reporting framework, (2) disclosures are adequate, and (3) the entity has justified that the principle is preferable, the auditor expresses an unmodified opinion. Otherwise, if the change is material, the misstatement results in expression of a qualified or an adverse opinion in the report for the year of change. A basis for modified opinion paragraph is added preceding the opinion paragraph. In the period of the change, the auditor also must add an emphasis-of-matter paragraph following the opinion paragraph to reflect the inconsistency. This paragraph is required in reports on financial statements in the period of change and in subsequent periods until the new principle is applied in all periods presented.

17.3 Uncertainties and Going Concern

8. An auditor most likely will express an unmodified opinion and will not add additional language to the report if the auditor

    A. Wishes to emphasize that the entity had significant transactions with related parties.

    B. Concurs with the entity's change in its method of computing depreciation.

    C. Discovers that supplementary information required by FASB has been omitted.

    D. Believes that there is a remote likelihood of a material loss resulting from an uncertainty.

Answer (D) is correct.
    REQUIRED: The condition under which an additional paragraph is not added to the report.
    DISCUSSION: Normally, an uncertainty does not require the auditor to add a paragraph to the report.
    Answer (A) is incorrect. Emphasis of a matter is accomplished with an additional paragraph added to the auditor's report. Answer (B) is incorrect. A change in the depreciation method is a change in estimate inseparable from a change in principle. If material, the change in principle requires an emphasis-of-matter paragraph. Answer (C) is incorrect. AU-C 730 requires the auditor to add an other-matter paragraph when supplementary information that is required by FASB or GASB has been omitted.

9. Management believes, and the auditor is satisfied, that a material loss probably will occur when pending litigation is resolved. Management is unable to make a reasonable estimate of the amount or range of the potential loss but fully discloses the situation in the notes to the financial statements. If management does not make an accrual in the financial statements, the auditor should express a(n)

    A. Qualified opinion due to a scope limitation.

    B. Qualified opinion due to a material misstatement.

    C. Unmodified opinion with an emphasis-of-matter paragraph.

    D. Unmodified opinion with no additional paragraph in the auditor's report.

Answer (D) is correct.
    REQUIRED: The auditor's reporting when a material loss is probable but not subject to estimation.
    DISCUSSION: If the auditor concludes that sufficient appropriate evidence supports management's assertions about the nature of a matter involving an uncertainty, an unmodified report is ordinarily appropriate.
    Answer (A) is incorrect. Inability to make a reasonable estimate of the potential loss is not a scope limitation. Answer (B) is incorrect. No material misstatement exists, an accrual of the loss contingency is not required in these circumstances, and full disclosure has been made. Thus, no report modification should be made. Answer (C) is incorrect. No basis for including an emphasis-of-matter paragraph to the report is given.

10. When an auditor concludes that substantial doubt exists about an entity's ability to continue as a going concern for a reasonable period of time, the auditor's responsibility is to

A. Prepare prospective financial information to verify whether management's plans can be effectively implemented.

B. Project future conditions and events for a period of time not to exceed 1 year following the date of the financial statements.

C. Express a qualified or adverse opinion, depending on materiality, because of the possible effects on the financial statements.

D. Consider the adequacy of disclosure about the entity's possible inability to continue as a going concern.

Answer (D) is correct.
REQUIRED: The auditor's responsibility given a substantial doubt about an entity's ability to continue as a going concern.
DISCUSSION: If the auditor reaches this conclusion after (1) identifying conditions and events that create such doubt and (2) evaluating management's plans to mitigate their effects, (s)he should consider the adequacy of disclosure and include an emphasis-of-matter paragraph (after the opinion paragraph) in the report that includes the words "substantial doubt" and "going concern." If disclosure is inadequate, the material misstatement requires modification of the opinion. By itself, however, the substantial doubt does not require a modified opinion paragraph or a disclaimer of opinion.
Answer (A) is incorrect. The auditor should consider management's plans but need not prepare prospective financial information. Answer (B) is incorrect. The auditor is not responsible for predicting future conditions or events. Answer (C) is incorrect. The opinion is not modified solely for a going-concern issue.

11. An auditor's report included the following paragraph relative to substantial doubt about a client's ability to continue as a going concern:

"The accompanying financial statements have been prepared assuming that the Company will continue as a going concern. If the Company is not able to renew the contract described in Note X, there may be substantial doubt about the company's ability to continue as a going concern."

Which of the following statements is true?

A. The paragraph should not refer to a note to the financial statements.

B. The report should not contain conditional language.

C. The report should refer to a qualification of the opinion.

D. The report should not use the phrase "substantial doubt."

Answer (B) is correct.
REQUIRED: The true statement about a report addressing a client's ability to continue as a going concern.
DISCUSSION: The report should not contain conditional language. "If the Company is not able to renew the contract . . ." is not permissible language.
Answer (A) is incorrect. The report may refer to a note that describes the issues. Answer (C) is incorrect. The opinion should not be qualified for a going-concern doubt. Rather, an emphasis-of-matter paragraph should be included in the report. Answer (D) is incorrect. The report should include the phrases "substantial doubt" and "going concern."

12. Green, CPA, concludes that there is substantial doubt about JKL Co.'s ability to continue as a going concern. If JKL's financial statements adequately disclose its financial difficulties, Green's auditor's report should

	Include a Paragraph Following the Opinion Paragraph	Specifically Use the Words "Going Concern"	Specifically Use the Words "Substantial Doubt"
A.	Yes	Yes	Yes
B.	Yes	Yes	No
C.	Yes	No	Yes
D.	No	Yes	Yes

Answer (A) is correct.
REQUIRED: The effect of a substantial doubt about the going-concern assumption.
DISCUSSION: An evaluation should be made as to whether substantial doubt exists about the entity's ability to continue as a going concern for a reasonable period of time (U.S. GAAP is 1 year from the date the statements are released or available to be released). If the auditor reaches this conclusion after identifying conditions and events that create such doubt and after evaluating management's plans to reduce their effects, (s)he should consider the possible effects on the statements and the adequacy of disclosure. (S)he also should include an emphasis-of-matter paragraph (after the opinion paragraph) in the report. The auditor should use language in the emphasis-of-matter paragraph that includes the phrases "substantial doubt" and "going concern." Also, the emphasis-of-matter paragraph should not use conditional language in expressing its conclusion about the existence of a substantial doubt. The substantial doubt is not a basis for a qualified or an adverse opinion, but a disclaimer is not precluded in the case of such a material uncertainty.

17.4 Comparative Financial Statements

13. When a predecessor auditor reissues the report on the prior period's financial statements at the request of the former client, the predecessor should

A. Indicate in the introductory paragraph of the reissued report that the financial statements of the subsequent period were audited by another CPA.

B. Obtain a representation letter from the auditor but not from management.

C. Compare the prior period's financial statements that the predecessor reported on with the financial statements to be presented for comparative purposes.

D. Add an additional paragraph to the reissued report stating that the predecessor has not performed additional auditing procedures on the prior period's financial statements.

Answer (C) is correct.
REQUIRED: The procedure performed by the predecessor auditor before reissuing a report.
DISCUSSION: The predecessor auditor should perform certain procedures before reissuing a report on prior-period financial statements. (S)he should (1) read the current period's financial statements, (2) compare the prior and current financial statements, (3) obtain a representation letter from the auditor stating whether (s)he has discovered matters having a material effect on (or requiring disclosure in) the statements reported on by the predecessor auditor, and (4) obtain a representation letter from management confirming past representations and stating whether post-balance-sheet events require adjustment of or disclosure in the financial statements.
Answer (A) is incorrect. The reissued report should not refer to another auditor. Answer (B) is incorrect. The predecessor auditor should obtain a representation letter from the auditor and from management. Answer (D) is incorrect. The report should not be modified unless the auditor's previous conclusions have changed.

14. When reporting on comparative financial statements, an auditor ordinarily should change the previously expressed opinion on the prior year's financial statements if the

A. Prior year's financial statements are restated to correct a material misstatement.

B. Auditor is a predecessor auditor who has been requested by a former client to reissue the previously issued report.

C. Prior year's opinion was unmodified and the opinion on the current year's financial statements is modified due to a change in accounting principle.

D. Reporting entity has changed as a result of the sale of a subsidiary.

Answer (A) is correct.
REQUIRED: The event that causes an auditor to change a previously expressed opinion.
DISCUSSION: If the previous opinion was modified because of a material misstatement, but the prior year's statements were restated to remove the basis for the modification, the updated report should express an unmodified opinion. The auditor's report should include an emphasis-of-matter paragraph that (1) states that the previously issued financial statements have been restated to correct a material misstatement and (2) refers to the entity's disclosure (AU-C 708).
Answer (B) is incorrect. If the predecessor's report is still appropriate, it normally should be reissued without revision. Answer (C) is incorrect. A change in accounting principle in the current period has no effect on the opinion expressed in the prior year. Answer (D) is incorrect. A change in the reporting entity resulting from a transaction or event, for example, a purchase or disposition of a subsidiary, does not require recognition in the auditor's report. Furthermore, such a transaction or event in the current year is not a circumstance that affects the prior period's statements. Thus, it presents no basis for modifying the opinion expressed on those statements.

15. Jewel, CPA, audited Infinite Co.'s prior-year financial statements. These statements are presented with those of the current year for comparative purposes without Jewel's auditor's report, which expressed a qualified opinion. In drafting the current year's auditor's report, the current auditor should

I.   Not name Jewel as the predecessor auditor
II. Indicate the type of opinion expressed by Jewel
III. Indicate the reasons for Jewel's qualification

A. I only.

B. I and II only.

C. II and III only.

D. I, II, and III.

Answer (D) is correct.
REQUIRED: The matter(s) included in an auditor's report.
DISCUSSION: The auditor should state in an other-matter paragraph (following the opinion paragraph and any emphasis-of-matter paragraph) (1) that the prior year's financial statements were audited by another auditor, (2) the date of the report, (3) the type of opinion expressed and the reasons for any modification, and (4) the nature of any emphasis-of-matter or other-matter paragraph. Furthermore, the predecessor auditor is not named.

16. Unaudited financial statements are presented in comparative form with audited financial statements in a document filed with the Securities and Exchange Commission. In accordance with the PCAOB's Auditing Standards, such statements should be

	Marked as "Unaudited"	Withheld until Audited	Referred to in the Auditor's Report
A.	Yes	No	No
B.	Yes	No	Yes
C.	No	Yes	Yes
D.	No	Yes	No

Answer (A) is correct.
    REQUIRED: The treatment of unaudited statements presented comparatively with audited statements in a document filed with the SEC.
    DISCUSSION: According to the PCAOB's Auditing Standards, when unaudited financial statements are presented in comparative form with audited statements in documents filed with the SEC, such statements should be clearly marked as "unaudited." They should not be referred to in the auditor's report or withheld until audited. NOTE: The source of authoritative guidance is the PCAOB's Auditing Standards, not the clarified SASs published by the AICPA. The PCAOB Standards apply to services for issuers.

17.5 Emphasis-of-Matter and Other-Matter Paragraphs

17. An other-matter paragraph is included in the auditor's report **except** when

A. The opinion on the prior-period statements has changed.

B. Required supplementary information is presented.

C. A predecessor auditor's report is not reissued.

D. The client has materially restated the prior year's comparative financial statements.

Answer (D) is correct.
    REQUIRED: The purpose for which an other-matter paragraph is inappropriate.
    DISCUSSION: An other-matter paragraph draws attention to a matter not required to be presented or disclosed in the financial statements that is relevant to users' understanding of the auditor's audit, responsibilities, or report. A correction of a material misstatement in previously issued financial statements requires the auditor to include an emphasis-of-matter paragraph. This matter is appropriately presented or disclosed in the financial statements and is fundamental to users' understanding.
    Answer (A) is incorrect. An auditor's opinion on prior-period statements reported on in connection with the current audit may have changed. If so, the auditor should make certain disclosures in an emphasis-of-matter or other-matter paragraph. Answer (B) is incorrect. An auditor should include an other-matter paragraph in the auditor's report to refer to the presentation of required supplementary information. Answer (C) is incorrect. The auditor should include an other-matter paragraph in the auditor's report when prior-period statements presented comparatively with the current period's statements were audited by a predecessor auditor whose report is not reissued.

18. In which situation is the auditor most likely **not** to include an emphasis-of-matter paragraph in the auditor's report?

A. An important audit procedure was performed.

B. The client suffered a major catastrophe.

C. Significant transactions with related parties were recorded.

D. Unusually important subsequent events occurred.

Answer (A) is correct.
    REQUIRED: The situation in which an emphasis-of-matter paragraph is not included in the auditor's report.
    DISCUSSION: An emphasis-of-matter paragraph is not used to describe an audit procedure. It is used to draw attention to a matter appropriately presented or disclosed in the financial statements that is fundamental to users' understanding. The following are examples of circumstances in which the auditor may need to include an emphasis-of-matter paragraph: (1) an uncertainty relating to the future outcome of unusually important litigation or regulatory action; (2) a major catastrophe that has had, or continues to have, a significant effect on the entity's financial position; (3) significant transactions with related parties; and (4) unusually important subsequent events.

19. An emphasis-of-matter paragraph is used in the auditor's report to draw users' attention to

    A. A material misstatement.

    B. A matter that is not presented or disclosed in the financial statements that is relevant to users' understanding of the audit.

    C. A matter that management wishes to highlight.

    D. A matter appropriately presented or disclosed in the financial statements.

Answer (D) is correct.

REQUIRED: The use of an emphasis-of-matter paragraph.

DISCUSSION: An emphasis-of-matter paragraph is used in the auditor's report to draw users' attention to a matter appropriately presented or disclosed in the financial statements that is fundamental to users' understanding of the financial statements.

Answer (A) is incorrect. A material misstatement requires a qualified or adverse opinion. Answer (B) is incorrect. An other-matter paragraph draws attention to a matter not required to be presented or disclosed in the financial statements that is relevant to users' understanding of the auditor's audit, responsibilities, or report. Answer (C) is incorrect. The auditor, not management, determines the content of the auditor's report.

20. A nonissuer's unaudited financial statements for the prior period are presented in comparative form with audited financial statements for the subsequent year. If the prior-period statements were reviewed,

I.   The report on the unaudited financial statements should be reissued.

II.   The report on the audited financial statements should include an other-matter paragraph.

    A. I only.

    B. II only.

    C. Neither I nor II.

    D. Either I or II.

Answer (D) is correct.

REQUIRED: The appropriate reporting when the prior-period's unaudited financial statements of a nonissuer are presented in comparative form with current-period audited financial statements.

DISCUSSION: A nonissuer's audited statements for the current period may be presented comparatively with the prior period's reviewed or compiled statements. If the prior period's report is not reissued, the auditor's current-period report should include an other-matter paragraph that states (1) the service performed in the prior period, (2) the date of the service, (3) a description of material modifications noted in the report, and (4) that the service was not an audit and did not provide a basis for an opinion (AU-C 700).

Access the Gleim CPA Premium Review System featuring SmartAdapt for exam-emulating multiple-choice questions and simulations with detailed answer explanations.

Learn more: gleim.com/CPApremium | 800.874.5346

STUDY UNIT EIGHTEEN
RELATED REPORTING TOPICS

(22 pages of outline)

This study unit addresses miscellaneous reporting issues. Subunit 18.1 applies the relevant standards to a review of interim (e.g., quarterly) financial information. The procedures and the report are similar to those of a review of annual statements of nonissuers (discussed in Study Unit 19). Subunits 18.2 and 18.3 relate to SEC engagements. The next four subunits (18.4 through 18.7) apply to information outside the basic financial statements. Subunit 18.8 addresses the auditor's responsibilities for financial statements prepared for use in other countries. Subunit 18.9 includes material about the accountant's responsibility when requested to provide an evaluation of, or a conclusion on, how accounting principles will be applied to specific transactions of a particular entity. Subunit 18.10 relates to audits of statements prepared in accordance with a special purpose framework (e.g., the tax basis or the cash basis). Subunit 18.11 addresses audits of historical information in the form of single statements or specific elements, accounts, or items. These may be prepared in accordance with a general or special purpose framework.

18.1 INTERIM FINANCIAL INFORMATION

1. Interim financial information (IFI) covers a period of (a) less than a full year or (b) the 12 months ending on a date other than fiscal year end.

   a. The IFI may be in the form of a complete set of statements.

      1) The applicable financial reporting framework (**framework**) should be the same one used in the annual statements.

         a) For example, the framework adopted by management may be U.S. GAAP, International Financial Reporting Standards, or a special purpose framework.

   b. The IFI also may be **condensed**.

      1) This IFI should be prepared in accordance with a framework appropriate for condensed IFI. Examples are the interim reporting standards of the FASB, SEC, or IASB.

2.   An auditor may review the IFI of an entity if the latest annual statements have been audited by the auditor or a predecessor. Moreover, the auditor

   a.   Should be engaged to audit the current-year statements, or

   b.   Should have audited the latest annual statements, if the successor auditor's engagement is not yet effective.

   NOTE: "Auditor" is used in this standard because the review of IFI is performed by an auditor of the annual statements.

3.   **Objective of a Review**

   a.   The objective of a review of IFI is to enable the auditor to state whether (s)he is aware of any material modifications needed for the IFI to be in accordance with the framework (also known as negative assurance).

   b.   A review primarily involves performing analytical and inquiry procedures. It does **not** involve (1) testing accounting records and the effectiveness of controls, (2) obtaining corroborating evidence, (3) applying certain other auditing procedures, or (4) becoming aware of all significant matters identified in an audit.

   c.   Thus, a review is **not** intended to (1) result in expression of an opinion, (2) provide assurance about internal control, or (3) identify significant deficiencies and material weaknesses in internal control (but these should be communicated to those charged with governance if identified).

4.   **Acceptance of Engagement**

   a.   Prior to acceptance, the auditor should request that management authorize the predecessor to fully respond to inquiries. (S)he should (1) evaluate the responses or (2) consider the implications if management refuses to authorize the predecessor to respond.

   b.   Also prior to engagement acceptance, the auditor should (1) determine that the framework is acceptable and (2) obtain an agreement with management about its responsibilities.

5.   **Agreement with Management**

   a.   Management is responsible for (1) fair presentation of IFI in accordance with the framework, (2) internal control that provides a reasonable basis for fair presentation, (3) giving the auditor unrestricted access to relevant information and persons within the entity, (4) including the report in any document containing IFI that indicates the IFI has been reviewed by the auditor, (5) providing a representation letter, and (6) adjusting the IFI for material misstatements.

      1)   The auditor's responsibility is to comply with applicable GAAS.

   b.   The agreement should include (1) the objectives, scope, and limitations of the engagement; (2) the responsibilities of management and the auditor; and (3) identification of the framework.

      1)   The agreement should be written, for example, in an **engagement letter**.

6.   **Auditor's Understanding of the Entity**

   a.   The auditor's understanding of the entity and its environment, including its **internal control**, should be sufficient to (1) identify types of misstatements, (2) consider the likelihood of their occurrence, and (3) select inquiries and analytical procedures.

b. This understanding may have been obtained from an audit of the entity's annual statements.

   1) But internal control over annual reporting may differ from that for interim reporting because accounting principles and practices also may differ. For example, IFI is based on estimated effective income tax rates.

      a) Nevertheless, the review is **not** intended to provide assurance about internal control or identify control deficiencies.

      b) However, the auditor cannot complete the review if control deficiencies are so significant that it is not feasible to perform effective review procedures.

c. Procedures to obtain the understanding should include

   1) Reading documentation of the prior audit and of prior reviews. The auditor specifically considers (a) corrected and uncorrected misstatements, (b) identified fraud risks (e.g., of management override), and (c) significant matters of continuing interest (e.g., control weaknesses).

   2) Reading the recent annual information and prior IFI.

   3) Considering current audit results.

   4) Inquiring of management about changes in the business or in internal control.

   5) Inquiring of the predecessor auditor in an initial review and reviewing his or her documentation, if permitted.

7. **Analytical Procedures**

   a. Analytical procedures should be applied to identify unusual relationships and items.

      1) The auditor's expectations developed in a review are less precise than in an audit, and management responses generally are not corroborated. The reasonableness and consistency of the responses are considered.

   b. Analytical procedures should include the following:

      1) Comparing the IFI with comparable information for the preceding interim period, if applicable, and with the corresponding period(s) in the previous year, considering knowledge about changes in the entity's business and specific transactions

      2) Considering plausible relationships among financial and, if relevant, nonfinancial information

      3) Comparing recorded amounts or ratios developed from recorded amounts with expectations developed by the auditor by identifying and using relationships that are reasonably expected to exist based on the auditor's understanding of the entity and the industry in which it operates

      4) Comparing disaggregated revenue data (e.g., monthly revenue of the current interim period with that of comparable prior periods)

8. **Inquiries and Other Procedures**

   a. The following inquiries and other procedures are required:

      1) Reading the minutes of meetings of shareholders, the board, and committees and inquiring about the results of meetings for which minutes are unavailable.

      2) Obtaining reports of auditors who have reviewed IFI of significant components of the entity or its investees. (If their reports are unissued, inquiries should be made.)

          3)   Inquiring of management about the following:

               a)   Unusual or complex situations

               b)   Significant recent transactions

               c)   Status of uncorrected misstatements

               d)   Knowledge of fraud

               e)   Deficiencies in control

               f)   Significant entries and other adjustments

               g)   Questions arising from application of review procedures

               h)   Events subsequent to the date of the IFI

               i)   Communications from regulators

               j)   Preparation of the IFI in accordance with the framework

               k)   Related parties and related party transactions

          4)   Reconciling the IFI and the accounting records.

          5)   Reading the IFI to consider, based on information coming to the auditor's attention, whether it is in accordance with the framework.

          6)   Reading other information accompanying the IFI.

    b.   Inquiries about **litigation, claims, and assessments** and the entity's ability to continue as a **going concern** ordinarily are not made unless the auditor becomes aware of reasons for such inquiries.

          1)   The auditor extends procedures if (s)he believes that the IFI is not in accordance with the framework. The auditor of the annual statements usually performs the review of the IFI and may be able to coordinate the engagements.

    c.   For all IFI and all periods covered, the auditor should request that management provide **written representations** as of the date of the report. Study Unit 14, Subunit 3, contains an example representation letter that addresses most of the same matters.

9. Evaluating Results

    a.   The auditor should **accumulate misstatements** unless they are clearly trivial.

          1)   Misstatements, including inadequate disclosure, are evaluated individually and in the aggregate to determine whether the IFI must be materially modified.

10. Auditor Communications

    a.   Possible matters communicated to management and those charged with governance include (1) the inability to issue a report because the review cannot be completed, (2) any material modifications of the IFI that should be made, (3) the auditor's awareness of material fraud or noncompliance with laws and regulations, (4) significant control deficiencies, and (5) certain other matters required to be communicated to those charged with governance.

    b.   Any discussion of the **quality** of the entity's accounting principles as applied to its interim reports is ordinarily limited to the effects of significant events, transactions, and changes in estimates considered in performing the review.

11. Example Review Report on IFI

    a.   The review report should be in **writing**.

    b.   The report should accompany the IFI if the entity refers to the auditor's review in a report, document, or written communication.

          1)   If management does not comply with a request to include the review report, the auditor should request that his or her name **not be associated** with the IFI or referred to.

    c.   Each page of the IFI must be clearly marked as unaudited.

d.   The auditor modifies the review report for material departures from GAAP or other frameworks. The modification describes the departure and, if feasible, states its effects.

   1)   If disclosure is inadequate, the auditor provides the necessary information.

e.   If modification of the review report is not sufficient to address the deficiencies in the IFI, the auditor should withdraw from the engagement.

EXAMPLE -- Auditor's Review Report

[Appropriate Addressee]

We have reviewed the accompanying [describe the interim financial information or statements reviewed] of ABC Company and subsidiaries as of September 30, 20X1, and for the three-month and nine-month periods then ended.

Management's Responsibility

The Company's management is responsible for the preparation and fair presentation of the interim financial information in accordance with [identify the applicable financial reporting framework; for example, accounting principles generally accepted in the United States of America]; this responsibility includes the design, implementation, and maintenance of internal control sufficient to provide a reasonable basis for the preparation and fair presentation of interim financial information in accordance with the applicable financial reporting framework.

Auditor's Responsibility

Our responsibility is to conduct our review in accordance with auditing standards generally accepted in the United States of America applicable to reviews of interim financial information. A review of interim financial information consists principally of applying analytical procedures and making inquiries of persons responsible for financial and accounting matters. It is substantially less in scope than an audit conducted in accordance with auditing standards generally accepted in the United States of America, the objective of which is the expression of an opinion regarding the financial information. Accordingly, we do not express such an opinion.

Conclusion

Based on our review, we are not aware of any material modifications that should be made to the accompanying interim financial information for it to be in accordance with [identify the applicable financial reporting framework; for example, accounting principles generally accepted in the United States of America].

Auditor's signature
Auditor's city and state
Date of the auditor's report

Stop and review! You have completed the outline for this subunit. Study multiple-choice questions 1 and 2 on page 391.

18.2 LETTERS FOR UNDERWRITERS AND CERTAIN OTHER REQUESTING PARTIES

1.   **Comfort Letters**

   a.   Independent auditors audit financial statements and schedules contained in registration statements filed with the SEC under the Securities Act of 1933. Because underwriters and others may be liable if a registration statement contains material misstatements or omissions, they seek to establish a defense against liability.

   1)   A defense is available under the act if a party demonstrates that a **reasonable investigation** provided reasonable grounds for believing that no material misstatements existed in the securities offering.

   2)   A comfort letter issued by an auditor in connection with a securities offering is one of the various ways of demonstrating that a reasonable investigation was made.

   a)   However, a comfort letter is not required by law and is not filed with the SEC. Furthermore, GAAS do not require an auditor to accept an engagement to issue a comfort letter.

b.   An auditor may issue a comfort letter in connection with financial statements included in a securities offering **only** to requesting parties. A **requesting party** is a specified party that has negotiated an agreement with the entity.

1) An underwriter may be a requesting party. An **underwriter** is a purchaser of an issue of securities for the purpose of public distribution.

2) Among the other requesting parties are those who are conducting a review process consistent with the **due diligence** process performed when a securities offering is registered.

3) A requesting party should provide either (a) a written attorney's opinion stating that the party has a due diligence defense or (b) a suitable representation letter.

a) When a requesting party other than an underwriter requests a comfort letter but does not provide a legal opinion or a representation letter, the auditor should **not** provide negative assurance. However, the comfort letter may describe the procedures that the requesting party asked the auditor to perform.

c.   Because the nature of a reasonable investigation has not been established, only the requesting party can determine what is sufficient. Thus, the assistance provided in a comfort letter is limited.

1) Auditors can comment only on matters to which their expertise is relevant, and the procedures permit the expression of, at most, negative assurance.

2.   **Form and Content**

a.   The letter ordinarily is **dated** on, or shortly after, the date the underwriting agreement is signed. The agreement specifies the cut-off date. Thus, the letter states that the described procedures did **not** cover the period from the cut-off date to the date of the letter.

b.   The letter should be **addressed** only to the requesting party (or that party and the entity) and should not be given to anyone else.

c.   The auditor should refer to, but **not repeat**, the report on the audited statements included in the securities offering.

d.   A typical comfort letter includes a statement about the auditor's **independence**.

e.   A typical comfort letter expresses, if applicable, an opinion on whether audited statements included in the securities offering **comply as to form,** in all material respects, with the applicable accounting requirements of the 1933 act and the related rules and regulations adopted by the SEC.

f.   The requesting party may request the auditor to **repeat** in the comfort letter the report on the audited statements. Because of the significance of the date of the auditor's report, the auditor must **not** agree to the request.

1) Moreover, the auditor must **not** agree to a request to provide **negative assurance** regarding the audit report.

a) Auditors have a statutory responsibility for their opinion as of the effective date of the securities offering. In addition, the significance of negative assurance is unclear, and such assurance might result in misunderstanding.

2) But the auditor should discuss the subject matter of any modification of the report.

3.   **Comments on Other Matters**

a.   The comments on information other than audited statements should describe the procedures performed by the auditor and the criteria specified by the requesting party. The auditor should **not**

1) State or imply that (s)he determined the procedures applied to be necessary or sufficient for the requesting party's purposes.

   2) Use terms of uncertain meaning (e.g., "check," "test," or "general review") unless the procedures are described.

   3) State that nothing else came to the auditor's attention that is of interest to the requesting party.

 b. An auditor should obtain an understanding of the entity's **internal control** when commenting on (1) unaudited IFI (including condensed IFI), (2) capsule information, (3) financial forecasts, or (4) subsequent changes.

   1) But no comment should be made on internal control.

 c. A typical comfort letter includes **negative assurance** on whether, if applicable, **unaudited IFI** included in the registration statement materially complies as to form with the 1933 act and SEC pronouncements.

   1) Moreover, negative assurance may be provided on whether any material modifications should be made to the unaudited IFI for them to conform with the applicable framework.

   2) But the auditor provides negative assurance on unaudited IFI included in the securities offering only if (s)he has performed a **review** in accordance with GAAS.

 d. **Capsule information** is (1) unaudited summarized IFI for periods subsequent to the periods covered by the audited statements or (2) unaudited IFI in the securities offering.

   1) The auditor may provide **negative assurance** on whether the capsule information is in accordance with the applicable framework if (a) the auditor has reviewed the underlying statements in accordance with GAAS and (b) the capsule information meets the framework's disclosure requirements.

 e. The auditor should not comment on **pro forma financial information** unless (s)he has acquired the appropriate level of knowledge. This topic is covered by AT 401, which is discussed in Study Unit 19, Subunit 7.

 f. To apply agreed-upon procedures to a **forecast** and comment on it in a comfort letter, the auditor must perform compilation procedures for a forecast and should attach the report to the comfort letter. Negative assurance on the results of such procedures may **not** be provided. Forecasts are covered by AT 301, which is discussed in Study Unit 19, Subunit 6.

 g. Comments on **subsequent changes** ordinarily apply to whether (1) a change has occurred in capital stock, (2) long-term debt has increased, or (3) other specified financial statement items have decreased during the change period (the period subsequent to the latest financial statements included in the registration statement that ends on the cut-off date).

   1) The auditor is usually requested to read minutes and make inquiries.

 h. A comfort letter should not comment on **tables, statistics, and other financial information** in the securities offering unless the information is (1) expressed in dollars (or percentages derived from such amounts) and obtained from records subject to internal control or (2) derived directly from the accounting records by analysis or computation.

   1) Comments should include (a) an identification of the information, (b) a description of the procedures performed, and (c) the findings.

   2) The term "presents fairly" should not be used.

   3) No comments on the compliance as to form of management's discussion and analysis (MD&A) with SEC rules should be made. Furthermore, no comments should be made on nonfinancial data in MD&A unless the auditor has examined or reviewed the MD&A.

i. The **concluding paragraph** of the comfort letter should state that it is solely for the information of the addressees and to assist the requesting parties with regard to the securities offering.

Stop and review! You have completed the outline for this subunit. Study multiple-choice questions 3 and 4 beginning on page 391.

18.3 FILINGS WITH THE SEC UNDER THE SECURITIES ACT OF 1933

1. **Responsibilities**

    a. **Management** is responsible for the financial representations contained in documents filed under the federal securities statutes.

    b. The **auditor's** responsibility is ordinarily similar to that for other types of reporting, but the statutes specify that responsibility in detail.

        1) For example, the Securities Act of 1933 imposes responsibility for false or misleading statements in an effective registration statement.

        2) The SEC has a **whistleblower** provision for informants other than the auditor. A whistleblower is a person who provides information to the SEC about a possible violation of securities laws. To be considered for an award, a whistleblower must voluntarily provide the SEC with original information that leads to monetary sanctions in excess of $1 million.

    c. The independent auditor has a responsibility as an auditing and accounting **expert** when his or her report is included in a registration statement. The 1933 act states that no person is liable

        1) If (s)he, after **reasonable investigation**, had reasonable grounds to believe that (a) the statements in the registration statement were true, and (b) no material fact required to be stated (or necessary to make the statements not misleading) was omitted.

        2) If the part of the registration statement for which (s)he had responsibility did **not fairly represent** his or her statement as an expert or was not a fair copy of or extract from his or her report or valuation as an expert.

    d. The standard of reasonableness is that required of a prudent individual in the management of his or her own property.

    e. The independent auditor whose report on audited financial statements is included in a registration statement has a statutory responsibility that is determined in light of the circumstances on the **effective date** of the registration statement.

        1) A report based on a review of unaudited interim financial information is **not deemed to be a report** or **part of the registration statement** for this purpose. The SEC requires that the prospectus contain language to this effect.

        2) If unaudited annual statements or unaudited interim information does not conform with the applicable framework, the auditor should request revision.

        3) The SEC requires that registrants obtain reviews of unaudited interim financial information by their independent auditors prior to filing **quarterly reports** in Form 10-Q or Form 10-QSB. But the SEC does not require an entity to include a review report on unaudited interim information in the registration statement if it does not state that the information has been reviewed.

    f. The independent auditor should be certain that his or her name is not being used in a way indicating his or her responsibility is greater than intended.

2. **Subsequent Events Procedures**

    a.   To sustain the burden of proof that the auditor has made a reasonable investigation, subsequent events procedures should be performed at or shortly before the **effective date of the registration statement**. These procedures are intended to identify events occurring between the date of the report and the effective date of the registration statement that require adjustment of, or disclosure in, the financial statements.

    b.   Following the date of the report, the independent auditor may rely mostly on **inquiries**. The auditor should

        1)   Apply the normal subsequent events procedures.

        2)   Read the prospectus and other pertinent portions of the registration statement.

        3)   Obtain written representations from management about whether (a) previous representations should be modified or (b) any events have occurred that require adjustment of, or disclosure in, the financial statements.

    c.   An auditor may have audited the statements for a prior period included in the registration statement but not those for the most recent period included in the registration statement.

        1)   This **predecessor** auditor is responsible for material subsequent events occurring after the date of the prior-period statements through a date at or shortly before the effective date of the registration statement.

    d.   If the auditor becomes aware of **subsequently discovered facts**, (s)he should consider their effect on the report.

        1)   If this consideration is not satisfactory, e.g., because management does not agree to a necessary revision of the statements, the auditor may need to withhold consent to the inclusion of the report.

Stop and review! You have completed the outline for this subunit. Study multiple-choice questions 5 and 6 on page 392.

Overview of the Reporting Responsibilities Covered in the Next Four Subunits

Subunit	AU-C Section	Type of Information/Example	Auditor's Procedures	Reporting Responsibility
18.4	AU-C 720	**Other**/Quarterly data	Read for consistency with financial statements	Add an other-matter paragraph to audit report only if other information is not consistent with financial statements
18.5	AU-C 730	**Required Supplementary**/Oil and gas reserve information	Apply limited procedures	Add an other-matter paragraph to audit report describing the auditor's responsibility
18.6	AU-C 725	**Supplementary in Relation to Statements**/Schedule of fixed assets	Audit	Refer to and report on fair presentation in audit report
18.7	AU-C 810	**Summary Financial Statements**/Summary of financial results	Determine whether consistent with audited financial statements	In a separate report, refer to audit report and state opinion about consistency with complete audited financial statements

18.4 OTHER INFORMATION IN DOCUMENTS CONTAINING AUDITED FINANCIAL STATEMENTS

1. **Other Information**

    a. Other information is financial or nonfinancial information (other than the financial statements and the auditor's report) that is included in a document containing audited statements and the auditor's report.

        1) An example of such a document is an annual report to owners.

        2) Examples of other information are reports by management on operations, financial summaries, and quarterly data.

        3) Examples of items that are not other information are press releases and analysts' briefings.

    b. "Other information" is a technical term that excludes information required to be included by a designated accounting standards setter.

        1) Thus, required supplementary information (RSI) is not other information. RSI is covered in the next subunit.

2. **Auditor's Objective**

    a. The auditor's responsibility is to respond appropriately when the other information may undermine the credibility of the statements and the auditor's report. However, unless otherwise required for a specific engagement, the opinion on the statements does not cover other information.

        1) Also, the auditor has no responsibility for determining whether it is properly stated.

3. **Material Inconsistencies**

    a. The auditor should read the other information to identify material inconsistencies with the audited statements.

        1) An inconsistency is a conflict with the audited information. It may create doubt regarding the audit conclusions.

        2) The auditor need not refer to the other information in the auditor's report. But (s)he may **disclaim** an opinion on it in an **other-matter** paragraph.

    b. A material inconsistency may be identified **prior** to the report release date that requires revision of the **audited statements**. If management refuses, the auditor should modify the opinion.

    c. A material inconsistency may be identified **prior** to the report release date that requires revision of the **other information**.

        1) If management refuses to revise the other information, the auditor should consult legal counsel.

        2) The auditor also should communicate the matter to those charged with governance and

            a) Include an other-matter paragraph in the auditor's report,
            b) Withhold the auditor's report, or
            c) Withdraw from the engagement.

    d. If a material inconsistency is identified **after** the report release date, and revision is needed, the guidance for subsequent discovery of facts existing at the report date applies.

    NOTE: The outline for subsequently discovered facts is in Study Unit 14, Subunit 2.

4. **Material Misstatements of Fact**

   a. A misstatement of fact is other information that is **unrelated** to matters in the audited statements and is incorrectly stated or presented.

      1) When management refuses to correct a material misstatement of fact, the auditor should notify those charged with governance. (S)he also should take any appropriate further action (e.g., consulting counsel, withholding the report, or withdrawing).

Stop and review! You have completed the outline for this subunit. Study multiple-choice questions 7 and 8 on page 393.

18.5 REQUIRED SUPPLEMENTARY INFORMATION (RSI)

1. RSI is information that the designated accounting standards setter has determined must accompany the basic financial statements.

   a. Thus, authoritative guidelines for its measurement and presentation have been prescribed.

2. **Procedures**

   a. The auditor should perform the following procedures:

      1) Inquire about

         a) Whether the RSI is within the guidelines,

         b) Whether methods of measurement or presentation have changed and the reasons for any change, and

         c) Any significant assumptions or interpretations.

      2) Compare the RSI for **consistency** with (a) the basic statements, (b) management's responses to inquiries, and (c) other audit evidence.

      3) Obtain management's **written representations** relevant to its responsibilities for RSI and compliance with guidelines.

3. **Reporting**

   a. The auditor should add an **other-matter** paragraph (following the opinion paragraph and any emphasis-of-matter paragraph) to the auditor's report to refer to RSI. If (1) RSI is not omitted, (2) prescribed guidelines are followed, and (3) required audit procedures are completed, the paragraph should include the following:

      1) A statement that identifies the RSI and the applicable reporting framework

      2) A statement that such information, although not part of the basic financial statements, is required to place them in context

      3) A statement that the auditor has applied certain limited procedures to the RSI in accordance with U.S. GAAS and a description of those procedures

      4) A statement that the auditor does not express an opinion or provide any assurance on the information and that limited procedures provide insufficient evidence

b.   The following is an example of an other-matter paragraph added to the auditor's report:

EXAMPLE -- Other-Matter Paragraph

Other Matter

[Identify the applicable financial reporting framework (for example, accounting principles generally accepted in the United States of America)] require that the [identify the required supplementary information] on page XX be presented to supplement the basic financial statements. Such information, although not a part of the basic financial statements, is required by [identify designated accounting standards setter] who considers it to be an essential part of financial reporting for placing the basic financial statements in an appropriate operational, economic, or historical context. We have applied certain limited procedures to the required supplementary information in accordance with auditing standards generally accepted in the United States of America, which consisted of inquiries of management about the methods of preparing the information and comparing the information for consistency with management's responses to our inquiries, the basic financial statements, and other knowledge we obtained during our audit of the basic financial statements. We do not express an opinion or provide any assurance on the information because the limited procedures do not provide us with sufficient evidence to express an opinion or provide any assurance.

---

c.   The paragraph should be revised when

1)   Some or all RSI is omitted,
2)   Measurement or presentation departs materially from prescribed guidelines or the auditor has unresolved doubts regarding such matters, or
3)   The auditor is unable to complete the prescribed procedures.

d.   Deficiencies in, or omissions of, RSI do not affect the opinion on the basic financial statements, and the auditor need not present the information if management fails to do so.

Stop and review! You have completed the outline for this subunit. Study multiple-choice question 9 on page 393.

18.6 SUPPLEMENTARY INFORMATION IN RELATION TO THE FINANCIAL STATEMENTS AS A WHOLE

1.   Supplementary information **(SI)** is presented outside the basic statements and is not necessary for the statements to be fairly presented in accordance with the applicable financial reporting framework.

a.   Examples include summaries extracted from the financial statements and statistical data.

2.   **Conditions for Reporting**

a.   An auditor ordinarily does not report on SI but may be engaged to do so.

b.   An auditor who is engaged to report on whether SI is fairly stated, in all material respects, in relation to the statements as a whole should determine that certain conditions are satisfied:

1)   The SI is derived directly from the underlying records used to prepare the statements and relates to the same period.
2)   The financial statements were audited, and the auditor issued a report that did not express an adverse opinion or disclaim an opinion.
3)   The SI will accompany the audited statements or be made readily available without further action by the entity (e.g., on the entity's website).

3.   **Agreement with Management**

a.   Management should understand its responsibilities for

1)   Preparing SI in accordance with applicable criteria,
2)   Providing written representations, and
3)   Including the auditor's report on the SI with the SI and the audited statements.

4. **Procedures**

   a. The following procedures to express an opinion on the SI are performed based on the **materiality level** used for the audit of the statements:

      1) Inquiring about the purpose of, and criteria for, the SI
      2) Determining conformity with the criteria
      3) Understanding methods of preparation
      4) Reconciling SI with underlying records or the statements
      5) Inquiring about significant assumptions or interpretations
      6) Evaluating the appropriateness and completeness of the SI
      7) Obtaining management's written representations about (a) responsibility for, and fairness of, presentation; (b) whether methods of measurement or presentation have changed; (c) assumptions or interpretations; and (d) ready availability of the SI

   b. The auditor need not perform **subsequent events** procedures on the SI.

5. **Reporting**

   a. When the SI and the audited statements are presented together, the auditor reports on the SI in (1) a separate report or (2) an other-matter paragraph following the opinion paragraph and any emphasis-of-matter paragraph. The following is an example of an other-matter paragraph:

EXAMPLE -- Other-Matter Paragraph for Supplementary Information
in Relation to the Financial Statements as a Whole

Other Matter

Our audit was conducted for the purpose of forming an opinion on the financial statements as a whole. The *[identify accompanying supplementary information]* is presented for purposes of additional analysis and is not a required part of the financial statements. Such information is the responsibility of management and was derived from and relates directly to the underlying accounting and other records used to prepare the financial statements. The information has been subjected to the auditing procedures applied in the audit of the financial statements and certain additional procedures, including comparing and reconciling such information directly to the underlying accounting and other records used to prepare the financial statements or to the financial statements themselves, and other additional procedures in accordance with auditing standards generally accepted in the United States of America. In our opinion, the information is fairly stated in all material respects in relation to the financial statements as a whole.

---

      1) If the SI and the audited statements are presented separately, a separate report should be issued.

6. The guidance above also applies, with any needed wording changes, when an auditor reports on whether RSI is fairly stated, in all material respects, in relation to the financial statements as a whole.

Stop and review! You have completed the outline for this subunit. Study multiple-choice questions 10 and 11 on page 394.

18.7 ENGAGEMENTS TO REPORT ON SUMMARY FINANCIAL STATEMENTS

1. This subunit addresses the auditor's responsibilities when reporting separately on summary financial statements. Such statements consist of historical information derived from financial statements audited in accordance with GAAS by the same auditor.

2. The auditor's objectives include forming an opinion on whether the summary statements are consistent, in all material respects, with the audited statements from which they are derived.

   a. This determination includes evaluating whether the summary statements are prepared in accordance with the criteria applied by management.

    b.   The auditor also should

        1)   Perform procedures necessary to form an opinion and

        2)   Clearly express that opinion through a written report that describes the basis for the opinion.

3.   The auditor should not accept an engagement to report on summary statements unless (s)he has been engaged to audit the statements from which they are derived.

4.   **Procedures**

    a.   The auditor should perform the following procedures:

        1)   Evaluate whether the summary statements (a) adequately disclose their nature and (b) identify the audited statements.

        2)   Evaluate whether the summary statements adequately disclose the applied criteria.

        3)   Determine whether the summary statements agree with, or can be recalculated from, the related information in the audited statements.

        4)   Evaluate whether the summary statements are prepared in accordance with the applied criteria.

        5)   Given the purpose of the summary statements, evaluate whether they (a) contain the necessary information and (b) are at an appropriate level of aggregation so that they are not misleading.

        6)   Request management to provide written representations in the form of a representation letter addressed to the auditor.

    b.   When the summary statements are not accompanied by the audited statements, the auditor should evaluate whether

        1)   They clearly describe where the audited statements are available, and

        2)   The audited statements are readily available to the intended users of the summary statements without further action by the entity, e.g., on a website.

            a)   They are not considered readily available if a request must be made by the user.

5.   **Opinion**

    a.   When an **unmodified** opinion on the summary statements is appropriate, the opinion should state that they are consistent, in all material respects, with the audited statements in accordance with the applied criteria.

        1)   If they are not, and management does not agree to the necessary changes, the auditor should express an **adverse** opinion.

            a)   The opinion paragraph should state that, because of the significance of the matter(s) described in the basis for adverse opinion paragraph, the summary statements are not consistent, in all material respects, with the audited statements.

            b)   A qualified opinion on summary statements is **not** appropriate.

    b.   When the auditor's report on the **audited statements** contains an **adverse** opinion or a **disclaimer** of opinion, the auditor should withdraw from the engagement.

    c.   If the auditor's report on the audited statements contains (1) a qualified opinion, (2) an emphasis-of-matter paragraph, or (3) an other-matter paragraph, the report on the summary statements should so state. Furthermore, it should describe the following:

        1)   The basis for the qualified opinion or additional paragraph in the report on the audited statements

        2)   The effect on the summary financial statements, if any

    d.   The auditor should **date** the auditor's report on the summary statements no earlier than (1) the date on which the auditor has obtained sufficient appropriate evidence on which to base the opinion and (2) the date of the auditor's report on the audited statements.

6.   **Report on Summary Statements**

    a.   The following are included in the report:

        1)   A title that includes the word "independent," for example, "Independent Auditor's Report on Summary Financial Statements"

        2)   Addressee

        3)   An introductory paragraph that

            a)   Identifies the summary statements on which the auditor is reporting, including the title of each statement

            b)   Identifies the audited statements from which the summary statements are derived

            c)   Refers to the auditor's report on the audited statements, the type of opinion it expresses, and the date of that report

            d)   Indicates that (1) the summary statements do not contain all the disclosures required by the framework applied in the preparation of the financial statements, and (2) reading the summary statements is not a substitute for reading the audited statements

        4)   A paragraph describing management's responsibility for the summary statements

        5)   A section describing the auditor's responsibility for expressing an opinion about whether the summary statements are consistent, in all material respects, with the audited statements based on the procedures required by U.S. GAAS. The procedures primarily involve

            a)   Comparing the summary statements with the related information in the audited statements from which they are derived and

            b)   Evaluating whether the summary statements are prepared in accordance with the applied criteria.

        6)   Opinion

        7)   Auditor's signature

        8)   Auditor's city and state

        9)   Date of the auditor's report

7.   **Other Considerations**

    a.   The auditor should evaluate whether any **unaudited** information presented with the summary statements is clearly differentiated from them.

    b.   The auditor should read **other information** included in a document containing the summary statements and the related auditor's report to identify material inconsistencies, if any, with the summary statements and the audited statements.

    c.   The auditor may become aware that the entity plans to state that the auditor has reported on summary statements in a document containing those statements. If the entity does not plan to include the related auditor's report, the auditor should request management to include it.

    d.   The auditor may learn that the entity plans to make a statement in a document that refers to (1) the auditor and (2) the derivation of the summary statements from the statements audited by the auditor. If the auditor has not reported on the summary statements, (s)he should become satisfied that users are not misled about the auditor's responsibility.

Stop and review! You have completed the outline for this subunit. Study multiple-choice questions 12 and 13 beginning on page 394.

18.8 FINANCIAL STATEMENTS PREPARED IN ACCORDANCE WITH A FINANCIAL REPORTING FRAMEWORK GENERALLY ACCEPTED IN ANOTHER COUNTRY

1. An auditor practicing in the U.S. may report on the financial statements of a **U.S. entity** prepared in accordance with a financial reporting framework generally accepted in another country for use outside the U.S.

   a. The auditor should clearly understand the purpose of the statements and obtain written representations from management.

   b. If the statements are for general use and the report form and content of the foreign country will be used, the auditor should consider any additional legal responsibilities.

   c. However, AU-C 910, *Financial Statements Prepared in Accordance with a Financial Reporting Framework Generally Accepted in Another Country*, does not apply to statements prepared in accordance with International Financial Reporting Standards (IFRS) issued by the International Accounting Standards Board (IASB).

      1) The reporting standards (e.g., AU-C 700 and AU-C 705) covered in Study Units 16 and 17 apply because the IASB is an AICPA-designated standards setter.

   d. Because the auditor should understand the entity's selection and application of accounting policies (AU-C 315), (s)he should understand the other accounting principles.

2. **Compliance with Auditing Standards of Another Country**

   a. An auditor engaged to audit financial statements prepared in accordance with a reporting framework generally accepted in another country may be requested to apply the auditing standards of that country or International Standards on Auditing (ISAs). This is acceptable if

      1) The auditor understands those standards
      2) The auditor uses the guidance in this standard for reporting

3. **Use Limited to Outside the United States**

   a. If the financial statements and auditor's report are intended for use only outside the United States, the auditor should report using either

      1) A U.S. form of report reflecting that the statements reported on have been prepared in accordance with a reporting framework generally accepted in another country. (Study Unit 16 contains the format of the basic U.S. report.)

         a) The introductory paragraph should refer to the note to the statements that describes their basis of presentation, including identification of the country of origin of the accounting principles.

      2) The report form and content of the other country (or, if applicable, as set forth in the ISAs).

   b. The auditor expresses an opinion on whether the financial statements are presented fairly in accordance with the framework of the other country.

4. **Use in the United States**

   a. If financial statements prepared in accordance with a reporting framework generally accepted in another country also are intended for use in the United States, the auditor should report using the U.S. form of report. This report includes an emphasis-of-matter paragraph

      1) Identifying the reporting framework used in the preparation of the financial statements,

2) Referring to the note in the statements that describes the framework, and

3) Indicating that the framework differs from accounting principles generally accepted in the U.S.

b. The auditor expresses an opinion on whether the financial statements are presented fairly within the framework of the other country.

Stop and review! You have completed the outline for this subunit. Study multiple-choice question 14 on page 395.

18.9 REPORTS ON APPLICATION OF REQUIREMENTS OF AN APPLICABLE FINANCIAL REPORTING FRAMEWORK

1. Management and others may consult with accountants to learn how to apply (a) accounting policies in a financial reporting framework (e.g., U.S. GAAP) to new transactions or (b) new accounting policies in a framework to existing transactions. They also may want to increase their knowledge of specific financial reporting issues.

2. **Applicability**

a. AU-C 915, *Reports on Application of Requirements of an Applicable Financial Reporting Framework*, should be applied by an accountant in public practice (reporting accountant), other than a continuing accountant, who has been requested to issue a **written report** on

1) The application of the requirements of a financial reporting framework to a specific transaction (completed or proposed) involving facts or circumstances of a specific entity or

2) The type of report that may be issued on a specific entity's statements.

b. AU-C 915 also applies to **oral advice** believed to be an important factor in the decisions about accounting principles made by a principal to the transaction.

c. AU-C 915 does not apply to

1) A continuing accountant's engagement to report on a specific entity's financial statements;

2) Assistance in litigation involving accounting matters or related expert testimony;

3) Professional advice provided to another public accountant; or

4) Position papers, such as (a) newsletters, (b) articles, (c) speeches, or (d) letters for the public record to standards-setting bodies.

d. The accountant need not be independent. But if (s)he is not, the report should state the lack of independence.

3. **Acceptance, Planning, and Performance**

a. Before accepting the engagement, the reporting accountant should consider the circumstances in which the report or advice is requested, the purpose, and the intended use.

1) An engagement to issue a written report should be accepted only when the transaction involves facts or circumstances of a specific entity, not a hypothetical transaction.

b. When planning and performing the engagement, the reporting accountant should

1) Obtain an understanding of the form and substance of the transaction(s) or the conditions relevant to the type of report that might be issued

2) Review the relevant requirements of the framework (e.g., U.S. GAAP)

3) Consult with other professionals or experts, if appropriate

4) Consider creditable precedents or analogies

5) Consult with the continuing accountant of the entity to determine the available relevant facts, including disputes with management

    c.   The reporting accountant should have an understanding with the requesting party that management

        1)   Acknowledges the reporting accountant's need to consult with the continuing accountant and

        2)   Upon request, will authorize the continuing accountant to respond fully.

4.   **Reporting**

    a.   The addressee of the accountant's written report is the requesting entity. The report should do the following:

        1)   Briefly describe the engagement and state that it was in accordance with AU-C 915.

        2)   Identify the specific entity; describe the transaction(s); state the facts, circumstances, and assumptions; and state the source of the information.

        3)   Describe the appropriate application of the framework (including the country of origin) to the specific transaction or type of report and, if appropriate, the reasons for the conclusion.

        4)   State that the responsibility for proper accounting is with the preparers of the statements, who should consult with their continuing accountant.

        5)   State that any difference in the facts, circumstances, or assumptions may change the report.

        6)   Include a separate paragraph the restricts the use of the report to specified and identified parties.

        7)   If appropriate, state any lack of independence.

Stop and review! You have completed the outline for this subunit. Study multiple-choice questions 15 and 16 on page 396.

18.10 AUDITS OF FINANCIAL STATEMENTS PREPARED IN ACCORDANCE WITH SPECIAL PURPOSE FRAMEWORKS

Background
Standards prior to the AICPA's Clarified Auditing Standards used the term "special reports" for the reporting described in the next two study units. They were "special" in the sense that the reports related to other types of reporting objectives.

1.   Auditors can report on the fairness of financial statements prepared in accordance with a special purpose framework.

2.   Special purpose frameworks include the following:

    a.   The **cash basis** is used to record cash receipts and cash payments.

    b.   The **tax basis** is used to file income tax returns.

    c.   The **regulatory basis** is used to comply with the requirements of a regulatory agency.

    d.   The **contractual basis** is used to comply with an agreement between the entity and a third party.

    e.   An **other basis** consisting of a definite set of logical, reasonable criteria that is applied to all material items in the statements.

3.   The cash, tax, regulatory, and other bases of accounting are commonly referred to as **other comprehensive bases of accounting (OCBOA)**.

4. The auditor obtains sufficient appropriate evidence, including evaluation of appropriate disclosures, to judge the fairness of the presentation.

    a. Statements also should be appropriately titled.

        1) For example, "Income Statement" and "Balance Sheet" are not appropriate titles for cash-basis statements. Instead, they may be labeled "Statement of Revenue Collected and Expenses Paid" or "Statement of Assets and Liabilities Arising from Cash Transactions."

    b. Moreover, the statements should include a summary of significant accounting policies and describe how the special purpose framework varies from GAAP.

5. **Auditor's Report**

    a. In addition to the requirements in AU-C 700, the report should

        1) Refer to management's responsibility to determine that the reporting framework is acceptable (if management has a choice).

        2) Describe the purpose of the statements (or refer to a note with that information) if the framework used is

            a) A regulatory or contractual basis or
            b) An other basis, and the use of the report is restricted.

    b. The auditor's report should have a basic format with the following items:

        1) Title -- Independent Auditor's Report

        2) Addressee -- For example, the entity or those charged with governance

        3) Introductory paragraph -- Identification of the entity, statement of the service performed (an audit), title of each financial statement, and the date or period of each statement

        4) Management's responsibility for the financial statements -- Description of responsibilities for preparation and fair presentation in accordance with the applicable framework, including relevant internal control, and for the determination that the framework is acceptable (if management has a choice)

        5) Auditor's responsibility -- Description of responsibilities for (a) expressing an opinion, (b) auditing in accordance with GAAS, (c) obtaining reasonable assurance, (d) assessing risks, (e) considering internal control, and (f) evaluating accounting policies and estimates and the overall presentation

        6) Opinion -- Opinion on fair presentation

        7) Auditor's signature -- Manual or printed

        8) Auditor's city and state -- Location of the auditor

        9) Date -- No earlier than when sufficient appropriate evidence was obtained

6. **Emphasis-of-Matter Paragraph**

    a. Except when regulatory-basis statements are intended for general use, this paragraph (titled "Basis of Accounting") should follow the opinion paragraph. It

        1) Identifies the special purpose framework,

        2) Refers to the note describing the framework, and

        3) States that the framework is not GAAP.

    b. The following is an example of an emphasis-of-matter paragraph included in a report on a cash-basis financial statement:

EXAMPLE -- Emphasis-of-Matter Paragraph

Basis of Accounting

We draw attention to Note X of the financial statements, which describes the basis of accounting. The financial statements are prepared on the cash basis of accounting, which is a basis of accounting other than accounting principles generally accepted in the United States of America. Our opinion is not modified with respect to this matter.

7. **Other-Matter Paragraph**

    a. Except when regulatory-basis statements are intended for general use, this paragraph (titled "Restriction on Use") should follow any emphasis-of-matter paragraph. It restricts the use of the report when the special purpose framework is

        1) A contractual basis of accounting,
        2) A regulatory basis of accounting, or
        3) An other basis of accounting (if measurement or disclosure criteria are suitable only for limited users or available only to the specified parties).

    b. The following is an example of an emphasis-of-matter paragraph and an other-matter paragraph included in a report on a regulatory-basis financial statement not intended for general use:

EXAMPLE -- Emphasis-of-Matter Paragraph and Other-Matter Paragraph

Basis of Accounting

We draw attention to Note X of the financial statements, which describes the basis of accounting. As described in Note X to the financial statements, the financial statements are prepared by ABC City on the basis of the financial reporting provisions of Section Y of Regulation Z of Any State, which is a basis of accounting other than accounting principles generally accepted in the United States of America, to meet the requirements of Any State. Our opinion is not modified with respect to this matter.

Restriction on Use

Our report is intended solely for the information and use of ABC City and Any State and is not intended to be and should not be used by anyone other than these specified parties.

---

8. **Regulatory Basis (General Use)**

    a. The auditor's report on regulatory-basis statements intended for general use does not include emphasis-of-matter and other-matter paragraphs.

        1) The auditor's report includes separate paragraphs expressing an opinion on fair presentation in accordance with (a) GAAP and (b) the special purpose framework, respectively.

    b. The following is an example:

EXAMPLE

Basis for Adverse Opinion on U.S. Generally Accepted Accounting Principles

As described in Note X of the financial statements, the financial statements are prepared by XYZ City on the basis of the financial reporting provisions of Section Y of Regulation Z of Any State, which is a basis of accounting other than accounting principles generally accepted in the United States of America, to meet the requirements of Any State.

The effects on the financial statements of the variances between the regulatory basis of accounting described in Note X and accounting principles generally accepted in the United States of America, although not reasonably determinable, are presumed to be material.

Adverse Opinion on U.S. Generally Accepted Accounting Principles

In our opinion, because of the significance of the matter discussed in the "Basis for Adverse Opinion on U.S. Generally Accepted Accounting Principles" paragraph, the financial statements referred to above do not present fairly, in accordance with accounting principles generally accepted in the United States of America, the financial position of each fund of XYZ City as of December 31, 20X1, or changes in financial position or cash flows thereof for the year then ended.

Opinion on Regulatory Basis of Accounting

In our opinion, the financial statements referred to above present fairly, in all material respects, the cash and unencumbered cash of each fund of XYZ City as of December 31, 20X1, and their respective cash receipts and disbursements, and budgetary results for the year then ended in accordance with the financial reporting provisions of Section Y of Regulation Z of Any State described in Note X.

Stop and review! You have completed the outline for this subunit. Study multiple-choice questions 17 and 18 beginning on page 396.

18.11 AUDITS OF SINGLE FINANCIAL STATEMENTS AND SPECIFIC ELEMENTS, ACCOUNTS, OR ITEMS OF A FINANCIAL STATEMENT

1. The objective of an audit of (a) a single financial statement or (b) a specific element, account, or item of a financial statement is to address the special considerations that are relevant to

    a. Acceptance of the engagement,
    b. Planning and performance of the audit, and
    c. Forming an opinion and reporting.

2. An **element** is defined for the purposes of AU-C 805, *Audits of Single Financial Statements and Specific Elements, Accounts, or Items of a Financial Statement*, as an **element, account, or item** of a financial statement.

3. A single financial statement or a specific element includes the related notes.

    a. The notes ordinarily include a summary of significant accounting policies and other explanatory information.

4. All relevant auditing standards apply for auditing an element or a single financial statement regardless of whether the auditor also audits the entity's complete set of statements.

    a. However, if the auditor did not audit those statements, (s)he should determine whether the audit of a single statement or a specific element in accordance with GAAS is feasible. The auditor also should determine whether (s)he can perform procedures on interrelated items.

5. For an audit of a single statement or a specific element, the auditor should obtain an **understanding** of

    a. The purpose for which the statement or element is prepared,
    b. The intended users, and
    c. Management's steps to ensure proper reporting.

6. In planning and performing the audit of a single statement or a specific element, the auditor should adapt all relevant auditing standards as necessary.

    a. Furthermore, the auditor should perform procedures on **interrelated items** as necessary to meet the objective of the audit. For example, sales and receivables, inventory and payables, and equipment and depreciation are interrelated.

        1) Thus, an auditor of a single statement may be unable to consider that statement in isolation.

7. **Audit of a Specific Element**

    a. The specific element may be, or may be based upon, the entity's **equity** or **net income**. The auditor should perform procedures necessary to obtain sufficient appropriate evidence to permit expression of an opinion on, respectively, (1) financial position and (2) financial position and results of operations.

        1) But the procedures need not address matters related to classification or disclosure that are not relevant to the audit of the specific element.

8. **Materiality**

    a. The auditor should determine materiality for the **single statement** being reported on, not for the complete set of statements.

    b. In an audit of one or more **specific elements**, the auditor should determine materiality for each element reported on, not the aggregate of all elements or the complete set of statements.

9. **Reporting**

    a.   If the auditor of the complete set of statements also audits a single statement or a specific element, (s)he should

        1)   Issue a separate auditor's report and express a separate opinion for each engagement.

        2)   Indicate in the report on a specific element the date of the auditor's report on the complete set of statements and the nature of the opinion expressed on those statements.

    b.   An audited single statement or an audited specific element ordinarily may be published with the entity's audited complete set of statements. But the presentation of the single statement or the specific element should be sufficiently differentiated from the complete set of statements.

    c.   If the auditor's opinion on an entity's complete set of statements is **modified**, the auditor should determine the effect on the auditor's opinion on a single statement or a specific element.

        1)   For example, a modified opinion due to **material misstatement** of the complete set of statements may be relevant to a specific element. In this case, an **adverse opinion** should be expressed on the element.

        2)   A modified opinion on the complete set of statements also may be due to an inability to obtain sufficient appropriate evidence. If this modified opinion is relevant to a specific element, the auditor should disclaim an opinion on the specific element.

    d.   The auditor's report on an entity's complete set of statements may include an **emphasis-of-matter** paragraph or an **other-matter** paragraph that is relevant to the audit of the single statement or the specific element.

        1)   In this case, the auditor should include a similar paragraph in the auditor's report on the single statement or the specific element.

    e.   An auditor may wish to express (1) an adverse opinion or disclaimer of opinion on the complete set of statements and (2) an unmodified opinion on a specific element. Doing so in the same auditor's report would contradict the adverse opinion or disclaimer and be equivalent to expressing a piecemeal opinion.

        1)   However, in the context of a separate audit of a specific element included in those statements, when the auditor considers it appropriate to express an unmodified opinion on the specific element, the auditor should do so only if

            a)   That opinion is expressed in an auditor's report that is neither published with nor accompanies the auditor's report containing the adverse opinion or disclaimer of opinion.

            b)   The specific element is not a major portion of the entity's complete set of statements or is not, or is not based upon, the entity's equity or net income.

Stop and review! You have completed the outline for this subunit. Study multiple-choice questions 19 and 20 on page 397.

QUESTIONS

18.1 Interim Financial Information

1. The objective of a review of interim financial information of an issuer is to provide an auditor with a basis for reporting whether

   A. A reasonable basis exists for expressing an updated opinion regarding the financial statements that were previously audited.

   B. Material modifications should be made to conform with generally accepted accounting principles.

   C. The financial statements are presented fairly in accordance with standards of interim reporting.

   D. The financial statements are presented fairly in accordance with generally accepted accounting principles.

Answer (B) is correct.
   REQUIRED: The objective of a review of interim financial information.
   DISCUSSION: The review provides the auditor with a basis for reporting whether (s)he is aware of material modifications that should be made for such information to conform with the applicable financial reporting framework. This objective differs significantly from that of an audit, which is to provide a basis for expressing an opinion (AU-C 930).
   Answer (A) is incorrect. The review of interim financial information does not provide a basis for expressing an opinion. Answer (C) is incorrect. Reporting on whether the statements are fairly presented is the expression of an opinion. Answer (D) is incorrect. Reporting on whether the statements are fairly presented is the expression of an opinion.

2. A modification of the auditor's report on a review of interim financial information is necessitated by which of the following?

   A. A substantial doubt about the entity's ability to continue as a going concern.

   B. Lack of consistency.

   C. Use of another auditor's report.

   D. Inadequate disclosure.

Answer (D) is correct.
   REQUIRED: The reason for modifying a review report on interim financial information.
   DISCUSSION: Modification of the report on a review of IFI is necessary if it is not, in all material respects, in accordance with the applicable reporting framework. If the departure is due to inadequate disclosure, the auditor should, if feasible, include the information in the report. But many circumstances that preclude the issuance of an unmodified report on audited statements do not cause a modification of a review report (AU-C 930).
   Answer (A) is incorrect. AU-C 930 specifically states that a substantial doubt about the entity's ability to continue as a going concern is not a cause for modification if appropriately disclosed. Answer (B) is incorrect. AU-C 930 specifically states that lack of consistency is not a cause for modification if appropriately disclosed. Answer (C) is incorrect. The use of the report of another auditor may result in, but does not require, modification of the report. After considering the guidance in AU-C 600 relating to component auditors, the auditor may be able to assume responsibility for the component auditor's work.

18.2 Letters for Underwriters and Certain Other Requesting Parties

3. Which of the following matters is covered in a typical comfort letter?

   A. Negative assurance concerning whether the entity's internal control activities operated as designed during the period being audited.

   B. An opinion regarding whether the entity complied with laws and regulations under Government Auditing Standards and the Single Audit Act.

   C. Positive assurance concerning whether unaudited condensed financial information complied with generally accepted accounting principles.

   D. An opinion as to whether the audited financial statements comply in form with the accounting requirements of the SEC.

Answer (D) is correct.
   REQUIRED: The item in a typical letter for underwriters.
   DISCUSSION: A typical comfort letter expresses an opinion on whether audited financial statements and schedules included in the securities offering comply as to form, in all material respects, with the applicable accounting requirements of the Securities Act of 1933 and the related published rules and regulations. However, the comfort letter does not state or repeat an opinion about the fairness of presentation of the statements.

4. In a comfort letter, an auditor may provide negative assurance about

- A. The absence of any significant deficiencies in internal control.

- B. Whether the entity's unaudited interim financial information complies as to form with the accounting requirements of the Securities Act of 1933.

- C. The results of procedures performed in compiling the entity's financial forecast.

- D. The compliance of the entity's registration statement with the requirements of the Securities Act of 1933.

Answer (B) is correct.
    REQUIRED: The negative assurance provided by a comfort letter.
    DISCUSSION: A typical comfort letter includes negative assurance on whether the unaudited interim financial information included in the registration statement complies as to form, in all material respects, with the applicable accounting requirements of the Securities Act of 1933 and rules and regulations of the SEC.
    Answer (A) is incorrect. The auditor should have knowledge of the client's internal controls but does not comment on them in the comfort letter. Answer (C) is incorrect. Practitioners do not provide limited assurance on forecasts. Answer (D) is incorrect. Auditors can comment only on matters to which their expertise is relevant. Compliance with aspects of the law is beyond that expertise.

18.3 Filings with the SEC under the Securities Act of 1933

5. An independent auditor's report is based on a review of interim financial information. If this report is presented in a registration statement, a prospectus should include a statement clarifying that the

- A. Auditor's review report is not a part of the registration statement within the meaning of the Securities Act of 1933.

- B. Auditor assumes no responsibility for subsequent events.

- C. Auditor's review was performed in accordance with rules and regulations adopted by the Securities and Exchange Commission.

- D. Auditor obtained corroborating evidence to determine whether material modifications are needed for such information to be in accordance with GAAP.

Answer (A) is correct.
    REQUIRED: The statement in a review report on IFI included in a registration statement.
    DISCUSSION: The auditor has reviewed interim information, and his or her report is presented or incorporated by reference in a registration statement. In these circumstances, the SEC requires that a prospectus containing a statement about the auditor's involvement clarify that the report is not a report on, or a part of, the registration statement within the meaning of sections 7 and 11 of the Securities Act of 1933. The prospectus should state that reliance on the report should be restricted given the limited procedures applied and that the auditor is not subject to the liability provisions of section 11.
    Answer (B) is incorrect. The registration statement contains audited financial statements. Thus, procedures should be extended from the date of the audit report to the effective date of the filing. Answer (C) is incorrect. The report might state that the independent public accountants have reported that they have applied limited procedures in accordance with professional standards for a review of such information. Answer (D) is incorrect. The auditor makes inquiries and applies analytical procedures to determine whether modifications are needed for financial information to be in accordance with the applicable framework. The auditor does not collect corroborating evidence in a review.

6. The Securities and Exchange Commission has authority to

- A. Prescribe specific auditing procedures to detect fraud concerning inventories and accounts receivable of companies engaged in interstate commerce.

- B. Deny lack of privity as a defense in third-party actions for gross negligence against the auditors of issuers.

- C. Determine accounting principles for the purpose of financial reporting by companies offering securities to the public.

- D. Require a change of auditors of governmental entities after a given period of years as a means of ensuring independence.

Answer (C) is correct.
    REQUIRED: The authority of the SEC.
    DISCUSSION: The SEC has the authority to regulate the form and content of all financial statements, notes, and schedules filed with the SEC and also the financial reports to shareholders if the company is subject to the Securities Exchange Act of 1934. The SEC has stated that financial statements conforming to FASB standards will be presumed to be in accordance with U.S. GAAP. However, the SEC reserves the right to substitute its principles for those of the accounting profession and to require any additional disclosures it deems necessary. The Sarbanes-Oxley Act of 2002 authorized the SEC to recognize as generally accepted any accounting principles established by a standards-setting body that meets the act's criteria.
    Answer (A) is incorrect. The SEC may not prescribe specific auditing procedures. The Public Company Accounting Oversight Board (PCAOB), established by the Sarbanes-Oxley Act, adopts auditing standards related to preparation of audit reports for issuers. Answer (B) is incorrect. The SEC may not deny lack of privity as a defense. Answer (D) is incorrect. The SEC may not require a change of auditors of governmental entities.

18.4 Other Information in Documents Containing Audited Financial Statements

7. When audited financial statements are presented in a document containing other information, the auditor

    A. Has an obligation to perform auditing procedures to corroborate the other information.

    B. Should express a qualified opinion if the other information is materially inconsistent with the statements.

    C. Should be aware of whether the other information contains a material misstatement of fact.

    D. Has no responsibility for the other information because it is not part of the basic financial statements.

Answer (C) is correct.

    REQUIRED: The auditor's responsibility for other information.

    DISCUSSION: A misstatement of fact is other information that is unrelated to matters in the audited statements and is incorrectly stated or presented. If material, it may undermine the credibility of the document containing the audited statements. When management refuses to correct a material misstatement of fact, the auditor should notify those charged with governance.

    Answer (A) is incorrect. The auditor should read, but need not corroborate, the other information. Answer (B) is incorrect. If the audited information is presented fairly, the opinion should be unmodified. However, if the other information needs revision, the auditor should request that management revise it. If revision is not made, (s)he should communicate the matter to those charged with governance and (1) modify the report to include an other-matter paragraph, (2) withhold use of the report, or (3) withdraw from the engagement. Answer (D) is incorrect. The auditor should read the other information to consider whether it is inconsistent with the audited financial statements.

8. An auditor concludes prior to the release date of the report that a material inconsistency exists in the other information in an annual report to shareholders. The report contains audited financial statements. If the auditor concludes that the financial statements do not require revision, but management refuses to revise or eliminate the material inconsistency, the auditor may

    A. Revise the auditor's report to include a separate other-matter paragraph describing the material inconsistency.

    B. Express a qualified opinion after discussing the matter with the client's directors.

    C. Consider the matter closed because the other information is not in the audited statements.

    D. Disclaim an opinion on the financial statements after explaining the material inconsistency in a separate other-matter paragraph.

Answer (A) is correct.

    REQUIRED: The auditor's response when management presents other information with a material inconsistency.

    DISCUSSION: If the other information contains a material inconsistency that requires revision, and management refuses to make the revision, the auditor should communicate the matter to those charged with governance. The auditor also should (1) revise the report to include an other-matter paragraph, (2) withhold use of the report, or (3) withdraw from the engagement.

    Answer (B) is incorrect. The opinion is expressed on the financial statements only. The inconsistency in the other information does not affect that opinion. Answer (C) is incorrect. The auditor may not ignore a material inconsistency in other information. Answer (D) is incorrect. The auditor's decision to disclaim an opinion is not affected by the other information.

18.5 Required Supplementary Information (RSI)

9. What is an auditor's responsibility for required supplementary information (RSI)?

    A. Include a disclaimer on the information only if the auditor is unable to apply limited procedures to it.

    B. Add an emphasis-of-matter paragraph to the auditor's report before the opinion paragraph.

    C. Apply limited procedures to the information and report its omission or the need for material modifications.

    D. Audit the RSI in accordance with applicable auditing standards.

Answer (C) is correct.

    REQUIRED: The auditor's responsibility for RSI.

    DISCUSSION: RSI differs from other information outside the basic statements because the designated accounting standard setter considers it to be an essential part of financial reporting for placing the basic financial statements in context. The auditor at minimum should apply limited procedures and report on the RSI in an other-matter paragraph that follows the opinion paragraph.

    Answer (A) is incorrect. The other-matter paragraph referring to RSI (by definition, not part of the basic statements) contains a disclaimer even if limited procedures are completed. Answer (B) is incorrect. An other-matter paragraph is added after the opinion paragraph. Answer (D) is incorrect. RSI need not be audited.

18.6 Supplementary Information in Relation to the Financial Statements as a Whole

10. Investment and property schedules are presented for purposes of additional analysis in a document outside the basic financial statements. The schedules are not required supplementary information. When the auditor is engaged to report on whether the supplementary information is fairly stated in relation to the audited financial statements as a whole, the measurement of materiality is the

A. Same as that used in forming an opinion on the basic financial statements as a whole.

B. Lesser of the individual schedule of investments or schedule of property by itself.

C. Greater of the individual schedule of investments or schedule of property by itself.

D. Combined total of both the individual schedules of investments and property as a whole.

Answer (A) is correct.
    REQUIRED: The measure of materiality.
    DISCUSSION: When reporting on whether supplementary information is fairly stated in relation to the statements as a whole, the measurement of materiality is the same as that used in forming an opinion on the basic financial statements taken as a whole. Accordingly, the auditor need not apply procedures as extensive as would be necessary to express an opinion on the information by itself.

11. The auditor is engaged to report on whether supplementary information is fairly stated in relation to the audited financial statements as a whole. Which of the following best describes the auditor's responsibility for this information if it is outside the basic financial statements and **not** deemed necessary to their fair presentation?

A. The auditor has no reporting responsibility concerning information accompanying the basic financial statements.

B. The auditor should report on the supplementary information only if the auditor participated in its preparation.

C. The auditor must disclaim an opinion on the information if it is supplementary information required by the applicable financial reporting framework.

D. The auditor should not express an opinion on the supplementary information if (s)he disclaimed an opinion on the financial statements.

Answer (D) is correct.
    REQUIRED: The auditor's reporting responsibility.
    DISCUSSION: Supplementary information is presented outside the basic statements and is not deemed necessary for their fair presentation in accordance with the applicable financial reporting framework. For example, it includes (1) additional details or explanations of items in or related to the statements, (2) consolidating information, (3) statistical data, and (4) historical summaries. The auditor should not express an opinion on the supplementary information if (s)he expressed an adverse opinion or disclaimed an opinion on the audited financial statements. Moreover, the auditor should have served as the group auditor of those statements.
    Answer (A) is incorrect. The auditor was engaged to report on the supplementary information. Answer (B) is incorrect. Management is responsible for preparing the supplementary information. Answer (C) is incorrect. The auditor is not precluded from performing an engagement to express an opinion on RSI. But the opinion on the audited financial statements does not cover RSI, absent a specific requirement in the agreement with the client.

18.7 Engagements to Report on Summary Financial Statements

12. The report on summary financial statements should indicate that the

A. Summary financial statements are prepared in conformity with a special purpose framework.

B. Procedures performed included evaluating whether they are prepared in accordance with the applied criteria.

C. Summary financial statements are fairly presented in all material respects.

D. The auditor expresses limited assurance that the financial statements conform with GAAP.

Answer (B) is correct.
    REQUIRED: The indication in a report on summary financial statements.
    DISCUSSION: The report on the summary statements describes, among other things, the procedures performed. They primarily include (1) comparing the summary statements with the related information in the audited statements and (2) evaluating whether the summary statements are prepared in accordance with the criteria applied by management.
    Answer (A) is incorrect. Summary financial statements are prepared on the same basis as the audited financial statements. Answer (C) is incorrect. Summary financial statements are to be presented consistently with the audited financial statements. Answer (D) is incorrect. The auditor expresses an opinion.

13. The auditor should not accept an engagement to report on summary statements **unless**

A. The auditor has been engaged to audit the financial statements from which the summary statements are derived.

B. The auditor issued an unmodified report on the statements from which the summary statements are derived.

C. The auditor takes responsibility for the summary financial statements.

D. A complete audit can be completed on the summary statements.

Answer (A) is correct.
    REQUIRED: The requirement to report on summary financial statements.
    DISCUSSION: Summary financial statements consist of historical information derived from financial statements audited in accordance with GAAS by the same auditor. The auditor should not accept an engagement to report on summary statements unless (s)he has been engaged to audit the statements from which they are derived. The report expresses an opinion on whether the summary statements are consistent, in all material respects, with the audited statements, in accordance with the applied criteria.
    Answer (B) is incorrect. The auditor may have expressed a qualified opinion on the audited statements or included an emphasis-of-matter or other-matter paragraph in the report. But the auditor should not report on the summary statements if an adverse opinion or disclaimer of opinion has been expressed on the audited statements. Answer (C) is incorrect. Management is responsible for the summary financial statements. Answer (D) is incorrect. An auditor applies procedures to determine whether the summary statements are consistent with the audited statements.

18.8 Financial Statements Prepared in Accordance with a Financial Reporting Framework Generally Accepted in Another Country

14. The financial statements of KCP America, a U.S. entity, are prepared for inclusion in the consolidated financial statements of its non-U.S. parent. These financial statements are prepared in accordance with a financial reporting framework generally accepted in the parent's country and are for use only in that country. Which is an appropriate report on the financial statements for KCP America's auditor to issue?

I.   A U.S. form of report (unmodified)

II. A U.S. form of report modified to report on the financial reporting framework of the parent's country

III. The report form of the parent's country

A. I only.

B. II only.

C. II and III only.

D. I, II, and III.

Answer (C) is correct.
    REQUIRED: The proper reporting on the financial statements of a U.S. entity prepared for inclusion in the consolidated financial statements of its non-U.S. parent.
    DISCUSSION: Financial statements may be prepared in accordance with a financial reporting framework generally accepted in another country. In these circumstances, if the statements are prepared for use only outside the U.S., the auditor may use either a U.S. form of report modified to report on the financial reporting framework of the other country or, if appropriate, the report form of the other country. An unmodified U.S. form of report is inappropriate because of the departures from GAAP contained in statements prepared in accordance with a financial reporting framework generally accepted in the other country.

18.9 Reports on Application of Requirements of an Applicable Financial Reporting Framework

15. Blue, CPA, has been asked to report on the application of a financial reporting framework to a specific transaction by an entity that is audited by another CPA. Blue may accept this engagement but should

A. Consult with the continuing accountant to obtain information relevant to the transaction.

B. Report the engagement's findings to the entity's audit committee, the continuing accountant, and management.

C. Disclaim any opinion on the application of the financial reporting framework to the hypothetical transaction.

D. Be independent of the client.

Answer (A) is correct.

REQUIRED: The responsibility of an accountant who is reporting on the application of a financial reporting framework to a specific transaction if (s)he is not the continuing accountant.

DISCUSSION: The reporting accountant should consult with the continuing accountant to determine the available facts relevant to a professional judgment. The continuing accountant may provide information not otherwise available to the reporting accountant. (S)he should (1) explain to the entity's management the need to consult with the continuing accountant, (2) request permission to do so, and (3) request authorization for the continuing accountant to respond fully.

Answer (B) is incorrect. The accountant's written report should be addressed to the requesting entity. Answer (C) is incorrect. The report should describe (1) the appropriate application of the financial reporting framework to the specific transaction and (2), if appropriate, the reasons for the conclusion, not an opinion or a disclaimer. Also, the engagement may not involve reporting on the application of the financial reporting framework to a hypothetical transaction. Answer (D) is incorrect. The accountant need not be independent. But if (s)he is not, the report should state the lack of independence.

16. In connection with a proposal to obtain a new client, an accountant in public practice is asked to prepare a written report on the requirements of an applicable financial reporting framework to a specific transaction. The accountant's report should include a statement that

A. Any difference in the facts, circumstances, or assumptions presented may change the report.

B. The engagement was performed in accordance with Statements on Standards for Consulting Services.

C. The guidance provided is for general use.

D. Nothing came to the accountant's attention that caused the accountant to believe that the application of the financial reporting framework to the facts is inappropriate.

Answer (A) is correct.

REQUIRED: The statement in a report on the application of a financial reporting framework to a specific transaction.

DISCUSSION: The accountant's report is addressed to the requesting party. The report should contain (1) a description of the engagement and a statement that it was performed in accordance with AU-C 915; (2) a description of the transaction and identification of the entity; (3) a description of the financial reporting framework applied (including its country of origin), the type of report that may be issued, and the reasons for the conclusion; (4) a statement that the responsibility for proper accounting is with the preparers of the financial statements; (5) statements of the facts, circumstances, and assumptions and their sources; (6) a statement that any difference in the facts, etc., may change the report; (7) an alert restricting the use of the report to specified parties; and (8), if the accountant is not independent, a statement of the lack of independence.

Answer (B) is incorrect. The accountant's report should state that the engagement is conducted in accordance with AU-C 915. Answer (C) is incorrect. The use of the report is restricted to specified parties. Answer (D) is incorrect. The report does not provide for limited assurance.

18.10 Audits of Financial Statements Prepared in Accordance with Special Purpose Frameworks

17. An auditor's report on financial statements prepared in accordance with the income tax basis of accounting should include all of the following **except**

A. Reference to the note to the financial statements that describes the basis of accounting.

B. A statement that the basis of accounting is other than GAAP.

C. An opinion as to whether the basis of accounting used is appropriate under the circumstances.

D. An opinion as to whether the financial statements are presented fairly, in all material respects, in accordance with the basis of accounting used for income tax purposes.

Answer (C) is correct.

REQUIRED: The item not in a report on statements prepared in accordance with a special purpose framework.

DISCUSSION: The auditor's report should include paragraphs or sections that (1) describe the financial statements; (2) state management's responsibility for the financial statements; (3) describe the auditor's responsibilities; (4) express an opinion on fair presentation in accordance with the income tax basis; and (5) identify in an emphasis-of-matter paragraph the basis of accounting, state that the basis is other than GAAP, and refer to the note that describes that basis. The auditor's responsibilities include evaluating the appropriateness of the accounting policies used. They do not include expression of an opinion on whether the basis of accounting used is appropriate under the circumstances.

18. When an auditor reports on financial statements prepared on an entity's income tax basis, the auditor's report should

A. Disclaim an opinion on whether the statements were examined in accordance with generally accepted auditing standards.

B. Not express an opinion on whether the statements are presented in conformity with income tax basis.

C. Include an explanation of how the results of operations differ from the cash receipts and disbursements basis of accounting.

D. State that the special purpose framework is a basis of accounting other than GAAP.

Answer (D) is correct.

REQUIRED: The content of a report on financial statements prepared on the income tax basis.

DISCUSSION: An emphasis-of-matter paragraph in an auditor's report on financial statements prepared in accordance with a special purpose framework, e.g., the income tax basis, should (1) state that the statements are prepared in accordance with the applicable framework, (2) refer to the note describing the framework, and (3) state that the special purpose framework is a basis other than GAAP. The special purpose framework may be (1) the tax basis, (2) the cash basis, (3) a regulatory basis, (4) a contractual basis, or (5) a definite set of logical and reasonable criteria applied to all material items in the statements.

Answer (A) is incorrect. The auditor applies GAAS in the engagement. Answer (B) is incorrect. The auditor expresses an opinion on whether the statements are presented in conformity with the income tax basis. Answer (C) is incorrect. A note in the financial statements should describe the special purpose framework, but the report need only refer to that note.

18.11 Audits of Single Financial Statements and Specific Elements, Accounts, or Items of a Financial Statement

19. Field is an employee of Gold Enterprises. Thomas Hardy, CPA, is asked to express an opinion on Field's profit participation in Gold's net income. Hardy may accept this engagement only if

A. Hardy also performs procedures on Gold's financial position and results of operations.

B. Gold's financial statements are prepared in accordance with GAAP.

C. Hardy's report is available for use only by Gold's other employees.

D. Field owns a controlling interest in Gold.

Answer (A) is correct.

REQUIRED: The condition for accepting an engagement to express an opinion on an employee's profit participation in the employer's net income.

DISCUSSION: If the auditor does not audit the complete set of statements, (s)he should determine whether it is feasible to (1) audit the profit participation and (2) perform procedures on interrelated items. If a specified element, account, or item is, or is based upon, an entity's net income or the equivalent, the auditor should perform the procedures needed to express an opinion on financial position and results of operations. The reason is that the profit participation interrelates with balance sheet and income statement accounts.

Answer (B) is incorrect. The financial statements could be based on a special purpose framework. Answer (C) is incorrect. The use of the report may be restricted, or the auditor may issue a general-use report. Answer (D) is incorrect. Whether Field owns a controlling interest in Gold is irrelevant.

20. For reporting purposes, the auditor should consider each of the following types of financial presentation to be a financial statement **except** the statement of

A. Retained earnings.

B. Operations by product lines.

C. Changes in the elements of working capital.

D. Revenue and expenses.

Answer (C) is correct.

REQUIRED: The presentation not a financial statement.

DISCUSSION: AU-C 805 defines financial statements as a structured representation of historical financial information, including related notes, intended to communicate an entity's economic resources and obligations at a point in time or the changes therein for a period of time in accordance with a financial reporting framework. The related notes ordinarily comprise a summary of significant accounting policies and other explanatory information. AU-C 805 lists various types of financial statements but excludes the statement of changes in working capital.

Answer (A) is incorrect. Statements of retained earnings are financial statements. Answer (B) is incorrect. Statements of operations by product lines are financial statements. Answer (D) is incorrect. Statements of revenue and expenses are financial statements.

 Access the Gleim CPA Premium Review System featuring SmartAdapt for exam-emulating multiple-choice questions and simulations with detailed answer explanations.

STUDY UNIT NINETEEN
PREPARATION, COMPILATION, REVIEW, AND ATTESTATION ENGAGEMENTS

(31 pages of outline)

Statements on Standards for Accounting and Review Services (SSARSs) are issued by the AICPA's Accounting and Review Services Committee (ARSC). SSARSs apply to engagements involving nonissuers, defined as all entities that are not issuers. **Issuers** (also known as public companies) (1) have registered securities under Section 12 of the Securities Exchange Act of 1934, (2) are required to report under Section 15 of that act, or (3) have filed a registration statement under the Securities Act of 1933 that has not become effective. Thus, SSARSs may be applied to all **nonpublic entities**.

The ARSC released Statement on Standards for Accounting and Review Services (Clarified) No. 21 (SSARS No. 21) in October 2014. It includes the following sections:

AR-C 60: General Principles for Engagements
AR-C 70: Preparation of Financial Statements
AR-C 80: Compilation Engagements
AR-C 90: Review of Financial Statements

SSARS No. 22, *Compilation of Pro Forma Financial Information* (AR-C 120), will supersede AR 120 in May 2017. It will be testable in July 2017. Materials in this study unit are based on AR 120 but will be updated prior to June 2017.

Subunits 19.5 through 19.8 cover various **Statements on Standards for Attestation Engagements**. They relate to services performed for a nonissuer that are beyond those for traditional historical financial statements.

19.1 GENERAL PRINCIPLES FOR SSARSs ENGAGEMENTS

1. **Introduction**

   a. The guidance for unaudited financial statements of nonissuers provides for three levels of service: (1) **preparations**, (2) **compilations**, and (3) **reviews**.

b.   The following table compares the preparation, compilation, and review services governed by SSARSs with an audit:

Issue	Preparation	Compilation	Review	Audit
Is assurance provided?	No	No	Limited	Positive
Is an engagement letter required?	Yes	Yes	Yes	Yes
Is independence required?	No[1]	No[2]	Yes	Yes
Is a report required?	No	Yes	Yes	Yes
May the financial statements be released to users other than management?	Yes	Yes	Yes	Yes
May the financial statements omit disclosures (notes)?	Yes	Yes	No	No

[1] No determination of independence is required.
[2] A determination of independence is required. The report is modified if the accountant is not independent.

GLEIM SUCCESS TIPS

Refer to the above table after you have studied each of the first 4 subunits in this study unit. It provides a quick review before taking the exam. The Auditing and Attestation part of the CPA exam includes many questions on preparation, compilation, and review topics. These subunits are especially important.

2.   **Accountant's Responsibilities**

a.   SSARSs describe responsibilities of the accountant for engagements to (1) prepare, (2) compile, or (3) review financial statements in accordance with the applicable financial reporting framework (typically GAAP). SSARSs should be adapted as necessary when those services are performed on **other historical or prospective** financial information. (But prospective financial information may be prepared or compiled but **not** reviewed.)

1)   The accountant is expected to follow any legal requirements. (S)he then can (a) evaluate whether completing the engagement according to SSARS requirements is possible and (b) complete the engagement accordingly. Thus, a redesign of the engagement may be necessary to ensure compliance with the relevant legal requirements.

b.   The CPA firm is required to have an effective **quality control** system. It should include a monitoring process designed to provide reasonable assurance that quality control policies and procedures are relevant, adequate, and operating effectively.

1)   Furthermore, all accountants on the engagement team should (a) comply with relevant ethical requirements and (b) exercise professional judgment and due care.

3.   **Acceptance and Continuation of Engagements**

a.   As a condition for accepting an engagement, the accountant should

1)   Determine whether professional competence is obtainable.
2)   Determine whether the financial reporting framework selected by management is acceptable.
3)   Obtain the agreement of management that it acknowledges and understands its responsibilities for

a)   Selecting the financial reporting framework.

        b) Designing, implementing, and maintaining internal control over financial reporting.

        c) Preventing and detecting fraud.

        d) Ensuring that the entity complies with laws and regulations.

        e) Maintaining accurate and complete records, documents, explanations, and other information.

        f) Providing access to all relevant information, including (1) information for preparing and fairly presenting the financial statements, (2) information the accountant may request, and (3) access to persons within the entity.

  b. An engagement should **not** be accepted if the accountant

    1) Believes that relevant ethical requirements will not be satisfied,

    2) Has a preliminary understanding that information needed to perform the engagement is likely to be unavailable or unreliable, or

    3) Doubts management's integrity.

  c. AR-C 60 does not address the agreement on the **terms** of the engagement. But, in an engagement to prepare, compile, or review financial statements, they should be documented in an **engagement letter** or other suitable form of written agreement. (Study Unit 3, Subunit 1, is relevant. It applies to pre-engagement acceptance activities.) The following are terms common to such engagements:

    1) The objective(s) of the engagement

    2) The responsibilities of management

    3) The responsibilities of the accountant, which, in a preparation, do not include issuing a report

    4) The limitations of the engagement

    5) That the engagement cannot be relied upon to disclose fraud, error, or noncompliance with laws or regulations

    6) Identification of the applicable reporting framework

4. **The Financial Reporting Framework**

  a. The applicable financial reporting framework **(framework)** includes accounting standards issued by an authorized or recognized standards-setting organization, e.g., the FASB, GASB, or IASB.

  b. The following are **special purpose** reporting frameworks:

    1) The **cash** basis is (a) a basis used to record cash receipts and disbursements or (b) a modification of the cash basis having substantial support. An example of a modification is recording depreciation on fixed assets, a substantial, noncash item.

    2) The **tax** basis is used to file the entity's tax return for the period covered by the financial statements.

    3) A **regulatory** basis is used to comply with the requirements or financial reporting provisions of a regulator with jurisdiction over the entity. An example is a basis that insurers use in accordance with the accounting practices prescribed or permitted by a state insurance commission.

    4) A **contractual** basis is used to comply with an agreement between the entity and one or more third parties other than the accountant.

    5) An **other** basis has a definite set of logical, reasonable criteria that is applied to all material items appearing in the financial statements.

  c. Special purpose frameworks other than the contractual basis are known as other comprehensive bases of accounting **(OCBOAs)**.

    d.   Many frameworks intend that financial statements provide information about the (1) financial position, (2) financial performance, (3) cash flows, and (4) related disclosures of an entity. For some other frameworks, a single financial statement and the related notes might be a complete set. The following are examples of a single financial statement, each of which includes related notes:

        1)   Balance sheet
        2)   Statement of income or statement of operations
        3)   Statement of retained earnings
        4)   Statement of cash flows
        5)   Statement of assets and liabilities
        6)   Statement of changes in owners' equity
        7)   Statement of revenue and expenses
        8)   Statement of operations by product lines

    e.   An accountant may (1) prepare, (2) compile, or (3) review a complete set of financial statements or a single statement (for example, a balance sheet). The statements may be for an annual or other period, depending on management's needs.

        1)   However, presenting statements other than for an annual period comparatively with statements for an annual period usually is inappropriate.

5.   **Understanding the Framework**

    a.   AR-C 60 does not specifically address the understanding of the framework. But the guidance for a preparation, compilation, or review includes the following:

        1)   The accountant should obtain an understanding of (a) the framework and (b) the **significant** accounting policies adopted by management.

        2)   The accountant is not prevented from accepting an engagement for an entity in an industry in which (s)he has **no** previous experience. The understanding may be obtained, for example, by consulting (a) AICPA guides, (b) industry publications, (c) financial statements of other entities in the industry, (d) textbooks and periodicals, (e) appropriate continuing professional education, or (f) individuals knowledgeable about the industry.

        3)   Obtaining the understanding satisfies the accountant's ethical obligation to perform services with competence (due care).

Stop and review! You have completed the outline for this subunit. Study multiple-choice questions 1 through 3 beginning on page 429.

19.2 PREPARATION OF FINANCIAL STATEMENTS

1.   **Nature of the Engagement**

    a.   A preparation engagement is a **nonattest** service that does **not** require the accountant to determine whether (s)he is **independent** of the entity. Furthermore, the accountant need **not**

        1)   Verify the accuracy or completeness of management's information,
        2)   Obtain evidence to express an opinion or a conclusion, or
        3)   Report on the financial statements.

    b.   The accountant's engagement **cannot** be relied upon to identify or disclose

        1)   Misstatements, including those caused by fraud or error, or
        2)   Wrongdoing (e.g., fraud) or noncompliance with laws and regulations.

    c.   The preparation service

        1)   Allows accountants to use software to generate client financial statements and release them to the client or third parties without attaching a report.

        2)   May be in conjunction with other services, such as a preparation of **interim** statements followed by an audit, review, or compilation of fiscal year-end statements.

2.   **Applicability**

    a.   AR-C 70 applies when an accountant in public practice is engaged to **prepare** financial statements. It does **not** apply when the accountant merely **assists** in their preparation (a bookkeeping service).

    b.   This guidance also applies, adopted as necessary, to the preparation of other historical or prospective information.

    c.   Thus, AR-C 70 applies to preparation of

        1)   Statements for use by the entity or a third party;

        2)   Statements prior to an audit or review by another accountant;

        3)   Statements to be presented with the entity's tax return;

        4)   Personal financial statements for presentation with a financial plan;

        5)   Single statements, such as a balance sheet or income statement, or statements that omit substantially all disclosures;

        6)   Statements outside of an accounting software system using the information in a general ledger; and

        7)   **Other historical or prospective** financial information, including

            a)   Specified elements, accounts, or items of a statement, such as schedules of rents, royalties, profit participations, or provisions for income taxes;

            b)   Supplementary information, whether or not such information is required;

            c)   Required supplementary information;

            d)   Pro forma financial information; and

            e)   Prospective financial information, including budgets, forecasts, and projections.

    d.   AR-C 70 does **not** apply if other AICPA pronouncements govern. Thus, it does not apply when an accountant prepares financial statements and is engaged to audit, review, or compile them. AR-C 70 also does **not** apply when the statements are **prepared**

        1)   Solely for submission to taxing authorities

        2)   For inclusion in written personal financial plans prepared by the accountant

        3)   In conjunction with litigation services involving pending or potential legal or regulatory proceedings

        4)   In conjunction with business valuation services

    e.   When an accountant does **not prepare** financial statements, AR-C 70 does **not** apply if the accountant merely

        1)   Maintains depreciation schedules;

        2)   Prepares or proposes certain adjustments, such as those applicable to deferred income taxes, depreciation, or leases;

        3)   Drafts financial statement notes; or

        4)   Enters general ledger transactions or processes payments (general bookkeeping) in an accounting software system.

3. **Independence**

   a. The accountant need **not** be independent of the client, and no disclosure is necessary if independence is impaired.

   b. An accountant's name is **not** required to be identified or associated with the financial statements, but the accountant may be identified if a disclaimer is attached.

4. **Preparation Procedures**

   a. The accountant should prepare the financial statements using the records, documents, explanations, and other information provided by management.

   b. The accountant need not (1) verify the accuracy or completeness of the information provided by management or (2) otherwise gather evidence to report (e.g., express an opinion or conclusion) on the fairness of the statements.

   c. The accountant may become aware that the information, including significant judgments, used to prepare the statements is incomplete, inaccurate, or otherwise unsatisfactory.

      1) In these circumstances, the accountant should request that management provide additional or corrected information.

      2) After discussions with management, the accountant may prepare statements that contain a **known departure** from the framework (including inadequate disclosure) and then should disclose the material misstatement.

         a) A **misstatement** may result from fraud or error. A misstatement is the difference between (1) the amount, classification, presentation, or disclosure of an item and (2) the amount, etc., required for the item to be fairly presented.

      3) A known departure ordinarily is disclosed in the notes but may be stated on the face of the statements.

EXAMPLE

Accounting principles generally accepted in the United States of America require that land be stated at cost. Management reported land at appraised value. If land had been reported at cost, the balances of the land account and shareholders' equity would have decreased by $500,000.

---

      4) Statements may be prepared that omit **substantially all disclosures** required by the framework unless the intent is to mislead users. The accountant should disclose the omission on the face of the statements or in a note.

         a) If some disclosures are omitted, the statements should include a heading such as **"Selected Information–Substantially All Disclosures Required by [the applicable financial reporting framework] Are Not Included."**

   d. When preparing statements in accordance with a **special purpose** framework, for example, the cash basis, the accountant should describe the framework on the face of the statements or in a note.

   e. The accountant may assist management in making **significant judgments**. For example, the accountant may (1) advise management on alternative significant accounting policies or (2) help management with significant judgments about accounting estimates.

      1) But management should understand and accept responsibility for significant judgments after discussions with the accountant.

5. **Notation on the Financial Statements**

   a. A preparation provides no assurance on the financial statements, and the accountant should include on **each page** (including notes) a notation that **no assurance is provided**.

      1) The notation is intended to avoid misunderstanding by users of the accountant's involvement, and the accountant's name is not required to be included.

      2) An alternative notation is that the financial statements have not been subjected to an audit, review, or compilation engagement, and no assurance is provided on them.

         a) Similar wording also is acceptable.

      3) If the accountant is **unable** to include a notation on each page of the financial statements, (s)he should (a) issue a disclaimer clarifying that no assurance is provided on the financial statements or (b) perform a compilation engagement.

EXAMPLE

The accompanying financial statements of XYZ Company as of and for the year ended December 31, 20XX, were not subjected to an audit, review, or compilation engagement by me (us) and, accordingly, I (we) do not express an opinion or a conclusion or provide any assurance on them.

Signature of accounting firm or accountant, as appropriate	<----------- May be manual, printed, or digital
Accountant's city and state	<----------- Accountant's office location
Date of the accountant's preparation disclaimer	<----------- Date of completion of preparation

---

6. **Other Presentation Considerations**

   a. The accountant should modify the titles on the statements when they are not in accordance with GAAP. For example, if the tax basis is the applicable framework, "balance sheet" should be replaced with a title similar to "Statement of Assets, Liabilities, and Equity – Income Tax Basis."

   b. When the statements do **not** include substantially all disclosures, the accountant should disclose the omission in the statements even though no accountant's report is presented. The following is an example of an appropriate notation on the face of the financial statements:

EXAMPLE

Management has elected to omit substantially all of the disclosures ordinarily included in financial statements prepared in accordance with the income tax basis of accounting. If the omitted disclosures were included in the financial statements, they might influence the user's conclusions about the company's assets, liabilities, equity, revenues, and expenses. Accordingly, these financial statements are not designed for those who are not informed about such matters.

---

   c. The accountant should **not** prepare financial statements that omit substantially all disclosures if the **intent is to mislead** users.

7. **Documentation**

   a. Documentation in connection with each preparation engagement should provide a clear understanding of the work performed and, at a minimum, include (1) the **engagement letter** and (2) a copy of the **financial statements**.

   b. Significant (1) consultations or (2) professional judgments made during the engagement may be documented.

Stop and review! You have completed the outline for this subunit. Study multiple-choice questions 4 though 7 beginning on page 430.

19.3 COMPILATION OF FINANCIAL STATEMENTS

1. **Scope and Objective**

    a.   The guidance for a compilation of financial statements also applies, adopted as needed, to other historical or prospective financial information.

    b.   The objective of a compilation is to apply accounting and financial reporting expertise to **assist management** in the presentation of financial statements without undertaking to obtain or provide any assurance on them. Unlike a preparation service, a compilation requires the accountant to

    1)   Determine whether (s)he is independent.
    2)   Report on the statements.
    3)   Disclose any lack of independence.
    4)   Associate his or her name with the statements. (It is included in the report.)

2. **Acceptance**

    a.   A compilation engagement should **not** be accepted unless the accountant obtains the agreement of management (typically in an engagement letter) that it acknowledges and understands its responsibility for

    1)   Preparing and fairly presenting financial statements and including all informative disclosures that are appropriate

    2)   Including the accountant's compilation report in any document containing financial statements if it indicates that the accountant has performed a compilation (unless a different understanding is reached)

3. **Compilation Procedures**

    a.   The accountant should **read** the statements after obtaining an understanding of the framework and significant accounting policies.

    b.   The accountant then considers whether the statements appear to be appropriate in form and free from obvious material misstatements.

    c.   The accountant is **not** required to make **inquiries** or perform **other procedures** to verify, corroborate, or review information supplied by the entity.

    1)   However, the accountant may have performed such inquiries or other procedures.

    2)   The (a) results of any procedures, (b) knowledge from prior engagements, or (c) statements themselves may cause the accountant to become aware that information provided by management is incorrect, incomplete, or otherwise unsatisfactory.

    a)   The accountant should bring such issues to the attention of management and request additional or corrected information.

    d.   If the accountant becomes aware that (1) the statements do not adequately refer to or describe the framework, (2) revisions of the statements are required for them to be in accordance with the framework, or (3) the statements are otherwise misleading, the accountant should propose the appropriate **revisions** to management.

    1)   For example, statements may be misleading if (a) the framework includes the assumption that the statements are prepared on the going concern basis, and (b) uncertainties about the entity's ability to do so are undisclosed.

    a)   If the accountant becomes aware of such uncertainties, (s)he may suggest additional disclosures.

    2)   But the existence of an adequately disclosed **uncertainty** does **not** require modification of the report.

e. The accountant should **withdraw** from the engagement and inform management of the reasons for withdrawing if

   1) (S)he is **unable to complete** the engagement because management has failed to provide records, documents, explanations, or other information, including significant judgments, as requested, or

   2) Management does **not** (a) make appropriate revisions proposed by the accountant or (b) disclose such departures in the statements, and the accountant determines not to disclose such departures in the compilation report.

f. When making withdrawal decisions, the accountant may wish to consult legal counsel.

g. Disclosure of items, such as an uncertainty, is not required in statements that omit substantially all disclosures required by the framework.

4. **Compilation Reports**

   a. The accountant should prepare a **written report** to accompany the statements. The compilation report consists of one paragraph. It should

      1) State that management (owners) is (are) responsible for the financial statements.

      2) Identify the statements.

      3) Identify the entity.

      4) Specify the date or period covered by the statements.

      5) State that the accountant performed the compilation engagement in accordance with SSARSs issued by the ARSC of the AICPA. (But the procedures performed and their results are not described in the report.)

      6) State that the accountant (a) did not audit or review the statements and (b) was not required to perform any procedures to verify the accuracy or completeness of the information provided by management. Accordingly, the accountant issues a **disclaimer**. (S)he does not express an opinion or a conclusion or provide any assurance on the statements.

      7) Include a manual, printed, or digital signature of the accountant or the accountant's firm.

      8) Include the city and state where the accountant practices.

      9) Include the date of the report, which should be the day that the accountant completed the required procedures.

   b. The accountant's written report may become unattached from the statements. Thus, (s)he may request that management refer on **each page** of the statements to the accountant's written report. Examples are

      1) "See Accountant's Report."

      2) "See Accountant's Compilation Report."

EXAMPLE -- Standard Compilation Report

Management is responsible for the accompanying financial statements of XYZ Company, which comprise the balance sheets as of December 31, 20X2 and 20X1 and the related statements of income, changes in stockholders' equity, and cash flows for the years then ended, and the related notes to the financial statements in accordance with accounting principles generally accepted in the United States of America. I (We) have performed compilation engagements in accordance with Statements on Standards for Accounting and Review Services promulgated by the Accounting and Review Services Committee of the AICPA. I (We) did not audit or review the financial statements, and I (we) was (were) not required to perform any procedures to verify the accuracy or completeness of the information provided by management. Accordingly, I (we) do not express an opinion or a conclusion or provide any form of assurance on these financial statements.

Signature of accounting firm or accountant, as appropriate   <------------ May be manual, printed, or digital
Accountant's city and state   <------------ Accountant's office location
Date of the accountant's compilation disclaimer   <------------ Date of completion of compilation

---

c. Neither the report nor the paragraph (paragraphs in a modified report) has a heading.

5. **Reporting on Statements Prepared Using a Special Purpose Framework**

    a. Unless the entity elects to omit substantially all disclosures, the accountant should modify the compilation report when the statements do **not** include

        1) A description of the special purpose framework, including a summary of significant accounting policies;

        2) An adequate description of how the special purpose framework materially differs from GAAP (but the effects of the differences need not be quantified); and

        3) Informative disclosures similar to those required by GAAP if the statements contain items that are the same as, or similar to, those in GAAP-based statements.

    b. The report should refer to management's responsibility for determining that the framework is acceptable. If a regulatory or contractual basis of accounting is used, the report also should describe the purpose for which the statements are prepared or refer to a note that contains that information.

    c. The report should include a **separate paragraph** that (1) indicates that the statements are prepared in accordance with the special purpose framework, (2) refers to the note to the statements that describes the framework (if applicable), and (3) states that the framework is a basis of accounting other than GAAP.

    d. The following is an example of a paragraph added to a report on statements prepared in accordance with a special purpose framework (i.e., the tax basis):

    EXAMPLE

    The financial statements are prepared in accordance with the tax basis of accounting, described in note 1 to the financial statements, which is a basis of accounting other than accounting principles generally accepted in the United States of America.

    ---

6. **Reporting When the Accountant Is Not Independent**

    a. An accountant who is not independent with respect to the entity should indicate his or her **lack of independence** in a final paragraph of the report.

    b. The following is an example of a paragraph indicating a lack of independence:

    EXAMPLE

    I am not independent with respect to XYZ Company.

    ---

    c. If the accountant elects to disclose the reasons independence is impaired, (s)he should include **all** the reasons.

    d. The following is an example of a paragraph indicating lack of independence:

    EXAMPLE

    I am not independent with respect to XYZ Company as of and for the year ended December 31, 20XX, because I had a direct financial interest in XYZ Company.

    ---

7. **Reporting on Financial Statements that Omit Substantially All Required Disclosures**

    a. An accountant should **not** report on statements that omit such disclosures if the omission was intended to **mislead** users.

    b. When the accountant reports on statements that omit disclosures, the report should state in a **separate paragraph** that

        1) Management has elected to omit substantially all disclosures (and the statement of cash flows, if applicable) required by the framework.

        2) The omitted disclosures might influence the user's conclusions if they (and the statement of cash flows, if applicable) were included in the statements.

        3) The statements are not designed for those who are not informed about such matters.

    c.   The following is an example paragraph that describes omitted disclosures:

EXAMPLE

Management has elected to omit substantially all the disclosures ordinarily included in financial statements prepared in accordance with accounting principles generally accepted in the United States of America. If the omitted disclosures were included in the financial statements, they might influence the user's conclusions about the company's assets, liabilities, equity, revenue, and expenses. Accordingly, the financial statements are not designed for those who are not informed about such matters.

---

    d.   The omission of one or more **notes**, when substantially all other disclosures are presented, should be treated in a compilation report like any other departure from the framework. The nature of the departure and its effects, if known, should be disclosed in the report as discussed in the following section.

8.   **Reporting Known Departures from the Applicable Financial Reporting Framework**

    a.   The accountant may become aware of a material departure from the framework (including inadequate disclosure). If (1) the statements are not revised or (2) the departure is not disclosed by the entity, the accountant should **modify** the compilation report by adding a separate paragraph to disclose the departure.

    b.   The **effects** of the departure should be disclosed if they (1) have been determined by management or (2) are readily known to the accountant.

    c.   The following is an example of a separate paragraph:

EXAMPLE

Accounting principles generally accepted in the United States of America require that land be stated at cost. Management has informed me that XYZ Company has stated its land at appraised value and that, if accounting principles generally accepted in the United States of America had been followed, the land account and stockholders' equity would have been decreased by $500,000.

---

    d.   If the effects of the departure are **not** known, the accountant is not required to determine its effects. But the report should state that the determination has not been made by management.

    e.   If modification of the compilation report is **not** adequate to indicate the deficiencies in the statements as a whole, the accountant should (1) **withdraw** from the engagement and (2) provide no further services with respect to those statements. (The accountant may want to consult legal counsel.)

    f.   The accountant **never** indicates in the compilation report that the statements do not conform with the framework. This conclusion can be formed only on the basis of an audit.

9.   **Supplementary Information**

    a.   When supplementary information accompanies financial statements, the accountant should clearly indicate the degree of responsibility, if any, (s)he is taking with respect to the information.

        1)   This indication may be in (a) an **other-matter** paragraph in the compilation report on the statements or (b) a **separate report** on the supplementary information.

    b.   An accountant who has performed a compilation of the statements **and** the supplementary information may elect to issue a separate report on the supplementary information. The separate report should state that the information is

        1)   Presented for additional analysis and is not required

        2)   The representation of management

        3)   Subject to the compilation engagement

        4)   Not audited or reviewed, and the accountant does not (a) express an opinion or a conclusion or (b) provide any assurance on the information

    c.   If the supplementary information was **not** compiled, the accountant also may elect to issue a separate report. The separate report should state that the supplementary information is

        1)   Presented for additional analysis and is not required

        2)   The representation of management

        3)   Not compiled and the accountant does not (a) express an opinion or a conclusion or (b) provide any assurance on the information

    d.   If a separate report is not presented, the disclosures discussed in this subunit are included in an other-matter paragraph of the compilation report.

10.   **Required Supplementary Information (RSI)**

    a.   If supplementary information is required, the accountant should explain one of the following in an **other-matter** paragraph:

        1)   RSI is included, and the accountant compiled it.

        2)   RSI is included, and the accountant did **not** compile, review, or audit the RSI.

        3)   RSI is omitted.

        4)   Some RSI is missing, and some is presented in accordance with prescribed guidelines.

        5)   The accountant has identified departures from prescribed guidelines.

        6)   The accountant has unresolved doubts about whether the RSI is presented in accordance with prescribed guidelines.

11.   **Compilation of Pro Forma Financial Information (To be updated June 2017)**

    a.   An accountant may assist management to compile pro forma financial statements and submit them to a third party.

        1)   An accountant, in certain cases, may do so without issuing a compilation report.

        2)   However, if the accountant has been engaged to report on such statements, a compilation report should be issued.

    b.   The accountant may agree to compile pro forma financial information only if it is contained in a document that includes (or incorporates by reference) the historical statements of the entity on which it is based.

    c.   The accountant should follow the guidelines for compiling and reporting on compiled financial statements.

12.   **Documentation of a Compilation Engagement**

    a.   The accountant should prepare documentation for each compilation engagement in sufficient detail to provide a clear understanding of the work performed.

    b.   The minimum presentation includes the following:

        1)   The engagement letter or other suitable written documentation of the understanding with management

        2)   A copy of the financial statements

        3)   A copy of the accountant's report

Stop and review! You have completed the outline for this subunit. Study multiple-choice questions 8 and 9 on page 431.

19.4 REVIEW OF FINANCIAL STATEMENTS

1. **Scope and Objective**

   a. The guidance for a review of financial statements also applies, as necessary, to reviews of other historical (but **not** prospective) financial information.

   b. The objective of a review of financial statements is to obtain **limited assurance** as a basis for reporting whether the accountant is aware of any material modifications that should be made to the statements for them to be in accordance with the reporting framework (e.g., GAAP).

   c. Limited assurance also is known as **negative assurance**, in contrast with the positive assurance provided by an audit.

   d. A review is performed primarily through **inquiry** and **analytical procedures**.

   e. The accountant **must be independent** of the entity when performing a review. If, during the review, the accountant determines that independence is impaired, (s)he should withdraw from the engagement.

      1) However, if the accountant lacks independence, (s)he may accept a new engagement to prepare or compile the statements.

2. **Communication with Management and Those Charged with Governance**

   a. The accountant should communicate appropriately **during the review** all related **significant** matters that merit the attention of (1) management and (2) those charged with governance.

      1) **Management** consists of persons with executive responsibility for the entity's operations.

      2) **Those charged with governance** include the persons or organizations (e.g., a corporate trustee) responsible for (a) overseeing the strategic direction of the entity and (b) the obligations related to the accountability of the entity (e.g., for oversight of financial reporting).

      3) Those charged with governance may include management personnel.

   b. Matters communicated include (1) the accountant's responsibilities and (2) significant findings. The following are examples of findings:

      1) Views about the entity's accounting practices

      2) The need to perform additional procedures

      3) Matters, such as fraud or noncompliance, that may require modification of the report

      4) Significant difficulties that may lead to withdrawal from the engagement

   c. Communication may be in the form of (1) inquiries while performing procedures or (2) other communications as part of having an effective dialogue to understand issues and develop a working relationship.

   d. The communication may be oral or written.

   e. The accountant normally is **not required** to communicate with those **outside the entity** unless required by law or regulation.

3. **Nature of a Review**

   a. The accountant should **possess or obtain** a sufficient **understanding** of the industry and knowledge of the entity.

      1) The understanding of the industry includes the accounting principles and practices generally used.

      2) The knowledge of the entity includes an understanding of (a) the entity's business and (b) its accounting principles and practices.

3) The understanding should suffice to (a) identify the **assertions** in the financial statements having a greater likelihood of material misstatement and (b) design procedures to address those risks.

4) A review is not as comprehensive as an audit. Thus, the accountant is not expected to (a) obtain an understanding of the entity's internal control, (b) assess fraud risks, (c) test the accounting records, (d) examine source documents, or (e) perform other audit procedures.

b. **Designing and Performing Review Procedures**

1) The accountant should (a) design and perform **analytical procedures**; (b) make **inquiries**; and (c) perform other procedures, as appropriate, to obtain **limited assurance**.

2) **Review evidence** is information used by the accountant to provide a reasonable basis for obtaining limited assurance.

3) The procedures to obtain review evidence should be based on the accountant's (a) understanding of the industry, (b) knowledge of the entity, and (c) awareness of risks.

a) The accountant should concentrate on assertions having increased risks of material misstatement (RMMs).

4. **Review Evidence – Analytical Procedures**

a. Analytical procedures are evaluations of financial information through analysis of plausible relationships among both **financial and nonfinancial data**.

1) They also include any necessary investigation of identified fluctuations or relationships that (a) are inconsistent with other relevant information or (b) differ significantly from expected values.

2) The accountant should apply analytical procedures to the financial statements to identify, and provide a basis for inquiry about, the relationships and individual items that (a) appear to be unusual and (b) may indicate a material misstatement.

3) The basic premise of analytical procedures is that plausible relationships among data may reasonably be expected to exist and continue in the absence of known conditions to the contrary.

b. Analytical procedures should

1) Compare the statements with comparable information for the **prior period**, considering knowledge about changes in the entity's business and specific transactions.

2) Consider plausible **relationships** among both **financial** and, when relevant, **nonfinancial** information.

3) Compare **recorded amounts**, or **ratios** developed from recorded amounts, with expectations developed from relationships within the entity or the entity's industry.

4) Compare **disaggregated revenue data**, as applicable.

c. When designing and performing analytical procedures, the accountant should

1) Determine the **suitability** of particular procedures.

2) Consider the **reliability** of the underlying data from which the expectations of recorded amounts or ratios are developed.

3) Develop an **expectation** of recorded amounts or ratios and evaluate whether it is sufficiently precise to provide limited assurance of identifying a material misstatement.

4) Determine the amount of any **difference** between recorded amounts and expected values that is **acceptable** without further investigation.

5) Compare the recorded amounts or ratios with expectations.

    d.   The following are examples of potentially useful analytical procedures:

        1)   Comparing revenues and expenses of the current period and the prior period

        2)   Comparing current statements with anticipated results, such as budgets and forecasts

        3)   Comparing current statement information with relevant nonfinancial information, such as hours worked or product shipped

        4)   Comparing the current-period and prior-period measures of (a) the current ratio, (b) receivables turnover, (c) inventory turnover, (d) depreciation to average fixed assets, (e) debt to equity, (f) gross profit percentage, and (g) net income percentage

        5)   Comparing ratios and indicators for the current period with those of entities in the same industry

        6)   Comparing disaggregated data, e.g., monthly or weekly amounts of (a) sales or (b) sales by product line, operating segment, or location, with data from prior periods or budgets

    e.   Analytical procedures may be performed at the **statement** level or the **detailed account** level.

        1)   Those at the statement level provide evidence to support overall conclusions. For example, the accountant may question whether the size of a warehouse can hold all of the reported inventory.

        2)   Those at the detailed account level provide evidence of potential account balance misstatement. For example, the accountant may compare monthly balances of receivables for the current year and prior year.

    f.   Analytical procedures may identify fluctuations or relationships that (1) are **inconsistent** with other relevant information or (2) differ significantly from expected values.

    g.   The accountant should investigate such differences by (1) **inquiring** of management and (2) performing **other** review procedures if necessary.

    h.   The following is an example of this process:

EXAMPLE

By applying an analytical procedure, the accountant discovered that the accounts receivable balance was greater than expected based on the prior year's balance. The accountant inquired of management about the reason. The response was that the cash receipts clerk was absent from work during the last week of the year. An inspection of the cash receipts records determined that cash receipts were not recorded for the last week. Accordingly, cash was understated and accounts receivable overstated. Based on this finding, management corrected the misstatement.

---

5.   **Review Evidence – Inquiries of Management**

    a.   The accountant should obtain review evidence by inquiring of members of management who have responsibility for **financial and accounting** matters related to the financial statements.

    b.   Inquiries should be made about matters the accountant considers necessary, such as the following:

        1)   Whether the statements have been prepared and fairly presented in accordance with the reporting framework consistently applied

        2)   Unusual or complex situations that may affect the statements

        3)   Significant transactions occurring or recognized during the period, particularly in the last several days of the period

        4)   The status of uncorrected misstatements identified during the previous review

        5)   Matters about which questions have arisen during the review

        6)   Events subsequent to the date of the statements that could have a material effect on their fair presentation

7) Knowledge of fraud or suspected fraud involving (a) management, (b) employees with significant roles in internal control, or (c) others if the fraud could materially affect the statements

8) Awareness of any allegations of fraud or suspected fraud affecting the entity

9) Whether management has disclosed all known or suspected noncompliance with laws and regulations that may affect the statements

10) Significant journal entries and other adjustments

11) Communications from regulatory agencies

12) Related parties and significant new related-party transactions

13) Any litigation, claims, and assessments (a) at the date of the balance sheet and (b) during the period from the balance sheet date to the date of management's response

14) Whether management believes that significant assumptions used in making accounting estimates are reasonable

15) Actions taken at meetings of shareholders, the board, or comparable meetings that may affect the statements

c. The accountant should consider the (1) reasonableness and consistency of the responses given, (2) results of other review procedures, and (3) accountant's knowledge of the entity's business. However, the accountant is **not required** to corroborate the responses.

6. **Review Evidence – Written Representations**

a. A **representation letter** addressed to the accountant should be obtained to confirm certain matters or to support other review evidence. (Study Unit 14, Subunit 3, provides an example.)

b. The letter typically is signed by members of management in key financial positions, such as the **chief executive officer** and the **chief financial officer**.

c. It should be dated as of the date of the review report.

7. **Review Evidence – Other Procedures**

a. The accountant should **read** the statements and consider whether any information has come to his or her attention to indicate that they are **not** in accordance with the framework.

b. The accountant also should (1) obtain evidence that the statements **agree or reconcile** with the **accounting records** and (2) read the reports of other accountants who have reported on significant components of the entity.

8. **Evaluating Evidence**

a. The accountant should accumulate **misstatements**, including inadequate disclosure.

b. The accountant should evaluate misstatements, individually and in the aggregate, to determine whether the statements should be materially modified for them to be in accordance with the framework.

c. The accountant may become aware that information is incorrect, incomplete, or otherwise unsatisfactory. The accountant then should

1) Request that management (a) consider the effect on the statements and (b) communicate the results of the consideration to the accountant.

2) Consider (a) the results and (b) whether they indicate that the statements may be materially misstated.

d. If the accountant believes that the statements may be materially misstated, (s)he should perform the **additional** procedures necessary to obtain **limited assurance**.

e. If the accountant concludes that the statements are materially misstated, the reporting guidance for known departures from the framework applies (item 11. on page 417).

    f.   Even if the accountant has no reason to believe that the statements are materially misstated, (s)he should evaluate whether the review evidence obtained is **sufficient and appropriate** to form a conclusion.

       1)   If it is not, the accountant should (a) extend the work performed or (b) perform other procedures that, in his or her professional judgment, are necessary.

       2)   The AICPA does **not** specify what additional (or other) procedures should be performed, but they might include tests of details, confirmations, and reconciliations.

9.   **Review Report**

    a.   A written review report in hard copy or electronic format should be presented that consists of

       1)   A title that includes the word **independent** to indicate clearly that it is the report of an independent accountant.

       2)   An addressee, as appropriate.

       3)   An introductory paragraph that

          a)   Identifies the entity whose financial statements have been reviewed.

          b)   States that the statements identified in the report were reviewed.

          c)   Identifies the statements.

          d)   Specifies the date or period covered by each statement.

          e)   States that a review primarily includes applying analytical procedures to management's (owner's) financial data and making inquiries of company management (owners).

          f)   States that a review is substantially less in scope than an audit, the objective of which is the expression of an opinion regarding the statements as a whole. Accordingly, the accountant does not express such an opinion.

       4)   A section with the heading **Management's Responsibility for the Financial Statements** that includes an explanation that management is responsible for the preparation and fair presentation of the statements in accordance with the applicable reporting framework. This responsibility includes the design, implementation, and maintenance of internal control sufficient to provide a reasonable basis for the presentation.

       5)   A section with the heading **Accountant's Responsibility** that includes the following statements:

          a)   The accountant's responsibility is to conduct the review in accordance with SSARSs promulgated by the Accounting and Review Services Committee of the AICPA.

          b)   The accountant believes that the review evidence obtained is sufficient and appropriate to provide a basis for the conclusion.

       6)   A concluding section with an appropriate heading, for example, **Accountant's Conclusion**. It includes a statement about whether the accountant is aware of any material modifications that should be made to the accompanying statements for them to be in accordance with the applicable reporting framework and identifies the country of origin of those accounting principles, if applicable.

       7)   The manual, printed, or digital signature of the accountant or the accountant's firm.

       8)   The city and state where the accountant practices.

       9)   The date of the review report. It should be dated no earlier than the date on which the accountant has completed procedures sufficient to obtain limited assurance.

    b.   The accountant should consider including a reference on each page of the financial statements, such as **See Independent Accountant's Review Report**.

    c.   A continuing accountant should **update** the report on one or more prior periods presented **comparatively** with those of the current period. An updated report considers information the continuing accountant has obtained during the current engagement and

        1)   Re-expresses the accountant's previous conclusions or

        2)   Depending on the circumstances, expresses different conclusions on the statements of a prior period as of the date of the current report.

    d.   The following is an example of a review report on comparative financial statements:

EXAMPLE -- Standard Review Report

Independent Accountant's Review Report

To the owners of XYZ Company

I (We) have reviewed the accompanying financial statements of XYZ Company, which comprise the balance sheets as of December 31, 20X2 and 20X1, and the related statements of income, changes in stockholders' equity, and cash flows for the years then ended, and the related notes to the financial statements. A review includes primarily applying analytical procedures to management's (owners') financial data and making inquiries of company management (owners). A review is substantially less in scope than an audit, the objective of which is the expression of an opinion regarding the financial statements as a whole. Accordingly, I (we) do not express such an opinion.

Management's Responsibility for the Financial Statements

Management (Owners) is (are) responsible for the preparation and fair presentation of these financial statements in accordance with accounting principles generally accepted in the United States of America; this includes the design, implementation, and maintenance of internal control relevant to the preparation and fair presentation of financial statements that are free from material misstatement whether due to fraud or error.

Accountant's Responsibility

My (Our) responsibility is to conduct the review engagement in accordance with Statements on Standards for Accounting and Review Services promulgated by the Accounting and Review Services Committee of the AICPA. Those standards require me (us) to perform procedures to obtain limited assurance as a basis for reporting whether I am (we are) aware of any material modifications that should be made to the financial statements for them to be in accordance with accounting principles generally accepted in the United States of America. I (We) believe that the results of my (our) procedures provide a reasonable basis for our conclusion.

Accountant's Conclusion

Based on my (our) reviews, I am (we are) not aware of any material modifications that should be made to the accompanying financial statements in order for them to be in accordance with accounting principles generally accepted in the United States of America.

Signature of accounting firm or accountant, as appropriate   <------------ May be manual, printed, or digital
Accountant's city and state   <------------ Accountant's office location
Date of the accountant's review report   <------------ Date of completion of review

---

10.   **Special Purpose Frameworks**

    a.   The accountant's review report on statements prepared in accordance with a special purpose framework (e.g., cash basis, tax basis, or a contractual or regulatory basis) should

        1)   Refer to management's responsibility for determining that the framework is acceptable.

        2)   Describe the purpose for which the statements are prepared or refer to a note that contains that information when they are prepared in accordance with a regulatory basis or a contractual basis.

        3)   Include an **emphasis-of-matter** paragraph, under an appropriate heading, that

           a)   Indicates that the statements are prepared in accordance with the special purpose framework,

           b)   Refers to the note that describes the framework, and

           c)   States that the framework is a basis of accounting other than GAAP.

   b.   The accountant should **modify** the review report if the statements do **not** include

        1)   A description of the framework

        2)   A summary of significant accounting policies

        3)   An adequate description of how the framework differs from GAAP

        4)   Informative disclosures similar to GAAP disclosures if items are included that are similar to items included in GAAP-based statements

11. Known Departures from the Framework

   a.   The accountant may become aware of a departure (including inadequate disclosure) that is material to the financial statements. If they are **not** revised, (s)he should consider whether modification of the report is adequate to disclose the departure.

        1)   If the accountant concludes that modification is **adequate**, the departure should be disclosed in a **separate paragraph** of the report under the heading Known Departures From Accounting Principles Generally Accepted in the United States of America (or other applicable framework).

           a)   The disclosure should include the **effects** of the departure if they (1) have been determined by management or (2) are known to the accountant as the result of his or her procedures.

           b)   If the effects of the departure have not been determined by management or are not known, the accountant is **not** required to determine the effects. In such circumstances, the accountant should state in the report that the determination has not been made.

           c)   The **Accountant's Conclusion** paragraph is modified to include the phrase ". . . except for the issue noted in the Known Departure From Accounting Principles Generally Accepted in the United States of America paragraph . . ."

           d)   The following is an example of the final two paragraphs in a report to disclose known departures from GAAP.

EXAMPLE

Accountant's Conclusion

Based on my (our) reviews, except for the issue noted in the Known Departure From Accounting Principles Generally Accepted in the United States of America paragraph, I am (we are) not aware of any material modifications that should be made to the accompanying financial statements in order for them to be in accordance with accounting principles generally accepted in the United States of America.

Known Departure From Accounting Principles Generally Accepted in the United States of America

As disclosed in Note X to these financial statements, accounting principles generally accepted in the United States of America require that inventory cost consist of material, labor, and overhead. Management has informed me (us) that the inventory of finished goods and work in process is stated in the accompanying financial statements at material and labor cost only, and that the effects of this departure from accounting principles generally accepted in the United States of America on financial position, results of operations, and cash flows have not been determined.

---

        2)   If modification of the report is **not adequate** to indicate the deficiencies in the statements as a whole, the accountant should **withdraw** from the engagement. The accountant also may wish to consult legal counsel.

b.   The accountant must **not** modify the report to state that the financial statements are not in accordance with the applicable framework. A review engagement provides no form of reporting that corresponds to an adverse opinion on audited financial statements. Thus, no **adverse** review report may be issued.

12.   **Fraud and Noncompliance**

a.   The accountant may become aware that **fraud** (including misappropriation of assets) might have occurred. (S)he then should communicate the matter as soon as practicable to the appropriate level of management (at a level above those involved with the suspected fraud, if possible).

b.   The accountant also may become aware of **noncompliance** that should be considered when preparing the financial statements. Unless the matter is clearly inconsequential, it should be communicated to management.

c.   If the fraud or noncompliance (1) involves senior management or (2) results in a material misstatement, the accountant should communicate the matter directly to those charged with governance.

d.   Management or those charged with governance (if appropriate) may not provide sufficient information that supports the conclusion that the statements are not materially misstated due to fraud or noncompliance.

1)   The accountant then should consider the need to obtain legal advice and take appropriate action, including potential withdrawal.

13.   **Emphasis-of-Matter and Other-Matter Paragraphs**

a.   An **emphasis-of-matter** paragraph is included in the review report (1) if required by SSARSs or (2) at the accountant's discretion.

1)   It refers to a matter that is **appropriately presented or disclosed** in the statements that, in the accountant's judgment, is fundamental to users' understanding and is a matter to which attention should be drawn.

2)   An accountant may add more than one such paragraph.

3)   The paragraph should have the heading **Emphasis-of-Matter** and follow the Accountant's Conclusion paragraph. The following are examples of matters that may be emphasized:

a)   Uncertainties
b)   That the entity is a component of a larger business enterprise
c)   That the entity has had significant transactions with related parties
d)   Unusually important subsequent events

b.   An **other-matter paragraph** is included in the report (1) if required by SSARSs or (2) at the accountant's discretion. It refers to a matter **other** than those presented or disclosed in the statements that, in the accountant's judgment, is relevant to (1) users' understanding of the review, (2) the accountant's responsibilities, or (3) the report.

1)   The paragraph should have the heading **Other Matter** and follow (a) the Accountant's Conclusion paragraph and (b) any emphasis-of-matter paragraph(s).

2)   Examples of other matters include the accountant's responsibility for (a) supplementary information included by management or (b) reporting on a regulatory requirement applying to the client.

14. **Ability to Continue as a Going Concern**

    a. During the review, evidence or information may come to the accountant's attention indicating an **uncertainty** about the entity's ability to continue as a going concern for a reasonable period of time. (The period specified by U.S. GAAP is 1 year from the date the statements are issued or are available to be issued.)

        1) If an uncertainty exists about an entity's ability to continue as a going concern, the accountant should request that management consider the **possible effects** on the statements, including the need for disclosure.

        2) After management communicates the results of its consideration of the possible effects, the accountant should consider the reasonableness of the conclusions, including the adequacy of disclosure.

            a) If the accountant determines that (1) management's conclusions are adequate and (2) the going concern uncertainty is appropriately presented and disclosed, (s)he may, but is **not** required, to include an **emphasis-of-matter** paragraph in the review report.

        3) The accountant may determine that (a) management's conclusions are unreasonable or (b) its disclosure is **not** adequate. These determinations should be included in a **Known Departures From the Reporting Framework** section of the report.

15. **Subsequent Events**

    a. Subsequent events occur between the date of the financial statements and the date of the review report.

    b. The accountant may identify evidence or information of a subsequent event that requires adjustment of, or disclosure in, the statements. The accountant then should request that management consider whether the subsequent event is appropriately reflected in the statements in accordance with the reporting framework.

    c. The accountant may determine that the subsequent event is **not** adequately accounted for or disclosed. These determinations should be included in a **Known Departures From the Reporting Framework** section of the report.

16. **Subsequently Discovered Facts**

    a. Subsequently discovered facts (1) become known to the accountant after the date of the review report and (2) might have caused a revision of the report if they had been known at that date.

    b. The accountant is **not** required to perform any procedures after the date of the report.

    c. However, if a subsequently discovered fact becomes known to the accountant **before the report release date**, (s)he should (1) discuss the matter with management and, when appropriate, those charged with governance and (2) determine whether the statements need revision and, if so, inquire how management intends to address the matter in the statements.

        1) If management **revises** the statements, the accountant should perform the necessary procedures on the revision.

            a) The accountant also should either (1) date the review report as of a later date or (2) include an additional date in the report on the revised statements that is limited to the revision (dual-date the report).

            b) **Dual-dating** indicates that the review procedures subsequent to the original date of the report are limited solely to the revision described in the relevant note to the statements.

        2) If management does **not revise** the statements when the accountant believes they should be revised, (s)he should modify the report as appropriate or consider withdrawal from the engagement.

d. A subsequently discovered fact may become known to the accountant **after the report release date**.

    1) The accountant should (a) discuss the matter with management and, when appropriate, those charged with governance and (b) determine whether the statements need revision and, if so, inquire how management intends to address the matter.

    2) If management does not take the appropriate action, the accountant should ensure that users do not rely on the accountant's report. For example, (s)he might notify users.

17. **Supplementary Information Accompanying the Statements**

a. Supplementary information, other than that required, is (1) presented outside the basic financial statements and (2) not considered necessary for fair presentation in accordance with the reporting framework.

b. The accountant should clearly indicate the degree of responsibility, if any, (s)he is taking with respect to such information in either (1) an **other-matter** paragraph in the report on the statements or (2) a **separate report** on the supplementary information.

c. If the accountant has **reviewed** the financial statements **and** the supplementary information, the other-matter paragraph or the separate report should state that

    1) The information is presented for additional analysis and is **not** required.

    2) The information is the representation of management.

    3) The accountant has reviewed the information.

        a) The accountant also should state, based on the review, whether (s)he can provide limited assurance.

    4) The accountant has not audited the information and does not express an opinion on it.

d. If the accountant has reviewed the statements but **not** the supplementary information, the other-matter paragraph or the separate report should state that

    1) The information is presented for additional analysis and is **not** required;

    2) The information is the representation of management; and

    3) The accountant has not audited or reviewed the information and does **not** express an opinion or a conclusion or provide any assurance on it.

18. **Required Supplementary Information (RSI)**

a. RSI is required by a designated accounting standards setter to accompany basic financial statements.

b. RSI is **not** part of those statements, but a designated standards setter considers it essential to place the statements in an appropriate operational, economic, or historical context. Also, authoritative guidelines for its measurement and presentation have been established. (An example is reserve information for oil and gas producers.)

c. The accountant should include an **other-matter** paragraph regarding RSI in the review report to explain one or more of the following, if applicable:

    1) RSI is included and was compiled or reviewed by the accountant.

    2) RSI is included and was **not** compiled, reviewed, or audited by the accountant.

    3) Some or all of the RSI is omitted.

    4) The accountant has identified departures from the prescribed guidelines.

    5) The accountant has unresolved doubts about whether the RSI is presented in accordance with prescribed guidelines.

19. **Review Documentation**

   a. Review documentation is the record of (1) review procedures performed, (2) relevant review evidence obtained, and (3) conclusions reached. (Other terms sometimes used are working papers or workpapers.)

   b. The accountant should prepare documentation that suffices to enable an experienced accountant, having no previous connection to the review, to understand

   1) The nature, timing, and extent of the procedures performed to comply with SSARSs;

   2) The results of the procedures performed and the evidence obtained; and

   3) Significant findings or issues arising during the review, the conclusions reached, and significant professional judgments made in reaching those conclusions.

   c. In addition, review documentation should include the following:

   1) The engagement letter or other suitable form of written agreement with management

   2) Communications to management and others about fraud or noncompliance with laws and regulations

   3) Communications with management about the accountant's expectation to include an emphasis-of-matter or other-matter paragraph in the report

   4) Communications with other accountants that have audited or reviewed the statements

   5) The representation letter

   6) A copy of the reviewed statements and the accountant's review report

20. **Change in Engagement From Audit to Review**

   a. An accountant engaged to audit the statements of a nonissuer may be requested to change the engagement to a review.

   1) The request may result from (a) a change in circumstances affecting the entity's need for an audit, (b) a misunderstanding about the nature of an audit or review, or (c) a restriction on the scope of the audit.

   2) Before an accountant engaged to perform an audit in accordance with GAAS agrees to change the engagement to a review, at least the following should be considered:

   a) The reason given for the request, especially the implications of a restriction on the scope of the engagement, whether imposed by management or by circumstances

   b) The additional audit effort required to complete the audit

   c) The estimated additional cost to complete the audit

   b. In **all** circumstances, if audit procedures are substantially complete, or the cost to complete the procedures is relatively insignificant, the accountant should **consider** the propriety of a change in the engagement.

   c. If the accountant (1) concludes that the change is reasonably justified and (2) complies with the standards applicable to a review, (s)he should issue an appropriate review report. The report should **not** refer to

   1) The original engagement,

   2) Any audit procedures that may have been performed, or

   3) Scope limitations that resulted in the change.

   d. If (1) the original engagement was to perform an audit and (2) management refused to allow the accountant to correspond with the entity's legal counsel, the accountant, except in rare circumstances, is precluded from accepting a review engagement.

21. **Reference to the Work of Other Accountants**

    a. Other accountants may have audited or reviewed the statements of significant components (e.g., subsidiaries). If the reporting accountant decides not to assume responsibility for the audit or review, (s)he should indicate in the review report (1) that the work was used and (2) the magnitude of the portion of the statements audited or reviewed by other accountants.

    b. Whether or not reference is made, the reporting accountant should communicate with the other accountants to determine that

        1) They are aware of the use of their work, and
        2) They are familiar with the reporting framework and applicable standards.

22. **Reporting when One Period is Audited**

    a. When the prior period statements were audited and the auditor's report is not reissued, the review report on the current statements should include an **other-matter** paragraph indicating

        1) That the statements of the prior period were audited;
        2) The date of the auditor's report;
        3) The type of opinion expressed;
        4) The substantive reasons for any modification of opinion; and
        5) That no auditing procedures were performed after the date of the previous report.

23. **Restricted Use of the Report**

    a. When the accountant concludes that the financial information reported on is suitable only for a **limited set of users**, the report should contain a separate paragraph that restricts the use of the report to those users.

Stop and review! You have completed the outline for this subunit. Study multiple-choice questions 10 though 13 beginning on page 432.

19.5 ENGAGEMENTS TO APPLY AGREED-UPON PROCEDURES

1. **Nature of the Engagement**

    a. An agreed-upon procedures engagement is one in which a practitioner is engaged by a client to issue a report of findings based on specific procedures performed on subject matter.

    b. **Specified parties** assume responsibility for the **sufficiency** of the procedures.

    c. The **report** is in the form of **procedures and findings**, and neither an opinion nor negative (limited) assurance should be provided.

    d. The **general, field work, and reporting standards** for attestation engagements apply. They are covered in Study Unit 1. However, a written assertion is generally not required in an agreed-upon procedures engagement unless specifically required by another attest standard.

2. **Procedures**

    a. **Appropriate procedures** include

        1) Inspection of specified documents for attributes
        2) Confirmation of specific information with third parties
        3) Comparison of documents or schedules with certain attributes
        4) Performance of mathematical computations or sampling

      b.   **Inappropriate procedures** include

         1)   Mere reading of the work performed by others to describe their findings
         2)   Evaluating the competency or objectivity of another party
         3)   Obtaining an understanding about a particular subject
         4)   General review, checking, or any other overly subjective procedure
         5)   Interpreting documents outside the scope of the practitioner's expertise

3.   The practitioner may perform an engagement provided that

      a.   (S)he is **independent**.
      b.   A specified party is responsible for the **subject matter** (or the client has a reasonable basis for providing a written assertion, if required).
      c.   The specified parties agree with the practitioner about the **procedures** to be performed.
      d.   The specified parties are responsible for the **sufficiency** of the procedures.
      e.   Procedures are expected to result in reasonably consistent **findings**.
      f.   **Criteria** to be used in the determination of findings are agreed upon.
      g.   Reasonably consistent subject matter **measurement** can be expected.
      h.   **Evidence** providing a reasonable basis for findings can be collected.
      i.   An agreement exists on **materiality** limits for reporting when applicable.
      j.   **Use** of the report is restricted to specified parties.

4.   To ensure that specified parties take **responsibility for the sufficiency of the procedures**, the practitioner should do one or more of the following:

      a.   Communicate directly with, and obtain affirmative acknowledgment from, the parties
      b.   Distribute the engagement letter to the specified parties
      c.   Distribute a draft of the anticipated report to the specified parties
      d.   Consider written requirements of the specified parties
      e.   Discuss procedures with appropriate representatives of the specified parties
      f.   Review contracts with or correspondence from the specified parties

5.   Attestation **documentation** (working papers) should be prepared.

EXAMPLE -- Report on Agreed-Upon Procedures

Independent Accountant's Report on Applying Agreed-Upon Procedures

To the Audit Committee and Managements of ABC, Inc., and XYZ Fund:

We have performed the procedures enumerated below, which were agreed to by the audit committees and managements of ABC, Inc., and XYZ Fund, solely to assist you in evaluating the accompanying Statement of Investment Performance Statistics of XYZ Fund (prepared in accordance with the criteria specified therein) for the year ended December 31, Year 1. XYZ Fund's management is responsible for the statement of investment performance statistics. This agreed-upon procedures engagement was conducted in accordance with attestation standards established by the American Institute of Certified Public Accountants. The sufficiency of these procedures is solely the responsibility of those parties specified in this report. Consequently, we make no representation regarding the sufficiency of the procedures described below, either for the purpose for which this report has been requested or for any other purpose.

[Include paragraphs to enumerate procedures and findings.]

We were not engaged to and did not conduct an examination, the objective of which would be the expression of an opinion on the accompanying Statement of Investment Performance Statistics of XYZ Fund. Accordingly, we do not express such an opinion. Had we performed additional procedures, other matters might have come to our attention that would have been reported to you.

This report is intended solely for the information and use of the audit committees and managements of ABC, Inc., and XYZ Fund and is not intended to be and should not be used by anyone other than these specified parties.

Signature   <----------- May be signed, typed, or printed
Date   <----------- Date completed engagement

Stop and review! You have completed the outline for this subunit. Study multiple-choice questions 14 and 15 on page 433.

19.6 FINANCIAL FORECASTS AND PROJECTIONS

1. **Prospective Financial Statements (PFSs)**

    a. PFSs consist of financial forecasts or projections, including summaries of significant assumptions and accounting policies. A practitioner must examine, compile, or apply agreed-upon procedures to PFSs if they are, or reasonably might be, expected to be used by another (third) party and if the practitioner

        1) Submits to the client or others PFSs that (s)he has assembled or assisted in assembling

        2) Reports on PFSs

    b. The practitioner must be **independent** to report on an examination or the results of agreed-upon procedures for PFSs. But the practitioner need not be independent to compile PFSs.

        1) However, the compilation report should be modified to include a separate paragraph disclosing the lack of independence.

        2) Also, the accountant is not prevented from disclosing the reason(s) that independence is impaired.

2. A **financial forecast** consists of PFSs that present, to the best of the responsible party's knowledge and belief, an entity's expected financial position, results of operations, and cash flows.

    a. It is based on the **responsible party's assumptions** reflecting conditions it expects to exist and the course of action it expects to take.

        1) The responsible party is usually management of the entity, but it may be a party outside the entity, such as a potential acquirer.

    b. It may be expressed in specific monetary amounts as a range or as a single point estimate of forecasted results. For a range, the responsible party selects key assumptions to form an interval within which it reasonably expects, to the best of its knowledge and belief, the item or items subject to the assumptions to actually fall.

3. A **financial projection** differs from a forecast. A projection is based on the responsible party's assumptions reflecting conditions it expects would exist and the course of action it expects would be taken, given one or more **hypothetical assumptions**.

    a. A projection is sometimes prepared to present one or more hypothetical courses of action for evaluation, as in response to a question such as, "What would happen if . . .?" A projection may be expressed as a point estimate or a range.

4. PFSs are for **general use** if they are for use by persons with whom the responsible party is not negotiating directly, e.g., in an offering statement of the party's securities.

    a. Only a compilation or examination of a **forecast** is appropriate for general use. Projections and all other presentations are for limited use.

    b. General use PFSs should portray expected results to the best of the responsible party's knowledge and belief.

5. **Limited use** of PFSs means use by the responsible party and those with whom that party is negotiating directly. Examples are use in a submission to a regulatory body or in negotiations for a bank loan. These third parties can communicate directly with the responsible party.

    a. Consequently, any type of PFSs that would be useful in the circumstances would be appropriate for limited use.

    b.   A projection is appropriate only for limited use. The reason is that the presentation of a projection is based on one or more hypothetical assumptions.

        1)   PFSs are appropriate for general use only if they portray, to the best of the responsible party's knowledge and belief, the expected results. A hypothetical assumption is a condition or course of action that is not necessarily expected to occur.

6.   **Examinations**

    a.   An examination evaluates the preparation of the statements, the support underlying the assumptions, and the presentation of the statements for conformity with AICPA guidelines.

    b.   It also involves issuance of a report stating the practitioner's opinion on whether the PFSs conform with AICPA guidelines and whether the assumptions provide a reasonable basis for (1) the forecast or (2) the projection given hypothetical assumptions.

    c.   If assumptions that appear to be significant at the time are not disclosed in the presentation, including the summary of assumptions, the practitioner should express an adverse opinion. Moreover, a practitioner should not examine a presentation that omits all such disclosures.

7.   **Compilations**

    a.   A compilation of PFSs, such as a financial forecast, involves (1) assembling, to the extent necessary, the statements based on the responsible party's assumptions; (2) performing required compilation procedures; and (3) issuing a compilation report.

    b.   The required procedures include (1) reading the statements and (2) considering whether they meet AICPA presentation guidelines and determining that the statements are not obviously inappropriate.

        1)   Other required procedures include (a) inquiries about accounting principles, (b) obtaining a list of significant assumptions and considering whether obvious omissions or inconsistencies exist, (c) testing the mathematical accuracy of the computations, and (d) obtaining written representations.

        2)   If the accountant inquired or performed procedures before and became aware of incorrect or unsatisfactory information, (s)he should request revised information from the entity. If the entity refuses to provide revised information, the accountant should **withdraw from the engagement**.

    c.   The standard report states that a compilation is limited in scope and does not enable the practitioner to express an opinion or any other form of assurance on the PFSs or the assumptions.

        1)   It adds that a compilation does **not include evaluation of the support** for the assumptions underlying the PFSs.

        2)   A report on a projection also should include a separate paragraph that limits the use of the presentation.

8.   **Agreed-Upon Procedures**

    a.   A practitioner may accept an engagement to apply **agreed-upon procedures** to PFSs if (s)he is **independent** and each of the following applies:

        1)   The specified parties agree to the procedures and take responsibility for their sufficiency.

        2)   Report use is limited to specified parties.

        3)   The statements include a summary of significant assumptions.

    b.   The report should state that the practitioner did not perform an examination and that other matters might have come to his or her attention if additional procedures had been performed.

        1)   It also should **disclaim an opinion** on conformity with AICPA presentation guidelines, etc.

        2)   The report lists the procedures performed and the related findings. It does not provide positive or limited assurance.

    c.   The guidance in Subunit 19.5 also is relevant.

9.   **Review**

    a.   The standard does not provide for the **review** form of engagement with regard to PFSs. Thus, it does not provide for the expression of limited assurance on them.

Stop and review! You have completed the outline for this subunit. Study multiple-choice questions 16 through 18 beginning on page 433.

19.7 REPORTING ON PRO FORMA FINANCIAL INFORMATION

1.   Pro forma financial information (PFFI) shows "what the significant effects on historical financial information would have been had a consummated or proposed transaction (or event) occurred at an earlier date." Examples of these transactions include

    a.   A business combination,

    b.   Disposal of a segment,

    c.   Change in the form or status of an entity, and

    d.   A change in capitalization.

2.   A practitioner may **examine or review** PFFI if three conditions are met:

    a.   The document containing the PFFI includes or incorporates by reference the complete historical statements for the most recent year available. Moreover, if the PFFI is for an interim period, the document also should include the interim historical information for that period.

    b.   If the PFFI has been examined, the historical financial statements on which it is based have been audited. If the PFFI has been reviewed, the historical financial statements have been audited or reviewed.

    c.   The reporting practitioner is appropriately knowledgeable about the accounting and financial reporting practices of each significant part of the combined entity.

3.   A compilation of the historical statements provides no assurance. Accordingly, it would not provide a basis for the accountant to examine or review the PFFI.

4.   The report on an examination should include an opinion (unmodified, qualified, or adverse).

    a.   It addresses whether

        1)   Management's assumptions provide a reasonable basis for the significant effects attributable to the transaction or event,

        2)   The pro forma adjustments give appropriate effect to the assumptions, and

        3)   The pro forma column reflects the proper application of those adjustments to the historical data.

    b.   Scope limitations, reservations about the assumptions or the presentation (including inadequate disclosure), and other matters may lead to modification of the opinion or a disclaimer.

5.   An issuer that discloses a material non-GAAP financial measure (a **pro forma release**) also must disclose the most directly comparable GAAP measure (SEC Regulation G).

Stop and review! You have completed the outline for this subunit. Study multiple-choice question 19 on page 434.

19.8 COMPLIANCE ATTESTATION

1. A practitioner may be asked to provide assurance about the entity's **compliance with specified requirements** (laws, regulations, rules, contracts, or grants). The engagement also may be directed toward the responsible party's **written assertion about compliance**. For example, management might make the assertion: "Z Company complied with the restrictive covenants in paragraph 20 of its Loan Agreement with Y Bank dated January 1, Year 1, as of and for the 3 months ended March 31, Year 1."

    a. The practitioner also may be asked to provide this type of assurance about the **effectiveness of internal control over compliance** with laws, regulations, etc.

2. The standard provides guidance for engagements related to reporting on compliance with requirements that are either **financial or nonfinancial**.

    a. The **general, field work, and reporting attestation standards** (AT 50) apply to this type of engagement.

    b. A compliance attestation does **not** provide a legal determination of an entity's compliance.

3. **Scope of Services**

    a. A practitioner may perform **agreed-upon procedures** or an **examination**. However, a practitioner should **not** perform a compliance attestation **review** service.

    b. In an **agreed-upon procedures engagement**, the subject matter (or an assertion about it) consists of (1) compliance with specified requirements, (2) the effectiveness of internal control over compliance, or (3) both.

        1) The users of the report decide the procedures to be performed by the practitioner and take responsibility for those procedures.

        2) The practitioner has **no obligation to perform other procedures**. However, if noncompliance comes to the practitioner's attention by other means, such information should be included in the report.

        3) The practitioner's report should be in the form of procedures and findings but should **not provide negative assurance** about whether an entity is in compliance or whether the responsible party's assertion is fairly stated.

        4) The **report**

            a) Has a **title** that includes the word **independent**
            b) Describes the **nature and scope** of the service
            c) **Limits use** to specified parties
            d) Is **signed** by the practitioner
            e) Is **dated** as of the completion of the agreed-upon procedures

    c. In an **examination** engagement, the subject matter (or an assertion about it) consists of compliance with specified requirements.

        1) The practitioner gathers evidence to support an opinion on whether an entity is in compliance, in all material respects, based on specified criteria.

4. **Conditions for Engagement Performance**

    a. For an **agreed-upon procedures** engagement, the responsible party should

        1) Accept responsibility for the entity's compliance with specified requirements and the effectiveness of the entity's internal control over compliance.

        2) Evaluate such compliance or effectiveness.

    b. For an **examination** of compliance with specified requirements, sufficient evidence (1) should exist or (2) can be developed to support management's evaluation. Furthermore, the **responsible party** should

        1) Satisfy the condition in item 4.a.1) above.
        2) Evaluate compliance with specified requirements.

    c.   To perform a compliance attestation engagement, the practitioner should obtain from the responsible party a **written assertion about compliance** with (1) specified requirements or (2) control over compliance.

5.   **Examination Engagement**

    a.   The purpose is to **express an opinion** on whether an entity is in compliance (or on whether the responsible party's assertion about such compliance is fairly stated), in all material respects, based on the specified criteria.

        1)   The practitioner must gather sufficient evidence to **reduce attestation risk** to an acceptably low level. Attestation risk is similar to the audit risk concept used in Statements on Auditing Standards.

    b.   The practitioner seeks to obtain **reasonable, not absolute, assurance** of compliance.

    c.   Based on the extent to which (s)he wishes to restrict attestation risk and the assessments of inherent risk and control risk, the practitioner determines the **acceptable level of detection risk**. This level will determine the nature, timing, and extent of the necessary compliance tests.

    d.   The consideration of **materiality** differs from that in an audit of financial statements in accordance with GAAS. The following should be considered:

        1)   The nature of the compliance requirements, which may not be quantifiable in monetary terms

        2)   The nature and frequency of noncompliance identified, with appropriate consideration of sampling risk

        3)   Qualitative considerations, including the needs and expectations of users

6.   **Performing an Examination Engagement**

    a.   The practitioner should use **due care** and exercise **professional skepticism** to achieve reasonable assurance that material noncompliance will be detected. The following summarizes the practitioner's **procedures and considerations** in an examination engagement:

        1)   Obtain an **understanding** of the specified compliance requirements.

        2)   **Plan** the engagement, including the potential use of specialists and internal auditors.

        3)   Obtain an **understanding** of the relevant portions of **internal control** over compliance to plan the engagement and to assess control risk. If control risk is to be assessed at a low level, tests of controls must be performed.

        4)   Perform **procedures** to provide reasonable assurance of detecting material noncompliance, including obtaining a **written representation letter** from the responsible party.

        5)   Consider **subsequent events**. (The requirement is similar to that established by AU-C 560, *Subsequent Events and Subsequently Discovered Facts*, for a financial statement audit.)

        6)   Form an **opinion**.

b. The practitioner's report on an examination should contain **introductory, scope, and opinion paragraphs**.

EXAMPLE -- Standard Report on Compliance with Specified Requirements Based on an Examination

Independent Accountant's Report

To: <----------- Addressed to Board of Directors or Shareholders

We have examined *[name of entity]*'s compliance with *[list of specified compliance requirements]* during the *[period]* ended *[date]*. Management is responsible for *[name of entity]*'s compliance with those requirements. Our responsibility is to express an opinion on *[name of entity]*'s compliance based on our examination.

Our examination was conducted in accordance with attestation standards established by the American Institute of Certified Public Accountants and, accordingly, included examining, on a test basis, evidence about *[name of entity]*'s compliance with those requirements and performing such other procedures as we considered necessary in the circumstances. We believe that our examination provides a reasonable basis for our opinion. Our examination does not provide a legal determination on *[name of entity]*'s compliance with specific requirements.

In our opinion, *[name of entity]* complied, in all material respects, with the aforementioned requirements for the year ended December 31, Year 1.

Signature <----------- May be signed, typed, or printed
Date <----------- Date completed examination

---

7. **Report Modifications**

a. **Material noncompliance.** When an examination discloses noncompliance with specified requirements that the practitioner believes have a material effect on the entity's compliance, the report should be modified.

   1) Depending on materiality, the practitioner should express either a **qualified** (except for) or an **adverse opinion** on compliance.

   2) An **explanatory paragraph** (before the opinion paragraph) should be added to the report.

b. **Scope limitations.** The practitioner should qualify or disclaim an opinion depending on materiality (e.g., if management refuses to provide a written representation letter).

c. **Report based, in part, on the report of another practitioner.** The practitioner should either refer to the other practitioner or issue the standard report [general guidance is provided by AU-C 600, *Special Considerations – Audits of Group Financial Statements (Including the Work of Component Auditors)*].

Stop and review! You have completed the outline for this subunit. Study multiple-choice question 20 on page 435.

QUESTIONS

19.1 General Principles for SSARSs Engagements

1. Statements on Standards for Accounting and Review Services (SSARSs) require an accountant to report when the accountant has

A. Photocopied client-prepared financial statements, without modification, as an accommodation to the client.

B. Provided a client with a financial statement format that does not include monetary amounts, to be used by the client in preparing financial statements.

C. Proposed correcting journal entries to be recorded by the client that change client-prepared financial statements.

D. Compiled, through the use of computer software, financial statements to be used by third parties.

Answer (D) is correct.
    REQUIRED: The situation in which an accountant must issue a report.
    DISCUSSION: Unlike a preparation, compilations and reviews require an accountant's report.
    Answer (A) is incorrect. Typing or reproducing client-prepared financial statements, without modification, as an accommodation to a client does not constitute a SSARSs service. Answer (B) is incorrect. Without monetary amounts, the presentation is not a financial statement. Answer (C) is incorrect. Journal entries are not a financial statement.

2. May an accountant accept an engagement to compile or review the financial statements of a not-for-profit entity if the accountant is unfamiliar with the specialized industry accounting principles but plans to obtain the required level of knowledge before compiling or reviewing the financial statements?

	Compilation	Review
A.	No	No
B.	Yes	No
C.	No	Yes
D.	Yes	Yes

Answer (D) is correct.

REQUIRED: The ability of an accountant to accept an engagement without the required level of knowledge.

DISCUSSION: The accountant may accept a compilation or review engagement for an entity in an industry with which the accountant has no previous experience. However, (s)he has a responsibility to obtain the required level of knowledge prior to completing the engagement.

3. In a SSARSs engagement, the accountant is responsible for selecting the

	Financial Reporting Framework	Procedures to be Applied in the Engagement
A.	No	No
B.	Yes	No
C.	No	Yes
D.	Yes	Yes

Answer (C) is correct.

REQUIRED: The responsibility of an accountant in a SSARSs engagement.

DISCUSSION: Management is responsible for selecting the financial reporting framework. The accountant is responsible for (1) determining whether the framework is acceptable and (2) selecting the procedures used in the engagement.

Answer (A) is incorrect. The accountant is responsible for selecting the procedures used in the engagement. Answer (B) is incorrect. Management is responsible for selecting the financial reporting framework, and the accountant is responsible for selecting the procedures used in the engagement. Answer (D) is incorrect. Management is responsible for selecting the financial reporting framework, and the accountant is responsible for determining whether the framework selected is acceptable.

19.2 Preparation of Financial Statements

4. Which of the following is a true statement about preparing financial statements in accordance with SSARSs?

A. The accountant must be independent.

B. The accountant's name must appear on the financial statements.

C. The financial framework must be GAAP.

D. Management must accept responsibility for the financial statements.

Answer (D) is correct.

REQUIRED: The true statement about preparing financial statements under SSARSs.

DISCUSSION: Management is responsible for (1) selection of the reporting framework, (2) internal control over financial reporting, (3) prevention and detection of fraud, (4) ensuring compliance with laws and regulations, and (5) maintaining accurate and complete information. Thus, management must accept responsibility for the financial statements.

Answer (A) is incorrect. The accountant need not be independent of the entity, and no disclosure is made if independence is lacking. Answer (B) is incorrect. AR-C 70 does not require an accountant's name to be identified or associated with the financial statements. But it also does not prohibit the identification of the accountant if a disclaimer is included with the financial statements. Answer (C) is incorrect. The statements may be prepared using any acceptable financial reporting framework.

5. In accordance with SSARSs, which of the following is an accurate comparison of a preparation service with a compilation service?

A. Both services require a full set of notes to be presented with the financial statements.

B. Only a compilation service requires an engagement letter.

C. Both services allow the financial statements to be released to outside users.

D. Both services require a report to be presented by the accountant.

Answer (C) is correct.

REQUIRED: The accurate comparison of a preparation service with a compilation service.

DISCUSSION: SSARSs allows release of financial statements for a preparation, compilation, or review service.

Answer (A) is incorrect. Neither a preparation nor a compilation requires management to present appropriate note disclosures. Answer (B) is incorrect. All SSARSs engagements require the accountant to obtain an engagement letter or other suitable form of written agreement. Answer (D) is incorrect. The preparation service does not require the accountant to present a report.

6. An accountant may complete an engagement to prepare financial statements under SSARSs even if

A. The accountant lacks professional competence.

B. Management uses an unacceptable financial reporting framework.

C. Management does not accept responsibility for the financial statements.

D. The accountant is not independent.

Answer (D) is correct.
   REQUIRED: The item not a condition for accepting a preparation engagement.
   DISCUSSION: The accountant need not (1) be independent or (2) determine whether (s)he is independent to prepare financial statements under SSARSs.
   Answer (A) is incorrect. The accountant must have or be able to obtain professional competence to complete the engagement. Answer (B) is incorrect. The accountant must determine whether management has selected an acceptable financial reporting framework. Answer (C) is incorrect. The accountant must obtain management's agreement that it acknowledges and understands its responsibilities for the financial statements.

7. In a preparation engagement, the financial statements should include a statement such as

A. "No assurance is provided."

B. "Use at your own risk."

C. "No accountant's report is presented."

D. "For management's use only."

Answer (A) is correct.
   REQUIRED: The statement in the financial statements when a preparation engagement is performed.
   DISCUSSION: A notation on each page (including notes) of financial statements prepared by an accountant should state, "No assurance is provided." The statement is intended to avoid misunderstanding of the accountant's involvement.
   Answer (B) is incorrect. The financial statements should state, "No assurance is provided." Answer (C) is incorrect. A preparation service does not result in an accountant's report. But the lack of a report is not noted on the statements. Answer (D) is incorrect. Prepared financial statements may be released to users other than management.

19.3 Compilation of Financial Statements

8. Compiled financial statements of a nonissuer intended for third-party use should be accompanied by a report stating that

A. The scope of the accountant's procedures has not been restricted in testing the financial information that is the representation of management.

B. The accountant assessed the accounting principles used and significant estimates made by management.

C. The accountant does not express an opinion or any other form of assurance on the financial statements.

D. A compilation consists principally of inquiries of entity personnel and analytical procedures applied to financial data.

Answer (C) is correct.
   REQUIRED: The language included in a compilation report.
   DISCUSSION: A compilation report contains a disclaimer stating that the accountant has not audited or reviewed the financial statements and does not express an opinion or any other form of assurance on them.
   Answer (A) is incorrect. A compilation does not entail testing the financial information. Answer (B) is incorrect. A financial statement audit, not a compilation, involves assessing the accounting principles used and the estimates made by management. Answer (D) is incorrect. A review, not a compilation, consists principally of inquiries and analytical procedures.

9. When compiling a nonissuer's financial statements, an accountant is **least** likely to

A. Perform analytical procedures designed to identify relationships that appear to be unusual.

B. Read the compiled financial statements and consider whether they appear to include adequate disclosure.

C. Omit substantially all of the disclosures required by generally accepted accounting principles.

D. Issue a compilation report on one or more, but not all, of the basic financial statements.

Answer (A) is correct.
   REQUIRED: The procedure least likely to be performed in a compilation.
   DISCUSSION: In a compilation engagement, the accountant is not required to make inquiries or perform analytical or other procedures to verify, corroborate, or review information supplied by the entity. However, analytical procedures are necessary in review and audit engagements.
   Answer (B) is incorrect. The accountant should read the compiled statements and consider whether they are free from obvious material errors, including inadequate disclosure. Answer (C) is incorrect. A compilation may omit substantially all disclosures required by the applicable reporting framework, provided the omission is clearly indicated in the report and, to the accountant's knowledge, is not done to mislead. Answer (D) is incorrect. An accountant may issue a compilation report on one or more, but not all, of the basic financial statements.

19.4 Review of Financial Statements

10. Which of the following should be the first step in reviewing the financial statements of a nonissuer?

A. Comparing the financial statements with statements for comparable prior periods and with anticipated results.

B. Completing a series of inquiries concerning the entity's procedures for recording, classifying, and summarizing transactions.

C. Obtaining a general understanding of the entity's organization, its operating characteristics, and its products or services.

D. Applying analytical procedures designed to identify relationships and individual items that appear to be unusual.

Answer (C) is correct.
   REQUIRED: The first step in reviewing the financial statements of a nonissuer.
   DISCUSSION: In a review, the accountant expresses limited assurance concerning the financial statements. In performing the review, the accountant should first obtain an understanding of the entity and the entity's industry. This will provide a foundation for completing the review.
   Answer (A) is incorrect. Comparing the financial statement with statements for comparable prior periods and with anticipated results is an analytical procedure, which is performed after obtaining an understanding of the business. Answer (B) is incorrect. Completing a series of inquiries concerning the entity's procedures for recording, classifying, and summarizing transactions is performed after obtaining an understanding of the entity's business. Answer (D) is incorrect. Applying analytical procedures designed to identify relationships and individual items that appear to be unusual is done after obtaining an understanding of the business.

11. Which of the following procedures should an accountant perform during an engagement to review the financial statements of a nonissuer?

A. Communicating control deficiencies discovered during the assessment of control risk.

B. Obtaining a client representation letter from members of management.

C. Sending bank confirmation letters to the entity's financial institutions.

D. Examining cash disbursements in the subsequent period for unrecorded liabilities.

Answer (B) is correct.
   REQUIRED: The procedure performed in a review.
   DISCUSSION: A review primarily consists of inquiries, analytical procedures, and management representations. In addition, the accountant must obtain a sufficient knowledge of the accounting principles and practices of the entity's industry and an understanding of the entity's business. The representations from management should encompass all statements and periods to be covered by the report. The representation letter should be signed by the current managers (usually the CEO and CFO or the equivalent) responsible for, and knowledgeable about, the matters covered (AR-C 90).
   Answer (A) is incorrect. Significant deficiencies and material weaknesses must be communicated in an audit, not a review. Answer (C) is incorrect. Confirmations to financial institutions are normally sent in an audit, not a review. Answer (D) is incorrect. Tests of details, e.g., tests of subsequent payments, are performed in an audit, not a review.

12. During an engagement to review the financial statements of a nonissuer, an accountant becomes aware that several leases that should be capitalized are not capitalized. The accountant considers these leases to be material to the financial statements. The accountant decides to modify the standard review report because management will not capitalize the leases. Under these circumstances, the accountant should

A. Express an adverse opinion because of the departure from GAAP.

B. Express no assurance of any kind on the entity's financial statements.

C. Emphasize that the financial statements are for limited use only.

D. Disclose the departure from GAAP in a separate paragraph of the accountant's report.

Answer (D) is correct.
   REQUIRED: The modification of a review report for a departure from GAAP.
   DISCUSSION: When a departure from GAAP precludes an unmodified review report, and modification of the standard report is sufficient to disclose the departure, the accountant should add an additional paragraph to the report disclosing the departure, including its effects on the financial statements if they have been determined by management or are known as the result of the accountant's procedures. The paragraph should have a heading such as "Known Departure From Accounting Principles Generally Accepted in the United States of America."
   Answer (A) is incorrect. Unless an audit has been conducted, an opinion may not be expressed. If modification of the report is not adequate to indicate the deficiencies, the accountant should withdraw from the engagement. Answer (B) is incorrect. The accountant provides limited assurance in a review report. Answer (C) is incorrect. A review report need not be limited in distribution.

13. Each page of a nonissuer's financial statements reviewed by an accountant may include the following reference:

- A. See Accountant's Review Report.
- B. Reviewed, No Accountant's Assurance Expressed.
- C. See Accompanying Accountant's Notes.
- D. Reviewed, No Material Modifications Required.

Answer (A) is correct.
   REQUIRED: The reference that may be on each page of financial statements reviewed by an accountant.
   DISCUSSION: The reviewed statements may become unattached from the review report. Thus, the accountant may consider including a reference to the report on each page of the statements. An example is "See Accountant's Review Report" (AR-C 90).
   Answer (B) is incorrect. A review report ordinarily expresses limited assurance. Answer (C) is incorrect. Notes are part of the financial statements, not the accountant's report. Answer (D) is incorrect. The review report states that the accountant is not aware of any modifications that should be made other than those indicated in the report.

19.5 Engagements to Apply Agreed-Upon Procedures

14. Negative assurance may be expressed when a practitioner is requested to apply agreed-upon procedures to specified

	Elements of a Financial Statement	Accounts of a Financial Statement
A.	Yes	Yes
B.	Yes	No
C.	No	No
D.	No	Yes

Answer (C) is correct.
   REQUIRED: The report in which negative assurance may be expressed.
   DISCUSSION: The practitioner does not express an opinion or negative assurance. Instead, the practitioner's report on agreed-upon procedures should be in the form of procedures and findings.

15. A practitioner may accept an agreed-upon procedures engagement to calculate the rate of return on a specified investment and verify that the percentage agrees with the percentage in an identified schedule provided that

- A. The practitioner's report does not enumerate the procedures performed.
- B. The practitioner accepts responsibility for the sufficiency of the procedures.
- C. Use of the practitioner's report is restricted.
- D. The practitioner is also the entity's continuing auditor.

Answer (C) is correct.
   REQUIRED: The condition of an engagement to apply agreed-upon procedures.
   DISCUSSION: An independent practitioner may accept such an engagement if (1) the specified parties agree to the procedures and take responsibility for their sufficiency, (2) the subject matter is subject to reasonably consistent measurement, (3) evidence is expected to exist providing a reasonable basis for the findings, (4) the use of the report is restricted, and (5) other conditions are met. The report should state that it is intended solely for the information and use of the specified parties and is not intended to be used and should not be used by anyone other than these specified parties.
   Answer (A) is incorrect. The procedures performed must be enumerated. Answer (B) is incorrect. The client or specified parties take responsibility for the sufficiency of the procedures. Answer (D) is incorrect. The practitioner need not be a continuing auditor.

19.6 Financial Forecasts and Projections

16. An examination of a financial forecast is a professional service that involves

- A. Compiling or assembling a financial forecast that is based on management's assumptions.
- B. Restricting the use of the practitioner's report to management and the board of directors.
- C. Assuming responsibility to update management on key events for 1 year after the report's date.
- D. Evaluating the preparation of a financial forecast and the support underlying management's assumptions.

Answer (D) is correct.
   REQUIRED: The accountant's responsibility in an examination of a financial forecast.
   DISCUSSION: An examination of a financial forecast entails evaluating the preparation of the statements, the support underlying the assumptions, and the presentation of the statements for conformity with AICPA guidelines (AT 301).
   Answer (A) is incorrect. An examination of a financial forecast involves providing assurance on the representations of management. Answer (B) is incorrect. An examination of a financial forecast need not be limited in its distribution. Answer (C) is incorrect. The practitioner need not assume responsibility to update management on key events after the issuance of the report.

17. Given one or more hypothetical assumptions, a responsible party may prepare, to the best of its knowledge and belief, an entity's expected financial position, results of operations, and cash flows. Such prospective financial statements are known as

    A. Pro forma financial statements.

    B. Financial projections.

    C. Partial presentations.

    D. Financial forecasts.

Answer (B) is correct.

    REQUIRED: The PFSs based on one or more hypothetical assumptions.

    DISCUSSION: PFSs include forecasts and projections. The difference between a forecast and a projection is that only the second is based on one or more hypothetical assumptions, which are conditions or actions not necessarily expected to occur.

    Answer (A) is incorrect. Pro forma statements are essentially historical, not prospective, statements. Answer (C) is incorrect. Partial presentations are not PFSs. They do not meet the minimum presentation guidelines. Answer (D) is incorrect. A financial projection, not a financial forecast, contains one or more hypothetical assumptions.

18. When an accountant compiles a financial forecast, the accountant's report should include a(n)

    A. Explanation of the differences between a financial forecast and a financial projection.

    B. Caveat that the prospective results of the financial forecast may not be achieved.

    C. Statement that the accountant's responsibility to update the report is limited to 1 year.

    D. Disclaimer of opinion on the reliability of the entity's internal controls.

Answer (B) is correct.

    REQUIRED: The statement included in an accountant's compilation report on a financial forecast.

    DISCUSSION: The standard report states that a compilation is limited in scope and does not enable the accountant to express an opinion or any other form of assurance. It adds that there will usually be differences between the forecasted and actual results (AT 301).

    Answer (A) is incorrect. The standard report does not define a forecast, a projection, or their differences. Answer (C) is incorrect. The practitioner's update responsibility is limited to the date of the report. Answer (D) is incorrect. A compilation engagement does not involve consideration of internal control.

19.7 Reporting on Pro Forma Financial Information

19. A practitioner's report on a review of pro forma financial information should include a

    A. Statement that the entity's internal control was not relied on in the review.

    B. Disclaimer of opinion on the financial statements from which the pro forma financial information is derived.

    C. Caveat that it is uncertain whether the transaction or event reflected in the pro forma financial information will ever occur.

    D. Reference to the financial statements from which the historical financial information is derived.

Answer (D) is correct.

    REQUIRED: The statement that should be included in a review of pro forma financial information.

    DISCUSSION: A practitioner's report on PFFI should include (1) an identification of the pro forma information, (2) a reference to the financial statements from which the historical financial information is derived and a statement as to whether such financial statements were audited or reviewed, (3) a statement that the review was made in accordance with standards established by the AICPA, (4) a caveat that a review is substantially less in scope than an examination and that no opinion is expressed, (5) a separate paragraph explaining the objective of PFFI and its limitations, and (6) the practitioner's conclusion providing limited assurance.

    Answer (A) is incorrect. The report should not mention internal control. Answer (B) is incorrect. The practitioner should disclaim an opinion on the pro forma financial information. Answer (C) is incorrect. The transaction may already have occurred.

19.8 Compliance Attestation

20. Practitioner was engaged by a group of pension recipients to apply agreed-upon procedures to financial data supplied by Pension written assertion about its compliance with contractual requirements to pay royalties. The report on these agreed-upon procedures should contain a(n)

- A. Disclaimer of opinion about the fair presentation of Employer's financial statements.
- B. List of the procedures performed (or reference to the) and Practitioner's findings.
- C. Opinion about the effectiveness of Employer's internal control over pension payments.
- D. Acknowledgment that the sufficiency of the procedures is solely Practitioner's responsibility.

Answer (B) is correct.

REQUIRED: The statement in a report on a compliance attestation engagement to apply agreed-upon procedures.

DISCUSSION: The practitioner's report should be in the form of procedures and findings but should not provide negative assurance about whether the entity is in compliance or whether the responsible party's assertion is fairly stated (AT 201).

Answer (A) is incorrect. The report should not contain a disclaimer of opinion on the fair presentation of Employer's financial statements. However, it should contain a paragraph stating that the independent accountant was not engaged to and did not perform an examination of the financial data related to the written assertion about compliance with contractual requirements to make pension payments. It also should state that (1) the objective of an examination would have been an expression of opinion on compliance with the specified requirements, and (2) no such opinion is expressed. Answer (C) is incorrect. An agreed-upon procedures engagement typically results in a summary of findings, not an opinion. Answer (D) is incorrect. The specified parties who agreed to the procedures are responsible for their sufficiency.

Candidates Love Gleim CPA Review

Check out the stories of some of the millions who have succeeded with Gleim.

From first hand experience, practicing the multiple-choice questions with Gleim will give you enough confidence and knowledge to pass each section. Using Gleim will have you well-prepared and conditioned for the exam.

– Thomas Najarian, CPA

The Gleim program was the answer I'd been looking for to finally conquer the exam. I've used other programs before and none of them compared to the step by step process Gleim used, which truly prepared me to conquer all four parts on my first try.

– Eric Murphy, CPA

The testing components simulate the actual exam, so I was completely comfortable with the exam setup when I took the actual exams.

– Tracy Caisse, CPA

STUDY UNIT TWENTY
GOVERNMENTAL AUDITS

(12 pages of outline)

The first subunit addresses *Government Auditing Standards*, the publication of the **Government Accountability Office (GAO)** that is fundamental to governmental auditing and is the basis for most of the related questions on recent CPA exams. Subunit 20.2 is based on an AICPA auditing standard and relates to opinions on whether an organization complies with applicable laws and regulations. The final subunit describes additional standards for audits of organizations that receive federal awards. The trend has been to increase the coverage of governmental auditing, so expect some questions on this material.

20.1 GOVERNMENT AUDITING STANDARDS

1.   The GAO establishes **generally accepted government auditing standards (GAGAS).** They are published in *Government Auditing Standards* (the Yellow Book).

   a.   GAGAS pertain to auditors' professional qualifications and the quality of their work, the performance of field work, and the characteristics of meaningful reporting.

   b.   *Government Auditing Standards* apply to engagements involving federal government entities, programs, activities, and functions. GAGAS also apply in audits of state and local governments and not-for-profit entities that receive federal awards. Moreover, contract terms or state and local laws may require the use of GAGAS.

   c.   GAGAS contain the following categories of professional requirements:

      1)   Auditors and audit organizations must comply with an **unconditional requirement** whenever it is relevant.

         a)   GAGAS use the word *must* to indicate an unconditional requirement.

      2)   Auditors and audit organizations must comply with a **presumptively mandatory requirement** whenever it is relevant except in rare circumstances.

         a)   GAGAS use the word *should* to indicate a presumptively mandatory requirement.

         b)   When a departure is necessary, auditors should perform alternative procedures to achieve the intent of the requirement.

         c)   The need to depart from a presumptively mandatory requirement is expected only when (1) it is for a specific procedure, and (2) the procedure would be ineffective in achieving the intent of the requirement.

2.   **Audits and Attestation Engagements**

   a.   **Financial Audits**

      1)   GAGAS incorporate by reference the AICPA's Statements on Auditing Standards (codified with the identifier AU-C).

      2)   **Financial statement audits** primarily determine whether financial statements are presented fairly, in all material respects, with an applicable financial reporting framework (typically GAAP).

         a)   GAGAS require related reporting on (1) internal control and (2) compliance with provisions of laws, regulations, contracts, and grant agreements.

    b)   The auditor conducting a governmental audit accepts a **greater scope** and assumes **more responsibility** than in an audit of a business entity.

3)   **Other types** of engagements provide for different levels of assurance and involve various scopes of work. They include the following:

    a)   Opinions on single financial statements, specified elements, accounts, or items of a financial statement

    b)   Issuing letters for underwriters and certain other requesting parties

    c)   Auditing compliance with requirements relating to government programs

b.   **Attestation Engagements**

1)   These engagements cover a broad range of financial or nonfinancial objectives. They involve examining, reviewing, or performing agreed-upon procedures on a subject matter or an assertion about a subject matter that is the responsibility of another party. GAGAS incorporate by reference the AICPA's *Statements on Standards for Attestation Engagements*. The following are examples of attestation engagements on which reports may be issued:

    a)   Internal control over financial reporting

    b)   Compliance with requirements of specified laws, regulations, rules, contracts, or grants

    c)   The effectiveness of internal control over compliance with specified laws, regulations, rules, contracts, or grants

    d)   Management's discussion and analysis (MD&A)

    e)   Prospective financial or performance information

    f)   Accuracy and reliability of performance measures

    g)   Quantity, condition, or valuation of assets

    h)   Allowability and reasonableness of proposed contract amounts based on detailed costs

    i)   Whether incurred final contract costs are supported by required evidence and comply with the contract terms

c.   **Performance Audits**

1)   These audits address many objectives, including assessing

    a)   Program effectiveness and results,
    b)   Economy and efficiency,
    c)   Internal control, and
    d)   Compliance with legal requirements.

2)   They also may provide prospective analysis, guidance, or summary information.

3.   **Additional Standards**

a.   The following are some of the more significant standards in addition to those of the AICPA incorporated by reference:

b.   **Independence.**

1)   Audit organizations and auditors must be independent in both mind and appearance.

2)   The standards develop a conceptual framework for independence similar to the AICPA's that requires auditors to

    a)   Identify threats to independence;

    b)   Evaluate the significance of the threats identified, both individually and in the aggregate; and

    c)   Apply safeguards as necessary to eliminate the threats or reduce them to an acceptable level.

        i)   For example, assuming management responsibilities for an auditee creates management participation threats that cannot be reduced to an acceptable level by safeguards. An example of a management responsibility that impairs independence if performed for an auditee is setting policies and strategic direction for the auditee.

c. **Ethical Principles**

    1)   The ethical principles that guide the work of auditors who conduct audits in accordance with GAGAS are (a) the public interest; (b) integrity; (c) objectivity; (d) proper use of government information, resources, and positions; and (e) professional behavior.

        a)   The public interest is the collective well-being of the community of people and entities the auditors serve. Observing integrity, objectivity, and independence assists auditors in serving the public interest and honoring the public trust. A distinguishing mark of an auditor is acceptance of responsibility to serve the public interest. This responsibility is critical in government. GAGAS embodies the concept of accountability for public resources.

        b)   Public confidence in government is strengthened when auditors perform their professional responsibilities with integrity. Integrity includes conducting audit work with an attitude that is objective, fact-based, nonpartisan, and nonideological with regard to audited entities and users of the auditors' reports. Within the constraints of laws, rules, or policies, communications are expected to be honest, candid, and constructive.

        c)   The credibility of auditing in the government sector is based on the auditors' objectivity in discharging their professional responsibilities. Objectivity includes independence of mind and appearance, maintaining an attitude of impartiality, having intellectual honesty, and being free of conflicts of interest.

        d)   Government information, resources, and positions are to be used for official purposes and not inappropriately for the auditor's personal gain or in a manner contrary to law or detrimental to the interests of the audited entity or the audit organization. This concept includes the proper handling of sensitive or classified information or resources.

        e)   High expectations for the auditing profession include compliance with all relevant obligations and avoidance of any conduct that might bring discredit to auditors' work. Professional behavior also includes an honest effort in performance of duties and professional services in accordance with the relevant standards.

d. **Continuing Professional Education.** Auditors who are involved in planning, directing, or reporting on GAGAS audits are required to acquire 80 hours of continuing education in related topics every 2 years. At least 24 hours of CPE should directly relate to governmental auditing.

e. **Quality Control and Assurance.** Each audit organization performing audits or attestation engagements in accordance with GAGAS must establish a system of quality control that is designed to provide the audit organization with reasonable assurance that the organization and its personnel comply with professional standards and applicable legal and regulatory requirements. The organization is required to have an external **peer review** at least once every **3 years**.

f. **Auditor Communication.** In addition to the AICPA requirements for auditor communication, auditors should communicate pertinent information that, in the auditors' professional judgment, needs to be communicated to individuals contracting for or requesting the audit and to cognizant legislative committees when auditors perform the audit pursuant to a law or regulation.

g. **Previous Audits and Attestation Engagements.** Auditors should evaluate whether the audited entity has taken appropriate corrective action to address findings and recommendations from previous engagements that could have a material effect on the financial statements or other financial data significant to the audit objectives.

h. **Developing Elements of a Finding.** When auditors identify findings, they should plan and perform procedures to develop the elements of the findings that are relevant and necessary to achieve the audit objectives. The elements needed for a finding depend on the objectives of the audit but include the following:

1) **Criteria.** The required or desired state (e.g., law or contract) or expectation with respect to the program or operation.

2) **Condition.** The situation that exists.

3) **Cause.** The reason or explanation for the condition.

4) **Effect or potential effect.** A clear, logical link to establish the impact or potential impact of the difference between the situation that exists (condition) and the required or desired state (criteria).

i. **Compliance with GAGAS.** The auditor's report should state that the audit was performed in accordance with GAGAS.

j. **Reporting on Internal Control and Compliance with Laws, Regulations, Contracts, and Grant Agreements**

1) The report (or separate reports) on financial statements should describe the scope of the auditor's testing of internal control over financial reporting and compliance with laws and regulations and grant or contract provisions. The report should state whether the tests provided sufficient, appropriate evidence to support opinions on internal control and on compliance. But assurance is not required to be stated.

2) Auditors should report all of the following:

a) Significant deficiencies and material weaknesses in internal control

b) Instances of fraud and noncompliance with provisions of laws or regulations that have a material effect on the audit and any other instances that warrant the attention of those charged with governance

c) Noncompliance with provisions of contracts or grant agreements that has a material effect on the audit

d) Abuse that has a material effect on the audit

k. **Reporting Views of Responsible Officials.** The auditors' report may disclose (1) deficiencies in internal control; (2) fraud; (3) noncompliance with provisions of laws, regulations, contracts, or grant agreements; or (4) abuse. Auditors then should obtain and report the views of responsible officials of the audited entity about the findings, conclusions, and recommendations as well as any planned corrective actions.

1) Abuse is deficient or improper behavior compared with what a prudent person considers reasonable and necessary. It is also misuse of position or authority for personal financial interests or those of a family member or business associate.

      l.   **Reporting Confidential or Sensitive Information.** If certain pertinent information is prohibited from public disclosure or is excluded from a report due to the confidential or sensitive nature of the information, auditors should disclose in the report that certain information has been omitted.

      m.   **Distributing Reports.** Audit organizations in government entities should distribute audit reports to (1) those charged with governance, (2) the appropriate officials of the audited entity, and (3) the appropriate oversight bodies or organizations requiring or arranging for the audits.

4.   **Examples of Reports**

EXAMPLE -- Auditor's Unmodified Report on General-Purpose Financial Statements

Independent Auditor's Report

To: <---------- Oversight Body

Report on the Financial Statements

We have audited the accompanying general-purpose financial statements of the City of Example, Any State, as of and for the year ended June 30, 20X1.

Management's Responsibility for the Financial Statements

Management is responsible for the preparation and fair presentation of these financial statements in accordance with accounting principles generally accepted in the United States of America; this includes the design, implementation, and maintenance of internal control relevant to the preparation and fair presentation of financial statements that are free from material misstatement, whether due to fraud or error.

Auditor's Responsibility

Our responsibility is to express opinions on these financial statements based on our audit. We conducted our audit in accordance with auditing standards generally accepted in the United States of America and the standards applicable to financial audits contained in *Government Auditing Standards*, issued by the Comptroller General of the United States. Those standards require that we plan and perform the audit to obtain reasonable assurance about whether the financial statements are free from material misstatement.

An audit involves performing procedures to obtain audit evidence about the amounts and disclosures in the financial statements. The procedures selected depend on the auditor's judgment, including the assessment of the risks of material misstatement of the financial statements, whether due to fraud or error. In making those risk assessments, the auditor considers internal control relevant to the entity's preparation and fair presentation of the financial statements in order to design audit procedures that are appropriate in the circumstances, but not for the purpose of expressing an opinion on the effectiveness of the entity's internal control. Accordingly, we express no such opinion. An audit also includes evaluating the appropriateness of accounting policies used and the reasonableness of significant accounting estimates made by management, as well as evaluating the overall presentation of the financial statements.

We believe that the audit evidence we have obtained is sufficient and appropriate to provide a basis for our audit opinion.

Opinion

In our opinion, the financial statements referred to above present fairly, in all material respects, financial position of the City of Example, Any State, as of June 30, 20X1, and the results of its operations and cash flows of its proprietary fund types and trust funds for the year then ended in accordance with accounting principles generally accepted in the United States of America.

Other Reporting Required by Government Auditing Standards

In accordance with *Government Auditing Standards*, we have also issued our report dated [date of report] on our consideration of the City of Example's internal control over financial reporting and on our tests of its compliance with certain provisions of laws, regulations, contracts, and grant agreements and other matters. The purpose of that report is to describe the scope of our testing of internal control over financial reporting and compliance and the results of that testing, and not to provide an opinion on internal control over financial reporting or on compliance. That report is an integral part of an audit performed in accordance with *Government Auditing Standards* in considering the City of Example's internal control over financial reporting and compliance.

Signature   <---------- May be signed, typed, or printed
Location   <---------- Auditor's city and state
Date   <---------- No earlier than the date on which the auditor has obtained sufficient appropriate evidence

---

EXAMPLE -- Auditor's Standard Combined Report on Internal Control and Compliance with Laws and Regulations (No Significant Weaknesses, Material Weaknesses, or Material Noncompliance)

Independent Auditor's Report

To: <---------- Oversight Body

We have audited, in accordance with the auditing standards generally accepted in the United States of America and the standards applicable to financial audits contained in *Government Auditing Standards* issued by the Comptroller General of the United States, the general-purpose financial statements of Example Entity, as of and for the year ended June 30, 20X1, and have issued our report thereon dated August 15, 20X1.

Internal Control over Financial Reporting

In planning and performing our audit of the financial statements, we considered Example Entity's internal control over financial reporting (internal control) to determine the audit procedures that are appropriate in the circumstances for the purpose of expressing our opinion on the financial statements, but not for the purpose of expressing an opinion on the effectiveness of Example Entity's internal control. Accordingly, we do not express an opinion on the effectiveness of Example Entity's internal control.

A deficiency in internal control exists when the design or operation of a control does not allow management or employees, in the normal course of performing their assigned functions, to prevent, or detect and correct, misstatements on a timely basis. A material weakness is a deficiency, or a combination of deficiencies, in internal control, such that there is a reasonable possibility that a material misstatement of the entity's financial statements will not be prevented, or detected and corrected on a timely basis. A significant deficiency is a deficiency, or a combination of deficiencies, in internal control that is less severe than a material weakness, yet important enough to merit attention by those charged with governance.

Our consideration of internal control was for the limited purpose described in the first paragraph of this section and was not designed to identify all deficiencies in internal control that might be material weaknesses or significant deficiencies. Given these limitations, during our audit we did not identify any deficiencies in internal control that we consider to be material weaknesses. However, material weaknesses may exist that have not been identified.

Compliance

As part of obtaining reasonable assurance about whether Example Entity's financial statements are free from material misstatement, we performed tests of its compliance with certain provisions of laws, regulations, contracts, and grant agreements, noncompliance with which could have a direct and material effect on the determination of financial statement amounts. However, providing an opinion on compliance with those provisions was not an objective of our audit, and accordingly, we do not express such an opinion. The results of our tests disclosed no instances of noncompliance or other matters that are required to be reported under *Government Auditing Standards*.

Purpose of this Report

The purpose of this report is solely to describe the scope of our testing of internal control and compliance and the results of that testing, and not to provide an opinion on the effectiveness of the entity's internal control or on compliance. This report is an integral part of an audit performed in accordance with *Government Auditing Standards* in considering the entity's internal control and compliance. Accordingly, this communication is not suitable for any other purpose.

Signature   <---------- May be signed, typed, or printed
Location   <---------- Auditor's city and state
Date   <---------- No earlier than the date on which the auditor has obtained sufficient appropriate evidence

---

Stop and review! You have completed the outline for this subunit. Study multiple-choice questions 1 through 11 beginning on page 448.

20.2 COMPLIANCE AUDITS

1. A compliance audit is a program-specific or organization-wide audit of compliance with requirements (laws, rules, regulations, contracts, or grants) that apply to government programs.

    a. It normally is performed with a **financial statement audit**.

2. **Scope**

    a. This guidance applies when an auditor performs a compliance audit in accordance with

        1) GAAS,

        2) Financial audit standards in *Government Auditing Standards*, and

        3) A **governmental audit requirement (GAR)** that requires an opinion on compliance.

    b. This guidance does **not** apply to an attestation engagement, including an examination of internal control over compliance. (AT 601 applies.)

3. **Management's Responsibilities**

    a. Identifying the entity's government programs and understanding and complying with the compliance requirements

    b. Establishing and maintaining effective controls over compliance

    c. Evaluating and monitoring compliance

    d. Taking necessary corrective action

4. **Audit Objectives**

    a. Obtain sufficient appropriate evidence to form an opinion and report at the level specified in the GAR on whether the entity complied, in all material respects, with the compliance requirements.

    b. Identify audit and reporting requirements in the GAR that supplement GAAS and *Government Auditing Standards* and perform and report on the related procedures.

5. The auditor, based on professional judgment, adapts AU-C sections for a **financial statement audit** for use in a compliance audit. But some do not apply, for example, AU-C 708, *Consistency of Financial Statements*.

6. **Materiality** levels, generally for a government program as a whole, are based on the GAR.

7. **Programs and Applicable Compliance Requirements (ACRs)**

    a. Based on the GAR, the auditor determines which government programs and ACRs identified by management to test.

8. **The Audit Process**

    a. An audit of compliance typically includes the following steps:

        1) Performing risk assessment procedures

        2) Assessing the risks of material noncompliance

        3) Performing further audit procedures in response to assessed risks

        4) Addressing supplementary audit requirements in the GAR

        5) Obtaining written management representations

        6) Performing subsequent events procedures

        7) Evaluating evidence and forming an opinion

        8) Reporting on compliance

        9) Documenting the audit

9. **Risk Assessment Procedures**

    a. The auditor should obtain a sufficient **understanding** of the ACRs and the entity's **internal control** over compliance to plan the audit.

    b. The auditor should **inquire** of management about whether findings and recommendations in reports or other communications resulting from previous audits or other monitoring relate to compliance.

10. Based on the results of the risk assessment procedures, the auditor should assess the **risks of material noncompliance**, whether due to fraud or error, for each ACR.

11. **Further Audit Procedures in Response to Assessed Risks**

   a. If the auditor identifies risks that have a **pervasive** effect on compliance, the auditor should develop an **overall response** to such risks.

   1) For example, the auditor may use more experienced staff or increase supervision.

   b. The audit should detect intentional and unintentional noncompliance. However, the auditor can obtain only **reasonable assurance** because of

   1) Performance of sampling procedures;
   2) Use of professional judgment;
   3) Availability of persuasive, not conclusive, evidence; and
   4) The inherent limitations of internal control, including the potential for collusion of entity employees.

   c. The auditor should perform further audit procedures, including **tests of details** (possibly including tests of transactions), to obtain sufficient appropriate evidence of compliance with each ACR.

   1) Risk assessment procedures, tests of controls, and analytical procedures alone are not sufficient to address the risks of material noncompliance.
   2) Furthermore, the use of analytical procedures as substantive procedures is generally less effective in a compliance audit than in a financial statement audit.

   d. **Tests of controls** should be performed if

   1) The auditor's risk assessment includes an expectation of operating effectiveness of controls related to the ACRs,
   2) Substantive procedures alone do not provide sufficient appropriate evidence, or
   3) Tests of controls over compliance are required by the GAR.

12. **Supplementary Audit Requirements**

   a. The auditor should determine whether audit requirements are specified in the GAR that supplement GAAS and *Government Auditing Standards* and perform the related procedures.

13. **Written Management Representations**

   a. The auditor should request written representations specific to the entity and the GAR. (These representations are parallel to those for a financial statement audit and are not repeated here.) Generally, those representations should include the following:

   1) Acknowledgment of management's responsibility for compliance
   2) Acknowledgment of management's responsibility for controls over compliance
   3) Declarations that all evidence has been made available and all instances of noncompliance have been provided to the auditor

14. **Subsequent Events**

   a. The auditor should perform audit procedures **up to the date of the auditor's report** to obtain sufficient appropriate evidence that all subsequent events related to compliance have been identified.

   b. Audit procedures include (1) considering the risk assessment and examples of noncompliance during the subsequent period and (2) inquiring of management.

15. **Evaluating Evidence and Forming an Opinion**

    a.   The auditor should evaluate the sufficiency and appropriateness of the audit evidence obtained and form an opinion (at the level stated by the GAR) on whether the entity complied, in all material respects, with the ACRs.

    b.   The auditor evaluates (1) **questioned costs**, (2) **likely questioned costs**, and (3) other material noncompliance.

16. **Reporting on Compliance**

    a.   The auditor may issue a separate report on compliance, or it may be included with a report on internal control over compliance required by the GAR.

    b.   Given **material noncompliance** with ACRs or a **restriction on the scope** of the audit, the auditor should **modify the opinion** in accordance with AU-C 705.

    c.   Even without a GAR to report on internal control, the auditor should communicate to management and those charged with governance the identified **significant deficiencies** and **material weaknesses** in internal control over compliance.

        1)   A material weakness in internal control over compliance is a deficiency, or combination of deficiencies, in internal control over compliance that results in a reasonable possibility that material noncompliance with a compliance requirement will not be prevented, or detected and corrected, on a timely basis.

        2)   A significant deficiency in internal control over compliance is a deficiency, or a combination of deficiencies, in internal control over compliance that is less severe than a material weakness, yet merits attention by those charged with governance.

    d.   The following is an example of a separate unmodified report:

EXAMPLE -- Auditor's Report on Compliance

Independent Auditor's Report

To: <---------- Oversight Body

Compliance

We have audited Example Entity's compliance with the *[identify the applicable compliance requirements or refer to the document that describes the applicable compliance requirements]* applicable to Example Entity's *[identify the government program(s) audited or refer to a separate schedule that identifies the program(s)]* for the year ended June 30, 20X1.

Management's Responsibility

Compliance with the requirements referred to above is the responsibility of Example Entity's management.

Auditor's Responsibility

Our responsibility is to express an opinion on Example Entity's compliance based on our audit. We conducted our audit of compliance in accordance with auditing standards generally accepted in the United States of America; the standards applicable to financial audits contained in *Government Auditing Standards* issued by the Comptroller General of the United States; and *[insert the name of the governmental audit requirement or program-specific audit guide]*. Those standards and *[insert the name of the governmental audit requirement or program-specific audit guide]* require that we plan and perform the audit to obtain reasonable assurance about whether noncompliance with the compliance requirements referred to above that could have a material effect on *[identify the government program(s) audited or refer to a separate schedule that identifies the program(s)]* occurred. An audit includes examining, on a test basis, evidence about Example Entity's compliance with those requirements and performing such other procedures as we considered necessary in the circumstances. We believe that our audit provides a reasonable basis for our opinion. Our audit does not provide a legal determination of Example Entity's compliance with those requirements.

Opinion

In our opinion, Example Entity complied, in all material respects, with the compliance requirements referred to above that are applicable to *[identify the government program(s) audited]* for the year ended June 30, 20X1.

Signature   <---------- May be signed, typed, or printed
Location   <---------- Auditor's city and state
Date   <---------- No earlier than the date on which the auditor has obtained sufficient appropriate evidence

17. **Documenting the Audit**

    a. The following should be documented by the auditor:

        1) Risk assessment procedures performed, including those related to understanding internal control over compliance

        2) Materiality levels and how they were determined

        3) Responses to the assessed risks of material noncompliance

        4) Procedures to test compliance with ACRs and their results, including tests of controls

        5) Compliance with supplementary GARs

Stop and review! You have completed the outline for this subunit. Study multiple-choice questions 12 through 15 beginning on page 452.

20.3 FEDERAL AUDIT REQUIREMENTS AND THE SINGLE AUDIT ACT

Background
Prior to 1984, agencies of the federal government that provided awards to state and local governments audited specific grants, contracts, subsidies, etc. This process often resulted in numerous audits of a recipient by various agencies and a wasteful duplication of effort. In other cases, large amounts of federal awards went unaudited.

1. In 1984, Congress passed the Single Audit Act (amended in 1996). It currently requires one (a single) audit or a program-specific audit of a nonfederal entity (e.g., state and local governments and nonprofit entities) that expends $750,000 or more of federal awards in 1 fiscal year.

    a. A **single audit** is required if the entity expends federal awards under more than one federal program. The single audit covers the operations of the entire entity or, at the option of the entity, may include a **series of audits** of the organizational subunits that expended or administered federal awards.

    b. Each **federal agency** must monitor the use of awards provided by the agency. Moreover, each **nonfederal agency** must be assigned a single federal agency to assess the quality of audits and provide technical assistance.

    c. **Reporting packages** are delivered to a federal clearinghouse. These packages include financial statements, audit reports, a schedule of expenditures of federal awards, and a corrective action plan.

    d. The **Office of Management and Budget (OMB)** prescribes policies and procedures for the single audit. Those policies and procedures are issued in OMB *Audit Requirements for Federal Awards* and the related **Compliance Supplement**.

    e. The audit focus is greater for **major programs**, which are selected on the basis of **risk-based criteria** subject to certain limitations based on dollar expenditures.

2. According to the Single Audit Act, the auditor must conduct the audit in accordance with GAGAS. The **scope of the audit** extends to

    a. Expressing or disclaiming an opinion on whether the **financial statements** are presented fairly, in all material respects, in conformity with GAAP. (This requirement includes reporting on **compliance** with laws and regulations and **internal control** for expenditures not covered explicitly below and on the following page.)

    b. Expressing or disclaiming an opinion on whether the **schedule of expenditures of federal awards** is presented fairly, in all material respects, in relation to the financial statements taken as a whole.

    c.   Performing procedures to obtain an **understanding of internal control** sufficient to plan the audit to support a low assessed level of control risk for **major programs**, planning **tests of controls** to support that assessment for the assertions relevant to compliance requirements for each major program, and performing **tests of controls**. (Planning and performing tests are not required if the controls are likely to be ineffective.)

        1)   The **report on internal control** related to the financial statements and major programs should describe the scope of testing and the results of tests and, if applicable, should refer to the **schedule of findings and questioned costs**.

        2)   **Control deficiencies** that are individually or cumulatively material should be identified.

    d.   Expressing or disclaiming **an opinion** on whether the **auditee has complied** with laws, regulations, and the provisions of contracts or grants that may have a direct and material effect on each major program.

    e.   Following up.

    f.   Reporting a schedule of findings and questioned costs.

3.   Compliance requirements applicable to awards made by many federal programs are covered in the **Compliance Supplement** (over 1,500 pages) to OMB *Audit Requirements for Federal Awards* (2 CFR 200). Its focus is on compliance requirements that could have a direct and material effect on a major program.

    a.   This supplement lists and describes the **types of compliance requirements** and related **audit objectives and procedures** that should be considered in every audit to which it relates. It also discusses objectives, procedures, and compliance requirements that are specific to **each federal program** included.

4.   Auditee **management** is responsible for **identifying federal awards** and the **related programs** and preparing a schedule of the expenditures of federal awards. The auditee also is responsible for (a) maintaining control over federal programs; (b) complying with laws, regulations, and the provisions of contracts and grants; (c) preparing financial statements; (d) ensuring that required audits are performed and submitted when due; and (e) following up and taking corrective action.

    a.   The auditee must submit to the **designated clearinghouse** a data collection form providing information about the auditee, its federal programs, and the results of the audit. Furthermore, the auditee must submit a **reporting package** that includes (1) financial statements, (2) a summary schedule of audit findings, (3) the auditor's reports, and (4) the corrective action plan.

    b.   Preparing the schedule of expenditures involves identifying and measuring expenditures. The following are examples:

        1)   Noncash assistance (e.g., donated surplus property or food stamps) must be measured at the fair value at the date of receipt or the assessed value determined by the federal agency.

        2)   Cash assistance includes government loans.

        3)   Free rent received as part of an award to carry out a federal program must be included in determining federal awards expended and is subject to audit.

            a)   But free rent by itself is not considered a federal award expended.

5. The auditor uses a **risk-based approach** in determining which federal programs are major programs. The criteria considered are (a) current and prior audit experience, (b) oversight by federal agencies and pass-through entities, (c) inherent risk, and (d) amounts of federal awards expended.

   a. A federal agency or pass-through entity may request that the auditee have a program audited as a **major program**.

   b. The auditor applies technical rules to determine which programs require audit focus.

6. Questioned costs result from an audit finding of (a) a violation or possible violation of a law, regulation, contract, grant, or agreement or document governing the use of federal funds, including matching funds; (b) inadequate documentation of costs at the time of the audit; or (c) costs that appear unreasonable and do not reflect the actions a prudent person would take in the circumstances. The **schedule of audit findings and questioned costs** includes any instances of (a) **known questioned costs** greater than $25,000 or (b) known questioned costs when likely questioned costs exceed $25,000 for compliance requirements for a major program.

   a. Moreover, **likely questioned costs** (a projection) must be considered when evaluating the effects of questioned costs on the audit opinion.

   b. **Audit findings** should be sufficiently detailed to permit the auditee to prepare a corrective action plan and to take such action.

7. For the purpose of **reporting an audit finding**, the auditor's determination of whether a **deficiency in internal control** is material or whether an **instance of noncompliance** is material is in relation to a **type of compliance requirement** for a major program or an **audit objective** identified in the OMB *Audit Requirements for Federal Awards* (2 CFR 200) Compliance Supplement.

   a. In contrast, materiality is considered in relation to the **financial statements** in an audit under GAAS.

8. Under the Single Audit Act, a federal agency or the U.S. Comptroller General may, upon request, obtain access to the auditor's **working papers** to (a) provide information for a quality review, (b) resolve audit findings, or (c) carry out oversight responsibilities. Access includes the right to obtain copies.

Stop and review! You have completed the outline for this subunit. Study multiple-choice questions 16 through 20 beginning on page 453.

QUESTIONS

20.1 Government Auditing Standards

1. An auditor was engaged to conduct a performance audit of a governmental entity in accordance with *Government Auditing Standards*. These standards do **not** require the auditor to report

A. The audit objectives and the audit scope and methodology.

B. All significant instances of noncompliance and instances of abuse.

C. The views of the audited program's responsible officials concerning the auditor's findings.

D. A concurrent opinion on the financial statements taken as a whole.

Answer (D) is correct.

REQUIRED: The action not required of an auditor engaged in a performance audit of a governmental entity in accordance with *Government Auditing Standards*.

DISCUSSION: Performance audits relate to assessing (1) program effectiveness and results; (2) economy and efficiency; (3) internal control; (4) compliance with legal requirements; or (5) providing prospective analysis, guidance, or summary information. There is no requirement that a financial audit be conducted simultaneously or concurrently with a performance audit.

2. Which of the following bodies issues standards for audits of recipients of federal awards?

A. Governmental Accounting Standards Board.

B. Financial Accounting Standards Board.

C. Government Accountability Office.

D. Governmental Auditing Standards Board.

Answer (C) is correct.

REQUIRED: The body that sets standards for audits of federal awards recipients.

DISCUSSION: The federal agency concerned with accounting and auditing standards for U.S. government programs and services is the Government Accountability Office. The GAO issues generally accepted government auditing standards.

Answer (A) is incorrect. The GASB promulgates standards for financial accounting and reporting by state and local governments. Answer (B) is incorrect. The FASB issues standards for financial accounting and reporting by nongovernmental entities. Answer (D) is incorrect. There is no Governmental Auditing Standards Board. The committee of the GAO that issues government auditing standards is the Advisory Council on *Government Auditing Standards*.

3. *Government Auditing Standards* relates to which of the services provided to government entities, programs, activities, and functions?

	Financial Audits	Nonaudit Services	Performance Audits
A.	Yes	Yes	No
B.	Yes	No	Yes
C.	Yes	Yes	Yes
D.	No	No	Yes

Answer (B) is correct.

REQUIRED: The scope of *Government Auditing Standards*.

DISCUSSION: *Government Auditing Standards* relates to financial audits and attestation engagements. Moreover, it relates to performance audits of (1) government entities, programs, activities, and functions and (2) government assistance administered by contractors, not-for-profit entities, and other nongovernmental activities. Although GAGAS are not applicable to nonaudit services, they state independence standards and describe the impact of nonaudit services on auditor independence.

4. An objective of a performance audit is to determine whether an entity's

A. Performance information is presented fairly.

B. Operational information is in accordance with generally accepted government auditing standards.

C. Financial statements present fairly the results of operations.

D. Specific operating units are functioning economically and efficiently.

Answer (D) is correct.

REQUIRED: The objective of a performance audit.

DISCUSSION: Performance audits include economy and efficiency audits. The objectives of these audits are to determine (1) whether the entity is acquiring, protecting, and using its resources economically and efficiently; (2) the causes of any inefficiencies; and (3) whether the entity has complied with laws and regulations concerning matters of economy and efficiency.

Answer (A) is incorrect. Reporting on the fairness of performance information is the subject of attestation engagements. Answer (B) is incorrect. The conduct of the audit and the audit report, not operational information, should be in accordance with *Government Auditing Standards*. Answer (C) is incorrect. Determining whether financial statements present fairly the results of operations is an objective of a financial statement audit.

5. When engaged to audit a governmental entity in accordance with *Government Auditing Standards*, an auditor prepares a written report on internal control over financial reporting

A. In all financial audits, regardless of circumstances.

B. Only when the auditor has noted significant deficiencies.

C. Only when requested by the governmental entity being audited.

D. Only when requested by the federal government funding agency.

Answer (A) is correct.

REQUIRED: The true statement about reporting on internal control.

DISCUSSION: *Government Auditing Standards* imposes more stringent reporting requirements than GAAS. For example, it mandates a written report on internal control over financial reporting in every audit. Furthermore, issuers must report on internal control. In contrast, GAAS require communication only if significant deficiencies or material weaknesses have been observed.

Answer (B) is incorrect. GAAS, not *Government Auditing Standards*, require communication only if significant deficiencies or material weaknesses have been observed. Answer (C) is incorrect. A written report should be prepared in all audits, regardless of circumstances. Answer (D) is incorrect. A written report should be prepared in all audits, regardless of circumstances.

6. Which of the following statements is a standard applicable to financial statement audits in accordance with *Government Auditing Standards* (the Yellow Book)?

A. An auditor should report on the scope of the auditor's testing of compliance with laws and regulations.

B. An auditor should assess whether the entity has reportable measures of economy and efficiency that are valid and reliable.

C. An auditor should report recommendations for actions to correct problems and improve operations.

D. An auditor should determine the extent to which the entity's programs achieve the desired results.

Answer (A) is correct.

REQUIRED: The scope of an audit under *Government Auditing Standards.*

DISCUSSION: According to additional government standards for financial statement audits, the report on the financial statements should either (1) describe the scope of the auditor's testing of compliance with laws and regulations and internal controls over financial reporting and present the results of those tests or (2) refer to separate report(s) containing that information. If the scope of the work performed is sufficient, an opinion on internal control and compliance can be expressed. In presenting the results of those tests, auditors should report (1) significant deficiencies and material weaknesses in internal control; (2) instances of fraud and noncompliance with provisions of laws or regulations that have a material effect on the audit and any other instances that warrant the attention of those charged with governance; (3) noncompliance with provisions of contracts or grant agreements that has a material effect on the audit; and (4) abuse that has a material effect on the audit. In some circumstances, auditors should report fraud and noncompliance directly to parties external to the audited entity.

Answer (B) is incorrect. Economy and efficiency are subjects of performance audits rather than financial audits. Answer (C) is incorrect. Advice may be provided on the correction of problems and the improvement of operations, but the auditor is not required to provide a report. Answer (D) is incorrect. Achievement of desired results is a subject of performance audits rather than financial audits.

7. In reporting on compliance with laws and regulations during a financial statement audit in accordance with *Government Auditing Standards*, an auditor should include in the auditor's report

A. A statement of assurance that all controls over fraud and compliance were tested.

B. Material instances of fraud and noncompliance that were discovered.

C. The materiality criteria used by the auditor in considering whether instances of noncompliance were significant.

D. An opinion on whether compliance with laws and regulations affected the entity's goals and objectives.

Answer (B) is correct.

REQUIRED: The issues included in an auditor's report in accordance with *Government Auditing Standards.*

DISCUSSION: An auditor's report, in accordance with *Government Auditing Standards*, should present (1) significant deficiencies and material weaknesses in internal control; (2) instances of fraud and noncompliance with provisions of laws or regulations that have a material effect on the audit and any other instances that warrant the attention of those charged with governance; (3) noncompliance with provisions of contracts or grant agreements that has a material effect on the audit; and (4) abuse that has a material effect on the audit.

Answer (A) is incorrect. No assurance need be provided that all controls over fraud and compliance were tested. Answer (C) is incorrect. The materiality criteria need not be reported. Answer (D) is incorrect. No opinion need be expressed.

8. Reporting on internal control under *Government Auditing Standards* differs from reporting under generally accepted auditing standards in that *Government Auditing Standards* requires a

A. Written report describing the entity's internal control activities specifically designed to prevent fraud and noncompliance.

B. Written report included with the audit report on financial statements describing significant deficiencies and material weaknesses in internal control.

C. Statement of negative assurance that the internal control activities not tested have an immaterial effect on the entity's financial statements.

D. Statement of positive assurance that internal control activities designed to detect material errors and fraud were tested.

Answer (B) is correct.

REQUIRED: The difference between *Government Auditing Standards* and GAAS regarding reports on internal control.

DISCUSSION: According to *Government Auditing Standards*, the report on the financial statements or a separate report should present any significant deficiencies and material weaknesses in internal control. However, the report need not provide any assurance on internal control design or effectiveness.

Answer (A) is incorrect. *Government Auditing Standards* does not require the auditor to list internal control activities specifically designed to prevent fraud or noncompliance. Answer (C) is incorrect. The auditor is not required to provide a statement of positive or negative assurance regarding internal control. However, positive assurance in the form of an opinion may be provided if the scope of the work is sufficient. Answer (D) is incorrect. The auditor is not required to provide a statement of positive or negative assurance regarding internal control. However, positive assurance in the form of an opinion may be provided if the scope of the work is sufficient.

9. Financial audits of certain governmental entities are required to be performed in accordance with generally accepted government auditing standards (GAGAS) as issued in *Government Auditing Standards*. These standards do **not** require, as part of an auditor's report, the inclusion of

A. A statement as to whether the tests performed provide sufficient appropriate evidence to support an opinion on internal control over financial reporting.

B. The significant deficiencies, with identification of material weaknesses.

C. Sampling methods used to test the controls designed to detect fraud whether or not material fraud is found.

D. A description of the scope of testing of internal control over financial reporting.

Answer (C) is correct.
    REQUIRED: The item not required by GAGAS to be identified in an audit report.
    DISCUSSION: The Government Accountability Office (GAO) issues *Government Auditing Standards* (the Yellow Book). GAGAS apply to financial audits, attestation engagements, and performance audits. GAGAS for financial audits incorporate by reference the AICPA's Statements on Auditing Standards (SAS) and also state requirements. However, they do not require that the report identify specific sampling techniques used to test the controls. Nevertheless, when presenting material fraud, auditors might consider the report contents standards for performance audits that pertain to, among other things, methodology. Thus, if sampling significantly supports the findings, the auditor might describe the sample design and state why it was chosen.
    Answer (A) is incorrect. Auditors should state whether tests provided sufficient appropriate evidence to support opinions on internal control over financial reporting and compliance with laws, regulations, contracts, or grant agreements. Answer (B) is incorrect. Auditors should communicate in writing on a timely basis significant deficiencies and material weaknesses identified during the audit. They are included in the GAGAS report on internal control over financial reporting. Answer (D) is incorrect. The report on the financial statements should describe the scope of testing of (1) compliance with laws, regulations, contracts, or grant agreements and (2) internal control over financial reporting. It should present the findings or refer to separate reports containing that information.

10. In reporting under *Government Auditing Standards*, an auditor most likely would be required to report a falsification of accounting records directly to a federal inspector general when the falsification is

A. Discovered after the auditor's report has been made available to the federal inspector general and to the public.

B. Reported by the auditor to the audit committee as a significant deficiency in internal control.

C. Voluntarily disclosed to the auditor by low-level personnel as a result of the auditor's inquiries.

D. Communicated by the auditor to the auditee and the auditee fails to make a required report of the matter.

Answer (D) is correct.
    REQUIRED: The time when an auditor is required to report externally under *Government Auditing Standards*.
    DISCUSSION: Under *Government Auditing Standards*, auditors should report fraud, noncompliance, and abuse directly to parties outside the auditee (for example, to a federal inspector general or a state attorney general) in two circumstances. These requirements are in addition to any legal requirements for direct reporting. First, if auditors have communicated such fraud, noncompliance, or abuse to the auditee and (s)he fails to report them, the auditors should communicate their awareness of that failure to the auditee's governing body. If the auditee does not make the required report as soon as practicable after the auditor's communication with its governing body, the auditors should report the fraud, noncompliance, or abuse directly to the external party specified in the law or regulation. Second, management is responsible for taking timely and appropriate steps to remedy fraud, noncompliance, or abuse that auditors report to it. When fraud, noncompliance, or abuse involves assistance received directly or indirectly from a government agency, auditors may have a duty to report it directly if management fails to take remedial steps. If auditors conclude that such failure is likely to cause them to depart from the standard report or resign from the audit, they should communicate that conclusion to the auditee's governing body. Then, if the auditee does not report the fraud, noncompliance, or abuse as soon as practicable to the entity that provided the government assistance, the auditors should report directly to that entity.

11. An auditor most likely will be responsible for communicating significant deficiencies in the design of internal controls

    A. To a court-appointed creditors' committee when the client is operating under Chapter 11 of the Federal Bankruptcy Code.

    B. To shareholders with significant influence (more than 20% equity ownership) when the deficiencies are deemed to be material weaknesses.

    C. To the Securities and Exchange Commission when the client is a publicly held entity.

    D. To specific legislative and regulatory bodies when reporting under *Government Auditing Standards*.

Answer (D) is correct.
    REQUIRED: The circumstance in which an auditor is likely responsible for communicating significant deficiencies in internal control.
    DISCUSSION: An auditor is required to include significant deficiencies and material weaknesses in internal control over financial reporting in a report prepared under *Government Auditing Standards*. The report is required to be distributed to those charged with governance, to the appropriate officials of the audited entity, and to the appropriate oversight bodies or organizations requiring or arranging for the audits.
    Answer (A) is incorrect. Management is responsible for providing audited financial statements to a creditors' committee. Answer (B) is incorrect. The auditor's report is included with the audited financial statements in the annual report, a document that is available to all shareholders. Answer (C) is incorrect. The opinion on internal control of an issuer discloses material weaknesses but not significant deficiencies.

20.2 Compliance Audits

12. In a compliance audit, the auditor's primary objective is to

    A. Determine that all instances of noncompliance are discovered and reported.

    B. Test and express an opinion on internal control over compliance.

    C. Obtain sufficient appropriate evidence to form an opinion on compliance.

    D. Provide management with recommendations for improvement over compliance.

Answer (C) is correct.
    REQUIRED: The auditor's primary objective in a compliance audit.
    DISCUSSION: The auditor's objective in a compliance audit is to obtain sufficient appropriate evidence to form an opinion and report at the level specified in the governmental audit requirement on whether the entity complied, in all material respects, with the applicable compliance requirements.
    Answer (A) is incorrect. Only instances of material noncompliance need be reported on. Answer (B) is incorrect. Although the auditor considers internal control in planning the audit, no opinion is required. Answer (D) is incorrect. An audit of compliance does not require the auditor to provide recommendations for improvement over compliance.

13. In an audit of an entity's compliance with applicable compliance requirements, an auditor obtains written representations from management acknowledging

    A. Its responsibilities for compliance, including disclosure of noncompliance.

    B. Implementation of controls designed to detect all noncompliance.

    C. Expression of positive assurance to the auditor that the entity complied with all applicable compliance requirements.

    D. Employment of internal auditors who can report their findings, opinions, and conclusions objectively.

Answer (A) is correct.
    REQUIRED: The representations obtained from management in a compliance audit.
    DISCUSSION: The auditor obtains written representations from management about its responsibilities for (1) understanding and complying with the compliance requirements and (2) establishing and maintaining controls that provide reasonable assurance that the entity administers government programs in accordance with the compliance requirements. Among other things, the auditor also requests representations that management has disclosed all known noncompliance with the applicable compliance requirements, including that subsequent to the period covered by the auditor's report.
    Answer (B) is incorrect. Management should disclose all known noncompliance. Given the inherent limitations of internal control, it cannot be expected to prevent or detect all noncompliance. Answer (C) is incorrect. In a compliance audit, management does not express an opinion that it has complied with all applicable compliance requirements. Answer (D) is incorrect. The entity will decide whether to employ internal auditors.

14. A material weakness in internal control over compliance arises when

A. At a minimum, a deficiency is important enough to merit attention by those charged with governance.

B. A reasonable possibility exists that material noncompliance will not be prevented or timely detected and corrected.

C. A risk of material noncompliance exists prior to the audit.

D. The design or operation of a control does not allow management or employees to detect noncompliance in the normal course of their duties.

Answer (B) is correct.
    REQUIRED: The definition of a material weakness.
    DISCUSSION: A material weakness in internal control over compliance is a deficiency, or combination of deficiencies, in internal control over compliance that results in a reasonable possibility that material noncompliance with a compliance requirement will not be prevented, or detected and corrected, on a timely basis.
    Answer (A) is incorrect. A significant deficiency in internal control over compliance is a deficiency, or a combination of deficiencies, in internal control over compliance that is less severe than a material weakness yet merits attention by those charged with governance. Answer (C) is incorrect. The risk of material noncompliance prior to the audit is the combination of the inherent risk of noncompliance and the control risk of noncompliance. Answer (D) is incorrect. A deficiency in internal control over compliance exists when the design or operation of a control over compliance does not allow management or employees, in the normal course of performing their assigned functions, to prevent, or detect and correct, noncompliance on a timely basis.

15. When an auditor is performing a compliance audit and identifies pervasive risks of material noncompliance, the auditor should

A. Withdraw from the engagement.

B. Develop an overall response to such risks.

C. Perform additional analytical procedures.

D. Issue a disclaimer of opinion.

Answer (B) is correct.
    REQUIRED: The auditor's response to pervasive risks of noncompliance.
    DISCUSSION: The auditor should develop an overall response to such risks. For example, the auditor may use more experienced staff or increase supervision.
    Answer (A) is incorrect. The auditor need not withdraw from the engagement and should attempt to mitigate risks by developing an overall response to such risks. Answer (C) is incorrect. The use of analytical procedures to gather substantive evidence is generally less effective in a compliance audit than it is in a financial statement audit. Answer (D) is incorrect. The auditor should attempt to mitigate risks by developing an overall response to such risks.

20.3 Federal Audit Requirements and the Single Audit Act

16. In an audit of compliance with requirements governing awards under major federal programs performed in accordance with the Single Audit Act, the auditor's consideration of materiality differs from materiality under generally accepted auditing standards. Under the Single Audit Act, materiality for the purpose of reporting an audit finding is

A. Calculated in relation to the financial statements taken as a whole.

B. Determined in relation to a type of compliance requirement for a major program.

C. Decided in conjunction with the auditor's risk assessment.

D. Ignored, because all account balances, regardless of size, are fully tested.

Answer (B) is correct.
    REQUIRED: The materiality determination under the Single Audit Act.
    DISCUSSION: Under the Single Audit Act, the emphasis of the audit effort is on major programs related to federal awards administered by nonfederal entities. According to OMB *Audit Requirements for Federal Awards* (2 CFR 200) Compliance Supplement adopted under the Single Audit Act, the schedule of findings and questioned costs includes instances of material noncompliance with laws, regulations, contracts, or grant agreements related to a major program. The auditor's determination of whether a noncompliance is material for the purpose of reporting an audit finding is in relation to a type of compliance requirement for a major program or an audit objective identified in the OMB 2 CFR 200 Compliance Supplement. Examples of types of compliance requirements include (1) activities allowed or unallowed; (2) allowable costs/cost principles; (3) cash management; (4) eligibility; (5) matching, level of effort, and earmarking; and (6) reporting.
    Answer (A) is incorrect. In a for-profit financial statement audit, materiality is related to the financial statements as a whole. Answer (C) is incorrect. Risk assessment is performed in planning the audit, but once the auditor makes a finding, the decision to report it is contingent on the materiality to the major program. Answer (D) is incorrect. Materiality should be considered in determining the appropriate tests to be applied.

17. A CPA has performed an examination of the general-purpose financial statements of Big City. The examination scope included the additional requirements of the Single Audit Act. When reporting on Big City's internal control over the administration of federal awards, the CPA should

    A. Communicate all control deficiencies related to all federal awards.

    B. Express an opinion on the systems used to administer awards under major federal programs and express negative assurance on the systems used to administer awards under nonmajor federal programs.

    C. Communicate significant deficiencies and material weaknesses that are material in relation to a type of compliance requirement for the federal program.

    D. Express negative assurance on the systems used to administer awards under major federal programs and express no opinion on the systems used to administer awards under nonmajor federal programs.

Answer (C) is correct.

    REQUIRED: The requirement of a report on internal controls used in administering awards under a federal program.

    DISCUSSION: Under the Single Audit Act, the auditor's determination of whether a deficiency in internal control is a significant deficiency or material weakness is in relation to a type of compliance requirement for a major program or an audit objective identified in the OMB *Audit Requirements for Federal Awards* (2 CFR 200) Compliance Supplement. The auditor also should identify all significant deficiencies and weaknesses.

    Answer (A) is incorrect. Only significant deficiencies and material weaknesses need be communicated. Answer (B) is incorrect. Although an auditor conducting a single audit is required to report on controls that relate to the systems used to administer awards under federal programs, the auditor is not required to provide assurance. Answer (D) is incorrect. Auditors are required to express an opinion (or disclaim an opinion) as to whether the auditee complied with laws, regulations, and the provisions of contracts or grant agreements that could have a direct and material effect on each major program.

18. Although the scope of audits of recipients of federal awards in accordance with federal audit regulations varies, audits under the Single Audit Act generally have which of the following elements in common?

    A. The auditor is to determine whether the federal financial assistance has been administered in accordance with applicable laws and regulations.

    B. The materiality levels are lower and are determined by the government entities that provided the federal awards to the recipient.

    C. The auditor should obtain written management representations that the recipient's internal auditors will report their findings objectively, without fear of political repercussion.

    D. The auditor is required to express both positive and negative assurance that fraudulent acts that could have a material effect on the recipient's financial statements are disclosed to the inspector general.

Answer (A) is correct.

    REQUIRED: The common element in federal audit regulations.

    DISCUSSION: According to the Single Audit Act, the scope of federal audits may vary, but the auditor should

1. Determine whether the financial statements are presented fairly, in all material respects, in conformity with GAAP.

2. Determine whether the schedule of expenditures of federal awards is presented fairly, in all material respects, in relation to the financial statements as a whole.

3. With respect to controls over compliance, obtain an understanding of those controls, assess control risk, and perform tests of controls unless the controls are ineffective.

4. Determine whether the nonfederal entity has complied with the provisions of laws, regulations, and contracts or grants that have a direct and material effect on each major program.

5. Report audit findings in a schedule of findings and questioned costs.

    Answer (B) is incorrect. Materiality is determined by the auditor in relation to a type of compliance requirement for a major program or an audit objective identified in the OMB *Audit Requirements for Federal Awards* (2 CFR 200) Compliance Supplement. Answer (C) is incorrect. Although the auditor should obtain written management representations, no specific requirements concerning the entity's internal auditors are stipulated. Answer (D) is incorrect. The auditor is required to report fraudulent acts but not to provide positive or negative assurance about them.

19. An auditor is auditing a nonfederal entity's administration of a federal award pursuant to a major program under the Single Audit Act. The auditor is required to

	Obtain Evidence Related to Compliance	Express or Disclaim an Opinion on Compliance
A.	Yes	Yes
B.	Yes	No
C.	No	Yes
D.	No	No

Answer (A) is correct.
REQUIRED: The auditor's responsibility in a compliance audit.
DISCUSSION: After an audit of a nonfederal entity that expends federal awards, the audit report on compliance should include an opinion or a disclaimer of opinion as to whether the auditee complied with the applicable compliance requirements, that is, with laws, regulations, rules, and the provisions of contracts or grants. This report also should describe identified noncompliance or refer to an accompanying schedule of noncompliance.

20. Wolf is auditing an entity's compliance with requirements governing a major federal program in accordance with the Single Audit Act. Wolf detected noncompliance with requirements that have a material effect on the program. Wolf's report on compliance should express

A. No assurance on the compliance tests.

B. Reasonable assurance on the compliance tests.

C. A qualified or adverse opinion.

D. An adverse opinion or a disclaimer of opinion.

Answer (C) is correct.
REQUIRED: The assurance about compliance given noncompliance with material requirements.
DISCUSSION: Under the Single Audit Act, the auditor should express an opinion on compliance with requirements having a direct and material effect on a major federal program or state that an opinion cannot be expressed. When the compliance audit detects noncompliance with those requirements that the auditor believes have a direct and material effect on the program, the auditor should express a qualified or adverse opinion. The auditor should state the basis for such an opinion in the report.
Answer (A) is incorrect. The auditor should express an opinion on compliance. Answer (B) is incorrect. The auditor's report should state that the audit was planned and performed to provide reasonable assurance about whether material noncompliance occurred. Answer (D) is incorrect. A disclaimer is not appropriate when the auditor has detected material noncompliance.

APPENDIX A
AUDITING AUTHORITATIVE
PRONOUNCEMENTS CROSS-REFERENCES

The following listing relates AU-C and other auditing pronouncements to the Gleim study unit(s) in which they are discussed. Note that the subject matter may be covered without specific reference to the pronouncement. Recall that the CPA exam does not test pronouncement numbers or titles.

Section No.	Gleim Study Unit	Statements on Auditing Standards
AU-C 200–299		**General Principles and Responsibilities**
200	1, 3	Overall Objectives of the Independent Auditor and the Conduct of an Audit in Accordance With Generally Accepted Auditing Standards
210	3	Terms of Engagement
220	1, 3	Quality Control for an Engagement Conducted in Accordance With Generally Accepted Auditing Standards
230	10	Audit Documentation
240	3	Consideration of Fraud in a Financial Statement Audit
250	3	Consideration of Laws and Regulations in an Audit of Financial Statements
260	9	The Auditor's Communication With Those Charged With Governance
265	9	Communicating Internal Control Related Matters Identified in an Audit
AU-C 300–499		**Risk Assessment and Response to Assessed Risk**
300	3	Planning an Audit
315	1, 3, 5-8	Understanding the Entity and Its Environment and Assessing the Risks of Material Misstatement
320	3	Materiality in Planning and Performing an Audit
330	8, 10	Performing Audit Procedures in Response to Assessed Risks and Evaluating the Audit Evidence Obtained
402	9	Audit Considerations Relating to an Entity Using a Service Organization
450	3	Evaluation of Misstatements Identified During the Audit
AU-C 500–599		**Audit Evidence**
500	4, 10-14	Audit Evidence
501	10-14	Audit Evidence—Specific Considerations for Selected Items
505	10-11	External Confirmations
510	3	Opening Balances—Initial Audit Engagements, Including Reaudit Engagements
520	3	Analytical Procedures
530	15	Audit Sampling
540	4, 13	Auditing Accounting Estimates, Including Fair Value Accounting Estimates, and Related Disclosures
550	4	Related Parties
560	14, 17	Subsequent Events and Subsequently Discovered Facts
570	14, 17	The Auditor's Consideration of an Entity's Ability to Continue as a Going Concern
580	14	Written Representations
585	*	Consideration of Omitted Procedures After the Report Release Date
AU-C 600–699		**Using the Work of Others**
600	17	Special Considerations—Audits of Group Financial Statements (Including the Work of Component Auditors)
610	4	The Auditor's Consideration of the Internal Audit Function in an Audit of Financial Statements
620	4	Using the Work of an Auditor's Specialist
AU-C 700–799		**Audit Conclusions and Reporting**
700	16-17	Forming an Opinion and Reporting on Financial Statements
705	16-17	Modifications to the Opinion in the Independent Auditor's Report
706	17	Emphasis-of-Matter Paragraphs and Other-Matter Paragraphs in the Independent Auditor's Report
708	17	Consistency of Financial Statements
720	18	Other Information in Documents Containing Audited Financial Statements
725	18	Supplementary Information in Relation to the Financial Statements as a Whole
730	18	Required Supplementary Information

*Not tested on the CPA exam

Section No.	Gleim Study Unit	Statements on Auditing Standards
AU-C 800–899		**Special Considerations**
800	18	Special Considerations—Audits of Financial Statements Prepared in Accordance With Special Purpose Frameworks
805	18	Special Considerations—Audits of Single Financial Statements and Specific Elements, Accounts, or Items of a Financial Statement
806	17	Reporting on Compliance With Aspects of Contractual Agreements or Regulatory Requirements in Connection with Audited Financial Statements
810	18	Engagements to Report on Summary Financial Statements
AU-C 900–999		**Special Considerations in the United States**
905	18	Alert That Restricts the Use of the Auditor's Written Communication
910	18	Financial Statements Prepared in Accordance With a Financial Reporting Framework Generally Accepted in Another Country
915	18	Reports on Application of Requirements of an Applicable Financial Reporting Framework
920	18	Letters for Underwriters and Certain Other Requesting Parties, as Amended
925	18	Filings With the U.S. Securities and Exchange Commission Under the Securities Act of 1933
930	18	Interim Financial Information
935	20	Compliance Audits
940	5, 9, 14	An Audit of Internal Control Over Financial Reporting That is Integrated with an Audit of Financial Statements
		Statements on Standards for Attestation Engagements
AT 20	1	Defining Professional Requirements in SSAEs
AT 50	1	SSAE Hierarchy
AT 101	1	Attest Engagements
AT 201	1, 19	Agreed-Upon Procedures Engagements
AT 301	1, 19	Financial Forecasts and Projections
AT 401	1, 19	Reporting on Pro Forma Financial Information
AT 601	1, 19	Compliance Attestation
AT 701	1	Management's Discussion and Analysis
AT 801	1, 9	Reporting on Controls at a Service Organization
		Statements on Standards for Accounting and Review Services
AR-C 60	1, 19	General Principles for Engagements Performed With Statements on Standards for Accounting and Review Services
AR-C 70	1, 19	Preparation of Financial Statements
AR-C 80	1, 19	Compilation of Financial Statements
AR-C 90	1, 19	Review of Financial Statements
AR 120	19	Compilation of Pro Forma Financial Information (Pre-Clarification)
		Statements on Quality Control Standards
QC 10	1, 3	A Firm's System of Quality Control
		Standards for Performing and Reporting on Peer Reviews
PR 100	1	Standards for Performing and Reporting on Peer Reviews
		Other Standards and References
	2	AICPA *Code of Professional Conduct*
	2	Sarbanes-Oxley Act of 2002
	2	Department of Labor: Auditor Independence
	20	*Government Auditing Standards* (Yellow Book)
	20	OMB Audit Requirements for Federal Awards (2 CFR 200)
	2	IFAC *Code of Ethics for Professional Accountants*
	5	The Committee of Sponsoring Organizations (COSO)

Section No.	Gleim Study Unit	Public Company Accounting Oversight Board Standards
1000		**General Principles and Responsibilities**
1001	1, 3	Responsibilities and Functions of the Independent Auditor
1005	1, 3	Independence
1010	1, 3	Training and Proficiency of the Independent Auditor
1015	1, 3	Due Professional Care in the Performance of Work
1100		**General Concepts**
1101	1, 3	Audit Risk
1105	4, 10-14	Audit Evidence
1110	1, 3	Relationship of Auditing Standards to Quality Control Standards
1200		**General Activities**
1201	1, 3	Supervision of the Audit Engagement
1205	17	Part of the Audit Performed by Other Independent Auditors
1210	4	Using the Work of a Specialist
1215	10	Audit Documentation
1220	1, 3	Engagement Quality Review
1300		**Auditor Communications**
1301	3, 9	Communications with Audit Committees
1305	9	Communications About Control Deficiencies in an Audit of Financial Statements
Audit Procedures		
2100		**Audit Planning and Risk Assessment**
2101	3	Audit Planning
2105	3	Consideration of Materiality in Planning and Performing an Audit
2110	1, 3, 5-8	Identifying and Assessing Risks of Material Misstatement
2200		**Internal Control over Financial Reporting**
2201	5, 9	An Audit of Internal Control over Financial Reporting That Is Integrated with an Audit of Financial Statements
2300		**Audit Procedures in Response to Risks – Nature, Timing, and Extent**
2301	8, 10	The Auditor's Responses to the Risks of Material Misstatement
2305	3	Substantive Analytical Procedures
2310	10, 11	The Confirmation Process
2315	15	Audit Sampling
2400		**Audit Procedures for Specific Aspects of the Audit**
2401	3	Consideration of Fraud in a Financial Statement Audit
2405	3	Illegal Acts by Clients
2410	4	Related Parties
2415	14, 17	Consideration of an Entity's Ability to Continue as a Going Concern
2500		**Audit Procedures for Certain Accounts or Disclosures**
2501	4, 13	Auditing Accounting Estimates
2502	4, 13	Auditing Fair Value Measurements and Disclosures
2503	4, 13	Auditing Derivative Instruments, Hedging Activities, and Investments in Securities
2505	14	Inquiry of a Client's Lawyer Concerning Litigation, Claims, and Assessments
2510	12	Auditing Inventories
2600		**Special Topics**
2601	9	Consideration of an Entity's Use of a Service Organization
2605	4	Consideration of the Internal Audit Function
2610	3	Initial Audits – Communications Between Predecessor and Successor Auditors
2700		**Auditor's Responsibilities Regarding Supplemental and Other Information**
2701	18	Auditing Supplemental Information Accompanying Audited Financial Statements
2705	18	Required Supplementary Information
2710	18	Other Information in Documents Containing Audited Financial Statements

Section No.	Gleim Study Unit	Public Company Accounting Oversight Board Standards
2800		**Concluding Audit Procedures**
2801	14, 17	Subsequent Events
2805	14	Management Representations
2810	3, 4, 8, 10-14	Evaluating Audit Results
2815	16, 17	The Meaning of "Present Fairly in Conformity with Generally Accepted Accounting Principles"
2820	17	Evaluating Consistency of Financial Statements
2900		**Post-Audit Matters**
2901	*	Consideration of Omitted Procedures After the Report Date
2905	14, 17	Subsequent Discovery of Facts Existing at the Date of the Auditor's Report

Auditor Reporting

Section No.	Gleim Study Unit	
3100		**Reporting on Audits of Financial Statements**
3101	16, 17	Reports on Audited Financial Statements
3110	16, 17	Dating of the Independent Auditor's Report
3300		**Other Reporting Topics**
3305	17, 18	Special Reports
3310	18	Special Reports on Regulated Companies
3315	18	Reporting on Condensed Financial Statements and Selected Financial Data
3320	16	Association with Financial Statements

Matters Relating to Filings Under Federal Securities Laws

4101	18	Responsibilities Regarding Filings Under Federal Securities Statutes
4105	18	Reviews of Interim Financial Information

Other Matters Associated with Audits

6101	18	Letters for Underwriters and Certain Other Requesting Parties
6105	18	Reports on the Application of Accounting Principles
6110	20	Compliance Auditing Considerations in Audits of Recipients of Governmental Financial Assistance
6115	9	Reporting on Whether a Previously Reported Material Weakness Continues to Exist

APPENDIX B
AICPA UNIFORM CPA EXAMINATION
BLUEPRINTS WITH GLEIM CROSS-REFERENCES

The AICPA has indicated that the Blueprints have several purposes, including to

- *Document the minimum level of knowledge and skills necessary for initial licensure.*
- *Assist candidates in preparing for the Exam by outlining the knowledge and skills that may be tested.*
- *Apprise educators about the knowledge and skills candidates will need to function as newly licensed CPAs.*
- *Guide the development of Exam questions.*

For your convenience, we have reproduced the AICPA's Auditing Blueprint. We also have provided cross-references to the study units and subunits in this book that correspond to the Blueprint's coverage. If one entry appears above a list, it applies to all items.

AUDITING AND ATTESTATION (AUD)

Area I – Ethics, Professional Responsibilities and General Principles (15-25%)

A. NATURE AND SCOPE

1. Nature and scope: audit engagements - 1.1-1.2
2. Nature and scope: engagements conducted under Government Accountability Office Government Auditing Standards - 1.3, 20.1
3. Nature and scope: non-audit engagements - 1.3-1.4

B. ETHICS, INDEPENDENCE AND PROFESSIONAL CONDUCT

1. AICPA Code of Professional Conduct - SU 2
2. Requirements of the Securities and the Exchange Commission and the Public Company Accounting Oversight Board - 2.7
3. Requirements of the Government Accountability Office and the Department of Labor - 2.7, 20.1

C. TERMS OF ENGAGEMENT

1. Preconditions for an engagement - 3.1
2. Terms of engagement and engagement letter - 3.1, 19.1, 19.4

D. REQUIREMENTS FOR ENGAGEMENT DOCUMENTATION - 10.3

E. COMMUNICATION WITH MANAGEMENT AND THOSE CHARGED WITH GOVERNANCE

1. Planned scope and timing of an engagement - 9.2
2. Internal control related matters - 9.1
3. All other matters - 9.2

F. COMMUNICATION WITH COMPONENT AUDITORS AND PARTIES OTHER THAN MANAGEMENT AND THOSE CHARGED WITH GOVERNANCE - 17.1, 20.1

G. A FIRM'S SYSTEM OF QUALITY CONTROL, INCLUDING QUALITY CONTROL AT THE ENGAGEMENT LEVEL - 1.5, 20.1

Area II – Assessing Risk and Developing a Planned Response (20-30%)

A.   PLANNING AN ENGAGEMENT - 3.2

  1.   Developing an overall engagement strategy
  2.   Developing a detailed engagement plan

B.   UNDERSTANDING AN ENTITY AND ITS ENVIRONMENT - 3.3

  1.   External factors, including the applicable financial reporting framework

  2.   Internal factors, including nature of the entity, ownership and governance structures and risk strategy

C.   UNDERSTANDING AN ENTITY'S INTERNAL CONTROL

  1.   Control environment and entity-level controls - 3.4
  2.   Flow of transactions and design of internal controls - 5.1-5.3, 6.1, 7.1
  3.   Implications of an entity using a service organization - 9.4
  4.   Information Technology (IT) general and application controls - 5.5, 6.4, 7.2, 7.5
  5.   Limitations of controls and risk of management override - 3.3, 5.1

D.   ASSESSING RISKS DUE TO FRAUD, INCLUDING DISCUSSIONS AMONG THE ENGAGEMENT TEAM ABOUT THE RISK OF MATERIAL MISSTATEMENT DUE TO FRAUD OR ERROR - 3.6

E.   IDENTIFYING AND ASSESSING THE RISK OF MATERIAL MISSTATEMENT, WHETHER DUE TO ERROR OR FRAUD, AND PLANNING FURTHER PROCEDURES RESPONSIVE TO IDENTIFIED RISKS

  1.   Impact of risks at the financial statement level - 3.3

  2.   Impact of risks for each relevant assertion at the class of transaction, account balance and disclosure levels - 8.1

  3.   Further procedures responsive to identified risks - 8.2

F.   MATERIALITY - 3.3

  1.   For the financial statements as a whole
  2.   Performance materiality and tolerable misstatement

G.   PLANNING FOR AND USING THE WORK OF OTHERS, INCLUDING GROUP AUDITS, THE INTERNAL AUDIT FUNCTION AND THE WORK OF A SPECIALIST - 4.1-4.2, 17.1

H.   SPECIFIC AREAS OF ENGAGEMENT RISK

  1.   An entity's compliance with laws and regulations, including possible illegal acts - 3.7, 20.1
  2.   Accounting estimates, including fair value estimates - 4.4
  3.   Related parties and related party transactions - 4.3

Area III – Performing Further Procedures and Obtaining Evidence (30-40%)

A.   UNDERSTANDING SUFFICIENT APPROPRIATE EVIDENCE - 1.1, 1.3, 10.1, 19.1

B.   SAMPLING TECHNIQUES - 15.1

C.   PERFORMING SPECIFIC PROCEDURES TO OBTAIN EVIDENCE

  1.   Analytical procedures - 3.5, 19.4
  2.   External confirmations - 10.2, 11.1
  3.   Inquiry of management and others - 10.1, 8.2
  4.   Observation and inspection - 8.1
  5.   Recalculation and reperformance - 10.1
  6.   All other procedures - 10.1

D. SPECIFIC MATTERS THAT REQUIRE SPECIAL CONSIDERATION

   1. Opening balances - 3.2
   2. Investments in securities and derivative instruments - 13.2
   3. Physical observation of inventory and inventory held by others - 12.2
   4. Litigation, claims and assessments - 14.1
   5. An entity's ability to continue as a going concern - 14.4
   6. Accounting estimates, including fair value estimates - 4.4

E. MISSTATEMENTS AND INTERNAL CONTROL DEFICIENCIES - 3.3, 10.1

F. WRITTEN REPRESENTATIONS - 14.3

G. SUBSEQUENT EVENTS AND SUBSEQUENTLY DISCOVERED FACTS - 14.2

Area IV – Forming Conclusions and Reporting (15-25%)

A. REPORTS ON AUDITING ENGAGEMENTS

   1. Forming an audit opinion, including modification of an auditor's opinion - 16.1, 16.4-16.5

   2. Form and content of an audit report, including the use of emphasis-of-matter and other-matter (explanatory) paragraphs - 16.2

   3. Examinations of internal control integrated with an audit of financial statements - 9.3

B. REPORTS ON ATTESTATION ENGAGEMENTS

   1. General standards for attestation reports - 19.6-19.8
   2. Agreed-upon procedures reports - 19.5
   3. Reporting on controls at a service organization - 9.4

C. ACCOUNTING AND REVIEW SERVICE ENGAGEMENTS

   1. Preparation engagements - 19.1-19.2
   2. Compilation reports - 19.1, 19.3
   3. Review reports - 19.1, 19.4

D. REPORTING ON COMPLIANCE - 19.8, 20.2

E. OTHER REPORTING CONSIDERATIONS

   1. Comparative statements and consistency between periods - 17.2

   2. Other information in documents with audited statements - 18.4

   3. Review of interim financial information - 18.1

   4. Supplementary information - 18.5

   5. Single statements - 18.11

   6. Special-purpose and other country frameworks - 18.1, 18.8

   7. Letters for underwriters and filings with the SEC - 18.2-18.3

   8. Alerts that restrict the use of written communication - 16.1

   9. Additional reporting requirements under Government Accountability Office Government Auditing Standards - 20.1

APPENDIX C
OPTIMIZING YOUR SCORE ON
THE TASK-BASED SIMULATIONS (TBSs)

Each section of the CPA exam contains multiple testlets of Task-Based Simulations. The number of TBS testlets and the number of TBSs in each testlet are the same for each exam section except BEC.

TBSs per Exam Section

	Testlet 3	Testlet 4	Testlet 5	Total
AUD	2	3	3	8
BEC	2	2	N/A*	4
FAR	2	3	3	8
REG	2	3	3	8

* Testlet 5 of BEC is Written Communications.

Task-Based Simulations are constructive response questions with information presented either with the question or in separate information tabs. Question responses may be in the form of entering amounts or formulas into a spreadsheet, choosing the correct answer from a list in a pop-up box, completing accounting or tax forms, or reviewing and completing or correcting a draft of a document. In the AUD, FAR, and REG exam sections, you will also have to complete a Research task, which requires you to research the relevant authoritative literature and cite the appropriate guidance as indicated. You will not have to complete a Research task in BEC.

It is not productive to practice TBSs on paper. Instead, you should use your online Gleim CPA Review Course to complete truly interactive TBSs that emulate exactly how TBSs are tested on the CPA exam. As a CPA candidate, you must become an expert on how to approach TBSs, how to budget your time in the TBS testlets, and the different types of TBSs. This appendix covers all of those topics for you and includes examples of typical TBSs. Use this appendix only as an introduction to TBSs, and then practice hundreds of exam-emulating TBSs in your Gleim CPA Review Course.

Task-Based Simulations -- Toolbar Icons and Operations

The following information and toolbar icons are located at the top of the testlet screen of each TBS. All screen shots are taken from the AICPA Sample Test (www.aicpa.org). The CPA exam, the Sample Test, and all screenshots are Copyright 2017 by the AICPA with All Rights Reserved. The AICPA requires all candidates to review the Sample Tests and Tutorials before sitting for the CPA exam.

1. **Exam Section and Testlet Number:** The testlet number will always be 3, 4, or 5 of 5 for the simulations.

2. **Time Remaining:** This information box displays how much time you have remaining in the entire exam. Consistently check the amount of time remaining to stay on schedule.

3. **Unsplit:** This icon, when selected, will unsplit the screen between two tabs.

4. **Split Horiz:** This icon, when selected, will split the screen horizontally between two tabs, enabling you to see, for example, both the simulation question and the help tab at the same time.

5. **Split Vertical:** This icon, when selected, will split the screen vertically between two tabs, enabling you to see, for example, both the simulation question and the help tab at the same time.

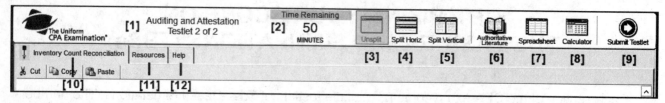

6. **Authoritative Literature:** The Authoritative Literature for AUD, FAR, and REG is available in every TBS testlet. You can use either the Table of Contents or the Search function to locate the correct guidance.

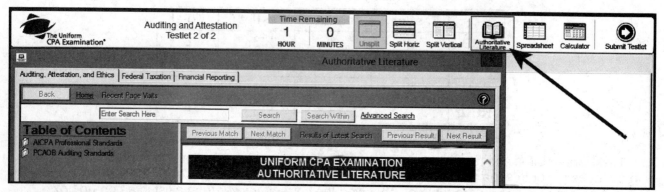

7. **Spreadsheet:** The spreadsheet operates like most others and is provided as a tool for complex calculations. You may enter and execute formulas as well as enter text and numbers.

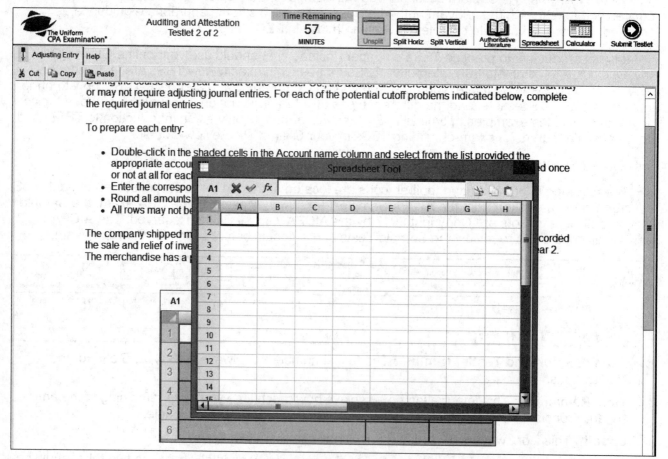

8. **Calculator:** The calculator provided is a basic tool for simple computations. It is similar to calculators used in common software programs.

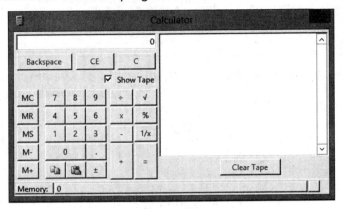

9. **Submit Testlet:** There are two options when you choose this icon from the toolbar.

   - In any of the first four testlets, you will be asked to select either Return to Testlet or Submit Testlet. Return to Testlet allows you to review and change your answers in the current testlet. Submit Testlet takes you to the next testlet.

   - In the final testlet, you will be asked to select either Return to Testlet or Quit Exam. Choose Quit Exam if you wish to complete the exam. You will not be able to return to any testlet, and you will not receive credit for any unanswered questions. To prevent accidentally ending your exam, you will be asked to verify your selection, or you can choose Go Back. Upon verifying you wish to End Exam, you will be required to leave the test center with no re-admittance.

10. **Work Tabs:** A work tab requires you to respond to given information. Each task will have at least one work tab (distinguished by a pencil icon), and each work tab will have specific directions you must read to complete the tab correctly. You must complete all the work tabs in each task to maximize your chance for full credit. The format of the work tab varies. You may encounter work tabs that require you to complete forms, fill in spreadsheets, or select an option from multiple choices. The TBSs on pages 475-488 are examples of each variety of work tab.

11. **Information Tabs:** An information tab gives you information to help with responding to work tabs. These tabs are generally labeled Resources or Exhibits and contain various resources and tools to use with the current work tab. An example is below.

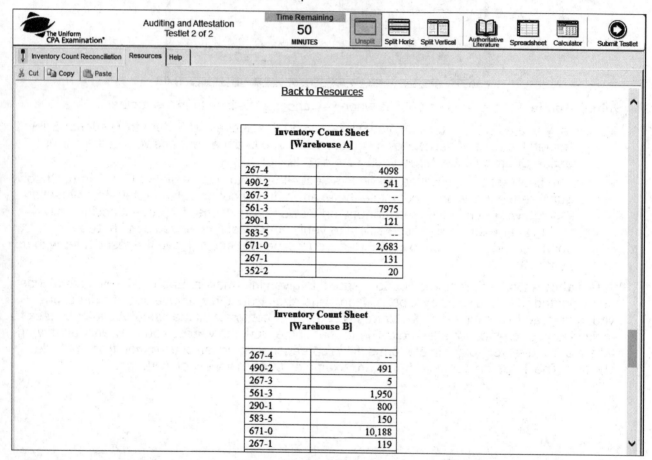

12. **Help:** This tab, when selected, provides a quick review of certain functions and tool buttons specific to the type of task you are working in. It will also provide directions and general information but will not include information related specifically to the test content.

The **navigation toolbar** below appears at the bottom of every TBS screen.

Clicking on a number takes you to that TBS; hovering over the number shows the name of the TBS. Clicking on the flag under a number marks the TBS. You can use the flag as a reminder to go back and check that TBS again if you have time.

Task-Based Simulation Answering Techniques

Do not be intimidated by TBSs. Just learn the material and practice answering the different question types. Knowing **how** to work through the simulations is nearly as important as knowing what they test.

You can maximize your score on the TBS testlets of each exam section by following these suggested steps for completing Task-Based Simulations.

A. **Budget your time so you can finish before time expires.**

1. Allot small segments of the total testing time to each specific task. We recommend you budget 18 minutes for each TBS.

2. Track your progress to ensure that you will have enough time to complete all the tasks.

3. Use our Time Allocation Table to determine the time at which you need to start and finish each TBS testlet.

B. **Devote the first few minutes to reading the directions and scanning each TBS.**

1. Spend no more than 3 minutes reading the directions and previewing the TBSs you received by clicking through the navigation bar at the bottom of the screen.

2. You will not need to spend any time on the directions for your second and third TBS testlets, so you can dedicate the full time (minus a minute for scanning to preview) to responding.

3. You will be familiar with the layout of the TBSs if you have been practicing with Gleim TBSs under exam conditions.

C. **Answer all the tasks within the time limit for each testlet.**

1. Read all information tabs (e.g., financial statements, memos, etc.) associated with the tab you are working on before you attempt to answer the simulation.

   a. We have included detailed directions on using exhibits as source documents in the next section on Document Review Simulations. Much of those instructions can also be used when answering regular TBSs that contain exhibits.

2. Do not skip any of the questions within a tab. Make an educated guess if you are unsure of the answer and set a reminder for yourself by clicking the flag icon under the number of the TBS in the navigation toolbar at the bottom of the screen. There is no penalty for incorrect answers, so do not move on without at least selecting your best guess.

D. **Spend any remaining time wisely to maximize your points.**

1. Ask yourself where you will earn the most points.

2. Move from task to task systematically, reviewing and completing each one. Focus specifically on any TBS you flagged.

3. Move on to the next TBS within the testlet or to the next testlet at the end of 18 minutes.

DOCUMENT REVIEW SIMULATIONS

Within the Task-Based Simulation testlets included in each CPA exam section, you may find a Document Review Simulation (DRS), which will be named Document Review. You are required to review various exhibits to determine the best phrasing of a particular document. The document will contain highlighted words, phrases, sentences, or paragraphs that may or may not be correct. You then must select answer choices that indicate which (if any) changes you believe should be made in the highlighted words, phrases, sentences, or paragraphs.

The DRSs always include the actual document you must review and correct, a help tab, and one or more information tabs. Information tabs vary from one DRS to the next because they contain the exhibits to be used as sources for your conclusions. For example, these exhibits may be financial statements, emails, letters, invoices, memoranda, or minutes from meetings. You must read each DRS tab so that you are always aware of the resources available.

Answering Document Review Simulations

A. **Familiarize yourself with every part of the DRS.**

Review each information tab so you know what information is available. If your subject-matter preparation has been thorough, you should be able to identify quickly the most relevant information in each part of the DRS.

B. **Address every underlined portion of text in the DRS.**

You must make an answer selection for every modifiable section of a DRS because each counts as a separate question. You will know an answer has been selected when you see that the white outline in the blue icon has changed to a white checkmark.

C. **Read the underlined section and answer choices carefully and completely.**

Each underlined portion of text may have five to seven answer choices that may include the options to revise the text, retain the original text, or delete the text. Verify that each word or amount is correct in your choice before making your final selection.

D. **Clearly understand the information in the exhibits.**

Quickly survey the various items; then analyze the most relevant facts specifically and refer to them to reduce the possible answer choices. Keep in mind that the relevant information may be presented or worded differently than the document you are revising.

E. **Double-check that you have officially responded to each underlined portion of text.**

If you have time, go through the entire DRS once more to confirm that every underlined section has a white checkmark next to it.

MANAGING TIME ON THE TBSs

Managing your time well during the CPA exam is critical to success, so you must develop and practice your time management plan before your test date. The only help you will receive during your actual CPA exam is a countdown of the hours and minutes remaining. When there are less than 2 minutes left in an exam section, the exam clock will begin to include the seconds, but you should be doing your final review by that point.

Each of the testlets on the exam is independent, and there are no time limits on individual testlets. Therefore, you must budget your time effectively to complete all five testlets in the allotted 4 hours.

The key to success is to become proficient in answering all types of questions in an average amount of time. When you follow our system, you'll have 2-16 minutes of total extra time (depending on the section) that you will be able to allocate as needed.

Each exam will begin with three introductory screens that you must complete in 10 minutes. (Time spent in the introductory screens does not count against the 240 minutes you get for the exam itself.) Then you will have two MCQ testlets. Each testlet contains half the total number of MCQs for that section (36/testlet for AUD, 31/testlet for BEC, 33/testlet for FAR, and 38/testlet for REG.). Based on the total time of the exam and the amount of time needed for the other testlets, you should average 1.25 minutes per MCQ.

The final three testlets in AUD, FAR, and REG will have eight TBSs each: two in Testlet #3, three in Testlet #4, and three in Testlet #5. BEC will have four TBSs in two testlets, then a final testlet of three Written Communications (WCs). We suggest you allocate approximately 18 minutes to answering each TBS. On BEC, budget 25 minutes for each of the three WCs (20 minutes to answer, 5 minutes to review and perfect your response).

To make the most of your testing time during the CPA exam, you will need to develop a time management system and commit to spending a designated amount of time on each question. To assist you, please refer to the Gleim Time Management System.

The table below shows how many minutes you should expect to spend on each testlet for each section. Remember, you cannot begin a new testlet until you have submitted a current testlet, and once you have submitted a testlet, you can no longer go back to it.

Time Allocation per Testlet (in minutes)

Testlet	Format	AUD	BEC	FAR	REG
1	MCQ	45	38*	41*	47*
2	MCQ	45	38*	41*	47*
3	TBS	36	36	36	36
15-Minute Break					
4	TBS	54	36	54	54
5	TBS/WC	54	75	54	54
Total		234	223	226	238
Extra Time		6	17	14	2
Total Time Allowed		240	240	240	240

*Rounded down

The exam screen will show hours:minutes remaining. Focus on how much time you have, NOT the time on your watch. Using the times above, you would start each testlet with the following hours:minutes displayed on-screen:

Completion Times and Time Remaining

	AUD	BEC	FAR	REG
Start	4 hours 0 minutes	4 hours 0 minutes	4 hours 0 minutes	4 hours 0 minutes
After Testlet 1	3 hours 15 minutes	3 hours 22 minutes	3 hours 19 minutes	3 hours 13 minutes
After Testlet 2	2 hours 30 minutes	2 hours 44 minutes	2 hours 38 minutes	2 hours 26 minutes
After Testlet 3	1 hour 54 minutes	2 hours 8 minutes	2 hours 2 minutes	1 hour 50 minutes
15-Minute Break				
After Testlet 4	1 hour 0 minutes	1 hour 32 minutes	1 hour 8 minutes	0 hours 56 minutes
After Testlet 5	0 hours 6 minutes	0 hours 17 minutes	0 hours 14 minutes	0 hours 2 minutes

Next, develop a shorthand for hours:minutes. This makes it easier to write down the times on the noteboard you will receive at the exam center.

	AUD	BEC	FAR	REG
Start	4:00	4:00	4:00	4:00
After Testlet 1	3:15	3:22	3:19	3:13
After Testlet 2	2:30	2:44	2:38	2:26
After Testlet 3	1:54	2:08	2:02	1:50
15-Minute Break				
After Testlet 4	1:00	1:32	1:08	0:56
After Testlet 5	0:06	0:17	0:14	0:02

The following pages of this appendix contain the AICPA TBS directions and the following nine example TBSs:

> Research
> Ratios: Numeric Entry
> Journal Entries: Numeric Entry and Drop-Down
> Risk Factors: Drop-Down 1
> Control Deficiencies: Drop-Down 2
> Bank Reconciliation: Drop-Down 3
> Misstatements: Drop-Down 4
> Review Report II: Drop-Down 5
> Document Review Simulation (DRS)

We have included a variety of TBS types, including Research, Drop-Down, Numeric Entry, and DRS, along with suggestions on how to approach each type. The answer key and our unique answer explanations for each TBS appear at the end of the appendix.

Again, do not substitute answering TBSs in your Gleim CPA Review Course with answering the TBSs presented here. Refer to these TBSs only for guidance on how to answer this difficult element of the exam. It is vital that you practice answering TBSs in the digital environment of our online course so that you are comfortable with such an environment during your CPA exam.

DIRECTIONS

Below and on the next page are reproductions of the Directions screen that appears at the beginning of each TBS testlet. Take the time now to read these directions line by line so that you do not have to spend time reading this screen when you take your exam. This preparation, along with completing numerous TBSs under exam conditions in the Gleim CPA Review Course, will help you refine your TBS-answering techniques.

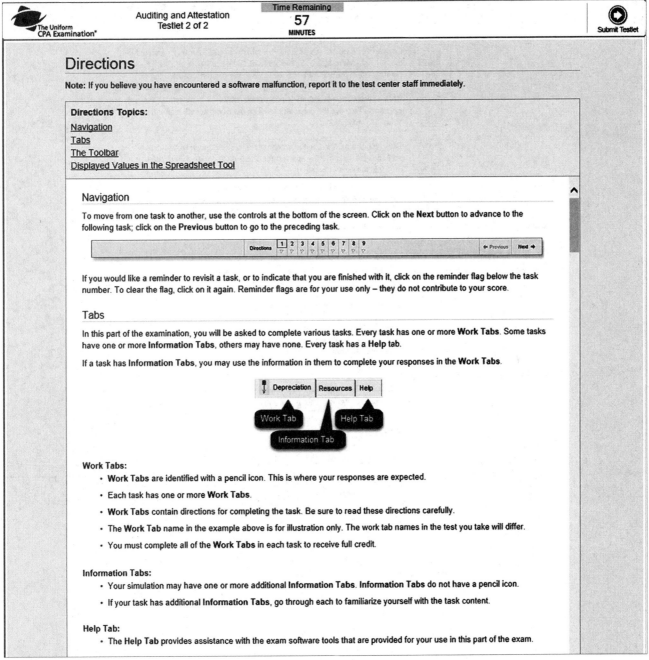

-- Continued on next page --

-- Continued

The Toolbar

The toolbar at the top of the screen shows the amount of time remaining for you to complete the examination. In addition, the following tools are available.

The **Authoritative Literature, Spreadsheet,** and **Calculator** buttons will NOT appear in written communication tasks in the BEC section of the exam.

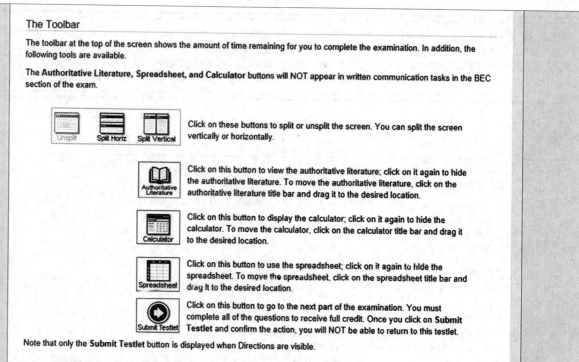

Click on these buttons to split or unsplit the screen. You can split the screen vertically or horizontally.

Click on this button to view the authoritative literature; click on it again to hide the authoritative literature. To move the authoritative literature, click on the authoritative literature title bar and drag it to the desired location.

Click on this button to display the calculator; click on it again to hide the calculator. To move the calculator, click on the calculator title bar and drag it to the desired location.

Click on this button to use the spreadsheet; click on it again to hide the spreadsheet. To move the spreadsheet, click on the spreadsheet title bar and drag it to the desired location.

Click on this button to go to the next part of the examination. You must complete all of the questions to receive full credit. Once you click on **Submit Testlet** and confirm the action, you will NOT be able to return to this testlet.

Note that only the **Submit Testlet** button is displayed when Directions are visible.

Displayed Values in the Spreadsheet Tool

If you type or calculate a value whose width exceeds the column width, not all characters will appear.

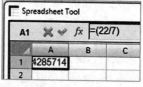

To see the entire value, adjust the column width.

RESEARCH

This type of TBS requires that you research within the Authoritative Literature, which is accessible from the top right corner of the TBS toolbar (shown below), to find the best supporting guidance for the presented scenario. Although there is only one question to answer in the Research TBS, it counts as much as a TBS with multiple questions, so you must treat it with the same gravity as any other TBS. Our suggested steps on how to answer this task type follow:

1. Read through the given scenario and identify key terms. In this scenario, the key terms are "XXX."
2. Type the key terms into the search box and click "Search."
3. Limit the results to the most relevant by analyzing the last portion of each result (e.g., in search result one, pay special attention to "XXX") in the context of your knowledge of the topic; e.g., ask yourself, "Does this result look like it would explain the XXX?"
4. If the first search does not yield the correct answer, restrict your search using the "Search Within" function.
5. Select the exact paragraph that corresponds to the given scenario and enter your response using the on-screen formatting prompts.

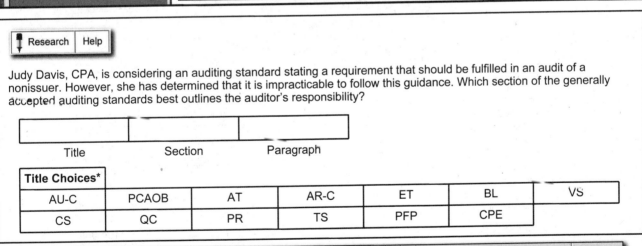

Judy Davis, CPA, is considering an auditing standard stating a requirement that should be fulfilled in an audit of a nonissuer. However, she has determined that it is impracticable to follow this guidance. Which section of the generally accepted auditing standards best outlines the auditor's responsibility?

Title	Section	Paragraph

Title Choices*

AU-C	PCAOB	AT	AR-C	ET	BL	VS
CS	QC	PR	TS	PFP	CPE	

*The following are the full titles for your reference:

AU-C:	Statements on Auditing Standards (Clarified)
PCAOB:	Public Company Accounting Oversight Board
AT:	Statements on Standards for Attestation Engagements
AR-C:	Statements on Standards for Accounting and Review Services (Clarified)
ET:	AICPA *Code of Professional Conduct*
BL:	Bylaws
VS:	Statements on Standards for Valuation Services

CS:	Statements on Standards for Consulting Services
QC:	Statements on Quality Control Standards
PR:	Standards for Performing and Reporting on Peer Reviews
TS:	Statements on Standards for Tax Services
PFP:	Statements on Responsibilities in Personal Financial Planning
CPE:	Continuing Professional Education

RATIOS: NUMERIC ENTRY

This type of TBS requires that you calculate and then respond with some kind of number, e.g., an amount of currency, a ratio, etc. The spreadsheet functions much like an Excel document would. Negative numbers should be entered using a leading minus sign and will be automatically formatted with parentheses. Some Numeric Entry TBSs may also have Drop-Down type responses required. The Drop-Down TBSs are in essence multiple-choice questions.

Ratios	Help

Adams Company
Balance Sheet
As of October 31, Year 2

Assets	
Cash	$ 240,000
Receivables	400,000
Inventory	600,000
Total current assets	$1,240,000
Plant and equipment - net	760,000
Total assets	**$2,000,000**
Liabilities and equity	
Accounts payable	$ 160,000
Notes payable	100,000
Other current liabilities	140,000
Total current liabilities	$ 400,000
Noncurrent debt	350,000
Common stock	750,000
Retained earnings	500,000
Total liabilities and equity	**$2,000,000**

Adams Company
Income Statement
For the 10 Months Ending October 31, Year 2

Sales		$ 3,000,000
Cost of goods sold		
Materials	$800,000	
Labor	700,000	
Overhead	300,000	1,800,000
Gross margin		$1,200,000
Selling expenses	$240,000	
General and administrative expenses	300,000	540,000
Operating income		$ 660,000
Minus interest expense		40,000
Income before taxes		$ 620,000
Minus federal income taxes		220,000
Net income		**$ 400,000**

-- Continued on next page --

 **-- Continued**

Given the year-to-date financial information, calculate the ratios. Enter the appropriate amounts in the shaded cells in the table below. Calculations should be rounded, if necessary, to the same number of places as the prior year's ratios, which are provided for comparative purposes only.

Ratio	Adams Company's Ratios for the 10 Months Ending 10/31/Year 2	Adams Company's Ratios for the 10 Months Ending 10/31/Year 1
1. Current ratio		2.5
2. Quick ratio		1.3
3. Accounts receivable turnover		5.5
4. Inventory turnover		2.5
5. Total asset turnover		1.2
6. Gross margin percentage		35%
7. Net operating margin percentage		25%
8. Times interest earned		10.3
9. Total debt to equity percentage		50%

JOURNAL ENTRIES: NUMERIC ENTRY AND DROP-DOWN

This TBS is an example of both Numeric Entry and Drop-Down type questions being asked in the same TBS.

| Journal Entries | Help |

During the course of the Year 2 audit of King Co., the auditor discovered potential cutoff and valuation problems that may or may not require adjusting journal entries. For each of the potential cutoff and valuation problems indicated below, complete the required journal entries.

To prepare each entry,

- Select from the Account Names Choices list the appropriate account name. If no entry is needed, select "No entry required." An account may be used once or not at all for each entry.
- Enter the corresponding debit or credit amount in the appropriate column.
- Round all amounts to the nearest dollar.
- All rows may not be required to complete each entry.

1. On January 1, Year 2, the company paid an insurance premium of $36,000 for the three following years. The entire payment was recognized as Year 2 insurance expense. No additional entry was made by the company in relation to this transaction. Record the necessary Year 2 adjustments, if any.

Account Name	Debit	Credit

2. In their response to the letter of audit inquiry for Year 2, the company's legal counsel indicated that a former employee has sued the company for $100,000. Management and counsel believe that a material loss probably will occur when pending litigation is resolved, and the reasonable estimate of the amount of range for the potential loss is $20,000 to $80,000. No amount within that range appears to be a better estimate that any other. No accrual was made in the financial statements regarding this suit. Record the necessary Year 2 adjustments, if any.

Account Name	Debit	Credit

3. On July 1, Year 2, the company received a 5-year loan of $100,000 from the bank. The loan bears a 10% interest that paid annually from July 1, Year 3. Accrued interest payable on the loan were not recorded at year end. Record the necessary Year 2 adjustments, if any.

Account Name	Debit	Credit

Account Names Choices
Cash
Cost of goods sold
Income tax expense
Insurance expense
Interest expense
Interest payable
Interest receivable
Inventory
Loss from contingent liability
No entry required
Payroll expense
Prepaid insurance expense
Provision for contingent liability
Shareholders' equity
Trade receivables

RISK FACTORS: DROP-DOWN 1

> The following five TBSs are all Drop-Downs, which are in essence multiple-choice questions. This type of task requires that you select a response from a list of choices. Some Drop-Down TBSs may also have Numeric Entry type responses required.

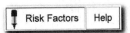

Bond, CPA, is considering the risk of material misstatement (RMM) at the financial statement level for Toxic Waste Disposal (TWD) Company for the year ended December 31, Year 6. TWD is a privately owned entity that contracts with municipal governments to remove environmental wastes. RMM at the financial statement level is influenced by a combination of factors related to management, the industry, and the entity.

Based only on the information in the table, select whether each factor below most likely increases, decreases, or has no effect on RMM. Each choice may be used once, more than once, or not at all.

Factor	Answer
1. This was the first year TWD operated at a profit since Year 2 because the municipalities received increased federal and state funding for environmental purposes.	
2. TWD's board of directors is controlled by Mead, the majority shareholder, who also acts as the chief executive officer.	
3. The internal auditor reports to the controller, and the controller reports to Mead.	
4. The accounting department has experienced a high rate of turnover of key personnel.	
5. TWD's bank has a loan officer who meets regularly with TWD's CEO and controller to monitor TWD's financial performance.	
6. TWD's employees are paid biweekly.	
7. Bond has audited TWD for 5 years.	
8. During Year 6, litigation filed against TWD in Year 1 alleging that TWD discharged pollutants into state waterways was dropped by the state. Loss contingency disclosures that TWD included in prior years' financial statements are being removed for the Year 6 financial statements.	
9. During December Year 6, TWD signed a contract to lease disposal equipment from an entity owned by Mead's parents. This related party transaction is not disclosed in TWD's notes to its Year 6 financial statements.	
10. During December Year 6, TWD increased its casualty insurance coverage on several pieces of sophisticated machinery from historical cost to replacement cost.	

Choices
A) Increase RMM
B) Decrease RMM
C) No effect

	1	2	3	4	5	6	7	8	9		
Directions	▽	▽	▽	▽	▽	▽	▽	▽	▽	◀ Previous	Next ▶

CONTROL DEFICIENCIES: DROP-DOWN 2

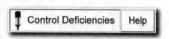

Land & Hale, CPAs, are auditing the financial statements of Stone Co., a nonissuer, for the year ended December 31, Year 1. Edwin Land, the engagement supervisor, anticipates expressing an unmodified opinion on May 20, Year 2. Ed Wood, an assistant on the engagement, drafted the auditor's communication of internal control related matters that Land plans to send to Stone's board of directors on May 30, Year 2. Land reviewed Wood's draft and indicated in the *Supervisor's Review Notes* that Wood's draft contained deficiencies.

Independent Auditor's Communication on Internal Control Related Matters

To Management and the Board of Directors:

In planning and performing our audit of the financial statements of Stone Co. as of and for the year ended December 31, Year 1, in accordance with auditing standards generally accepted in the United States of America, we considered Stone Co.'s internal control over financial reporting (internal control) as a basis for designing our auditing procedures for the purpose of expressing our opinion on the financial statements and for the purpose of expressing an opinion on the effectiveness of the Company's internal control.

Our consideration of internal control was for the limited purpose described in the preceding paragraph and can be expected to identify all deficiencies in internal control that might be significant deficiencies or material weaknesses. As discussed below, we identified a deficiency in internal control that we consider to be significant.

A deficiency in internal control exists when the design or operation of a control does not allow the auditors, in the normal course of performing their assigned functions, to prevent, or detect and correct, misstatements on a timely basis. A "significant deficiency" is a deficiency, or a combination of inconsequential deficiencies, in internal control that is less severe than a material weakness, yet important enough to merit attention by those charged with governance.

We consider the following to be a significant deficiency in internal control: failure to safeguard assets, particularly inventory stored at remote locations. The potential effect of this deficiency is that inventory reported on the balance sheet may not exist. An unmodified opinion was expressed on the financial statements.

This communication is intended solely for the information and use of management and the Board of Directors of Stone Co. and is not intended to be and should not be used by anyone other than these specified parties.

Land & Hale, CPAs
Chicago, Illinois
May 30, Year 2

-- Continued on next page --

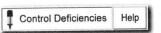 **-- Continued**

For each item, indicate in the shaded column whether Wood's original draft is correct, Land's modification is correct, or neither Wood's original draft nor Land's modification is correct.

Land's Modifications	Answer
In the first paragraph:	
1. The communication should refer to "our consideration of the internal controls."	
2. The communication should indicate that providing assurance on internal control is not the purpose of the consideration of internal control.	
3. The communication should refer to "conformity with generally accepted accounting principles."	
In the second paragraph:	
4. The communication should use the term "failures" rather than "deficiencies."	
5. The statement "can be expected to identify all deficiencies" should be changed to "can be expected to identify most deficiencies."	
In the third paragraph:	
6. The definition of a control deficiency should be replaced with a definition of internal control.	
7. The phrase "does not allow the auditors" should be replaced with "does not allow the audit committee."	
8. The term "inconsequential" should be changed to "minor."	
9. The communication should define "material weakness."	
In the fourth paragraph:	
10. The report should state that significant deficiencies were identified but should not identify them.	
11. The communication should include the actual effects of noted deficiencies, not the potential effects.	
In the final paragraph:	
12. The restriction on the communication's use is inappropriate because other parties ordinarily would receive the communication.	
13. The communication should refer to an opinion on the financial statements if a modified opinion was expressed.	
14. The communication should indicate that the auditor is not responsible for updating the communication for events or circumstances occurring after the date of the communication.	
Dating the report:	
15. The communication should be dated on the same date as the financial statements.	

Choices
A) Wood's original draft is correct
B) Land's modification is correct
C) Neither Wood's original draft nor Land's modification is correct

BANK RECONCILIATION: DROP-DOWN 3

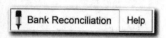

You are collecting evidence in your audit of a client's cash receipts and cash disbursements. To properly test management's assertions about the balances in the financial statements, you are preparing to perform substantive testing of the cash cycle.

The following is a bank reconciliation prepared by your client, who has a September 30 year end:

General Company
Bank Reconciliation
1st National Bank of U.S. Bank Account
September 30, Year 1

Balance per bank			$28,375
Deposits in transit			
9/29/Year 1		$4,500	
9/30/Year 1		1,525	6,025
			34,400
Outstanding checks			
# 988	8/31/Year 1	2,200	
#1281	9/26/Year 1	675	
#1285	9/27/Year 1	850	
#1289	9/29/Year 1	2,500	
#1292	9/30/Year 1	7,225	(13,450)
			20,950
Customer note collected by bank			(3,000)
Error: Check #1282, written on 9/26/Year 1			
for $270, was erroneously charged by bank			
as $720; bank was notified on 10/2/Year 1			450
Balance per books			$18,400

Assume the following:

- The client prepared the bank reconciliation on 10/2/Year 1.
- The bank reconciliation is mathematically accurate.
- The auditor received a cutoff bank statement dated 10/7/Year 1 directly from the bank on 10/11/Year 1.
- The 9/30/Year 1 deposit in transit, outstanding checks #1281, #1285, #1289, and #1292, and the correction of the error regarding check #1282 appeared on the cutoff bank statement.
- The auditor assessed the risk of material misstatement for cash as high.

-- Continued on next page --

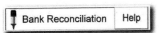 Bank Reconciliation Help   **-- Continued**

Based on the bank reconciliation, select from the list provided one or more procedures (as indicated) for each of the following items that the auditor most likely should perform to gather sufficient, competent, and relevant evidence. Each choice may be used once, more than once, or not at all.

Item	*Answer(s)*				
1. Balance per bank – **select 2 procedures**					
2. Deposits in transit – **select 5 procedures**					
3. Outstanding checks – **select 5 procedures**					
4. Customer note collected by bank – **select 1 procedure**					
5. Error – **select 2 procedures**					
6. Balance per books – **select 1 procedure**					

Choices
A) Trace to cash receipts journal.
B) Trace to cash disbursements journal.
C) Compare with 9/30/Year 1 general ledger.
D) Confirm directly with bank.
E) Inspect bank credit memo.
F) Inspect bank debit memo.
G) Ascertain reason for unusual delay.
H) Inspect supporting documents for reconciling item not appearing on cutoff statement.
I) Trace items on the bank reconciliation to cutoff statement.
J) Trace items on the cutoff statement to bank reconciliation.

MISSTATEMENTS: DROP-DOWN 4

The year under audit is Year 2.

During the audit of accounts payable, you detected misstatements previously undetected by the client. All misstatements were related to Year 2. For each of the liability misstatements shown below, select from the lists provided the most appropriate item.

- In Column I, select the audit procedure that was most likely used to detect the misstatement.
- In Column II, select the internal control that most likely could prevent or detect this type of misstatement in the future.

Audit procedures and internal controls may be selected once, more than once, or not at all.

Misstatement	Column I: Audit Procedure Used to Detect Misstatement	Column II: Internal Control that Could Prevent or Detect Misstatement in the Future
1. An accounts payable clerk misplaces year-end invoices for raw materials that were received on December 21, Year 2, and therefore liabilities were not recorded.		
2. The company tends to be careless in recording payables in the correct period.		
3. The company has the same person approving pay requests and preparing checks.		
4. The company's receiving department misplaces receiving reports for purchases of raw materials at year end, and therefore liabilities were not recorded.		

Column I Selection List

A) From the January Year 3 cash disbursements journal, select payments and match to corresponding invoices.

B) Review the cash disbursements journal for the month of December Year 2.

C) On a surprise basis, review the receiving department's filing system and test check quantities entered on December Year 2 receiving reports to packing slips.

D) Identify open purchase orders and vendors' invoices at December 31, Year 2, and investigate their disposition.

E) Request written confirmation from the accounts payable supervisor that all vendor invoices have been recorded in the accounts payable subsidiary ledger.

F) Investigate unmatched receiving reports dated prior to January 1, Year 3.

G) Compare the balances for selected vendors at the end of Year 2 and Year 1.

H) Determine that credit memos received 10 days after the balance sheet date have been recorded in the proper period.

I) Select an unpaid invoice and ask to be walked through the invoice payment process.

Column II Selection List

A) The purchasing department supervisor forwards a monthly listing of matched purchase orders and receiving reports to the accounts payable supervisor for comparison to a listing of vouched invoices.

B) The accounts payable supervisor reviews a monthly listing of open purchase orders and vendors' invoices for follow-up with the receiving department.

C) Copies of all vendor invoices received during the year are filed in an outside storage facility.

D) All vendor invoices are reviewed for mathematical accuracy.

E) On a daily basis, the receiving department independently counts all merchandise received.

F) All vendor invoices with supporting documentation are canceled when paid.

G) At the end of each month, the purchasing department confirms terms of delivery with selected vendors.

H) Separate the functions of accounts payable and cash disbursements.

I) A clerk is responsible for matching purchase orders with receiving reports and making certain they are included in the proper month.

REVIEW REPORT II: DROP-DOWN 5

Help

Jordan & Stone, CPAs, audited the financial statements of Tech Co., a nonissuer, for the year ended December 31, Year 1, and expressed an unmodified opinion. For the year ended December 31, Year 2, Tech issued comparative financial statements. Jordan & Stone reviewed Tech's Year 2 financial statements and Kent, an assistant on the engagement, drafted the accountants' review report below. Land, the engagement supervisor, decided not to reissue the prior year's auditor's report.

Land reviewed Kent's draft presented below and indicated in the *Supervisor's Noted Deficiencies* on the next page that 13 deficiencies were in Kent's draft.

We have reviewed and audited the accompanying balance sheets of Tech Co. as of December 31, Year 1 and Year 2, and the related statements of income, changes in stockholders' equity, and cash flows for the years then ended. A review is substantially less in scope than an audit, the objective of which is the expression of an opinion regarding the financial statements as a whole. Accordingly, we do not express such an opinion.

Management's Responsibility for the Financial Statements

Management is responsible for the preparation and full presentation of the financial statements in accordance with accounting principles generally accepted in the United States of America and for designing, implementing, and maintaining internal control relevant to the preparation and fair presentation of the financial statements.

Accountant's Responsibility

Our responsibility is to conduct the review in accordance with Statements on Standards for Accounting and Review Services issued by the American Institute of Certified Public Accountants. Those standards require us to perform procedures to obtain significant assurance that there are no material modifications that should be made to the financial statements. We believe that the results of our procedures provide a reasonable basis for our conclusion.

Accountant's Conclusion

Based on our study, we are not aware of any material modifications that should be made to the accompanying financial statements in order for them to be in conformity with accounting principles generally accepted in the United States of America. Because of inherent limitations in a review engagement, this report is intended for the information of management and should not be used for any other purpose.

Other Matter

The financial statements for the year ended December 31, Year 1, were audited by us, and our report was dated March 2, Year 2. We have no responsibility for updating that report for events and circumstances occurring after that date.

Jordan and Stone, CPAs
Anytown, Anystate
March 1, Year 3

For each noted deficiency, indicate whether Kent's draft is correct, Land's noted deficiency is correct, or neither Kent's draft nor Land's noted deficiency is correct. Each item in the answer list may be used once, more than once, or not at all.

-- Continued on next page --

| Review Report II | Help | **-- Continued** |

Supervisor's Noted Deficiencies	**Answer**
1. The reference to the prior year's audited financial statements should be in a separate paragraph.	
2. All the current-year basic financial statements are not properly identified in the first (introductory) paragraph.	
3. The first paragraph should state that a review includes primarily applying analytical procedures to management's financial data and making inquiries of company management.	
4. In the second paragraph, "full presentation" should be replaced with "accurate presentation."	
5. The reference should be to the PCAOB, not the American Institute of Certified Public Accountants in the third paragraph.	
6. The phrase "to obtain significant assurance" in the third paragraph should be replaced with "to obtain limited assurance."	
7. The last sentence in the third paragraph that begins, "We believe that the results . . ." should be deleted.	
8. The fourth paragraph should begin, "Based on our evidence . . ."	
9. No restriction on the distribution of the accountant's review report should be included in the fourth paragraph.	
10. The reference should be "material misstatements," not to "material modifications" in the fourth paragraph.	
11. An indication of the type of opinion expressed on the prior year's audited financial statements should be included in a separate paragraph.	
12. An indication that no auditing procedures were performed after the date of the report on the prior year's financial statements should be included in a separate paragraph.	
13. No reference to "updating that report for events and circumstances occurring after that date" should be included in the fourth (separate) paragraph.	

Choices

A) Kent's draft is correct.

B) Land's noted deficiency is correct.

C) Neither Kent's draft nor Land's noted deficiency is correct.

DOCUMENT REVIEW SIMULATION (DRS)

> This type of TBS requires that you analyze certain words or phrases in a document to decide whether to (1) keep the current text, (2) replace the current text with different text, or (3) delete the text. You must review various exhibits (e.g., financial statements, emails, invoices, etc.; see the second row of tabs in the image below) presented with the original document in order to find the information necessary for each response.

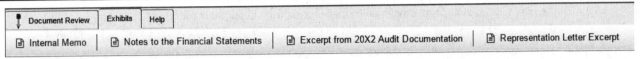

You are auditing Gasey Bats, a nonissuer. This is a continuing audit for the fiscal year ended 12/31/X2. Certain issues in the audit documentation noted by your audit supervisor may affect the completion of the audit. She has sent you an email with questions, which are numbered and are followed by the response you are planning to make. Using the information from the exhibits presented on the following pages, select the option from the list provided that corrects the underlined portion of each of your answers. If the underlined text is already correct in the context of the document, select *[Original Text]* from the list.

From: Audit Supervisor
To: You
Sent: Monday, March 28, 20X3
Subject: Audit Questions for Gasey Bats

1. What do you believe our position should be regarding the issue identified in the draft of Note L?
The issue identified in Note L will require <u>an "except for" modification of the 20X2 audit opinion.</u>

- [A] *[Original Text]* an "except for" qualification of the 20X2 audit opinion.
- [B] no modification of the 20X2 audit report regarding the issue.
- [C] addition of an emphasis-of-matter paragraph in the 20X2 audit report.
- [D] addition of a footnote to the 20X2 audit report describing the misstatement.
- [E] additional clarification by management, including the cause of the misstatement, in the note.

2. Should any additional information be provided by management in the draft of Note N?
Note N also should include a statement that <u>the prior year's balance sheet for 20X1 has been restated for comparative purposes.</u>

- [A] *[Original Text]* the prior year's balance sheet for 20X1 has been restated for comparative purposes.
- [B] no future reference will be made to the three separate cash accounts.
- [C] no cash was lost during the reclassification process.
- [D] the effect of the reclassification on the income statement was minimal.
- [E] internal control was improved by the reclassification.

3. Does the language in the draft of Note C require us to modify our opinion?
Yes. The issue in the note that may require us to modify the opinion is <u>that the related party is not specifically named.</u>

- [A] *[Original Text]* that the related party is not specifically named.
- [B] the statement that the transaction was consummated on terms that were equivalent to those in an arm's-length transaction with a nonrelated party.
- [C] the reference to an assumed mortgage of $450,000 without stating who holds the mortgage.
- [D] that the specific building that was acquired is not identified in the note.
- [E] that the reason for the acquisition is not explained in the note.

4. Should we require management to correct the misstatement of accounts payable that we discovered and noted in the internal memo from the CEO to the Accountant?
<u>Because we discovered the misstatement, it must be corrected. Otherwise, we will modify our audit opinion.</u>

- [A] *[Original Text]* Because we discovered the misstatement, it must be corrected. Otherwise, we will modify our audit opinion.
- [B] We should require management to correct the misstatement, although it will not affect our audit report.
- [C] We should require management to correct the misstatement. Otherwise, we will withhold our audit report.
- [D] We need not require management to correct the misstatement in the current year.

-- Continued on next page --

-- **Continued**

5. What will happen if we do not confirm the receivable discussed in working paper G-1?

<u>We should not complete the audit until we confirm the receivable.</u>

- • [A] *[Original Text]* We should not complete the audit until we confirm the receivable.
- • [B] We may have to qualify the audit opinion because of a scope limitation.
- • [C] We may have to include an emphasis-of-matter paragraph in our audit report.
- • [D] We may have to ask management to write off the receivable to bad debts before we issue our report.

6. Should the management representation letter include a representation by management of its responsibility for internal control to prevent and detect fraud?

<u>No, it is our responsibility to detect fraud during the audit.</u>

- • [A] *[Original Text]* No, it is our responsibility to detect fraud during the audit.
- • [B] Yes, and I will add a sentence stating that management is responsible for the development and application of controls to prevent and detect fraud.
- • [C] Yes, but management has asked that we delete that statement, and we have appropriately done so.
- • [D] No, the letter is silent as to the responsibility for fraud prevention and detection.
- • [E] No, the statement, "The effects of all known actual or possible litigation and claims have been accounted for and disclosed in accordance with U.S. GAAP," covers this issue.

7. The management representation letter states, "All events subsequent to the date of the financial statements and for which U.S. GAAP requires adjustment or disclosure have been adjusted or disclosed." Should "subsequent to the date of the financial statements" be changed to "subsequent to the date of the audit?"

<u>Yes, I will change the draft of the letter.</u>

- • [A] *[Original Text]* Yes, I will change the draft of the letter.
- • [B] Yes, we can make the change, but the dates are the same.
- • [C] No, we require information about subsequent events up to the date of the audit report.
- • [D] No, I will remove the entire sentence from the draft.
- • [E] No, but the word "events" should be changed to "actual transactions."

DRS: EXHIBITS

Gasey Bats
Internal Memo
11/30/X2

From: James Icanno, CEO
To: Darlene Kasper, Accountant

The auditors have uncovered an error that results in an overstatement of accounts payable for the year. They have indicated that the misstatement is not material. Since correcting this error requires considerable effort, we will not make the correction until next year.

Draft of several notes that are intended to be included in the financial statements

Note C

The acquisition of the building reported in the current year's financial statements at a cost of $800,000 was from a related party. Gasey Bats assumed the existing mortgage of $450,000 on the property. We have concluded that the transaction was consummated on terms that were equivalent to those in an arm's-length transaction with a nonrelated party.

Note L

A material misstatement in inventory was identified that resulted in a $280,000 decrease in inventory from 20X1 to 20X2. The comparative 20X1 statements have been restated and an adjustment to retained earnings has been made to reflect this correction.

Note N

The 20X1 balance sheet presented three bank accounts in current assets: Cash – Mid Bank, Cash – South Bank, and Cash – Overland Trust. These accounts have been reclassified for 20X2 as one account, Cash.

G-1
3/20/X3

[Your Initials]

Confirmations related to receivables due from the government of Tobago were not returned, and follow-up efforts were not effective. The account is current, and payments on the account have been made during the past year. We believe that it is necessary to confirm this account in order to obtain sufficient, appropriate evidence.

The amount of the receivable at 12/31/X2 is $495,000. We believe that this amount is material to the financial statements, but the effect is not pervasive.

The following is a section from the draft of the management representation letter that has been prepared for Gasey Bats. The letter will be requested to be signed by the CEO and the CFO.

Financial Statements

- We have fulfilled our responsibilities, as set out in the terms of the audit engagement dated 2/1/X2, for the preparation and fair presentation of the financial statements in accordance with U.S. GAAP.
- We acknowledge our responsibility for the design, implementation, and maintenance of internal control relevant to the preparation and fair presentation of financial statements that are free from material misstatement.
- Significant assumptions used by us in making accounting estimates, including those measured at fair value, are reasonable.
- Related party relationships and transactions have been appropriately accounted for and disclosed in accordance with the requirements of U.S. GAAP.
- All events subsequent to the date of the financial statements and for which U.S. GAAP requires adjustment or disclosure have been adjusted or disclosed.
- The effects of all known actual or possible litigation and claims have been accounted for and disclosed in accordance with U.S. GAAP.

ANSWERS 1 OF 4

1. Research (1 Gradable Item)

Answer: AU-C 200.25

AU-C Section 200 -- *Overall Objectives of the Independent Auditor and the Conduct of an Audit in Accordance With Generally Accepted Auditing Standards*

Defining Professional Responsibilities in GAAS

.25 GAAS use the following two categories of professional requirements, identified by specific terms, to describe the degree of responsibility it imposes on auditors:

- Unconditional requirements. The auditor must comply with an unconditional requirement in all cases in which such requirement is relevant. GAAS use the word "must" to indicate an unconditional requirement.
- Presumptively mandatory requirements. The auditor must comply with a presumptively mandatory requirement in all cases in which such a requirement is relevant except in rare circumstances discussed in paragraph .26. GAAS use the word "should" to indicate a presumptively mandatory requirement.

2. Ratios (9 Gradable Items)

1. Current ratio	3.1	($1,240,000 ÷ $400,000)
2. Quick ratio	1.6	[($1,240,000 − $600,000) ÷ $400,000]
3. Accounts receivable turnover	7.5	($3,000,000 ÷ $400,000)
4. Inventory turnover	3.0	($1,800,000 ÷ $600,000)
5. Total asset turnover	1.5	($3,000,000 ÷ $2,000,000)
6. Gross margin percentage	40%	($1,200,000 ÷ $3,000,000)
7. Net operating margin percentage	22%	($660,000 ÷ $3,000,000)
8. Times interest earned	16.5	[($400,000 + $40,000 + $220,000) ÷ $40,000]
9. Total debt to equity percentage	60%	[($400,000 + $350,000) ÷ ($750,000 + $500,000)]

3. Journal Entries (12 Gradable Items)

1. A cutoff test verifies that transactions have been recorded in the proper period. The amount of $36,000 is an insurance premium for 3 years. Thus, Year 2 insurance expense and prepaid insurance expense are 1/3 and 2/3 of this amount, respectively.

Account Name	Debit	Credit
Prepaid insurance expense	$24,000	
Insurance expense		$24,000

2. Because the loss is probable and can be reasonably estimated, it should be accrued if the amount is material. If the estimate is stated within a given range and no amount within that range appears to be a better estimate than any other, the minimum of the range should be accrued.

Account Name	Debit	Credit
Loss from contingent liability	$20,000	
Provision for contingent liability		$20,000

3. Since the loan was received in the middle of the year, the interest on loan is accrued for half of the year and calculated as follows: $5,000 = $100,000 × 10% × 0.5.

Account Name	Debit	Credit
Interest expense	$5,000	
Interest payable		$5,000

4. Risk Factors (10 Gradable Items)

1. **B) Decrease RMM.** Continued losses indicate an increase in risk. However, the turnaround into a profitable organization will likely decrease the risk of material misstatement in the financial statements for the auditor.

2. **A) Increase RMM.** One set of opportunity risk factors for misstatements arising from fraudulent financial reporting involves ineffective monitoring of management. One such risk factor is domination of management by a single person or small group (in a non-owner managed business) without compensating controls. A compensating control in that circumstance is effective oversight by the board or audit committee of the financial reporting process and internal control.

ANSWERS 2 OF 4

3. <u>A) Increase RMM.</u> Ideally, the internal auditor should report to the audit committee of the board of directors. If the internal auditor reports to operating management, the risk of material misstatement is increased.

4. <u>A) Increase RMM.</u> When management turnover is high, particularly of senior accounting personnel, the risk of material misstatement is increased.

5. <u>B) Decrease RMM.</u> Oversight by external parties, e.g., a bank loan officer, provides some assurance to the auditor and decreases the risk of material misstatement.

6. <u>C) No effect.</u> Paying employees biweekly likely has little effect on the risk of material misstatement.

7. <u>B) Decrease RMM.</u> A continuing engagement in which the auditor has had experience with management is likely to be less risky than a first-time audit.

8. <u>B) Decrease RMM.</u> The settlement of lawsuits filed against the client likely decreases the risk that the financial statements are misstated.

9. <u>A) Increase RMM.</u> A set of opportunity risk factors for misstatements arising from fraudulent financial reporting involves the nature of the industry or the entity's operations. One such risk factor is the existence of significant related party transactions not in the ordinary course of business or with entities not audited or audited by another firm.

10. <u>C) No effect.</u> The change in insurance coverage for specific assets will not likely change the risk of material misstatement.

5. Control Deficiencies (15 Gradable Items)

1. <u>A) Wood's original draft is correct.</u> The auditor's written communication should refer to planning and performing our audit.

2. <u>B) Land's modification is correct.</u> The communication should indicate that internal control was considered for the purpose of designing the audit and expressing an opinion on the financial statements but not for expressing an opinion on the effectiveness of internal control.

3. <u>A) Wood's original draft is correct.</u> The communication relates to control deficiencies, not whether the financial statements are in accordance with the applicable reporting framework.

4. <u>A) Wood's original draft is correct.</u> The purpose is to communicate significant deficiencies and material weaknesses. Thus, it is appropriate to refer to control deficiencies in the communication.

5. <u>C) Neither Wood's original draft nor Land's modification is correct.</u> The AICPA's illustrative written communication states that the consideration of internal control "was not designed to identify all deficiencies in internal control that might be significant deficiencies or material weaknesses."

6. <u>A) Wood's original draft is correct.</u> The AICPA's illustrative written communication states the definition of a control deficiency to place significant deficiencies in the correct context.

7. <u>C) Neither Wood's original draft nor Land's modification is correct.</u> The phrase should refer to "management or employees," not to "the auditors" or "the audit committee."

8. <u>C) Neither Wood's original draft nor Land's modification is correct.</u> The definition of significant deficiency does not include the terms "inconsequential" or "minor."

9. <u>B) Land's modification is correct.</u> The communication defines "material weakness" and, if relevant, "significant deficiency."

10. <u>A) Wood's original draft is correct.</u> The specific significant deficiencies should be described in the communication.

11. <u>A) Wood's original draft is correct.</u> The report should include the potential effects of any identified significant deficiencies and material weaknesses.

12. <u>A) Wood's original draft is correct.</u> The communication is intended for use by management, those charged with governance, and others within the organization. If the entity must provide such a communication to a governmental authority, it should specifically refer to that authority. Moreover, it is not intended to be used and should not be used by anyone other than these specified parties.

13. <u>C) Neither Wood's original draft nor Land's modification is correct.</u> The communication does not identify the type of opinion that was expressed on the financial statements.

14. <u>A) Wood's original draft is correct.</u> The communication should not contain a statement about the auditor's responsibility for updating the communication. The auditor has no such obligation.

15. <u>A) Wood's original draft is correct.</u> The communication is best made at the audit report release date, but it should be made no later than 60 days after the audit report release date.

ANSWERS 3 OF 4

6. Bank Reconciliation (16 Gradable Items)

1. <u>D) Confirm directly with bank and I) Trace items on the bank reconciliation to cutoff statement.</u> The balance per bank should be confirmed directly with the bank using a "Standard Form to Confirm Account Balance Information with Financial Institutions." Moreover, the cutoff bank statement gives the balance per bank at September 30, Year 1.

2. <u>A) Trace to cash receipts journal, G) Ascertain reason for unusual delay, H) Inspect supporting documents for reconciling item not appearing on cutoff statement, I) Trace items on the bank reconciliation to cutoff statement, and J) Trace items on the cutoff statement to bank reconciliation.</u> Each deposit should be supported by an entry in the cash receipts journal. The 9/29/Year 1 deposit in transit should be investigated to determine the reason for the delay. It should have been reported on the cutoff bank statement. The deposits in transit on the bank reconciliation should be compared with items in the cutoff bank statement to test for their existence. In addition, a test should be performed in the opposite direction. The deposits in transit on the cutoff bank statement should be compared with items in the bank reconciliation to test the completeness of the deposits in transit.

3. <u>B) Trace to cash disbursements journal, G) Ascertain reason for unusual delay, H) Inspect supporting documents for reconciling item not appearing on cutoff statement, I) Trace items on the bank reconciliation to cutoff statement, and J) Trace items on the cutoff statement to bank reconciliation.</u> Each check should be supported by an entry in the cash disbursements journal. Check #988 should be investigated to determine the reason for its delay in clearing and to determine why it did not appear on the cutoff bank statement. Outstanding checks on the bank reconciliation should be compared with the cutoff bank statement to test the existence of the outstanding checks. In addition, a test should be performed in the opposite direction. Outstanding checks on the cutoff bank statement should be compared with the bank reconciliation to test for the completeness of the listed outstanding checks.

4. <u>E) Inspect bank credit memo.</u> The problem involves reconciling the balance per bank to the balance per books. The proceeds of the customer note collected by the bank increased the balance per bank, so the amount of the note must be subtracted to arrive at the balance per books. The amount collected on the note can be verified by inspecting the bank's credit memo. The bank credited the customer's account (a liability to the bank) when it collected the proceeds of the note.

5. <u>E) Inspect bank credit memo and I) Trace items on the bank reconciliation to cutoff statement.</u> The credit memo issued in October should be inspected and the credit given to the customer for $450 should be compared with the cutoff bank statement.

6. <u>C) Compare to 9/30/Year 1 general ledger.</u> The balance per books should be compared with the 9/30/Year 1 cash balance in the general ledger.

7. Misstatements (8 Gradable Items)

	Column I	Column II
1.	F)	A)
2.	A)	I)
3.	I)	H)
4.	D)	B)

1. <u>F) Investigate unmatched receiving reports dated prior to January 1, Year 3.</u> Receiving reports should be matched with purchase orders and vendor invoices as support for a payment voucher. Investigating unmatched documents would uncover the failure to prepare a voucher.

    <u>A) The purchasing department supervisor forwards a monthly listing of matched purchase orders and receiving reports to the accounts payable supervisor for comparison to a listing of vouched invoices.</u> Comparing an independent listing of matched purchase orders and receiving reports with vouched invoices would detect a lost document in accounts payable.

2. <u>A) From the January Year 3 cash disbursements journal, select payments and match to corresponding invoices.</u> A cutoff test that evaluates transactions recorded at or near year end would detect transactions recorded in the improper period.

    <u>I) A clerk is responsible for matching purchases orders with receiving reports and making certain they are included in the proper month.</u> Having an employee responsible for making certain that transactions are recorded in the proper period would be a control to help ensure proper cutoff.

3. <u>I) Select an unpaid invoice and ask to be walked through the invoice payment process.</u> A walkthrough of the process would allow the auditor to identify weaknesses in the system.

    <u>H) Separate the functions of accounts payable and cash disbursements.</u> Separation of the approval and custody functions is a control to mitigate risks in a payment system.

4. <u>D) Identify open purchase orders and vendors' invoices at December 31, Year 2, and investigate their disposition.</u> To detect missing or lost receiving reports, the auditor should identify open purchase orders and vendors' invoices at December 31, Year 2, and investigate their disposition.

    <u>B) The accounts payable supervisor reviews a monthly listing of open purchase orders and vendors' invoices for follow-up with the receiving department.</u> A useful control would be to have the accounts payable supervisor review a monthly listing of open purchase orders and vendors' invoices for follow-up with the receiving department.

ANSWERS 4 OF 4

8. Review Report II (13 Gradable Items)

1. B) Land's noted deficiency is correct. The prior-period statements were audited, and the report was not reissued. Thus, the current period's report should include an other-matter paragraph indicating (a) that the prior-period statements were audited; (b) the date of the report on those statements; (c) the opinion expressed; (d) the substantive reasons for any modification of the opinion; and (e) that no audit procedures were performed after the date of the previous report.

2. A) Kent's draft is correct. The basic financial statements are properly identified in the introductory paragraph.

3. B) Land's noted deficiency is correct. The first paragraph describes, in general, the procedures performed in review.

4. C) Neither Kent's draft nor Land's noted deficiency is correct. The phase included in the report should be "fair presentation."

5. A) Kent's draft is correct. The identification of the applicable guidance should refer to the Accounting and Review Services Committee of the American Institute of Certified Public Accountants.

6. B) Land's noted deficiency is correct. A review provides limited assurance.

7. A) Kent's draft is correct. The statement, "We believe that the results of our procedures provide a reasonable basis for our conclusion." should be included.

8. C) Neither Kent's draft nor Land's noted deficiency is correct. The fourth paragraph should begin, "Based on our review . . ."

9. B) Land's noted deficiency is correct. A review report ordinarily is not limited regarding either its use or distribution. Exceptions are the use of measurement or disclosure criteria (a) suitable only for a limited number of users or (b) available only to specified parties.

10. A) Kent's draft is correct. The report should refer to "material modifications" to the financial statements.

11. B) Land's noted deficiency is correct. The opinion expressed on the audited financial statements should be described in the other-matter paragraph.

12. B) Land's noted deficiency is correct. The paragraph describing the prior year's audit should indicate that no auditing procedures were performed after the audit report date.

13. B) Land's noted deficiency is correct. The review report should not refer to updating the prior-period report.

9. Document Review (7 Gradable Items)

1. C) addition of an emphasis-of-matter paragraph in the 20X2 audit report. The audit report should include an emphasis-of-matter paragraph drawing attention to the issue.

2. A) [Original Text] the prior year's balance sheet for 20X1 has been restated for comparative purposes. A reclassification results in restating the prior statements to reflect the change and to make the statements comparable, which should be included in the note.

3. B) the statement that the transaction was consummated on terms that were equivalent to those in an arm's-length transaction with a nonrelated party. The auditor is not likely to be able to obtain evidence to support the statement that the transaction was consummated on terms that were equivalent to those in an arm's-length transaction with a nonrelated party. Thus, it should be removed, or the auditor should modify the audit opinion, due to a scope limitation.

4. D) We need not require management to correct the misstatement in the current year. Immaterial misstatements need not be corrected for the financial statement to be fairly presented.

5. B) We may have to qualify the audit opinion because of a scope limitation. Failure to obtain sufficient appropriate evidence may be a scope limitation that results in a qualified opinion or a disclaimer. In this case, the failure is material but not pervasive. Thus, modifying the opinion because of a scope limitation is appropriate. Disclaiming an opinion is appropriate if the potential effects of the scope limitation are pervasive.

6. B) Yes, and I will add a sentence stating that management is responsible for the development and application of controls to prevent and detect fraud. Management should acknowledge its responsibilities in the representation letter. Consequently, it should state its responsibility for the design, implementation, and maintenance of internal control to prevent and detect fraud.

7. C) No, we require information about subsequent events up to the date of the audit report. Audit evidence is collected up to the date of the report including evidence for events after the balance sheet date that could affect the current year's statements. The date of the report is no earlier than the date on which the auditor obtained sufficient appropriate audit evidence to support the opinion.

INDEX